Helping Children Learn Mathematics

Fifth Edition

Robert E. Reys
University of Missouri

Marilyn N. Suydam
Ohio State University

Mary M. Lindquist
Columbus State University

Nancy L. Smith
Emporia State University

JOHN WILEY & SONS, INC.
NEW YORK · CHICHESTER · WEINHEIM · BRISBANE · SINGAPORE · TORONTO

The paper in this book was manufactured by a mill whose forest management programs include sustained yield harvesting of its timberlands. Sustained yield harvesting principles ensure that the number of trees cut each year does not exceed the amount of new growth.

Library of Congress Cataloging-in-Publication Data
Helping children learn mathematics.—5th ed. / Robert E. Reys . . .
[et al.]
     p.   cm.
   Rev. ed. of: Helping children learn mathematics / Robert E. Reys,
Marilyn N. Suydam, Mary Montgomery Lindquist. 4th ed. c1995.
   Includes bibliographical references and index.
   ISBN 0-471-36536-X
   1. Mathematics—Study and teaching (elementary).   I. Reys, Robert
E.   II. Reys, Robert E. Helping children learn mathematics.
QA135.5.R49   1998
372.7'044—dc21   97-15924
                                                   CIP

Printed in the United States of America

10   9   8   7   6   5   4   3   2   VHP   02   01   00   99

Contents

Preface   *vii*

1 The Changing Elementary School Mathematics Program   1

Introduction   1

What Is Mathematics?   2

What Determines the Mathematics Being Taught?   2
- Needs of the Subject   2
- Needs of the Child   3
- Needs of Society   4

What Mathematics Should Be Taught?   4

What Forces Affect the Curriculum?   8
- Educational Organizations   8
- Research   10
- Technology   10
- Threats to National Security and the Economy   10
- Government   10
- Textbooks   11
- Testing   11

What Curricular Content Has Been Proposed as Essential?   11
- The Drill Load of Arithmetic   12
- Key Concepts for Postwar Programs   12
- Skills Essential for Enlightened Citizens   12
- Essential Skill Areas   12

Ongoing Curricular Concerns   14

A Glance at Where We've Been   14

Things to Do: From What You've Read   15

Things to Do: Going Beyond This Book   15

Selected References   15

2 Understanding How Children Learn Mathematics   17

Introduction   17

How Do Children Learn Mathematics?   17
- Building Behavior   18
- Constructing Understanding   19

What Mathematical Knowledge Should Be Learned?   20

Implications of What We Know about Learning Mathematics   22

Recommendations for Teaching from What We Know about Learning Mathematics   31

A Glance at Where We've Been   32

Things to Do: From What You've Read   33

Things to Do: Going Beyond This Book   33

Children's Corner   34

Selected References   34

3 Planning for Mathematics Instruction   36

Snapshot of a Lesson   36

Introduction   37

An Overview: Six NCTM Professional Standards   37

The Importance of Planning   39

Levels of Planning   40

Components of a Lesson Plan   41

Grouping for Instruction   42

Points to Consider in Planning and Teaching   44
- The Importance of Questions   45
- The Use of Manipulative Materials   45
- The Role of Drill and Practice   46

Evaluation   47
- Diagnosis   47
- Remediation   47
- Equity   48

Using the Strategic Moment   48

A Glance at Where We've Been   49

Things to Do: From What You've Read   49

Things to Do: Going Beyond This Book   49

Selected References   49

4 Assessing for Learning   52

Introduction   52

Ways to Gather Evidence   54
- Observation   54
- Questioning   54

Interviewing 55
Performance Tasks 55
Self-Assessments 56
Work Samples 57
Portfolios 57
Writings 57
Written Tests 58
Achievement Tests 60

Ways to Keep Records and to Communicate about Assessments 61
Recording the Information 61
Communicating the Information 63

A Glance at Where We've Been 65
Things to Do: From What You've Read 66
Things to Do: Going Beyond This Book 66
Selected References 66

5 Problem Solving 68

Snapshot of a Lesson 68
Introduction 69

What Is a Problem and What Is Problem Solving? 70

How Can Problem Solving Be Taught Effectively? 71
Time 72
Planning 72
Resources 73
Technology 74
Class Management 74

What Problem-Solving Strategies Should Be Taught? 75
Act It Out 76
Make a Drawing or Diagram 77
Look for a Pattern 77
Construct a Table 78
Account Systematically
for All Possibilities 78
Guess and Check 79
Work Backward 80
Identify Wanted, Given, and
Needed Information 80
Write an Open Sentence 80
Solve a Simpler or Similar Problem 80
Change Your Point of View 81

The Importance of Looking Back 81
Generalize 82
Check the Solution 82
Find Another Way to Solve It 82
Find Another Solution 82
Study the Solution Process 82

Using Problem-Solving Opportunities 82

How Can Problem Solving Be Assessed? 83
Observations 83
Interviews 84
Inventories and Checklists 84
Paper-and-Pencil Tests 84

A Glance at Where We've Been 84
Things to Do: From What You've Read 84
Things to Do: Going Beyond This Book 85

Children's Corner 85
Selected References 85

6 Development of Number Sense and Counting 88

Snapshot of a Lesson 88
Introduction 89

Prenumber Concepts 90
Classification 90
Patterns 94
Comparisons 95
Conservation 97
Group Recognition 98

Counting 98
Counting Principles 99
Counting Stages 100
Counting Strategies 100
Counting Practice 102

Early Number Development 104
Developing Number Benchmarks 104
Making Connections 106

Cardinal, Ordinal, and Nominal Numbers 109

Writing Numerals 110

A Glance at Where We've Been 111
Things to Do: From What You've Read 111
Things to Do: Going Beyond This Book 112
Children's Corner 112
Selected References 113

7 Developing Number Sense with Numeration and Place Value 115

Snapshot of a Lesson 115
Introduction 117

Our Numeration System 117
Thinking Place Value 117
Grouping or Trading 117
Nature of Place Value 118
Modeling 120

Developing Place Value 121
A Place to Start 121
Counting and Patterns 128
Regrouping and Renaming 130

Reading and Writing Numbers 132

Estimation and Rounding 136
Estimation 136
Rounding 137

A Glance at Where We've Been 139
Things to Do: From What You've Read 141
Things to Do: Going Beyond This Book 141
Children's Corner 142
Selected References 142

8 Beginning Whole-Number Operations: Basic Facts 144

Snapshot of a Lesson   144
Introduction   145
Prerequisites   146
    Counting   146
    Concrete Experiences   146
    Problem-Solving Context   147
    Language   147
Models for the Operations   147
    Addition and Subtraction   147
    Multiplication and Division   149
Mathematical Properties   151
The Basic Facts   152
    Get Ready: The Starting Place   154
    Get Set: Presenting the Basic Facts   154
    Go: Mastering the Basic Facts   166
A Glance at Where We've Been   168
Things to Do: From What You've Read   169
Things to Do: Going Beyond This Book   170
Children's Corner   170
Selected References   170

9 Computational Alternatives— The Need to Reach a Balance 173

Snapshot of a Lesson   173
Introduction   174
Computational Tools   175
    Calculators   176
    Mental Computation   178
    Computational Estimation   183
    Front-End Estimation   184
    Adjusting or Compensating   185
    Flexible Rounding   186
    Compatible Numbers   187
    Clustering   188
Choosing Estimation Strategies   189
A Glance at Where We've Been   190
Things to Do: From What You've Read   192
Things to Do: Going Beyond This Book   192
Selected References   193

10 Extending Whole-Number Operations: Algorithms 195

Snapshot of a Lesson   195
Introduction   196
    Role of Materials in Learning Algorithms   197
    Importance of Place-Value Ideas   197

Addition   198
    Column Addition   199
    Higher-Decade Addition   200
Subtraction   201
    Zeros in the Sum   203
Multiplication   204
    Multiplication with One-Digit Multipliers   204
    Multiplication with Two-Digit Multipliers   205
    Multiplying by 10 and Multiples of 10   207
    Multiplying with Zeros   209
    Multiplication with Large Numbers   209
Division   209
    Division with Remainders   210
    Division with One-Digit Divisors   211
    Division with Two-Digit Divisors   214
Checking   215
Choosing Appropriate Ways   216
A Glance at Where We've Been   216
Things to Do: From What You've Read   216
Things to Do: Going Beyond This Book   217
Children's Corner   217
Selected References   217

11 Exploring Geometry 220

Snapshot of a Lesson   220
Introduction   221
Solid Geometry   221
    Describing and Classifying Objects   222
    Constructing and Then Exploring and Discovering   224
    Relating Three Dimensions to Two   226
Plane Geometry   228
    Properties of a Shape   228
    Names of Geometric Shapes   235
    Relationships between Shapes   236
    Classification Schemes   238
A Glance at Where We've Been   240
Things to Do: From What You've Read   240
Things to Do: Going Beyond This Book   241
Children's Corner   241
Selected References   241

12 Measuring 243

Snapshot of a Lesson   243
Introduction   244
Teaching Measurement   246
    Identifying Attributes   247
    Units of Measure   250
    Instruments for Measuring   253
    Formulas for Measuring   255
Comparing Measurements   259
    Equivalences   259
    Conversions   260

Estimating Measurements 261
Connecting Attributes 262
   Area and Shape 262
   Volume and Shape 263
   Perimeter and Area 263
   Volume and Surface Area 264
   Perimeter and Dimensions 264
   Metric Relations 264
A Glance at Where We've Been 265
Things to Do: From What You've Read 266
Things to Do: Going Beyond This Book 266
Children's Corner 267
Selected References 267

13 Developing Fractions and Decimals 268

Snapshot of a Lesson 268
Introduction 269
Conceptual Development of Fractions 269
   Three Meanings of Fractions 270
   Models of the Part–Whole Meaning 271
   One Way to Introduce Fractions 272
   Ordering Fractions 275
   Equivalence of Fractions 276
   Mixed Numbers and Improper Fractions 278
Operations with Fractions 280
   Addition and Subtraction 280
   Multiplication 283
   Division 285
Development of Decimals 286
   Relationship to Common Fractions 286
   Relationship to Place Value 289
   Ordering and Rounding Decimals 290
Decimal Operations 290
   Addition and Subtraction 291
   Multiplication and Division 291
A Glance at Where We've Been 293
Things to Do: From What You've Read 294
Things to Do: Going Beyond This Book 294
Children's Corner 294
Selected References 294

14 Ratio, Proportion, and Percent 296

Snapshot of a Lesson 296
Introduction 297
Ratios 298
Proportions 300
Percents 302
   Understanding Percents 305
   Applying Percents 308
A Glance at Where We've Been 310
Things to Do: From What You've Read 310
Things to Do: Going Beyond This Book 311

Children's Corner 311
Selected References 312

15 Using Data 314

Snapshot of a Lesson 314
Introduction 316
Graphing 317
   Picture Graphs 318
   Pie, or Circle, Graphs 318
   Bar Graphs 319
   Line Graphs 319
   Stem-and-Leaf Plots and Box Plots 319
   Graphical Roundup 321
   Teaching Tips 322
Statistics 324
   Averages 324
   The Mean 324
   The Median 325
   The Mode 326
Probability 327
   Probability of an Event 328
   Randomness 331
   Independence of Events 332
A Glance at Where We've Been 333
Things to Do: From What You've Read 334
Things to Do: Going Beyond This Book 334
Children's Corner 335
Selected References 335

16 Searching for Patterns and Relationships 337

Snapshot of a Lesson 337
Introduction 338
Patterns and Relationships 338
   Repeating Patterns 338
   Growing Patterns 341
   Relationships 342
Number Theory 344
   Benefits of Teaching Number Theory 344
   Specific Number Theory Topics 346
A Glance at Where We've Been 352
Things to Do: From What You've Read 353
Things to Do: Going Beyond This Book 354
Children's Corner 354
Selected References 355

Appendix A: Summary of NCTM Recommendations 356

Appendix B: Blackline Masters 359

Appendix C: Publishers and Distributors 387

Index 388

Preface

This fifth edition of *Helping Children Learn Mathematics* coincides with one of the most exciting times in the history of mathematics education. Change is everywhere. The release of the *Curriculum and Evaluation Standards for School Mathematics* and *Professional Standards for Teaching Mathematics* by the National Council of Teachers of Mathematics has stimulated unprecedented activity in mathematics education. These publications have orchestrated major changes affecting the elementary school mathematics curriculum, standardized tests, and teacher education. Some important changes have already been made, many are being made, and still others are in the planning stages. As a teacher of mathematics in elementary school, you will not only be a part of these changes, but also will have an opportunity to lead the way.

Helping Children Learn Mathematics has been written as a part of this mathematics education movement. This book is intended for those of you who are or who will be teachers of mathematics in elementary school. It is designed to help you help children learn mathematical concepts and skills, as well as important problem-solving techniques. In the process it will challenge your thinking and further stimulate your interest in mathematics.

Helping Children Learn Mathematics is divided into two main parts. The first part (Chapters 1–5) provides a base for understanding the changing mathematics curriculum and how children learn it. It offers some guidelines for planning and evaluating instruction. Attention is directed to problem solving and assessment, both of which have pro-

found implications for mathematics teaching at all levels. Their importance is reflected throughout the book as they are integrated into various chapters.

The second part (Chapters 6–16) discusses teaching strategies, techniques, and learning activities related to specific mathematical topics. Emphasis is on using models and materials to develop concepts and understanding so that mathematics learning is indeed meaningful. We believe that meaning is most effectively established by helping students discuss mathematics as they move from concrete materials and examples to generalizations and abstractions.

Helping Children Learn Mathematics is a unique resource. Here are thirteen (a baker's dozen) features designed to make this book particularly useful:

1. **Problem Solving.** Problem solving, the single most important and challenging basic skill in mathematics, is addressed in a separate chapter (Chapter 5). This chapter discusses various problem-solving strategies and also presents a wide variety of problems with which the strategies are useful. You will also find a problem-solving spirit reflected in the Lesson Cards and Activity Cards, as well as in many of the discussions throughout the book.

2. **Snapshots of a Lesson.** Snapshots of a Lesson provide a brief look into a variety of mathematical lessons at different grade levels. All of the content-specific chapters (Chapters 6–16) open with one of these Snapshots to remind you of the realities of teaching. The Snapshots both demonstrate many effective classroom practices and illustrate

the vital role that you play as the teacher in leading and promoting students to talk and learn about mathematics.

3. **Lesson Cards and Activity Cards.** Lesson Cards and Activity Cards are used to highlight a wide variety of instructional ideas. Lesson Cards summarize key questions and could serve as a skeletal outline for a specific lesson. Activity Cards focus on specific mathematical topics but are student oriented so they can be explored independently by children. Seventy-eight Activity Cards, or about half of those used in the textbook, are duplicated in a separate manual titled *Activity Cards for Helping Children Learn Mathematics* (ISBN 0-471-36525-4). The perforated edges and larger format enable future teachers and children to work effectively with each exercise. This booklet can be shrinkwrapped with the main text (ISBN 0-471-37637-X) or purchased separately. Here is a sample Activity Card; the checkmark in the upper right corner indicates that this Activity Card appears in the separate manual:

Activity Card 8–11

Multig

▼ Use the playing board here or make a larger one on heavy construction paper. Each player needs some buttons, macaroni, or chips for markers.

Don't forget the spinner. You can't play this game without it!

1. Take turns. Spin twice. Multiply the 2 numbers. Find the answer on the board. Put a marker on it.

2. Score 1 point for each covered ◊ that touches a side or corner of the ◊ you cover.

3. If you can't find an uncovered ◊ to cover, you lose your turn.

4. Opponents may challenge any time before the next player spins.

5. The winner is the player with the most points at the end of 10 rounds.

4. **Research Base.** A research base has been threaded throughout. As a teacher, you are often called on to provide a rationale for curricular or instructional decisions, and we think you will find this integration of relevant research, along with its implications, useful.

5. **Technology.** Technology, such as the calculator, is widely available to everyone—including young students. We recommend that calculators be used in schools, and we have integrated calculator activities throughout the book. As different uses of technology are experienced, their potential for stimulating learning becomes more obvious, and technology is used more freely and creatively.

6. **Computational Alternatives.** Computational alternatives—mental computation, estimation, written techniques, as well as calculators—are explicitly discussed in Chapter 9. Technology has increased the importance of students making wise choices among the computational alternatives, and we have included a new chapter that provides a balanced discussion of them.

7. **Encouraging Children to Construct Meaning.** As written techniques are developed, attention has been given to the value of encouraging young students to create, invent, construct, or use written methods that are meaningful for them. Much learning and understanding can be gained from exploring alternative algorithms, including some of the traditional algorithms that are part of our culture. However, tedious computational algorithms, such as long division, are de-emphasized. We believe that meaningful operations with numbers must be established, but our development focuses on understanding and facility with the computational alternatives and pays less attention to the painfully laborious task of crunching large numbers.

8. **Cultural and Gender Equity.** Equity—treating students of different sexes as well as different ethnic and cultural backgrounds similarly, with equal expectations—is an important issue in mathematics classes. We have reflected equity and provisions for individual differences in many ways—from the wide range of student abilities portrayed in the Snapshots of a Lesson to the Lesson Cards and Activity Cards. Our use of calculators and our integration and discussion of research findings provide further insight into equity issues as well as other individual differences. We think such discussions will be helpful in implementing a mathematical envi-

ronment that is positive and productive for everyone.

9. **Use of Children's Literature.** Literature is a powerful ally in learning and one that has often been under-used in mathematics classes. We have made direct efforts to identify books that might be effectively used to complement and supplement mathematics learning. In some cases, we have cited and discussed specific books within the text. In others, we have identified titles of books we have found useful in the Children's Corner, which appears at the end of many chapters.

10. **Things to Do.** Things to Do are found near the end of each chapter. These sections have been divided into two parts. One section relates directly to this book and is subtitled "From What You've Read." The other section is subtitled "Going Beyond This Book" and often includes explorations into other resources and references as well as some microteaching with children. All of the Things to Do embody our active learning/teaching approach to mathematics. These experiences are designed to engage you in inquiring and thinking about mathematics—investigations that will provide the greater understanding and insight that is needed to be a successful teacher.

11. **References.** Many helpful references (some new, some old—but all relevant) are listed at the end of each chapter to document research, as well as further illustrate ideas and other points made within the chapter. Some of these works discuss ideas that have been mentioned but space did not allow us to develop them to the extent we would like. Others elaborate and extend ideas that will promote greater insight and understanding.

12. **Resources.** We have provided addresses and phone numbers of major publishers and distributors of mathematics materials in Appendix C. Many valuable instructional resources exist to help you teach mathematics. The commercial manipulatives shown and used in this book, or mentioned in the end-of-chapter references, are available from different sources. It is useful to have catalogs from these publishers and distributors to learn what is available and how much the materials cost.

13. **Blackline Masters.** In our teaching, we have found certain materials to be frequently useful in a variety of ways. A number of these materials are included as blackline masters in Appendix B. These pages can be used as masters to make multiple copies for your students or to make a transparency for an overhead projector. As you teach and use these materials, we welcome feedback from you about other masters you would like to see in future editions.

Helping Children Learn Mathematics is not a workbook, but it is an ideabook. We believe that you will learn much from reading and talking about what you have read. The NCTM *Standards* have identified communication as an important part of mathematics learning, and this book is designed to encourage and facilitate communication.

It is not possible—or desirable—to establish exact steps to follow in teaching mathematics. Too much depends on what is being taught, to whom, and at what levels. In your classroom, it is you who will ultimately decide what to teach, to whom to teach it, how to teach it, and the amount of time to spend. This book will not answer all of these questions for you, but we think you will find it very helpful in making wise decisions as you guide elementary school students in their learning of mathematics. We believe this book will be a valuable teaching resource that can be used again and again in your classroom long after the course has been completed.

As we complete this fifth edition of *Helping Children Learn Mathematics,* we welcome Nancy Smith to the author team. Nancy is an experienced elementary teacher and has also prepared the Instructor's Manual for our book.

We wish to acknowledge the many family members, friends, colleagues, and students who have contributed in various ways. We thank our mathematics education colleagues who have shared particular insight and helpful suggestions—especially Barbara Reys, University of Missouri, and Douglas Grouws, University of Iowa.

We acknowledge the help of specific reviewers of the fifth edition, including Daniel Brahier, Bowling Green State University; Claire J. Graham, Framingham State University; Janet Handler, Mount Mercy College; Susan E. Johnson, Northwestern College; William Merrill, Central Michigan University; Don Ploger, Florida Atlantic University; and Thomas A. Romberg, University of Wisconsin. We also wish to recognize the help of reviewers for previous editions, including Roda P. Amaria, Salem State College; Bernard Arnez, Southwest Missouri State University; Tom Bassarear, Keene State College; Grace M. Burton, University of North Carolina, Wilmington; Bert Crossland, University of North Texas; Bob M. Drake, University of Cincinnati; Jane E. Drucker, Temple University; Marvel Froemming,

Moorhead State University; Ellen Hines, Northern Illinois University; Robert L. Jackson, University of Minnesota, Twin Cities; W. Tad Johnston, University of Maine; Mary Kabiri, Lincoln University; Rick Kruschinsky, University of St. Thomas; Robert Matulis, Millersville University; Kay Meeks, Ball State University; Lucy Orsan, Kean College; Jacelyn Marie Rees, McNeese State University; Mary Ellen Schmidt, The Ohio State University; Juan Vazquez, Missouri Southern State College; Margaret C. Wyckoff, University of Maine, Farmington; and Bernard R. Yvon, University of Maine.

We especially thank our students for their willingness to read earlier drafts of this book and provide helpful comments and suggestions. And we also thank the many teachers and professors who have talked with us and written to us with ideas designed to extend this book's usefulness. We have tried to incorporate many of their suggestions into this fifth edition. We extend to each of you an invitation to continue to share your thoughts and communicate your suggestions for future changes. To facilitate that exchange, you may contact any of us; send an e-mail to cirr@showme.missouri.edu, or contact us via snail mail if you prefer. Regardless of how you choose to communicate, your ideas and suggestions are both encouraged and appreciated.

R. E. R.
M. N. S.
M. M. L.
N. L. S.

1

The Changing Elementary School Mathematics Program

 ## Introduction

Soon you will be walking into a classroom, responsible for helping a group of children learn mathematics—as well as many other things. What mathematics will you be teaching? How will you teach it? This book will help you gain a clearer understanding of the answers to those two questions.

You will also be asking other questions, as all teachers must, including these:

- What mathematical knowledge and understanding will the children in my classroom have as they begin the year?
- What mathematical ideas do they need to learn?
- What am I expected to teach?
- How can each child, different in many ways from the others, be taught so that he or she will learn?

The answers to such questions provide the framework for the elementary school mathematics program in each classroom. From them, you can outline specific objectives to be accomplished, organize instructional materials, and plan daily lessons. No matter what age children you teach, you will probably have several general goals:

- To help children learn specific mathematical content (facts, skills, and concepts)

- To help children learn how to apply mathematical ideas to solve problems
- To foster a positive attitude toward mathematics

Developing lessons that teach a range of mathematical content to the children in your class will be considered in later chapters of this book. Our first concern is with the curriculum—the scope and sequence of the mathematics program—that has evolved through the years and is continuing to change.

You will find that you are entering the teaching field at a particularly exciting time. The curriculum in mathematics, as well as in many other subject areas, is being adapted to the changing needs of our society, changing knowledge about how children learn, and changing viewpoints of mathematics, many of which have been brought about by technology.

The National Council of Teachers of Mathematics (NCTM), the largest organization for teachers of mathematics in the world, has been at the forefront in laying the foundation for this curricular change. In 1989, the NCTM published the first of three sets of standards designed to provide goals for curriculum, instruction, and assessment. We will discuss these in more detail later in this chapter, and you will find references to them throughout the book. They are affecting the teaching of mathematics in the 1990s and promise to have a long-range impact as we move into the twenty-first century.

● What Is Mathematics?

Frequently, people equate mathematics and arithmetic. Arithmetic is concerned with numbers. When considering the mathematics curriculum, some people focus on the computational skills of arithmetic—addition, subtraction, multiplication, and division with whole numbers, fractions, and decimals—and believe that these constitute the full set of competencies that children must have in mathematics. However, mathematics involves far more than computation.

1. Mathematics is a *study of patterns and relationships.* Children need to become aware of recurring ideas and of relationships between and among mathematical ideas. These relationships and ideas provide a unifying thread throughout the curriculum, because each topic is interwoven with others that have preceded it. Children must come to see how one idea is like or unlike others already learned. For instance, children in second grade can consider how one basic fact (say 3 + 2 = 5) is related to another basic fact (say 5 − 3 = 2). Or children in later grades can consider the effect that changing the perimeter of a figure has on its area.

2. Mathematics is a *way of thinking.* It provides us with strategies for organizing, analyzing, and synthesizing data, largely but not exclusively numerical. People who are comfortable with mathematics use it as they meet everyday problems. For example, some people write an equation to solve an everyday problem. Others form tables to record information or to develop an analogy with several related items.

3. Mathematics is an *art,* characterized by order and internal consistency. Many children think of mathematics as a confusing set of discrete facts and skills that must be memorized. Because teachers tend to focus on developing the skills required to "do" mathematics, they may forget that children need to be guided to recognize and appreciate the underlying orderliness and consistency as they construct their own understanding of mathematics.

4. Mathematics is a *language,* using carefully defined terms and symbols. These terms and symbols enhance our ability to communicate about science, real-life situations, and mathematics itself.

5. Mathematics is a *tool.* It is what mathematicians use, and it is also used by everyone in the course of daily life. Thus, children can come to appreciate why they are learning the facts, skills, and concepts that the school program involves.

They, too, can use mathematics to solve both abstract and practical problems, just as mathematicians do. Mathematics is useful or even a prerequisite for many occupations and vocations.

● What Determines the Mathematics Being Taught?

Mathematics plays a prominent role in the elementary school program. It is second only to reading in the amount of time devoted to it and in the amount of money spent for curricular materials. Its importance is, in fact, reflected in the degree of concern about it recurrently voiced by parents and other members of the public.

What is this curriculum about which people are concerned? There is no national curriculum guide for elementary school mathematics in the United States. Yet there has been a great deal of similarity in the content of most elementary school mathematics textbook series. Both state and local curriculum guides (where they exist) tend to parallel this same content. There are some differences in sequence, but for the most part there has been a surprising degree of agreement on the order in which topics will be introduced.

How did this consensus come about? Three general factors influence the mathematics curriculum and play roles in its evolution:

- Needs of the subject
- Needs of the child
- Needs of society

Needs of the Subject

The nature of mathematics has helped to determine what is taught and when it is taught in elementary grades. Whole numbers are the basis for many mathematical ideas; moreover, experiences with them arise long before children come to school. Thus, whole-number work is stressed first. Work with rational numbers logically follows work with whole numbers. Such seemingly "natural" sequences are the result of long years of curricular evolution. This process has involved much analysis of what constitutes a progression from easy to difficult, based in part on what is deemed necessary at one level for the development of ideas at later levels.

Once a curriculum is in place for a long time, however, people tend to consider it the only proper sequence. Thus, to omit a topic or to change the sequence of topics often involves a struggle for acceptance.

Sometimes the process of change is aided by an event, such as when the Soviet Union sent the first Sputnik into orbit. The shock of this evidence of another country's technological superiority sped curriculum change in the United States. The "new math" of the 1950s and 1960s was the result, and millions of dollars were channeled into mathematics and science education to strengthen school programs.

Mathematicians became integrally involved, and because of their interests and the perceived weaknesses of previous curricula, they developed curricula based on the needs of the subject. Emphasis was shifted from social usefulness to such unifying themes as the structure of mathematics, operations and their inverses, systems of notation, properties of numbers, and set language. Not only was new content added at the elementary school level, but also some old topics were introduced at lower grade levels.

Mathematics continues to change; new mathematics is created and new uses of mathematics are discovered. Technology has made some mathematics obsolete and has opened the door for other mathematics. No one knows exactly what mathematics will be needed for the twenty-first century, but it is clear that students will need to know how to reason mathematically and how to apply mathematical thinking to a wide range of situations.

Needs of the Child

Clearly, the mathematics curriculum has been influenced by beliefs about how children learn. Until the early years of this century, mathematics was taught to train "mental faculties" or provide "mental discipline." Struggling with mathematical procedures was thought to exercise the mind, helping it work more effectively.

Around the turn of the century, mental discipline was replaced by *connectionism*, dominated by the thinking of Edward Thorndike. The stimulus–response theory, which deemed it necessary to establish strong bonds or connections, resulted in an emphasis on speed and accuracy, attained by repeated drill. Much stress was placed on identifying specific skills to be mastered and on the relative difficulty of the various topics. Precise placement of topics seemed vital, leading to such practices as introducing 7×3 a full year before introducing 3×7. Standardized tests were developed and normed so that children could be graded according to their attainment of mathematical skills. In turn, teachers resorted to endless drill in an attempt to ensure high scores on the tests.

In reaction to the strictures of a drill-based program, and under the influence of writers such as John Dewey, the Progressive Movement in the 1920s advocated *incidental learning*. It was believed that children would learn as much arithmetic as they needed and would learn it better if arithmetic was not systematically taught. The teacher was to make use of situations as they occurred and to create situations in which arithmetic would arise.

During the late 1920s, a committee of school superintendents and principals from midwestern cities surveyed pupils to find out when topics were mastered (Washburne 1931). They then suggested the mental age at which each topic should be taught. Thus, subtraction facts under 10 were to be taught to children with a mental age of 6 years 7 months and facts over 10 at 7 years 8 months; subtraction with borrowing or carrying was to be taught at 8 years 9 months. The Committee of Seven had a strong impact on the sequencing of the curriculum for years to come.

Another change in thinking occurred in the mid-1930s, as *field,* or *Gestalt, theory* was advanced. Greater emphasis was placed on a planned program to encourage the development of insight and the understanding of relationships, structure, patterns, interpretations, and principles. This contributed to a shift to concern for *meaning and understanding*, with William Brownell as a prominent spokesperson. Learning was seen as a meaningful process. The value of drill was noted, but it was placed after understanding; drill no longer was the major means of sequencing the curriculum and providing instruction.

Changes in psychology have continued. Educators have come to believe that the developmental level of the child is also a factor in determining the sequence of the curriculum. Topics cannot be taught until a child is developmentally ready to learn them. Or, from another point of view, topics must be taught in such a way that children at a given developmental level are ready to learn them.

Increasingly, educators' attention is drawn to the evidence that children *construct* their own knowledge; to help children learn mathematics, teachers must be aware of how the children have constructed mathematics from their experiences both in and out of school. Such ideas and inferences have been taken into consideration as the curriculum has evolved. These factors will be considered in Chapter 2.

Needs of Society

The practicality and usefulness of mathematics in everyday situations and in many vocations has also affected what is taught and when it is taught. This has been true since colonial times, when mathematics was considered necessary primarily for clerks and bookkeepers. The curriculum was limited to counting, the simpler procedures for addition, subtraction, and multiplication, and some knowledge of measures and of fractions. Much of the computation was with denominate numbers involving measures in commercial use (such as 3 feet 5 inches).

By the late nineteenth century, business and commerce had increased to the point that mathematics was considered important for everyone. The arithmetic curriculum expanded to include such topics as percentage, ratio and proportion, powers, roots, and series.

The emphasis on teaching what was needed for use in occupations continued into the twentieth century. One of the most vocal advocates of *social utility* was Guy Wilson (1948). He and his students conducted numerous surveys to determine what arithmetic was actually used by carpenters, shopkeepers, and other workers. He believed that the "dominating" aim of the school mathematics program should be to teach those skills, and only those skills.

We have already noted the outburst of public concern in the 1950s, when the desire to improve the curriculum so that the United States wouldn't fall behind in the "space race" resulted in a wave of curriculum development and research in mathematics. Much of this effort was focused on the mathematically talented student. In the mid-1960s, however, concern was also expressed for the disadvantaged student as U.S. society renewed its search for equality of opportunity. With these changes—in fact, with *each* change—more and better mathematical achievement was promised.

In the 1970s, when it became apparent that once again the promise had not fully materialized, there was another swing in the curricular curve. Renewed emphasis was placed on skills needed for "survival" in the real world. The minimal-competency movement stressed the basics. As embodied in sets of objectives and in tests, the basics were considered to be primarily addition, subtraction, multiplication, and division with whole numbers and fractions. Thus, the skills needed by children in colonial times were again considered by many to be the sole necessities for children living in a world with calculators and computers.

As we move toward the twenty-first century, we see dramatic changes in the needs of society. No longer will it suffice for only a few to be mathematically literate. Our society needs a citizenry and a work force that can solve problems, reason mathematically, process and interpret data, and communicate in a technological world. Changes in mathematics programs are needed in order to prepare students for life in today's society.

● What Mathematics Should Be Taught?

In 1989, the National Council of Teachers of Mathematics took a decisive step toward improving the teaching of mathematics with the publication of *Curriculum and Evaluation Standards for School Mathematics*. This work represents the current major effort "to create a set of standards to guide the revision of the school mathematics curriculum and its associated evaluation" (NCTM 1989, p. 1) in order to develop a mathematically literate citizenry, and the *Curriculum and Evaluation Standards* are to be used "to ensure quality, to indicate goals, and to promote change" (p. 2).

At each grade level, the NCTM *Standards* emphasize problem solving, communicating mathematics in a range of representational modes, mathematical reasoning, and mathematical connections. These emphases reflect the assumptions from which the content-specific standards for each grade level were developed.

Figure 1–1 provides a synthesis of the assumptions behind the thirteen standards for grades K through 4, which are shown in Figure 1–2. Similarly, Figure 1–3 synthesizes the assumptions underlying the thirteen standards for grades 5 through 8, which are given in Figure 1–4. (Note that there is also a set of standards for grades 9 through 12.)

The K–4 curriculum should
- Be conceptually oriented
- Actively involve children in doing mathematics
- Emphasize the development of children's mathematical thinking and reasoning abilities
- Emphasize the application of mathematics
- Include a broad range of content
- Make appropriate and ongoing use of calculators and computers

Figure 1–1 ● **Assumptions underlying NCTM standards for grades K–4**   (Reprinted with permission from *Curriculum and Evaluation Standards for School Mathematics*, © 1989 by the National Council of Teachers of Mathematics.)

NCTM Curriculum Standards for School Mathematics: Grades K–4

1. Mathematics as Problem Solving: Students will
   - Use problem-solving approaches to investigate and understand mathematical content
   - Formulate problems
   - Develop and apply strategies to solve a wide variety of problems
   - Verify and interpret results
   - Acquire confidence in using mathematics meaningfully

2. Mathematics as Communication: Students will
   - Relate physical materials, pictures, and diagrams to mathematical ideas
   - Reflect on and clarify their thinking about mathematical ideas and situations
   - Relate their everyday language to mathematical language and symbols
   - Realize that representing, discussing, reading, writing, and listening to mathematics are a vital part of learning and using mathematics

3. Mathematics as Reasoning: Students will
   - Draw logical conclusions about mathematics
   - Use models, known facts, properties, and relationships to explain their thinking
   - Justify their answers and solution processes
   - Use patterns and relationships to analyze mathematical situations
   - Believe that mathematics makes sense

4. Mathematical connections: Students will
   - Link conceptual and procedural knowledge
   - Relate various representations of concepts or procedures to one another
   - Recognize relationships among different topics in mathematics
   - Use mathematics in other curriculum areas
   - Use mathematics in their daily lives

5. Estimation: Students will
   - Explore estimation strategies
   - Recognize when an estimate is appropriate
   - Determine the reasonableness of results
   - Apply estimation in working with quantities, measurement, computation, and problem solving

6. Number Sense and Numeration: Students will
   - Construct number meanings through real-world experiences and use of physical materials
   - Understand our numeration system by relating counting, grouping, and place-value concepts
   - Develop number sense
   - Interpret the multiple uses of numbers encountered in the real world

7. Concepts of Whole-Number Operations: Students will
   - Develop meaning for the operations by modeling and discussing a rich variety of problem situations
   - Relate mathematical language and symbolism of operations to problem situations and informal language
   - Recognize that a wide variety of problem structures can be represented by a single operation
   - Develop operation sense

8. Whole-Number Computation: Students will
   - Model, explain, and develop reasonable proficiency with basic facts and algorithms
   - Use a variety of mental computation and estimation techniques
   - Use calculators in appropriate computational situations
   - Select and use computation techniques appropriate to specific problems and determine whether results are reasonable

9. Geometry and Spatial Sense: Students will
   - Describe, model, draw, and classify shapes
   - Investigate and predict results of combining, subdividing, and changing shapes
   - Develop spatial sense
   - Relate geometric ideas to number and measurement ideas
   - Recognize and appreciate geometry in their world

10. Measurement: Students will
    - Understand attributes of length, capacity, weight, area, volume, time, temperature, and angle
    - Develop the process of measuring and concepts related to units of measurement
    - Make and use estimates of measurement
    - Make and use measurements in problems and everyday situations

11. Statistics and Probability: Students will
    - Collect, organize, and describe data
    - Construct, read, and interpret displays of data
    - Formulate and solve problems that involve collecting and analyzing data
    - Explore concepts of chance   *(continues)*

Figure 1–2 • NCTM curriculum standards for grades K–4 (From *Curriculum and Evaluation Standards for School Mathematics,* NCTM 1989. Used by permission.)

12. **Fractions and Decimals:** Students will
    - Develop concepts of fractions, mixed numbers, and decimals
    - Develop number sense for fractions and decimals
    - Use models to relate fractions to decimals and to find equivalent fractions
    - Use models to explore operations of fractions and decimals
    - Apply fractions and decimals to problem situations

13. **Patterns and Relationships:** Students will
    - Recognize, describe, extend, and create a wide variety of patterns
    - Represent and describe mathematical relationships
    - Explore use of variables and open sentences to express relationships

Figure 1–2 ● **Continued**

Throughout this book you will notice references to points highlighted or stressed by the NCTM *Standards,* and they are referred to in many current articles as well. The *Standards* have exciting promise for helping teachers to reshape the mathematics curriculum and how it is taught. Moreover, they include some specific suggestions on what emphases in the curriculum should be decreased and increased (see Appendix A).

The curriculum and evaluation standards were followed by the release of *Professional Standards for Teaching Mathematics* (NCTM 1991). The focus of this second set of standards is on providing guidance for how mathematics should be taught, envisioning a different kind of teaching from the way many teachers themselves were taught. Five major shifts are needed "to move from current practice to mathematics teaching for the empowerment of students," including shifts:

- Toward classrooms as mathematical communities—away from classrooms as simply a collection of individuals
- Toward logic and mathematical evidence as verification—away from the teacher as the sole authority for right answers
- Toward mathematical reasoning—away from merely memorizing procedures
- Toward conjecturing, inventing, and problem solving—away from an emphasis on mechanistic answer finding
- Toward connecting mathematics, its ideas, and its applications—away from treating mathematics as a body of isolated concepts and procedures (NCTM 1991, p. 3)

A third set of NCTM standards focuses on assessment. These standards promote the criteria that teachers and others can use to develop assessment practices that will aid all students in developing mathematical power. As Figure 1–5 indicates, these standards are concise: vignettes and examples in the document show how teachers and others can use the standards as alternative ways of assessing mathematics learning. We will discuss all these standards further in Chapter 4. Thus, the scope of the curriculum, ways of helping children learn that content, and means of ascertaining whether these have been effective are integrated to provide guid-

- Problem situations should serve as the context for mathematics.
- Communication with and about mathematics and mathematical reasoning should permeate the curriculum.
- A broad range of topics should be taught, with connections among them emphasized.
- Technology, including calculators, computers, and videotapes, should be used when appropriate.
- Learning activities should incorporate topics and ideas across standards.
- Learning should engage students both intellectually and physically: they must become active learners.
- Classroom activities should provide students with the opportunity to work individually and in small and large groups.
- Every classroom should have ample sets of manipulative materials, resource materials on problems and ideas for explorations, calculators, and computers.

Figure 1–3 ● **Assumptions underlying NCTM standards for grades 5–8** (From *Curriculum and Evaluation Standards for School Mathematics,* NCTM 1989. Used by permission.)

NCTM Curriculum Standards for School Mathematics: Grades 5–8

1. Mathematics as Problem Solving: Students will

    - Use problem-solving approaches to investigate and understand mathematical content
    - Formulate problems from situations within and outside mathematics
    - Develop and apply a variety of strategies to solve problems, with emphasis on multistep and non-routine problems
    - Verify and interpret results
    - Generalize solutions and strategies to new problem situations
    - Acquire confidence in using mathematics meaningfully

2. Mathematics as Communication: Students will

    - Model situations using oral, written, concrete, pictorial, graphical, and algebraic methods
    - Reflect on and clarify thinking about mathematical ideas and situations
    - Develop common understandings of mathematical ideas, including the role of definitions
    - Use the skills of reading, listening, and viewing to interpret and evaluate mathematical ideas
    - Discuss mathematical ideas and make conjectures and convincing arguments
    - Appreciate the value of mathematical notation and its role in the development of mathematical ideas

3. Mathematics as Reasoning: Students will

    - Recognize and apply deductive and inductive reasoning
    - Understand and apply reasoning processes, with special attention to spatial reasoning and reasoning with proportions and graphs
    - Make and evaluate mathematical conjectures and arguments
    - Validate their own thinking
    - Appreciate the pervasive use and power of reasoning as a part of mathematics

4. Mathematical Connections: Students will

    - See mathematics as an integrated whole
    - Explore problems and describe results using graphical, numerical, physical, algebraic, and verbal mathematical models or representations
    - Use a mathematical idea to further understanding of other mathematical ideas

    - Apply mathematical thinking and modeling to solve problems arising in other disciplines
    - Value the role of mathematics in our culture and society

5. Number and Number Relationships: Students will

    - Understand, represent, and use numbers in a variety of equivalent forms in problem situations
    - Develop number sense for whole numbers, fractions, decimals, integers, and rational numbers
    - Understand and apply ratios, proportions, and percents
    - Investigate relationships among fractions, decimals, and percents
    - Represent numerical relationships in one- and two-dimensional graphs

6. Number Systems and Number Theory: Students will

    - Understand and appreciate the need for numbers beyond the whole numbers
    - Develop and use order relations for whole numbers, fractions, decimals, integers, and rational numbers
    - Extend understanding of whole-number operations to fractions, decimals, integers, and rational numbers
    - Understand how the basic arithmetic operations are related; develop and apply number theory concepts

7. Computation and Estimation: Students will

    - Compute with whole numbers, fractions, decimals, integers and rational numbers
    - Develop, analyze, and explain procedures for computation and techniques for estimation
    - Develop, analyze, and explain methods for solving proportions
    - Select and use an appropriate method for computing from among mental arithmetic, paper and pencil, calculator, and computer methods
    - Use computation, estimation, and proportions to solve problems
    - Use estimation to check the reasonableness of results

8. Patterns and Functions: Students will

    - Describe, extend, analyze, and create a wide variety of patterns   *(continues)*

Figure 1–4 • NCTM curriculum standards for grades 5–8   (From *Curriculum and Evaluation Standards for School Mathematics,* NCTM 1989. Used by permission.)

- Describe and represent relationships with tables, graphs, and rules
- Analyze functional relationships to explain how a change in one quantity results in a change in another
- Use patterns and functions to represent and solve problems

9. Algebra: Students will

- Understand the concepts of variable, expression, and equation
- Represent situations and number patterns with tables, graphs, verbal rules, and equations, and explore the interrelationships
- Analyze tables and graphs to identify properties and relationships
- Develop confidence in solving linear equations using concrete, informal, and formal methods
- Investigate inequalities and nonlinear equations informally
- Apply algebraic methods to solve a variety of problems

10. Statistics: Students will

- Systematically collect, organize and describe data
- Construct, read, and interpret tables, charts, and graphs
- Make inferences and convincing arguments based on data analysis
- Evaluate arguments based on data analysis
- Develop an appreciation for statistical methods as powerful means for decision making

11. Probability: Students will

- Model situations by devising and carrying out experiments or simulations to determine probabilities
- Model situations by constructing a sample space to determine probabilities

- Appreciate the power of using a probability model by comparing experimental results with mathematical expectations
- Make predictions based on experimental or theoretical probabilities
- Develop an appreciation of the pervasive use of probability in the real world

12. Geometry: Students will

- Identify, describe, compare, and classify geometric figures
- Visualize and represent geometric figures with special attention to developing spatial sense
- Explore transformations of geometric figures
- Represent and solve problems using geometric models
- Understand and apply geometric properties and relationships
- Develop an appreciation of geometry as a means of describing the physical world

13. Measurement: Students will

- Extend understanding of the process of measurement
- Estimate, make and use measurements to describe and compare phenomena
- Select appropriate units and tools to measure to the degree of accuracy required in a particular situation
- Understand the structure and use of systems of measurement
- Extend understanding of the concepts of perimeter, area, volume, angle measure, capacity, and weight and mass
- Develop the concepts of rates and other derived and indirect measurements
- Develop formulas and procedures for determining measures to solve problems

Figure 1–4 ● **Continued**

ance for changing mathematics instruction to meet the needs of the 1990s and beyond.

● **What Forces Affect the Curriculum?**

As we have noted, the curriculum is affected by the needs of society, the student, and the subject, mathematics. The NCTM *Standards* illustrate

that the curriculum can also be affected by other factors.

Educational Organizations

In addition to the NCTM, other educational organizations have at times established commissions, panels, or committees to provide a status report on the curriculum (or some aspect of it) and to develop recommendations for proposed change. A report

NCTM Assessment Standards for School Mathematics

1. The Mathematics Standard
   - Assessment should reflect the mathematics that all students need to know and be able to do.

2. The Learning Standard
   - Assessment should enhance mathematics learning.

3. The Equity Standard
   - Assessment should promote equity.

4. The Openness Standard
   - Assessment should be an open process.

5. The Inferences Standard
   - Assessment should promote valid inferences about mathematics learning.

6. The Coherence Standard
   - Assessment should be a coherent process.

Figure 1–5 • **NCTM assessment standards** (From NCTM 1995. Used by permission.)

NCTM Recommendations in *An Agenda for Action*—1980

1. Problem solving must be the focus of school mathematics in the 1980s.
2. The concept of basic skills in mathematics must encompass more than computational facility.
3. Mathematics programs must take full advantage of the power of calculators and computers at all grade levels.
4. Stringent standards of both effectiveness and efficiency must be applied to the teaching of mathematics.
5. The success of mathematics programs and student learning must be evaluated by a wider range of measures than conventional testing.
6. More mathematics study must be required for all students and a flexible curriculum with a greater range of options should be designed to accommodate the diverse needs of the student population.
7. Mathematics teachers must demand of themselves and their colleagues a high level of professionalism.
8. Public support for mathematics instruction must be raised to a level commensurate with the importance of mathematical understanding to individuals and society.

Figure 1–6 • **Recommendations in *An Agenda for Action*** (From NCTM 1980. Used by permission.)

that had a decided impact in the 1970s was prepared by the National Advisory Committee on Mathematical Education (NACOME). It provided an extensive overview and analysis of school mathematics in kindergarten through grade 12. The curriculum reforms of 1955 to 1975 were analyzed and new curricular emphases considered. Both curriculum content and curriculum development were addressed. In introducing its recommendations on content, the report noted:

> Curriculum content, subject to the flux of accelerating change in all areas of our society, cannot be viewed as a fixed set of goals or ideas; it must be allowed to emerge, ever changing, responsive to the human and technological lessons of the past, concerns of the present, and hopes for the future. With this in mind, no definitive curriculum can ever be recommended. (NACOME 1975, p. 138)

Five years after the NACOME report, the NCTM issued a set of recommendations in the form of *An Agenda for Action: Recommendations for School Mathematics of the 1980s* (NCTM 1980). The eight recommendations in the agenda are listed in Figure 1–6.

The emphasis on problem solving and the use of calculators and computers is clear in the NCTM recommendations.

In the 1980s, public concern was heightened by a series of reports, most notably *A Nation at Risk: The Imperative for Educational Reform* (National Commission on Excellence in Education 1983), which linked economic difficulties with problems in our schools. The wave of concern led to the formation of the Mathematical Sciences Education Board in 1985. Composed of organizations involved in mathematics education, the Board strives to provide national leadership in promoting needed changes in curriculum, instruction, and evaluation. The efforts in the 1980s culminated in the release of the NCTM *Standards* (NCTM 1989, 1991, 1995), which represent the latest steps in ongoing efforts to provide for children a mathematics program to meet current and anticipated needs.

Research

Research has also influenced curriculum change. Research-based knowledge can be of help in implementing such change. A noteworthy example is the testing program of the National Assessment of Educational Progress (see Lindquist et al. 1989; Kenney and Silver 1997; Mullis et al. 1991). These assessments, occurring at intervals of several years, have provided evidence on how well students are learning certain content (for example, addition) and how poorly they are doing on other content (for example, problem solving). Concern about weakness in the latter has been voiced by many educators, and problem solving continues to be a leading candidate for curriculum change.

Another example is provided by international assessments of mathematical achievement. The most recent of these is the Third International Mathematics and Science Study (TIMSS), providing information collected from 1991 to 1995 in more than 40 countries (*Pursuing Excellence* 1996). It has five different parts: (1) assessments of student achievement at five grade levels; (2) questionnaires for students, teachers, and schools at those grades; (3) analyses of textbooks and curriculum guides; (4) videotapes of classroom instruction in the United States, Germany, and Japan; and (5) case studies of the educational context in those three countries.

Overall, U.S. eighth graders were slightly below the average mathematics achievement of students from other countries. They were above average in probability and statistics, average in algebra and arithmetic, but below average in geometry and measurement. Thus, this indicates that more attention should be given to such topics as geometry and measurement.

Technology

Technology is changing people's everyday lives, so it is not surprising that technology should affect what goes on in schools. Although television, videotapes, and other technology have played some role in mathematics instruction, computing technology has clearly played the biggest role.

Since the mid-1970s, the availability of low-cost calculators has resulted in debates about their usefulness and, indeed, about whether they should be used at all in schools. The NCTM and other mathematics organizations have taken a strong stand in support of their use, a position that is strongly supported by research (Hembree and Dessart 1986).

When the microcomputer began to enter schools around 1980, it was warmly embraced by mathematics teachers and students. Its usefulness in teaching mathematics had been apparent from work with previous generations of computers, and it appeared to be less threatening to established curriculum and practices than did the calculator (Suydam 1988).

In both cases, however, the usefulness of computer hardware rested with the availability of appropriate applications and software, and with teachers knowing how to use it effectively. The NCTM *Standards* (1989) repeated its previous statements that the use of calculators and computers must be integrated into mathematics instruction at all grade levels.

Threats to National Security and the Economy

War is a threat to national security that has affected the mathematics curriculum. During World Wars I and II, concerns about the mathematical competency of draftees led to inquiries about change. In addition, wars have tended to generate new applications of mathematics and even new mathematics, thus spurring curriculum revision.

We have already noted the threat raised when the Soviet Union launched the first Sputnik. This event challenged the United States as the world's scientific leader and resulted in the massive curriculum development effort of the late 1950s. The "new math" projects resulted in cooperation among mathematics educators, mathematicians, and psychologists to develop new curricular materials.

In the 1980s, a concern about security arose from perceived threats to the economy. This concern involved the amount of mathematics children in other countries—especially the Soviet Union and Japan—were being taught in school and how well they were doing on tests in comparison to children in the United States. Fear arose that a better mathematics background might give other countries an advantage, especially in terms of technology, and an ability to do better than the United States in applying mathematics for economic gains. Thus, a "national goal" was articulated that this country should become "number one" in the world in science and mathematics in the 1990s.

Government

The major curriculum development projects initiated in the late 1950s had federal funding for all or part of their activities. For the first time, federal agencies became involved in curriculum development on a massive scale, and they attempted to fund a variety of types of projects in order to provide alternatives, rather than to control the direction of the development activities.

In addition to the funding provided by federal agencies such as the National Science Foundation and the National Institute of Education, which were responsible for funding multitudes of research, curriculum development, teacher training, and equipment proposals, legislation provided other funds. For example, the National Defense Education Act provided money for equipment to schools, and the Elementary and Secondary Education Acts supplied funds for improving instructional programs. Money was specifically earmarked for remedial teachers in such areas as mathematics. More recently, the Eisenhower Grants program has provided funds to assist teachers in improving mathematics instruction in their classrooms and also to enhance their professional development. Still other projects and programs are being developed in the 1990s with funding from the National Science Foundation.

Textbooks

Textbooks are the primary determinant of the mathematics curriculum that is actually being taught. State curriculum guides present an outline that can be filled in by use of a textbook; local guides resemble textbooks in scope and sequence.

The evidence indicates that there appears to be a rather firm adherence to "covering the material" in the text, although sections that teachers do not consider important (and that may be given little attention on standardized tests) may be ignored. Nevertheless, the textbook does influence what is learned. Different patterns of achievement have been associated with the use of different textbooks.

For the past several decades, textbooks have shown support for the NCTM recommendations and standards. Their advertisements particularly highlighted problem solving after the appearance of *An Agenda for Action* (NCTM 1980), and have similarly indicated the changes made to incorporate major points from each of the sets of standards. Naturally enough, what appeared on the textbook pages varied—yet a message of change was being carried to the teachers and, to some extent, has influenced what they do in their classrooms.

The textbook analysis conducted by the TIMSS in 1993 indicated that curriculum guides and textbooks in the U.S. contain more topics at each grade level through grade 8 than do those in other countries, and there is less emphasis on each topic at any grade level (*Pursuing Excellence* 1996). Many topics are introduced and kept in the curriculum much longer than in other countries. For example, U.S. students in grades 7 and 8 spent time reviewing and drilling on arithmetic. Thus, they had less opportunity to study other important topics.

Testing

Tests can be a means of controlling a curriculum or instigating curricular change. If schools rely on the results of tests for certain purposes, then they want their students to do well on those tests. To accomplish this goal, they must teach the content that the tests cover. Thus, when the College Entrance Examination Board included "new math" content on its test, schools were forced to consider that new content seriously.

Tests can also act to retard curricular change, however, by excluding new content. Thus, efforts to effect widespread use of calculators were hindered because tests (as well as textbooks) were slow to reflect the existence of new procedures. However, calculators have become more commonplace in testing in the 1990s.

Competency tests provide another example of tests acting to retard curricular change. Such tests have tended to focus on computation, thereby increasing the importance of computational skill rather than decreasing it, contrary to recommendations in the NCTM *Standards* of 1989 and many other sets of recommendations, as well.

One of the first tasks set by the Mathematical Sciences Education Board in 1985 was to study in depth the role of testing, with a view toward changing both attitudes toward testing, and current testing practices. A high priority for the Board was to encourage the inclusion of new content and new methods, so that tests would evaluate thinking skills. Many states have since developed assessment projects to explore alternative means of assessment. Chapter 4 of this book discusses of a variety of techniques to use in assessing learning, and the references list a number of articles and books that can help teachers make changes consistent with their goals.

● What Curricular Content Has Been Proposed as Essential?

Long before the NCTM *Standards* (NCTM 1989, 1991) stressed the need to select "important" content to teach, attention had been periodically focused on what curricular content is essential for all students. Four sets of suggestions that emerged at different times were based on the assumption that school mathematics programs must meet societal needs by preparing individuals to live and work in the adult world.

The Drill Load of Arithmetic

This program was proposed by Guy Wilson on the basis of his surveys of the arithmetic actually used by workers. He concluded that

> 90 percent of adult figuring is covered by the four fundamental processes, addition, subtraction, multiplication, and division [of whole numbers]. Simple fractions, percentage, and interest, if added to the four fundamental processes, will raise the percentage to over 95 percent. (Wilson 1948, p. 337)

Thus, Wilson arrived at "a very simple load for drill mastery." For example, for addition he proposed that all children master 100 primary facts, 300 related decade facts, 80 other facts needed for multiplication to 9 × 9, simple columns and examples with sums to 39 + 9, and U.S. money.

Key Concepts for Postwar Programs

World War II not only revealed the need for mathematical competencies at many levels, but also led to the development of new mathematical ideas and new applications of mathematics. The Commission on Postwar Plans of the NCTM (1947) developed a list of twenty-nine key concepts that defined functional competence for junior high school mathematics students.

In addition to such topics as computation, percents, ratio, square root, and geometric concepts, the key concepts in the guidance report prepared by the commission included estimation, tables and graphs, statistics, algebra, and trigonometry. Practicality was also reflected in the report's "first steps in business arithmetic" and "stretching the dollar."

Skills Essential for Enlightened Citizens

Another NCTM committee was appointed in 1970 to draw up a list of basic mathematical competencies, skills, and attitudes necessary for citizens in contemporary society (Edwards et al. 1972). The

committee's report noted continuing changes in mathematics and the impact of new technology.

This committee presented a detailed list of skills and competencies needed by the majority of adults, characteristics of mathematics as a system, and understandings about the role of mathematics in society. These ideas broadened the scope of what the mathematics curriculum should encompass and suggested that mathematics should be taught not merely as a collection of facts and skills, but as a necessary and enjoyable component of living.

Essential Skill Areas

In response to what mathematics educators perceived as a potentially dangerous narrowing of the mathematics curriculum by those advocating a "return to the basics" in the 1970s, the National Council of Supervisors of Mathematics prepared its "Position Paper on Basic Mathematical Skills" (NCSM 1977). This position paper argued that far more than computational skills were needed, and it identified ten basic skill areas and rationalized the expanded definition of basic skills as follows:

> The present technological society requires use of such skills as estimating, problem solving, interpreting data, organizing data, measuring, predicting, and applying mathematics to everyday situations. The changing needs of society, the explosion of the amount of quantitative data, and the availability of computers and calculators demand a redefining of the priorities for basic mathematics skills. (NCSM 1977, p. 1)

This position statement was revised to incorporate twelve areas of essential mathematics, with a reaffirmation of the importance of each for students in the next century (NCSM 1989). There is much agreement between the items on this list, which is given in Figure 1–7, and the NCTM *Standards*. The NCSM's position paper also included a statement on the learning environment, which mirrors many of the items in the NCTM's *Professional Standards,* as discussed in Chapter 3.

Changing needs are reflected in the four sets of suggestions discussed in this section. To Wilson, what was actually used in vocations provided the basis for determining curriculum. To the Postwar Commission, the use of mathematics as a tool in other subject areas was decisive in defining mathematical literacy for all who can possibly attain it. The suggestions of Edwards et al. went far beyond computation and were to some extent paralleled by

NCSM Components of Essential Mathematics

1. Problem Solving: Learning to solve problems is the principal reason for studying mathematics. Problem solving is the process of applying previously acquired knowledge to new and unfamiliar situations. Solving word problems in texts is one form of problem solving, but students also should be faced with non-text problems. Problem-solving strategies involve posing questions, analyzing situations, translating results, illustrating results, drawing diagrams, and using trial and error. Students should see alternate solutions to problems; they should experience problems with more than a single solution.

2. Communicating Mathematical Ideas: Students should learn the language and notation of mathematics. For example, they should understand place value and scientific notation. They should learn to receive mathematical ideas through listening, reading, and visualizing. They should be able to present mathematical ideas by speaking, writing, drawing pictures and graphs, and demonstrating with concrete models. They should be able to discuss mathematics and ask questions about mathematics.

3. Mathematical Reasoning: Students should learn to make independent investigations of mathematical ideas. They should be able to identify and extend patterns and use experiences and observations to make conjectures (tentative conclusions). They should learn to use a counterexample to disprove a conjecture, and they should learn to use models, known facts, and logical arguments to validate a conjecture. They should be able to distinguish between valid and invalid arguments.

4. Applying Mathematics to Everyday Situations: Students should be encouraged to take everyday situations, translate them into mathematical representations (graphs, tables, diagrams, or mathematical expressions), process the mathematics, and interpret the results in light of the initial situation. They should be able to solve ratio, proportion, percent, direct variation, and inverse variation problems. Not only should students see how mathematics is applied in the real world, but they should observe how mathematics grows from the world around them.

5. Alertness to the Reasonableness of Results: In solving problems, students should question the reasonableness of a solution or conjecture in relation to the original problem. Students must develop the number sense to determine if results of calculations are reasonable in relation to the original numbers and the operations used. With the increase in the use of calculating devices in society, this capability is more important than ever.

6. Estimation: Students should be able to carry out rapid approximate calculations through the use of mental arithmetic and a variety of computational estimation techniques. When computation is needed in a problem or consumer setting, an estimate can be used to check reasonableness, examine a conjecture, or make a decision. Students should acquire simple techniques for estimating measurements such as length, area, volume, and mass (weight). They should be able to decide when a particular result is precise enough for the purpose at hand.

7. Appropriate Computational Skills: Students should gain facility in using addition, subtraction, multiplication, and division with whole numbers and decimals. Today, long, complicated computations should be done with a calculator or computer. Knowledge of single-digit number facts is essential, and using mental arithmetic is a valuable skill. In learning to apply computation, students should have practice in choosing the appropriate computational method: mental arithmetic, paper-pencil algorithm, or calculating device. Moreover, there are everyday situations that demand recognition of, and simple computation with, common fractions. In addition, the ability to recognize, use, and estimate with percents must also be developed and maintained.

8. Algebraic Thinking: Students should learn to use variables (letters) to represent mathematical quantities and expressions; they should be able to represent mathematical functions and relationships using tables, graphs, and equations. They should understand and correctly use positive and negative numbers, order of operations, formulas, equations and inequalities. They should recognize the ways in which one quantity changes in relation to another.

9. Measurement: Students should learn the fundamental concepts of measurement though concrete experiences. They should be able to measure distance, mass (weight), time, capacity, temperature, and angles. They should learn to calculate simple perimeters, areas, and volumes. They should be able to perform measurement in both metric and customary systems using the appropriate tools and levels of precision.

10. Geometry: Students should understand the geometric concepts necessary to function effectively in the three-dimensional world. They should have knowledge of concepts such as parallelism, perpendicularity, congruence, similarity, and symmetry. Students should know properties of simple plane and solid geometric figures. Students should visualize and verbalize how objects move in the world around them using terms such as slides, flips, and turns. Geometric concepts should be explored in settings that involve problem solving and measurement.

11. Statistics: Students should plan and carry out the collection and organization of data to answer questions in their everyday lives. Students should know how to construct, read, and draw conclusions from simple tables, maps, charts, and graphs. They should be able to present information about numerical data such as measure of central tendency (mean, median, mode) and measures of dispersion (range, deviation). Students should recognize the basic uses and misuses of statistical representation and inference.

12. Probability: Students should understand elementary notions of probability to determine the likelihood of future events. They should identify situations where immediate past experience does not affect the likelihood of future events. They should become familiar with how mathematics is used to help make predictions such as election results, business forecasts, and outcomes of sporting events. They should learn how probability applies to research results and to the decision-making process.

Figure 1–7 • Components of essential mathematics (From National Council of Supervisors of Mathematics 1988. Used by permission.)

the essential mathematics listed by the NCSM. Each proposal is based on the assumption that a mathematically literate population is not only desirable but vital to both society and the individual. Current efforts by the NCTM, the Mathematical Sciences Education Board, and other organizations on promoting standards are based on this same assumption.

● Ongoing Curricular Concerns

At any point in time certain curricular concerns are unresolved. The curriculum is in a constant state of change. Therefore,

> curriculum work is a never-ending process. There needs to be ongoing assessment of the content, ways of treating the content, and the effects of the curriculum on students. (Trafton 1980, p. 13)

Today the curriculum is changing because the content and skills that students must have to meet societal needs have changed. In addition, new evidence about better ways of teaching is continually being found.

Promoting acceptance of the NCTM standards with enhanced curriculum content for all students, along with changing teaching practices and learning activities, is the focus of the most attention among educators. Perhaps among parents and other lay community members, however, enhancing achievement test results is of higher priority.

That the two are not incompatible must be made clear to and by both groups. At stake is a fundamental change in how mathematics is viewed—not as boring, sterile, and difficult, but as exciting exploration with practical uses every day for everyone. Clearly, how mathematics is taught will have much to do with such changing perceptions, and this will influence the scope of the curriculum.

Change does not come easily or quickly in our schools. Hatfield and Price (1992, p. 36) note that "not every district or every school or every teacher is now ready for the massive change envisioned in the *Curriculum and Evaluation Standards*. Some actions, however, can and should be taken in preparation for change." For example,

- Include problem-solving situations and applications in teaching wherever possible.
- Encourage students to write about mathematics.

- Create opportunities for students to discuss mathematics and make sense of mathematics in cooperative-learning situations.
- Engage students in an active process of learning in which they create and discover mathematics concepts.
- Teach mathematics concepts using manipulatives and hands-on materials.
- Offer activities that encompass various learning styles and instructional formats to stimulate learning in students of all ability levels.
- Incorporate mathematics into other curricular areas to form mathematical connections.
- Use various formal and informal assessment techniques.
- Extend your personal growth and professional development by attending in-service workshops and professional meetings related to mathematics, reading professional journals, and sharing ideas with others.
- Increase the use of such technology as calculators and computers as an integral part of mathematics instruction.
- Facilitate learning by posing questions, asking students to clarify and justify their ideas, and challenging students to seek assistance from one another.
- Sharply reduce the number of worksheets that emphasize memorizing rules, procedures, and formulas.

▶ A Glance at Where We've Been

The mathematics curriculum is continually changing to reflect the needs of the subject, the child, and society. This chapter gave examples of such changes. It also considered seven other forces that affect the curriculum: educational organizations, research, technology, threats to national security and the economy, government, textbooks, and testing.

At intervals throughout U.S. history recommendations have been made as to content considered essential for all students. This chapter presented four sets of such suggestions to indicate their changing (and enlarging) scope. The *Curriculum and Evaluation Standards for School Mathematics* (NCTM 1989), with their promise for having a substantial impact on the curriculum, were summarized.

THINGS TO DO:
From What You've Read

1. What types of information can help you decide what mathematics to teach to a given group of children?

2. Give an illustration (in addition to those in this chapter) of how mathematics is a study of patterns and relationships, a way of thinking, an art, and a language.

3. Several educators have noted that the curriculum is in a continuous process of change in order to maintain balance as the needs of the subject, the child, and society pull it first one way and then another. Discuss this comment.

4. Discuss the role that testing can play in regard to the curriculum.

5. What elementary school curriculum content appears to have been constant for the past 100 years? Why? Is this likely to remain true? Why or why not?

6. Identify some ways that a healthy economy stimulates curriculum changes in mathematics.

7. Which unresolved curriculum concerns do you consider most important? Why?

THINGS TO DO:
Going Beyond This Book

1. Many countries have a national curriculum. Does a national curriculum exist in the United States?

2. Obtain a copy of the *Curriculum and Evaluation Standards for School Mathematics* (NCTM 1989). Choose one of the topics summarized in Figure 1–2 or Figure 1–4 (for example, "Mathematics as Communication") and present its major ideas to your class.

3. Work with a small group of students in your class. List and describe patterns and relationships you believe are important to your understanding of mathematics. Indicate which ones you believe should be included in the elementary school mathematics curriculum. Save this list until the end of the course and see how well it reflects your thinking then.

Selected References

Carpenter, Thomas; Coburn, Terrence G.; Reys, Robert E.; and Wilson, James W. *Results from the First Mathematics Assessment of the National Assessment of Educational Progress.* Reston, Va.: NCTM, 1978.

Carpenter, Thomas P.; Corbitt, Mary Kay; Kepner, Henry S., Jr.; Lindquist, Mary Montgomery; and Reys, Robert E. *Results from the Second Mathematics Assessment of the National Assessment of Educational Progress.* Reston, Va.: NCTM, 1981.

Commission on Post-War Plans of the NCTM. "Guidance Report of the Commission on Post-War Plans." *Mathematics Teacher,* 40 (July 1947), pp. 315–339.

DeVault, M. Vere, and Weaver, J. Fred. "Forces and Issues Related to Curriculum and Instruction, K–6." In *A History of Mathematics Education in the United States and Canada,* Thirty-Second Yearbook (ed. Phillip S. Jones). Washington, D.C.: NCTM, 1970.

Driscoll, Mark J. "The Teacher and the Textbook." In *Research within Reach: Elementary School Mathematics.* Reston, Va.: NCTM, 1981.

Edwards, E. L., Jr.; Nichols, Eugene D.; and Sharpe, Glyn H. "Mathematical Competencies and Skills Essential for Enlightened Citizens." *Arithmetic Teacher,* 19 (November 1972), pp. 601–607.

Hatfield, Mary M., and Price, Jack. "Promoting Local Change: Models for Implementing NCTM's *Curriculum and Evaluation Standards.*" *Arithmetic Teacher,* 39 (January 1992), pp. 34–37.

Hembree, Ray, and Dessart, Donald J. "Effects of Hand-held Calculators in Precollege Mathematics Education: A Meta-Analysis." *Journal for Research in Mathematics Education,* 17 (March 1986), pp. 83–99.

Kenney, Patricia Ann, and Silver, Edward A. (eds.). *Results from the Sixth Mathematics Assessment of the National Assessment of Educational Progress.* Reston, Va.: NCTM, 1997.

Lindquist, Mary M.; Brown, Catherine A.; Carpenter, Thomas P.; Kouba, Vicky L.; Silver, Edward A.; and Swafford, Jane O. *Results from the Fourth Mathematics Assessment of the National Assessment of Educational Progress.* Reston, Va.: NCTM, 1989.

Mullis, I. V. S.; Dossey, J. A.; Owen, Eugene U.; and Phillips, G. W. *The States of Mathematics Achievement: NAEP's 1990 Assessment of the Nation and the Trial Assessment of the States.* Washington, D.C.: NCES, 1991.

National Advisory Committee on Mathematical Education. *Overview and Analysis of School Mathematics Grades K–12.* Washington, D.C.: Conference Board of the Mathematical Sciences, 1975.

National Assessment of Educational Progress. *The Third National Mathematics Assessment: Results, Trends, and Issues.* Denver: National Assessment of Educational Progress, 1983.

National Commission on Excellence in Education. *A Nation at Risk: The Imperative for Educational Reform.* Washington, D.C.: U.S. Government Printing Office, 1983.

National Council of Supervisors of Mathematics. "Position Paper on Basic Mathematical Skills." *Arithmetic Teacher,* 25 (October 1977), pp. 18–22.

National Council of Supervisors of Mathematics. "Essential Mathematics for the 21st Century." *Arithmetic Teacher,* 37 (September 1989), pp. 44–46.

National Council of Teachers of Mathematics. *An Agenda for Action: Recommendations for School Mathematics of the 1980s.* Reston, Va.: NCTM, 1980.

National Council of Teachers of Mathematics. *Curriculum and Evaluation Standards for School Mathematics.* Reston, Va.: NCTM, 1989.

National Council of Teachers of Mathematics. *Professional Standards for Teaching Mathematics.* Reston, Va.: NCTM, 1991.

National Council of Teachers of Mathematics. *Assessment Standards for School Mathematics.* Reston, Va.: NCTM, 1995.

Pursuing Excellence: A Study of U.S. Eighth-Grade Mathematics and Science Teaching, Learning, Curriculum, and Achievement in International Context. Washington, D.C.: National Center for Education Statistics, 1996.

Suydam, Marilyn N. "The Case for a Comprehensive Mathematics Curriculum." *Arithmetic Teacher,* 26 (February 1979), pp. 10–11.

Suydam, Marilyn N. "Review of Research: Computers in Mathematics Education, K–12." In *Computers in Mathematics Classrooms.* Reston, Va.: NCTM, 1988.

Trafton, Paul R. "Assessing the Mathematics Curriculum Today." In *Selected Issues in Mathematics Education* (ed. Mary Montgomery Lindquist). Chicago: National Society for the Study of Education, and Reston, Va.: NCTM, 1980, pp. 9–26.

Van de Walle, John A. "Implementing the *Standards*: Redefining Computation." *Arithmetic Teacher,* 38 (January 1991), pp. 46–51.

Washburne, Carleton. "Mental Age and the Arithmetic Curriculum: A Summary of the Committee of Seven Grade Placement Investigations to Date." *Journal of Educational Research,* 23 (March 1931), pp. 210–231.

Wilson, Guy M. "The Social Utility Theory as Applied to Arithmetic, Its Research Basis, and Some of Its Implications." *Journal of Educational Research,* 41 (January 1948), pp. 321–337.

2

Understanding How Children Learn Mathematics

 Introduction

How is mathematics learned? This important question has no simple answer. Teachers provide their "answers" through classroom practices. In fact, every instructional activity within the classroom expresses the teacher's view of learning. The way in which lessons are planned, topics presented, and questions handled reflects how learning is perceived and influences what happens in classrooms.

Consider this exchange about the amount of homework needed:

STUDENT: Do we have to do all thirty exercises on this page?

TEACHER: Yes, do every one of them. Why do you think they are there if we are not supposed to do them?

A common pitfall in assignments is too much practice too soon. Research confirms that students rarely need all the practice provided in a textbook. Far more important than the quantity of exercises done is the developmental instruction that precedes them and the distribution of practice that follows (Koehler and Grouws 1992).

Because teachers' beliefs about the learning process make such a difference in the classroom, a thoughtful study and understanding of how mathematics is learned should have high priority for every elementary teacher. The purpose of this chapter is to build on your previous knowledge from educational psychology and stimulate your thinking about how children learn mathematics.

● How Do Children Learn Mathematics?

Early in the twentieth century, John Dewey asserted that learning comes from experience and active involvement by the learner. Much has been discovered since then about how children learn mathematics, but the importance of meaningful experience remains unchallenged. More recently Jean Piaget argued that learners actively construct their own knowledge. This view of learning, known as *constructivism*, suggests that rather than simply accepting new information, students interpret what they see, hear, or do in relation to what they already know.

Thus, a middle-grade child who concludes that 0.285 is greater than 0.4 because "0.285 has more digits" is building on what he or she already knows about whole numbers and interprets the information about decimals in light of this previous knowledge. The student had constructed knowledge, but this example is a reminder that the constructed knowledge is not always correct.

More will be said about constructivism later, but first let's examine key elements of two major theories of how children think and learn. Each view holds implications for learning and teaching mathematics. One of these views has long been associated with mathematics learning (behaviorism), while the other has been shown to be helpful in promoting meaningful learning (constructivism).

Building Behavior

Behaviorism has its roots in stimulus–response and conditioned learning. This theory asserts that behavior can be shaped through rewards and punishments. Over the years, it has marshaled a number of distinguished advocates, including Edward L. Thorndike, B. F. Skinner, and Robert Gagne. However, no learning theorists today argue for an exclusively behaviorist approach to mathematics learning. Behaviorism has had a significant impact on mathematics programs, but the strict adherence to a behaviorist approach to mathematics learning in elementary school is clearly inappropriate.

One of the major tenets of behaviorism is reinforcement, which is practice promoting the desired behavior. The value and power of meaningful practice is well documented; however, research has reported negative effects associated with excessive practice, premature practice, or practice without understanding (Koehler and Grouws 1992). Such practice often leads to a fear or dislike of mathematics and an attitude that mathematics doesn't need to make sense when, in fact, sense making of mathematics is a major goal of mathematics learning. In our judgment, behaviorist psychology must be considered by teachers, but used wisely. Keeping this point in mind, let's examine behaviorism a bit more closely to see why.

The hierarchical nature of mathematics makes it a popular candidate for a behaviorist approach. The first step in such an approach is to state precisely the objective, or goal, of instruction. This statement gives teachers direction in planning instruction and gives the student clear expectations—both valuable outcomes that are consistently supported by research. Once an objective has been clearly stated, behaviorists recommend that the prerequisites for achieving that goal be identified and used as building blocks in planning instruction.

Consider the following example.

Objective:

Correctly use the formula $A = \frac{1}{2}ba$ to find the area of a triangle.

Some prerequisite questions are:

What is area?

What is base?

What is altitude?

What is a triangle?

Clear answers to these prerequisite questions are necessary if the objective is to be reached. However, this particular task analysis could be extended to include these questions:

How do you multiply by a fraction?

How do you multiply by whole numbers?

Thus, it is hard to imagine constructing a complete task analysis for any objective, no matter how simple it may seem. It is obvious that important prerequisites must be considered in preparing lessons, but teachers must be guided by common sense, not by zeal to construct "the definitive task analysis."

Behaviorism is useful in clarifying goals and focusing learning outcomes. Although forming behaviorally oriented objectives may be useful, such objectives often focus on low-level knowledge that may involve virtually no mathematical thinking. Behaviorism can be good or bad—the key is balance. As teachers we must maintain a balanced focus which attends to cognitive processes and important skills.

An examination of mathematics programs discloses a heavy influence of behaviorism as students are "shown" algorithms, and mathematical relationships are "illustrated" on the textbook pages. The influence of a behaviorist orientation can also be found in daily, unit, grade, and program objectives.

The behaviorist approach does have some attractive features: it provides instructional guidelines, allows for short-term progress, and lends itself well to accountability pressures. However, a real and constant danger in using a behaviorist approach is to focus on simple, short-term objectives that are easily measured. This approach can produce mastery of specific objectives, but it lacks the critical connections that make the so-called "knowledge" meaningful and useful. Often the emphasis on short-term objectives results in other things being deemphasized, and these "other things" generally include long-term goals and higher-level cognitive processes such as problem solving.

Behaviorism needs to be refocused to have a positive effect on mathematics learning. It is possible for behaviorism to provide more learner involvement and promote higher-level thinking in mathematics. This possibility is illustrated by the use of many behaviorally oriented verbs—such as *explore, justify, represent, solve, construct, discuss, use, investigate, describe, develop,* and *predict*—in the NCTM *Standards* (NCTM 1989, p. 17). Each of these verbs encourages critical thinking and requires an active role for children in doing and eventually learning mathematics.

Behaviorism does need to be refocused, but even then, it is indefensible to rely exclusively on behaviorism to guide mathematics instruction. For this reason, we now turn to a different interpretation of how children learn.

Constructing Understanding

The notion of meaningful learning advanced by William Brownell during the first half of the twentieth century was a forerunner of constructivism. Brownell conceived of mathematics as a closely knit system of ideas, principles, and processes—a structure that should be the cornerstone for learning mathematics. Connections among concepts should be established so that "arithmetic is less a challenge to the pupil's memory and more a challenge to his [or her] intelligence" (Brownell 1935, p. 32).

In recent years, research has consistently confirmed that isolated "learnings" are not retained (Hiebert and Carpenter 1992). Mathematics can and should make sense. If it does, it has meaning and is understood as a discipline with order, structure, and numerous relationships; and it is likely to be called upon in a variety of problem-solving situations. Meaningful learning provides the base for mathematical connections highlighted in the NCTM *Standards* (1989) and *Addenda Series* (NCTM 1991–93). Meaningful learning is also an integral part of constructivism.

In addition to Brownell, Jean Piaget, Jerome Bruner, and Zoltan Dienes have each contributed to the growth of constructivism. Many of the major recommendations for teaching mathematics advocated by the *Professional Standards for Teaching Mathematics* (NCTM 1991) are based on how children learn mathematics, and there is strong support for change from the traditional behavioralist approach to constructivism. In fact, "educational research offers compelling evidence that students learn mathematics well only when they *construct* their own mathematical understanding" (National Research Council 1989, p. 58). What does it mean for students to construct their mathematical knowledge? Three basic tenets on which constructivism rests provide an answer to this question.

1. Knowledge is not passively received; rather, knowledge is actively created or invented (constructed) by students. Piaget (1972) suggested that mathematics is made (constructed) by children, not found like a rock nor received from others as a gift.

2. Students create (construct) new mathematical knowledge by reflecting on their physical and mental actions. They observe relationships, recognize patterns, and make generalizations and abstractions as they integrate new knowledge into their existing mental structure (Dienes 1960).

3. Learning reflects a social process in which children engage in dialogue and discussion with themselves as well as others (including teachers) as they develop intellectually (Bruner 1986). This tenet suggests that students are involved not only in manipulating materials, discovering patterns, inventing their own algorithms, and generating different solutions, but also in sharing their observations, describing their relationships, explaining their procedures, and defending the processes they followed.

Clearly, these tenets have significant implications for learning and teaching mathematics. The tenets also suggest that constructivism is a process that takes time and reflects several developmental stages.

Research has documented that children's level of mathematical development provides a window of opportunity for a range of learning activities. At each stage of development, the lower limit of this window of opportunity rests on previous concepts and skills that have been established, while the upper limit is determined by tasks that can be successfully completed only with step-by-step instruction. Learning activities and experiences that fall within this range, or window of opportunity, have been identified by the Russian psychologist Lev Vygotsky (1978) as being within a child's *zone of proximal development*.

Research suggests that learning activities that fall within a child's zone of proximal development have a high probability of success, whereas engaging in activities outside of the zone have much less likelihood of success. The challenge provided by Vygotsky is to know our students well and have a reasonably good understanding of these zones.

Theories of learning suggest that it is a natural process. Learning is active and internally monitored; it is a process of acquiring, discovering, and constructing meaning from experience. The process results in learning that is filtered through the student's unique knowledge base, thoughts, perceptions, and feelings.

Although the levels of development are characterized differently by Piaget, Bruner, and Dienes, as outlined in Figure 2–1, the frameworks proposed by

Levels of Thinking by Elementary School Children as Characterized by Piaget	Levels of Developmental Learning as Characterized by Bruner	Levels of Mathematical Learning as Characterized by Dienes
Formal Operational: Considers the possible rather than being restricted to concrete reality. Capable of logical thinking that allows children to reflect on their own thought processes.	**Symbolic:** Manipulation of symbols. Child manipulates and/or uses symbols irrespective of their enactive or iconic counterparts.	**Formalization:** Provides an ordering of the mathematics. Fundamental rules and properties are recognized as structure of the system evolves. **Symbolization:** Describes the representation in language and/or mathematical symbols. **Representation:** Provides a peg on which to hang what has been abstracted. Images and pictures are used to provide a representation.
Concrete Operational: Thinking may be logical but is perceptually oriented and limited to physical reality.	**Iconic:** Representational thinking based on pictures, images, or other representations. Child is involved with pictorial and/or verbal information based on the real world.	**Generalization:** Patterns, regularities, and commonalities are observed and abstracted across different models. These structural relationships are independent of the embodiments.
Pre-Operational: Represents action through thought and language but is prelogical in development.	**Enactive:** Firsthand manipulating, constructing, or arranging of real-world objects. Child is interacting directly with the physical world.	**Free Play:** Interacts directly with physical materials within environment. Different embodiments provide exposure to the same basic concepts, but at this stage few commonalities are observed.

Advanced — Early (left axis)   *Abstractions — Introductory* (right axis)

Figure 2–1 ● **Frameworks of the learning process**

each are remarkably similar. A careful examination of these frameworks reveals that:

- Children are actively involved in the learning process and opportunities for talking about (communicating) their ideas is essential.
- Several characteristic and identifiable stages of thinking exist, and children progress through these as they grow and mature.
- Learning proceeds from the concrete to the abstract. Here we need to keep in mind that "concrete" is a relative term. To one child, joining two blocks and four blocks is concrete but 2 + 4 is not; another child may view 2 + 4 as concrete and $x + y$ as abstract.
- Symbols and formal representation of mathematical ideas follow naturally from the concrete level, but only after conceptualization and meaningful understanding have been established.

Taken collectively, theories about how children learn help considerably in planning instruction and developing curricula. They provide a strong argument for using appropriate models and concrete materials to illustrate mathematical concepts and for actively involving students in the learning process. A major instructional implication is that teachers should explain new information in terms of knowledge students already possess. This idea raises a critical question—what mathematics do students need?

● What Mathematical Knowledge Should Be Learned?

The importance of skills versus concepts in mathematics learning has long been debated. Such debates create a false dichotomy that plays one against the other. The truth is that skills (procedural knowledge) and concepts (conceptual knowledge) are both necessary for expertise in mathematics. As teachers, we need to understand what constitutes procedural and conceptual knowledge and the importance of helping students make connections and establish meaningful relationships between them.

Procedural knowledge is based on a sequence of actions, often involving rules and algorithms; *conceptual knowledge,* on the other hand, is based on connected networks that link relationships and discrete pieces of information (Hiebert and Lefevre 1986). Computation provides the setting for much procedural knowledge, since algorithms can be acquired through a prescribed, step-by-step sequence of procedures. These procedures can be acquired with understanding or can be applied rotely. For example, to compute 23 + 49, one might use a series of regroupings to apply a written algorithm and produce a sum of 72; or one might add 20 and 40 to get 60 and then add 12 more to get 72; or one could use the related mental computation of 23 + 50 = 73, and then subtract 1 to get 72. Each of these "algorithms" illustrate procedural knowledge, and each can be developed with meaning and understanding.

However, it is also possible to learn the same algorithms as a series of steps devoid of meaning. For example, 23 + 49 could be memorized as "add the 3 and the 9 to get 12. Bring down the 2 and carry the 1. . . ." Such rote learning has no place in school mathematics; yet it highlights one of the ever-present dangers associated with algorithms. Research suggests that students with highly developed rules for manipulating symbols are reluctant to connect these rules to other representations that might give them meaning (Wearne and Hiebert 1989). Other research reports that once elementary students learn procedures to do written computation, they are more likely to use the written rather than mental procedures (Reys and Barger 1994). These studies remind us that once particular procedures are established and practiced, they become fixed, and the process makes later acquisition of understanding using the procedures less likely.

While procedural knowledge may provide a rule or definition to answer a specific question, the resulting knowledge might be limited or devoid of important connections. For example, in response to a question—what is a square?—a student might respond correctly—"a square has four congruent sides and four right angles"—but without further probing, we don't know if other relationships—such as a square is a rectangle, a parallelogram, a regular polygon, or an equilateral quadrilateral—also exist. Awareness of these relationships requires conceptual knowledge that may not be evident from the initial response.

Conceptual and procedural knowledge can and should be developed with meaning and understanding. Although the nature of conceptual knowledge requires the establishment of meaningful relationships and connections, it is possible to develop procedural knowledge without regard for meaning. For example, "invert the divisor and multiply" will produce a correct result for the quotient of two fractions. A student may be able to apply this procedure but have no way to explain why it works. If only the answer is important, then the student has no desire to learn why the algorithm works.

Conceptual knowledge requires the learner to be active in thinking about relationships and making connections, along with making adjustments to accommodate the new learning with previous mental structures. On the other hand, procedural knowledge can be acquired in a more passive mode, as when a certain procedure is demonstrated or illustrated and the student is required only to imitate the technique. Later, the consequence of such rote learning is observed as the student grasps for a set of steps, a rule, or a formula to apply in some algorithmic manner. The student's ability to properly use procedural knowledge relies completely on memory, which may be inadequate to make the necessary recall due to a lack of connections and networks between conceptual and procedural knowledge. When this happens, errors occur. Students possessing only procedural knowledge have limited means of detecting and correcting errors and unreasonable answers.

As teachers, we need to acknowledge the importance of procedural and conceptual knowledge in mathematics learning. The need to help students establish connections and relationships between conceptual and procedural knowledge is great, and current research (Hiebert and Carpenter 1992) suggests that understanding and connections (conceptual knowledge) should come before proficiency in skills (procedural knowledge). Any discussion of what mathematics should be learned must include discussion of the way it is taught. This fact is elegantly captured in the statement, "What students learn is fundamentally connected with how they learn it" (NCTM 1991, p. 21).

Now let's turn to some specific instructional implications to help students build connections and learning bridges as they explore and learn mathematics.

● Implications of What We Know about Learning Mathematics

Teaching occurs only to the extent that learning occurs. Therefore, effective teaching of mathematics rests heavily on considerations about how children learn. The process of building bridges from the concrete to the symbolic and helping children cross them is at the heart of good teaching—and it is a continual challenge.

The practical principles for teaching mathematics given in this section are based on a blend of research, teaching experience, and thinking about how children learn mathematics. Because each principle addresses a specific issue, they are presented separately, and no priority of importance is suggested by the order in which they are listed.

Principle 1: Actively involve students.

This principle is based on the conviction that active involvement will encourage students to make sense out of what they are doing and thereby develop greater understanding of mathematics. Recall the ancient Chinese proverb:

> I hear and I forget;
> I see and I remember;
> I do and I understand.

It reflects the importance of active involvement as a cornerstone on which students construct their own mathematical meaning. Active involvement may provide for physical activity but always demands mental activity. It takes many forms, including interaction of children and teachers, hands-on experience with manipulatives, and use of special learning materials such as textbooks or technology. One of the daily challenges of teaching is to provide experiences that will encourage, promote, and reward active involvement.

Suppose, for example, you were developing a lesson on volume. One approach might be to provide a formula for finding the volume of a right prism: $V = bhl$. You could show students drawings of various right prisms and then ask students to use the formula to compute the volume for each.

4 ft.

3 ft.

8 ft.

An active approach to developing volume is shown in Activity Card 2–1. Here children are provided with some blocks and asked to build different boxes (right prisms). As they build the boxes, they begin to relate the dimensions of the boxes to their volumes. The need to multiply the dimensions becomes clear, so the formula for the volume of a box evolves naturally from this active involvement. Children are involved in using models, making decisions, and thinking about mathematics, rather than methodically applying a formula. Such active involvement is exemplified in illustrated vignettes in the *Professional Standards for Teaching Mathematics* (NCTM 1991) and in the NCTM's *Addenda Series*, (NCTM 1991–93).

Principle 2: Learning is developmental.

Effective and efficient learning of mathematics doesn't just happen. Children learn best when

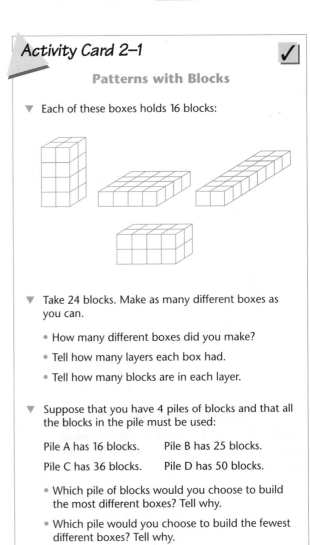

Activity Card 2–1 ✓

Patterns with Blocks

▼ Each of these boxes holds 16 blocks:

▼ Take 24 blocks. Make as many different boxes as you can.

* How many different boxes did you make?
* Tell how many layers each box had.
* Tell how many blocks are in each layer.

▼ Suppose that you have 4 piles of blocks and that all the blocks in the pile must be used:

Pile A has 16 blocks.   Pile B has 25 blocks.

Pile C has 36 blocks.   Pile D has 50 blocks.

* Which pile of blocks would you choose to build the most different boxes? Tell why.
* Which pile would you choose to build the fewest different boxes? Tell why.

mathematical topics are appropriate for their developmental level and presented in an enjoyable and interesting way that challenges their intellectual development. This instructional task is a challenging one—it takes time and must be planned. The NCTM Standards state:

> Emphasizing mathematical concepts and relationships means devoting substantial time to the development of understandings. It also means relating this knowledge to the learning of skills by establishing relationships between the conceptual and procedural aspects of the tasks. The time required to build an adequate conceptual base should cause educators to rethink when children are expected to demonstrate a mastery of complex skills. (1989, p. 17)

The teacher plays a critical role in establishing a rich environment to explore mathematics at an appropriate developmental level. The teacher also provides the necessary direction to help children recognize relationships, make connections, and talk about mathematics.

It takes time to extract mathematics from real-life experiences and concrete materials. Yet this time is well spent, since it helps develop a lasting facility not only to think about mathematics, but also to think mathematically.

Principle 3: Build on previous learning.

Mathematics must be organized so that it is appropriate and understandable to students. Because mathematics includes both conceptual and procedural knowledge, the challenge is not only to develop these types of knowledge, but also to establish relational understanding between them. In no other discipline is previous knowledge and learning more critical. For example, it is fruitless to try to estimate a distance in kilometers if you don't know what a kilometer is.

The mathematics program in a K–8 textbook series is organized both to provide continuous development and to help students to understand the basic structure of mathematics. Scope-and-sequence charts provide an overview of how a particular program is arranged. A careful examination of such a chart will reveal how a sequence of activities is organized in a spiral approach.

Ideally, the *spiral approach* provides many opportunities over time to develop and broaden concepts. More specifically, it incorporates and builds on earlier learning to help guide the child through continued, but increasingly more intricate, study of related topics. Angle measurement, for example, is informally introduced in primary grades and returned to many times. When the concept of angle reappears in later grades, greater levels of sophistication are required. The diagram in Figure 2–2 shows how previous experience is used to develop the concept.

There is, however, a danger associated with the spiral approach to curriculum that should be recognized. Although in theory the spiral mathematics curriculum provides for continuous growth and development, in reality many topics are revisited each year without appreciable change in the intellectual level of treatment. Consequently, much valuable time is spent each year treading water, as topics are merely reviewed, rather than continuing an exploration that builds on prior learning or introduces new topics.

This problem is highlighted in one study that reported that the average percentage of new content in three popular fourth-grade mathematics textbooks was just 44 percent (Flanders 1987). More recently, the Third International Mathematics and Science Study (TIMSS) reported that mathematics programs in the United States reflect more review of topics from year to year than other countries, such as Germany and Japan (TIMSS, 1996). Such repetition is detrimental because it turns students off. It robs both teachers and students of the excitement inherent in exploring fresh and new mathematics. It also diverts large amounts of instructional time

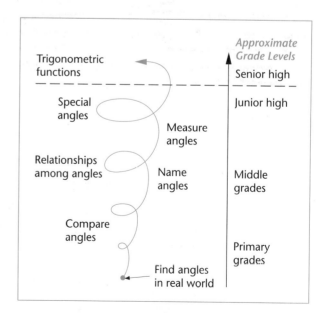

Figure 2–2 • Spiral approach for learning about angles

from new learning to reviewing familiar concepts, which means that fewer new ideas can be experienced each year.

The spiral approach holds profound implications for learning and teaching. Instructional planning must consider the prerequisites for success on the current lesson, and the teacher must check to see if students have them. It is not unusual to find students who have skipped, never learned, forgotten, or incorrectly learned prerequisite topics. Detecting these weaknesses early and quickly allows the inclusion of reviews, so that later lesson development is not hampered by students' lack of prerequisites.

Just as we must know what has happened in earlier grades, we must look ahead to what will be expected of our students tomorrow, next month, and next year. Third-grade teachers must know what has happened in kindergarten, first grade, and second grade, as well as what will be expected of their students in later years. This broad perspective helps each of us to better understand and appreciate the importance of our role. It also demands that we guard against learning gaps in mathematics and, whenever they are detected, do our best to fill them.

Principle 4: Communication is integral.

Models, manipulatives, and real-world examples provide many opportunities for thinking, talking, and listening. The importance of communication in mathematics learning is demonstrated by the fact that communication is one of only four NCTM standards that are highlighted in all grade levels. This emphasis means that "students should have many opportunities to use language to communicate their mathematical ideas. . . . Opportunities to explain, conjecture and defend one's ideas orally and in writing can stimulate deeper understandings of concepts and principles" (NCTM 1989, p. 78). Talking and writing about mathematics is an integral part of learning mathematics.

Although precision is valued in mathematics, precision in mathematical language is a product of learning; it is not necessarily a tool for the learning of mathematics. As teachers, we must be careful about pushing for too much precision in language too soon. Students at all levels should talk about mathematics before they are expected to communicate mathematics symbolically. Just as speaking precedes writing for children, so should the oral language of mathematics precede symbolization. Both student-to-student communication and student-to-teacher communication are important in the learning process.

In talking about mathematics, students are likely to provide valuable insights into their thinking and understanding. This talk may take different forms. For example, consider two second graders who are responding to the following question:

Today is February 9—how many days are left in the month?

Student-to-Student Communication

WILLIAM: The answer is 21.

WHITNEY: I got 19.

WILLIAM: How did you get that?

WHITNEY: I said 9 plus 10 is 19 and 10 more is 29. That is one too many days, so it is 19. How did you get 21?

WILLIAM: I subtracted . . . [he proceeds to write

$$\begin{array}{r} 28 \\ -\ 9 \\ \hline \end{array}$$

and then says] I messed up. I subtracted 8 from 9 instead of 9 from 28. You're right, it is 19.

This kind of talking between students is natural and provides many opportunities for explanations, justifications, and sharing of methods. As teachers, we may often be unaware of such conversations, but we should do all we can to stimulate and encourage student-to-student communication.

Consider now the following student–teacher interaction as a fourth-grade class is exploring primes and composite numbers by building rectangles with tiles.

Student-to-Teacher Communication

BOB: So every even number is composite.

TEACHER: What about two?

This question stimulates additional thinking and will encourage Bob to justify this overgeneralization.

Raising questions, and challenging answers that have been proposed by students, are excellent ways to stimulate thinking and talking about mathematics and create a classroom that encourages students to engage in communication. Such interaction allows students opportunities to talk about their ideas, get feedback for their thinking, and hear other points of view. Thus, students learn from one another as well as from teachers.

In writing about mathematics, students provide insight into what they are thinking and what they understand. It may be helpful to write prompts to help students get started. For example,

I think the answer is . . .
Another way to do it is . . .
The thing I liked best was . . .
I still don't understand . . .

Children can and will tell us much about what they know and don't know. In the process, they are developing some important communication skills. Talking and writing about mathematics makes it more alive and more personal, thus heightening student interest. Reading and listening carefully to what is being said, as well as noticing what is not being said, allows us to better tailor our teaching.

Principle 5: Good questions facilitate learning.

Students can and should ask questions of each other. Students can and should ask questions of teachers, and teachers can and should ask questions of students. Questions are a vital element of the learning process. Teachers need to know when to ask a question and what kinds of questions to ask. The teacher also needs to know when to answer a question and when to ask another question that will facilitate the answering of the original question.

In theory, there are no bad questions. Some that are raised may be unnecessary because they have just been answered—but the person asking was not paying attention. Some questions may be stated poorly and may be misunderstood. Some questions may be more appropriate at another time. There may be times, for example, when low-level questions with a unique answer are appropriate (for example, "What is seven times six?"), but at other times, more open-ended questions are most effective ("About how many tennis balls will fit in our room?"). Our attention here (and in further discussion of questions in Chapter 3) is to focus on the need for good questions that stimulate thinking and learning.

What are good questions? Good questions take a variety of different forms, but are generally characterized by their potential to encourage critical thinking, establish relationships, and promote meaningful connections.

Here are some examples of several different types of good "generic" questions that need to be an integral part of mathematics learning:

What would be a reasonable estimate for the answer?

How did you solve that problem?

Can you solve that a different way?

What is different about these solutions?

What pattern do you see?

Can you explain that a different way?

What pattern can you construct?

Explain how . . . ?

Explain why . . . ?

What are some possible solutions for . . . ?

What is another example of . . . ?

Are there other patterns . . . ?

What do you think would happen if . . . ?

What do you still not understand about . . . ?

How would you help someone else understand?

How is . . . related to . . . ?

How is this . . . related to . . . that we studied earlier?

How would you use this . . . to . . . ?

How does . . . affect . . . ?

How are . . . and . . . similar?

How are . . . and . . . different?

All of these questions are appropriate for either students or teachers to ask. It is important that, as teachers, we be sensitive to the need to raise good questions and encourage our students to do so as well.

Principle 6: Manipulatives aid learning.

Manipulative materials and models assume a critical role in helping students learn mathematics throughout elementary school (Suydam 1986). By their very nature, mathematical thoughts are abstract, so any model that embodies them is imperfect and has limitations. The model is not the mathematics—at best, it illustrates the mathematical concept under consideration. Helping children link, connect, or establish meaningful bridges from the model to the mathematics is a challenge, but a rewarding struggle (Hiebert 1989).

Suppose you were developing the concept of a circle. A plate could be used to illustrate this concept, but it would also illustrate many other mathematical concepts: area, boundary, circumference, and diameter, to name but a few. When a concept is being formed, the learner has no way of knowing which attributes characterize it. Thus, irrelevant variables (design on the plate, its attractive finish, a chip or crack) may be the only things "seen." It will not be clear exactly what characterizes a circle.

Other models, such as coins or jar lids, could be introduced, but the focus might still be on the interior rather than the boundary of these models. Additional models, such as a rim of a wheel, a bike tire, a ring, and the core from a roll of paper towels, would reinforce the roundness associated with a circle but would also make it clear that a circle is associated with the outer edge or boundary of the models (see Figure 2–3). Research has shown that mildly attracting attention to the important attributes will enhance learning, so one might take a piece of chalk or a water-soluble pen and mark around the outer part of the coin or plate to highlight the circle.

The use of perceptually different models, such as those shown in Figure 2–3, is called multiple embodiment, or *multi-embodiment*. The more different the models look, the more likely the students are to extract only the common characteristics and make abstractions. It is foolhardy to make abstractions from a single model in mathematics. Multi-embodiment encourages students to abstract, but to do so with discretion. It also decreases the likelihood of a mathematical concept's being uniquely associated with a particular model. Such associative learning can occur whenever a single model is used to illustrate a mathematical concept.

Although research has documented the value of providing multi-embodiments, important questions remain. For example, how long should a model be used? The length of time that a model is used depends on both the student and the content. It is, however, safe to say that, in general, too little time is spent with a model. That is, students are rushed (or dragged) too quickly through firsthand experiences with models and then confronted with symbolizations. Students need to feel comfortable with a model and observe as well as talk about the key mathematical features it embodies. Even at this stage, leaving a model doesn't mean that it will never be used again. In fact, the same model may be used at various levels throughout elementary school to develop new and/or more sophisticated concepts.

Mathematical learning depends heavily on abstraction and generalization. The multi-embodiment principle rests on the value of experiencing a mathematical concept in a variety of different physical settings. Within each embodiment, many attributes or characteristics appear. The use of *mathematical variability* ensures that, within a given embodiment, various mathematical features are allowed to change. Many different examples and nonexamples are needed before generalizations can be made.

Let's reconsider one of the embodiments of a circle—the plate shown in Figure 2–3—to develop the concept of a circle. In order to dispel the attention given to physical features, such as size, design, or chips, several different kinds of plates could be used. Hopefully, this experience with variability would refocus attention on the plate's roundness. The model is unchanged, but examples within it are varied. These changes within a given model enhance the prospects of the learner's focusing on only the significant mathematical attributes.

Similarly, if rings are used, different designs, styles, and materials will provide a reminder that the rings model a circle. It is also advisable to point out that some rings don't model a circle.

For example, consider this "adjustable ring":

Although it is a ring, it does not model a circle. Such *nonexamples* play an important role in concept formulation. An oval serving platter could be used with the plates to provide a nonexample within that multi-embodiment.

Research confirms that students learn more when presented with a combination of examples and nonexamples of a mathematical concept than with examples alone (Hiebert and Carpenter 1992). Implementation of mathematical variability provides opportunities to vary examples and include nonexamples.

Principle 7: Metacognition affects learning.

Metacognition refers to what one knows or believes about oneself as a learner and how one controls and adjusts one's behavior. Students need to become aware of their strengths, weaknesses, and typical behaviors and of the repertoire of procedures and

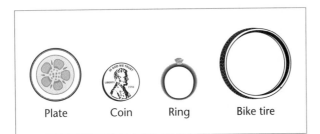

Figure 2–3 ● **Some models of a circle**

strategies that they use to learn and do mathematics and, more specifically, solve problems.

Metacognition is a form of looking over your own shoulder—observing yourself as you work and thinking about what you are thinking. Competent problem solvers are efficient at keeping track of what they know and of how well or poorly their attempt to solve a problem is proceeding. They continuously ask,

What am I doing?

Why am I doing it?

How will it help me?

A growing research base suggests that what students know or believe about themselves as mathematics learners not only greatly affects their performance, but also influences their behavior as they do mathematics (Campione et al. 1988).

Examples of metacognitive knowledge range from knowing that practice improves task proficiency and that drawing a picture often helps in understanding a problem, to knowing that "I get scared when I see a word problem." Metacognitive knowledge often helps students control and adjust behavior. Thus, if Sheena knows that she has frequently made keystroking errors with her calculator, she is more likely to work slowly and to check on the reasonableness of her calculator answers.

The development of metacognition requires that children observe what they know and what they do and reflect on what they observe. Encouraging students to "think about their thinking" is an important ingredient of mathematics learning. Teachers can do several things to help students develop this metacognitive awareness.

- Make explicit how they themselves work when solving problems. Teachers often present complete polished solutions to students, which may hide many critical decisions made while planning the lesson. For example, consider the following questions:

  Why did you do that?

  How did you know not to use that information?

  Why did you decide to estimate?

  Such questions are routinely addressed by teachers in preparing lessons, but students are not often made aware of this background. There is value in sharing some of the behind-the-scenes decision making with students.

- Point out to students various aspects of problem solving, such as the following:

  Some problems take a long time to solve.

  There may be more than one right answer to a problem.

  Some problems can be solved several different ways.

  You don't have to solve problems the way the teacher does.

- Students should also be encouraged to become more aware of metacognition and the need to think about their mathematical thinking. For example, teachers might ask students to discuss the following:

  What mathematics problems do you like best? Tell why.

  What mathematics problems are most difficult?

  What can you do to improve as a solver of these problems?

  What do you do when you find a mathematics problem that you don't know how to do?

  What errors do you make most often in mathematics? Why do you think you make them?

Principle 8: Teacher attitudes are vital.

Students' attitudes toward mathematics are a byproduct of learning and are linked to both motivation and success in mathematics. Students' values, including attitudes, are greatly influenced by teachers. Teachers who enjoy teaching mathematics and share their interest and enthusiasm for the subject tend to produce students who like mathematics (Renga and Dalla 1993).

Thus, if teachers' words or actions suggest that boys, or students of Asian background, for example, are likely to excel in mathematics, then a message of differentiated expectation has been sent to girls, or to students who are from a different ethnic background. However, if it is made clear that mathematics exists in every culture and that high achievement is expected of all students regardless or race or gender, then a different message is sent. The power of this message of "mathematics for everyone" is documented by research consistently confirming that teacher expectations greatly affect student performance (Koehler and Grouws 1992).

Similarly, if the mathematics instruction places heavy emphasis on computational skills, students will view computation as very important. However, if teachers reward creative solutions or approaches to problems, then students will develop respect for divergent thinking. Further, if teachers make it clear that critical thinking and problem solving is valued and respected, then critical thinking and problem solving will be viewed as important by students. Establishing what is important and valued within each mathematics classroom greatly influences not only what is learned and how it is learned, but students' attitudes toward mathematics as well.

Principle 9: Experiences influence anxiety.

Mathematics anxiety, or "mathophobia," is a fear of mathematics or an intense negative feeling about mathematics. Some classic symptoms of mathematics anxiety (such as poor performance, misunderstandings, and dislike of mathematics) are shown in Figure 2–4. Other negative emotions may be reflected by insecurity, as well as fears of failure, punishment, ridicule, or stigmatizing labels. In some students, mathematics anxiety may be reflected as a negative attitude toward mathematics or as a negative emotional reaction to mathematics.

Mathematics anxiety is often associated with how mathematics is learned. Research suggests that primary-grade children are generally positive about mathematics, yet the likelihood of mathematics anxiety increases as children move into middle school and junior high school (Renga and Dalla 1993). The students who experience mathematics anxiety tend to take less mathematics during secondary school, thereby blocking their access to many careers.

What can be done about mathematics anxiety? Research indicates that, unless action is taken or help provided, the level of anxiety does not lessen on its own (Hart and Walker 1993), so the best strategy is prevention or early detection. The following suggestions address the need to help students cope with the problem of mathematics anxiety.

● Emphasize meaning and understanding rather than memorization. Mathematics learning must be characterized by sense making—that is, the mathematics learned must make sense to the learner. Children attempting to memorize math-

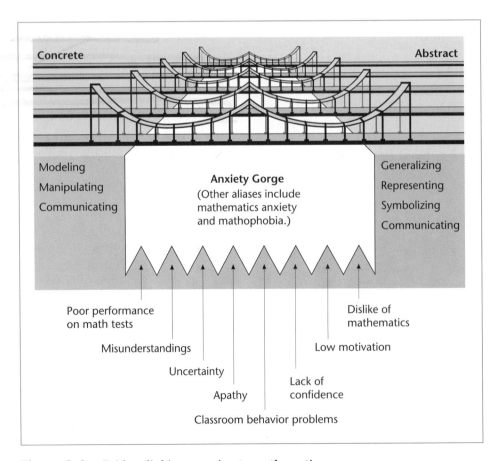

Figure 2–4 ● **Bridges linking meaning to mathematics**

ematics without understanding are likely to fall into the "anxiety gorge" in Figure 2–4. Helping students make connections between concrete models and either conceptual or procedural knowledge facilitates understanding and promotes greater learning success.

- Model problem-solving strategies rather than presenting a finished solution. Encourage students to offer suggestions, try their ideas, and see what happens. Help students realize that incorrect strategies and steps are a natural part of problem solving. Remind students that in the long run the problem-solving journey is more important than the resulting answer. This focus on the process rather than the answer helps reduce anxiety associated with "wrong" answers.

- Provide mathematical experiences that are interesting and challenging, but that allow children to be successful. Self-confidence results from successful experiences in learning mathematics.

- Help all students appreciate the power, usefulness, and importance of mathematics. Make it clear that success in mathematics is for everybody, and avoid any suggestion that different mathematics expectations are associated with race or gender.

- Show an enjoyment for mathematics.

- Maintain and project a positive attitude toward mathematics and students.

- Encourage students to tell you how they feel about mathematics. What do they like? Why do they like it? This self-reflective (or metacognitive) diagnosis can help you detect symptoms of mathematics anxiety.

- Be careful not to emphasize speed tests or drills in your classroom. Some children enjoy the challenge of competition. Others are uncomfortable with timed pressure; for these students, timed races breed apprehension and fear of mathematics.

- Use diagnostic techniques to identify students experiencing particular difficulty or in need of special help, and provide this help quickly to get them back on track.

Principle 10: Gender aptitudes are equal.

A complex assortment of social forces produce or influence gender inequities related to mathematics. For example, parents of young children may express different expectations in mathematics classes for their sons than for their daughters. School counselors may subtly discourage girls from pursuing mathematical careers. Such factors may contribute to fewer girls taking advanced mathematics courses, which may prematurely foreclose, or at least delay, options for careers in mathematics, science and technical fields.

Research suggests that teachers may actually treat boys differently from girls in the classroom. For example, teachers may call on boys more often in mathematics classes than girls, and teachers may be less likely to praise girls than boys for correct responses and less willing to prompt girls who gave wrong answers (Leder 1992). Teachers also are more likely to attribute boys' failure to a lack of motivation than they are girls' failure. Girls may take such criticism to heart and think this is a true indicator of their talent in mathematics.

Risk taking, or the willingness of students to take a chance in answering a question they are not certain of, may influence gender differences on tests. Research suggests that the format of the test may produce gender differences. Numerous studies have reported that boys gamble more than girls in choosing answers to questions that they are not sure of, and this may be rewarded by higher scores (Ramos and Lambating 1996). More specifically, multiple choice tests tend to favor males because these objective tests often focus on small bits of knowledge, require a choice of one right answer with no chance to explain the choice, and exist in a competitive environment that girls find more stressful, whereas more open-ended responses favor girls because they are less stressful and allow for more creative complex answers.

Although both boys and girls experience "learned helplessness," girls are particularly susceptible to this syndrome. Learned helplessness is the belief that the individual cannot control outcomes and is destined to fail without the existence of a strong safety net. Learned helplessness includes feelings of incompetence, lack of motivation and low self-esteem. It usually develops from what is perceived as failure or lack of success in learning, and it is often associated with mathematics. Students feel there is little sense in trying because the opportunity for success is beyond their control.

Although strong efforts to confront and eliminate gender biases have been made, providing gender equality for learning mathematics remains a challenge. Among successful actions taken by teachers to address gender inequities are:

- Having equally high expectations for both boys and girls, and clearly communicating these expectations to both students and their parents.

- Engaging both boys and girls in answering difficult questions, raising questions and communicating their mathematical thinking, and making sure boys don't dominate either the class discussion or the teacher's time.

- Calling attention to female role models in mathematics and science, as well as helping students become increasingly aware of the career opportunities for people with strong mathematics backgrounds.

- Communicating with parents the importance of encouraging and supporting their daughters to aspire to and persist in nontraditional fields, such as studying mathematics.

- Discussing learned helplessness with people having problems and developing ways to prevent or help remedy the situation (Renga and Dalla 1993).

- Providing a variety of ways (different testing formats, interviews, and portfolios) to assess student performance.

Principle 11: Retention can improve.

A very important aspect of learning is *retention*. For example, if students can read a clock in class but not when they get home, their retention of this skill is so limited that it is virtually useless. Retention reflects the amount of knowledge kept, skill maintained, or problem-solving behaviors consistently exhibited.

Forgetting is a problem in all disciplines, but the cumulative nature of mathematics increases its importance. Forgetting occurs over a summer, a spring vacation, a weekend, a day, or even shorter periods. The graph in Figure 2–5 shows that skills and specific knowledge are subject to dramatic changes. Factual knowledge, such as the answers to the following questions, is quickly forgotten when it isn't used regularly.

What is a prime number?

State the transitive property.

Skills, such as how to do the following exercises, are also quickly lost without regular maintenance.

What is the quotient of ⅔ and ⅕?

Use the formula for a trapezoid.

Thus, classroom and achievement tests often report very volatile levels of performance on mathematical skills and knowledge.

The skill of problem solving, on the other hand, is less susceptible to big declines, and performance is more stable over time. One reason is that problem solving is a complex behavior requiring a number of higher-level thinking processes. Such processes take time to develop, but once established are retained longer than other skills and often improve as time goes by.

Retention is an important goal in mathematics education. Instructional efforts must recognize the importance of retention and try to maximize it. How can retention be improved? Research suggests several ways.

1. Meaningful learning is the best way to shore up retention. All phases of mathematics (knowledge, skills, and problem solving) that have been developed with meaning and learned with understanding are retained longer.

2. Connections help children see how mathematical ideas are related. Mathematical topics must not be taught in isolation as discrete topics, but they must be developed in conjunction with problem solving and applications that cut across several areas whenever possible. For example, consider this problem, which could be viewed as arithmetic:

Find the sum of the first 20 odd counting numbers.

If students simply use a calculator to find the sum of 1 + 3 + 5 + 7 + . . . 39, a golden opportunity to use problem solving to establish connections is missed. A teacher might use Activity Card 2–2 to involve students in gathering and organizing data, then searching for patterns and discussing them, and later generalizing and expressing their findings symbolically. This process uses arithmetic, patterns, problem solving, and algebra to help generalize and make a prediction with a formula.

Another teacher might use Activity Card 2–3, which provides a visual means of developing the

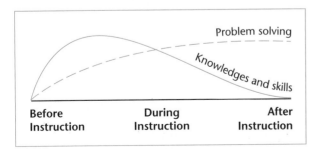

Figure 2–5 ● **Typical learning retention curve**

Activity Card 2–2

Patterns with Numbers

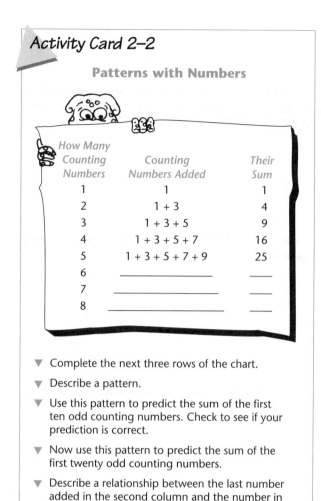

How Many Counting Numbers	Counting Numbers Added	Their Sum
1	1	1
2	1 + 3	4
3	1 + 3 + 5	9
4	1 + 3 + 5 + 7	16
5	1 + 3 + 5 + 7 + 9	25
6	_____	___
7	_____	___
8	_____	___

▼ Complete the next three rows of the chart.

▼ Describe a pattern.

▼ Use this pattern to predict the sum of the first ten odd counting numbers. Check to see if your prediction is correct.

▼ Now use this pattern to predict the sum of the first twenty odd counting numbers.

▼ Describe a relationship between the last number added in the second column and the number in the first column.

Activity Card 2–3

Using Patterns ✓

▼ These drawings suggest some patterns:

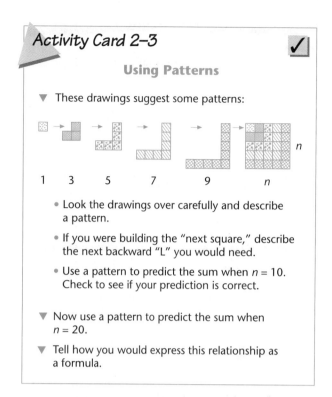

1   3   5   7   9 n

• Look the drawings over carefully and describe a pattern.

• If you were building the "next square," describe the next backward "L" you would need.

• Use a pattern to predict the sum when $n = 10$. Check to see if your prediction is correct.

▼ Now use a pattern to predict the sum when $n = 20$.

▼ Tell how you would express this relationship as a formula.

3. Periodic (weekly and monthly) reviews of selected key ideas contribute substantially to the quantity of mathematics retained. A regular maintenance program removes rustiness and provides important reinforcement and refreshers that improve immediate performance, contribute to higher levels of learning, and improve retention.

● Recommendations for Teaching from What We Know about Learning Mathematics

The principles from the previous section provide ideas related to learning in general, and to mathematics learning in particular. We propose the following recommendations that we think will be useful in planning instructional activities consistent with our knowledge of how children learn. Here are some (a baker's dozen) of our recommendations to guide instructional planning and learning.

1. Establish a mathematics class motto: "Do only what makes sense to you." This motto will encourage students to question, reflect, and seek explanations that make sense to them. It will pave the way for constructing knowledge that is meaningful and understood by them.

same mathematical concept. Here the visual pattern suggested by the geometric representation suggests an algebraic relationship that connects arithmetic, geometry, and algebra together in a natural way. After completing either activity, students have constructed knowledge (both conceptual and procedural) about finding the sum of odd counting numbers that involved models, patterns, and generalizations. These students are experiencing the power of mathematics as discussed in the *Professional Standards for Teaching Mathematics* (NCTM 1991).

Activity Cards 2–2 and 2–3 provide experiences that move from the concrete to the symbolic and help establish connections. These activities help connect the concrete to the abstract and should not be viewed as mutually exclusive, but rather reinforcing. Research documents the value of establishing these connections to not only gain better understanding but also to promote greater retention and recall.

2. Provide rich learning situations to involve students. Interesting problems are more stimulating and effective in promoting mathematics. Typically, these situations are driven by real-world applications that involve, connect, integrate, and use many different mathematical concepts and skills. Check problem contexts to ensure that the situations have a broad appeal to both genders and to different cultural backgrounds. Although some sports may have strong appeal to boys, the same sports may "turn off" girls. Select a balance of problem situations to appeal to different groups and involve your students in choosing the contexts.

3. Make reading an integral part of mathematics. Many children's books offer starting points for mathematical thinking and rich mathematics lessons. Such books help make interdisciplinary connections that stimulate student interest and provide reminders of the power and usefulness of mathematics. These books can provide the context for a variety of rich mathematical experiences.

4. Use models and manipulatives to explore problems and provide concrete experiences that will help children build their mathematical thinking. Provide a variety of different models (through multi-embodiments). Allow children ample time to become familiar with the materials, and help children construct knowledge as they make connections between the models and materials.

5. Encourage children to talk about their mathematical thinking as well as to listen and respond to other students' ideas. Interaction among children provides them opportunities to talk about their ideas, obtain feedback, and learn other points of view. Students can learn from one another as well as the teacher.

6. Make writing an integral part of learning mathematics. Writing is a natural extension of talking and provides valuable insight into students' thinking and communication skills.

7. Provide a safe and intellectually stimulating environment for learning mathematics. Incorrect answers and conceptual errors are natural as children construct their mathematical knowledge. Children uninhibited with concerns about intuitive responses and faulty answers are more likely to observe patterns, make conjectures, engage in discussions, and take risks when doing mathematics. Make sure children do only what makes sense to them. If they "don't get it," they should not be doing it!

8. Maintain high expectations for every child regardless of gender or cultural background. Make it clear that you expect all children to be successful in mathematics, and be careful to involve both boys and girls in all aspects of mathematics learning.

9. Accept the fact that confusion, partial understanding, and some frustration are a natural part of the process of learning mathematics. All students will not learn everything at the same time, nor will they all demonstrate the same level of proficiency. Learning mathematics is a long-term process. Sometimes progress is slow; at other times, it is reflected in moments of insight such as "I've got it!" or "Now I understand."

10. Make sure students realize that processes are valued. Focusing on answers places the priority on the end result. As teachers, we must explore behind the scenes to learn where the answer came from. For much mathematics learning, the most important element is the process—that is, the way you got the answer. This focus on process requires communication, which may be oral explanations or notes in journals.

11. Project a positive attitude toward mathematics. Children are influenced by their teachers. If a teacher has mathematics anxiety, this feeling is likely to influence students' feelings. Make it clear that you value mathematics, and help children become aware of the importance of mathematics.

12. Encourage children to reflect on their learning. Metacognition is an important part of the learning process. Individual reflection or interaction with others (both teachers and peers) encourages students to communicate and explain their thinking.

13. Use classroom organizations that facilitate learning. Whole-class instruction and cooperative small-group work have both been demonstrated to be effective ways to promote mathematics learning. The challenge for teachers is to know when and how to use them effectively.

▶ A Glance at Where We've Been

Mathematics learning can and must have meaning. This statement is the cornerstone of all instructional planning and teaching.

Conceptual and procedural knowledge are essential elements of mathematics learning, but decades of research have revealed no single best path to their development. There is, however, a strong and growing research base from learning theories to guide the learning process. These theories recognize the importance of the concrete level and offer effective ways to help children learn mathematics with meaning and understanding.

Research and experience suggests that there is significant value in children constructing their own knowledge and that the teacher plays an important role in facilitating such construction. In addition to hands-on experiences, children learn from telling, explaining, clarifying, making conjectures, and reflecting on what they have done. They also learn from watching, listening, reading, following directions, imitating, and practicing. All of these experiences contribute to learning mathematics; teachers have the responsibility of deciding the proper balance of these experiences.

We know that mathematics learning is influenced by factors specific to the individual, such as previous experience, environmental influences, maturation, ability, and motivation. Consequently, no single comprehensive learning theory can be unequivocally applied to all students at all levels for all mathematical knowledge. We also know that mathematics learning is a slow process that requires years of development. We know that many individual differences exist and that the rate of learning varies greatly among children. Given these variables, the essential role of teachers is to help children construct mathematical knowledge that is meaningful to them. In performing this role, teachers must make countless decisions to plan appropriate learning activities, establish an inviting classroom environment, and organize the classroom to ensure that all children are actively participating in experiencing, learning, abstracting, and constructing mathematics that is meaningful to them.

▶ THINGS TO DO: *From What You've Read*

1. List some characteristics of mathematics anxiety. Discuss how the use of learning bridges can save victims from the "anxiety gorge."

2. Provide some examples to help distinguish between procedural and conceptual knowledge in mathematics.

3. Give an example of meaningful learning in mathematics. Then give an example of nonmeaningful learning. State in your own words what distinguishes them.

4. Examine the learning frameworks in Figure 2–1. Tell how the models proposed by Piaget, Bruner, and Dienes are alike. How are they different?

5. Identify the three tenets on which constructivism is based.

6. State in your own words what the zone of proximal development is. Do you think it is important? Tell why.

7. What is metacognition? Examine Activity Card 2–2 or 2–3. Describe how metacognition might be used to think about your thinking during that activity.

8. Why is it important to have children talk about the mathematics they are learning? Tell how talking about mathematics relates to the NCTM standard on "mathematics as communication."

9. Do you think the learning principles are equally appropriate for early childhood and middle school students? Tell why or why not.

10. Describe some specific steps that teachers can take to improve retention of mathematics learning.

▶ THINGS TO DO: *Going Beyond This Book*

1. Select a topic from a scope-and-sequence chart for a current elementary mathematics textbook series. Describe how this topic is spiraled. For example, at what grade level is it introduced? How many years is it spiraled? During what year(s) does it receive the heaviest instructional attention?

2. Choose a mathematics textbook series. Find a common topic (such as geometry) for two consecutive grade levels. Examine the contents of the two chapters. Identify examples of new content that is introduced. Identify examples of old content that is reviewed. Would you say the content overlaps too much? Defend your position.

3. Select a topic from a first-, second-, or third-grade textbook series. Read all the related suggested activities described in the teacher's manual. What concrete materials were used? Is multi-embodiment reflected in these materials?

4. Examine an article discussing gender/race as related to learning mathematics, such as Renga and Dalla (1993) or Ramos and Lambating (1996) or Sumrall (1995). Describe significant issues raised, and implications for you as a teacher.

5. Observe a mathematics lesson and make a list of good questions that you heard during the lesson.

6. Read one of the articles from *Teaching and Learning Mathematics in the 1990s* (Cooney and Hirsch 1990). Describe how the implementation of ideas in this article would affect how you teach.

7. Check the TIMSS web page (either http://www.ed.gov/NCES/timss/index.htm or via the NCTM http://www.nctm.org) for the information and related publications. Read one of the reports and share something that you think would be of interest to other teachers.

8. Examine one of the vignettes from the *Professional Standards for Teaching Mathematics* (NCTM 1991). Present this vignette to your classmates, and discuss its value in helping you help children learn mathematics.

9. Obtain a publication from the Math/Science Network (Lawrence Hall of Science, University of California, Berkeley, CA 94720), such as *Math for Girls and Other Problem Solvers* or *Use Equals To Promote the Participation of Women in Mathematics*. Review one of their publications and share your reactions.

10. Describe how children's books such as the *American Women in Science Biographies* series listed in the Children's Corner might encourage more young students to take additional mathematics and consider careers in science.

11. Examine the book *Encouraging Girls in Mathematics: The Problem and the Solution,* by Brush (1980). Describe some things you can do in your teaching to help encourage girls to study mathematics.

12. View one of the video tapes in the *Connecting the Past with the Future: Women in Mathematics and Science* series (Judith Olson, Project Director, Western Illinois University, Macomb, IL 61455). Describe some ways in which this experience might help encourage more girls to study mathematics.

13. Tell how books such as *Mathematicians Are People, Too* promote interest in humanizing mathematics. Do you think this personalization helps promote more interest in learning mathematics? Tell why.

14. Examine the NCTM Yearbook *Multicultural and Gender Equity in the Mathematics Classroom* (Trentacosta and Kenney, 1997). Read one of the articles, then identify and discuss several specific implications for mathematics teaching.

15. Examine the book by Edeen et al. (1990) and report how you might use it to develop ideas for bulletin boards that would make women in mathematics more visible. Do you think helping children learn more about women's contributions in mathematics is an important instructional goal? Tell why.

▼▼▼▼▼▼▼▼▼▼▼▼▼▼▼▼▼▼▼▼▼▼▼▼

Children's Corner

Verheyden-Hilliard, Mary Ellen. *American Women in Science Biographies* (5 books). Bethesda, Md.: Equality Institute, 1988.

Edeen, Susan; Edeen, John; and Slachman, Virginia. *Portraits for Classroom Bulletin Boards: Women Mathematicians.* Palo Alto, Calif.: Dale Seymour Publications, 1990.

Reimer, Luetta, and Reimer, Wilbert. *Mathematicians Are People, Too,* 2 vols., Palo Alto, Calif.: Dale Seymour Publications, 1990.

Selected References

Boling, Ann Neaves. "They Don't Like Math? Well, Let's Do Something." *Arithmetic Teacher,* 38 (March 1991), pp. 17–19.

Brownell, William A. "Psychological Considerations in the Learning and the Teaching of Arithmetic." In *The Teaching of Arithmetic,* Tenth Yearbook (ed. W. D. Reeves). Reston, Va.: NCTM, 1935, pp. 1–31.

Bruner, Jerome. *Actual Minds, Possible Worlds.* Cambridge, Mass.: Harvard University Press, 1986.

Brush, L. *Encouraging Girls in Mathematics: The Problem and the Solution.* Cambridge, Mass.: ABT Books, 1980.

Buxton, Laurie. *Math Panic.* Portsmouth, N.H.: Heineman and Boynton/Cook, 1991.

Campione, Joseph C.; Brown, Ann L.; and Connell, Michael L. "Metacognition: On the Importance of Understanding What You Are Doing." In *The Teaching and Assessing of Mathematical Problem Solving* (eds. Randall I. Charles and Edward A. Silver). Reston, Va.: NCTM, 1988, pp. 93–114.

Carpenter, Thomas P. "Research on the Role of Structure in Thinking." *Arithmetic Teacher,* 32 (February 1985), pp. 58–60.

Clements, Douglas H. "Constructivist Learning and Teaching." *Arithmetic Teacher,* 38 (September 1990), pp. 34–35.

Cobb, Paul. "The Tension between Theories of Learning and Instruction in Mathematics Education." *Educational Psychologist,* 23 (1988), pp. 87–103.

Cooney, Thomas J., and Hirsch, Christian R. (eds.). *Teaching and Learning Mathematics in the 1990s,* 1990 Yearbook. Reston, Va.: NCTM, 1990.

Dienes, Zoltan P. *Building Up Mathematics.* London: Hutchinson Education, 1960.

Dossey, John A. "Learning, Teaching and Standards." *Arithmetic Teacher,* 35 (April 1988), pp. 20–21.

Feldt, Constance Curley. "Becoming a Teacher of Mathematics: A Constructive, Interactive Process." *Mathematics Teacher,* 86 (May 1993), pp. 400–403.

Fennema, Elizabeth; Peterson, Penelope L.; Carpenter, Thomas P.; and Lubinski, Cheryl. "Teacher Attributions and Beliefs about Girls, Boys and Mathematics." *Educational Studies in Mathematics,* 21 (February 1990), pp. 55–69.

Flanders, James R. "How Much of the Content in Mathematics Textbooks Is New?" *Arithmetic Teacher,* 35 (September 1987), pp. 18–23.

Garafalo, Joe. "Metacognition and School Mathematics." *Arithmetic Teacher,* 34 (May 1987), pp. 22–23.

Ginsburg, Herbert P., and Baron, Joyce. "Cognition: Young Children's Construction of Mathematics," In *Research Ideas for the Classroom: Early Childhood Mathematics* (ed. Robert J. Jensen). Reston, Va.: NCTM, and New York: Macmillan, 1993, pp. 3–21.

Hart, Laurie E., and Walker, Jamie. "The Role of Affect in Teaching and Learning Mathematics." In *Research Ideas for the Classroom: Middle Grades Mathematics* (ed. Douglas T. Owens). Reston, Va.: NCTM, and New York: Macmillan, 1993, pp. 22–38.

Hiebert, James. "Children's Mathematics Learning: The Struggle to Link Form and Understanding." *Elementary School Journal,* 84 (May 1984), pp. 496–513.

Hiebert, James. "The Struggle to Link Written Symbols with Understandings: An Update." *Arithmetic Teacher,* 36 (March 1989), pp. 38–44.

Hiebert, James, and Carpenter, Thomas P. "Learning and Teaching with Understanding." In *Handbook of Research on Mathematics Teaching and Learning* (ed. Douglas Grouws). New York: Macmillan, 1992, pp. 65–97.

Heibert, James, and Lefevre, P. "Conceptual and Procedural Knowledge in Mathematics: An Introductory Analysis." In *Conceptual and Procedural Knowledge: The Case of Mathematics* (ed. James Hiebert). Hillsdale, N.J.: Lawrence Erlbaum Associates, 1986, pp. 1–27.

Kamii, Constance, and Lewis, Barbara A. "Constructivism and First-Grade Arithmetic." *Arithmetic Teacher,* 38 (September 1990), pp. 36–37.

Kloosterman, Peter, and Gainey, Patricia Haynes. "Students' Thinking: Middle Grade Mathematics." In *Research Ideas for the Classroom: Middle Grades Mathematics* (ed. Douglas T. Owens). Reston, Va.: NCTM, and New York: Macmillan, 1993, pp. 3–21.

Koehler, Mary S. "Classroom, Teachers and Gender Issues in Mathematics." In *Mathematics and Gender* (eds. Elizabeth Fennema and Gilah C. Leder). New York: Teachers College Press, 1990, pp. 128–148.

Koehler, Mary S., and Grouws, Douglas A. "Mathematics Teaching Practices and Their Effects." In *Handbook of Research on Mathematics Teaching and Learning* (ed. Douglas Grouws). New York: Macmillan, 1992, pp. 115–126.

Leder, Gilab C. "Mathematics and Gender: Changing Perspectives." In *Handbook of Research on Mathematics Teaching and Learning* (ed. Douglas Grouws). New York: Macmillan, 1992, pp. 597–622.

Long, Madeleine J., and Ben-Hur, Meir. "Informing Learning through the Clinical Interview." *Arithmetic Teacher,* 38 (March 1991), pp. 44–46.

Morrow, Jean; Schrock, Connie; and Buchman, Debbie. " 'Real People': A Fifth-Grade Class Investigates the Lives of Mathematicians." *Mathematics Teaching in the Middle School,* 1(4) (January–March 1995) pp. 274–282.

National Council of Teachers of Mathematics. *Curriculum and Evaluation Standards for School Mathematics.* Reston, Va.: NCTM, 1989.

National Council of Teachers of Mathematics. *Professional Standards for Teaching Mathematics.* Reston, Va.: NCTM, 1991.

National Research Council. *Everybody Counts: A Report to the Nation on the Future of Mathematics Education.* Washington, D.C.: National Academy Press, 1989.

Nichols, Rosalie S., and Kurtz, V. Ray. "Gender and Mathematics Contests." *Arithmetic Teacher,* 41 (January 1994), pp. 238–239.

Piaget, Jean. *To Understand Is to Invent.* New York: Grossman, 1972.

Ramos, Ismael, and Lambating, Julia. "Risk Taking: Gender Differences and Educational Opportunity." *School Science and Mathematics,* 96(2) (February 1996), 94–98.

Renga, Sherry, and Dalla, Lidwins. "Affect: A Critical Component of Mathematical Learning in Early Childhood." In *Research Ideas for the Classroom: Early Childhood Mathematics* (ed. Robert J. Jensen). Reston, Va.: NCTM, and New York: Macmillan, 1993, pp. 22–39.

Reys, Barbara J., and Barger, Rita. "Mental Computation: Issues from the United States Perspective." In *Computational Alternatives for the 21st Century: Cross Cultural Perspectives from Japan and the United States* (ed. Robert E. Reys and Nobuhiko Nohda). Reston, Va.: NCTM, 1994, pp. 31–47.

Sawada, Diayo. "Mathematical Symbols: Insight through Invention." *Arithmetic Teacher,* 32 (February 1985), pp. 20–22.

Shumway, Richard J. "Students Should See 'Wrong' Examples: An Idea from Research on Learning." *Arithmetic Teacher,* 21 (April 1974), pp. 344–348.

Sumrall, William J. "Reasons for the Perceived Images of Scientists by Race and Gender of Students in Grades 1–7." *School Science and Mathematics,* 95(2) (February 1995), 83–90.

Suydam, Marilyn N. "Manipulative Materials and Achievement." *Arithmetic Teacher,* 33 (February 1986), p. 10.

Third International Mathematics and Science Study (TIMSS). *U.S. National Research Center Report No. 7,* East Lansing, Mich.: TIMSS U.S. National Research Center, Michigan State University, December 1996. http://ustimss.msu.edu/

Trentacosta, Janet, and Kenney, Margaret J. (eds.). *Multicultural and Gender Equity in the Mathematics Classroom.* 1997 Yearbook of the National Council of Teachers of Mathematics. Reston, Va.: NCTM, 1997.

Vygotsky, Lev. *Mind in Society.* Cambridge: Harvard University Press, 1978.

Wearne, Diane, and Hiebert, James. "Cognitive Changes during Conceptually Based Instruction on Decimal Fractions." *Journal of Educational Psychology,* 81 (1989), pp. 507–513.

Weaver, J. Fred. "What Research Says: The Learning of Mathematics." *School Science and Mathematics,* 87 (January 1987), pp. 66–69.

Wheatley, Grayson H. "Constructivist Perspectives on Science and Mathematics Learning." *Science Education,* 75 (1991), pp. 9–21.

3

Planning for Mathematics Instruction

▶ *Snapshot of a Lesson*

What We Did Today

Today math was about problems with BIG
numbers. We worked in pairs. Tim worked with
me. We got a problem to solve. We could use any
stuf in the room. base ten blocks, cubes, rods,
links, or any thing else. Tim and I used links at
first. Then we used blocks becuase it was easyer
to keep track of the numbers. We argude about how to start.

After we got our answer we wrote about how we
did it. Then we met with three other pairs of kids that
got the same problem. We talked about how we got our
ansers. Nobody had solved the same way but that w
was OK. Some of the other ways were neat.

We all put our ways of doing it into a folder.
with the problem on the cover. I want to do some
of the other problems to see if my way is like anybody else.

▶ Introduction

At the heart of good teaching lies planning. Children learn best from lessons that are interesting and carefully organized, that are directed by thoughtful questions, and that are enriched by activities and materials that give them the opportunity to develop ideas about mathematics. Research indicates that careful development of ideas, with clear explanations, careful questioning, and manipulative materials, is particularly important in teaching mathematical content (Bush et al. 1977; Sowell 1989; Thornton 1977).

Teachers plan mathematics lessons in a variety of ways. Some teachers just list the objectives they want children to attain, or at least take a step toward attaining. Some jot down key questions they want to ask. Some teachers lay out the materials for children to use or run off the worksheet that they will give the children. Others read the comments in the teacher's guide to the textbook. All of these approaches require teachers to think through what they plan to do.

Few teachers have the time to write out a complete, detailed plan for every mathematics lesson they teach. Some do it occasionally, when they know the idea they want to teach must be developed especially carefully. For beginning teachers, however, writing detailed lesson plans is particularly worthwhile. Careful planning helps to make the initial experiences good ones, not only for the children but also for the beginning teacher.

Lesson plans give you the security of knowing what you will do and say, of having interesting activities and materials ready for the children's use, and of anticipating what the children might do. A detailed lesson plan also gives you a way of judging how well the lesson went. Even though you might not have been able to follow the plan precisely, it helps you evaluate your behaviors and assess the actions and responses of the children. Moreover, through writing detailed plans you learn how to plan "in your head."

● An Overview: Six NCTM Professional Standards

The *Professional Standards for Teaching Mathematics* (NCTM 1991) focus on the teaching and learning of mathematics. Six standards in the first section encompass the core dimensions.

Standard 1, shown in Figure 3–1, focuses on *tasks:* "the projects, questions, problems, construc-

---

**NCTM Standard 1:
Worthwhile Mathematical Tasks**

The teacher of mathematics should pose tasks that are based on

- Sound and significant mathematics
- Knowledge of students' understandings, interests, and experiences
- Knowledge of the range of ways that diverse students learn mathematics

and that

- Engage students' intellect
- Develop students' mathematical understandings and skills
- Stimulate students to make connections and develop a coherent framework for mathematical ideas
- Call for problem formulation, problem solving, and mathematical reasoning
- Promote communication about mathematics
- Represent mathematics as an ongoing human activity
- Display sensitivity to, and draw on, students' diverse background experiences and dispositions
- Promote the development of all students' dispositions to do mathematics

Figure 3–1 • Standard focusing on tasks (From *Professional Standards for Teaching Mathematics,* NCTM 1991, p. 25. Used by permission.)

---

tions, applications, and exercises in which students engage" (p. 20). These tasks must encourage students "to reason about mathematical ideas, to make connections, and to formulate, grapple with, and solve problems. . . . Good tasks nest skill development in the context of problem solving" (p. 32).

Standards 2, 3, and 4, which are shown in Figure 3–2, concern *discourse:* "the ways of representing, thinking, talking, and agreeing and disagreeing that teachers and students use to engage in those tasks" (p. 20). The role of the teacher as the orchestrator of this process is first discussed, followed by the role of the student and the tools that enhance discourse. A flow of ideas, with interactions not only from teacher to student, but also from student to teacher and student to student, using a variety of modes, is

NCTM Standard 2:
The Teacher's Role in Discourse

The teacher of mathematics should orchestrate discourse by

- Posing questions and tasks that elicit, engage, and challenge each student's thinking
- Listening carefully to students' ideas
- Asking students to clarify and justify their ideas orally and in writing
- Deciding what to pursue in depth from among the ideas that students bring up during a discussion
- Deciding when and how to attach mathematical notation and language to students' ideas
- Deciding when to provide information, when to clarify an issue, when to model, when to lead, and when to let a student struggle with a difficulty
- Monitoring students' participation in discussions and deciding when and how to encourage each student to participate

NCTM Standard 3:
Students' Role in Discourse

The teacher of mathematics should promote classroom discourse in which students

- Listen to, respond to, and question the teacher and one another
- Use a variety of tools to reason, make connections, solve problems, and communicate
- Initiate problems and questions
- Make conjectures and present solutions
- Explore examples and counterexamples to investigate a conjecture
- Try to convince themselves and one another of the validity of particular representations, solutions, conjectures, and answers
- Rely on mathematical evidence and argument to determine validity

NCTM Standard 4:
Tools for Enhancing Discourse

The teacher of mathematics, in order to enhance discourse, should encourage and accept the use of

- Computers, calculators, and other technology
- Concrete materials used as models
- Pictures, diagrams, tables, and graphs
- Invented and conventional terms and symbols
- Metaphors, analogies, and stories
- Written hypotheses, explanations, and arguments
- Oral presentations and dramatizations

Figure 3–2 • **Standards focusing on discourse** (From *Professional Standards for Teaching Mathematics,* NCTM 1991, pp. 35, 45, 52. Used by permission.)

expected in order to help every child learn more mathematics.

The *environment* is the focus of Standard 5, which is shown in Figure 3–3. It is concerned with the physical setting and more: "If we want students to learn to make conjectures, experiment with alternative approaches to solving problems, and construct and respond to others' mathematical arguments, then creating an environment that fosters these kinds of activities is essential" (p. 56).

Standard 6, in Figure 3–4, considers *analysis:* "the systematic reflection in which teachers engage . . . how well the tasks, discourse, and environment foster the development of every student's mathematical literacy and power" (p. 20). Such analyses are a primary source of information for planning and improving instruction during the course of a lesson and as lessons build during the year.

NCTM Standard 5:
Learning Environment

The teacher of mathematics should create a learning environment that fosters the development of each student's mathematical power by

- Providing and structuring the time necessary to explore sound mathematics and grapple with significant ideas and problems
- Using the physical space and materials in ways that facilitate students' learning of mathematics
- Providing a context that encourages the development of mathematical skill and proficiency
- Respecting and valuing students' ideas, ways of thinking, and mathematical dispositions

and by consistently expecting and encouraging students to

- Work independently or collaboratively to make sense of mathematics
- Take intellectual risks by raising questions and formulating conjectures
- Display a sense of mathematical competence by validating and supporting ideas with mathematical argument

Figure 3–3 • **Standard focusing on environment** (From *Professional Standards for Teaching Mathematics,* NCTM 1991, p. 57. Used by permission.)

**NCTM Standard 6:
Analysis of Teaching and Learning**

The teacher of mathematics should engage in ongoing analysis of teaching and learning by

- Observing, listening to, and gathering other information about students to assess what they are learning

- Examining effects of the tasks, discourse, and learning environment on students' mathematical knowledge, skills, and dispositions

in order to

- Ensure that every student is learning sound and significant mathematics and is developing a positive disposition toward mathematics

- Challenge and extend students' ideas

- Adapt or change activities while teaching

- Make plans, both short- and long-range

- Describe and comment on each students' learning to parents and administrators, as well as to the students themselves

---

Figure 3–4 ● **Standard focusing on analysis** (From *Professional Standards for Teaching Mathematics,* NCTM 1991, p. 63. Used by permission.)

Other sections of the *Professional Standards for Teaching Mathematics* (NCTM 1991) discuss the evaluation of the teaching of mathematics, the professional development of teachers of mathematics, and the support and development of mathematics teachers and teaching. Clearly, these sections should also interest you, and we urge you to read them.

We have focused on the first six standards because they so clearly will affect your planning for mathematics instruction. They emphasize the important decisions that a teacher makes in teaching. As you read the rest of this chapter, reflect on the potential effect of these standards on your planning—and teaching.

● The Importance of Planning

Planning for mathematics instruction is important for a number of reasons.

1. Planning establishes definite goals and helps to ensure that all essential content will be included, whether you are considering the year's work, a unit's work, or a day's work. The purposes of each lesson will be delineated clearly to help you to avoid omissions and mistakes.

2. Planning permits scheduling work in feasible units of time and in a sensible sequence. The amount of time allotted to teaching a particular topic is determined on the basis of relative importance and relative difficulty. The sequence of topics is determined on the basis of the specific mathematics content and the developmental level of the children. Mathematics appears to be more highly sequenced than some other bodies of knowledge. For example, it is difficult to teach how to multiply with fractions before children know how to multiply with whole numbers.

On the other hand, sometimes a particular sequencing is not as mandatory as it seems. For instance, for many years, it was considered mandatory to delay instruction on decimals until after instruction on whole numbers was well under way—that is, until the intermediate grades. As children use calculators, however, they encounter decimals much earlier, and we find that they can learn decimal ideas before the intermediate grades.

Developmental level must also be considered, however. For example, a child who is at the concrete operations level, where ideas must be rooted in concrete illustrations and it is difficult to manipulate abstract relationships, would find it difficult (if not impossible) to learn with understanding how to find the volume of a cube.

3. Planning helps to ensure that a lesson begins interestingly and involves each child, throughout the time. Time is relatively flexible in most elementary schools, with no ringing of bells to signify that students are to move on to the next class. Nevertheless, there are constraints such as lunch time or another subject that must be taught. Often, however, you will be able to allow more time than you'd originally planned for a lesson in which the children are totally involved or in which they need more help in grasping an idea. Sometimes you will be able to end a lesson sooner than you'd thought because they have learned the content quickly or have had difficulty so that you need to reconsider how to teach them.

4. Planning aids in holding the children's interest and attention, whether they are working as a total class, in small groups, or individually. We know from research that "time-on-task" is associated with achievement gains. That is, the more time a student spends actively engaged in tasks related to the topic, the more he or she achieves on a test of that content. Thus, the teacher's goal is to have the children

spend as much as possible of the time available for mathematics instruction actually working on content. Moreover, children actively involved are less likely to create discipline problems.

5. Planning helps to avoid unnecessary repetition, while ensuring necessary repetition for review and practice. In most schools, with most textbooks, you will be using a spiral approach, in which mathematical ideas and skills are taught at several points in a year or over a several-year period, as discussed in Chapter 2. At each encounter a topic should be approached in more depth. As you plan, you will need to consider the extent to which your pupils are ready for another look at a topic they have previously encountered. Sometimes you will want to delay instruction on a particular topic. But be wary of scheduling all the instruction on a given topic for a single period of time. Children may need the "time between" to assimilate it.

Some schools take a "mastery learning" approach, in which children are to master each topic or skill before they go on to the next. This approach has decided advantages, not the least of which may be achievement—but it also has some disadvantages, not the least of which is that children who do not learn a skill may be "stuck" at that point in the curriculum, unable to go on to new mathematical ideas with which they might be more successful. Frequently, a later topic will provide practice related to the earlier idea, and then the child learns it. The advantage of having all children master prerequisite topics before they go on to new material must be carefully weighed against the disadvantages—and efforts must be made to compensate for those disadvantages.

6. Planning creates a feeling of confidence for you. You know what you want to do, and your class will recognize that you are prepared. If you think about the "good teachers" you have had, you will probably recognize that they were well prepared for teaching. As Rathmell (1994) indicates:

> Planning for instruction that promotes the development of children's thinking and reasoning about mathematics not only helps them make sense of the content they are studying but also helps them learn ways of thinking that later will enable them to make sense of *new* content. (p. 290)

The focus in the classroom will shift from a teacher-directed effort to develop proficiency with skills to a student-centered one involving discussions about solution strategies and reasonableness.

Moreover, assessment and instruction will be naturally integrated, as teachers observe groups working, listen to explanations of solutions, or interpret written reports.

Data from another source should also be considered. The Third International Mathematics and Science Study (TIMSS) indicated that the structure of mathematics lessons in the United States and Germany is similar: the teacher instructs students in a concept or skill and solves sample problems with the class; then students practice solving similar problems on their own while the teacher assists individual students (*Pursuing Excellence* 1996). Typical lessons in Japan, however, have a different structure: the teacher poses a thought-provoking problem, then students struggle with the problem and present ideas or solutions to the class, which discusses these solution methods. The underlying mathematical concepts are articulated before students practice similar problems.

Lessons in the United States and Germany concentrate on skill acquisition, or teaching students to do something, while in Japan the focus is on understanding mathematical concepts. Over twice as much time in U.S. and German classrooms includes practice on routine procedures. (However, many Japanese students practice skills in paid tutoring sessions after school.) Japanese students spent the majority of their time inventing new solutions and being engaged in conceptual thinking about mathematics.

Analysis of TIMSS data suggests that what occurs in schools is critical to students' learning. The specific topics taught and how these topics are presented and developed shapes what students learn and are able to do. Rather than the focused coherence seen in other countries, U.S. lessons often consist of "episodic encounters" between students and curricular content. Topics and concepts are presented in a fragmented and disjointed manner in which underlying themes or principles are either not identified or merely stated but not developed.

● Levels of Planning

You must plan more than each day's mathematics lesson. At the beginning of the school year, you will need to consider what you want to have the children in your class accomplish during the year. These goals are not something you must develop on your own. Most schools prepare scope-and-sequence charts or guides, or they rely on the ones provided with the textbook series they use.

You should be familiar with your school's scope-and-sequence guide or chart before you do any planning. Such materials are designed to ensure that a child will be taught the desired range of content across grade levels. It would also be wise to check with your principal and other teachers to determine whether any changes have been made to meet the needs of children in your school, and to learn what flexibility you will have in making changes for your class.

Suggestions for planning with a textbook and yet maintaining the spirit of the suggestions made in the *Curriculum and Evaluation Standards for School Mathematics* (NCTM 1989) are offered by Schmalz (1990, 1994). She suggests, for instance, that the first topic to be taught should be one of which most of the students are unsure. Avoiding the obvious review, which seems boring to many students, is only one of her reasons.

After ascertaining the goals of mathematics instruction and the order in which topics will be taught, you will need to consider the approximate amounts of time you want to spend on each phase of the curriculum in terms of its relative importance. This allotment helps you to fit in all the mathematics content you want to include. If you want to include additional time for problem solving, for example, indicate that in your planning.

The goals for the year need to be considered by textbook units or chapters and the specific objectives to be taught about each topic. The school's curriculum guide or the textbook's planning chart will help you here—and with the decision about the amount of time you assign to teaching each topic, which is again important. Most mathematics textbooks contain 130–150 lessons. Given the typical 180-day school year, you may have some opportunity to spend extra time on some topics or to teach topics not included in the textbook.

In planning for a unit or chapter, you begin by outlining, in sequence, what topics are to be taught and how much time you will spend on each. Next you outline what you want to accomplish each week, and then you are ready to develop daily lesson plans. Some schools require teachers to maintain a lesson plan book in which they note the objectives (and sometimes other details as well) for each day's lessons for a week. Even if this practice is not required, it is a good idea. It keeps you aware of progress toward the goals for the year and gives you a guide to follow each day. You cannot expect to follow it exactly. However, it serves as a guide, and as you plan each week you can review the progress of the children in your class and then vary or pace the content to be taught to meet their individual needs. Or you can plan to teach different content to small groups or individuals.

● Components of a Lesson Plan

The *Professional Standards for Teaching Mathematics* (NCTM 1991, p. 25) suggests:

> Teachers should choose and develop tasks that are likely to promote the development of students' understanding of concepts and procedures in a way that also fosters their ability to solve problems and to reason and communicate mathematically. Good tasks are ones that do not separate mathematical thinking from mathematical concepts or skills, that capture students' curiosity, and that invite them to speculate and to pursue their hunches.

These guidelines must be incorporated into the lesson plans you prepare for a particular mathematical topic. As you prepare the plan, you need to do several things.

- State clearly the objective or objectives. What mathematical skill or idea are you trying to teach? What do you want the children to learn? Is the purpose to introduce a new topic, develop understanding, or provide review? What do the children already know? Do they have the necessary prerequisites?

- Decide how the class is to be organized. Should the lesson involve the total class, small groups, and/or individual work?

- Determine the procedures to be followed. What teaching strategy will be most effective? What type of motivation will capture the children's interest and attention? What must be reviewed to relate this lesson to previous work? What will you do and what will the children do? What questions will you ask? How will you and the children interact? What varied activities will be incorporated? What materials will you and the children use? How will the materials and activities be tailored to meet individual needs? Should practice be assigned—and if so, will it be from the textbook, from worksheets, or from a follow-up activity? Will there also be homework? What and how much? (The assignment of homework depends on school policy. You will need to check what role homework has in your school.)

- Decide how much time to spend on each part of the lesson. What is the lesson's relative importance in terms of the time available, as well as the difficulty it might present to the children?

- Decide how you will assess or evaluate—both as the lesson proceeds and after it is completed. What should you look for during the lesson? How will you and the children know what they have learned? Will writing be involved? Will each child meet with some success during the lesson?

- Write the plan for the lesson. Putting your plan into writing will help you clarify many of your ideas and also give you a record that can be used in evaluating the lesson and in planning subsequent lessons. Moreover, if you diverge from the plan, you will be able to pinpoint the point of divergence and return later to pick up where you left off.

Middleton and Goepfert (1996) divide these ideas into a nine-step "process for developing lesson plans" (pp. 62–63). Their main points (which are supplemented with subtopics and questions) are:

1. Pick a topic.
2. Determine the prior knowledge of the students.
3. State the goals clearly.
4. Determine the instructional sequence.
5. Decide on the methods of classroom organization.
6. Map out the procedures to be followed.
7. Decide how much time to spend on each part of the lesson.
8. Decide on the assessment techniques you will use.
9. Write down the lesson plan.

Such lists may make it seem that lesson planning is a cut-and-dried process and one in which each lesson is teacher-directed. Instead, use them as a set of points to be considered. As we move toward lessons that follow the guidelines in the NCTM *Professional Standards* (NCTM 1991), we need to approach planning as a process that evolves from what the children have learned and are learning, not merely from what we expect them to learn. Lappan (1993, p. 524) states:

No other decision that teachers make has a greater impact on students' opportunity to learn and on their perceptions about what mathematics is than the selection or creation of the tasks with which the teacher engages the students in studying mathe-

matics. Here the teacher is the architect, the designer of the curriculum.

Expanding on this idea, Reys and Long (1995) suggest that good tasks

- Are often authentic in that they come from the students' environment
- Are challenging yet within students' reach
- Pique the students' curiosity
- Encourage students to make sense of mathematical ideas
- Encourage multiple perspectives and interrelated mathematical ideas
- Nest skill development in the context of problem solving

Teacher's guides to textbooks provide a variety of ideas for teaching a lesson incorporating the textbook page. Often a three-step lesson plan is followed.

1. *Before using the textbook:* Prerequisites, motivation, and activities developing the concept (often using manipulative materials) are described.

2. *Using the textbook:* The mathematical concept is developed systematically through pictures and words, with examples for practice.

3. *After using the textbook:* Suggestions are given for follow-up activities, such as seatwork and games. Many guides also provide suggestions for remediation, enrichment, and variation for children with learning disabilities and other special needs.

You can select from these types of guides and enhance them with ideas from other sources.

● Grouping for Instruction

There are three basic patterns of grouping for mathematical instruction:

- Whole class, with teacher guidance
- Small group, either with teacher guidance or with pupil leaders
- Individuals working independently

The first pattern is probably used most often, yet small-group work can mean that children work on content that is focused on their particular needs and at the same time learn to work together to solve problems.

Here are some guidelines to aid you in determining which grouping pattern to use.

1. Use large-group instruction:
   - If the topic is one that can be presented to all pupils at approximately the same point in time (that is, if all pupils have the prerequisites for understanding the initial presentation)
   - If pupils need continuous guidance from the teacher in order to attain the knowledge, skill, or understanding

2. Use small-group instruction:
   - If pupils can profit from pupil-to-pupil interaction with less teacher guidance
   - If exploration and communication about mathematics are being encouraged
   - If cooperative learning skills and effects are being fostered

3. Use individual instruction:
   - If pupils can follow a sequence or conduct an activity on their own
   - If individual practice for mastery is the focus

The kind of teaching envisioned by the NCTM *Professional Standards* (NCTM 1991) is probably very different from the kind of teaching you experienced. The emphasis is shifting from a teacher-directed classroom to one in which students are actively involved in learning. The teacher is, of course, still in control, but involves the students through discussions and activities, usually by incorporating much small-group work. Presentations and discussions with the whole class have not disappeared, but we have learned that children learn much more effectively when they work with materials to solve problems and talk about their results with each other.

Farivar and Webb (1994) point out that, "Simply putting students in small groups will not guarantee that they will interact in ways that are beneficial to learning" (p. 521). They draw on extensive research to outline how students learn how to "use one another" as resources for doing mathematics, by developing skills in communication, team building, small-group socialization, and helping.

At times, the instruction is teacher directed. This approach has been found to be particularly effective in teaching basic skills to young students and those who are slow-learning or otherwise "educationally at risk" (Thornton and Wilson 1993). These learners succeed better with structured activities, close supervision, and active, teacher-led instruction. Even so, most effective teachers combine whole-class, direct instruction with cooperative learning, and other student-centered modes of instruction. For example, a teacher might develop new material with the whole class and allow children to break up for individual or small-group work during part of the period for one or more activities. The class is then brought together for a teacher-mediated discussion so that children can hear ideas from students in other groups. The teacher ends the discussion by providing closure on the lesson for the day. This method of integrating whole- and small-group work has proved more effective than direct instruction alone for developing higher-level thinking skills (Thornton and Wilson 1993, p. 275).

Guidelines from research that can help teachers to merge active student learning with active mathematics teaching include the following:

- Be proactive by constructing detailed long- and short-range plans [and] by checking prerequisite concepts or skills.
- Make students aware of the major objective(s) of the lesson.
- Spend at least half of the period developing material in a way that *actively* engages all students and emphasizes understanding.
- Involve students in important problem solving, estimation, mental math, and mathematical extensions related to the lesson.
- Communicate the expectation that, if students attend, they will be able to master the material.
- Be clear; provide relevant examples as well as nonexamples.
- Ask many "why," "how," and other high-level questions.
- Be organized; maintain a brisk pace to foster time-on-task.
- Allow time for guided seatwork before independent seatwork.
- Regularly assign a small amount of homework (or seatwork) to develop fluency with knowledge or skills previously mastered, to stimulate thinking about the next day's lesson, or to provide open-ended challenges. (Thornton and Wilson 1993, p. 274)

Research has indicated the effectiveness of such student-centered learning modes as cooperative learning and peer teaching or tutoring (Thornton and Wilson 1993). Cooperative learning involves setting a group goal and having students collaborate in groups to help each other. Those who have experienced it find that it brings a sense of relief that the burden for coming up with an answer is not solely on the individual. He or she can learn *from* the group as well as contributing *to* the group, and both actions result in more positive attitudes.

The lesson might begin with the teacher meeting with the whole class to provide an overall perspective, present new material, pose problems or questions for investigation, and clarify directions for the group activity. The class then divides into small groups, usually with four members each. Students work together cooperatively in each group, discussing the problem or question, making and testing conjectures, verifying that each student is satisfied that the group answer is reasonable. This communication of ideas with one another is especially valuable in the learning process: The students help each other learn mathematical ideas. The teacher moves from group to group, providing assistance by asking thought-provoking questions as needed (Davidson 1990).

Despite the additional planning and class time needed for cooperative learning,

> it seems easy to justify the time spent when one considers the positive factors: increase in mathematical communication, the social support for learning mathematics, an opportunity for all students to experience success in mathematics, the possibility that several approaches to solving a problem might arise, and the opportunity to deal with mathematics through and discussion of meaningful problems. (Fitzgerald and Bouck 1993, pp. 251–252)

Cooperative learning may evolve to two children working together to teach each other in a peer-teaching situation. The process of teaching—of deciding how to help someone else learn—promotes the learning of both children.

Whatever the structure of lesson—whether it is more teacher-directed or more student-centered—the teacher orchestrates the classroom discourse by "deciding when to provide information, when to clarify an issue, when to model, when to lead, and when to let students struggle with a difficulty" (NCTM 1991, p. 35). You learn to make these decisions through planning and through experience. Research indicates that no one mode of instruction

can be considered best. Teachers should learn many instructional modes and use them when appropriate. The NCTM *Professional Standards* urge teachers to consider the goal, the task, and the students—that is, to ask what will best help them learn.

● Points to Consider in Planning and Teaching

In recent years much attention has been directed toward what actually goes on in classrooms and what factors are correlated with higher achievement. One research review described four categories of student responses that were correlated with achievement and suggested ways teachers can organize and present instruction to encourage such responses (Anderson 1981):

1. **Attention ("time-on-task" behavior).** When instruction is designed so that active participation in the learning activity is demanded, students' attention is usually higher. Having all children, for example, hold up a card giving the sum of two numbers is better than having only one child give the answer. Teachers' strategies for selecting students to participate during discussions also influence attention and active participation. A teacher who calls only on volunteers to answer questions soon finds that other children stop paying attention.

2. **Initiative.** Learning is most efficient when children can identify points where they need help and then obtain it. Willingness to initiate contact with the teacher promotes learning. Some teachers discourage student-initiated contacts by lower-achieving students, who may interrupt at inconvenient times and with queries that are not directed toward the task. Thus, these students are unable to get help when they need it. Teachers who are very specific about desired student behavior are more successful in promoting achievement. They let slower learners as well as other students know when they can and should demonstrate initiative, thus encouraging this behavior.

3. **Understanding.** Students who believe a task is worthwhile and understand clearly how to complete it are more likely to persist at it. Teachers further students' understanding when they are explicit about how work should be done and what the reasons are for doing it.

4. **Success.** Not surprisingly, success in daily classroom tasks has been positively related to long-

term achievement. Teachers can promote success in a number of ways.

- Assignments should be matched to students' abilities.
- Work in progress should be monitored and prompt feedback provided (if a child makes an error and does not realize it, it may affect performance on the remainder of the task).
- Checking times should be incorporated into classroom activities (for example, by circulating through the room to look over children's shoulders as they work and being available to answer questions).

In studies to identify patterns of behaviors that make a difference in students' learning of mathematics at the fourth-grade level, one group of researchers found that necessary skills for effective whole-class instruction include the ability to explain material clearly, to structure seatwork problems for the class, and to respond to individual students' need for help (Good et al. 1983). Good teachers expect and even demand work and achievement from students and move through the curriculum quickly, thus increasing time-on-task. Students approach the teachers readily to ask for help and are more likely to get developmental, nonevaluative, and task-relevant feedback.

The Importance of Questions

Questions can be aimed at checking children's knowledge of a fact or their ability to perform a skill. These are relatively low-level questions. At a higher level are questions requiring the analysis or synthesis of information—as when we ask a child to explain why a procedure works. In mathematics lessons, teachers often use questions of the first type and only infrequently those of the latter type (Evertson et al. 1980). Although use of fact-checking, lower-level questions may be correlated with the ability of children to score high on some achievement tests, it gives the child an erroneous picture of mathematics as involving only short answers, with one correct answer per question. We need to encourage children to do more talking about mathematics—why a procedure works, what would happen if something were changed in the problem, how the mathematics could be applied in a real-life situation.

As you plan a lesson, give thought to the types of questions you want to ask. Try to include a range of them, with more requiring children to think rather than merely to supply a fact from memory or to perform a learned procedure. Encourage them to make conjectures, to examine the validity of their thoughts, and to consider how they would convince someone else that they are right (Burns 1985). Ask such questions as:

Who has a different solution?

Can you find another way to explain that?

Why do you think that's true?

Vacc (1993) proposes three types of questions: factual, reasoning, and open questions with a wide range of acceptable answers. Her aim is in accord with the *Professional Standards* (NCTM 1991, pp. 3–4), which look at five categories of questions that teachers should ask.

- In the first category are questions that help students work together to make sense of mathematics: "What do others think about what Janine said?" and "Can you convince the rest of us that that makes sense?"
- The second category contains questions that help students rely more on themselves to determine whether something is mathematically correct: "Why is that true?" and "How did you reach that conclusion?"
- The third category of questions seeks to help students learn to reason mathematically: "How could you prove that?" and "What assumptions are you making?"
- The fourth category focuses on helping students learn to conjecture, invent, and solve problems: "What would happen if . . . ?" and "Do you see a pattern?"
- The questions in the fifth category relate to helping students connect mathematics, its ideas, and its applications: "How does this relate to . . . ?" and "Have we ever solved a problem like this one before?"

The Use of Manipulative Materials

All through this book, we stress the importance of having children use manipulative materials. Although it has not yet shown why, research indicates that lessons using manipulative materials have a higher probability of producing greater mathematical achievement than do lessons without such materials (Sowell 1989; Suydam and Higgins 1977).

Handling the materials appears to help children construct mathematical ideas and retain them.

Thompson (1994) points out that some discrepant findings in research stem from the fact that some "concrete materials do not automatically carry meaning for students" (p. 557). Like many others, he suggests that the focus must continually be on *understanding*. Clements and McMillen (1996) were also concerned with what "concrete" means, and report evidence on the value of computer manipulatives as concrete. Furthermore, research indicates that student learning is enhanced when the children connect real-world situations, manipulatives, pictures, and spoken and written symbols.

When planning a lesson involving manipulatives, Ross and Kurtz (1993, p. 256) suggest the teacher should be certain that:

1. Manipulatives have been chosen to support the lesson's objectives
2. Significant plans have been made to orient students to the manipulatives and corresponding classroom procedures
3. The lesson involves the active participation of each student
4. The lesson plan includes procedures for evaluation that reflect an emphasis on the development of reasoning skills

One of the challenges a teacher faces is how to store the materials so that they can be found and used easily (Suydam 1990). Shelves and small plastic boxes (or dishpans) help to make them manageable. Children should be able to reach and remove things easily themselves, without assistance from the teacher. It is also helpful to:

● Color code or label the materials and put a matching code or label on the appropriate storage space.

● Prepackage manipulatives into sets for one student, two students, or a small group.

● Put extra pieces into a "spare parts" container.

● Package sets of materials in durable individual containers, such as heavy plastic bags or transparent containers.

● Store individual sets of materials in "trays," such as box lids, shallow plastic pans, or stackable vegetable bins.

To help children who are disorganized, you might use materials with built-in organization (such as bead frames or an abacus) or materials that fit together (such as Unifix cubes) rather than separate objects such as lima beans or blocks. Or use containers that keep counters separated, such as egg cartons, muffin tins, or mats with clearly delineated spaces.

There is one more thing to consider: have the children pass out and collect the materials as much as possible. You don't have to do it all!

The Role of Drill and Practice

It should be obvious that students need drill and practice in order to be able to perform a desired behavior or procedure at will. Just as we practice learning to walk or drive a car, we practice basic addition facts or how to multiply fractions. The choice is not if, but when. Research has long indicated that drill and practice should follow, not precede, the development of meaning (Brownell and Chazal 1935). Research also indicates that drill-and-practice activities should not consume as much time as developmental work that helps children to understand an idea or procedure (Suydam and Weaver 1981).

Workbooks published to accompany textbook series provide practice on the content presented in the textbook, lesson by lesson. Whether to assign this practice material (perhaps in addition to the practice already presented in the textbook itself) is a decision you must make in terms of children's needs. Keep in mind that they must understand an idea or procedure before they are asked to practice it. On the other hand, practicing a skill that has already been mastered can be harmful if children become bored. Therefore, it is advisable to include practice on previously learned topics as a small but regular component of each practice session.

Many teachers use worksheets in place of workbooks. When these are purchased, they are little different from workbooks. But when the teacher prepares them with the needs of particular children in mind, they can become a valuable tool. They can be used to aid slower learners by providing practice on subskills, to challenge faster learners with extension activities, and to provide personalized practice for the whole class.

Many games can also be used to provide practice. They offer a motivating format and a competitive aspect that many children love. An example of such a game is Bingo—by changing the rules slightly, you can make it into a game that provides practice on place value ("the number has 3 tens and 2 ones") or for one of the operations ("the number is the sum of

50 and 24") or for geometric ideas ("the number of sides in a hexagon").

● Evaluation

Assessment should be an integral aspect of mathematics instruction. Teachers need to ascertain whether they have taught what they think they have taught and whether each child has learned what they think he or she has learned. Teachers evaluate for several purposes:

1. To assess the mathematics program in the classroom and in the school
2. To assess the mathematics achievement of the children in each classroom
3. To diagnose individual strengths and weaknesses

In the process, teachers may well ask such questions as

- Is the content appropriate for the students?
- How well are they progressing toward the goals and objectives?
- Are they able to apply their knowledge and skills in new situations?
- Do they enjoy doing and using mathematics?

Among the procedures teachers use are observations, interviews, inventories and checklists, tests, reports from parents, samples of students' work collected in portfolios, and attitude scales. Increasingly, writing is being incorporated into mathematics as a means of helping children reflect on what they have learned, as well as providing another means of enabling teachers to gauge both student learning and their own effectiveness. Chapter 4 provides a detailed discussion of assessment.

In the final analysis, all the evaluative information teachers collect is useful as they plan lessons. They know more about the achievement and progress of each child, as well as what his or her individual needs are.

In addition, many teachers have found it helpful to keep an evaluative record of the effectiveness of their lessons. They jot down notes in their planbooks or their teacher's guides about the things that went well and the things that didn't during each lesson. These notes help them to plan the following year. You may think you will remember what happened, but you will probably forget without such notes.

Diagnosis

To meet the needs of children learning mathematics, you must first determine what their strengths and weaknesses are, using one or more of the procedures mentioned here or using a specific diagnostic test. The results of such evaluation are used to place students in instructional materials, to group students for instruction, and to decide just what needs to be taught or retaught to individuals and to the class. Guidelines for diagnosis in mathematics include the following (Driscoll 1981a):

1. Make sure that a child's apparent mathematical deficiency is really a deficiency.
2. Remember that each child progresses through several stages of development before reaching an adult conceptual level.
3. Strengthen your diagnosis with the liberal use of manipulative materials.
4. Don't lose sight of the emotional side of students in your diagnosis.
5. Be both flexible and patient in piecing together an accurate picture of a child's thinking.
6. Maintain a climate of acceptance.
7. Distinguish between errors that are random and those that occur more systematically.

Both observations and interviews are highly effective in revealing behaviors not noticeable from paper-and-pencil tests. But tests are also useful tools in diagnosis, especially when you analyze how the child reached an answer, not merely what the final score was.

Remediation

Effective remediation begins with effective diagnosis. Once you have a clear picture of a child's needs, you can plan activities to provide the missing prerequisites that are at the source of a difficulty, develop the understanding that has been missed, provide the practice that is needed, and give the encouragement that is so vital in effective remediation.

At times you will be able to group pupils who need help on a particular point; at other times you will need to work with individuals. Research has provided some pointers for effective remediation (Driscoll 1981b):

1. Involve the child in planning his or her remedial program.

2. Design remedial instruction to be different from previous instruction.

3. Provide multisensory experiences.

4. Guide the child from a concrete, intuitive understanding of mathematical ideas toward being able to represent his or her understanding verbally and symbolically.

5. Encourage the child to estimate answers.

6. Have the child use a calculator.

Equity

We want to provide equal opportunity to learn mathematics, equal educational treatment, and equal educational outcomes for every child. The *Professional Standards* (NCTM 1991, p. 4) state:

By "every child" we mean specifically—

* Students who have been denied access in any way to educational opportunities as well as those who have not

* Students who are African American, Hispanic, Native American, and other minorities as well as those who are considered to be a part of the majority

* Students who are female as well as those who are male

* Students who have not been successful in school and in mathematics as well as those who have been successful

We will discuss throughout this book strategies that promote this goal, and you will find a number of references to help you (for example, see Cuevas and Driscoll 1993). We will focus here on the third group, girls, because it seems that so often their equitable treatment is taken for granted. Yet research indicates that teachers often treat girls very differently from boys during mathematics instruction. Girls get asked fewer questions, and generally those questions demand short answers, rather than reflective, problem-solving types of thinking. Thus, girls are not encouraged to think as reflectively about mathematics, and they are not encouraged to believe that they can do mathematics as well as boys can.

In your classroom, be sure to consider such specific actions as the following, all indicated by research:

* Ask girls and boys the same types of questions, and ask probing, follow-up questions of both girls and boys.

* Ask girls and boys the same number of questions.

* Have girls and boys do the same tasks, including equal opportunities to develop visualization skills.

* Have girls and boys work in cooperative learning groups at least some of the time.

* Praise girls and boys in the same way for the same achievement.

* Provide both female and male role models for situations and careers that involve mathematics.

A number of sources can provide you with materials. For instance, the EQUALS Program* has published problem-solving activities and a curriculum for grades 1–8. The Equity Institute† has easy-to-read books suitable for grades 1–4 and a 15-minute videotape.

● Using the Strategic Moment

Despite careful planning, teachers must make many minute-to-minute decisions. It would be very sad if you did not take advantage of a situation because you had not planned for it (see Figure 3–5). Making use of teachable or strategic moments and events is imperative.

To some extent, you can encourage strategic moments by the way you arrange the environment—by bringing in something new and therefore exciting, for instance. You must know what concepts you

---

Several first-grade children come into the room all excited by the parade they saw yesterday, with "hundreds" and "thousands" of marchers. You've planned a lesson on measurement for that day. What do you do?

All the traffic lights in town are off. Why? The computer has failed. You've planned a lesson on multiplication with two-digit numbers. Do you discuss the computer's role in society instead?

You are teaching a lesson on estimation. You have the class use calculators to find 3762.5 × 795.6 quickly. A child asks, "Why is there no zero after the decimal point in the answer?" Do you continue the lesson on estimation?

Figure 3–5 • Some examples of strategic moments

---

*EQUALS Program, 240 Lawrence Hall, University of California, Berkeley, Calif. 94720.
†The Equity Institute, P.O. Box 30245, Bethesda, Md. 20824.

want to teach and how these develop for the children in your class—and then recognize the strategic moment when it arises.

Experience will also help you as you make the many on-the-spot decisions that are a part of teaching. You will learn what works and what doesn't. Try to define for yourself the goals you want to attain and how to attain them, and try to work within that framework. Consider how children develop and learn. Observe the children in your class as individuals, and watch for their errors and their successes. These observations will help you diagnose their needs and plan their instruction. And when you know your children well, you will be more ready to see and grasp strategic moments and make valid decisions.

 ## A Glance at Where We've Been

Planning lies at the heart of good teaching. Planning helps to ensure that all essential content will be included, permits scheduling the work in feasible periods of time and in a sensible sequence, helps to control the pace of a lesson, aids in holding children's attention, helps to avoid unnecessary repetition while ensuring necessary review and practice, and creates a feeling of confidence for you. Planning must be done for the year, the unit, and the day. Lesson plans should include clearly stated objectives, procedures, and evaluation. There are certain guidelines to aid in determining which grouping pattern to use (large-group, small-group, or individual instruction).

Observations in classrooms have indicated the importance of children's attention, initiative, understanding, and success to their achievement. Also critical are the teacher's skill in questioning, the use of manipulative materials, and the role of drill and practice. Evaluation procedures are another integral part of mathematics instruction. Finally, using strategic moments is important.

 ## THINGS TO DO: From What You've Read

1. Why is planning important?
2. What must be considered as you plan?
3. What should be included in a daily lesson plan?
4. Write a lesson plan for the "Snapshot of a Lesson" at the beginning of Chapter 10.

5. Plan how to evaluate learning resulting from the lesson at the beginning of Chapter 8.
6. What were the objectives of the lesson described in this chapter's Snapshot of a Lesson? How were the NCTM standards concerning problem solving, communication, reasoning, and connections involved?
7. In the Snapshot, the problem the two children solved wasn't given. Write or find a problem that could have been used, and then write their report on how they solved it. Finally, write about how they solved it in a different way.

 ## THINGS TO DO: Going Beyond This Book

1. Compare two different scope-and-sequence charts for a particular grade level. How does the scope of the content included differ? What proportion is the same? How does the sequence differ?
2. Select a content topic. Compare the way it is taught in two different textbooks.
3. Select a content topic. Follow its development through three grade levels in a textbook series. Trace what is review and what is new development of mathematical content.
4. Select a topic and plan a week's work for it.
5. Design a lesson in which children will work in cooperative learning groups.
6. Observe in a classroom, recording the way teacher and pupils interact. What proportion of time does the teacher talk? What types of questions are asked? Is there evidence that children learned?
7. Consider the suggestions for planning and grouping offered by Larson (1983). Talk over these suggestions with a classroom teacher, and then write a summary of the ideas you want to try in your classroom.
8. Read the NCTM standard on the learning environment in the *Professional Standards* (NCTM 1991, pp. 57–61). Compare the kind of teaching portrayed there with what you recall from your elementary school experiences or what you have observed in a school recently.

Selected References

Anderson, Linda M. "Short-Term Student Responses to Classroom Instruction." *Elementary School Journal,* 82 (November 1981), pp. 97–108.

Artzt, Alice F., and Newman, Claire M. *How to Use Cooperative Learning in the Mathematics Class.* Reston, Va.: NCTM, 1990.

Bright, George W. "Understanding Children's Reasoning." *Teaching Children Mathematics,* 3 (September 1996), pp. 18–22.

Brownell, William A., and Chazal, Charlotte B. "The Effects of Premature Drill in Third-Grade Arithmetic." *Journal of Educational Research,* 29 (September 1935), pp. 17–28.

Burns, Marilyn. "The Role of Questioning." *Arithmetic Teacher,* 32 (February 1985), pp. 14–16.

Burns, Marilyn. "What I Learned from Teaching Second Grade." *Teaching Children Mathematics,* 3 (November 1996), pp. 127–124.

Bush, A. J.; Kennedy, J. J.; and Cruickshank, D. R. "An Empirical Investigation of Teacher Clarity." *Journal of Teacher Education,* 28 (March–April 1977), pp. 53–58.

Bush, William S., and Kincer, Lisa A. "The Teacher's Influence on the Classroom Learning Environment." In *Research Ideas for the Classroom: Early Childhood Mathematics* (ed. Robert J. Jensen). Reston, Va.: NCTM, and New York: Macmillan, 1993, pp. 311–328.

Clements, Douglas H., and McMillen, Sue. "Rethinking 'Concrete' Manipulatives." *Teaching Children Mathematics,* 2 (January 1996), pp. 270–279.

Cuevas, Gilbert, and Driscoll, Mark (eds.). *Reaching All Students with Mathematics.* Reston, Va.: NCTM, 1993.

Davidson, Neil. *Cooperative Learning in Mathematics: A Handbook for Teachers.* Reading, Mass.: Addison-Wesley, 1990.

Driscoll, Mark J. "Diagnosis: Taking the Mathematical Pulse." In *Research within Research: Elementary School Mathematics.* Reston, Va.: NCTM, 1981a.

Driscoll, Mark J. "Unlocking the Mind of a Child: Teaching for Remediation in Mathematics." In *Research within Reach: Elementary School Mathematics.* Reston, Va.: NCTM, 1981b.

Evertson, Carolyn M.; Emmer, Edward T.; and Brophy, Jere E. "Prediction of Effective Teaching in Junior High Mathematics Classrooms." *Journal for Research in Mathematics Education,* 11 (May 1980), pp. 167–178.

Farivar, Sydney, and Webb, Noreen M. "Helping and Getting Help—Essential Skills for Effective Group Problem Solving." *Arithmetic Teacher,* 41 (May 1994), pp. 521–525.

Fennell, Francis (Skip). "Mainstreaming and the Mathematics Classroom." *Arithmetic Teacher,* 32 (November 1984), pp. 22–27.

Fitzgerald, William M., and Bouck, Mary Kay. "Models of Instruction." In *Research Ideas for the Classroom: Middle Grades Mathematics* (ed. Douglas T. Owens). Reston, Va.: NCTM, and New York: Macmillan, 1993, pp. 244–258.

Good, Thomas L.; Grouws, Douglas A.; and Ebmeier, Howard. *Active Mathematics Teaching.* New York: Longman, 1983.

Kelly, Margaret. "A Script for a Mathematics Lesson." *Arithmetic Teacher,* 38 (December 1990), pp. 36–39.

Koehler, Mary Schatz, and Prior, Millie. "Classroom Interactions: The Heartbeat of the Teaching/Learning Process." In *Research Ideas for the Classroom: Middle Grades Mathematics* (ed. Douglas T. Owens). Reston, Va.: NCTM, and New York: Macmillan, 1993, pp. 280–298.

Lappan, Glenda. "What Do We Have and Where Do We Go from Here?" *Arithmetic Teacher,* 40 (May 1993), pp. 524–526.

Larson, Carol Novillis. "Organizing for Mathematics Instruction." *Arithmetic Teacher,* 31 (September 1983), pp. 16–20.

Liedtke, Werner. "Diagnosis in Mathematics: The Advantages of an Interview." *Arithmetic Teacher,* 36 (November 1988), pp. 26–29.

Lindquist, Mary Montgomery. "Assessing through Questioning." *Arithmetic Teacher,* 35 (January 1988), pp. 16–18.

Long, Madeleine J., and Ben-Hur, Meir. "Informing Learning through the Clinical Interview." *Arithmetic Teacher,* 38 (February 1991), pp. 44–46.

Madsen, Anne L., and Baker, Kendella. "Planning and Organizing the Middle Grades Mathematics Curriculum." In *Research Ideas for the Classroom: Middle Grades Mathematics* (ed. Douglas T. Owens). New York: Macmillan, 1993, pp. 259–279.

Meyers, Marcee J., and Burton, Grace M. "Yes You Can . . . Plan Appropriate Instruction for Learning Disabled Students." *Arithmetic Teacher,* 36 (March 1989), pp. 46–50.

Mueller, Delbert W. "Building a Scope and Sequence for Early Childhood Mathematics." *Arithmetic Teacher,* 33 (October 1985), pp. 8–11.

National Council of Teachers of Mathematics. *Curriculum and Evaluation Standards for School Mathematics.* Reston, Va.: NCTM, 1989.

National Council of Teachers of Mathematics. *Professional Standards for Teaching Mathematics.* Reston, Va.: NCTM, 1991.

Pursuing Excellence: A Study of U.S. Eighth-Grade Mathematics and Science Teaching, Learning, Curriculum, and Achievement in International Context. Washington, D.C.: National Center for Education Statistics, 1996.

Rathmell, Edward C. "Planning for Instruction Involves Focusing on Children's Thinking." *Arithmetic Teacher,* 41 (February 1994), pp. 290–291.

Reys, Barbara J., and Long, Vena M. "Teacher as Architect of Mathematical Tasks." *Teaching Children Mathematics,* 1 (January 1995), pp. 296–299.

Ross, Rita, and Kurtz, Ray. "Making Manipulatives Work: A Strategy for Success." *Arithmetic Teacher,* 40 (January 1993), pp. 254–257.

Scheibelhut, Carolyn. "I Do and I Understand, I Reflect and I Improve." *Teaching Children Mathematics,* 1 (December 1994), pp. 242–246.

Schmalz, Rosemary. "The Mathematics Textbook: How Can It Serve the Standards?" *Arithmetic Teacher,* 38 (September 1990), pp. 14–16. Reprinted in *Arithmetic Teacher,* 41 (February 1994), pp. 330–332.

Sowell, Evelyn J. "Effects of Manipulative Materials in Mathematics Instruction." *Journal for Research in Mathematics Education,* 20 (November 1989), pp. 498–505.

Suydam, Marilyn N. *Evaluation in the Mathematics Classroom.* Colombus, Ohio: ERIC Clearinghouse for Science, Mathematics and Environmental Education, 1987.

Suydam, Marilyn. "Planning for Mathematics Instruction." In *Mathematics for the Young Child* (ed. Joseph N. Payne). Reston, Va.: NCTM, 1990.

Suydam, Marilyn N., and Higgins, Jon L. *Activity-Based Learning in Elementary School Mathematics: Recommendations from Research.* Columbus, Ohio: ERIC Clearinghouse for Science, Mathematics and Environmental Education, 1977.

Suydam, Marilyn N., and Weaver, J. Fred. *Using Research: A Key to Elementary School Mathematics.* Columbus, Ohio: ERIC Clearinghouse for Science, Mathematics and Environmental Education, 1981.

Third International Mathematics and Science Study (TIMSS). *U.S. National Research Center Report No. 7,* East Lansing, Mich.: TIMSS U.S. National Research Center, Michigan State University, December 1996. http://ustimss.msu.edu/

Thompson, Alba G., and Briars, Diane J. "Implementing the Standards: Assessing Students' Learning to Inform Teaching: The Message in NCTM's Evaluation Standards." *Arithmetic Teacher,* 37 (December 1989), pp. 22–26.

Thompson, Patrick W. "Research into Practice: Concrete Materials and Teaching for Mathematical Understanding." *Arithmetic Teacher,* 41 (May 1994), pp. 556–558.

Thornton, Carol A., and Wilson, Sandra J. "Classroom Organization and Models of Instruction." In *Research Ideas for the Classroom: Early Childhood Mathematics* (ed. Robert J. Jensen). Reston, Va.: NCTM, and New York: Macmillan, 1993, pp. 269–293.

Thornton, Carol D. "An Evaluation of the Mathematics-Methods Program Involving the Study of Teaching Characteristics and Pupil Achievement in Mathematics." *Journal for Research in Mathematics Education,* 8 (January 1977), pp. 17–25.

Vacc, Nancy Nesbitt. "Questioning in the Mathematics Classroom." *Arithmetic Teacher,* 41 (October 1993), pp. 88–91.

Vacc, Nancy Nesbitt. "Planning for Instruction: Barriers to Mathematics Discussion." *Arithmetic Teacher,* 41 (February 1994), pp. 339–341.

4

Assessing for Learning

 Introduction

In this chapter, we examine ways to assess what students understand and how they feel about mathematics. Such assessment allows teachers to make careful decisions about helping students learn. As you proceed through the remainder of this book, we encourage you to think about the ways in which you could assess what you learn, as you are learning it.

You were introduced to the *Assessment Standards for School Mathematics* (NCTM 1995) through a listing of the six assessment standards in Chapter 1. These standards are short, but powerful, statements that you can use to make judgments about your assessments. The first standard focuses on the mathematics. You should ask yourself if you are assessing mathematics that is important for students to learn. Although this may sound like a rhetorical question, it is not. Often the easiest aspects of mathematics to assess are the most trivial. You will need to plan assessments that tap important mathematics in ways that are meaningful to children.

The second standard asks if your assessments enhance the opportunity for students to learn mathematics. Have you thought of tests as a way to help in the learning, or as a hurdle to jump? Assessing should be integral to learning, not something separate. Children will learn what we value in mathematics. For example, if we think that problem solving is important and yet never or rarely assess problem solving, students will soon conclude that it is not an important part of their learning. Result: they will not become problem solvers.

There are many questions that you could ask yourself about the third standard, the equity standard. As you strive to help all children learn mathematics, look carefully at your assessment procedures and ask questions such as these:

- What opportunities has each student had to learn the mathematics being assessed?
- How does the assessment help students demonstrate their best work?
- How have the effects of bias been minimized throughout the assessment? (NCTM 1995, p. 16)

These three standards and the other three (openness, inferences, and coherence) call for some fundamental shifts in how we in the classroom and how externally opposed assessments view assessment (see Table 4–1).

In this chapter, however, we will focus on the aspects of assessment that will assist you in the classroom. If you are equating assessment with testing, then begin to think in a broader way. It is more than testing. Assessment of mathematical learning may be thought of as the process of gathering evidence about student's knowledge of, ability to use, and disposition toward mathematics, and of making inferences from that evidence for a variety of purposes (NCTM 1995, p. 3). You will need to plan your assessments, gather evidence in many ways such as those discussed in this chapter, interpret the evidence, and use the results.

Table 4–1 • **Major shifts in assessment practices**

Toward	*Away From*
• Assessing students' full mathematical power	• Assessing only students' knowledge of specific facts and isolated skills
• Comparing students' performance with established criteria	• Comparing students' performance with that of other students
• Giving support to teachers and credence to their informed judgment	• Designing "teach-proof" assessment systems
• Making the assessment process public, participatory, and dynamic	• Making the assessment process secret, exclusive, and fixed
• Giving students multiple opportunities to demonstrating their full mathematical power	• Restricting students to a single way of demonstrating their mathematical knowledge
• Developing a shared vision of what to assess and how to do it	• Developing assessment by oneself
• Using assessment results to ensure that all students have the opportunity to achieve their potential	• Using assessment to filter and select students out of the opportunities to learn mathematics
• Aligning assessment with curriculum and instruction	• Treating assessment as independent of curriculum or instruction
• Basing inferences on multiple sources of evidence	• Basing inferences on restricted or single sources of evidence
• Viewing students as active participants in the assessment process	• Viewing students as the objects of assessment
• Regarding assessment as continual and recursive	• Regarding assessment as sporadic and conclusive
• Holding all concerned with mathematics learning accountable for assessment results	• Holding only a few accountable for assessment results

(Reprinted with permission from *Assessment Standards for School Mathematics,* © 1995 by the National Council of Teachers of Mathematics.)

We will focus on two of the purposes described in the *Assessment Standards* (NCTM 1995), making instructional decisions and monitoring student progress. You will be making many instructional decisions. As with any decision, the better informed that we are, the wiser the choices we usually make. The six assessment standards suggest the following shifts in making instructional decisions:

1. A shift toward integrating assessment with instruction (to provide data for moment-by-moment instructional decisions) and away from depending on scheduled testing (generally useful only for delayed instructional decisions).

2. A shift toward using evidence from a variety of assessment formats and contexts for determining the effectiveness of instruction and away from relying on any one source of information.

3. A shift toward using evidence of every student's progress toward long-range goals in instructional planning and away from planning for content coverage with little regard for students' progress. (NCTM 1995, p. 45)

As we monitor student progress, there are also several shifts in assessment practice being called for by the *Assessment Standards.*

4. A shift toward judging the progress of each student's attainment of mathematical power and away from assessing students' knowledge of specific facts and isolated skills.

5. A shift toward communicating with students about their performance in a continuous, comprehensive manner, and away from simply indicating whether or not answers are correct.

6. A shift toward using multiple and complex assessment tools (such as performance tasks, projects, writing assignments, oral demonstrations, and portfolios), and away from sole reliance on answers to brief questions on quizzes and chapter tests.

7. A shift toward students learning to assess their own progress, and away from teachers and external agencies as the sole judges of progress. (NCTM 1995, p. 29)

The number of shifts listed in this opening section is an indication of the need for change in many of our assessment practices. This will come through time and open minds; this chapter is an opportunity for you to begin asking yourself questions considering how you will assess students in order to make decisions and monitor progress.

● Ways to Gather Evidence

There are many different ways to gather information about the abilities, dispositions, and interests of students. The type of information and how to obtain it depend on the purpose for which it will be used. You first need to ask yourself what mathematics learning you want to assess.

For example, if you want to assess the principle discussed in Chapter 2—that mathematics learning should be meaningful—then you will want to find out whether students have attached meaning to what they are doing by observing them and by asking questions that elicit their level of understanding. If you want your students to be persistent and willing to approach problems in a variety of ways, then you will assess these characteristics through problems of a challenging nature. If you want your students to be able to communicate well and to work well with others, as discussed in Chapter 2, then you will make those characteristics part of your assessment procedure.

In this section, we consider several different techniques for obtaining information to assess students' learning and their dispositions according to the NCTM's vision. We also will look at some combinations of methods—for example, giving a written test and then asking individual children to explain how they arrived at the solution.

Observation

Although you naturally will know how to observe your students, practice and planning will help you to hone your observation skills. For example, it is helpful to plan what you will observe on a given day. Suppose you are teaching first grade and your students are solving problems involving addition facts. You may want to observe and record which students are using physical materials, which are doing most of the problems mentally, which are using thinking strategies (which will be discussed in Chapter 9), and which are relying on memorized facts. At times, you may plan to observe only one student in a cooperative group setting:

Does José jump right in or wait for others to begin?

Is he willing to listen?

Does he accept or challenge the ideas of others?

Is he willing to play different roles within the group?

Is he persistent? Does the problem interest him?

From such observations, you can gain insight into a student's attitude and disposition toward mathematics. This knowledge, in turn, can help you plan ways to encourage strengths and work on weaknesses.

Sometimes, you may want to observe students when they are engaged in tasks:

What does the frown on Rhonda's face mean?

Why is the cluster of students at the back table off the task?

How is Roger attempting to arrive at an answer?

Which students in the class do not appear to be grasping the new concept?

Your notes about what you have observed will be useful not only for anecdotal records that you can use for assessment and for planning, but your observations themselves also can help you decide what to do immediately while you are leading a discussion or presenting a new concept.

Questioning

Observation is complemented and enlightened by asking questions. For example, suppose Rhonda was frowning during a sixth-grade class in which students were investigating the decimal representations of fractions using calculators. The calculator has shown these results:

$$\frac{1}{9} = 0.1111111$$

$$\frac{2}{9} = 0.2222222$$

$$\frac{3}{9} = 0.3333333$$

You know that Rhonda is a confident and capable mathematics student, so what might be the cause of the frown? In this case, a direct question to Rhonda about what is puzzling her is appropriate. In other cases, asking a direct question such as "What don't you understand?" may not help because a less-confident or less-capable student may not know how to formulate his or her puzzlement. You may need to ask a series of questions to probe for the cause.

For example, suppose a middle-school student, Raymond, thinks that ⅑ equals 0.1111111 because the calculator shows it. To help Raymond understand that this result is an approximation, you may need to ask Raymond the following questions.

What does ⅑ mean?

If Raymond responds that it means one of nine equal parts of a whole, you could proceed in this manner:

Can you draw a sketch and label the parts with both notations (fractional and decimal)?

Each part is equal to ⅑, so what is the total of all nine parts?

Each part is equal to 0.1111111, so what is the total of all nine parts? Is this one?

Is it near to one?

If Raymond responds that ⅑ means one divided by nine, then you might have him divide 1 by 9 using paper and pencil to see there is always a remainder no matter how many places you carry out the division.

Asking good questions is an art that needs to be developed and practiced. When you teach through questioning, you actively involve students and know more about what they are thinking. In planning your lessons, you should think of questions that will help you gauge whether students are understanding the mathematics, whether they are approaching a problem in different ways, whether they can generalize, or whether they can explain their thinking.

For example, look at the lesson that opens Chapter 14, and examine the questions that Mr. Flores asked. The questions about which students took the most and the least shots are low-level questions that do not give you much information. The questions about who is the best shot, however, elicit a great deal of information about students' thinking and their understanding of the mathematics. Remember that students need time to think about their answers to such questions. Practice waiting silently.

Interviewing

Interviewing is a combination of questioning and observing, usually done with one student in a quiet place. It is a powerful way to learn about a student's thinking and to give her or him some special attention. Key factors in a successful interview are establishing rapport with the child, accepting responses without judging, and encouraging the child to talk and explain.

Although you will not have time to interview all of your students each day or even each week, choose a few to interview each week until you have had a chance to talk with each individually. Teachers are often surprised at how students value the private time with them and how much they learn in a short time about the individual student.

Before interviewing a student, you need a basic plan of what you want to investigate, what materials you will need, what questions you will ask, and when and how you will record the information. You may want to have alternative paths to take if the interview proceeds in different ways. Figure 4–1 shows a plan and some notes the teacher made in preparation for interviewing some of her third-grade students.

Performance Tasks

In a class that is alive with problem solving and investigations, many valuable opportunities will arise to observe students working on performance tasks. In fact, the only way we can assess some skills will be through performance tasks. For example, if one objective is for children to know how to measure with a ruler, then they need to be assessed doing such measuring. Questions on written tests that line up a picture of a ruler with the object do not reveal much about the actual skill of measuring.

Performance tasks often mirror the real world, are open-ended, and require time for grappling with a problem. It often is helpful to pair children when observing performance of such tasks so that you can hear their conversation as they work. In planning, you will want to list of some of the areas you want to observe as the pairs work on appropriate tasks.

Here are three areas you might plan to observe and examples of the notes you might make while observing the performance task in Activity Card 2–1.

1. Strategy: Used trial and error

Organized by length (or height or width)

Found and used patterns

Made other comparisons

Used a combination of strategies

Interview: Place Value

Reminders: Don't teach!
Listen - let them do.
- How would you show a friend?
- How would you tell your sister?

Materials: Proportional models (Unifix cubes and base-10 blocks), paper and pencil

Questions to Probe

Can the child model various numbers with different models?

Does the child understand the symbol?

Does the child understand regrouping?

Are these understandings with tens extended to hundreds?

Tasks *(Be flexible - ask more if needed)*

1. Show me 24.
   - Can you show with cubes?
   - Can you show with base-10 blocks?
   - Is there another way?

   Repeat with 40.

   Show me 37. (Group the cubes into tens, if the child did not).
   - How do you know that is 37?

   This is 37.
   - What if I gave you 10 more cubes?
   - How many would you have?
   - How do you know?

2. Let's look again at this many cubes (37). (Write the number.)
   - What does the seven mean? Can you show me with cubes?
   - What does the three mean? Can you show me with cubes?

3. Begin with 37 as 3 tens and 7 ones. Trade a ten for 10 ones.
   - How many do you have now?
   - Do you have more cubes than 37? Why or why not?

4. Extend the above to hundreds if child has tens.

Extension: Check to see how many different ways the child can show 136.

Figure 4–1 • Example teacher plan and notes for interviewing third graders

2. Result: Found few (or all) combinations
Found the connection to factors of the number
Found (did not find) the formula
Able (unable) to describe the procedure

3. Attitude: Worked well together
Curious, explored other shapes, other numbers
Remained engaged
Enthusiastic

As indicated in Chapter 3, emphasis on worthwhile mathematical tasks is a core dimension of the *Professional Standards for Teaching Mathematics* (NCTM 1991). Figure 3–1 gives the standard describing the type of tasks and the goals of this focus on task performance. You may want to begin with simple tasks and then build up to longer, more complicated ones. Often you will be surprised at the tenacity of very young children on a task that is engaging them; you should not rule out richer tasks for this age.

Self-Assessments

Students are often the best assessors of their own work and feelings. When students evaluate their own work, the responsibility for their learning is theirs. You can begin the self-assessment process by having students validate their own thinking or their answers to selected exercises. For example, in a nonthreatening way, you could ask Dwayne to show you how he arrived at the answer in the following case:

$$\begin{array}{r} 28 \\ \times\,46 \\ \hline 168 \\ 122 \\ \hline 290 \end{array}$$

You will also want to ask him to explain how he obtained the answer to this problem:

$$\begin{array}{r} 24 \\ \times\,39 \\ \hline 216 \\ 72 \\ \hline 936 \end{array}$$

It is important to ask about correct answers as well as incorrect ones so that children do not think that they are questioned only when something is wrong. Only asking about incorrect answers will not help build their self-esteem or establish the feeling that they have control of the mathematics.

Students can also analyze each others' strategies for solving problems. As they listen to and discuss how another student or group of students solved a problem, they will begin to see different ways to proceed and to make judgments about which way makes the most sense to them, which seems easier or different, and which leads to stumbling blocks. Not only will they learn from such discussions and self-assessments, but you will also learn a lot about the students.

No one is better at assessing how a student feels about a given task than the student who is doing it. You may want to give a simple attitude inventory. However, you probably will learn more from young children by asking them to complete tasks such as the following.

- If mathematics were a color (a food or a toy), what would it be? Why?
- Draw a picture of what mathematics looks (feels) like to you.
- If you were telling a friend about the favorite thing you do in mathematics class, what would you tell him or her?

You can learn much about older children's view of mathematics through discussions. Several questions suggested by Spangler (1992) included the following:

- If you and a friend got different answers to the same problem, what would you do?
- If you were playing "Password" (one-word clues) and you wanted a friend to guess the word mathematics, what clues would you give?
- How do you know when you have solved a problem correctly?

Work Samples

Work samples can include written assignments, projects, and other student products that you collect and evaluate. Figure 4–2 reproduces the work of four children on problem (19) in Chapter 5. Figure 4–3 provides one analytic scoring scale for assessing children's work in problem solving on three measures, and Table 4–2 shows the scores for each child on the three measures in Figure 4–3.

There are, in fact, many different schemes for scoring problem solving, and each involves judgment. For example, try scoring the papers in Figure 4–3 using the same analytic scoring scale to see whether you agree with the scorer in Table 4–2. (You may well disagree, but you should be able to justify your position.)

Perhaps more important than scoring children's work is analyzing it to see what you can learn about the students. Looking again at the work of the four students in Figure 4–3, for example, we could conclude that only Suzy searched for more than one answer to the problem.

Portfolios

Portfolios have been used for evaluations of art works for a long time, but only recently has there been an emphasis on using this technique in mathematics. A student's mathematics portfolio might include such things as special problem-solving tasks, writings, investigations, projects, and reports. These could be presented through a variety of media, including paper and pencil, audio or video-tapes, and computer disks.

If you have your students keep portfolios, you will need to make many decisions:

What will be included?

Where will they be kept?

How often will you give feedback?

Will you grade them?

Once you have determined these things, portfolios can be a rich source of information for you and your students.

An additional benefit of portfolios is their value as a self-assessment tool for students. It is important for students to date the entries so that they can see their growth over the year. It is also helpful if they describe the task and reflect on it.

Writings

The NCTM *Standards* call for more emphasis on communication in mathematics, and student writings as a form of communication can provide another source for assessment. You may want students to keep a journal or add writing to other assignments.

A simple way to begin is to ask students to write about what they understood and did not understand for one assignment, how they felt about an ac-

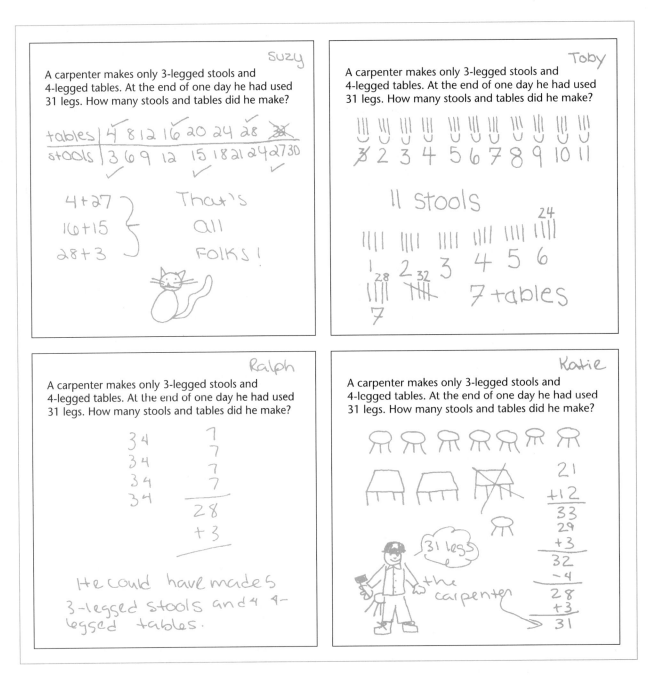

Figure 4–2 • **Samples of children's problem-solving work**

tivity, what they learned today in class, or what they like about math. Your creativity in providing suggestions will help spark theirs. For example, you might ask them to write a letter to a friend about math class or to write a poem about triangles. As writing becomes a part of math class, you can use it to assess children's knowledge of and attitudes toward mathematics.

Written Tests

Tests can inform and guide your instruction, rather than being simply the determinants of a grade. Students learn from tests, but too often the lessons they learn may not be those intended. When too much emphasis is placed on written tests, students can learn that they do not have to know why some pro-

---

Analytic Scoring Scale

Understanding the Problem

0: Complete misunderstanding of the problem

1: Part of the problem misunderstood or misinterpreted

2: Complete understanding of the problem

Planning a Solution

0: No attempt, or totally inappropriate plan

1: Partially correct plan based on part of the problem being interpreted correctly

2: Plan could have led to a correct solution if implemented properly

Getting an Answer

0: No answer, or wrong answer based on an inappropriate plan

1: Copying error, computational error, partial answer for a problem with multiple answers

2: Correct answer and correct label for the answer

Figure 4–3 • **A scale for scoring problem solving** (Reprinted with permission from Charles, Lester, and O'Daffer, *How to Evaluate Progress in Problem Solving,* © 1987 by the National Council of Teachers of Mathematics.)

Table 4–2 • **Scoring for children's work in Figure 4–2 using the scale in Figure 4–3**

	Understanding the Problem	Planning a Solution	Getting an Answer	Total
Suzy	2	2	2	6
Toby	1	1	0	2
Katie	2	2	1	5
Ralph	2	2	2	6

cedure works, to explain how they solved a problem, or to be able to solve word problems, since a passing grade may be obtained without ever doing these things.

Carefully constructed and correctly analyzed tests can tell us a lot about students. For example, the children's papers in Figure 4–4 are for a simple test on subtraction of two-digit numbers, but they reveal a lot about the students. Notice how many of them missed the problems with zeros. If the first or seventh item had not been on the test, the teacher might not have realized that Jim regroups—and then ignores—even when regrouping is not necessary. (Try analyzing the kinds of errors the other students made and what characterizes each student.)

Most paper-and-pencil tests will not give you the opportunity to learn how a student arrived at an answer. One way to gain more insight is to ask the students to explain in writing what they did. If children are accustomed to explaining orally in class, then this task will be easier for them, and you will receive more meaningful explanations. Ask for explanations on a few items, and accept them in the children's language. Otherwise, they will soon learn to parrot explanations that are meaningless to them.

There is no reason why paper-and-pencil tests cannot include estimation items and require manipulatives and calculators. These tests can also permit the use of textbooks or notebooks, ask thought-provoking questions, and require students to connect new learnings to previous ones. They need not be races against time in which the students regurgitate all they remember from the week or about the procedure last taught.

Thoughtful, well-constructed tests are one way—often a very efficient way—to gather information. Alone, they will not give a complete assessment of students' knowledge, but they can add one more piece to the puzzle.

Edie

27	94	60	41	52
− 14	− 37	− 48	− 26	− 39
13	57	12	15	13

80	76	57	66	92
− 25	− 53	− 49	− 8	− 16
55	23	8	58	76

Steve

27	94	60	41	52
− 14	− 37	− 48	− 26	− 39
13	63	28	25	23

80	76	57	66	92
− 25	− 53	− 49	− 8	− 16
65	23	12	2	84

Mary Beth

27	94	60	41	52
− 14	− 37	− 48	− 26	− 39
13	57	28	25	23

80	76	57	66	92
− 25	− 53	− 49	− 8	− 16
65	23	18	58	86

Jim

27	94	60	41	52
− 14	− 37	− 48	− 26	− 39
13	67	22	25	23

80	76	57	66	92
− 25	− 53	− 49	− 8	− 16
65	23	18	518	76

Becky

27	94	60	41	52
− 14	− 37	− 48	− 26	− 39
13	58	12	15	14

7 8 9 10 11 12 13 14   9 10 11 12

80	76	57	66	92
− 25	− 53	− 49	− 8	− 16
65	23	8	60	77

59   58

30 40 50 60 70 80

HSM

27	94	60	41	52
− 14	− 37	− 48	− 26	− 39
13	57	28	15	13

80	76	57	66	92
− 25	− 53	− 49	− 8	− 16
65	23	8	58	76

Herbie

27	94	60	41	52
− 14	− 37	− 48	− 26	− 39
13	57	12	15	13

80	76	57	66	92
− 25	− 53	− 49	− 8	− 16
		8	68	76

Brad

27	94	60	41	52
− 14	− 37	− 48	− 26	− 39
13	56	18	14	12

80	76	57	66	92
− 25	− 53	− 49	− 8	− 16
65	23	7	57	75

Fran

27	94	60	41	52
− 14	− 37	− 48	− 26	− 39
13	57	12	67	91

80	76	57	66	92
− 25	− 53	− 49	− 8	− 16
55	29	106	8	76

Figure 4–4 • Samples of children's papers for a written test of subtraction

Achievement Tests

At some point you will undoubtedly be asked to administer standardized or state-wide tests. The results of these are often received too late to be applied to instruction that year, but they can be used to take a look at your instruction in general. For example, if you see that your students did poorly in measurement, then you need to rethink what you are doing in that area.

Remember that norm-referenced tests are designed to spread children across the whole normal distribution. There will always be 50 percent of the students below average and 50 percent above average. Thus, some items on such tests are not intended for everyone at a grade level to do correctly. The fact that an item on multiplying fractions appears on a fourth-grade test does not mean that this is a recommended skill for all students at this level.

Achievement tests are changing. Some allow the use of calculators, some are asking questions in an open format rather than multiple choice format, some are asking for explanations, and some are including problem-solving situations.

If you help your students learn in a way that is meaningful to them, and build their confidence and the attitude that they can do mathematics, then you will not have to worry about the results of achievement tests.

● Ways to Keep Records and to Communicate about Assessments

It is important to keep both informal and formal records of students' learning and their disposition toward mathematics. The type of records you keep may depend on the school system, but you can keep additional ones of your own.

A word of caution: do not become burdened with a multitude of records, but do keep enough that you can reflect on your students' progress and can justify any major decisions about them or what to teach. The type of records you keep also will depend on the ways you report information to students, to parents, and to the school administration.

Recording the Information

Teachers are aware of a multitude of things about their students and keep many informal records about them. For example, you will know that Treena is always willing to answer in math class, that Joshua does not work well with Katrina, that Yong knows how to compute but seems to lack understanding about when and why certain operations are used, and that Cary is often absent on math test days. But maybe you need to jar your memory about Rachel before her parents come for the next parent conference. Or maybe you are thinking about changing the composition of cooperative groups and wondering if Jerry and Richard worked well together in the past.

Because of the volume of information about students that may be useful, it is often helpful as well as necessary to record some of it. Several techniques for recording information are described here. You may find others or modify these to suit your needs.

Checklists Checklists may be used in a variety of ways to record individualized information about students' understandings, attitudes, or content

achievement. They may be simply lists that are marked in different ways, rating scales, or annotated checklists (see Figures 4–5, 4–6, 4–7, and 4–8). The beauty of checklists is that they can be adapted to your situation and, in fact, may help you think about your goals and the needs of each child you are teaching.

You cannot spend all your time keeping records, so select a few significant aspects of students' learning and attitudes and target a few children each day. For example, you may want to observe and keep records about children working in cooperative groups one week and focus on individual children's understanding of a new topic the next week.

If you use a checklist, you will want to keep it handy so that you can make quick entries as children are engaged in tasks. If you wait until the end of the day, you may forget some of the day's gems or be too preoccupied with other tasks to jot them down.

If you are recording information that is meant only for you, keep the checklist away from the eyes of your students. Be especially sensitive to children's feelings. A public checklist that shows the progress of each class member's skill attainment may be a great boost for those at the top but quite detrimental to those at the bottom, who often need the most encouragement.

Student Files Many teachers keep a record of students' learning in the form of a file of work samples from each. If children are keeping their own portfolios, those may suffice, so that you do not need to keep additional samples of their work in your own student files. In either case, you may want to keep a summary profile for each child, like the one shown in Figure 4–9. Sometimes the school's format for reporting to parents will require that you keep such a record.

Class Records Often the only class record is the grade book. Although it may be necessary to keep such a record, you must realize the limitations of a grade book. Alternatively, you could modify it with shorthand entries of your choosing to tell you more than attendance; grades on assignments, quizzes, and tests; and cumulative grades.

You could also supplement the grade book with a cumulative checklist made from your daily or weekly checklists. You can determine which items to include by reviewing the usefulness and frequency of your entries in these earlier checklists. The cumulative checklist will then give you a picture of the class as a whole and help you plan.

Figure 4–5
This checklist of student participation in math class activities is useful for tracking which children need to be encouraged to participate and which need to be supported in their involvement. For example, as Brenda's teacher, you would see that she has worked at the math centers and has been responsible for materials, and you could use this information as a reminder to support her interest by making her a group leader.

MATH CLASS PARTICIPATION

NAME	DATE: March	Center A	Center B	Center C	Group Leader	Group Recorder	Group Reporter	Bulletin Board	Materials	Other
Atkins, Willie		2	4	6	5	13	10	✓	✓	MCounts
Bero, Chuck		9	10	11	10	5			March	
Connel, Brenda		2	3	5			10		✓	
Cosby, Kim				2		5		✓	✓	
Coroi, Troy		11	10	9	5		13	✓	March	MCounts
Foster, Greg		12		2		10	5		✓	
Hale, Carol		2	4	6	13	5		✓	✓	
Jones, Tempie			12	13				March		
Jones, Zelda		10	9	6			5		March	
McGee, Leslie		6	4		5	13		march	✓	
Mory, Kelly		11		12	13	10		✓		
Navarro, Sarita			10	4	10			✓	march	
Nelson, Clara		5	6	2			5	March	✓	
Odom, Ruby			2		5		13		✓	
Pak, Yong		12	11	10	13				March	
Porter, Jessie			5		10	5		March		
Roy, Lulu		10		12			10			
Stewart, Scott			2				5	✓		
Tucker, Enoka		11		3	5	13		March		MCounts
Watt, Mary Lee		10	2	3		5	10	March		
Weaver, J. T.		12	2	5	10			✓		
White, Emma		3		5	13	10		✓		MCounts
Wortaszek, Sam		4	10	3		10	5	March		
Yi, Sik				11	10					
Zuber, Albert			11				10			

Figure 4–6
This annotated checklist is useful for recording classroom observations as well as actions the teacher took when necessary. Such checklists are also useful for providing reminders of points to discuss when communicating with parents and students.

CLASS OBSERVATION
Class 5th period   Week Feb. 6-10/13-17

NAMES	COMMENTS	ACTION NEEDED	ACTION TAKEN
Atkins, Willie			
Bero, Chuck	Needs a challenge	✱	Yes
Connel, Brenda			
Cosby, Kim	No homework for 3 days	✱	Called
Coroi, Troy			
Foster, Greg			
Hale, Carol	Doing much better with fractions – fraction bars helped		
Jones, Tempie			
Jones, Zelda	What a difference in geometry – good spatial sense		
McGee, Leslie			
Mory, Kelly			
Navarro, Sarita			
Nelson, Clara	Wants to be on math team next year – mother says yes ✱		Called mother
Odom, Ruby			
Pak, Yong			
Porter, Jessie	Spend some time with Jessie – he can do this		
Roy, Lulu			
Stewart, Scott	Is beginning to work well in a group		
Tucker, Enoka			
Watt, Mary Lee			
Weaver, J. T.			
White, Emma			
Wortaszek, Sam			
Yi, Sik	Loves group work – helps with language		
Zuber, Albert			

Figure 4–7
This annotated checklist is used to record the teacher's observations of group work. Notes such as these can help the teacher in assessing group interactions and to make decisions on how to group students for future work.

GROUP OBSERVATION	DATE	TASK	COMMENTS	DATE	TASK	COMMENTS
GROUP A	1/18	Problem: Quarter Change	Group worked well together – would not stop until they had all the possibilities			
John						
Caryl						
Luther						
Jara						
GROUP B						
Todd						Need to observe!
Kate						
David						
Cathy						
GROUP C	1/18	Problem: Quarter Change	Need to watch, that Brandi doesn't take over – talk with her – give some questions to ask	1/22	Data	Brandi made a real effort to obtain the ideas from others – they arrived at a neat different question
Tamia						
Larry						
Maude						
Brandi						
GROUP D		Data: What's My Favorite?	Chose TV programs – finally focused on G-4 – were on task			
Otis						
Sandra						
Gloria						
Chon ho						
GROUP E	1/22	Data: Favorite	Could not agree on topic – all wanted their own	1/24	Same	
Renea						
Lisa						
Tamio						
Gary						

Figure 4–8
This checklist of student dispositions is helpful in determining which students might need special activities or encouragement to help boost their confidence or perseverance in problem solving, for example. It can also be used for support in parent conferences or in discussions with students.

STUDENT DISPOSITIONS — CLASS: 3rd Grade Math — MONTH: October	Helen	Art	Whit	Beverly	Anita	Jim
Confidence						
Is sure of answer	✓			✓		
Knows how to proceed	✓			✓		
Flexibility						
Will change direction	If prodded ✓		✓		✓	
Tries several ways			✓			
Perseverance						
Stays with task	✓					
Enjoys involved problems		✓		✓		
Curiosity						
Wants to find out why		✓	✓	✓		✓
Challenges						
Sharing						
Works well with others		✓				✓
Shows leadership				✓		

Other Notes You may also want to keep records of activities you have tried, articles you have read, ideas you want to try, and other anecdotal records. If you are using a textbook, then consider using stick-on notes to record comments and ideas that you do not want to forget.

Look at the collection of notes taken from a fifth-grade teacher's book in Figure 4–10. A few min-utes doing this kind of annotating may save much time the next year.

Communicating the Information

Most teachers have three main audiences to whom the information they have gathered will be communicated. Each group—students, parents, and admin-

```
Student Profile in Mathematics K–4

Date  Feb.
Student  Jeremy Gelder              Teacher  Matt Bell              Grade  2

Content Areas
  Number Sense & Numeration   Still sees numbers as ones – needs to develop place value
  Estimation   Good feel for numbers – size of quantities
  Concepts of Operations   Good problem solver
  Computation
  Geometry & Spatial Sense   Geometry he loves
  Measurement
  Statistics & Probability
  Fractions & Decimals
  Patterns & Relationships   Better at spatial patterns
Math Power
  Problem Solving   Likes to think in creative ways
  Reasoning
  Communication   Explains well
  Connections
  Concepts   Developing
  Procedures   Doesn't like to follow procedures – invents his own
Dispositions
  Confidence   Growing
  Flexibility
  Perseverance   On many tasks
  Curiosity   Great
  Reflection
Other Comments
```

Figure 4–9 ● **Student profile**

istration—will receive different amounts of information in different ways.

To Students Much of your communicating of information to students will be done orally or through actions, but you also will be writing comments on work samples, portfolios, tests, journals, or other forms of assessment materials. And, perhaps, you will give a letter or number grade. All these communications influence children's feelings about the value of different aspects of mathematics, their expectations of what they can accomplish, and their sense of their own worth.

Be positive and fair. Use information from your checklists or from student portfolios when letting each student know whether he or she is meeting expectations, and look for ways to demonstrate to each that he or she can do what is expected. Finally, remember that it is important that children grow in

their ability to self-assess. One of your goals should be to help children become independent learners. If they always have to rely on you to validate their work and their thinking, they will not reach this goal.

To Parents You will be reporting to parents both in written form and orally. The format of these reports is often determined by the school system, but you are responsible for the quality. You will grow in your ability to communicate with parents, but it is important from the beginning that you keep records and use them to illustrate or justify your oral and written comments.

Parent conferences are also times for gathering information. Parents often provide insights about their children that may not be evident to you in the classroom. And the information you glean from them should be included in notes in your student files.

Figure 4–10 • **A sampling of stick-on notes from a fifth-grade teacher's textbook**

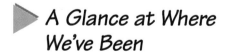

To the School Administration When you begin teaching, you will need to find out what type of records are required in your school and how they are used.

- Does the administration expect written reports on each child?
- Is there an official checklist?
- Is the class grade record sufficient?
- Is information on students passed to the next teacher, kept in a permanent file, or used to make tracking decisions?
- Is the information used in teacher evaluations?

The type and use of records vary from school to school, so it is necessary to find out about your own situation. When you know how the records are to be used, you will be better able to provide information that is suitable for particular uses.

▶ A Glance at Where We've Been

Assessment is an integral part of teaching. This chapter looks at student assessment to help you make informed decisions about instruction and monitoring student progress. There are many ways to gather, analyze, and present the information from assessments.

The different ways to gather information range from informal observations to formal achievement tests. Collecting information about students' learning is only one goal. The other is to collect information regarding their dispositions toward mathematics. Information needs to be recorded in some way so you can analyze it. There are several techniques for recording and communicating information.

Assessment can make a difference in how you help your students learn mathematics. You can use it in a positive way to encourage the children to become independent learners, to modify your instruction, and to communicate with parents.

THINGS TO DO:
From What You've Read

1. What recommendations for shifts in assessment (Table 4–1) are most closely connected to the classroom?

2. A narrow view is that assessment in mathematics focuses on how well students can carry out procedures in a limited amount of time. Describe a broader view of mathematics assessment.

3. Describe some different ways to make assessments. Which require children to respond orally?

4. Identify an error pattern in the work of at least four of the students in Figure 4–4.

5. What can you learn from a student interview?

6. What records could you keep to assist with a parent conference?

7. Give one idea for keeping a record of your class.

8. What is the purpose of student assessment?

9. Make a plan of how you would assess students in your class on one of the standards given in Figures 1–2 and 1–4.

THINGS TO DO:
Going Beyond This Book

1. Watch the videotape *A Look at Children's Thinking* (Richardson 1990) or a similar video on interviewing students. Describe what you learned from the students and the interviewer.

2. Read one of the articles on interviewing listed in the Selected References. Design an interview and use it with three students. Describe what you learned about each student.

3. Collect a set of problem-solving papers from students. Analyze and score them using the analytic scale in Figure 4–3.

4. Develop a test that involves the use of manipulatives.

5. Analyze a test in an elementary mathematics textbook. Would it make a difference if the students used calculators? What items would you need to change?

6. Analyze a test in an elementary mathematics textbook to determine whether it requires writing about mathematics. If not, what changes could you make so that it would do so?

7. Observe one or two students during a mathematics class. Describe what you observed. If you were to work with these students in mathematics, what course of action would you take?

8. Try a performance task with a couple of students. Make a list of observations and use it as the basis for your description of the children's performance. You may find samples in *Measuring Up: Prototypes for Mathematics Assessment* (Mathematical Sciences Education Board, 1993).

9. Examine a standardized test. Does it allow use of calculators? Identify examples of good and poor questions, and explain your opinions.

Selected References

California Mathematics Council. *Assessment Alternatives in Mathematics: An Overview of Assessment Techniques That Promote Learning.* Berkeley, Calif.: EQUALS, 1989.

Charles, Randall; Lester, Frank; and O'Daffer, Phares. *How to Evaluate Progress in Problem Solving.* Reston, Va.: NCTM, 1987.

Clark, H. Clifford, and Nelson, Marvin N. "Evaluation: Be More Than a Scorekeeper." *Arithmetic Teacher,* 38 (May 1991), pp. 15–17.

Clarke, David J.; Clarke, Doug M.; and Lovitt, Charles J. "Changes in Mathematics Teaching Call for Assessment Alternatives." In *Teaching and Learning Mathematics in the 1990s,* 1990 Yearbook (ed. Thomas J. Cooney). Reston, Va.: NCTM, 1990.

Garnett, Cynthia M. "Testing—Do Not Disturb? A Parent's View of Testing." *Arithmetic Teacher,* 39 (February 1992), pp. 8–10.

Harvey, John G. "Using Calculators in Mathematics Changes Testing." *Arithmetic Teacher,* 38 (March 1991), pp. 52–54.

Kamii, Constance, and Lewis, Barbara Ann. "Achievement Tests in Primary Mathematics: Perpetuating Lower-Order Thinking." *Arithmetic Teacher,* 38 (May 1991), pp. 4–9.

Labinowicz, Ed. "Assessing for Learning: The Interview Method." *Arithmetic Teacher,* 35 (November 1987), pp. 22–25.

Lambdin, Diana V., and Walker, Vicki L. "Planning for Classroom Portfolio Assessment." *Arithmetic Teacher,* 41 (February 1994), pp. 318–324.

Lambdin, Diana V.; Kehle, Paul E.; and Preston, Ronald V. *Emphasis on Assessment: Readings from NCTM's School-Based Journals.* Reston, Va.: NCTM, 1996.

Lester, Frank, and Kroll, Diana L. "Assessing Student Growth in Mathematical Problem Solving." In *Assessing Higher Order Thinking in Mathematics* (ed. Gerald Kulm). Washington, D.C.: American Association for the Advancement of Science, 1990.

Lindquist, Mary M. "Assessing through Questioning." *Arithmetic Teacher,* 35 (January 1988) pp. 16–18.

Mathematical Sciences Education Board. *Measuring Up: Prototypes for Mathematics Assessment.* Washington, D.C.: National Academy Press, 1993.

Mathematical Sciences Education Board. *Measuring What Counts: A Conceptual Guide for Mathematics Assessment.* Washington, D.C.: National Academy Press, 1993.

Moon, C. Jean. "Connecting Learning and Teaching through Assessment." *Arithmetic Teacher,* 41 (September 1993), pp. 13–15.

Mumme, Judy. *Portfolio Assessment in Mathematics.* Santa Barbara, Calif.: Regents of the University of California, 1990.

National Council of Teachers of Mathematics. *Curriculum and Evaluation Standards for School Mathematics.* Reston, Va.: NCTM, 1989.

National Council of Teachers of Mathematics. *Professional Standards for Teachers of Mathematics.* Reston, Va.: NCTM, 1991.

National Council of Teachers of Mathematics. *Assessment Standards for School Mathematics.* Reston, Va.: NCTM, 1995.

Peck, Donald M.; Jencks, Stanley M.; and Connell, Michael L. "Improving Instruction through Brief Interviews." *Arithmetic Teacher,* 37 (November 1989), pp. 15–17.

Richardson, Kathy. "Assessing Understanding." *Arithmetic Teacher,* 35 (February 1988), pp. 39–41.

Richardson, Kathy. *A Look at Children's Thinking. Assessment Videos for K–2 Mathematics.* Norman, Okla.: Educational Enrichment, 1990.

Robinson, G. Edith, "Assessing for Learning: The Purposes of Testing." *Arithmetic Teacher,* 35 (September 1987), p. 33.

Smith, Jacque. "Assessing Children's Reasoning: It's an Age-Old Problem." *Teaching Children Mathematics,* 1 (May 1996), pp. 524–528.

Spangler, Denise A. "Assessing Students' Beliefs about Mathematics." *Arithmetic Teacher,* 40 (November 1993), pp. 148–52.

Stenmark, James K. (ed.). *Mathematics Assessment: Myths, Models, Good Questions, and Practical Suggestions.* Reston, Va.: NCTM, 1991.

Trafton, Paul. "Assessing for Learning: Tests—A Tool for Improving Instruction." *Arithmetic Teacher,* 35 (December 1987), pp. 17–18.

Weaver, J. Fred. "Big Dividends from Small Interviews." *Arithmetic Teacher,* 2 (April 1955), pp. 40–47.

Webb, Norman (ed.). *Assessment in the Mathematics Classroom,* 1993 Yearbook. Reston, Va.: NCTM, 1993.

Zawojewski, Judith. "Polishing a Data Task: Seeking Better Assessment." *Teaching Children Mathematics,* 1 (February 1996), pp. 372–378.

Zawojewski, Judith, and Richard Lesh. "Scores and Grades: What Are the Problems? What Are the Alternatives." *Teaching Children Mathematics,* 1 (May 1996), pp. 776–779.

5

Problem Solving

 ## Snapshot of a Lesson

One day Mary Roberts read this story to her sixth-grade class:

Libby was walking up the stairs to her apartment.

"Hi, Libby," said Veronica. Veronica had just moved into the building and was in Libby's class at school. "Do you want to come over until dinner?"

"Sure," said Libby. "Just let me put these keys away."

"Why do you have so many keys?" asked Veronica.

"Because I walk dogs after school. Their owners work and I let myself into their apartments. I have five keys—one key fits each door."

"Oh," said Veronica. "By the way, did you finish the math homework?"

"Those word problems? Sure. I finished them in school. Get your math paper. I'll show you a trick. Then you can finish them in a flash," said Libby.

Veronica got her paper and started to read the first problem aloud.

Libby interrupted. "You're wasting time reading the whole problem. All you have to do is look for the key word or words. They always tell you how to solve the problem. Just like the right key always opens the right apartment door."

"Are you sure?" asked Veronica.

"Positive. For example, look at number one. You see the word *more*. So you add. The answer is $55."

Veronica wasn't sure that Libby was correct. The problem read: "Joe has $15. He needs $40 to buy a new bike. How much more money does he need?"

"But $55 doesn't seem like the right answer. How can Joe need $55 more if the bike only costs $40?" asked Veronica.

"Hmmm . . . it always worked before," said Libby. "Let's try number two. The key words are *took away*. Whenever it says less or take away, you subtract. The answer is 10."

Veronica carefully read the problem to herself: "There were 12 baseball cards missing from Susan's set. Then her brother took away 2. How many are missing now?"

Veronica could see that the answer was 14.

"Maybe I'll finish these problems after dinner. Then I'll have more time to read each problem carefully," said Veronica.

"Suit yourself," said Libby. "But you're doing it the hard way."

When she had finished, Mrs. Roberts asked her class two questions:

1. Do you agree with Libby? Why or why not?

2. What do you think happened the next day in Libby's class?

▶ *Introduction*

Every day, each of us must solve problems. We continually face situations in which there is an obstacle between us and something we want, and we must overcome or remove that obstacle. Not all the problems we face are mathematical, of course. Therefore, our goal as elementary teachers is to help children learn to solve a wide spectrum of problems. We help them to learn word attack and comprehension skills in reading, to use inquiry skills in science, analyze the reasons why events occurred in social studies, and cope with social interactions. And in mathematics, we present story or word problems and applications.

Increasingly, we present situations to children so they must first identify a problem or problems within the situation and then decide how to go about finding a solution. We need to develop children's ability to use various techniques and strategies for solving problems. Knowledge, skills, and understandings are important elements of mathematical learning, but it is in problem solving that the child synthesizes these components in order to answer a question, make a decision, or achieve a goal.

As the story about Libby and Veronica illustrates, we do not always produce problem solvers. Libby's problem-solving approach epitomizes the way many children attack problems. Look for the numbers and the key words, and then go! They have decided there is no need to read, much less understand, the problem. They try to get an answer in the quickest way possible. Even after being wrong twice, Libby is still convinced her way is better than Veronica's. After all, it works at other times.

Teachers have difficulty teaching children how to solve problems, and children have difficulty learning to solve them. Some of the difficulty arises because "finding the answer" has been viewed as the sole objective. Children often misuse a technique intended to aid in problem solving because of this focus on the answer, just as Libby misuses the key words. Increasingly, we have to recognize that the *process* of solving problems is of primary importance. When answers are stressed, children may learn to solve particular problems. When the process is stressed, children are more likely to learn how to attack other problems.

Although problem solving has been of concern for many years, renewed attention was focused on it by several widely read reports. In 1988, the National Council of Supervisors of Mathematics prepared its second position paper on essential mathematics. The first component of these papers (see Figure 1–6) focuses on problem solving—"the principal reason for studying mathematics."

In *An Agenda for Action: Recommendations for School Mathematics of the 1980s* (NCTM 1980; see Figure 1–5) and again in the *Curriculum and Evaluation Standards for School Mathematics* issued by NCTM in 1989, the emphasis on problem solving is strongly reaffirmed as "the central focus of the mathematics curriculum." Moreover, the *Standards* (NCTM 1989, p. 23) state:

> Problem solving is not a distinct topic but a process that should permeate the entire program and provide the context in which concepts and skills can be learned.

Problem solving is a way of teaching. This means it involves more than the presentation of word problems; it involves the way we encourage children to approach mathematical learning. A situation is posed, as in a word problem, then there is a search for a resolution, very often using some of the same processes or procedures as are used in solving a word problem. But the situation that is posed often has a mathematical basis beyond the application of some procedures. It usually involves the teacher as the poser of the situation and as a poser of questions that may provoke some thought; but primarily it involves the student in a search for a reasonable solution or solutions.

One group of researchers proposes that:

> students should be allowed to make the subject problematic . . . allowing students to wonder why things are, to inquire, to search for solutions, and to resolve incongruities. It means that both curriculum and instruction should begin with problems, dilemmas, and questions for students. (Hiebert et al. 1996)

Franke and Carey (1997) are among those who have begun the process of documenting the changes in children's perceptions about mathematics when they are taught in an environment reflecting the spirit of the NCTM Standards, the Cognitively Guided Instruction program. The first graders they studied "perceived of mathematics as a problem-solving endeavor in which many different strategies are considered viable and communicating mathematical thinking is an integral part of the task" (p. 8). In a study of another problem-centered mathematics program, after two years in the program third graders scored significantly higher on standardized measures of computational proficiency and conceptual understanding and held stronger beliefs about the importance of finding their own or different ways to solve problems than those in "textbook classes" (Wood and Sellers 1996).

Increasingly, problem solving as a way of teaching is merging with problem solving as only a curriculum component—although they have always overlapped. Yet here we will focus primarily on the latter—on word problems, because they still exist and still can provide students with knowledge that will help them in taking a problem-solving approach to other mathematics and to real-life concerns.

Problem solving has been the focus of numerous books, collections of materials, and research studies. But many questions continue to be raised about the nature and scope of problem solving.

- What is a problem and what does problem solving mean?
- How can problem solving be taught effectively?
- What problem-solving strategies should be taught?
- How can problem solving be evaluated?

This chapter addresses these questions.

● What Is a Problem and What Is Problem Solving?

A *problem* involves a situation in which a person wants something and does not know immediately what to do to get it. If a problem is so easy that children know how to obtain the answer or know the answer immediately, there is really no problem at all.

To gain skill in solving problems, one must have many experiences in doing so. Research indicates that children who are given many problems to solve score higher on problem-solving tests than children who are given few. This finding has led many textbooks and teachers to offer a problem-solving program that simply presents problems—and nothing more.

Children have often been expected to learn how to solve problems merely by solving problems, with virtually no guidance or discussion of how to do it. Thus, a typical page in a children's textbook might begin with exercises such as the following:

3194	5479	6754
5346	3477	8968
+ 8877	+ 6399	+ 7629

Next would appear "story problems" such as the following:

(A) 7809 people watched television on Monday.

9060 people watched on Tuesday.

9924 people watched on Wednesday.

How many people watched in the three days?

That such story problems are really problems for most children is debatable.

In effect, they are exercises with words around them. The biggest difficulty lies in doing the computation. The choice of what computation to perform is obvious. Do what you have been doing most recently. If the past week's work has been on addition, solve the problems by adding; if the topic has been division, then find two numbers in the word problem and divide. The problems generally provide practice on content just taught, with the mathematics placed in a more-or-less "real-world" setting. It is little wonder that children taught in this way flounder on tests, where problems are not grouped so conveniently by operation.

Consider, as an alternative, the following problem—and try it yourself.

(B) Begin with the digits:

1 2 3 4 5 6 7 8 9

Use each of them at least once, and form three four-digit numbers with the sum of 9636.

To obtain a solution (or solutions), the children will have the desired practice in addition—but they will have to try many possibilities. They will be aided in reaching a solution if they apply some mathematical ideas. For instance, knowing that the sum of three odd numbers is odd will lead them to avoid placing 1, 3, and 5 all in the ones place. The children have the prerequisites for solving the problem—but the solution is not immediately apparent. They may have to guess and check a number of possibilities.

The decision to add the three numbers in word problem (A) presents little if any challenge to most children in terms of determining what to do. The problem is merely a computational exercise, providing practice with addition. The children know what to do because the pattern has been set by the examples before it. With problem (B), however, they will probably have to try several alternatives. Interest in obtaining a solution or solutions and acceptance of the challenge of trying to do something you have not done before (but believe you can do) are key aspects of problem solving.

Whether a problem is truly a problem or merely an exercise depends on the person faced with it. For example, tying a shoelace is no longer a problem for you, but it is for a three-year-old. What is a problem for Ann now may not be a problem for her in three weeks, or it may not be a problem now for Armando. Problems that you select for children must truly be seen as problems.

Many teachers are prone to select only problems that can be solved immediately, which often means the problems are too easy for children. Children form the idea that problems should be solved readily—so a problem where the route to solution is not immediately apparent is viewed as "impossible." Finding the right level of challenge for students is not easy—but you can do so by trying out a range of problems, providing time, then encouraging students to explore many ways around the obstacles initially posed. Don't underestimate their abilities. Wienberg (1996) comments on her fear that a problem was too difficult for her second-grade class—and how amazed she was at their strategies for solving the problem.

A distinction is sometimes made between routine and nonroutine problems. *Routine problems* involve an application of a mathematical procedure in much the same way as it was learned. *Nonroutine problems* often require more thought because the choice of mathematical procedures to solve them is not as obvious.

Results from national assessments have shown that the majority of students have difficulty with any nonroutine problem that requires some analysis or thinking. Students are generally successful in solving routine one-step problems like those found in most textbooks. They have great difficulty, however, in solving multistep or nonroutine problems. National assessment results have indicated that:

> the primary area of concern should not be with simple one-step verbal problems, but with nonroutine problems that require more than a simple application of a single arithmetic operation. (Carpenter et al. 1981, p. 147)

Results from the sixth assessment indicate that students at all three grade levels (4, 8, and 12) performed well on addition and subtraction word problems set in familiar contexts and involving only one step or calculation (Kenney and Silver 1997). Eighth- (and twelfth-) grade students did well on multiplication and division problems involving one step as long as one of the factors was a whole number. Difficulties arose when fourth-grade students applied an incorrect strategy of "when in doubt, add," and when some students at all three grade levels, but especially grade four, attempted to solve multistep problems as though they involved a single step.

Unfortunately, in many mathematical programs, problem solving has been limited to finding the answers to word problems in textbooks. Mathematical problem solving involves more. Whenever children are faced with providing a solution to a task they have not mastered, they are solving a problem.

● How Can Problem Solving Be Taught Effectively?

Because problem solving is so difficult to teach and to learn, researchers have devoted much attention to it over the years. Their work has focused on characteristics of problems, on characteristics of those who are successful or unsuccessful at solving problems, and on teaching strategies that may help children to be more successful at problem solving. On the basis of this research, several broad generalizations can be made (Suydam 1982):

- Problem-solving strategies can be specifically taught, and, when they are, not only are they used more, but students also achieve correct solutions more frequently.

- No *one* strategy is optimal for solving all problems. Some strategies are used more frequently than others, with various strategies being used at different stages of the problem-solving process.

- Teaching a variety of strategies (in addition to providing an overall plan for how to go about problem solving) provides children with a repertoire from which they can draw as they meet a wide variety of problems. They should be encouraged to solve different problems with the same strategy and to discuss why some strategies are appropriate for certain problems.

- Students need to be faced with problems in which the way to solve them is not apparent, and they need to be encouraged to test many alternative approaches.

● Children's problem-solving achievements are related to their developmental level. Thus, they need problems at appropriate levels of difficulty.

A strong problem-solving program builds on the natural, informal methods that the child has when entering school. Many of the best problem-solving situations come from everyday happenings. "How many more chairs will we need if we're having five visitors and two children are absent?" or "How many cookies will we need if everyone is to have two?" may be of concern to a group of first-graders. "Who has the higher batting average, Benny or Marianne?" or "What's the probability of our class winning the race?" may be urgent questions for a group of fifth-graders.

A problem-solving approach should pervade the mathematics curriculum. Teachers need to use problem situations to introduce new topics, as a continuing thread throughout instruction, and as a culmination to ascertain whether children can apply what they have learned. To teach problem solving effectively, teachers need to consider the time involved, planning aids, needed resources, the role of technology, and how to manage the class.

Time

Effective teaching of problem solving demands time. Attention must be focused on the relationships in the problem and on the thinking processes involved in reaching a solution. Thus, students must have time to "digest," or mull over, a problem thoroughly—time to understand the task, time to explore avenues of solution, time to think about the solution. Moreover, teachers need to encourage students to extend the amount of time they are willing to work on a problem before giving up. It takes more time to tackle a problem that you do not know how to solve than to complete an exercise where you know how to proceed. (Consider problems (A) and (B) on page 70: how long did it take you to solve each?)

Some time for problem solving is already included as part of the mathematics program. Additional time can be gained by organizing instructional activities so that some of the time allotted for practicing computational and other skills is directed toward problem solving. This approach is logical, since students use such skills and thus practice them as they solve many problems.

Planning

Instructional activities and time must be planned and coordinated so that students have the chance to tackle numerous problems, to learn a variety of problem-solving strategies, and to analyze, write about, and discuss their methods of attack. You will probably use a textbook when you teach mathematics; therefore, you need to consider how to use it most effectively to help you teach problem solving. For instance, you might identify your objectives for using problem-solving materials in the textbook, examine the entire book for problems to use, regroup textbook materials to suit your objectives, use the textbook to develop questions to ask about problem solving, extend textbook problems with materials you develop yourself, and make use of "challenge problems" (found in some textbooks) with all children (Le Blanc 1982; Meiring 1979).

As you plan, consider including problems with the following characteristics.

● Problems that contain superfluous or insufficient information:

(C) A bag contains 2 dozen cookies for 99¢. Andy bought 3 bags. How many cookies did she get?

(D) Terry would like to be as tall as his uncle, who is 6 ft. 4 in. How much more must Terry grow?

● Problems that involve estimation:

(E) Anita has 75¢. Does she have enough money to buy a candy bar costing 35¢ and a notebook costing 49¢?

● Problems that require students to make choices about the degree of accuracy required:

(F) Kurt is helping his father build a pen for his rabbit. He finds three pieces of lumber in the garage that they can use for the frame. One piece is 8 feet long; the other two are each 7 feet long. What is the largest size pen that they can build?

● Problems that involve practical applications of mathematics to consumer or business situations.

(G) Which is the better buy, a 6-ounce jar of jelly for $1.79 or a 9-ounce jar for $2.79?

● Problems that require students to conceptualize very large or very small numbers:

(H) Have you lived one million hours?

● Problems that are based on students' interests or events in their environment or can be personalized by adding their names:

(I) Some of you play soccer every Tuesday. If today were Wednesday, January 21st, on what date would you play next?

● Problems that involve logic, reasoning, testing of conjectures, and reasonableness of information:

(J) Three children guessed how many jelly beans were in a jar. Their guesses were 80, 75, and 76. One child missed by 1. Another missed by 4. The other child guessed right. How many jelly beans were in the jar?

● Problems that have no mathematical answer (but seem to):

(K) There are 125 sheep and 5 dogs in a flock. How old is the shepherd?

● Problems that are multistep or require the use of more than one strategy to attain a solution:

(L) Ellie had 95¢. She spent 34¢ for popcorn and 50¢ for the movies. How much does she have left?

● Problems that require decision making as a result of the outcome (perhaps there are many answers—or no answers):

(M) Is a traffic light needed in front of the school?

In addition, you should try to include problems that are open ended. Such problems have no one "correct" answer, but rather an answer that depends on the approach taken. Each solution is, however, expected to be reasonable. Such problems are especially appropriate for cooperative group work and should be followed with a class discussion in which the mathematical ideas and planning skills are explored and students get a chance to clarify their thinking and validate their decisions.

(N) You have just been given $20, and you have decided to plan a special outing for your family. Where will you go? Plan a schedule for the day. What time will you get to your destination? What time will you leave? How long will you stay? What will you do? Will $20 be enough money to cover all activities? If not, how much more money will you need?*

(O) Your group has decided to plan a track-and-field competition. What events would be fun? What equipment will you need? Where and when should different events be held so that they will not interfere with each other? Develop a map and time schedule for the competition. How will you collect and display data from the events to determine winners?*

(P) Squares are made by using matchsticks as shown in the picture. When the number of squares is eight, how many match sticks are used?*

(Q) How many marbles are in the picture? Find the answer in as many different ways as you can.*

Resources

Although many textbooks include a range of word problems, you will find it helpful to acquire additional problems to stimulate and challenge your students. Fortunately, there are many sources of problems; the list of references at the end of this chapter includes several such sources. In addition, you can do the following:

● Collect potential problems from newspapers, magazines, and so on.

(R)

America's 30 Most Densely Packed Cities . . .

Among cities with 1980 population of 100,000 or more —

	Area (sq. mi.)	People Per Square Mile
1. New York	302	23,453
2. Jersey City	13	16,934
3. Paterson, N.J.	8	16,623
4. San Francisco	46	14,633
5. Newark	24	13,662
6. Chicago	228	13,174
7. Philadelphia	136	12,413
8. Boston	47	11,928
9. Yonkers, N.Y.	18	10

*Problems (N) and (O) are from Chancellor and Porter (1994, pp. 304–305); problems (P) and (Q) are from Becker (1992).

- Write problems yourself (possibly using ideas from newspapers or from events in your community).

- Make use of situations that arise spontaneously, particularly questions children raise ("How tall is that building?").

- Attend problem-solving sessions at professional meetings.

- Share problems with other teachers.

- Have children write problems to share with each other (Kliman and Richard 1992; Silverman et al. 1992).

   (S) From a picture of items for sale (with prices), have children make up one problem using addition and one problem using subtraction.

- Make videotapes to bring real-life problem situations into the classroom (Kelly and Wiebe 1993; Cognition and Technology Group 1993).

It is not too soon to start a problem file, with problems grouped or categorized so you can locate them readily. File them by mathematical content, by strategies, by how you are going to use the file. Laminating the cards permits them to be used over and over by students for individual or small-group problem solving.

Technology

Ever since calculators dropped in price and it became feasible to use them throughout the school program, their potential for increasing problem-solving proficiency has been recognized. Many problems can now deal with more realistic numbers rather than with numbers that come out even. Calculators also help us to shift attention from computation to problem solving. However, research has indicated that use of calculators will not necessarily improve problem-solving achievement (Suydam 1982). The student must still be able to determine *how* to solve a problem before he or she can use a calculator to attain the solution.

Research also indicates that children tend to use more strategies when they use calculators (Wheatley 1980). The main reason is that the time once spent on performing calculations can be spent on extending the use of problem-solving strategies. More problems also can be considered when calculations are no longer as burdensome. Consider using calculators whenever they:

- Extend a child's ability to solve problems

- Eliminate tedious computations and decrease anxiety about inability to do computations correctly

- Allow time to devote extended attention to a problem or to consider more problems

- Allow consideration of more complex problems or of problems with realistic data

- Provide motivation and confidence that a problem can be solved

Computers also can be an important problem-solving tool. As with calculators, computers allow for the processing of problems with realistic data. But computers also can be used to present problems of different types—for instance, problems involving graphics and graphing.

Many fine software programs provide a variety of problem-solving experiences. Some, such as What Do You Do with a Broken Calculator? involve computation; others, such as The Factory and The Super Factory, address spatial visualization. Still others, such as Math Shop, provide direct experiences with problem solving. The Cruncher teaches spreadsheet skills for solving such real-life problems as how many weeks of allowance equal a new CD player.

Logo and BASIC, still available to students in some schools, also can provide rich problem-solving experiences. These languages encourage students to think about what will happen, try it and see what happens, and then try something else. Activity Card 5–1 illustrates how mathematical ideas can be "explored mentally" and then verified with a computer. Activity Card 5–2 uses BASIC to challenge students to explore some important mathematical concepts with arithmetic patterns and then to verify and extend them.

Class Management

When you teach problem solving, you will find it useful at times to teach the whole class, to divide the class into small groups, or to have children work individually or with one other child. Large-group activities are effective for presenting and developing a new problem-solving strategy and for examining a variety of strategies for solving the same problem. You can focus children's attention on a problem's components, pose questions to help them use one strategy or find one solution, lead them to use other

Activity Card 5–1

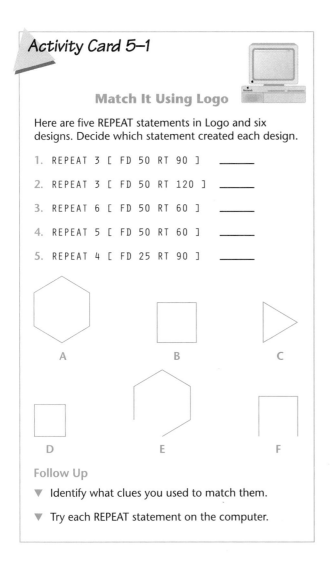

Match It Using Logo

Here are five REPEAT statements in Logo and six designs. Decide which statement created each design.

1. `REPEAT 3 [ FD 50 RT 90 ]` _____

2. `REPEAT 3 [ FD 50 RT 120 ]` _____

3. `REPEAT 6 [ FD 50 RT 60 ]` _____

4. `REPEAT 5 [ FD 50 RT 60 ]` _____

5. `REPEAT 4 [ FD 25 RT 90 ]` _____

Follow Up

▼ Identify what clues you used to match them.

▼ Try each REPEAT statement on the computer.

Activity Card 5–2

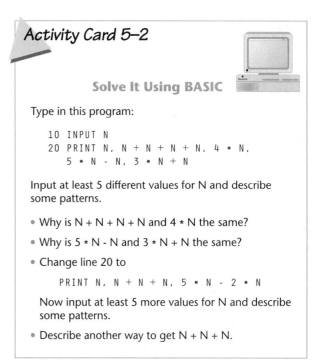

Solve It Using BASIC

Type in this program:

```
10 INPUT N
20 PRINT N, N + N + N + N, 4 * N,
   5 * N - N, 3 * N + N
```

Input at least 5 different values for N and describe some patterns.

- Why is N + N + N + N and 4 * N the same?
- Why is 5 * N - N and 3 * N + N the same?
- Change line 20 to

  `PRINT N, N + N + N, 5 * N - 2 * N`

  Now input at least 5 more values for N and describe some patterns.

- Describe another way to get N + N + N.

strategies or find other solutions, and encourage them to generalize from the problem to other problems. Individuals may suffer, however, because the faster students will tend to come up with answers before others have had a chance to consider the problem carefully. Moreover, what may be a problem to some students may appear trivial or impossibly difficult to others. Discussions about problem solving are feasible with large groups, but the process of solving problems should be practiced in small groups as well as individually.

Small-group instruction makes it possible to group students by problem-solving ability and interests. They have the opportunity to work cooperatively at an appropriate level of difficulty in this type of group. Their anxiety level is lowered as they all work together, discussing problems, sharing ideas, debating alternatives, and verifying solu-

tions. In small groups, students can generally solve more problems than when working alone, although the groups may take longer on each problem. Research indicates that, when groups discuss problem meanings and solution paths, they achieve better results than when they are told how to solve the problem (Suydam and Weaver 1981). Groups are clearly a means of promoting communication about mathematics.

When pairing children to work together, you may want to pair children of comparable abilities or of slightly different abilities so that one child can teach the other. Both children can end up learning from a peer-teaching situation.

Some problem solving should be done individually. The child can progress at his or her own rate and use the strategies with which he or she is comfortable. You will also want to have in the classroom sources of problems to which individual children can turn in their free time: a bulletin board, a problem corner, or a file of problems (Van de Walle and Thompson 1981).

● What Problem-Solving Strategies Should Be Taught?

You cannot consider problem solving without finding numerous references to the contribution of

George Polya (1973). He proposed a four-stage model of problem solving:

1. *Understand* the problem.
2. *Devise* a plan for solving it.
3. *Carry out* your plan.
4. *Look back* to examine the solution obtained.

This model forms the basis for the problem-solving approach used in most elementary school mathematics textbooks. Such an approach, which focuses on teaching students to SEE, PLAN, DO, and CHECK, can help students see problem solving as a process consisting of several interrelated actions. Students have a guide to help them attack a problem because actions are suggested that will lead them to the goal.

However, the model can be misleading. Except for simple problems, it is rarely possible to take the steps in sequence. Students who believe they can proceed one step at a time may find themselves as confused as if they had no model. Moreover, the steps are not discrete; nor is it always necessary to take each step. As students try to understand a problem, they may move unnoticed into the planning stage. Or, once they understand the problem, they may see a route to a solution without any planning. Moreover, the stages do not always aid in finding a solution. Many children become trapped in an endless process of read, think, reread—and reread—and reread—until they give up.

Specific strategies are needed to help children move through the model (Polya himself delineates many of these). Many textbooks provide lists of the strategies presented at various grade levels. These strategies are tools for solving problems, whereas the four-stage model is a blueprint of the points that must be covered.

In this section, we will consider a number of problem-solving strategies. This list is only one way of organizing and listing these strategies. It is not exhaustive, yet it provides a set of strategies that seem particularly useful and can be applied in a wide variety of problem settings.

A plan is needed for introducing the strategies; it is not feasible for a teacher to introduce them all in a given year. Children need time to gain confidence in applying each. The plan also will ensure that students are exposed to the range of strategies you want them to learn, and that they have the opportunity to practice them at an appropriate level. Thus, you may decide to introduce "act it out" and "make a drawing" in grade 1, "look for a pattern" and "solve a simpler or similar problem" in grade 2,

and so on. No one sequence is best. In successive grade levels, children will practice and use the strategies they have already learned. For a plan from one school district, see Tobin (1982).

Textbooks also outline the scope and sequence for any strategies included in the series. Use this outline to compare the scope of your textbook's program with what you want to implement. Then you can devise a plan, if necessary, for extending children's learning beyond what the textbook covers.

The discussion that follows includes a number of illustrative problems, covering a range of mathematical topics and grade levels, that could be used to develop each problem-solving strategy. Usually a problem also can be solved with another strategy; it is rare that a problem can be solved by one and only one strategy. For this reason, a repertoire of strategies is useful. (On the other hand, not all strategies can be used effectively to solve a given problem.) Often more than one strategy must be used to solve a problem; thus, students may begin to "consider all possibilities," but find they need to record them in a table. By becoming familiar with possible strategies, a student acquires a repertoire that can be drawn on to start to attack a problem. And making a start is often the most difficult point. Moreover, when one strategy fails, the child has others to turn to—thus enhancing his or her confidence that a path to a solution can be found.

As you read, do stop and try to solve the problems!

Act It Out

This strategy helps children to visualize what is involved in the problem. They actually go through the actions, either themselves or by manipulating objects. This physical action makes the relationships among problem components clearer in their minds.

When teaching children how to use the act-it-out strategy, it is important to stress that other objects may be used in place of the real thing. Obviously, real money is not needed when a problem involves coins—only something labeled "25¢" or whatever. Because children are adept at pretending, they probably will suggest substitute objects themselves. Make sure they focus their attention on the actions rather than on the objects per se.

Many simple real-life problems can be posed as you develop the act-it-out strategy in the early grades:

(1) Six children are standing at the teacher's desk. Five children join them. How many children are at the teacher's desk then?

The value of acting it out becomes clearer, however, when the problems are more challenging:

(2) Suppose you have 7 coins in your pocket that add up to $1.00. What are the coins?

(3) A man buys a horse for $60, sells it for $70, buys it back for $80, and sells it for $90. How much does the man make or lose in the horse-trading business?

(4) Gum balls cost 1¢ each. There are gum balls of 5 different colors in the machine. You can't see them, because it's dark. What would be the least number of pennies you'd have to spend to be sure of getting at least 3 gum balls of the same color?

(5) I counted 7 cycle riders and 19 cycle wheels go past my house this morning. How many bicycles and how many tricycles passed?

Make a Drawing or Diagram

Probably within the past week or so you have used the drawing strategy to help you solve a real-life problem. Perhaps you had to find someone's house from a complicated set of directions, so you drew a sketch of the route. Or maybe you were rearranging a room and drew a diagram of how the furniture was to be placed. This strategy provides a way of depicting the information in a problem to make the relationships apparent.

When teaching this strategy, stress to the children that there is no need to draw detailed pictures. Encourage them to draw only what is essential to tell about the problem. For example, the appearance of the bus, the pattern of the upholstery, the presence of racks above the seats, and similar details are irrelevant in drawing a picture that will help to solve the bus problem:

(6) A bus has 10 rows of seats. There are 4 seats in each row. How many seats are there on the bus?

(7) You enter an elevator on the main floor. You go up 6 floors, down 3 floors, up 9 floors, down 7 floors, up 8 floors, down 2 floors, down 5 more floors. Then you get off the elevator. On what floor are you?

(8) How much carpet would we need to cover our classroom floor?

(9) When you buy stamps at the post office, they are usually attached to each other. How many different ways can three stamps be attached?

(10) It takes 3 minutes to saw through a log. How long will it take to saw the log into 4 pieces?

(11) A patch of lilly pads doubles its size each day after it starts growing in a pond. If a pond was completely covered just today, what part of it was covered in lily pads five days ago?

At times you can reverse this strategy by presenting a picture for which the children have to make up a problem:

(12)

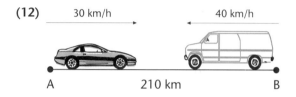

Look for a Pattern

In many early learning activities, children are asked to identify a pattern in pictures or numbers. When pattern recognition is used to solve problems, it involves a more active search. Often students will construct a table then use it to look for a pattern.

(13) Triangle dot numbers are so named because the number of dots can be used to form a triangle with an equal number of dots on each side:

What triangle dot number has 10 dots on a side? What triangle dot number has 195 dots on a side?

(14) How long would it take to spread a rumor in a town of 90,000 people if each person who heard the rumor told it to 3 new people every 15 minutes?

(15) Little Island has a population of 1,000 people. The population doubles every 30 years. What will the population be in 30 years? 60 years? 300 years? When will the population be over a million? over a billion?

(16) An explorer found some strange markings on a cave wall. Can you find and complete the pattern?

Construct a Table

Organizing data into a table helps children to discover a pattern and to identify information that is missing. It is an efficient way to classify and order large amounts of information or data, and it provides a record so that children need not retrace nonproductive paths or do computations repeatedly to answer new questions.

> **(17)** Can you make change for a quarter using only 9 coins? only 17? only 8? How many ways can you make change for a quarter?
>
> **(18)** How many ancestors have you had in the last 400 years?
>
> **(19)** A carpenter makes only 3-legged stools and 4-legged tables. At the end of one day he had used 31 legs. How many stools and how many tables did he make?
>
> **(20)** Ann, Jan, and Nan all like pizza. One likes her pizza plain. One likes pizza with mushrooms. One likes pizza with anchovies. Which kind of pizza does each girl like? Here are three clues:
>
> 1. Ann doesn't know the girl who likes her pizza plain.
> 2. Jan's favorite kind of pizza is cheaper than pizza with mushrooms.
> 3. The one who likes mushrooms is Ann's cousin.
>
> **(21)** Your teacher agrees to let you have 1 minute of recess on the first day of school, 2 minutes on the second day, 4 minutes on the third day, and so on. How long will your recess be at the end of 2 weeks?

Notice that the mathematical idea involved in problem (21) can be stated in terms of other situations. Such reformulation can alter the difficulty level of the problem. It can also give children practice in recognizing similarities in problem structure—an ability that appears to be closely allied to good problem-solving skills. Here is one alternative to that problem:

> **(22)** Suppose someone offers you a job for 15 days. They offer you your choice of how you will be paid. You can start for 1¢ a day and double the new amount every day. Or you can start for $1 and add $1 to the new amount every day. Which would you choose? Why?

Textbooks frequently teach part of the table-constructing strategy. They have students read a table or complete a table already structured. It is important for students to learn to read a table, and thus problems such as this one are presented:

> **(23)** Here is a bus schedule. What time does the bus from New York arrive? [Ask other questions about arrival, departure, and traveling times.]

But it is also vital that children learn how to construct a table. They need to determine for themselves what its form should be (for example, how many columns are needed), what the columns or rows should be labeled, and so on. For this purpose, you can present problems that require children to collect information and then organize it into a table in order to report it.

> **(24)** Make a table that shows how many cars pass through the traffic lights at each intersection by the school.

Account Systematically for All Possibilities

This strategy is sometimes used with "look for a pattern" and "construct a table." Children don't always have to examine all possibilities—rather, they have to account for all in some systematic way. They may be able to organize the possibilities into categories and then dismiss some classes of possibilities before beginning a systematic search of the remaining ones. Sometimes, however, they do need to actually check all possibilities.

> **(25)** In how many different ways can a bus driver get from Albany to Bakersville? The driver always moves toward Bakersville.

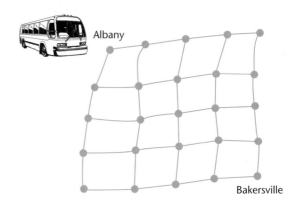

> **(26)** In how many ways can you add 8 odd numbers to get a sum of 20? (You may use a number more than once.)

(27) Ask a friend to think of a number between 1 and 10. Find out what number it is by asking him or her no more than five questions that can be answered only by yes or no. How many questions would you need to ask to find a number between 1 and 20? between 1 and 100?

(28) If each letter is a code for a digit, what is the following addition problem? Use 1, 2, 3, 6, 7, 9, and 0.

$$\begin{array}{r} \text{SUN} \\ + \text{FUN} \\ \hline \text{SWIM} \end{array}$$

(29) You need 17 lb. of fertilizer. How many bags of each size do you buy to obtain at least 17 lb. at the lowest cost?

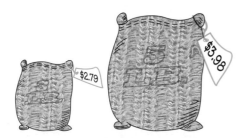

Guess and Check

For years, children have been discouraged from guessing. They have been told, "You're only guessing," in a derisive tone. But guessing is a viable strategy when they are encouraged to incorporate what they know into their guesses, rather than doing "blind" or "wild" guessing.

An educated guess is based on careful attention to pertinent aspects of the problem, plus knowledge from previous related experiences. There is some reason to expect to be "in the right ballpark." Then the child must check to be sure.

(30) Suppose it costs 19¢ to mail a postcard and 29¢ for a letter. Bill wrote to 12 friends and spent $2.98 for postage. How many letters and how many postcards did he send?

(31) Cut the circular region into two parts that have the same area but are not congruent.

(32) Place the numbers 1 through 9 in the cells so that the sum in each direction is 15.

(33) Margie hit the dart board with 4 darts. Each dart hit a different number. Her total score was 25. Which numbers might she have hit to make that score?

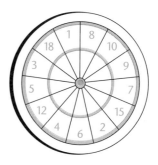

(34) This box has a volume of 2880 cubic centimeters. Find another box with the same volume.

(35) Use the numbers 1 through 6 to fill the 6 circles. You may use each number only once. Each side of the triangle must add up to 9.

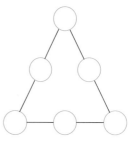

Work Backward

Some problems are posed in such a way that children are given the final conditions of an action and are asked about something that occurred earlier. In other problems, children may be able to determine the endpoint and work backward (many mazes are like that).

(36) Complete the following table:

			3		
	12		11	15	
6		6			7
2			5	9	
					13
5					14

(37) If two whole numbers have a sum of 18 and a product of 45, what are the numbers?

(38) Sue baked some cookies. She put one-half of them away for the next day. Then she divided the remaining cookies evenly among her three sisters so each got 4. How many cookies did she bake?

Identify Wanted, Given, and Needed Information

This strategy has long been used in some textbook series, and research evidence indicates that it is valuable to many children. Instead of just "doing something with the numbers in a problem," they are encouraged to sort out relevant and irrelevant information. They select those facts that are needed from what is available. Most real-life problems are "messy," and a first task is to identify the information that you have, determine the goal for which you are headed, and ascertain the information you will need to reach that goal. Then you need to determine the question to be answered, select specific information necessary for solution, and choose the appropriate process.

An adjunct to this information-oriented strategy is to provide experiences in which the child must formulate the question to be answered. This situation parallels many everyday problems, where you must ask questions before you begin working on a solution.

Children also need to solve problems for which they must collect information or data. The typical textbook problem gives all the necessary facts. For everyday situations you often must obtain necessary data. Problems such as the following from *The USMES Guide* (Unified Science and Mathematics in the Elementary School Project 1974) provide these types of situations:

(39) Challenge: Determine which brand of a product is the best buy for a certain purpose.

(40) Challenge: Recommend and try to have a change made which would improve the safety and convenience of a pedestrian crossing near your school.

Write an Open Sentence

The open-sentence (or equation) strategy is often taught in textbooks; in some, in fact, it is the only strategy taught. Research indicates that it is useful (Suydam and Weaver 1981), but not so useful that it should be taught exclusively. Once you can write an open sentence, you probably can solve the problem—true; but writing the sentence in the first place may be difficult. Thus, some problems cannot be solved easily with this strategy, and sometimes other problem-solving strategies may be needed first to clarify the problem. In particular, children must be able to perceive a relationship between given and sought information in order to write the sentence. Also, children need to learn that more than one sentence may be formed to solve some problems.

(41) An ant travels 33 cm in walking completely around the edge of a rectangle. If the rectangle is twice as long as it is wide, how long is each side?

(42) Two-thirds of a number is 24 and one-half of the number is 18. What is the number?

(43) Jorge put $3 in his bank account today. Now he has $55 in the bank. How much money did he have in the bank yesterday?

Solve a Simpler or Similar Problem

Some problems are made difficult by large numbers or complicated patterns, so the way to solve them is unclear. For such a problem, making an analogous but simpler one may aid in ascertaining how to solve it. Thus, for the following problem, you might have second or third graders first consider what they would do if Cassie had 3¢ and Kai had 5¢:

(44) Cassie saved $3.56. Kai saved $5.27. How much more money has Kai saved?

You may need to break some problems down into manageable parts. When problems require a series of actions, children often fail to recognize the need to answer one question before another can be answered. They need help in identifying the questions that must be answered.

Many kinds of problems are interrelated. Knowing how to solve one problem usually means that children can solve another problem that is somewhat similar. The insight and understanding that permit them to solve more complicated problems are built through solving easier problems, where relationships are easier to see and possibilities for solving can be readily considered. Momentarily, children can set aside the original problem to work on a simpler one; if that problem can be solved, then the procedure used can be applied to the more complicated problem.

(45) Place the numbers 1 to 19 into the 19 circles so that any three numbers in a row will give the same sum.

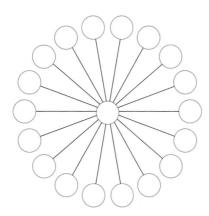

(46) How thick is a sheet of paper? Find the answer using only a ruler as your measuring instrument.

Often children need to restate a problem, expressing it in their own words. Sometimes this repetition will indicate points at which they do not understand the problem, and you can then help them to clarify it. At other times, the rephrasing will help them to ascertain what the problem means or requires, so that they see a possible path of solution. Rephrasing can be a way of getting rid of unimportant words or of changing to words that are more easily understood. Try rewording each of the following problems so that children will understand the terms.

(47) Find 3 different integers such that the sum of their reciprocals is an integer.

(48) I bought some items at the store. All were the same price. I bought as many items as the number of cents in the cost of each item. My bill was $2.25. How many items did I buy?

Change Your Point of View

Often this strategy is used after several others have been tried without success. When children begin to work on most problems, they tend to adopt a particular point of view or make certain assumptions. Often they quickly form a plan of attack and implement it to determine whether it produces a plausible solution. If the plan is unsuccessful, they tend to return to the problem with the same point of view to ascertain a new plan of attack. But there may be some faulty logic that led them to adopt that point of view. They need to try to redefine the problem in a completely different way. Encourage them to ask themselves such questions as, "What precisely does the problem say and not say? What am I assuming that may or may not be implied?"

Problem (20), the pizza problem, is one version of a set of logic problems that are useful in presenting this strategy. Following are some other problems that most students will rather quickly attack in a particular way. Only when it is apparent that an incorrect answer has been obtained (or no answer) will they see the value of looking at the problem from another point of view.

(49) How many squares are there on a checkerboard?

(50) Without lifting your pencil from the paper, draw four straight line segments through the 9 dots.

(51) A state with 750 schools is about to begin a "single elimination" basketball tournament—one loss and you're out. How many games must be played to determine a champion?

● The Importance of Looking Back

Some of the best learning about problem solving may occur after the problem solution has been attained. It is important to think about how a problem is solved. In fact, research indicates that time spent discussing and reconsidering their thinking may be more important than any other strategy in helping children become better problem solvers (Suydam and Weaver 1981). Thus, this step, which should be included regularly in instructional planning, may focus on one or more helpful strategies.

Generalize

The generalization strategy is used to extend the solution to broader and more far-reaching situations. Analyzing the structural features of a problem rather than focusing only on details often results in insights more significant than the answer to the specific situation posed in the problem. According to research (Suydam 1987), being able to see similarities across problems is one of the characteristics of good problem solvers.

> **(52)** First solve: A boy selling fruit has only three weights and a double pan balance. But with them he can weigh any whole number of pounds from 1 pound to 13 pounds. What weights does he have? Then consider: should he buy a fourth weight? How many additional weighings could be made with the four weights?

> **(53)** When five consecutive numbers are added together their sum is 155. Find the numbers. How can this problem be symbolized so that other totals could be considered?

Getting children to focus on the relationships involved in a problem and then generalizing can sometimes be accomplished by giving children problems without numbers:

> **(54)** A store sells ping-pong balls by the box. For the amount of money Maria has, she can buy a certain number of boxes. What price does she pay per ball?

Check the Solution

Checking has long been advocated as a way to help children pinpoint their errors—provided they do not simply make the solution and the check agree. One way of checking is going through the procedures again. Another is verifying the reasonableness of the answer. Is it a plausible answer to the question posed in the problem? Estimating the answer before obtaining the solution will aid in this verification process.

Find Another Way to Solve It

Most problems can be solved with many different strategies. Use of each adds to an understanding of the problem. You have probably felt uncomfortable with the classification of some of the problems in this chapter under one or another strategy. But even for each of the problems where you felt the classification was satisfactory, there is probably another way each could be solved. (Try it and see!)

Find Another Solution

Too often, children are given problems for which there is one and only one correct solution. Almost all textbook problems are like that. In real-life situations, however, there may be two or more answers that are acceptable (depending, sometimes, on the circumstances or the assumptions). You probably noticed that some of the problems given here have several solutions. For many others, such as the following, each person tackling the problem will have a different answer:

> **(55)** Find out how many days (or minutes) old you are.

Study the Solution Process

This strategy aims to help the child put the problem into perspective: the thinking used at each stage, the facts that were uncovered, the strategies that were employed, and the actions that were productive and nonproductive. Again, giving a problem without numbers helps children to focus on the process they follow, as well as the relationships in the problem, as they describe how they would go about finding the answer. Different students can also be asked to share with the group the varying ways in which they proceeded to reach the same solution. Having children write about how they solved a problem also adds to their understanding of the problem-solving process.

● Using Problem-Solving Opportunities

This chapter has presented a variety of problems. We have noted the possible use of nonverbal problems, embodied in pictures or materials. Real-world problems arise in a variety of modes, offering many opportunities for teaching. Make use of problems posed spontaneously by children or by situations in which you find yourself. Bring in games that present good problem-solving situations, games that will present children with the opportunity to use many different strategies. Have children work cooperatively in small groups. And be aware that personalizing problems—for instance, by substituting the names of children in your class—can help many children to accept problems that otherwise would seem remote or uninteresting.

Throughout your instruction, you need to encourage enjoyment in solving problems. You have helped children achieve this sense of enjoyment in part when they begin to believe that they *can* solve a problem. They need an atmosphere in which they feel both free and secure. Your positive attitude toward problem solving will stimulate a similar attitude on the part of the children.

● How Can Problem Solving Be Assessed?

It is more difficult to assess children's problem-solving skills than many other skills in the mathematics curriculum. The NCTM Standards (1989, p. 209) state:

> The assessment of students' ability to use mathematics in solving problems should provide evidence that they can:
>
> - Formulate problems
> - Apply a variety of strategies to solve problems
> - Solve problems
> - Verify and interpret results
> - Generalize solutions

To assess problem solving, we need to go beyond the open-ended or multiple-choice format of a paper-and-pencil test. Chapter 4 describes the assessment process, and many of the points to follow are discussed in Chapter 4. We present them here as well, because it is so important that assessment be considered a vital component of teaching children to be problem solvers.

It takes a long time to develop problem-solving skills. Therefore, assessment is a long-term process, not accomplished solely with short-term measures. It needs to be continuous over the entire school mathematics program (Charles et al. 1987).

Assessment of problem solving should be based on your goals, using techniques consistent with those goals. If the mathematics program encompasses the ability to solve both routine and non-routine problems, then assessment measures must include both types of problems. If the program includes emphasis on the process of problem solving, then assessment measures must incorporate ways of evaluating children's use of the process.

As you plan each lesson, consider how you will determine whether or not its objectives have been attained. Paper-and-pencil measures have a place in this type of evaluation. But consider, also, such procedures as these:

- Presenting students with a problem-solving situation and observing how they meet it
- Interviewing students
- Having students describe to a group how they solved a problem
- Having one student teach another how to solve a problem

You will need to assess as you go along, because you will want to ascertain children's understanding and nonunderstanding, for guidance in developing the next lesson. Remember that problem solving cannot be learned in any one lesson. The process must develop and thus be assessed over time.

Observations

As children work individually or in small groups, you can move about the room, observing them as they work, listening as they talk among themselves, making notes, questioning, offering suggestions. Focus on how each goes about the task of solving a problem. You might want to consider the following points:

- Is there evidence of careful reading of the problem?
- Do individual children seem to have some means of beginning to attack a problem?
- Do they apply a strategy, or do they try to use the last procedure you taught?
- Do they have another strategy to try if the first one fails?
- How consistent and persistent are they in applying a strategy?
- Are careless errors being made, and if so, when and why?
- How long are they willing to keep trying to solve a problem?
- How well are they concentrating on the task?
- How quickly do they ask for help?

- What strategies does each child use most frequently?
- Do they use manipulative materials? How?
- What do their behaviors and such factors as the expressions on their face indicate about their interest and involvement?

Then make a brief note—an anecdotal record—that describes the situation and the behaviors you have observed.

Interviews

An interview is an attempt to remove the limitations of writing—your own limitations in developing a written test item and the child's in developing a written answer. An interview lets you delve further into how a student goes about solving a problem. You can follow the child's thought patterns as he or she describes what is done and why.

Basically, you need to present the student with a problem; let the student find a solution, describe what he or she is doing; and question the student, eliciting specific details on what he or she is doing and why. Make notes as the student works and talks. Sometimes it is helpful to have an exact record of the replies.

You may want to have a student use a tape recorder when working alone. Or have a group of students discuss various ways of solving a problem. You can play the tape back later and analyze students' thinking more carefully and from a different perspective than if you are involved in the interview.

Inventories and Checklists

An inventory can be used to check on what a student knows about problem-solving strategies. You might give students one or several problems and ask them to solve each with a specified strategy or to solve each using two or three specified strategies. Your aim is to find out whether or not the student can apply each strategy—not what the answer to the problem is. You can also record your observations on a checklist, which then serves as an inventory.

Paper-and-Pencil Tests

You will also want to use written tests to assess children's ability to solve problems. Make sure that those you develop follow the guidelines of your problem-solving program—that is, select good problems that are interesting and challenging, allow sufficient time for the process, and so on. Of particular interest are paper-and-pencil tests that assess the stages of problem solving (see Schoen and Oehmke 1980; Charles et al. 1987).

Evaluation should be an ongoing component of the problem-solving program. You use it not just to assess where students are, but also to help you plan what to do next. If children do not use a strategy you have taught, you need to consider why, and then try again. If they try to use a strategy, you have evidence on how well they use it and whether they need more practice. Do not let evaluation become just a recording process. It is a way of helping you solve the problem of how to teach problem solving more effectively!

▶ A Glance at Where We've Been

Problem solving should pervade the mathematics curriculum. Children need many experiences with problems that they do not immediately know how to solve. Moreover, they should be taught to use a variety of problem-solving strategies, providing them with a repertoire from which they can draw. You will need to provide not only a large resource of good problems, but also enough time for problem solving. Your instruction must coordinate textbook materials with the use of calculators and other technology, as well as large-group, small-group, and individual work.

An overall strategy for approaching problems is desirable (understand, plan, carry out, look back), plus specific strategies that give children ways to begin to attack a problem. This chapter has described such strategies, provided sample problems, and discussed the assessment of problem solving by means of observations, interviews, inventories, and tests.

▶ THINGS TO DO: From What You've Read

1. What other questions might Mary Roberts pursue with her class after reading the story that opens this chapter?

2. Describe why Polya's four-step plan is inadequate for helping students become good problem solvers. Why is it useful?

3. Discuss: "We don't teach textbook word problems any more because no one has to solve that kind of problem."

4. Identify levels (such as primary or intermediate) for problems presented in the chapter.

5. Identify problems in the chapter for which calculators would be useful.

6. Answer true or false, then defend your answer: "Before solving a problem, pupils should be required to draw a picture of it."

7. Solve problems (5), (11), and (41) using two different strategies for each.

8. Why isn't finding the answer the final step in solving a problem?

9. Look again at problems (11) and (13). What do you notice? Can you find other pairs or sets of problems with the same characteristic?

▶ THINGS TO DO: Going Beyond This Book

1. Choose a problem from this chapter and pose it to two children. Identify the strategies each child uses, and write an evaluation of their efforts.

2. Start a file with problems from this chapter and add other problems, especially nonroutine ones. Categorize them in the way you find most useful.

3. Make up problems using newspaper or magazine articles. Add them to your file.

4. Think of your activities for the past week. List the problem-solving strategies you used to solve each of five mathematical problems you faced.

5. Search textbooks for a particular grade level. Find at least one problem that could be solved by using the following strategies: make a drawing or diagram, act it out, and solve a simpler or similar problem.

6. Choose a content topic for a particular grade level. Make up at least one interesting problem for that topic that can be solved by each of these strategies: look for a pattern, make a drawing or diagram, and construct a table.

7. Plan a bulletin board focused on problem solving.

8. Obtain catalogs from software companies; select promising software to promote problem solving.

9. Check a textbook for a list of the problem-solving strategies taught. Write an evaluation of it.

10. Read Knapp and Peterson (1995). Choose one of the teachers whose comments about teaching are reported and share the notable perceptions with your class.

▼▼▼▼▼▼▼▼▼▼▼▼▼▼▼▼▼▼▼▼▼▼▼▼▼▼

Children's Corner

Allington, Richard L., and Krull, Kathleen. *Thinking.* Milwaukee, Wis.: Raintree Publications, 1980.

Anno, Mitsumasa. *Anno's Math Games.* New York: Philomel Books, 1987.

Anno, Mitsumasa. *Anno's Math Games II.* New York: Philomel Books, 1989.

Burns, Marilyn. *Math for Smarty Pants.* Boston: Little, Brown, 1982.

Burns, Marilyn. *The I Hate Mathematics! Book.* Boston: Little, Brown, 1975.

Butrick, Lyn McClure. *Logic for Space Age Kids.* Athens, Ohio: University Classics, 1984.

Fehr, Howard. *Number Patterns Make Sense.* New York: Holt, Rinehart & Winston, 1965.

Hayes, Cyril, and Hayes, Dympna. *Number Mysteries.* Milwaukee, Wis.: Penworthy Publishing, 1987.

Lipscomb, Susan Drake, and Zuanich, Margaret Ann. *BASIC Fun: Computer Games, Puzzles, and Problems Children Can Write.* New York: Avon Books, 1982.

Phillips, Louis. *263 Brain Busters: Just How Smart Are You, Anyway?* New York: Penguin Books, 1985.

Sharp, Richard M., and Metzner, Seymour. *The Sneaky Square and 113 Other Math Activities for Kids.* Blue Ridge Summit, Pa.: TAB Books, 1990.

Selected References

Becker, Jerry P. (ed.). *Report of U.S.–Japan Cross-National Research on Students: Problem Solving Behaviors.* Carbondale, Ill.: Southern Illinois University, 1992.

Bledsoe, Gloria J. "Hook Your Students on Problem Solving." *Arithmetic Teacher,* 37 (December 1989), pp. 16–20.

Brown, Sue. "Integrating Manipulatives and Computers in Problem-Solving Experiences." *Arithmetic Teacher,* 38 (October 1990), pp. 8–10.

Bruni, James V. "Problem Solving for the Primary Grades." *Arithmetic Teacher,* 29 (February 1982), pp. 10–15.

Campbell, Patricia F. "Using a Problem-Solving Approach in the Primary Grades." *Arithmetic Teacher,* 32 (December 1984), pp. 11–14.

Carpenter, Thomas P.; Corbitt, Mary Kay; Kepner, Henry S., Jr.; Lindquist, Mary Montgomery; and Reys, Robert E. *Results from the Second Mathematics Assessment of the National Assessment of Educational Progress.* Reston, Va.: NCTM, 1981.

Cemen, Pamala Byrd. "Developing a Problem-Solving Lesson." *Arithmetic Teacher,* 37 (October 1989), pp. 14–19.

Chancellor, Dinah, and Porter, Jeanna. "Calendar Mathematics." *Arithmetic Teacher,* 41 (February 1994), pp. 304–305.

Charles, Randall, and Lester, Frank. *Teaching Problem Solving: What, Why & How.* Palo Alto, Calif.: Dale Seymour Publications, 1982.

Charles, Randall; Lester, Frank; and O'Daffer, Phares. *How to Evaluate Progress in Problem Solving.* Reston, Va.: NCTM, 1987.

Ciochine, John G., and Polivka, Grace. "The Missing Link? Writing in Mathematics Class!" *Mathematics Teaching in the Middle School,* 2 (March–April 1997), pp. 316–320.

Cognition and Technology Group at Vanderbilt University. "The Jasper Experiment: Using Video to Furnish Real-World Problem-Solving Contexts." *Arithmetic Teacher,* 40 (April 1993), pp. 474–478.

Didactics and Mathematics. Palo Alto, Calif.: Creative Publications, 1978.

Duea, Joan, and Ockenga, Earl. "Classroom Problem Solving with Calculators." *Arithmetic Teacher,* 29 (February 1982), pp. 50–51.

Everybody Counts: A Report to the Nation on the Future of Mathematics Education. Washington, D.C.: National Academy Press, 1989.

Ford, Margaret I. "The Writing Process: A Strategy for Problem Solvers." *Arithmetic Teacher,* 38 (November 1990), pp. 35–38.

Franke, Megan Loef, and Carey, Deborah A. "Young Children's Perceptions of Mathematics in Problem-Solving Environments." *Journal for Research in Mathematics Education,* 28 (January 1997), pp. 8–25.

Gilbert-Macmillan, Kathleen, and Leitz, Steven J. "Cooperative Small Groups: A Method for Teaching Problem Solving." *Arithmetic Teacher,* 33 (March l986), pp. 9–11.

Grouws, Douglas (ed.). *Handbook of Research on Mathematics Teaching and Learning.* New York: Macmillan, 1993.

Grouws, Douglas A. "Critical Issues in Problem Solving Instruction in Mathematics." In *Proceedings of the China–Japan–U.S. Seminar on Mathematical Education* (eds. Dianzhou Zhang, Toshio Sawada, and Jerry P. Becker). Carbondale, Ill.: Southern Illinois University, 1996, pp. 70–93.

Hembree, Ray, and Marsh, Harold. "Problem Solving in Early Childhood: Building Foundations." In *Research Ideas for the Classroom: Early Childhood Mathematics* (ed. Robert J. Jensen). Reston, Va.: NCTM, and New York: Macmillan, 1993, pp. 151–170.

Hiebert, James; Carpenter, Thomas P.; Fennema, Elizabeth; Fuson, Karen; Human, Piet; Murray, Hanlie; Olivier, Alwyn; and Wearne, Diana. "Problem Solving as a Basis for Reform in Curriculum and Instruction: The Case of Mathematics." *Educational Researcher* 25 (May 1996), pp. 12–21.

Holbrook, Helen, and Van de Walle, John A. "Patterns, Thinking, and Problem Solving." *Arithmetic Teacher,* 34 (April 1987), pp. 6–12.

Immerzeel, George. *Iowa Problem Solving Project Resource Decks.* Cedar Falls, Iowa: University of Northern Iowa, 1978.

Kelly, M. G., and Wiebe, James H. "Using the Video Camera in Mathematical Problem Solving." *Arithmetic Teacher,* 41 (September 1993), 41–43.

Kenney, Patricia Ann, and Silver, Edward A. (eds.). *Results from the Sixth Mathematics Assessment of the National Assessment of Educational Progress.* Reston, Va.: NCTM, 1997.

Kliman, Marlene, and Richards, Judith. "Writing, Sharing, and Discussing Mathematics Stories." *Arithmetic Teacher,* 40 (November 1992), pp. 138–141.

Knapp, Nancy F., and Peterson, Penelope L. "Teachers' Interpretations of 'CGI' After Four Years: Meanings and Practices." *Journal for Research in Mathematics Education,* 26 (January 1995), pp. 40–65.

Knifong, J. Dan, and Burton, Grace M. "Understanding Word Problems." *Arithmetic Teacher,* 32 (January 1985), pp. 13–17.

Kroll, Diana Lambdin, and Miller, Tammy. "Insights from Research on Mathematical Problem Solving in the Middle Grades." In *Research Ideas for the Classroom: Middle Grades Mathematics* (ed. Douglas T. Owens). Reston, Va.: NCTM, and New York: Macmillan, 1993, pp. 58–77.

Kroll, Diana Lambdin; Masingila, Joanna O.; and Mau, Sue Tinsley. "Cooperative Problem Solving: But What about Grading?" *Arithmetic Teacher,* 39 (February 1992), pp. 17–23.

Krulik, Stephen, and Rudnick, Jesse A. *The New Sourcebook for Teaching Reasoning and Problem Solving in Elementary School.* Boston: Allyn and Bacon, 1995.

Krulik, Stephen, and Reys, Robert E. (eds.). *Problem Solving in School Mathematics.* 1980 Yearbook. Reston, Va.: NCTM, 1980.

Krulik, Stephen. "Problem Solving: Some Considerations." *Arithmetic Teacher,* 25 (December 1977), pp. 51–52.

LeBlanc, John F. "Teaching Textbook Story Problems." *Arithmetic Teacher,* 29 (February 1982), pp. 52–54.

Leitze, Annette Ricks. "Connecting Process Problem Solving to Children's Literature." *Teaching Children Mathematics,* 3 (March 1997), pp. 398–406.

Lindquist, Mary Montgomery. "Problem Solving with Five Easy Pieces." *Arithmetic Teacher,* 25 (November 1977), pp. 7–10.

Lubinski, Cheryl Ann. "The Influence of Teachers' Beliefs and Knowledge on Learning Environments." *Arithmetic Teacher,* 41 (April 1994), pp. 476–479.

Mathematics Resource Project. Palo Alto, Calif.: Creative Publications, 1977.

Meiring, Steven P. *Problem Solving . . . A Basic Mathematics Goal.* Columbus, Ohio: Ohio Department of Education, 1979. White Plains, N.Y.: Dale Seymour Publications.

Middleton, James A. and Goepfert, Polly. *Inventive Strategies for Teaching Mathematics: Implementing Standards for Reform.* Washington, D.C.: American Psychological Association, 1996.

Morris, Janet. *How to Develop Problem Solving with a Calculator.* Reston, Va.: NCTM, 1981.

National Council of Supervisors of Mathematics. "Essential Mathematics for the 21st Century." *Arithmetic Teacher,* 37 (September 1989), pp. 44–46.

National Council of Teachers of Mathematics. *An Agenda for Action: Recommendations for School Mathematics of the 1980s.* Reston, Va.: NCTM, 1980.

National Council of Teachers of Mathematics. *Curriculum and Evaluation Standards for School Mathematics.* Reston, Va.: NCTM, 1989.

National Council of Teachers of Mathematics. *Reaching Higher: A Problem-Solving Approach to Elementary School Mathematics.* Reston, Va.: NCTM, 1990.

Polya, George. *How to Solve It.* Princeton, N.J.: Princeton University Press, 1973 (1945, 1957). Worth, Ill.: Creative Publications.

Rosenbaum, Linda; Behounek, Karla Jeanne; Brown, Les; and Burcalow, Janet V. "Step into Problem Solving with Cooperative Learning." *Arithmetic Teacher,* 36 (March 1989), pp. 7–11.

Sanfiorenzo, Norberto R. "Evaluating Expressions: A Problem-Solving Approach." *Arithmetic Teacher,* 38 (March 1991), pp. 34–35.

Schoen, Harold L., and Oehmke, Theresa. "A New Approach to the Measurement of Problem-Solving Skills." In *Problem Solving in School Mathematics, 1980* (eds. Stephen Krulik and Robert E. Reys). Reston, Va.: NCTM, 1980, pp. 216–227.

Silverman, Fredrick L.; Winograd, Ken; and Strohauer, Donna. "Student-Generated Story Problems." *Arithmetic Teacher,* 39 (April 1992), pp. 6–12.

Suydam, Marilyn N. "Indications from Research on Problem Solving." In *Teaching and Learning: A Problem-Solving Focus* (ed. Frances R. Curcio). Reston, Va.: NCTM, 1987, pp. 99–114.

Suydam, Marilyn N., and Weaver, J. Fred. *Using Research: A Key to Elementary School Mathematics.*

Columbus, Ohio: ERIC Clearinghouse for Science, Mathematics and Environmental Education, 1981.

Suydam, Marilyn N. "Update on Research on Problem Solving: Implications for Classroom Teaching." *Arithmetic Teacher,* 29 (February 1982), pp. 56–60.

Thornton, Carol A., and Bley, Nancy S. "Problem Solving: Help in the Right Direction for LD Students." *Arithmetic Teacher,* 29 (February 1982), pp. 26–27, 38–41.

Tobin, Alexander. "Scope and Sequence for a Problem-Solving Curriculum." *Arithmetic Teacher,* 29 (February 1982), pp. 62–65.

Unified Science and Mathematics in the Elementary School Project. *The USMES Guide.* Newton, Mass.: Education Development Center, 1974.

Van de Walle, John A., and Thompson, Charles S. "Fitting Problem Solving into Every Classroom." *School Science and Mathematics,* 81 (April 1981), pp. 289–297.

Weinberg, Susan. "Going Beyond Ten Black Dots." *Teaching Children Mathematics,* 2 (March 1996), pp. 432–435.

Wheatley, Charlotte L. "Calculator Use and Problem-Solving Performance." *Journal for Research in Mathematics Education,* 11 (November 1980), pp. 323–334.

Wilson, John W. "The Role of Structure in Verbal Problem Solving." *Arithmetic Teacher,* 14 (October 1967), pp. 486–497.

Wood, Terry, and Sellers, Patricia. "Assessment of a Problem-Centered Mathematics Program: Third Grade." *Journal for Research in Mathematics Education,* 27 (May 1996), pp. 337–353.

Worth, Joan. "Problem Solving in the Intermediate Grades: Helping Your Students Learn to Solve Problems." *Arithmetic Teacher,* 29 (February 1982), pp. 16–19.

Yancey, Anna V.; Thompson, Charles S.; and Yancey, John S. "Children Must Learn to Draw Diagrams." *Arithmetic Teacher,* 36 (March 1989), pp. 15–19.

Developing Number Sense and Counting

 Snapshot of a Lesson

Key Ideas for an Early Lesson on Numbers

1. Maintain and/or improve skill in small-group recognition.
2. Increase awareness of number patterns.
3. Develop counting skills.

Necessary Materials

Overhead projector and about 20 counters or beans.

Orientation

The children are learning to recognize by sight the number of objects in small groups. The teacher, Miss Chen, spends a few minutes each day on this activity. She has just placed four beans on the face of the overhead. She turns on the overhead for two seconds, then turns it off.

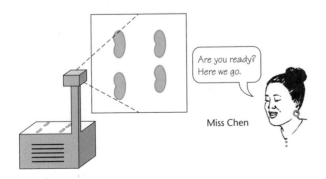

MISS CHEN: How many beans did you see?

Less than half the children raise their hands, so Miss Chen decides to do it again. This time nearly all the children raise their hands.

> MISS CHEN: How many beans? Barry?
>
> BARRY: Four.

One child, Susan, is in obvious disagreement, so Miss Chen calls on her.

> SUSAN: Five.
>
> MISS CHEN: O.K., let's check. I will turn on the overhead and Susan can count the beans for us.

Susan counts the images.

> SUSAN: There are only four. When I saw the pattern, I thought there was one in the middle.
>
> MISS CHEN: I am glad Susan is looking for patterns. That is the key to recognizing groups of things. Let's try another one and be sure to look for patterns.

Miss Chen places five beans on the overhead, turns it on for two seconds, then turns it off.

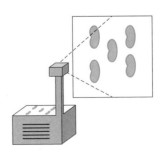

MISS CHEN: How many beans?

All the children have a hand up; Miss Chen points to one of them, who says five. The others agree.

MISS CHEN: We will try one more.

Miss Chen places five beans on the overhead in a different arrangement. She then turns it on for two seconds.

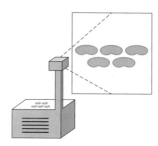

MISS CHEN: How many beans did you see? Bonny?

BONNY: Five, but it looks different than the other five.

SUSAN: It is different because there are six. It fits the pattern for six.

MISS CHEN: Let's check it.

Miss Chen turns the projector on, and Bonny confirms there are five. Susan and many other children are looking for patterns, but their recognition skills need sharpening. They see part of a pattern but are not sensitive to small differences. That's why this activity is used for a couple of minutes each day.

MISS CHEN: Thanks, Bonny, there are only five. We really have to watch those patterns carefully. That's enough for today.

Many children groan and plead for more. They really enjoy this activity, but Miss Chen realizes the value of not overdoing a good thing. Therefore, she is careful not to "burn them out" with too much at one time. Even though the children don't realize it, this activity reviews counting and increases their readiness for addition and subtraction.

Introduction

Number sense, like common sense or horse sense, is difficult to define or express simply. It refers to an intuitive feel for numbers and their various uses and interpretations. Number sense also includes the ability to compute accurately and efficiently, to detect errors, and to recognize results as reasonable. People with number sense are able to understand numbers and use them effectively in everyday living (McIntosh et al. 1992).

The NCTM *Curriculum and Evaluation Standards for School Mathematics* (1989, p. 38) describe children with good number sense as those who:

- Thoroughly understand number meanings
- Have developed multiple relationships among numbers
- Recognize the relative magnitude of numbers
- Know the relative effect(s) of operating on numbers
- Develop referents for measures of common objects and situations in their environments

These ideas regarding number sense are reminiscent of Brownell's ideas about meaningful learning (see Chapter 2). The vision of the NCTM *Standards* regarding number sense is that students need to develop concepts meaningfully, so they can use numbers effectively both in and out of school. Helping students to develop such number sense requires appropriate modeling, posing process questions, encouraging thinking about numbers, and in general creating a classroom environment that nurtures number sense.

Let's explore several examples of number sense in action. What does the number 5 mean to young children? It can mean many things. It might be their current age or their age next year. It might be how old they were when they started kindergarten. Figure 6–1 illustrates a few uses and interpretations of the number 5 suggested by young children. Other children would provide different examples. In fact, the examples in Figure 6–1 might be different for the same children tomorrow because children's concept of numbers continuously grows and changes. A few examples illustrating the multidimensional nature of number sense for older children are shown in Figure 6–2.

It should be understood that number sense is not a finite entity that a student either has or does not have. Its development is a lifelong process. In an effort to facilitate the development of number sense

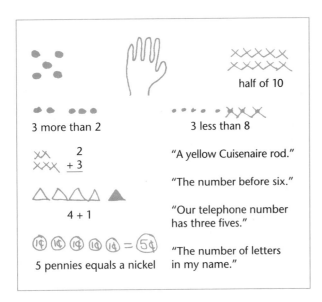

Figure 6–1 • The meanings of the number five suggested by young children

in elementary school, the NCTM has published several books on number sense as part of the *Addenda* series (Burton et al. 1993; Reys et al. 1991).

Children begin to develop some sense about numbers long before they begin to count. For example, young children can answer these kinds of questions:

How old are you? [two]

What channel should we watch? [thirteen]

On what floor is your father's office? [four]

How many sisters do you have? [one]

Such early experiences introduce the number names as well as their symbols—13 on the channel indicator or 4 on the elevator. These names and symbols are memorized through sound and sight recognition and provide an important beginning, but a child's knowledge of these alone does not indicate the child's grasp of number.

For one thing, these experiences underscore a very important characteristic of number. It is an abstraction. It can't be adequately illustrated in just one situation. The multiple meanings of 5 illustrated in Figure 6–1 demonstrate how quickly the concept of "five" becomes associated with different situations. Research into how children develop number sense makes it clear that the more varied and different their experiences, the more likely it is that they will abstract number concepts from their experiences (Payne and Huinker 1993). Helping

children further their development of number and number sense has a high instructional priority. The goal of this chapter is to stimulate your thinking about number sense and its development during the early stages of prenumber experiences and counting.

• Prenumber Concepts

Numbers are everywhere, and thus even young children have a vast amount of early number experiences, as was shown in Figure 6–1. Many of these experiences do not rely on numbers per se, but provide the basis for building early number concepts and the foundation for later skills. Such experiences are called *prenumber experiences* and, as teachers, we often need to help children take advantage of them. Different steps are involved in developing prenumber concepts that will lead eventually to meaningful counting skills and number sense. Although the learning paths that children take are bound to differ greatly, they all begin with classifying whatever is to be counted.

Classification

Classification is fundamental to learning about the real world and can be done with or without numbers. For example, children can be separated into groups of boys and girls (which is classification) without considering number. Yet classification skills are prerequisite to any meaningful number work. If we want to know how many girls are in the class, we must be able to recognize (that is, classify) the girls. Thus, before children can count, they must know what to count, and classification helps identify what is to be counted. Opportunities to sort and classify help children sharpen their classification and thinking skills.

Young children learn to distinguish between dogs and cats, reptiles and mammals, toys they enjoy and those they never use. These distinctions are examples of classification in action. Classification not only helps children make some sense of things around them, but also helps them become flexible thinkers. Classifying objects in different ways fosters the development of thinking skills.

As children classify or sort materials, such as buttons, (Whitten, 1989) they must decide whether or not each object has the given characteristic. If children disagree on how an object should be sorted, it forces them to defend their answers and perhaps further clarify how the classification process was done. At this point, there may be no counting as

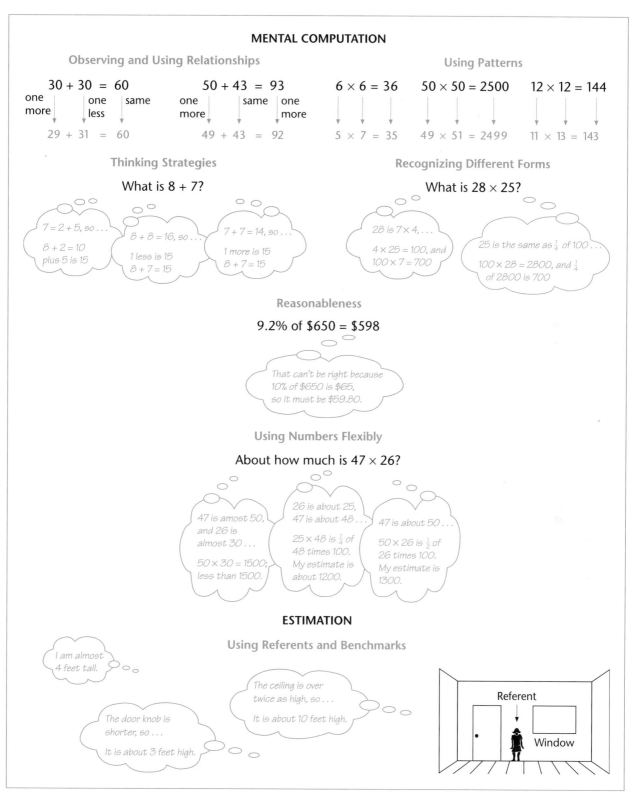

Figure 6–2 • Some examples of number sense in action

materials are classified—yet words such as *more, few, many, most,* and *none* will likely be used in describing the resulting collections.

Classification allows us to reach general agreement on what is to be counted. For example, consider a pile of buttons and the questions: How many plastic buttons have two holes? The answer is a number that tells *how many*. When a number is used in this way, it is called a *cardinal number*. However, before finding the specific cardinal number, we must first decide which buttons are plastic and how many of them have exactly two holes. Once this classification is done, then the members to be counted are well defined, and the results should be the same.

Stories provide opportunities for classification. Books such as *Where's Waldo?* by Martin Handford challenge students to find Waldo in a vast and often complex picture containing many different things. Such search-and-find challenges provide practice in visual discrimination as well as in classification.

Attribute blocks, sometimes called *logic blocks,* provide an excellent model for classification activities as well as developing logical thinking. These blocks can be made from cardboard (see Appendix B for an attribute block master), but are also commercially available in wood or plastic. They differ in several attributes, including color, shape, and size. Consider, for example, the twenty-four pieces shown in Appendix B and Activity Card 6–1. These pieces illustrate three attributes:

Size: Large, Small (L, S)

Color: Blue, White, Gray (B, W, G)

Shape: Square, Triangle, Pentagon, Circle (S, T, P, C)

The first block can be described in words as the "Large Blue Square" or symbolically as LBS. As children manipulate the blocks and describe them, they begin to make natural connections between the concrete model and different ways of representation. Many of the twenty-four pieces are alike in some attributes, but no two pieces are alike in all attributes, which provides opportunities for "Who am I?" games, as presented in Activity Card 6–1. Such activities encourage children to think logically and develop communication skills. In the process, children informally explore fundamental notions, including matching, comparison, shape, sets, subsets, and disjoint sets as well as set operations.

Communication and language can be further developed as the set operations of union and intersec-

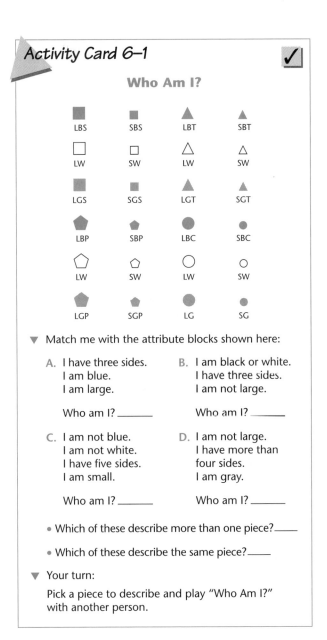

Activity Card 6–1

Who Am I?

▼ Match me with the attribute blocks shown here:

A. I have three sides.
I am blue.
I am large.

Who am I? _____

B. I am black or white.
I have three sides.
I am not large.

Who am I? _____

C. I am not blue.
I am not white.
I have five sides.
I am small.

Who am I? _____

D. I am not large.
I have more than
four sides.
I am gray.

Who am I? _____

● Which of these describe more than one piece? _____

● Which of these describe the same piece? _____

▼ Your turn:

Pick a piece to describe and play "Who Am I?" with another person.

tion are encountered. The combining, or union, of *disjoint sets* (sets with no members in common) is a natural model for addition. The logical connection *or* can be used to develop the union of two or more sets. For example, as Figure 6–3 shows, the union of triangles and squares produces a set that contains all attribute blocks that are either triangles *or* squares.

The intersection of sets can be used to explore the logical connective *and*. Using the attribute blocks, we could examine the pieces that are pentagons *and* blue. Children might place these in yarn loops as shown in Figure 6–4. This arrangement also allows children to identify other subsets, such as pieces that

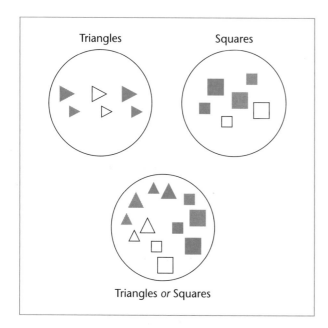

Figure 6–3 • The union of two sets

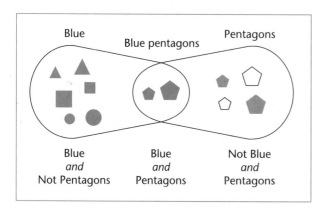

Figure 6–4 • The intersection of two sets

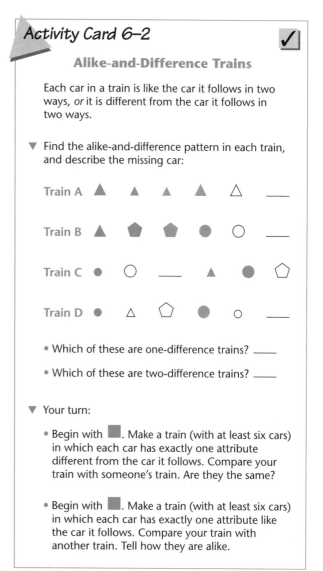

are blue and not pentagons. Using *not* to describe a relationship is an important step in development.

The logical connectives *and, or,* and *not* can be used to help children classify pieces according to their attributes. For example, the "alike and difference trains" shown in Activity Card 6–2 provide opportunities for students to use attribute blocks to classify and to search for patterns and use logical thinking as well. Children at all grade levels can benefit from structured activities with these materials.

Attribute blocks almost guarantee student involvement, but they also require teachers to assume an active role. When children are engaged in activities with attribute blocks, directed questions and probes can provide clues about their thinking pro-

cesses. Observing children's actions reveals much about their maturity. For example, when asked to choose a piece that is blue and a triangle, one child might choose a blue piece but not a triangle. Another might select a triangle that is not blue. These responses may only reflect poor listening skills. However, additional questioning may show the two children don't understand what the word "and" means or are unable to keep two different attributes in mind simultaneously. Carefully observing and questioning children as they are using these materials will help you better understand what they are thinking, which in turn will help you design more appropriate learning activities.

Many different experiences are needed to sharpen children's observation skills and provide them with the basis on which the notion of numbers is built. Consider another example, in which children are asked to count money:

How much money is this?

Three, if coins are counted

Seven, if cents are counted

This example provides a reminder that a number name alone, such as three or seven, is rarely reported. In this case, "three coins" tells us both *cardinality* (that is, how many) and what was actually counted. This example also provides another reminder that what is to be counted must be well defined or clearly understood. If there is any confusion about what is being counted, then counting discrepancies are certain to happen.

Such discrepancies occur in many different forms but are particularly troublesome with a number line. Two children standing on a number line that has been made from a roll of adding machine tape and fastened to the floor provide an example:

Barb   Scott

We can ask,

How far is it from Barb to Scott?

Is it 4? or 3? or 5?

The solution depends on what is to be counted:

Should the intervals between the dots be counted?

Should the dots be counted?

All of the dots?

Research confirms that confusion between dots and intervals often contributes to later misunder-

standing with a number line (Sowder 1992). Confusion over what should be counted is a classification problem that must be solved before meaningful counting can begin. Thus, classification is a very important step in developing number sense and early counting skills (Payne and Huinker 1993).

Patterns

Mathematics is the study of patterns. Creating, constructing, and describing patterns require problem-solving skills and constitute an important part of mathematics learning. Patterns can be based on geometric attributes (shapes, properties), relational attributes (sequence, function), physical attributes (color, length, number), or affective attributes (like, dislike). Sometimes patterns combine several attributes. For example, a child's list of favorite colors provides a pattern involving physical attributes (color) and affective attributes (like).

Paper, cubes, attribute blocks, pattern blocks, and other manipulatives provide opportunities for children to stack, arrange, and order objects in various ways. Number sense and mathematical exploration grow from such patterning. In the early grades, patterns help children develop number sense, ordering, counting, and sequencing (Coburn et al. 1992). Later, patterns are helpful in developing thinking strategies for basic facts, as will be discussed in Chapter 8. As children grow older, their experiences with patterns accelerate as they explore graphing, number theory, and geometry (Phillips et al. 1991). Patterns, as with puzzles, are usually intellectually inviting and stimulating for people of all ages.

Exploring patterns requires active mental involvement and often physical involvement. The opportunities to do patterning are limitless, but there are several different types of pattern activities that children should encounter regularly. Let's consider four different ways that patterns might be used in developing mathematical ideas.

Copying a Pattern Children are shown a pattern and then asked to make one "just like it." The original pattern might take many different forms. For example, children might be given a string with beads and asked to make the same pattern:

Or pattern blocks could be laid out for children to copy:

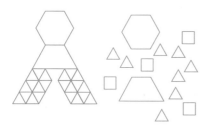

This experience requires students to choose the same pieces and arrange them in the same order. Or one could model a figure on a geoboard (see Appendix B for a geoboard master)

and ask children to copy the figure on an empty geoboard.

Finding the Next One The trains in Activity Card 6–2 illustrate problems where children "find the next one." In that case, "the next one" was the next car in the train. Consider a somewhat easier pattern suggested by "stairs" of Cuisenaire rods:

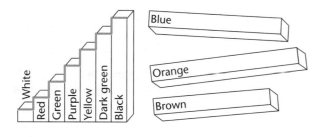

Children might be asked to find the next rod for the staircase. This find-the-next activity naturally leads to continuing or extending the pattern.

Extending a Pattern Children are shown a pattern and asked to continue it. For example, an initial pattern can be made with blocks, and children can be asked to continue the pattern:

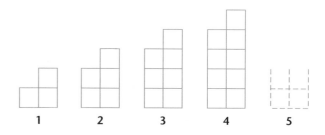

Notice how this visual pattern might serve as the foundation for exploring several important mathematical ideas. It could lead to classifying odd numbers. It could be used to observe something common about the representations—that they are all a rectangle plus one. This latter observation might lead to the algebraic generalization $2N + 1$ to describe odd numbers.

Making Their Own Patterns Children need opportunities to create their own patterns and are eager to do so. Sometimes the patterns they make are highly creative and reveal insight into their mathematical thinking.

Language and communication are important elements of patterning activities. Children should be encouraged to "think out loud" as they search for patterns. Ask them to tell why they selected a certain piece, or why they did what they did. Sometimes children "see" different patterns than we anticipate. As teachers, we must try to learn and understand children's patterns and encourage them to share their thinking.

Comparisons

Comparison of quantities is another important step toward counting and is also essential in developing number awareness. Comparisons are plentiful in classrooms as children use materials. Teacher-led activities frequently provide opportunities for comparisons, with questions such as

> Does everyone have a piece of paper?
>
> Are there more pencils or desks?

These questions either directly or indirectly involve comparisons, which may lead to the very important and powerful mathematical notion of one-to-one correspondence.

Look at Figure 6–5A and consider this question: are there more hearts or gingerbread cookies? Counting would provide a solution, particularly with the cookies scattered on a plate. However, if the cookies are arranged in an orderly fashion (Fig-

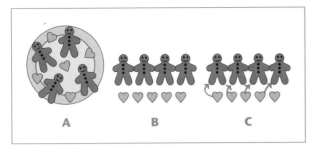

Figure 6–5 • Models for counting (A) versus comparison (B) with one-to-one correspondence (C)

ure 6–5B), we can make direct comparisons and answer the question without counting. Sometimes placing connectors (laying string or yarn; drawing lines or arrows) provides a visual reminder of the one-to-one correspondence that underlies many comparisons, as in Figure 6–5C.

When making comparisons, students must be able to discriminate between important and irrelevant attributes. In Figure 6–6A, for example, who has more leaves—Bonnie or Sammy? The leaves are very different; their sizes, shapes, and colors vary. Still, the procedure for setting up a correspondence is the same.

To ensure that members of two sets are arranged in an orderly fashion for comparison, a method that is sometimes helpful involves using pieces of square paper or index cards. In this case placing each leaf on a card and then stacking the cards on a common base as in Figure 6–6B provides a helpful framework. This method provides a graphical representation of

the information, allowing quick and accurate visual comparisons.

Several different but equally valid verbal descriptions may be used for the example given in Figure 6–6:

> Bonnie has more leaves than Sammy.
>
> Sammy has fewer leaves than Bonnie.

Children need to become familiar with descriptions of relationships such as *more than, less (fewer) than,* and *as many as.* A grasp of these terms is followed by more explicit characterization:

> Bonnie has one more leaf than Sammy.
>
> Sammy has one less leaf than Bonnie.

In these cases, the notion of order and succession are being developed. Children must come to realize that 4 is the number between 5 and 3 as well as one more than 3 and 1 less than 5. Understanding of such relationships can evolve naturally as comparisons are made and discussed.

When comparisons are made among several different things, ordering is involved. For example, children can print their first names on some grid paper:

Then they can physically compare their names with others' names to answer questions such as these:

> Who has the longest name?
>
> Who has the shortest name?
>
> Can you find someone with a name the same length as yours?
>
> Can you find someone whose name has one more (less) letter than your name?

Ordering often requires several comparisons, and a graph might help organize the information. The graph in Figure 6–7 was constructed by classifying children's names according to length. It summarizes much information and presents it in an organized form. The graph could be used to answer the previous questions and additional questions such as these:

> Which length name is most popular?
>
> Greg wasn't here today. Where should his name go on our graph?
>
> Can you think of anyone you know who has a shorter name than Tim?

Figure 6–6 • A framework for comparison that eliminates irrelevant attributes

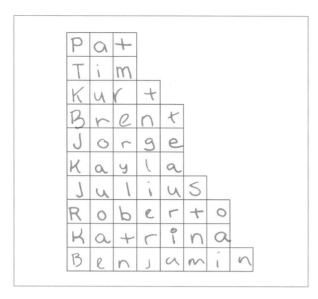

Figure 6–7 • **Classification of children's names on a graph for comparison**

As more things are ordered, the ordering process becomes more complicated, and most children need some guidance to be able to order things efficiently. That's why organizational techniques, such as graphing (see Chapter 15), are particularly helpful and will contribute toward the early development of numbers.

Conservation

The phenomenon of *conservation of number*—that a given number does not vary—reflects how children think. We need to be aware of the symptoms of the lack of conservation of number in children and its implications for early number development and counting. This phenomenon occurs in different forms, but we'll look at an example involving counting and numbers.

Two rows of blocks are arranged side by side, and a teacher and a five- or six-year-old child look at them together:

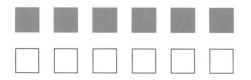

The teacher, asking the child to make a comparison to decide whether there are more white blocks or blue blocks, initiates the following dialogue.

T: How many blue blocks?
S: (Counting them) Six.
T: How many white blocks?
S: (Counting again) Six.
T: Are there more blue blocks or white blocks?
S: They are the same.

Now the teacher spreads out the white blocks as follows:

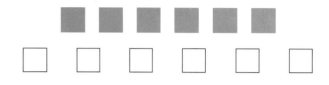

T: How many blue blocks now?
S: Six.
T: How many white blocks now?
S: Six.
T: Are there more blue blocks or white blocks?
S: More white blocks.
T: I thought you said there were six blue and six white.
S: I did, but this six (pointing to row of white blocks) is bigger.

This example illustrates a typical case where a young child thinks a number varies and depends on arrangement or configuration. Here the child believes that stretching out the row makes it longer; the fact that the number remains the same creates no conflict. Look at the following grouping of marbles.

Some children count six in each of these groups but report one group has more. For adults it seems inconceivable that "this six" could be more than "that six," but as this and other examples in this book show, children's logic and adults' logic are very different.

The phenomenon of conservation was described by Jean Piaget and has been the subject of much research (Payne and Huinker 1993). Rarely do children conserve number before five or six years of age. Children up to this age don't realize that moving the objects in a set has no effect on the number of the objects. Thus, many children in kindergarten or first and second grade—and sometimes in higher grades—are nonconservers. A child can be very adept at counting and remain naive about conservation. Whenever this happens, instructional activities (such as the different configurations of five objects on the overhead in the opening Snapshot Lesson) should be used to increase the child's awareness of the invariance of number. In the Children's Corner listing at the end of this chapter, books such as *Bears on Wheels* (Berenstain and Berenstain 1969) are great for counting and provide insight into how children count.

Group Recognition

The patterns encountered in classifying and making comparisons provide many number- sense experiences. In fact, prior to actually counting, children are aware of small numbers of things: one nose, two hands, three wheels on a tricycle. Research shows that most children entering school can identify quantities of three things or less by inspection alone without the use of counting techniques (Payne and Huinker 1993). In fact, one instructional goal for first-grade students is to develop immediate recognition of groups of up to five or six. Sight recognition of quantities up to five or six is important for several reasons:

1. It saves time. Recognition of the number in a small group is much faster than counting each individual member of that group.

2. It is the forerunner of some powerful number ideas. Children who can name small groups give evidence of knowing early order relations, such as 3 is more than 2 and 1 is less than 4. Some may also realize that 3 contains a group of 2 and a group of 1.

3. It helps develop more sophisticated counting skills. Children who recognize the number in a small group will more quickly begin counting from that point.

4. It accelerates the development of addition and subtraction. Early work with these operations involves manipulation with objects. Being able to recognize the quantity in a small group will free children of the burden of counting small quantities to be joined or removed and allow them to concentrate on the action of the operation.

The teacher in the opening Snapshot Lesson used beans and the overhead projector to develop sight recognition. The overhead projector allowed careful control of time so that the children could not count individual beans. The teacher placed the beans in different arrangements to encourage children to identify different patterns—and to do so quickly. Several different approaches were demonstrated as the children counted. Sight recognition is also evidenced by children's skills in reading the number of dots on the face of a die or on a domino. In fact, both of these materials provide natural as well as interesting models for developing and practicing this skill.

As children grow older, their ability to recognize quantities continues to improve but it is still very limited. Few adults can recognize by inspection groups of more than 6 or 8, and even these groups must be in common patterns such as those found on playing cards or dominoes. For example, look at these birds:

How many birds do you see? Each picture shows 12 birds, but you probably used different processes to count them. The picture at the left provides no clear groups, so you could either count every bird or perhaps immediately identify the numbers in some subset of the birds and then count the rest. In the other two pictures, some natural groupings are suggested: four groups of 3 and two groups of 6. It is even more difficult to recognize larger groupings without counting or forming some subsets of numbers. Nevertheless, small-group recognition is a powerful ally in counting larger groups.

● Counting

Patterns facilitate the counting process. However, there are no sound patterns within the first twelve number names. Children learn these number names by imitating adults and older children. As young children practice counting, they often say nonconventional sequences of number names. It is not unusual to hear a young child count "one, two, five, eight, fifteen, twenty, six, hundred." This counting may sound strange, but it is perfectly natural. It reflects the child's struggle to remember both the number names and their order, both of which are necessary to count.

Eventually children may count apples, blocks, cards, rocks, stones, twigs, even petals on a flower. Try counting the petals on the flowers shown in Figure 6–8. They provide a very interesting setting for practicing counting and remind us that numbers are everywhere in nature.

Items such as blocks or petals are *discrete objects*—that is, materials that lend themselves well to handling and counting. *Continuous quantities*, such as the amount of water in a glass or the weight of a person, are measured rather than counted (see Chapter 12).

What is counting? It is a surprisingly intricate process by which children call number values by name. A close look at the counting process shows that finding how many objects are present involves two distinct actions. A child must say the number-name series, beginning with one, and point to a different object as each number name is spoken. Children exhibit several different but distinct stages of counting, which we will discuss later in this chapter.

Counting Principles

How do children count? Let's look at an actual counting situation. Suppose seven shells are to be counted. A child who is what we will call a "rational counter" says each number name as the shells are counted, as indicated in Figure 6–9. The last number named, "seven," reports the total.

As adults, we probably cannot recall our own struggle with counting. Yet observing young children can remind us how counting strategies vary and are developed sequentially over a period of years (Fuson 1988). Here are four important principles on which the counting process rests:

1. Each object to be counted must be assigned one and only one number name. As shown in Figure 6–9, a one-to-one correspondence between each block and the number-name was established.

2. The number-name list must be used in a fixed order every time a group of objects is counted. The child in the figure started with "one" and counted "two, three, . . . , seven," in a specific order. This is also known as the stable order rule.

3. The order in which the objects are counted doesn't matter (this is known as the order irrelevance rule). Thus the child can start with any object and count them in any order.

4. The last number-name used gives the number of objects. This principle is a statement of the *cardinality rule*, which connects counting with *how many*. Regardless of which block is counted first or the order in which they are counted, the last block named always tells the number.

Figure 6–8 • Models from nature for counting practice

These principles help us recognize the levels of children's counting skills. Careful observation of children, coupled with a good understanding of these principles, will pinpoint counting errors. Once the trouble is diagnosed, instruction can focus on the specific problem.

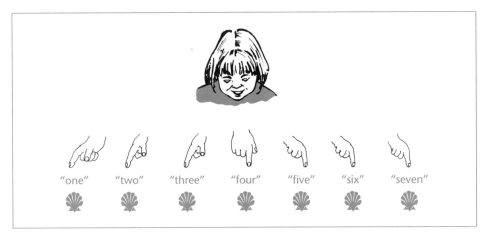

Figure 6–9 ● **Rational counting: Correct sequence, with correct correspondence**

Counting Stages

There are several identifiable counting stages, and each reflects one or more of the counting principles. For example, some children may count the objects correctly and still not know how many objects have been counted. In response to the question "How many shells are on the table?" a child might correctly count "one, two, three, four, five, six, seven," as shown in Figure 6–9, and yet be unable to answer the question. This child does not realize that the last number named tells how many.

Rote Counting A child using rote counting knows some number names, but not necessarily the proper sequence, as shown in Figure 6–10A. In this case, the child provides number names, but these names are not in correct counting sequence. Research shows that such children may "count" the same objects several times and use a different counting sequence each time (Fuson 1988).

Rote counters may know the proper counting sequence, but they may not always be able to maintain a correct correspondence between the objects being counted and the number names. Figure 6–10B shows an example in which the rote counter is saying the number-names faster than pointing, so that number-names are not coordinated with the shells being counted. Rote counters may say the number-names until they perceive all the objects as being counted. It is also possible that the rote counter points faster than saying the words, as illustrated in Figure 6–10C. This rote counter is pointing to the objects, but is not providing a name for each of them.

Thus, rote counters may not have their number-names in the proper sequence, or they may not consistently provide a number-name for each object being counted. A one-to-one correspondence may not be shown, which is a critical distinction between rote and rational counting. Using a one-to-one correspondence in counting represents significant progress and establishes one of the prerequisites to rational counting.

Rational Counting In rational counting, the child gives a correct number-name as objects are counted in succession. However, in rational counting the child not only uses one-to-one correspondence in counting, but also is able to answer the question about the number of objects being counted. In fact, rational counters exhibit all four counting principles.

Rational counting is an important skill for every primary-grade child. Children notice their own progress in developing this skill and become proud of their accomplishments. Early in first grade, some children will count to 10, others to 20, some to 50, and a few to over 100 (Fuson 1988). No upper limit should be imposed, although a goal of 100 is clearly reasonable for most children by the end of first grade. Instruction should provide regular practice and encourage each child to count as far as he or she can.

Counting Strategies

Once mastery of rational counting to 10 or 20 has been reached, more efficient and sophisticated counting strategies should be encouraged.

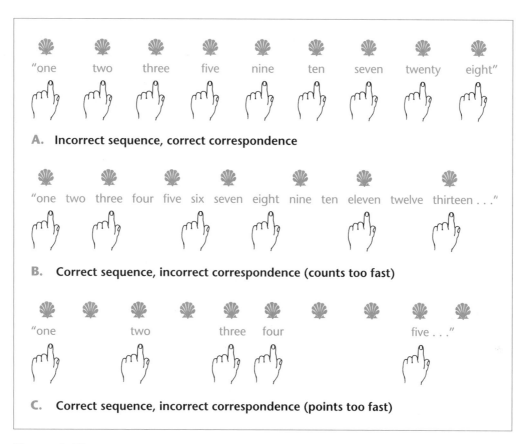

Figure 6–10 • Rote counting errors

Counting On In counting on, the child gives correct number names as counting proceeds and can start at any number and begin counting. For example, the child can begin with 8 pennies and count "nine, ten, eleven"; or begin with 78 pennies and count "seventy-nine, eighty, eighty-one"; or begin with 98 pennies and count "ninety-nine, one hundred, one hundred one." Counting-on practice leads children to the discovery of many valuable patterns. Counting on is also an essential strategy for developing addition.

Counting Back When children count back, they give correct number names as they count backward from a particular point. For example, to count back to solve the problem, "Bobbie had 22 rabbits and 3 were lost," a child might count "twenty-one, twenty, nineteen" and conclude there were 19 left. At an early stage, counting back can be related to rockets blasting off (counting down—five, four, three, two, one, blast off); later it becomes helpful in developing subtraction.

Many children find it very difficult to count backward, just as many adults find it difficult to recite the alphabet backward. The calculator provides a valuable instructional tool to help children improve their ability to count backward. Many children are surprised to learn that it is as easy to count backward on a calculator as it is to count forward.

Instruction in counting should include practice counting backward as well as forward. Counting backward, "Five, four, three, two, one," helps children establish sequences and relate each number to another in a different way. Activity Card 6–3 provides an activity that integrates such practice with pattern recognition.

Skip Counting In skip counting, the child gives correct names, but instead of counting by ones, counts by twos, fives, tens, or other values. The starting point and direction are optional. In addition to providing many patterns, skip counting provides readiness for multiplication and division.

Skip counting, coupled with counting on and counting back, provides excellent preparation for counting change. Thus, given the coins shown, children would be encouraged to choose the largest-

Activity Card 6–3

Hunting for Numbers

▼ Look at this chart:

1	2	3	4	5	6	7	8	9	10
11	12	13	14	15	16	17	18	19	20
21	22	23	24	25	26	27	28	29	30
31	32	33	34	35	36	37	38	39	40
41	42		44	45	46	47	48	49	50
51	52	53	54	55	56	57	58	59	60
61	62	63	64	65	66	67	68	69	70
71	72	73	74	75	76	77	78	79	80
81	82	83	84	85	86	87	88	89	90
91	92	93	94	95	96	97	98	99	100

- What is hidden by the ■?
- What number is after ■?
- What number is before the ■?

▼ Put a ● on any number.

- Begin at ●: Count forward five.
- Begin at ● again: Count backward five.

▼ Put a ▲ on a different number.

- Begin at ▲: Count forward five.
- Begin at ▲ again: Count backward five.

▼ Tell about any patterns you see.

valued coin and then begin counting on—"twenty-five, thirty, thirty-five, forty."

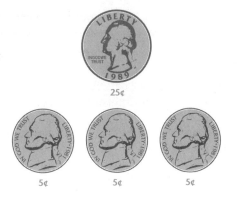

Counting change is a very important skill whose usefulness children recognize. It holds great appeal for them. It should be introduced and extended as far as possible in the primary grades. Interestingly enough, most of the difficulties associated with counting change can be traced to weaknesses in counting. This finding suggests that teachers should take advantage of every opportunity to encourage accurate and rapid counting.

Counting Practice

Counting practice should include counting on and counting back by ones. Situations that encourage thoughtful counting often present problems embedded in real world models. These situations may provide practice in counting either forward or backward. For example:

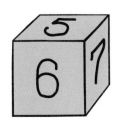

If the six numbers on the cube must be consecutive (i.e., whole numbers in order for the cube)—

> Name some possible numbers that could be on the six faces of this cube.
>
> What is the smallest possible number on the cube?
>
> What is the largest possible number on the cube?

This problem requires counting, but it also encourages higher-level thinking and logical reasoning. For example, questions such as, "Is there more than one correct answer?" should be raised and discussed. The problem also illustrates that unique answers don't always exist. These experiences may even encourage children to formulate similar problems.

A number of books listed in the Children's Corner, such as *Anno's Counting Book* and *Anno's Counting House* by Mitsumasa Anno and *I Can Count the Petals of a Flower* by John and Stacy Wahl, provide a variety of rich and stimulating contexts for counting. Other books, such as *How Many Snails? A Counting Book* by Paul Giganti, focus on numerical relationships. These books are very useful for counting-based discussions between children and adults. For example, *Anno's Counting Book* provides a sequence of pictures of different scenes of the house where little people move from one house to another. Initially the teacher/parent can ask questions such as:

How many children are in the house?

How many are boys?

How many are girls?

How many are wearing hats?

How many are on the second floor?

Starter questions are provided to encourage active participation and maintain a high level of interest. After students start counting, not only are many new things to count identified, but important aspects of early number sense also are experienced.

Practice in skip counting from 1 and other start numbers, including 0, contributes to developing good counting skills and greater number sense. The hundred chart is an ideal model for practicing skip counting, as in Activity Card 6–4. Here finding patterns and problem solving are integrated with the counting practice.

Research has shown some predictable trouble spots for children when counting. For example, children often slow down, hesitate, or stop when they reach certain numbers, such as twenty-nine. However, as soon as they establish the next number as thirty, their counting pace quickens, until they are ready to enter the next decade (set of ten). Bridging the next century (set of one hundred) poses a similar challenge. As children count ". . . one hundred ninety-eight, one hundred ninety-nine," they may pause and be uncertain how to name the next number. Bridging to the next ten or hundred are among the common transitional points of counting difficulty identified by Labinowicz (1985):

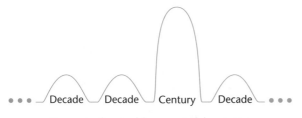

Bumps in the road for successful counters

Not only is the calculator a valuable instructional tool that helps children improve their ability to count, but it also is a powerful counting tool that they love to explore. Early counting with the calculator should emphasize the physical link between pressing the keys and watching the display. Because

the display changes constantly, the students begin to recognize patterns. Calculator counting involves a physical activity (pressing a key each time a number is counted), through which students relate the size of a number to the amount of time needed to count.

Children are usually surprised to find that it is as easy to count by any number on the calculator as to count by ones. A calculator can start at zero and count by ones (Activity Card 6–5) or begin at any starting point and skip count by any number (Activity Cards 6–6 and 6–7). Calculators can also easily count backward (Activity Card 6–8).

Estimation is a natural part of counting, and Activity Card 6–5 encourages students to estimate the time it takes to count by ones to 100 and 1,000 with the calculator. By expanding this activity, students will come to realize that it takes about the same amount of time to count to 1,000 by ones as to count to 1,000,000 by 1,000 or to 100 by 0.01. Such

Activity Card 6–5

Counting
On . . . and On . . . and On . . .

- How long did it take to count from 1 to 100? _____

- Guess how long it will take to count from 1 to 1,000. _____

- Count from 1 to 1,000. How long did it take? _____

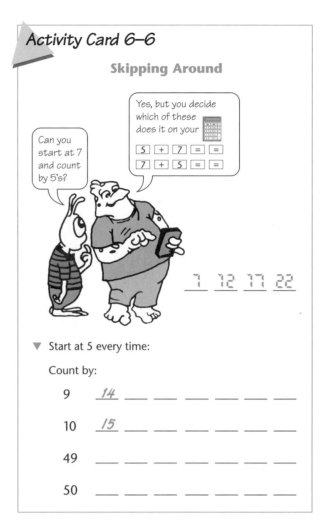

Activity Card 6–6

Skipping Around

▼ Start at 5 every time:

Count by:

9	_14_	__	__	__	__	__
10	_15_	__	__	__	__	__
49	__	__	__	__	__	__
50	__	__	__	__	__	__

Early Number Development

Comparing and counting experiences help children develop early foundations for number sense. Today's children also have had many experiences, primarily while watching television (*Sesame Street,* for example), that develop counting skills. Classroom instruction for early number development should be designed to build on these experiences.

Developing Number Benchmarks

Number benchmarks are perceptual anchors that become internalized from many concrete experiences, often accumulated over many years. The numbers 5 and 10 (the number of fingers on one and two hands) provide two early number benchmarks. Children recognize four fingers as being one less

counting experiences develop important place-value concepts and contribute to number sense.

Counting from a particular number or by a certain number leads students to see many patterns. For example, Activity Card 6–6 helps students recognize that adding 49 to a number is the same as adding 50 and subtracting 1, which is a powerful pattern often used in mental computation. Calculator counting opens exciting mathematical explorations and promotes both critical thinking and problem solving.

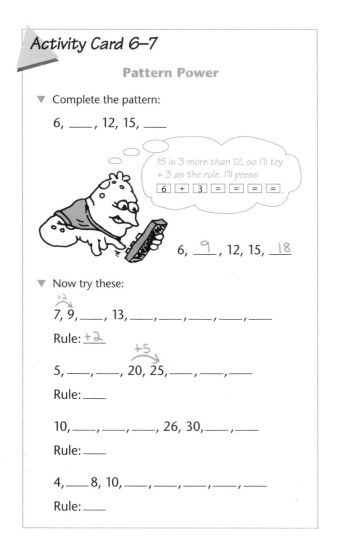

Activity Card 6–7

Pattern Power

▼ Complete the pattern:

6, ____, 12, 15, ____

15 is 3 more than 12, so I'll try + 3 as the rule. I'll press [6] [+] [3] [=] [=] [=] [=].

6, _9_, 12, 15, _18_

▼ Now try these:

7, 9, ____, 13, ____, ____, ____, ____, ____   (+2)

Rule: _+2_

5, ____, ____, 20, 25, ____, ____, ____   (+5)

Rule: ____

10, ____, ____, ____, 26, 30, ____, ____

Rule: ____

4, ____ 8, 10, ____, ____, ____, ____, ____

Rule: ____

Activity Card 6–8

Counting Backward

Can you make your count like this?

Sure. See if this makes your count backwards [10] [−] [1] [=] [=] [=] *If it doesn't work on your try other ways until it counts.*

10, 9, 8, 7, 6, . . .

▼ Try these:

15 − 1 = _14_ , _13_ , ____ , ____ , ____ , ____

20 − 2 = _18_ , ____ , ____ , ____ , ____ , ____

35 − 3 = ____ , ____ , ____ , ____ , ____ , ____

than five and eight being three more than five or two less than ten:

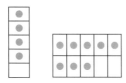

"one less than five"   "three more than five" "two less than ten"

The five-frame (5 × 1 array) and the ten-frame (5 × 2 array) utilize these early benchmarks:

In Japan, the early benchmarks of 5 and 10 are later used with the ten-frame and the Japanese *soroban* (which is similar to an abacus) to promote counting, quick recognition of quantities, and mental computation (Shigematsu et al. 1994).

Activity Card 6–9 illustrates an activity that encourages the development of benchmark numbers. Because the goal is to develop an intuitive sense of the anchor number (not laborious counting), these early activities show numbers of dots that are significantly different from the anchor.

Of course, many different anchors can be drawn from children's experiences. You might show a bowl of peanuts and ask, "About how many can you hold in one hand?" Change the contents of the bowl to other things, such as erasers, centimeter cubes, marbles, or balls. As children grow older, they should be comfortable and skilled with more and more benchmark numbers. The early number-sense activities with 5 and 10 as anchors can naturally be extended to anchors of 20 or 100, as shown in Activity Card 6–10.

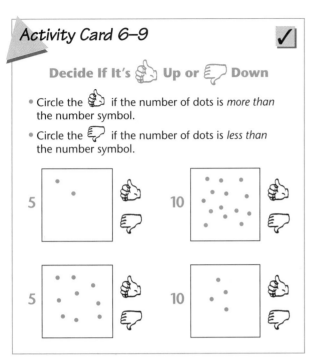

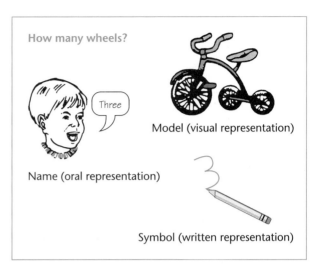

Figure 6–11 ● **A number development model linking visual, oral, and written representations**

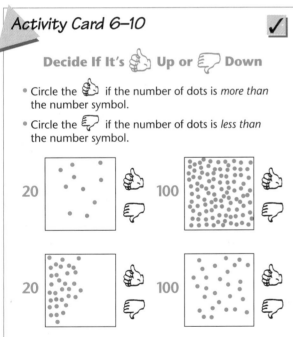

and written symbol. It is also important to provide different configurations of dots, blocks, and other objects, as well as different forms of the numerals, such as *3* and 3, to broaden their experiences.

Many valuable relationships are established as the numbers 1 through 5 are developed, but none are more useful than the notions of *one more* and *one less.* These connections are fundamental in early counting and also in learning place value with larger numbers. The notions *one more* and *one less* evolve from many different real-world experiences, such as these:

David has one less cookie than Jean-Paul.

Mira has one more apple than Beth.

They have one less player on their team.

Their group has one more girl than our group.

The concepts of *one more* and *one less* can be modeled in different ways. Figure 6–12 shows three such models. These arrangements provide a basis for developing the concept of 5 as well as discussing *one more* or *one less.* Using these models for discussion will help children establish important connections that link numbers such as 4 and 5. For example, children might say,

The yellow rod is one step longer than the purple rod.

The five card is just like the four card except it has an extra dot in the middle.

Having many experiences with such models and patterns helps children abstract numbers and establish useful connections between them.

Making Connections

The development of the numbers 1 through 5 will be principally done through sight recognition of patterns, coupled with immediate association with the oral name and then the written symbolization. For example, as Figure 6–11 illustrates, a picture of a tricycle and the question, "How many wheels?" can be used to develop the number 3. It is important that the number of wheels be linked to both oral name

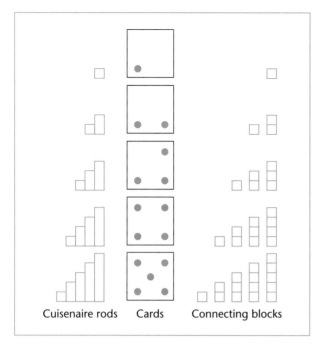

Figure 6–12 • **Three models for *one more* or *one less***

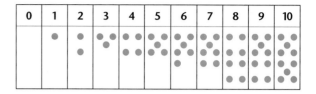

The dots on the cards and the trains of blocks in Figure 6–12 provide clear reminders of the numbers represented and the notion of *one more* or *one less*. Both the staircase of rods and the trains of blocks vividly illustrate not only these concepts but also an important, yet subtle, difference between the models. The staircase of rods illustrates the concept of *more,* but it is not absolutely clear how much more until the length of the rods has been made clear. If we used a single rod without identifying a unit rod, it would not be possible to associate the rod with a unique number. Thus, the rods are a very different model for developing numbers than the dot cards or trains of blocks.

Some models illustrate zero more clearly than others. For example, a rod of length zero is more difficult to grasp than a card with zero dots. Care should be taken to introduce zero as soon as it becomes natural to do so, using models appropriate for the purpose. Help children distinguish between zero and nothing by encouraging the use of zero to report the absence of something. For example, when reporting the score of a game, it is better to say "Cardinals three, Bears zero" than to say "three to nothing."

As the numbers through 10 are developed, it is important that various patterns among them be discovered, recognized, used, and discussed. Many patterns suggesting many different relationships are shown in this number chart:

For example, the number 7 is shown by 5 dots and 2 more dots. The number 10 is composed of two groups of 5 dots. It is also useful to explore other patterns.

On the number chart, 6 is shown as 5 dots and 1 dot, but other representations are possible, as shown in Figure 6–13, and they should be explored and discussed with students. Part (B) of Figure 6–13, for example, shows that 6 can be represented as one group of 3, one group of 2, and one group of 1. It can also be shown as two groups of 3, as in parts (A) and (D), or three groups of 2, as in part (C). No mention is made of addition or multiplication in this context, but such observations provide helpful connections when these operations are developed.

Similar illustrations and applications of the numbers 7 through 10 should be presented. For example, 7 days in a week may suggest a natural grouping; 8 vertices (corners) of a cube suggest two groups of 4; and the number of boxes in a tic-tac-toe grid suggest three groups of 3.

Most children realize very early that 10 is a very special number. At the early stage of number development, the most unusual thing about 10 is that it is the first number represented by two digits, 1 and 0. In addition to having 10 fingers and toes, children encounter the number 10 in many situations such as in playing games and changing money.

These experiences can be extended to include discussion about different representations of 10:

Can you find two groups of 5?

Can you find five groups of 2?

Does the group of 4, 3, 2, and 1 remind you of bowling?

The number 10 provides the cornerstone for our number system, and its significance is developed further in Chapter 7.

A ten-frame is certainly one of the most effective models for facilitating patterns, developing group

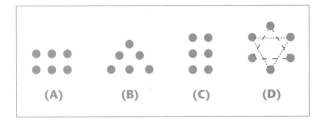

Figure 6–13 • **Some representations of 6**

Figure 6–14 • **Representations of 8 on a ten-frame**

recognition of numbers, and building an understanding of place value. The ten-frame can be made from an egg carton shortened to contain ten boxes, or it may simply be outlined on paper or tagboard (see ten-frame in Appendix B). This frame is a powerful organizer and helps provide the base for many thinking strategies and mental computation. Initially, children might use counters to make different representations of the same number in the ten-frame, as illustrated in Figure 6–14. Encountering a variety of groupings on the ten-frame should stimulate discussion about different patterns.

Figure 6–15 shows some of the connections that might be constructed as children examine different representations on the ten-frame. These relationships encourage children to think flexibly about numbers, thereby promoting greater number sense. Experiences with the ten-frame also facilitate the de-

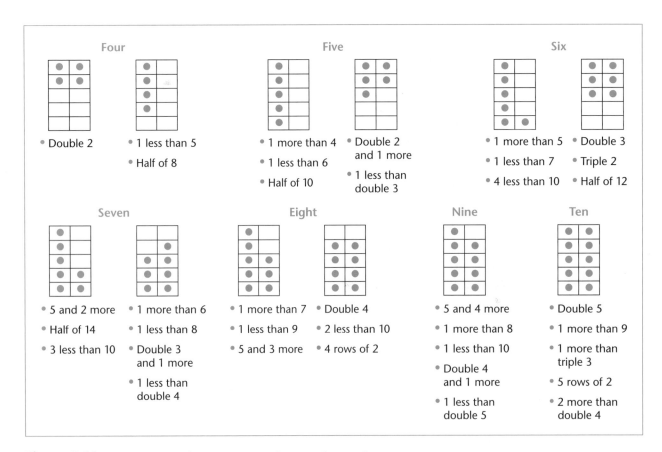

Figure 6–15 • **Connections from representations on the ten-frame**

velopment of addition, subtraction, multiplication, and division, as well as place value.

● Cardinal, Ordinal, and Nominal Numbers

We have discussed some important considerations in number development. The emphasis has been on finding a correct number name for a given group. This aspect of number provides a *cardinal number*, which answers the question "How many?" Another important aspect of number emphasizes arranging things in an order and is known as *ordinal number*; it answers the question "Which one?"

An emphasis on ordering, seriating, or arranging things in a given sequence leads to ordinal numbers. The order may be based on any criterion such as size, time of day, age, or position in a race. Once an order is established, however, the counting process not only produces a set of number names, but also names each object according to its position. Thus, in counting the rungs on the ladder in Figure 6–16, number 1 is first, 2 is second, 3 is third, and so on.

Research shows that many children know some ordinal numbers such as first, second, and third before they begin school (Payne and Huinker 1993). Encounters with statements such as the following provide early and valuable experience with ordinal numbers.

The first letter of the alphabet is A.

Bob is second in line.

Cary was third in the race.

It is important that the development of early number concepts provides children with opportunities to learn both ordinal and cardinal numbers. Don't worry about which to teach first; just be sure both are given attention.

It is possible for a child to recognize a pattern of 4 beans but not be able to count to 4 correctly. Such a child could give the cardinal number 4 to answer the question, "How many beans do you see?"

For this child, the notion of cardinal number is very limited but has preceded the use of ordinal number in counting. Such instances are rare, and, when they do occur, they are limited to small numbers.

The second counting principle presented earlier suggests that counting cannot occur until a child knows which number-name comes first, which second, and so on, even though (as mentioned in the third principle) the order in which things are counted is not important. The only way for the ordinal aspect of number to be present is for the things counted to be seen in order.

A knowledge of ordinal relationships, along with logical thinking, leads to more challenging experiences, such as that offered in Activity Card 6–11. These questions are guaranteed to generate much discussion as they help children further clarify notions of ordinal numbers.

Another aspect of number provides a label or classification and is known as *nominal*. Examples are

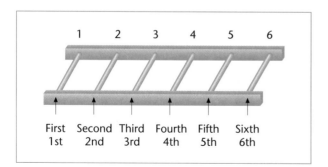

Figure 6–16 • **A counting model for ordinal numbers**

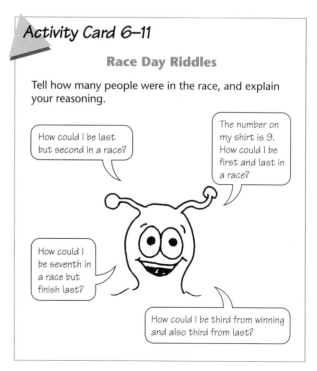

the number on a player's uniform, the license plate of a car, a postal zip code, and a telephone number. The nominal numbers provide essential information for identification but do not necessarily utilize the ordinal or cardinal aspects of the number.

When using cardinal, ordinal, and nominal numbers, children do not need to distinguish between the terms. Distinctions can be made informally by asking questions within problem situations such as

How many pieces are on the chess board?

Which pawn is third?

Where is the queen?

These questions not only help children think about numbers but also illustrate that numbers have different uses.

● Writing Numerals

The NCTM *Standards* (1989) recommend that the writing of numerals by young children should receive less attention; instead, young children should focus their attention on number development and relationships among numbers. These recommendations are based on research studies that document that young children typically have difficulty writing numerals as well as letters (Payne and Huinker 1993). The lack of development of the small muscles needed to write presents one problem, and the limited eye–hand coordination of many young children constitutes another difficulty. Both of these make it difficult or impossible for young children to write numerals. If children are pressured into premature symbolization, it can create unnecessary frustrations and anxieties.

Many children initiate early writing of numerals on their own, and they get a feeling of great accomplishment from it, which is great. However, research shows that children learn these writing skills much more quickly as second graders than in kindergarten!

First graders can usually recognize a number symbol and say it correctly long before they write it. However, when it is time for writing numerals, children should be supervised closely to ensure that proper skills are being formed and poor habits avoided. They should begin by tracing the digits:

0 1 2 3 4 5 6 7 8 9

Textbooks provide guidance to children in different forms. Usually a starting point is indicated as well as the direction:

2	2	2	2	'			

Encourage children to draw the appropriate number of objects beside the numeral being written to help them connect the number concept with its symbolic representation. We recommend that, when children are learning to write numerals, the writing skill be developed aside from "mathematics." Thus, children should master this skill and use it freely before applying it in written computational situations; otherwise, the writing task consumes all their concentration, and they forget about the mathematics being done.

Many children develop the necessary writing skills on their own. These youngsters need only monitoring and maybe some occasional guidance. Others, however, need systematic step-by-step procedures to help them. Although there is no one best way to form a numeral, there are some patterns that may help. Guiding a child's hand until the child takes the initiative in writing helps him or her get started. Later, outlines of numerals for children to trace is helpful. Here are some additional suggestions; these will not be necessary in all cases, but some children will profit from them.

1. Cut out shapes of numerals. Use the overhead projector to project a numeral on the chalkboard or wall and have a child trace the numeral's silhouette.

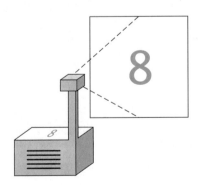

2. As one child is tracing the projected numeral, have class members trace it in the air. As the tracing is being done, describe it verbally such as "go to the right and then down." This activity can be

extended to using only dots to form the outline or pattern for the children to follow.

3. Have a child who can make numerals stand behind someone who cannot. Ask the skilled child to use a finger and gently "write" a numeral on the other child's back. The child in front should identify the numeral and write it on the chalkboard, trace it on the wall, or write it in the air. This approach calls on the tactile sense and helps some children better develop their writing skills.

It feels like a three!

4. Use numerals that have been cut from sandpaper and pasted to cards, or take some cord and glue it in the shape of numerals. Place a mark on each numeral to show the child where to begin tracing it with his or her finger. This approach is particularly helpful with children who persist in reversing numerals.

5. Cover numerals to be traced with a transparency. Then give the child a water-soluble pen and have him or her practice tracing the numerals.

6. For children having difficulty writing numerals, a calculator is helpful. The calculator display provides a visual reminder of a number's symbolization and removes the burden of writing complicated numerals.

The fact that numerals take different forms also should be mentioned, but not belabored.

4 **4** ⅞ ⁴

Some familiarity with these forms will help avoid confusion when a 4 appears as a printed number or as a digital display on a clock or calculator. The wide use of digital numbers in everyday living demands planned instruction to make children familiar with them.

A Glance at Where We've Been

Good number sense is a prerequisite to all later computational development. Young children need to recognize small groups of objects (up to 5 or 6) by sight and name them properly. Activities involving sight recognition of the numbers of objects in small groups provide many opportunities to introduce and use key terms such as *more, less, after, before, one more,* and *one less.* To foster a better number sense, instruction on the numbers through 5 should focus on patterns and develop recognition skills. Models such as the ten-frame provide a powerful tool for helping children explore and construct relationships for numbers to 10 and beyond.

Counting skills are started before children begin school but must be developed by careful and systematic instruction before written work is appropriate. Counting processes reflect various levels of sophistication, beginning with rote counting, and eventually leading to rapid skip counting forward and backward. Although the four counting principles are established in the primary grades, counting skills are extended in the intermediate grades and often are further refined throughout our lives.

Competence with and understanding of the numbers 0 through 10 are essential for meaningful later development of larger numbers. The relation of the sets of objects, the number-names, the written symbols, and the order between numbers must be well understood. This knowledge is the basis for the successful study of elementary mathematics, and it prepares children for the necessary understanding of large numbers and place value.

THINGS TO DO: From What You've Read

1. What are some characteristics of number sense? Why is number sense difficult to define?

2. Describe why classification is an important pre-number skill.

3. Suppose you send a note home to parents encouraging them to help their child improve sight-recognition skills. One parent responds, "Why should my child learn to recognize a group of 5? After all, you can just count them." How would you respond?

4. Four fundamental principles of counting were identified in this chapter. Describe in your own words what each means and why it is necessary.

5. Several different stages of counting exist. Distinguish between rote and rational counting.

6. What is meant by conservation of number? Why is its development an important part of number sense?

7. Describe how the following activity could help children sharpen their understanding of ordinal and cardinal numbers.

   How many ordinal numbers are in this sentence? "The 500 residents of Centerville celebrated the 100th anniversary of the town's founding by setting off a $200 fireworks display at the corner of Fifth and Broadway on January 1st."

8. Describe how counting could be used to answer these questions:

   How many floors are between the seventh and fifteenth floors?

   If Alfinio has read to the bottom of page 16, how many pages must he read to reach the top of page 21?

9. Describe how the ten-frame serves as a useful model for early number development.

▶ **THINGS TO DO:**
   Going Beyond This Book

1. Examine *Number Sense and Operations* (Burton et al. 1993), *Developing Number Sense in Middle Grades* (Reys et al. 1991), or the *SENSE* series (McIntosh et al. 1997). How do these books characterize number sense? Report on several instructional activities designed to foster number sense.

2. Select a patterning activity from *Patterns* (Coburn et al. 1992) or *Patterns and Functions* (Phillips et al. 1991) that would be appropriate for primary grades. Describe how you would prepare for, use, and extend this activity.

3. Examine the chapter "Concepts of Number" by Van de Walle (1990) in *Mathematics for the Young Child*. Describe three different instructional activities for promoting early number sense.

4. Read "Bring on the Buttons" (Whitin 1989) and describe some ways in which buttons could be used to develop classification skills.

5. The February 1989 issue of *Arithmetic Teacher* focused on number sense. Select an article from this special issue and report how it addressed developing number sense.

6. Read "A Proposed Framework for Examining Basic Number Sense" (McIntosh et al. 1992). Summarize the key components of this framework and provide an example of each.

7. Examine a textbook series published in 1997 or later. Describe how calculators are used to develop counting skills in the first three grades.

8. Compare two current textbook series.
   a. Find how far each series expects children to be able to count when they begin first grade and when they complete first grade.
   b. Find examples of activities designed to develop number sense. Describe the activities and identify the grade level. Do you think these activities would be effective? Tell why.
   c. Find an example of a visual pattern that is connected to numbers and arithmetic.

9. Observe some young children (ages 4 to 7) counting. Describe how the four counting principles are reflected in their actions.

10. Examine one of the books from the Children's Corner. Describe how this book might be used to develop counting and classification skills.

11. Review *The Wonderful World of Mathematics: A Critically Annotated List of Children's Books in Mathematics* (Thiessen and Matthias 1992). Find three multicultural books related to counting that are highly recommended.

12. Read one of the vignettes in the *Professional Standards for Teaching Mathematics* (NCTM 1991) that involves early development of number. Describe the role of the teacher.

13. Read the book *How Many Snails: A Counting Book* (Giganti 1988). Then read the article by Whitin, Mills, and O'Keefe (1994) to see how this book was used to explore mathematical problem solving. Discuss how the project was done and how the examples of children's work provides insight into their development of number sense.

14. View a segment from the video tape series *Number Sense Now!* (Fennell 1992). Discuss ways in which this tape might help students become more sensitive to the importance and power of number sense.

▼▼▼▼▼▼▼▼▼▼▼▼▼▼▼▼▼▼▼▼▼▼▼▼

Children's Corner

Anno, Mitsumasa. *Anno's Counting Book.* New York: Thomas Y. Crowell, 1977.

Anno, Mitsumasa. *Anno's Counting House.* New York: Philomel Books, 1982.

Berenstain, Stanley, and Berenstain, Janice. *Bears on Wheels.* New York: Random House, 1969.

Carter, David A. *How Many Bugs in A Box?* New York: Simon & Schuster, 1988.

Dee, Rudy. *Two Ways to Count to Ten.* New York: Henry Holt, 1988.

Feelings, Muriel. *Maja Means One: A Swahili Counting Book.* New York: Dial Books for Young Readers, 1971.

Giganti, Paul. *How Many Snails? A Counting Book.* New York: Greenwillow Books, 1988.

Handford, Martin. *Where's Waldo?* Boston: Little, Brown, 1987.

Hawkins, Colin, and Hawkins, Jacqui. *How Many Are in This Old Car? A Counting Book.* New York: G.P. Putnam's Sons, 1988.

Hoban, Russell, and Selig, Sylvie. *Ten What? A Mystery Counting Book.* New York: Scribner's, 1975.

Kingsley, Emily Perl; Moss, Jeffrey; Stiles, Norman; and Wilcox, Daniel. *Sesame Street One, Two, Three Story Book.* New York: Random House, 1973.

Nozaki, Akihiro, and Anno, Mitsumasa. *Anno's Hat Tricks.* New York: Philomel Books, 1985.

Pluckrose, Henry. *Numbers.* New York: Franklin Watts, 1988.

Robinson, Shari. *A First Number Book.* New York: Grossett & Dunlap, 1981.

Thomson, Ruth. *All about 1, 2, 3.* Milwaukee: Stevens Publishing, 1986.

Wahl, John, and Wahl, Stacy. *I Can Count the Petals of a Flower.* Reston, Va.: NCTM, 1976.

Yeoman, John. *Sixes and Sevens.* New York: Macmillan, 1974.

Zaslavsky, Claudia. *Count on Your Fingers African Style.* New York: Crowell Publishers, 1980.

Selected References

Baratta-Lorton, Mary. *Mathematics Their Way.* Palo Alto, Calif.: Addison-Wesley, 1976.

Burton, Grace; Mills, Ann; Lennon, Carolyn; and Parker, Cynthia. *Number Sense and Operations.* Reston, Va.: NCTM, 1993.

Coburn, Terrence G.; Bushey, Barbara J.; Holton, Liana C.; Latozas, Debra; Mortimer, Debbie; and Shotwell, Deborah. *Patterns.* Reston, Va.: NCTM. 1992.

Fennell, Francis. *Number Sense Now!* (video tape and guidebook). Reston, Va.: NCTM, 1992.

Fuson, Karen C. "Adding by Counting on with One Handed Finger Patterns." *Arithmetic Teacher,* 35 (September 1987), pp. 38–41.

Fuson, Karen C. *Children's Counting and Concepts of Number.* New York: Springer-Verlag, 1988.

Howden, Hilde. "Teaching Number Sense." *Arithmetic Teacher,* 36 (February 1989), pp. 6–11.

Huntsberger, John P. "Using Attribute Blocks with Children." *Science and Children,* 15 (January 1978), pp. 23–25.

Kroll, Diana Lambdin, and Yabe, Toshiaki. "A Japanese Educator's Perspective on Teaching Mathematics in the Elementary School." *Arithmetic Teacher,* 35 (October 1987), pp. 36–43.

Labinowicz, Ed. *Learning from Children: New Beginnings for Teaching Numerical Thinking.* Menlo Park, Calif.: Addison-Wesley, 1985.

McIntosh, Alistair; Reys, Barbara J.; and Reys, Robert E. "A Proposed Framework for Examining Basic Number Sense." *For the Learning of Mathematics,* 12 (November 1992), pp. 2–8.

McIntosh, Alistair; Reys, Barbara; and Reys, Robert. *Number SENSE, Simple Effective Number Sense Experiences: Grades 1–2 & 3–4,* Palo Alto, Calif.: Dale Seymour Publications, 1997.

National Council of Teachers of Mathematics. *Curriculum and Evaluation Standards for School Mathematics.* Reston, Va.: NCTM, 1989.

National Council of Teachers of Mathematics. *Professional Standards for Teaching Mathematics.* Reston, Va.: NCTM, 1991.

Payne, Joseph N., and Huinker, DeAnn M. "Early Number and Numeration." In *Research Ideas for the Classroom: Early Childhood Mathematics* (ed. Robert J. Jensen). Reston, Va.: NCTM, and New York: Macmillan 1993, pp. 43–70.

Phillips, Elizabeth; Gardella, Theodore; Kelly, Constance; and Stewart, Jacqueline. *Patterns and Functions.* Reston, Va.: NCTM, 1991.

Reys, Robert E.; Bestgen, Barbara J.; Coburn, Terrence G.; Marcucci, Robert; Schoen, Harold L.; Shumway, Richard J.; Wheatley, Charlotte L.; Wheatley, Grayson, H.; and White, Arthur L. *Keystrokes: Calculator Activities for Young Students: Counting and Place Value.* Palo Alto, Calif.: Creative Publications, 1980.

Reys, Barbara J.; Barger, Rita; Bruckheimer, Maxim; Dougherty, Barbara; Hope, Jack; Lembke, Linda; Markovitz, Zvia; Parnas, Andy; Reehm, Sue; Sturdevant, Ruthi; and Weber, Marianne. *Developing Number Sense in the Middle Grades.* Reston, Va.: NCTM, 1991.

Ritchart, Ron. *Making Numbers Make Sense: A Source Book for Developing Numeracy.* Menlo Park, Calif.: Addison-Wesley, 1994.

Shigematsu, K.; Iwasaki, H.; and Koyama, M. "Mental Computation: Evaluation, Curriculum and Instructional Issues from the Japanese Perspective." In *Computational Alternatives for the 21st Century: Cross Cultural Perspectives from Japan and the United States* (eds. Robert E. Reys and Nobubiko Nohda). Reston, Va.: NCTM, 1994.

Sowder, Judith, and Schappelle, Bonnie. Number Sense-Making, *Arithmetic Teacher,* 41(6) (February 1994), pp. 342–345.

Sowder, Judith T. (1992). Estimation and number sense. In D. A. Grouws (Ed.), *Handbook of Research on Mathematics Teaching and Learning* (pp. 371–389). New York: Macmillan.

Suydam, Marilyn. "The Process of Counting." *Arithmetic Teacher,* 33 (January 1987), p. 29.

Thiessen, Diane, and Matthias, Margaret (eds.). *The Wonderful World of Mathematics: A Critically Annotated List of Children's Books in Mathematics.* Reston, Va.: NCTM, 1992.

Thompson, Charles S. "Number Sense and Numeration in Grades K–8." *Arithmetic Teacher,* 37 (September 1989), pp. 22–24.

Thornton, Carol A., and Tucker, Sally C. "Lesson Planning: The Key to Developing Number Sense." *Arithmetic Teacher,* 36 (February 1989), pp. 18–21.

Thornton, Carol A.; Jones, Graham A.; and Neal, Judy L. "The 100s Chart: A Stepping Stone to Mental Mathematics." *Teaching Children Mathematics,* 1(8) (April 1995), pp. 480–483.

Welchman-Tischler, Rosamand. *How to Use Children's Literature to Teach Mathematics.* Reston, Va.: NCTM, 1992.

Van de Walle, John. "Concepts of Number." In *Mathematics for the Young Child* (ed. Joseph N. Payne). Reston, Va.: NCTM, 1990, pp. 62–87.

Whitin, David J. "Bring on the Buttons." *Arithmetic Teacher,* 36 (January 1989), pp. 4–6.

Whitin, David J. "Number Sense and the Importance of Asking 'Why'?" *Arithmetic Teacher,* 36 (February 1989), pp. 26–29.

Whitin, David J., Mills, Heidi, and O'Keefe, Timothy. Exploring Subject Areas with a Counting Book, *Teaching Children Mathematics,* 1(3) (November 1994), pp. 170–177.

Developing Number Sense with Numeration and Place Value

 ## Snapshot of a Lesson

Key Ideas for a Primary-Grade Lesson on Place Value

1. Develop number sense by using tens (bean sticks) for a quick benchmark estimate.

2. Illustrate the place-value concept with two different models.

3. Provide concrete representation of two-digit numbers and their corresponding symbolization.

Necessary Materials

• *Bean Sticks:* Each child should have a set of 10 bean sticks and a small pile of loose beans. (A bean stick is a tongue depressor or popsicle stick on which ten lima or butter beans are glued. Children should each make their own bean sticks, thereby convincing themselves that there are indeed ten beans on a stick. Gluing on the beans will also instill a pride in ownership of the sticks.) The teacher also needs some loose beans and a set of beansticks.

• *Place-Value Mat:* Each child should have a place-value mat and a water-soluble pen. (A place-value-mat is a piece of heavy construction paper that has been laminated so children can write on it. It has two columns—for tens and ones.) The teacher needs a transparency of a place-value mat for use on the overhead projector.

Tens	Ones

Orientation

In previous lessons, these second graders have been counting by ones and tens, as well as counting on (by ones). This lesson continues to develop number sense and place value, as the children count the sticks and beans in several different ways. (For example, they count the sticks first and then the separate beans or count the beans first and then the sticks—which is more difficult for the children but an important skill to develop.) To encourage students to decide about how many beans there are without counting, Mrs. Golden places the bean sticks and four beans on the overhead, turns it on for only a couple of seconds, and then turns it off.

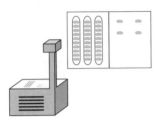

MRS. GOLDEN: Did you see more than 30?

Tranh raises his hand immediately.

TRANH: Yes.

MRS. GOLDEN: Tell us how you knew that so quickly. Did you count them?

TRANH: No, I didn't need to count. There are 3 sticks—that makes 30. There are also some other beans, so I know there are more than 30.

MRS. GOLDEN: Are there more than 40?

SANDRA: No. You have 30, but there are not 10 more beans to make 40, so I know there are not more than 40.

MRS. GOLDEN: Good. Now let's count them together.

Mrs. Golden points to appropriate pieces as the children count.

MRS. GOLDEN: Now, let's start with the beans instead of the sticks and count them a different way.

Mrs. Golden again points to appropriate pieces as the children count.

MRS. GOLDEN: Does it matter how you count the beans?

DERREK: No, you get the same answer. But it's easier for me to start with the sticks first.

MRS. GOLDEN: That's fine, Derrek. We will learn to count in different ways, but you should use what is easiest for you. Now everyone try modeling the number with beans and then writing this number on our number mats.

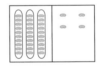

Tens	Ones
3	4

Before continuing, Mrs. Golden checks for any difficulties in modeling the number or writing the correct numerals. Writing the numerals on the place-value mat helps children naturally associate the symbol with the model, and understand the significance of place value in a concrete way.

MRS. GOLDEN: Here are some practice numbers for you to pair and share:

    25   52   forty-one   89

I want you to take turns and show each of them on your mat to your partner one at a time. Be sure to model the number with your beans and sticks first and then write the number on your mat. When you finish, ask your partner to check the number before you clear the mat. Then your partner does the next one and you check it.

Introduction

"Children must understand numbers if they are to make sense of the ways numbers are used in their everyday world . . . and an understanding of place value is crucial" (*Curriculum and Evaluation Standards for School Mathematics,* NCTM 1989, p. 38). Place value is a cornerstone of our numeration system, but this system is multicultural; it is "ours" only to the extent that it is a part of our cultural heritage. History tells us that "our numeration system" is really the result of continuous development and refinement over many centuries.

Called the Hindu-Arabic system, the number system we use was probably invented in India by the Hindus and transmitted to Europe by the Arabs, but many different countries and cultures contributed to its development.

● Our Numeration System

Our numeration system has four very important characteristics:

1. *Place value:* The position of a digit represents its value; for example, the 2 in $23 names "twenty" and has a different mathematical meaning from the 2 in $32, which names "two."
2. *Base of ten:* The term *base* simply means a collection. Thus, in our system, 10 is the value that determines a new collection, and the system has ten digits, 0 through 9.
3. *Use of zero:* A symbol for zero exists and allows us to represent symbolically the absence of something; for example, 309 shows the absence of tens in a number containing hundreds and ones.
4. *Additive property:* Numbers can be summed with respect to place value; for example, 123 names the number that is the sum of 100 + 20 + 3.

These properties make the system efficient and contribute to the development of number sense. That is, once these characteristics are understood, the formation and interpretation of numbers—either large or small—is a natural development.

Thinking Place Value

Place value is an essential feature of our number system. In fact, place value, together with base ten, allows us to manipulate, read, and symbolize both large and small numbers. The power of place value

can and should be developed early. For example, each of the piles shown has the same number of buttons. Decide how many buttons are in each pile.

Which pile would you use to decide how many? Explaining which pile and telling why that pile was chosen leads to a discussion of how grouping by tens facilitates counting and organizing larger quantities.

The ten-frame (Appendix B) provides a convenient model for counting, grouping, and eventually representing two-digit numbers. It is a natural model for place value and often provides valuable mental imagery for children in naming and distinguishing between two numbers. For example, Mrs. Golden asked the children to illustrate 25 and 52:

This exercise alerts students to the physical differences between these values, which are formed with the same digits but are different because of place value.

Grouping or Trading

Children in the first three grades need experience in counting piles of objects; trading for grouped tens, hundreds, and thousands; and talking about the results. The fourth national mathematics assessment reported that third-grade students had not mastered grouping and place value (Kouba et al. 1989). The Snapshot Lesson at the beginning of this chapter demonstrated how students might count and model different numbers. The bean sticks and ten-frame thus provide two early models for counting and grouping. As children work with these models, they need piles of materials (beans, buttons, cubes, or other counters) to practice counting and grouping. Activity Card 7–1 provides some early guided practice in grouping by tens. It helps establish connections between trading by tens and place value.

Trading and grouping by tens help develop number sense and provide opportunities for problem solving. Activity Card 7–2 illustrates another grouping experience that facilitates counting and trading. Although it may be easy to decide which group has more or less when the values differ greatly (as between B and the others), it may be very difficult when the values differ only slightly (as between A and C). This activity shows how grouping by tens facilitates visual comparisons. It also provides valuable experiences in counting, trading, and place value.

Asking children to group by tens as they count the larger piles serves several valuable purposes. First, if a child loses count, correction is often easier if these smaller groups have been formed. It is also easier to check for errors by inspecting groups of 10 than to recount the entire pile. However, the most important purpose of this practice is that it shows children how an unknown quantity can be organized into a form that can be interpreted by inspection. This process of grouping by tens is the framework for place value.

Nature of Place Value

A thorough understanding of place value is necessary if computational algorithms for addition, subtraction, multiplication, and division are to be learned and used in a meaningful way. Development of place value promotes number sense, which facilitates estimation and sharpens a sense of reasonableness about computational results. Place value rests on two key ideas.

1. Explicit grouping or trading rules are defined and consistently followed. These ideas are implicit in the bulletin board display shown in Figure 7–1. Such a display provides a constant reminder of the importance of grouping by tens to place value. Our base-ten system is characterized by trading 10 ones for 1 ten (or 1 ten for 10 ones), 10 tens for 1 hundred, 10 hundreds for 1 thousand, and so on. The two-way direction of these trades (for example, 10 tens for 1 hundred or 1 hundred for 10 tens) should be stressed because there are times when each type of trade must be used. It also should be noted that sim-

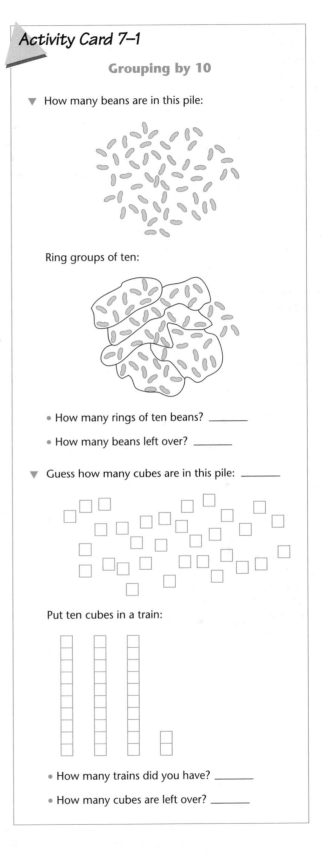

Activity Card 7–1

Grouping by 10

▼ How many beans are in this pile:

Ring groups of ten:

- How many rings of ten beans? _____
- How many beans left over? _____

▼ Guess how many cubes are in this pile: _____

Put ten cubes in a train:

- How many trains did you have? _____
- How many cubes are left over? _____

Activity Card 7–2

Trading for 10

▼ Look at these three groups of beans:

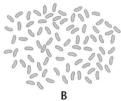

A   B   C

• Which group has the most?

Could you decide without counting?

Do you know exactly how many are in that group without counting? Tell why.

• Which group has the least?

Could you decide without counting?

Do you know exactly how many are in that group without counting? Tell why.

▼ Some of the beans have been traded and are now arranged in tens and ones:

• Does trading help you decide which group has the most? Tell why.

• Does trading help you know exactly how many are in that group without counting? Tell why.

▼ On your own:

Show a group of 34 beans in box D.

Trade for 10 and show the 34 beans arranged by tens and ones in box E.

Which is the easiest to count?

Show 84 beans the easiest way you can.

What is the quickest way to count 84 beans?

D   E

---

ilar trades are followed with numbers less than one—decimals. Thus, 1 can be traded for 10 tenths (or 10 tenths for 1), 10 hundredths for 1 tenth (or 1 tenth for 10 hundredths), and so on.

2. The position of a digit determines the number being represented. For example, the 2 in 3042 and the 2 in 2403 represent completely different quantities: 2 ones in 3042 and 2 thousands in 2403. Furthermore, the zero plays a similar yet different role in each of these numbers. It has positional value in each case, but it reports the lack of a quantity for that place. Although the notion of zero will continue to be expanded and developed throughout elementary school mathematics, children should experience the role of zero in place value early and often.

In our number system, place value means that any number can be represented using only 10 digits (0–9). Think about the problems of representing numbers without place value! Each number would require a separate and unique symbol. Our memory storage would quickly be exceeded, and we would probably have to use only the few numbers with symbols we could remember. Nevertheless, place value is difficult for some children to grasp. Oral counting or rote recitation of numbers by young children is often interpreted as understanding of place value. Yet many children who can count correctly have absolutely no concept of place value. In most cases, the confusion or misunderstanding can be traced to a lack of counting and trading experiences with appropriate materials and the subsequent

Figure 7–1 • **A bulletin board display for place value**

recording of these results. Early and frequent hands-on counting activities, similar to those described in Chapter 6, are essential in establishing this concept.

Place-value concepts are encountered before starting school. For example, many children distinguish between the one- and two-digit numbers on a channel indicator of a television, a timer for a microwave oven, and house or apartment numbers. Children learn early that apartments 201 and 102 are different.

Modeling

Hands-on experience with manipulatives is essential in establishing and developing the concept of place value. Research suggests that instruction should focus on concrete models that are connected to oral descriptions and symbolic representations of the models (Thompson 1990; Wearne and Hiebert 1994). Bean sticks and the ten-frame provide two effective models for developing place value.

Figure 7–2 illustrates some additional physical models that are effective in helping students understand not only place value but larger numbers as well. All of the models shown in Figure 7–2 represent the same three-digit number, 123. The value of using different embodiments is that a child will be less likely to associate place value with a particular model. In fact, a key instructional goal is to develop concepts to a level that does not depend on any one physical model, instead providing for abstraction of the commonalty among all models.

Models may be either proportional or nonproportional, but all are based on groups of 10. In proportional models for base ten, such as popsicle sticks, the material for 10 is ten times the size of the material for 1; 100 is ten times the size of 10, and so on. Measurement provides another proportional model. For example, a meter stick, decimeter rods, and centimeter cubes can be used to model any three-digit number.

Nonproportional models, such as money, do not maintain any size relationships. Ten pennies are bigger than a dime, but are fair trade in our monetary system. Ten dimes are the same as a dollar, but they are not proportional. These ideas introduce children to a level of abstraction based entirely on trading rules. Young students often focus on proportionality, which is why they are often willing to trade a dime for one or two pennies, or why they prefer to have a few dimes rather than a dollar bill.

Although both types of embodiments are important and should be represented, proportional models are more concrete; and we recommend that children use and clearly understand them before moving on to nonproportional models.

Of the nonproportional models shown in Figure 7–2, the abacus and the counters are very similar. In each model, different colored beads or counters provide the basis for trading. For example, 10 white beads (or counters) might be traded for 1 black, 10 black for 1 blue, and so on. Use of a trading mat can help keep the counters in order. The beads on an abacus are arranged in a fixed order. The color dis-

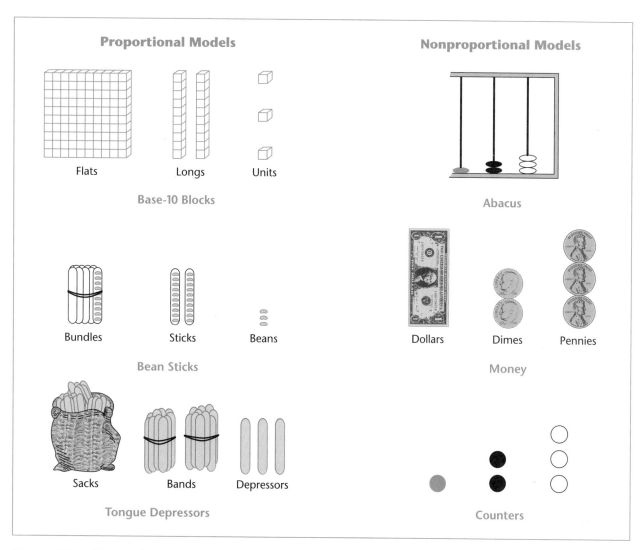

Figure 7–2 • **Place-value models**

tinction is important for the early establishment of proper trades, but it should be dropped as soon as possible so that attention will shift from color of the beads or counters to their position. It is only the position of the bead counter that has long-range significance.

• Developing Place Value

A Place to Start

In developing place value and establishing number names, it is far better to skip beyond the teens and start with the larger numbers. The names for the numbers 11 through 19 are not consistent with the names for other numbers, even though the symbolization or visual pattern is wholly consistent. The

numbers 11 through 19 do not exhibit the place-value characteristic in their names that other numbers do. To do so, they would have to be renamed onety-one (1 ten and 1 one), onety-two, . . . , onety-nine, which would make them consistent with larger numbers, such as forty-one, forty-two, . . . , forty-nine. In many other countries, such as Japan, the naming pattern for the numbers 11 through 19 is consistent with the naming of larger numbers. This feature reinforces place value early and helps Japanese children name the teen numbers (Yoshikawa 1994).

What does a number such as 25 mean? It is important that children have the capability of thinking of numbers in various ways. With such number sense, 25 might be thought of several different ways. When multiplying, a square array of 5 × 5 may come to mind. When thinking of money, several combinations of coins, such as 25 pennies, 2 dimes and 5 pennies, 5 nickels, and 1 quarter may be envisioned. With certain items, such as eggs, 1 more than 2 dozen and 4 six-packs plus 1 are two different representations of the quantity 25. With metric measures, 25 centimeters might be thought of as 2 decimeters and 5 centimeters. However, it could also be thought of as 0.25 or ¼ meter. Children with good number sense know when a particular form is useful.

Of course, if place value is to be called upon, the tens and ones model is needed. It might use money (2 dimes and 5 pennies) or another model, such as bean sticks. With the bean sticks, 25 could be represented several different ways:

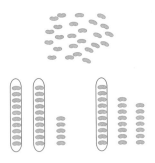

Which way is better? It depends on what is to be done with the 25 beans because there are times when each form may be useful. The grouping at the top, for example, would be easier to divide among several people. Either of the groupings on the bottom would be easier to count.

The notion of representing a quantity with the least number of pieces for a particular model is critical in place value. Establishing its importance at an early stage will eliminate some later errors such as:

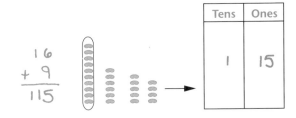

Because 10 or more of something (namely, ones) exist on the place-value mat, a trade must be made. Making the ten-for-one trade results in the least number of pieces and thus 25 becomes the only representation that is meaningful:

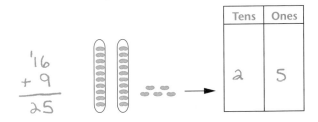

Figure 7–3 highlights the advancement from a concrete model to symbolic representation. The bridges from the physical models to the symbolic representation must be crossed back and forth many times if meaningful learning is to occur.

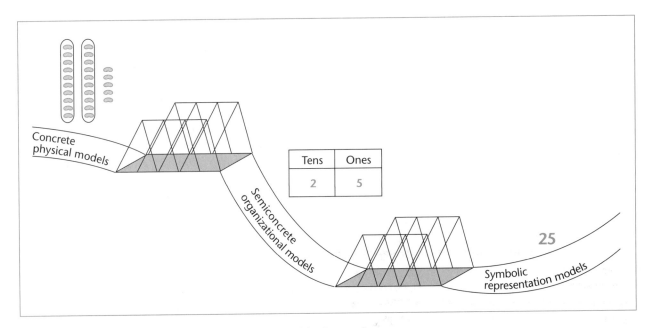

Figure 7–3 ● **From the concrete to the symbolic with place value**

Careful attention must be given to linking modeling with the language. As children become fluent in talking about their models, it will become natural to them to describe 25 in different ways.

Many children reverse the digits of numbers. Although this error is generally caused by carelessness, it may be symptomatic of a disability known as *dyslexia*. In either case, it is very important that children understand the consequences of such reversals. That's why Mrs. Golden included the first two practice numbers at the end of the Snapshot Lesson at the beginning of this chapter.

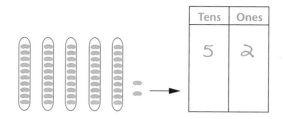

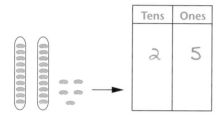

How many tens? [2]

How many ones? [5]

Name this number. [25]

Although the same digits are used, the resulting numbers—25 and 52—are very different. Children should compare the modeled numbers and talk about them in an effort to better appreciate the magnitude of the differences.

The base-10 blocks, together with the place-value mat, as shown in Figure 7–4, can be used to model the additive property and illustrate expanded notation. A variety of strips, such as those in Figure 7–4, which connect the base-10 blocks to number symbols in an expanded form, can be used effectively to review key ideas.

A hundred chart (Appendix B) also can be used to develop place-value concepts. Activity Cards 7–3 and 7–4 highlight different activities designed to develop a greater awareness and understanding of place value and to improve mental computation.

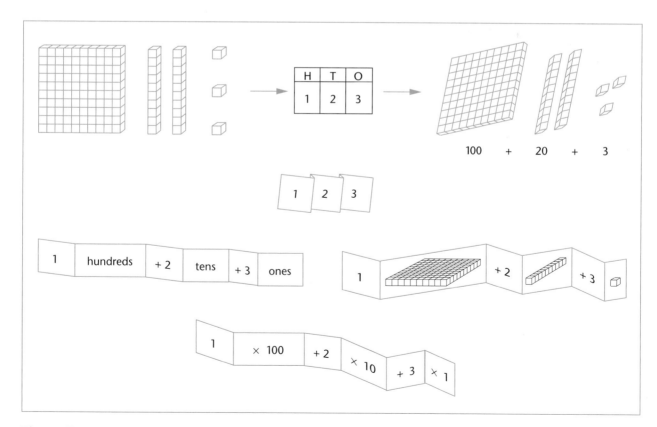

Figure 7–4 • **Connecting models and symbols that reinforce place value**

Activity Card 7–3

Exploring the Hundred Chart

▼ Look at this chart:

1	2	3	4	5	6	7	8	9	10
11	12	13	14	15	16	17	18	19	20
21	22	23	24	25	26	27	28	29	30
31	32	33	34	35	36	37	38	39	40
41	42	43	44	45	46	47	48	49	50
51	52	53	54	55	56	57	58	59	60
61	62	63	64	65	66	67	68	69	70
71	72	73	74	75	76	77	78	79	80
81	82	83	84	85	86	87	88	89	90
91	92	93	94	95	96	97	98	99	100

↑ Fifth column

- Tell why you think it is called a hundred chart.
- Describe a pattern you see in the chart.
- Tell something that is alike for all the numbers in the fifth column.
- How are numbers in the fourth and sixth columns alike? Different?

▼ Try this:

- Cut out a piece like .

- Take and lay it on the chart:

1	2	3	4	5	6	7	8	9	10
11	12	13	14	15	16	17	18	19	20
21	22	23	24	25	26	27	28	29	30
31	32	33	34	35		37	38	39	40
41	42	43	44	45		47	48	49	50
51	52	53	54			57	58	59	60
61	62	63	64	65	66	67	68	69	70
71	72	73	74	75	76	77	78	79	80
81	82	83	84	85	86	87	88	89	90
91	92	93	94	95	96	97	98	99	100

- Ask a friend to find the numbers covered without peeking under the piece.
- Do it again with different shapes, like and .

Activity Card 7–4

Find That Number!

▼ Use this hundred chart:

1	2	3	4	5	6	7	8	9	10
11	12	13	14	15	16	17	18	19	20
21	22	23	24	25	26	27	28	29	30
31	32	33	34	35	36	37	38	39	40
41	42	43	44	45	46	47	48	49	50
51	52	53	54	55	56	57	58	59	60
61	62	63	64	65	66	67	68	69	70
71	72	73	74	75	76	77	78	79	80
81	82	83	84	85	86	87	88	89	90
91	92	93	94	95	96	97	98	99	100

- Pick a number and count 10 more.

  Where did you stop? ____

- Pick a number and count 20 more.

  Where did you stop? ____

- Pick a number and count 50 more.

  Predict where you would stop. ____

- Tell how you can use the hundred chart to mentally add 30 to a number.

▼ Here is only a part of a hundred chart:

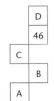

- Use what you know about a hundred chart to find the values:

  A ____ B ____ C ____ D ____

- Tell how you found C.
- Could you find C in more than one way? Explain your answer.

Lesson Card 7–1 highlights an activity that extends the modeling to three-digit numbers and provides some opportunities to order numbers according to place value. Modeling three-digit numbers establishes the importance of position for each digit more clearly. It provides an early reward for

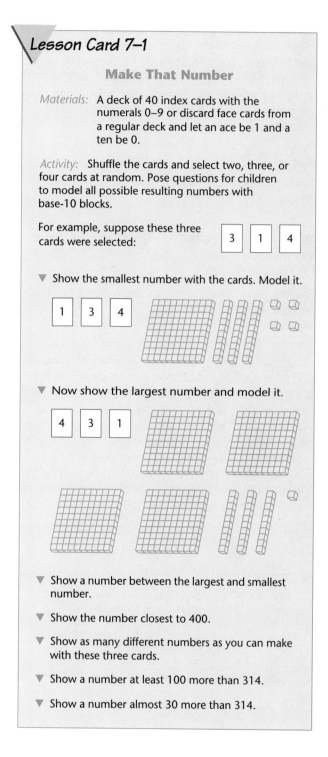

looking at the "front-end" (lead) digits of a number. For example, when students are asked to show the number closest to 400 in Lesson Card 7–1, they can concentrate on the values with 4 hundreds. Further, when asked to show a number at least 100 more than 314, students can focus on hundreds and ig-

nore the other digits. This ability to focus on certain digits in numbers is an important part of number sense.

Activity Card 7–5 reinforces place value and also provides practice in important mental computational skills. Scores are found by counting the darts in each circle, which provides practice counting by ones, tens, and hundreds, and then computing the totals.

A calculator provides many opportunities to practice and develop important place-value concepts. Wipe Out is a place-value game that involves either addition or subtraction using a calculator. The goal is to change (wipe out) a predetermined digit by subtracting or adding a number. This activity can be made into a competitive game for two people. The players take turns entering a number and naming a specific digit the other player must change to 0.

For example, Kelly enters 431, naming the 3 to be wiped out:

Tanya wipes out the 3 by subtracting 30, which also leaves the other digits unchanged:

A player scores a point for changing the digit to 0 on the first try. A record of the game in table form reinforces the process of identifying the correct place value:

WIPE OUT RECORD   Name: Tanya

Entered	Wiped Out	Keys Pressed	Display	Score
431	3	-30	401	1
24	4	+6	30	1
849	8	-800	49	1
206	2	-200	6	1

A variation of Wipe Out that has been developed focuses more attention on the place value of the digits (Hopkins 1992). In this variation, which can be played with or without a calculator, the teacher chooses a multidigit number with no two digits the same, such as 5849. The teacher identifies a digit (for example, the 5 in 5849) to be "wiped out," and students must try to change only that digit to 0 by using one operation. Students are called upon until the correct answer is given, and points are awarded according to their responses.

Response	Scoring
Student names operation and number: "Subtract five."	Teacher scores 2 points.
Student names operation and number: "Subtract five, zero, zero, zero")	Teacher scores 1 point.
Student names operation and number: "Subtract five thousand."	Class scores 2 points.

Although Wipe Out or a variation of it can be played without a calculator, it is much more exciting with one. Children don't get bogged down with computation. The focus remains on place value. Furthermore, they are often surprised by what happens when they make a place-value error, which increases their place-value understanding.

The challenge of the "wipe-out" type of activities is illustrated by a question included on a recent national assessment shown in Figure 7–5. The figure

---

Question: Laura wanted to enter the number 8375 into her calculator. By mistake, she entered the number 8275. Without clearing the calculator, how could she correct her mistake?

Satisfactory Responses:

1. 8275 + 100 = 8375

2. She could add 100 more.

3. If she subtracted 100 she could add 200.

Figure 7–5 • **An example from a national assessment test that reinforces the connection between "wipe-out" type calculator game and mental computation skills**

shows this open-ended question along with examples of satisfactory responses. Although calculators were available, the decision as to whether or not to use a calculator was made by each student. However, more than 60 percent of the fourth graders made no response or provided an incorrect response. This performance level indicates the value of the "wipe-out" type of activities and reminds us that connections need to be established between such activities and mental computations.

Research reports that many children lack an understanding of the relative sizes of numbers greater than 100 (Payne and Huinker 1993). This results from many factors, one of which may be the lack of opportunities to model which help children develop a visual awareness of the relative size of numbers. Large numbers can be modeled using variations of the models shown in Figure 7–2. For the base-10 blocks, lay another place-value mat to the left of the mat holding hundreds, tens, and

ones. This thousands mat holds thousands, ten-thousands, and hundred-thousands. Figure 7–6 provides another demonstration of how two numbers can have the same digits but be very different. How are 2130 and 1032 alike and different? As children engage in discussion to answer this question, their knowledge of place value and their sense of numbers will grow. Using the same digits to represent different numbers helps children appreciate the importance of representing the place values accurately. Although the numbers 2130 and 1032 use the same digits, the models that represent these numbers are dramatically different (see Appendix B). This type of experience helps develop number sense and alerts children to the importance of the front-end, or lead, digits, which in this case denote thousands.

As the number of digits increases, children should be encouraged to focus on the front-end digits. The front-end digits are used when comparing

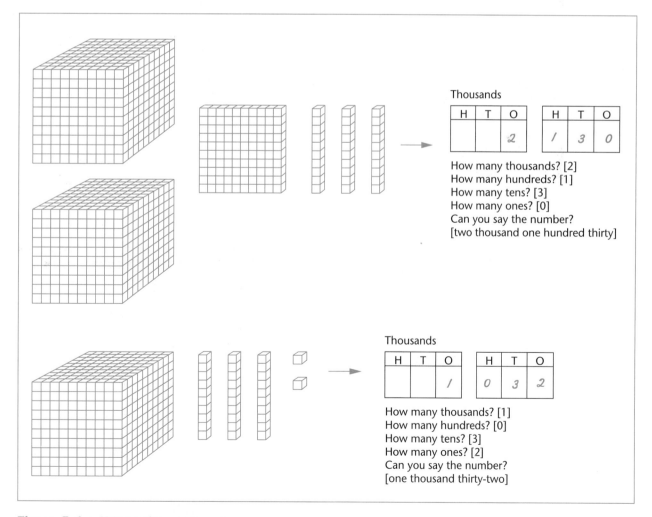

Figure 7–6 • Using a thousands mat

and ordering numbers, as well as when computing mentally and estimating:

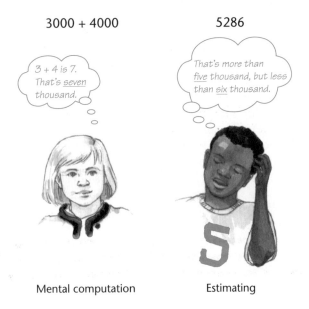

3000 + 4000

3 + 4 is 7. That's seven thousand.

Mental computation

5286

That's more than five thousand, but less than six thousand.

Estimating

The front-end approach can be naturally extended and applied to larger numbers. Activity Card 7–6 provides a slightly different approach to establishing the front-end of a number. The last task asks students to construct two five-digit numbers that have the same three front-end digits. This task helps students compare and order larger numbers.

Try this problem:

Norway has an area of 125,181 square miles.

New Mexico has an area of 121,400 square miles.

Greece has an area of 50,944 square miles.

Why is it easy to tell which has the least area?

Can you tell which is the greatest area by comparing the first front-end digit? The first two front-end digits? The first three front-end digits?

Which has the greatest area?

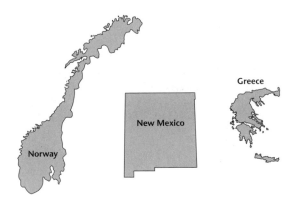

Greece

New Mexico

Norway

Activity Card 7–6

Create a Creature

Here is a three-digit number creature.

4 3 1

A 4 is on the front end.

▼ Make a three-digit number creature with a 5 on the front end.

(A) ⬜⬜⬜

Make a three-digit number creature with a different number on the front end.

(B) ⬜⬜⬜

• Which is greater? _____

▼ Make a six-digit number creature with any number on the front end.

(C) ⬜⬜⬜⬜⬜⬜

Make a different six-digit number creature with the same front-end digit.

(D) ⬜⬜⬜⬜⬜⬜

• Which is greater? _____

▼ Make 2 five-digit number creatures where the first 3 front-end digits are the same.

(E) ⬜⬜⬜⬜⬜
(F) ⬜⬜⬜⬜⬜

• Which is greater? _____

This problem reminds students of the importance of place value when comparing numbers. For example, the front-end approach is used only when the numbers have the same number of digits. It is not needed to compare 125,181 square miles with 50,944 square miles, because the numbers of digits are different.

Counting and Patterns

As noted in Chapter 6, calculators are useful in counting and pattern recognition. Seeing each value displayed on the calculator helps students develop important insight into what digits are changing and when. For example, as Figure 7–7 shows, when counting on the calculator by ones, children observe that the digit on the right (ones place) changes every time they "count," while the next digit (tens place) changes less frequently, and it takes much counting to change the third digit (hundreds place).

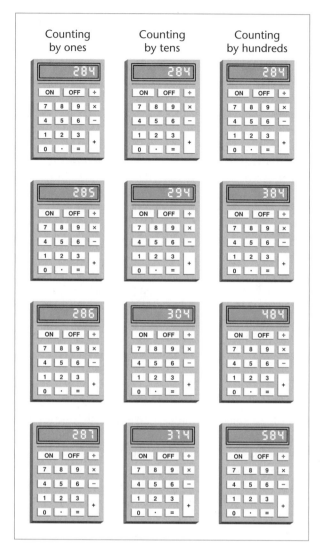

Figure 7–7 • **Calculator counting to illustrate place-value patterns**

Calculator counting provides many opportunities to discuss patterns related to place value. Such counting can also contribute to a better grasp of large numbers, thereby helping to develop students' number sense. For example, in Chapter 6, Activity Card 6–5 asked pupils to record how long it took to count from 1 to 1,000 by ones. Students might also be asked to find how long it takes to count from 1 to 1,000,000 by thousands.

Many pupils are surprised to learn that it takes about the same time. One fourth grader said, "That means there are as many thousands in one million as ones in one thousand." This is a profound observation—of the type that leads to a better understanding of both place value and large numbers, and also reflects a growing sense of numbers.

As Figure 7–7 shows, counting on by tens or by hundreds never changes the ones place. However, when counting by tens, the tens place changes on each count and the next digit (hundreds) changes every ten counts. Observing these patterns in counting larger and larger numbers helps students recognize place-value properties. Activity Card 7–7 utilizes calculators and patterns to help students add multiples of 100. Similar exercises should be provided with other powers of ten.

Computers are also powerful counters. Activity Card 7–8 shows how a short program can be used for computer counting and mathematics learning. Many place-value patterns are observed as the computer counts. For example, as you look from right to left, the digits are easier to read as the numbers scroll by on the computer screen. These screen shots of

consecutive numbers show several place-value changes.

12388	12395
12389	12396
12390	12397
12391	12398
12392	12399
12393	12400
12394	12401

Activity Card 7–8

Can Your Computer Count?

Type this BASIC program in your computer.

```
10 FOR N=0 TO 50 STEP 10
20 PRINT N
30 NEXT N
```

When you RUN this program, you get

```
0
10
20
30
40
50
```

Eureka! I made it count!

1. How long does the computer take to "count" to 50 by 10?

2. What change would you make in the program to count to 500 by 100? Try it and see how long the computer takes.

3. How long does the computer take to count to 1000 by 1? by 10?

4. How long does the computer take to count to 1,000,000 by 1? First estimate your answer and then try it to find out.

5. How long does the computer take to count to 1,000,000 by 10? Estimate the answer before you try it.

6. How long does the computer take to count to 1,000,000 by 100? by 1000? Estimate your answer first.

7. How do your answers to questions 3 and 6 compare?

In Activity Card 7–8, modification of the program to answer questions two through six stimulates thinking and logical reasoning, and students also are called upon to use their estimation skills. The activity in this card demonstrates another of the ways in which technology can be used to help students develop number sense.

The hundred chart provides another useful model for counting and pattern recognition related to place value. Activities involving counting with multiples of 10, as in Activity Cards 7–9 and 7–10, further develop students' number sense and provide practice in important mental computation skills. (See Appendix B for copies of several master charts.)

For example, 43 + 30 can be determined by counting mentally 43, 53, 63, 73 and is a natural by-product of counting by tens on the hundred chart in Activity Card 7–9. Further, 43 + 29 can be found by counting 43, 53, 63, 73 and then dropping back one to 72. Counting by tens and then dropping back or bumping up illustrate how to adjust numbers and be flexible when using and thinking about numbers.

Regrouping and Renaming

Counting suggests many patterns, but one of the most important for young children is observing what happens when the number after 9 (or 19, 29, etc.) is modeled. Trading occurs in every case. The pattern involved in bridging from one decade to another should be recognized and clearly understood by children.

Regrouping and place value are intertwined in later development of computation. Regrouping happens whenever bridging occurs, as from 1 ten to another (such as 29 to 30) or from 1 hundred to another (such as 799 to 800). Regrouping also happens when 6 tens 7 ones are considered as 5 tens 17 ones, or 245 is thought of as 24 tens 5 ones, or 40 pennies are traded for 4 dimes. The importance of clearly understanding the regrouping process cannot be overstressed. Understanding is most likely to develop when children experience this bridging with physical models and practice trading and regrouping.

Whenever trading occurs, there are accompanying changes in how the number is recorded. An understanding of this symbolization requires many experiences with problems involving trading and the related recording process. Figure 7–8 shows how regrouping affects digits and place value.

Figure 7–9 further illustrates the regrouping process with two different models. Similar models with larger numbers should be used as soon as children have grasped the trading principles involving

Activity Card 7–9

The Power of 10 on the Hundred Chart

1	2	3	4	5	6	7	8	9	10
11	12	13	14	15	16	17	18	19	20
21	22	23	24	25	26	27	28	29	30
31	32	33	34	35	36	37	38	39	40
41	42	43	44	45	46	47	48	49	50
51	52	53	54	55	56	57	58	59	60
61	62	63	64	65	66	67	68	69	70
71	72	73	74	75	76	77	78	79	80
81	82	83	84	85	86	87	88	89	90
91	92	93	94	95	96	97	98	99	100

▼ Count by 10:

- Start on any square in the first three rows.
- Count forward 10 squares, and tell where you stopped.
- Start at a different square, and count forward 10 squares.
- After you have done this several times, tell about a pattern that you found.
- Describe a quick way to count "ten more" on this hundred chart.

▼ Count by 9:

- Start on any square in the first three rows.
- Count forward 9 squares. Tell where you stopped.
- After you have done this several times, tell about a pattern that you found.
- Describe a quick way to count "nine more" on this chart.

▼ Connect the patterns:

- Does knowing how to add by 10 help you add by 9?

Activity Card 7–10

The Power of 10 on the Thousand Chart

10	20	30	40	50	60	70	80	90	100
110	120	130	140	150	160	170	180	190	200
210	220	230	240	250	260	270	280	290	300
310	320	330	340	350	360	370	380	390	400
410	420	430	440	450	460	470	480	490	500
510	520	530	540	550	560	570	580	590	600
610	620	630	640	650	660	670	680	690	700
710	720	730	740	750	760	770	780	790	800
810	820	830	840	850	860	870	880	890	900
910	920	930	940	950	960	970	980	990	1000

▼ Count by 10:

- Start on any square in the first three rows.
- Count forward 10 squares, and tell where you stopped.
- Start at a different square, and count forward 10 squares.
- After you have done this several times, tell about a pattern that you found.
- Describe a quick way to count "a hundred more" on this thousand chart.

▼ Count by 100:

- Tell how you could use the thousand chart to add 300 to 240.
- Tell how you could use the thousand chart to add 290 to 240.

▼ Connect the charts:

- Tell how using the hundred chart helps you use the thousand chart.

ones, tens, and hundreds. In fact, it is this extension process that demonstrates the power of mathematical abstraction. Extending to thousands should be done with proportional models to illustrate the dramatic size increase that continues to occur as new places are used. Children will soon recognize that it becomes very cumbersome to model large numbers with proportional models (see Powers of Ten in Appendix B).

The calculator can be used with very large numbers. Computers also provide many opportunities to develop larger numbers, such as the counting

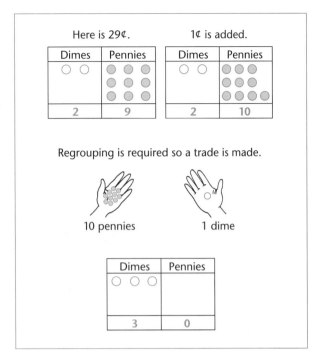

Figure 7–8 • **Nonproportional model illustrating relation between regrouping and place value**

program in Activity Card 7–8. Minor variations of this program (such as finding how long the computer takes to count to one million or one billion) can help students develop a better grasp of large numbers.

● Reading and Writing Numbers

Reading and writing numbers are symbolic activities and should follow much modeling and talking about numbers. That's why the NCTM *Standards* (1989) recommend that less attention be given to "reading, writing and ordering numbers symbolically." The key word is *symbolically*. This recommendation alerts us to the danger of a premature focus on symbols. A sustained development of number sense should precede the reading and writing of numbers. This approach ensures that the symbols the students are writing and reading are meaningful to them.

Now let's consider some ways in which understanding place value helps develop the reading and writing of numbers. Let us again take the example of the number 123. We can identify the places (hundreds, tens, ones) as well as the value of each (1, 2, 3). We know that the 1 means one hundred. We also

know that 23 is both 2 tens 3 ones and 23 ones, and that 123 is 1 hundred 2 tens 3 ones; 12 tens 3 ones; and 123 ones.

These representations may be shown on the place-value mat:

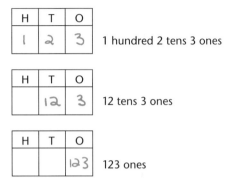

The skill of reading numbers in different ways (and the understanding of the grouping that allows this to be done) can be useful in many operations with whole numbers. For example, re-reading provides a nice stepping stone to mental computation; more specifically, it leads to multiplying a number by 10:

Although it seems logical to write number words as they sound, this procedure can lead to difficulty. If this were done, sixty-one would be incorrectly written as 601 and one hundred twenty-three as 100203. The exercise in the Snapshot Lesson where children were asked to show forty-one was aimed at detecting this error. If a child made this mistake, the teacher could use the place-value mat as a model to demonstrate:

Modeling several numbers on the mat will help clarify this notion.

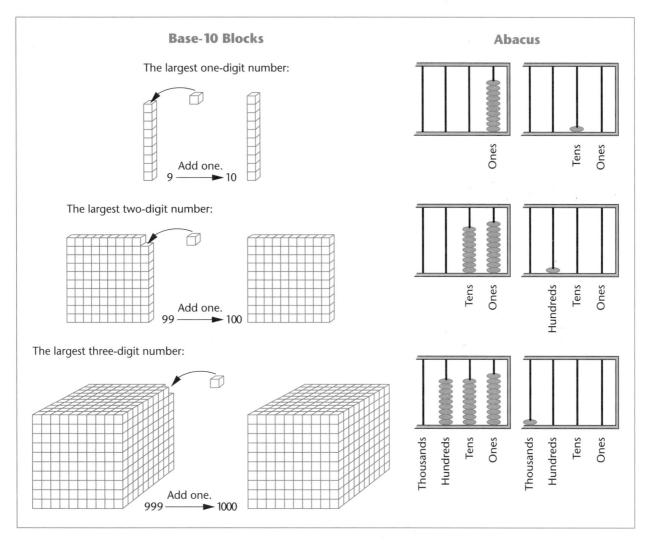

Figure 7–9 • **Proportional and nonproportional models illustrating some relationships between regrouping and place value**

Similar problems exist in naming and representing larger numbers. Consider the following questions from a national assessment:

The census showed that three hundred fifty-six thousand, ninety-seven people lived in Middletown. Written as a number, the population is

350,697
356,097
356,907
356,970

What number is four hundred five and three tenths?

45.3
405.3
453
4005.3

About 70 percent of fourth graders and 90 percent of eighth graders correctly connected the place-value language and symbolic representation. Yet research shows that number sense development lags behind language (McIntosh et al. 1992). Children need to make sense of large numbers in order to read and write them. The calculator counting (Activity Card 6–7) and computer counting (Activity Card 7–8) activities are useful. Open-ended questions such as those shown in Activity Card 7–11 encourage children to guess and make estimates. As they share their answers and talk about different ways of understanding millions and billions, their number sense grows. Reading books listed in the Children's Corner, such as *If You Made a Million* (Schwartz 1989) and *In One Day* (Parker 1984), gives children additional insight and appreciation of larger numbers.

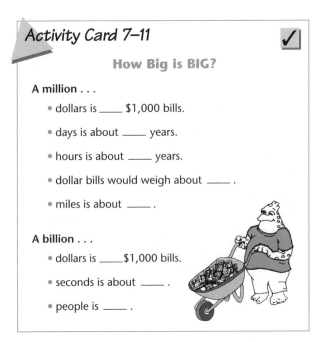

Activity Card 7–11 ✓

How Big is BIG?

A million . . .

• dollars is _____ $1,000 bills.

• days is about _____ years.

• hours is about _____ years.

• dollar bills would weigh about _____ .

• miles is about _____ .

A billion . . .

• dollars is _____ $1,000 bills.

• seconds is about _____ .

• people is _____ .

It Is helpful for students to link some of the models to larger numbers. For example, the students might begin with a one cubic centimeter block. If they then make a cubic meter box, that box will hold one million cubic centimeter cubes, as illustrated in Figure 7–10.

Base-10 blocks also can be used to help students make the connection between the concrete model

Figure 7–10 • Children constructing a cubic meter box (Photo by Gene Sutphen.)

and the symbolic representation, as in Figure 7–11. This model helps mentally "see" that 10 thousand is a long piece made up of 10 cubes, where each cube is 1 thousand. Although this model can be constructed with physical models, children quickly appreciate the power of constructing mental images to represent larger numbers.

When students begin to develop an intuitive grasp of larger numbers and begin to use millions and billions intelligently, they are ready to write and read these larger numbers. Place-value mats can be naturally expanded to represent larger numbers:

Billions			Millions			Thousands			Ones		
H	T	O	H	T	O	H	T	O	H	T	O

In order to develop facility in reading large numbers, children need careful instruction and practice in actually naming them aloud. For example, would you read 12,345,678 as "one ten-million two million three hundred-thousand four ten-thousand" and so on? Certainly not! You would use the period names and read it as "twelve million, three hundred forty-five thousand, six hundred seventy-eight." This example is a clear application of an organizing strategy: the digits within each period are read as hundreds, tens, and ones, as with "three hundred forty-five thousand." For this reason, children need to think of larger numbers (those of more than three digits) in blocks of three digits.

Recognition and understanding of the hundreds, tens, and ones pattern provide a powerful organizational strategy that can be called upon in naming numbers. Only the key terms—ones, tens, and hundreds—along with the recognition of the periods for thousands, millions, and billions are needed to name very large numbers.

Did you know that in many countries commas are not used to separate blocks of three digits? Instead, for example, the number 2,346,457 is written as 2 346 457. The blocks of digits remain visible but are separated by spaces rather than commas. Some newspapers, journals, and textbooks in the United States now print numbers this way. This change has instructional implications for both reading and writing numbers. In particular, children must become even more sensitive to the importance of writing numbers clearly and distinctly.

Speaking of reading and writing, newspapers provide a rich context to explore numbers of all

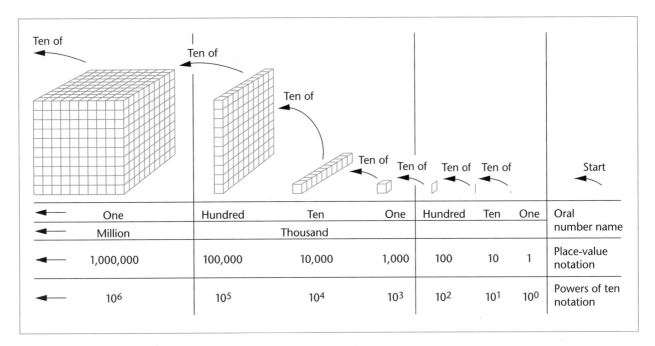

Figure 7–11 • **Connecting the symbolic representation of one million with a concrete model** (Adapted from Labinowicz 1989.)

	One	Hundred	Ten	One	Hundred	Ten	One	Oral number name
	Million	Thousand						
	1,000,000	100,000	10,000	1,000	100	10	1	Place-value notation
	10^6	10^5	10^4	10^3	10^2	10^1	10^0	Powers of ten notation

sizes. Examine a newspaper and highlight all of the numbers reported in headlines and related stories. We were surprised at the high frequency in which numbers occurred. It reminds us of the importance of developing notions of place value and number sense. Activity Card 7–12 provides one way for students to become more sensitive to the frequent use of numbers in newspapers, and some related activities to engage students in writing about them.

Naming numbers is clearly an important skill. Yet with the widespread use of calculators, a more efficient way to read multidigit numbers is being used. For example, 32,764 is read as "three two seven six four" and 4.3425 as "four point three four two five." Each of these readings is correct and much easier to say than the respective periods. There is the danger that children will say the digits without any realization of the value of the numbers involved, but such interpretations are not necessary at every stage of the problem-solving process. If it is only desired to copy a number displayed on a calculator, then a direct translation of digits is without a doubt the best way to read the number. Rather than requiring children to read numbers in a specific way, it is far better to recognize the value of each technique and encourage children to choose wisely—namely, to select the technique that is most appropriate for a given situation.

Activity Card 7–12

Making More Sense of Numbers by Reading and Writing

Use a front page of a daily newspaper:

1. Find a headline or sentence that contains a number.

2. Is the number exact or an estimate? How can you tell?

3. Rewrite the headline or sentence without the number.

   • Does this change the meaning?

   • Do you like the headline with or without the number best? Tell why.

4. Does a newspaper article always have at least one number in it?

5. How many articles on your front page can you find that do not include a number?

● Estimation and Rounding

An important aspect of developing number sense is recognizing that some numbers are approximate (such as our national debt) and some are exact (such as the number of people killed in a fatal airplane crash). Approximate values are associated with estimation, often involving rounding, and are encountered regularly in our daily lives.

Estimation

Estimation provides a natural way to develop number sense and place-value concepts. Children love to estimate, and they enjoy many types of estimating situations that challenge their skills:

> About how many balloons could fill this room?
>
> About how many pennies tall are you?
>
> About how many dollar bills can you lift?

These types of questions stimulate thinking and invite involvement.

In this section, our focus is on estimating quantities. This experience provides an important foundation for number sense and place value, but practice situations must be well chosen. If the number of objects is small, it is natural to count and un-

necessary to estimate. However, when the number becomes large and tedious or too time-consuming to count, then estimates are useful.

Research has demonstrated that children use several different techniques for estimating, and there is a wide range of performance at each grade level. Providing opportunities for children to share strategies is an effective way to help children develop competence and confidence in estimating (Sowder 1992).

Figure 7–12 illustrates three different thinking processes students use in making an estimate. Students also should be encouraged to share their thinking strategies. Sharing may offer insight into not only the thinking processes used but also any misconceptions held by the students.

Experience in making comparisons of different quantities is important at every grade level. Activity Card 7–13 provides two types of estimation experiences, each of which fosters number sense. Part A provides an opportunity to make visual comparisons, and part B provides an opportunity to visualize the impact of place value resulting from 10, 20, and 100.

Benchmarks are a very important and useful tool in estimating (see Figure 6–2). If you know your own height, for example, that information can help you estimate someone else's height. You can decide if the other person is taller or shorter than you are,

Figure 7–12 • **Examples of children's thinking when making an estimate**

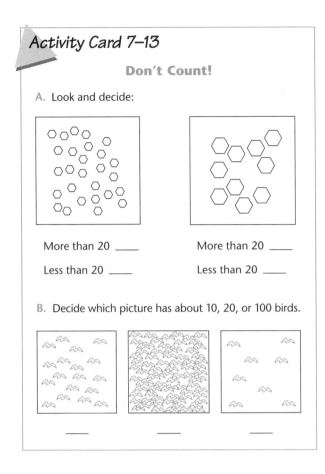

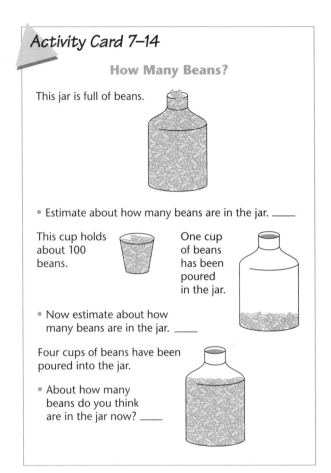

and this decision helps you make an estimate. In this case, you have used your height as a benchmark for comparison.

Good estimation skills require the development of number sense; thus, they evolve slowly over time. The foundation for estimation includes counting, models, and meaningful interpretations of real-life encounters with numbers of all sizes. For example, the bulletin board display shown in Figure 7–13 provides some benchmarks that can help children better grasp the relationships between small and large numbers when estimating length. Frequent practice with the lower portion of the display provides an enjoyable activity that helps develop both estimation skills and number sense.

The benchmark principle is used in many different ways. Activity Card 7–14 demonstrates how providing additional information (new benchmarks) can be helpful in producing closer estimates. It is important that students make initial estimates and then refine or adjust these in light of new information. For example, Activity Card 7–14 produces a "trail" of estimates, with each estimate reflecting

changes resulting from new benchmarks. This trail encourages students to continue to think about numbers and provides teachers with insight into their thinking.

Rounding

As students estimate, they become more comfortable with numbers that are not exact. Thus, early estimation of quantity and use of benchmarks provide some useful preparation for rounding numbers.

Rounding is an important skill that integrates understanding of approximate values with place value and naming numbers. Numbers are usually rounded to make them easier to use or because exact values are unknown. How numbers are rounded depends on the uses that will be made of the rounded numbers. For example, attendance at a major league baseball game may be 54,321. Although the attendance could be rounded to the nearest ten (54,320) or the nearest hundred (54,300), it is more likely to be reported as "about 54,000" or "over 50,000" or "less

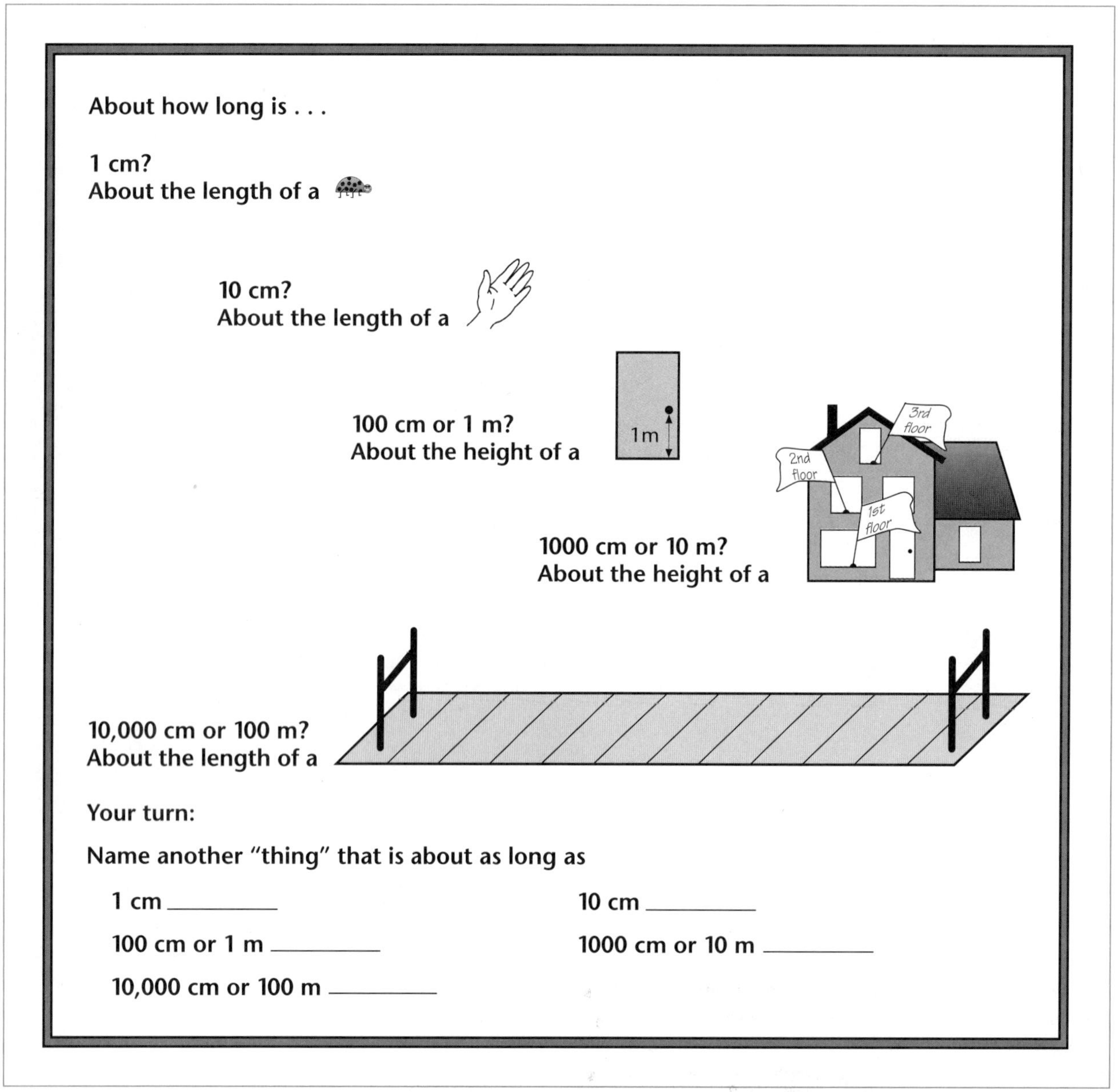

About how long is . . .

1 cm?
About the length of a

10 cm?
About the length of a

100 cm or 1 m?
About the height of a

1m

1000 cm or 10 m?
About the height of a

3rd floor

2nd floor

1st floor

10,000 cm or 100 m?
About the length of a

Your turn:

Name another "thing" that is about as long as

1 cm _____   10 cm _____

100 cm or 1 m _____   1000 cm or 10 m _____

10,000 cm or 100 m _____

Figure 7–13 ● **A bulletin board display to develop benchmarks of length**

than 60,000" because these values are convenient and a little easier to comprehend and remember.

As they develop rounding skills, children should come to realize that rounding "rules" may vary and are not universal. For example, here are two different rules from current textbooks for rounding a number ending in 5:

(a) Increase the previous digit by 1.
(b) If the digit preceding the 5 is even, leave the 5 alone; if it is odd, increase the 5 to the next even digit.

In either case, 75 would round to 80. However, 85 would round to 90 using rule (a) and 80 using rule (b). Neither rule is "right" or "best," but this variability across textbooks can confuse children. Checking to make sure students understand the specific rules of rounding that are to be used avoids some of the confusion.

Regardless of the rounding rule used, the precision of the rounded numbers reflects the problem context. For example, a meter stick could serve as a number line. Consider this train of Cuisenaire rods, with 7 decimeter rods and 4 centimeter rods:

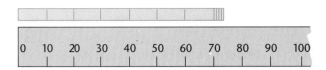

Is the train closer to 7 or 8 decimeters?

Is it closer to 0 or 1 meter?

If we round to the nearest decimeter, then the length is 7 decimeters. If we round to the nearest meter, the length is 1 meter. How numbers are rounded depends on how the values will be used. For example, if we were to cut a strip of cloth to cover this train, it would be foolish to round to the nearest decimeter and cut a length of 7 decimeters, but a meter of cloth would provide plenty of material to cover the train. Children must think about numbers before rounding them and not just indiscriminately apply rounding rules. That is why the NCTM *Standards* (1989) recommend that "rounding numbers out of context" be given decreased attention in school mathematics.

Even in a context, interpretation of rounded numbers is challenging, as illustrated by this national assessment question:

> The length of a dinosaur was reported to have been 80 feet (rounded to the nearest 10 feet). What length other than 80 feet could have been the actual length of the dinosaur?

Several different answers, such as 76 or 84 feet, were acceptable. Only 20 percent of the fourth graders and less than half of the eighth graders reported an acceptable answer. This performance shows that interpreting a rounded result needs to be addressed in elementary and middle grades.

The base-10 blocks provide a natural method for developing rounding skills with larger numbers. Questions such as these focus attention on the quantity and the idea of *closer to,* which is essential in rounding:

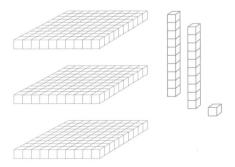

Is this more than three hundred? [yes]

Is this more than four hundred? [no]

Is this closer to three or four hundred? [closer to three hundred]

This model can also be extended to help children become more aware that 350 is halfway between 300 and 400.

A roller coaster is another model that could be used to develop rounding skills (see Activity Card 7–15). The labeling shown on the roller coaster provides an effective tool if children understand the number line. Children know what happens when the coaster stops at certain points. The model also suggests that something special happens at the top: The coaster could roll either way. This observation provides an opportunity to discuss a rule of rounding, such as "if the number ends in 5, you go over the hump to the next valley." In rounding, attention is given to the back-end digit or digits, as illustrated in Activity Card 7–16.

Perhaps the biggest difficulty related to rounding is knowing whether to round to the nearest ten, hundred, thousand, or whatever. Normally this decision depends on the purpose of rounding and the context of the problem. Students should view rounding as something that not only makes numbers easier to handle, but, most importantly, also makes sense.

Activity Card 7–16 encourages students to think about advantages as well as consequences of rounding numbers. Meaningful rounding (knowing how much precision is necessary and what to round to) will improve through practice in many different problem contexts.

▶ A Glance at Where We've Been

Children must have a clear understanding of our number system if they are going to be mathematically literate. They must be able to distinguish characteristics of our number system, the role of zero, the additive property of numbers, a base of ten, and place value. Many counting and trading experiences (particularly grouping by tens) are necessary.

As children develop their skills with the aid of various models (such as bean sticks, base-10 blocks, and an abacus), they need to learn how to organize the results in some systematic fashion and record them. Place-value mats serve as a visual reminder of the quantities involved and provide a bridge toward

Activity Card 7–15

Take a Ride on the Number Line

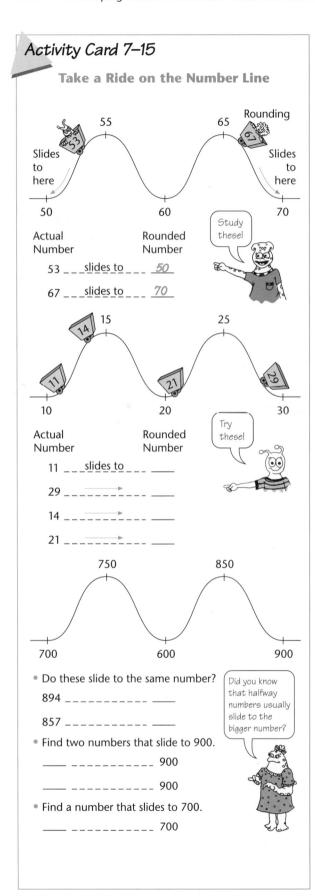

Study these!

Actual Number		Rounded Number
53	slides to	50
67	slides to	70

Try these!

Actual Number		Rounded Number
11	slides to	___
29		___
14		___
21		___

• Do these slide to the same number?

894 _____ ___

857 _____ ___

• Find two numbers that slide to 900.

___ _____ 900

___ _____ 900

• Find a number that slides to 700.

___ _____ 700

Did you know that halfway numbers usually slide to the bigger number?

Activity Card 7–16 ✓

Deciding Which Way to Round

▼ These prices could be rounded different ways:

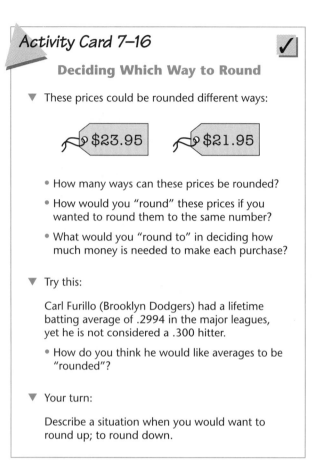

$23.95 $21.95

• How many ways can these prices be rounded?
• How would you "round" these prices if you wanted to round them to the same number?
• What would you "round to" in deciding how much money is needed to make each purchase?

▼ Try this:

Carl Furillo (Brooklyn Dodgers) had a lifetime batting average of .2994 in the major leagues, yet he is not considered a .300 hitter.

• How do you think he would like averages to be "rounded"?

▼ Your turn:

Describe a situation when you would want to round up; to round down.

the symbolic representation of larger numbers. Establishing these bridges from the concrete to the abstract is the heart of good teaching. It is particularly critical in developing place value, whose importance is second to none in all later development of number concepts.

Place-value concepts are developed over many years. The trading rules help plant the seeds early, but recognition of the power and importance of place value is developed, refined, extended, and expanded throughout the study of mathematics. Estimation provides a natural setting for students to experience larger numbers and develop place-value concepts via rounding.

Systematic study of place value over a long period is essential. For example, review of important place-value concepts must be provided as computation is being established. This type of study also provides an opportunity not only to maintain but also to extend many place-value concepts learned earlier. The point is that place value is not just taught for a couple of days in one or two grades; rather, systematic instruction on place value must be planned and integrated throughout the elementary school mathematics program.

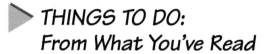

THINGS TO DO:
From What You've Read

1. Identify four characteristics of our number system. Select one characteristic and make a visual representation of it.

2. Show how 201 and 120 would be represented with three different place-value models.

3. Distinguish between proportional and nonproportional models. Name an example of each.

4. Tell why trading activities are so important with respect to place value. Describe several materials that could be used for trading.

5. Estimation provides many opportunities to explore place value. Describe an estimation activity that would encourage students to think about 10, 100, 1,000, and 10,000 and distinguish among these values.

6. Describe some ways that benchmarks are used in estimating length and quantity.

7. Describe ways in which modeling, reading, and writing numbers can be used to get children actively involved in talking about mathematics and linking concrete materials with their symbolic representations.

8. It has been suggested that centuries and decades can be used to demonstrate some notions of place value. Describe how this could be done.

9. Examine Lesson Card 7–1. Show the six different numbers that could be made with the three cards. Which is closest to 400? Which number less than 400 is next closest to 400?

10. Use your calculator. Enter the largest number possible in the display and name this number. How many digits does it have? Add one to this number and describe what your calculator does.

THINGS TO DO:
Going Beyond This Book

1. Find a scope-and-sequence chart for an elementary mathematics textbook series. Is place value identified as a strand? If so, are place-value concepts included at all grade levels? Identify the grades where place value receives the most attention.

2. Examine a primary-level mathematics textbook. How many different place-value models are illustrated? Which model is used the most? Do you think the textbook provides a good choice of models? Defend your position.

3. Examine an elementary mathematics textbook series. Find where rounding is introduced. Summarize the rounding rules that are provided. Trace the development of rounding to tens, hundreds, thousands, and so on. Are children given problems that encourage them to decide how to round, or are they told, for example, to "round to the nearest hundred"?

4. Read "Some Aids for Teaching Place Value" by Jensen and O'Neil (1981). Compare and contrast the place-value models discussed with those illustrated in Figure 7–2.

5. Different models exist for helping children develop a concept of large numbers. Each of the articles (Bickerton-Ross, 1988; Ellis, 1979; Harrison, 1985; Joslyn, 1990; Makurat, 1977; Parker & Widmer, 1991; Thompson 1989) shows and describes useful physical models. Examine one or more of the articles and describe the approach taken to help children better understand large numbers.

6. Select either *Number Sense and Operations* (Burton et al. 1993), *Developing Number Sense in the Middle Grades* (Reys et al. 1991) or SENSE (McIntosh et al. 1997). Choose an activity that you think would be useful to help students develop a better understanding of large numbers and demonstrate how you would implement the activity.

7. Read "A Two-Dimensional Abacus—The Papy Minicomputer" by Van Arsdel and Lasky (1972). Is this a proportional or nonproportional model? Describe how it would be used to represent several three-digit numbers.

8. Read the article "Ancient Systems of Numeration —Stimulating, Illuminating" by Cowle (1970) or "Numeration Systems and Their Classroom Roles" by Rudnick (1968). Describe a project that could be used to provide enrichment for several able students.

9. Make bean sticks for base five. Describe how to demonstrate any number up to 24 with your bean sticks and loose beans. Alternatively, use pennies and nickels for base five, and describe how you would show all numbers up to 24.

10. Examine one of the books from the Children's Corner at the end of this chapter. Would you encourage children to use this book? Tell why and when.

11. Examine *The Wonderful World of Mathematics: A Critically Annotated List of Children's Books in Mathematics* (Thiessen and Matthias 1992). Find a book related to place value that is highly recommended. Read the book with some children and describe how they react.

▼▼▼▼▼▼▼▼▼▼▼▼▼▼▼▼▼▼▼▼▼▼▼▼

Children's Corner

Berry, David. (1994). The Rajah's Rice: A Mathematical Folktale from India. New York: W. H. Freeman & Company.

Demi. *Demi's Count the Animals 1-2-3.* New York: Gossett Dunlap, 1986.

Diagram Group. *Comparisons.* New York: St. Martin's Press, 1980.

Howard, Katherine. *I Can Count to One Hundred . . . Can You?* New York: Random House, 1979.

Parker, Tom. *In One Day.* Boston: Houghton Mifflin, 1984.

Paulos, John Allen. *Innumeracy.* New York: Hill and Wang, 1989.

Schwartz, David M. *How Much Is a Million?* New York: Lothrop, Lee and Shepard Books, Division of William Morrow, 1985.

Schwartz, David M. *If You Made a Million.* New York: Lothrop, Lee and Shepard Books, Division of William Morrow, 1989.

Selected References

Beattie, Ian D. "The Number Namer: An Aid to Understanding Place Value." *Arithmetic Teacher,* 33 (January 1986), pp. 24–29.

Bickerton-Ross, Linda. "A Practical Experience in Problem Solving: A '10,000' Display." *Arithmetic Teacher,* 35 (December 1988), pp. 14–15.

Bobis, Janette F. "Using a Calculator to Develop Number Sense." *Arithmetic Teacher,* 38 (January 1991), pp. 42–45

Bove, Sandra. "Place Value: A Vertical Perspective." *Teaching Children Mathematics,* 1(9) (May 1995), pp. 542–546.

Brumaugh, Frederick L. "Big Numbers in a Classroom Model." *Arithmetic Teacher,* 19 (November 1981), pp. 18–19.

Burns, Marilyn N. *Mathematics with Manipulatives: Base Ten Blocks* (videotape). New Rochelle, N.Y.: Cuisenaire Co., 1988.

Burton, Grace et al. *Number Sense and Operations.* Reston, Va.: NCTM, 1993.

Cowle, Irving M. "Ancient Systems of Numeration—Stimulating, Illuminating." *Arithmetic Teacher,* 17 (May 1970), pp. 413–416.

Curcio, Frances R., and Zarnowski, Myra. "Revisiting the Powers of 2." *Teaching Children Mathematics,* 2(5) (January 1996), pp. 300–304.

Ellis, Glen. "Reader Reflections: How Large Is a Billion?" *Mathematics Teacher,* 72 (May 1979), p. 324.

Fennell, Francis. Number Sense Now! (video tape and guidebook) Reston, Va.: NCTM 1992.

Gluck, Doris. "Helping Students Understand Place Value." *Arithmetic Teacher,* 38 (March 1991), pp. 10–13.

Harrison, Marilyn, and Harrison, Bruce. "Developing Numerations Concepts and Skills." *Arithmetic Teacher,* 33 (February 1986), pp. 18–21.

Harrison, William B. "How to Make a Million." *Arithmetic Teacher,* 32 (September 1985), pp. 46–47.

Hopkins, Martha H. "Wipe Out Refined." In *Calculators in Mathematics Education,* 1992 Yearbook (eds. James T. Fey and Christian R. Hirsch). Reston, Va.: NCTM, 1992.

Jensen, Rosalie, and O'Neil, David R. "Some Aids for Teaching Place Value." *Arithmetic Teacher,* 29 (November 1981), pp. 6–9.

Joslyn, Ruth E. "Using Concrete Models to Teach Large Number Concepts." *Arithmetic Teacher,* 38 (November 1990), pp. 6–9.

Kouba, Vicky L.; Carpenter, Thomas P.; and Swafford, Jane O. "Number and Operations." In *Results from the Fourth Mathematics Assessment of the National Assessment of Educational Progress* (ed. M. Lindquist). Reston, Va.: NCTM, 1989.

Labinowicz, Ed. *Learning from Children: New Beginnings for Teaching Numerical Thinking.* Menlo Park, Calif.: Addison-Wesley, 1985.

McIntosh, Alistair; Reys, Barbara J.; and Reys, Robert E. "A Proposed Framework for Examining Basic Number Sense." *For the Learning of Mathematics,* 12 (November 1992), pp. 2–8.

McIntosh, Alistair; Reys, Barbara; and Reys, Robert (1997). *Number SENSE: Simple Effective Number Sense Experiences: Grades 3–4 & 4–6,* Palo Alto, Calif.: Dale Seymour Publications.

Makurat, Phillip A. "A Look at a Million." *Arithmetic Teacher,* 25 (December 1977), p. 23.

National Council of Teachers of Mathematics. *Curriculum and Evaluation Standards for School Mathematics.* Reston, Va.: NCTM, 1989.

National Council of Teachers of Mathematics. *Professional Standards for Teaching Mathematics.* Reston, Va.: NCTM, 1991.

Parker, Janet, and Widmer, Connie. "How Big Is a Million?" *Arithmetic Teacher,* 39 (September 1991), pp. 38–41.

Payne, Joseph N., and Huinker, DeAnn M. "Early Number and Numeration." In *Research Ideas for the Classroom: Early Childhood Mathematics* (ed. Robert J. Jensen). Reston, Va.: NCTM, and New York: Macmillan, 1993, pp. 43–70.

Phillips, Elizabeth; Gardella, Theodore; Kelly, Constance; and Stewart, Jacqueline. *Patterns and Functions.* Reston, Va.: NCTM, 1991.

Rathmell, Edward C., and Leutzinger, Larry P. "Number Representations and Relationships." *Arithmetic Teacher,* 38 (March 1991), pp. 20–23.

Reys, Barbara J.; Barger, Rita; Bruckheimer, Maxim; Dougherty, Barbara; Hope, Jack; Lembke, Linda; Markovitz, Zvia; Parnas, Andy; Reehm, Sue; Sturdevant, Ruthi; and Weber, Marianne. *Developing Number Sense in the Middle Grades.* Reston, Va.: NCTM, 1991.

Reys, Robert E.; Bestgen, Barbara J.; Coburn, Terrence G.; Marcucci, Robert; Schoen, Harold L.; Shumway, Richard J.; Wheatley, Charlotte L.; Wheatley, Grayson, H.; and White, Arthur L. *Keystrokes: Calculator Activities for Young Students: Counting and Place Value.* Palo Alto, Calif.: Creative Publications, 1980.

Ritchhart, Ron. *Making Numbers Make Sense: A Sourcebook for Developing Numeracy.* Menlo Park, Calif.: Addison-Wesley, 1994.

Rinker, Ethel. "Eight-Ring Circus: A Variation in the Teaching of Counting and Place Value." *Arithmetic Teacher,* 19 (March 1972), pp. 209–216.

Ronshausen, Nina L. "Introducing Place Value." *Arithmetic Teacher,* 25 (January 1978), pp. 38–40.

Rudnick, Jesse A. "Numeration Systems and Their Classroom Roles." *Arithmetic Teacher,* 15 (February 1968), pp. 138–147.

Sowder, Judith. "Estimation and Number Sense." In *Handbook of Research on Mathematics Teaching and Learning* (ed. Douglas Grouws). New York: Macmillan, 1992, pp. 371–389.

Thiessen, Diane, and Matthias, Margaret (eds.). *The Wonderful World of Mathematics: A Critically Annotated List of Children's Books in Mathematics.* Reston, Va.: NCTM, 1992.

Thompson, Charles S. "Number Sense and Numeration in Grades K–8." *Arithmetic Teacher,* 37 (September 1989), pp. 22–24.

Thompson, Charles S. "Place Value and Larger Numbers." In *Mathematics for the Young Child* (ed. Joseph N. Payne). Reston, Va.: NCTM, 1990, pp. 89–108.

Thornton, Carol A.; Jones, Graham A.; and Neal, Judy L. "The 100s Chart: A Stepping Stone to Mental Mathematics," *Teaching Children Mathematics,* 1(8) (April 1995), pp. 480–483.

Van Arsdel, Jean, and Lasky, Joanne. "A Two-Dimensional Abacus—The Papy Minicomputer." *Arithmetic Teacher,* 19 (October 1972), pp. 245–451.

Wearne, Diane, and Hiebert, James "Place Value and Addition and Subtraction," *Arithmetic Teacher,* 41(5) (January, 1994), pp. 271–275.

Yoshikawa, Shigeo. "Computational Estimation: Curriculum and Instructional Issues from the Japanese Perspective." In *Computational Alternatives for the 21st Century: Cross Cultural Perspectives from Japan and the United States* (eds. Robert E. Reys and Nobubiko Nohda). Reston, Va.: NCTM, 1994.

Beginning Whole-Number Operations: Basic Facts

8

 Snapshot of a Lesson

Purpose

To provide initial experiences with multiplication (as repeated addition) and division (as repeated subtraction).

Needed Materials

Flannelboard or magnetic board; flannel or magnetic "candies": 20 small yellow, 15 medium orange, and 12 large red; discs for each child: 25 yellow, 20 orange, and 15 red.

Procedures

Read this story to children, stopping to ask questions and model each situation on the board:

Once upon a time there was a little old lady who lived in a little old house in the middle of a little old town. She was such a nice little old lady that all the children who lived in the town liked to come to visit her. For a special treat, she would often give them candy. She had three kinds, each wrapped in a different color:

- small yellow ones
- medium orange ones
- large red ones

[Put a sample of each on the board.]

She let the children choose the kind they wanted, but she realized there could be a problem—everyone might want the largest. So she made a rule: each child could have

- 4 yellow, or
- 3 orange, or
- 2 red

[Put each grouping on the board.]

1. One day 3 children came to visit. They all took red candies. Who can show how many pieces one child took? How many the children took altogether?

[Expected response: 2 + 2 + 2 = 6; possibly 3 groups of 2, 3 twos are 6, or 3 × 2 = 6. Have child show and count.]

2. 2 children took red.
   (a) How many pieces?
   (b) How do you know?
   (c) Is there any other way to know?

[Ask questions (a), (b), (c) for the next examples. After several with whole group watching the board, have each child use discs.]

3. 3 children—orange

4. 2 children—yellow

5. 4 children—orange

6. 3 children—yellow.

7. If needed:

   2 children—orange

   4 children—yellow

8. 6 children—3 took yellow, 3 red

9. 4 children—2 took red, 2 orange

10. 5 children—2 took orange, 3 yellow

11. If needed:

    5 children—all took yellow

    6 children—all took red

Suppose the old lady had 8 pieces of yellow candy. How many children could choose yellow? How do you know?

[After several examples with board, have each child solve with discs.]

1. 15 orange

2. 10 red

3. 12 red

4. 12 yellow

5. 12 orange

6. 9 orange

7. 8 red

Practice

Worksheet paralleling lesson [use to evaluate]:

3 children.
All took red.
Make a drawing.

Extension

1. If the old lady gave away 2 candies, how many children came? What color candies did she give? What if she gave 9 candies? 15?

2. Pretend you see boots all lined up outside a classroom. How many children are in the room if there are 18 boots and each child left boots?

3. Ask children to make up similar problems.

 ## Introduction

The Snapshot Lesson incorporates several essential components of a well-planned classroom activity involving computation. First and foremost, it involves the student in an active way in manipulating objects to answer questions. It provides problem-solving experiences that promote reasoning and discussion. "How do you know?" is an important question because it encourages students to think about "why" and not just "what." Also, computational ideas are posed in a potentially real situation.

These components are important in elementary school mathematics lessons, particularly as understanding of the relevance and meaning of computational ideas is being developed. An understanding of addition, subtraction, multiplication, and division and knowledge of the basic facts for each of these operations provide a foundation for all later

work with computation. To be effective in this later work, children must develop broad concepts for the operations. This development is more likely to happen if each operation is presented through a multi-embodiment approach using various physical models. Such experiences help children recognize that an operation can be used in several different types of situations. Children also must understand the properties that apply to each operation and the relationships between operations.

Learning the basic facts is one of the first steps children take as they refine their ideas about each operation. By using the facts, plus an understanding of place value and mathematical properties, a child can perform any addition, subtraction, multiplication, or division with whole numbers. Understanding the operations and having immediate recall of number facts are essential in doing estimation, mental computation, and pencil-and-paper algorithms; they continue to be essential as calculators and computers are used. Without such devices, the basic facts form the building blocks for performing more difficult, multidigit calculations; with calculational devices, the basic facts provide a means of quickly checking the reasonableness of answers.

Moreover, knowing the basic facts lets children perform calculations or estimate answers in many everyday situations where it would be slower to use a calculator. So, no matter what type of computation a child is using—mental computation, estimation, paper-and-pencil computation, or a calculator— quick recall of the basic facts for each operation is essential.

● Prerequisites

Ultimately, the instructional goal is that children not only know how to add, subtract, multiply, and divide, but, more importantly, know *when* to apply each in a problem-solving situation. Children also should be able to recall the basic facts quickly when needed.

How do we help them to attain these skills and understandings? We begin by finding out what each child knows. Then we capitalize on this knowledge as we help them to continue to build on the number concepts they have already constructed (Kouba and Franklin 1993). Most children entering school will be ready in some ways and not ready in others for formal work on the operations. Of the prerequisites for such work, four seem particularly important.

Counting

Children use counting to solve problems involving addition, subtraction, multiplication, and division long before they come to school, as research has indicated (Baroody and Standifer 1993; Suydam and Weaver 1981). Any problem with whole numbers can be solved by counting, provided there is sufficient time. Because there is not always the time to solve problems by counting, children need to be able to use more efficient operations and procedures that help them cope with more difficult computation. Figure 8–1 illustrates this idea by comparing the counting method with the multiplication operation.

Counting nevertheless remains an integral aspect of children's beginning work with the operations. They need to know how to count forward, backward, and by twos, threes, and other groups

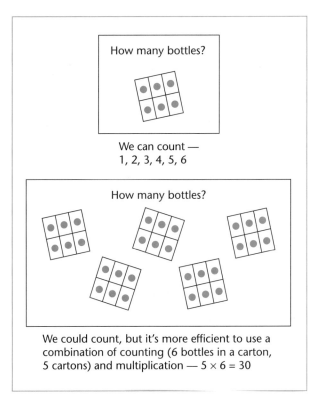

Figure 8–1 ● **An example showing the efficiency of using operations**

(see Chapter 6). They need to count as they compare and analyze sets and arrays as they affirm their initial computational results. But they need more than counting to become proficient in computing.

Concrete Experiences

Children need to have many experiences in real-life situations and in working with physical objects in order to develop understandings about the operations. Research has indicated that work with actual physical objects promotes achievement for most children (Sowell 1989; Suydam and Higgins 1977). Understanding improves if they can relate mathematical symbols to some experience they have had or can visualize. A basic fact cannot be learned with meaning unless it has been experienced in a situation that gives it meaning.

Manipulative materials serve as a referent for later work with the operations, as well as constructing the basic facts. They also provide a link to connect each operation to real-world problem-solving situations. And whenever a child wants to be sure that an answer is correct, materials can be used for confirmation.

Problem-Solving Context

As with other mathematical content, a problem-solving context or situation should be used in the introductory stages and all along the way until practice for mastery is the only goal. We want children to think of mathematics as problem solving—as a means by which they can resolve problems through applying what they know, constructing possible routes to reach solutions, and then verifying that the solutions are plausible. We want them to realize that mathematics is a tool that has real-life applications. Most children already know that computation is used in everyday life. We want to connect the mathematics lesson to those experiences. But we also want them to realize that $6 \times 8 = \square$ or $9 + 2 = \square$ also may be problems—ones that they can resolve. We want them to have the attitude, "I don't know the answer but I can work it out" (Thornton and Smith 1988).

Language

Children need to talk about mathematics; experiences to develop meanings need to be put into words. Manipulative materials and problems can be vehicles for talking about mathematics. Such discussion of mathematics is a critical part of meaningful learning. All early phases of instruction on the operations and basic facts should reflect the important role language plays in their acquisition. The *Curriculum and Evaluation Standards for School Mathematics* (NCTM 1989) discusses the roles of language in great depth in presenting the recommendations on communication and thus provides a valuable source of additional information.

Frequently, the move to symbols is made too quickly, and the use of materials dropped too soon. Instead, the use of materials should both precede and then parallel the use of symbols. Recording of symbols should be done as materials are manipulated. As illustrated in the lesson that opened this chapter, language should be used to describe what is happening in a given situation. Then and only then will children see the relation of the symbols to the manipulation of materials and to the problem setting (Carey 1992).

The language that is learned as children communicate about what they are doing and what they see happening as they use materials help them to understand the symbolism related to the operations. Thus, the referent for each symbol is being strengthened. Children should begin their work with operations after having had a variety of experiences about

which they have talked among themselves and with the teacher. They need to be encouraged to continue talking about the mathematical ideas they meet as they work with the operations. And, as soon as feasible, they need to put their ideas on paper—by drawings alone at first, then by writing explanations (when they can write).

● **Models for the Operations**

Development of the basic facts and later work with multidigit examples are based on a clear understanding of the operations. Models help children to understand addition, subtraction, multiplication, and division by representing the situation and portraying the action involved in an operation.

The four operations are clearly different, but there are relationships among them that children must come to understand:

- Addition and subtraction are inverse operations; that is, one undoes the other:

$$5 + 8 = 13 \longleftrightarrow 13 - 5 = 8$$

- Multiplication and division are inverse operations:

$$4 \times 6 = 24 \longleftrightarrow 24 \div 4 = 6$$

- Multiplication can be viewed as repeated addition:

$$4 \times 6 \longleftrightarrow 6 + 6 + 6 + 6$$

- Division can be viewed as repeated subtraction:

$$24 \div 6 \longleftrightarrow 24 - 6 - 6 - 6 - 6$$

These relationships can be developed through careful instruction with a variety of different experiences.

Addition and Subtraction

Figure 8–2 illustrates a variety of models that can be used to represent addition. In each, the idea that addition means "finding how many in all" is depicted.

The models for addition also can be used for subtraction. Each can be applied in the three situations that lead to subtraction.

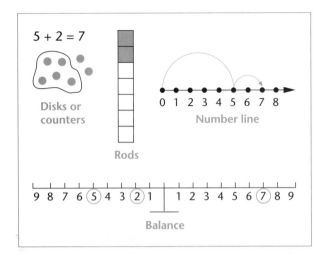

Figure 8–2 • Some models for addition

1. Separation, or take away, involves having one quantity, removing a specified quantity from it, and noting what is left. Research indicates that this subtraction situation is the easiest for children to learn (Gibb 1956). However, persistent use of the words *take away* results in many children assuming they apply to the *only* subtraction situation and leads to misunderstanding of the other two situations.

> Peggy had 7 balloons. She gave 4 to other children. How many did she have left?

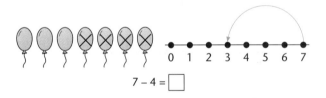

2. Comparison, or finding the difference, involves having two quantities, matching them one-to-one, and noting the quantity that is the difference between them.

> Peggy had 7 balloons. Richard had 4 balloons. How many more balloons did Peggy have than Richard did?

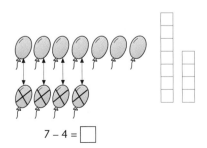

3. "How many more are needed" involves having the total quantity, knowing one of the parts, and ascertaining the remaining part.

> Peggy had 7 balloons. Four of them were red and the rest were blue. How many were blue?

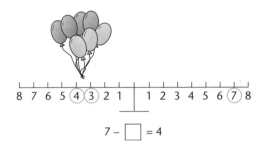

The importance of providing many varied experiences in which children use physical objects to model or act out examples of each operation cannot be overemphasized. The lesson at the beginning of this chapter provided one such experience. It illustrates a way to involve each child in forming equal-sized groups. Writing symbols for each action is not essential at this early stage. Moving, counting, and questioning are the important components.

Lesson Card 8–1 and Activity Card 8–1 illustrate slightly more symbolic activities. The children solve problems in a variety of ways using the dot sticks, followed by individual practice. Similar activities can be done with the abacus, rods, or other objects.

Initially, symbols are given as a complement to the physical manipulation of objects. They are a way of showing the action with the materials and should be introduced along with the materials. As the work progresses, the amount of symbolization you offer and encourage will increase. The symbols should always be introduced in conjunction with a concrete material or model.

The number line is used in some textbooks as a model for addition and subtraction, but it must be used with caution. The second national mathematics assessment indicated that there is misunderstanding of how to use and interpret this model (Carpenter et al. 1981). For example, consider this number line:

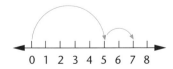

About twice as many nine-year-olds responded that "5 + 7" was pictured as did those responding

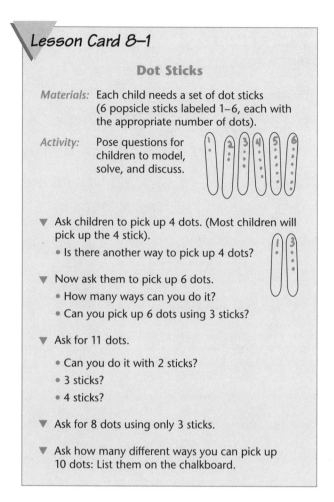

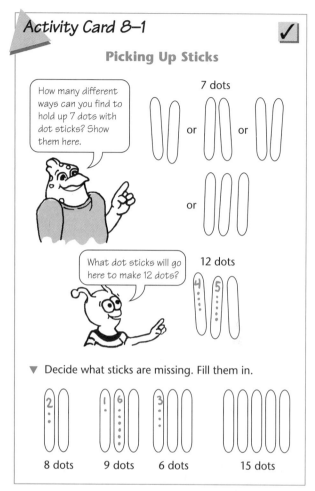

with the correct answer, "5 + 2 = 7." The same error was made by 39 percent of the thirteen-year-olds. Carpenter et al. (1981, p. 19) suggested:

> Since the model does not seem to clearly suggest the operation, the meaning must be developed or misunderstandings may occur. The mathematics curriculum should be constructed to ensure that students have a meaningful development of the basic operations. Certainly, many types of models can help this development, but they must be carefully selected and meaningfully taught.

Whatever model is used to illustrate the ideas of addition and subtraction, the desired components are clear:

1. Use a variety of problem settings and manipulative materials to act out and model the operation.

2. Provide representations of objects in pictures, diagrams, and drawings to move a step away from the concrete toward symbolization.

3. Use symbols to illustrate the operation.

In this way, children move through experiences from the concrete to the semiconcrete to the abstract, linking each to the others.

Multiplication and Division

The three components for addition and subtraction are also followed for multiplication and division. Many different models can be used to represent multiplication. Figure 8–3 illustrates the three most commonly used models: (1) equivalent groups of objects, which is often used by teachers to relate multiplication to repeated addition, (2) the number line, and (3) the array, in which equivalent groups are joined together. Research indicates that children do best when they can use various representations for all multiplication and division situations and can explain the relationships among those representations (Kouba and Franklin 1995).

Occasionally, multiplication is considered in terms of Cartesian products (Quintero 1985). For example, consider the number of different sundaes

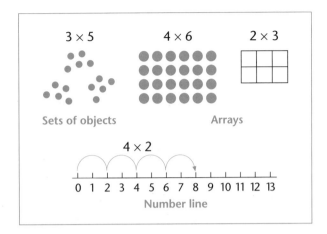

Figure 8–3 ● Commonly used models for multiplication

possible with four different ice cream flavors and two toppings:

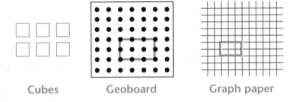

The array model for multiplication can be especially effective. It may serve as a natural extension to children's prior work in making and naming rectangles using cubes, geoboards, or graph paper:

These illustrations show a 2-by-3 or 3-by-2 rectangle. Thus, each contains six small squares. Asking children to build and name numerous rectangles with various numbers is a good readiness experience for the concept of multiplication. Activity Cards 8–2 through 8–5 illustrate several experiences designed for this purpose.

Just as sets of objects, the number line, and arrays are useful in presenting multiplication, they can be useful in representing division, with the relationship to repeated subtraction frequently shown. However,

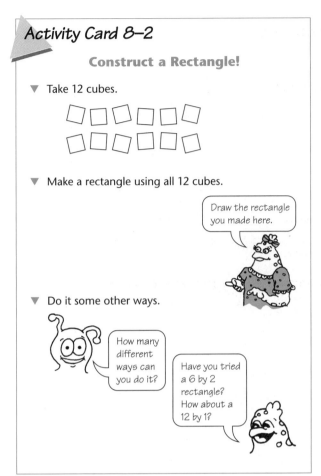

for division, two different types of situations must be considered: measurement and partition.

1. In *measurement* situations, one knows the number in each group and must determine the number of groups.

   Jenny had 12 candies. She gave 3 to each person. How many persons got candies?

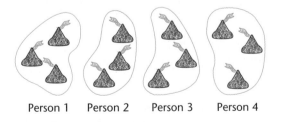

2. *Partition*, or sharing, situations are those in which a group is separated into a given number of equivalent groups and one seeks the number in each group.

Activity Card 8–3 ✓

Rectangles and More Rectangles!

▼ How many ways can you make a rectangle with this many cubes?

▼ List the ways:

1 cube ☐

_____

2 cubes ☐ ☐

_____

3 cubes ☐ ☐ ☐

_____
_____

4 cubes ☐ ☐ ☐

_____
_____

5 cubes ☐ ☐ ☐ ☐ ☐

_____
_____

8 cubes ☐ ☐ ☐ ☐ ☐ ☐ ☐ ☐

_____
_____
_____
_____

Activity Card 8–4 ✓

How Many Squares in a Rectangle?

▼ Draw a 3 × 4 rectangle:

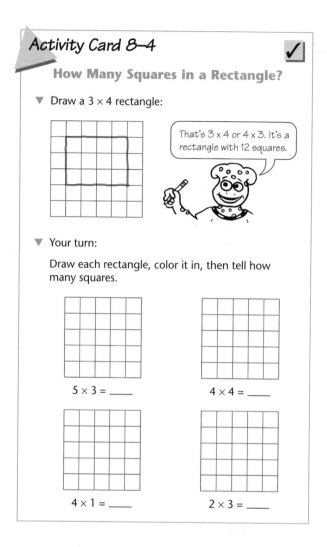

That's 3 x 4 or 4 x 3. It's a rectangle with 12 squares.

▼ Your turn:

Draw each rectangle, color it in, then tell how many squares.

5 × 3 = _____   4 × 4 = _____

4 × 1 = _____   2 × 3 = _____

Gil had 15 shells. If he wanted to share them equally among 5 friends, how many should he give to each?

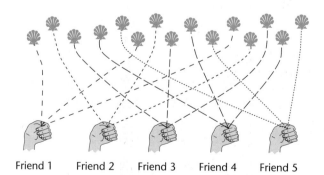

Friend 1   Friend 2   Friend 3   Friend 4   Friend 5

Partitioning is very difficult to show in a diagram, but relatively easy to have children act out. Dealing cards for a game is another instance of a partition situation.

It is not necessary for children to learn the terms and to name problems as measurement or partition situations. To identify when a problem requires division is vital, however, and that means being able to identify both types of situations as division situations. Lesson Card 8–2 illustrates an early activity that can be used to introduce the idea of division to children in a meaningful way.

● Mathematical Properties

An understanding of the mathematical properties that pertain to each operation is vital to the child's understanding of the operation and how to use it. This understanding is not a prerequisite to work with operations, but it must be developed as a part of the understanding of the operations.

Activity Card 8–5

Rolling for Rectangles!

▼ Use this pattern to make 2 cubes.

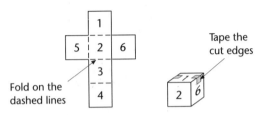

Fold on the dashed lines

Tape the cut edges

▼ Use your cubes and a sheet of graph paper to play.

• Roll your cubes, then make a rectangle having that size.

• Keep rolling until you fill the paper.

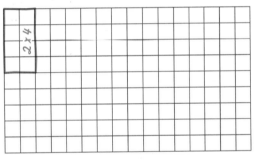

Lesson Card 8–2

Lots of Links

Materials: 20 links (or other counters) for each child; an overhead projector

Activity: Discuss with children different ways to separate the links into equal-sized groups.

▼ Scatter 12 links on an overhead projector.

• How can we place these links into equal-sized groups? (6 groups of 2, 4 groups of 3, 1 group of 12, etc.)

• How many different ways can we do it?

▼ Scatter 15 links on the projector.

• How many different ways can these links be split into equal-sized groups?

• What happens if we try dividing 12 links into groups of 5?

CCCCC   CCCCC   CC   2 groups and 2 leftovers

▼ Focus on numbers that can be divided into equal-sized groups without "leftovers":

• Which of these numbers can be divided into groups of 3 without having leftovers?

8 4 7 3 18

Try each one.

• Name a number that will have no leftovers if we divide it into groups of 5. How many numbers like this can you name?

• Name a number that will have 1 leftover if we divide it into groups of 5. Can you name 3 numbers like this?

In elementary school, children are not expected to state these properties precisely or identify them by name. Rather, the instructional goal is to help them understand the commutative, associative, distributive, and identity properties and to use them when it is efficient. Table 8–1 gives the meaning of each property, states what children should understand, and provides examples to illustrate how the property can make learning and using the basic facts easier.

Understanding these properties implies knowing when they apply. For example, both addition and multiplication are commutative, but neither subtraction nor division is:

$$7 - 3 \text{ is } not \text{ equal to } 3 - 7$$

$$28 \div 7 \text{ is } not \text{ equal to } 7 \div 28$$

Many children have difficulty with the idea of commutativity. They tend to "subtract the smaller number from the larger" or to "divide the larger number by the smaller" regardless of their order. Care needs to be taken to ensure that they construct correct notions.

● The Basic Facts

As children develop concepts of the meanings of the operations, instruction begins to focus on certain

Table 8–1 • Mathematical properties for elementary-school children

Property	Mathematical Language	Child's Language	How It Helps
Commutative	For all numbers *a* and *b*: $a + b = b + a$ and $a \times b = b \times a$	If 4 + 7 = 11, then 7 + 4 must equal 11, too. If I know 4 × 7, I also know 7 × 4.	The number of addition or multiplication facts to be memorized is reduced from 100 to 55.
Associative	For all numbers *a*, *b*, and *c*: $(a + b) + c = a + (b + c)$ and $(ab)c = a(bc)$	When I'm adding (or multiplying) three or more numbers, it doesn't matter where I start.	When more than two numbers are being added (or multiplied), combinations that make the task easier can be chosen. For example, 37 × 5 × 2 can be done as 37 × (5 × 2) or 37 × 10 rather than (37 × 5) × 2.
Distributive	For all numbers *a*, *b*, and *c*: $a(b + c) = ab + ac$	8 × (5 + 2) is the same as (8 × 5) + (8 × 2). 24 ÷ 3 is the same as (12 ÷ 3) + (12 ÷ 3).	Some of the more difficult basic facts can be split into smaller, easier-to-remember parts. For example, 8 × 7 is the same as (8 × 5) + (8 × 2) or 40 + 16.
Identity	For any whole number *a*: $a + 0 = a$ and $a \times 1 = a$	0 added to any number is easy; it's just that number. 1 times any number is just that number.	The 19 addition facts involving 0 and the 19 multiplication facts involving 1 can be easily remembered once this property is understood and established.

number combinations. These are generally referred to as the *basic facts:*

- *Basic addition facts* each involve two one-digit addends and their sum. There are one hundred basic addition facts.

- *Basic subtraction facts* rely on the inverse relationship of addition and subtraction for their definition. The one hundred basic subtraction facts result from the difference between one addend and the sum for all one-digit addends.

- *Basic multiplication facts* each involve two one-digit factors and their product. There are one hundred basic multiplication facts.

- *Basic division facts* rely on the inverse relationship of multiplication and division. There are only ninety basic division facts. Because division by zero is not possible, there are no facts with zero as the divisor.

Development and mastery of the addition and subtraction facts begins in kindergarten or first grade and continues as multiplication and division facts are developed and practiced.

Some children, however, have not mastered the facts several years later. Children's difficulty in attaining this competency may have two causes for which teachers can provide help. (A third cause—a learning disability—can make it virtually impossible for a child to memorize the facts; however, use of a calculator allows a child with a learning disability to proceed with learning mathematics. Or, as research by Clark and Kamii (1996) indicates for multiplication, the children may not have developed the ability to think multiplicatively.) First, the underlying numerical understandings may not have been developed. Thus, the process of memorizing the facts becomes merely manipulation of symbols. Second, the skill of memorizing itself may not be taught by teachers or understood by children, resulting in inefficient strategies. Teachers can do something about both of these lacks:

● Start from where the children are: *Get ready.*

● Build understandings: *Get set.*

● Focus on how to memorize: *Go.*

Get Ready: The Starting Place

Many children come to school knowing some basic facts. For instance, the chances are great that they can say "one and one are two," "two and two are four," and maybe even "five and five are ten." They may know that 2 and 1 more is 3, and that 6 and "nothing more" is still 6. But they probably don't know that 6 + 7 = 13. Nor do they have a clear concept of the meanings of symbols such as + and =.

Similarly, they may know that if you have 3 and take away 2, you have only 1 left. But they probably won't know 3 − 2 = 1 (or "three minus two equals one"). They may know that buying three pieces of gum at 5¢ each will cost 15¢, but they won't know that 3 × 5 = 15. They may know that eight cookies divided among four children means that each child will get two cookies, but they won't know that 8 ÷ 4 = 2.

In other words, they can solve simple problems involving facts, but they are not likely to be able to either recognize or write the facts. Nor do many children understand *why* 5 + 5 = 10 or realize that 4 + 2 = ☐ asks the same question as:

$$
\begin{array}{r}
4 \\
+\,2 \\
\hline
\end{array}
$$

It is our task to help them organize what they know, construct more learning to fill in the gaps, and, in the process, develop meaning.

We need to begin by determining what each child knows, using responses from group discussions, observations of how each child works with materials and with paper-and-pencil activities, and individual interviews. Many teachers use an inventory at the beginning of the year, administered individually to younger children and in a questionnaire format in later grades. The purpose of such an inventory is to discover:

● Whether the children have the concept of an operation: "What does it mean to add?" "Why did you subtract?" "When can you multiply?"

● What basic facts they understand (demonstrated by drawing a picture to illustrate or by writing the fact for an illustration)

● What strategies they use to find the solution to combinations: "How did you know 7 + 9 = 16?"

● What basic facts they have memorized

We use such information to plan instruction. Do some children need more work with manipulative materials to understand what multiplication means? Do some children need help in seeing the relationship of 17 − 8 and 8 + 9? Do some children need to be taught that counting on from a number is quicker than counting each number? Which children need regular practice in order to master the facts? We can group them to meet individual needs (as suggested in Chapter 3) and provide activities and direct instruction to fill in the missing links and strengthen understanding and competency. The calculator can be one of the tools. Research has indicated that the development of basic facts is enhanced through calculator use.

Get Set: Presenting the Basic Facts

The emphasis in helping children to learn the basic facts is on aiding them in organizing their thinking and seeing relationships among the facts. Children should use strategies for remembering the facts prior to drill for memorizing them.

The basic facts have been classified as "easy" or "difficult" in a variety of studies (Suydam and Weaver 1981). But relative difficulty is not a simple matter to determine with accuracy; generally the facts with both addends or factors greater than five are more difficult for most children, but what is difficult for an individual child is really the important point. Although many textbooks, workbooks, and computer programs emphasize practice on the generally difficult facts, many also encourage the child to keep a record of those facts that are difficult for him or her and suggest extra practice on those. The teacher should suggest or reinforce this idea.

Some research has focused on the use of mathematical properties and analysis of relationships among the facts to determine the order in which to present them to children and ways of helping children understand them (Suydam and Weaver 1981). It should be kept in mind, however, that no one order for teaching the basic facts has been shown to be superior to any other order. Thus, the teacher can use professional judgment about what each group of children needs, choosing to use or not use the sequence in a given textbook.

How can the basic facts for an operation be organized meaningfully? Many textbooks present facts in small groups (for example, facts with sums to 6: 0 + 6 = 6, 1 + 5 = 6, 2 + 4 = 6, and so forth). Other textbooks organize the facts in "families" (for example, facts in the "2-3-5 family" are 3 + 2 = 5, 2 + 3 = 5, 5 – 3 = 2, and 5 – 2 = 3). Still other textbooks organize the facts by "thinking strategies" (for example, all facts where 1 is added, or containing "doubles" such as 7 + 7).

A variety of thinking strategies can be used to recall the answer to any given fact. Thinking strategies are efficient methods for determining answers on the basic facts. The more efficient the strategy, the more quickly the student will be able to construct the correct answer for the sum, difference, product, or quotient of two numbers and, eventually, memorize these facts so he or she can quickly recall them.

Research has shown that certain thinking strategies help children learn the basic facts (Rathmell 1978; Thornton and Smith 1988). Understanding of the facts develops in a series of stages characterized by the thinking children use. Some of these thinking strategies involve using concrete materials or counting. Others are more mature in the sense that a known fact is used to figure out an unknown fact. We want to help children develop these mature, efficient strategies to help them recall facts.

Many children rely heavily on counting—in particular, finger counting—and fail to develop more efficient ways of recalling basic facts. For example, a child may count 4 fingers and then 5 more to solve 4 + 5. This strategy is perfectly acceptable for a while. However, this counting process should not be repeated every time 4 + 5 is given. We want the child to move to counting on from 4, to thinking "4 + 4 = 8, so 4 + 5 is 9" or other strategies. Eventually, we want the child to memorize "4 + 5 = 9" for quick recall.

Some children discover new thinking strategies on their own, but many children need explicit instruction. In the following sections, thinking strategies and ways to teach them are illustrated.

Thinking Strategies for Addition Facts The one hundred basic facts for addition are shown in Figure 8–4. They are not presented to children in this completed form; rather, the children gradually and sys-

+	0	1	2	3	4	5	6	7	8	9
0	0	1	2	3	4	5	6	7	8	9
1	1	2	3	4	5	6	7	8	9	10
2	2	3	4	5	6	7	8	9	10	11
3	3	4	5	6	7	8	9	10	11	12
4	4	5	6	7	8	9	10	11	12	13
5	5	6	7	8	9	10	11	12	13	14
6	6	7	8	9	10	11	12	13	14	15
7	7	8	9	10	11	12	13	14	15	16
8	8	9	10	11	12	13	14	15	16	17
9	9	10	11	12	13	14	15	16	17	18

Figure 8–4 • The 100 basic facts for addition

tematically learn the facts and may fill in or check them off on the chart.

Lesson Card 8–3 presents questions that a teacher might use to help children see the orderliness of the basic addition facts. This overview will help children see their goal as they begin to memorize.

The thinking strategies that can be used when teaching basic addition facts include commutativity; adding 0, 1, and doubles; counting on; and adding to 10. For many facts, more than one strategy is appropriate.

1. *Commutativity* The task of learning the basic addition facts is simplified because of the commutative property. Changing the order of the addends does not affect the sum. Children encounter this idea when they note that 2 blue objects and 3 white objects form the same quantity as 3 blue objects and 2 white objects:

In work with the basic addition facts, children will see or write, for example:

$$\begin{array}{c} 2 \\ +5 \end{array} \quad \text{and} \quad \begin{array}{c} 5 \\ +2 \end{array}$$

or

$$2 + 5 = \boxed{} \quad \text{and} \quad 5 + 2 = \boxed{}$$

Lesson Card 8-3

The Big Picture

Materials: Activity sheet for each child; a transparency of it for use on the overhead projector.

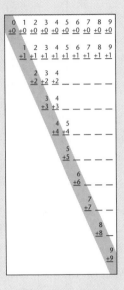

Activity: To discover the orderliness of the basic addition facts to be memorized.

▼ Ask each child to study carefully examples on the activity sheet.

- What is alike about the examples?
- What patterns are apparent?

▼ Discuss the top row of examples—those involving 0. Have the children fill in each of the sums.

▼ Discuss the second row of examples.

- Why isn't $\overset{0}{\underline{+1}}$ included? (It is in the top row).
- How can each sum be found quickly? (By counting on one).

▼ Look at the diagonal containing these facts:

0	1	2	3	4	5	6	7	8	9
+1	+1	+2	+3	+4	+5	+6	+7	+8	+9

- Find the sum.

▼ On the overhead projector, quickly fill in the remaining sums. Then focus attention on the entire table.

- What patterns are apparent?
- What is the largest sum? What are its addends?
- What is the smallest sum? What are its addends?
- Ask children to circle all examples whose sum is 8.
- Where are they?
- What patterns do you see in the addends?
- Why isn't $\overset{5}{\underline{+7}}$ in the chart?

▼ Continue discussing patterns as long as you feel your children are benefitting from the experience. Encourage the children to understand that all the basic facts to be memorized are included on this sheet.

We want them to realize that the same two numbers will have the same sum, no matter which comes first. We want them to be able to put this idea into their own words; they do not need to know the term *commutative property*. We want them to use the idea as they work with basic facts, not merely parrot a term.

We encourage the use of commutativity by using materials such as a chain of loops:

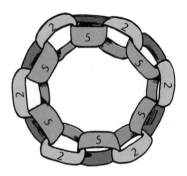

Have the children note that 5 is followed by 2 and 2 is followed by 5 all around the chain. The chain can be turned as they read and add:

$$5 + 2 = 7, \ 2 + 5 = 7, \ 5 + 2 = 7, \dots$$

The calculator also can help children verify that the order of the addends is irrelevant. Have them key into their calculators

$$5 + 8 = \qquad \text{and} \qquad 8 + 5 =$$

Use a variety of combinations, so the idea that the order does not affect the outcome becomes evident. Activity Card 8–6 presents another way of helping them develop and use the idea of commutativity.

The blank boxes in Figure 8–5 indicate that forty-five addition facts remain to be learned after children apply commutativity.

2. *Strategies for 0, 1, and Doubles* The strategy for *adding zero* applies to facts that have zero as one addend. These facts are learned as a generalization. Zero added to any number does not change the number. This idea follows from many concrete examples in which children see that any time they add "no more" (zero) they have the same amount. Activities then focus on this pattern:

○   1 + 0 = ☐   0 + 1 = ☐

○ ○   2 + 0 = ☐   etc.

○ ○ ○   3 + 0 = ☐

○ ○ ○ ○   4 + 0 = ☐

Activity Card 8–6 ✓

Arranging and Rearranging

▼ Use some counters and string for the rings to make this arrangement:

A   B

- How many counters are in Ring A? _____
- How many counters are in Ring B? _____

▼ Rearrange your counters and rings to show the same numbers, and then move 1 counter from Ring A to Ring B.

- How many counters are now in Ring A? _____
- How many counters are in Ring B? _____

▼ See how many different ways you can put 10 counters in the two rings.

- Use your counters and rings, and list the ways here:

  4+6   _____   _____   _____

  _____   _____   _____   _____

  _____   _____   _____

- Plot the ways you listed on graph paper:

Did you know that those x's are for 3 + 7 and 4 + 6?

+	0	1	2	3	4	5	6	7	8	9
0	0	1	2	3	4	5	6	7	8	9
1		2	3	4	5	6	7	8	9	10
2			4	5	6	7	8	9	10	11
3				6	7	8	9	10	11	12
4					8	9	10	11	12	13
5						10	11	12	13	14
6							12	13	14	15
7								14	15	16
8									16	17
9										18

Figure 8–5 • Addition facts derived by the commutative thinking strategy

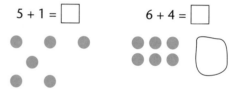

$5 + 1 = \boxed{}$ $6 + 4 = \boxed{}$

Recognition of the pattern is then encouraged:

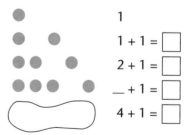

1

$1 + 1 = \boxed{}$

$2 + 1 = \boxed{}$

$\_ + 1 = \boxed{}$

$4 + 1 = \boxed{}$

Doubles are basic facts in which both addends are the same number, such as 4 + 4 or 9 + 9. Most children learn these facts quickly, often parroting them before they come to school. They can profit from work with objects followed by drawings:

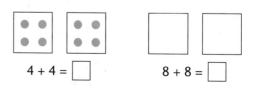

$4 + 4 = \boxed{}$ $8 + 8 = \boxed{}$

Adding one to a number is easy for most children. In fact, most learn this idea before they come to school, and they only have to practice the recognition and writing of it rather than develop initial understanding. To reinforce their initial concept, experiences with objects come first, followed by such paper-and-pencil activities as these:

Another strategy, *one more or one less* (sometimes called "near doubles"), can be used for the facts that are one more or one less than the doubles:

Think

$7 + 8 = \square$ $7 + 7 = 14$
So $7 + 8$ is one more.
$7 + 8 = 15$

Think

$7 + 6 = \square$ $7 + 7 = 14$
So $7 + 6$ is one less.
$7 + 6 = 13$

Lesson Card 8–4 shows one way of presenting this strategy.

The four thinking strategies in this section can be used with the addition facts shown in Figure 8–6.

+	0	1	2	3	4	5	6	7	8	9
0	0	1	2	3	4	5	6	7	8	9
1	1	2	3	4	5	6	7	8	9	10
2	2	3	4	5						
3	3	4	5	6	7					
4	4	5		7	8	9				
5	5	6			9	10	11			
6	6	7				11	12	13		
7	7	8					13	14	15	
8	8	9						15	16	17
9	9	10							17	18

Figure 8–6 ● **Addition facts derived by commutativity and the 0, 1, and doubles strategies**

Lesson Card 8–4

Nearly Double

Materials: Flannelboard or magnetic board and disks for each child

Activity: To develop the addition strategy of 1 more or 1 less with doubles.

▼ Have children put a group of 6 disks on the board:

▼ Have them add a second group of 6.

● How many in each group?

● How many in all?

▼ Have children add one more disk to the second group:

● How many in the first group?

● How many in the second group?

● How many in all?

▼ Write the equation on the chalkboard:

$6 + 7 = 13$

3. *Counting On* The strategy of *counting on* is most easily used when one of the addends is 1, 2, or 3. For example,

Think

$2 + 6 = \square$ $6 \ldots 7 \ldots 8$
$2 + 6 = 8$

Initially, children will probably count all objects in a group, as noted in Chapter 6.

1,   2,   3,   4,   5, . . .   6,   7,   8,

They need to learn to start with the larger addend, 5, and count on, 6, 7, 8. (Notice that understanding of the commutative property is assumed.) Research indicates that young children will count on, but not necessarily from the larger addend (Ginsberg 1977). Thus, the strategy must be taught to many children using activities such as this one:

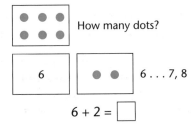

A ten-frame can also help in teaching this strategy:

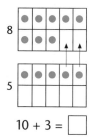

$$10 + 3 = \boxed{}$$

The research of Funkhouser (1995) indicates that working with the five-frames as a base and then moving to ten-frames may be particularly helpful for children with learning disabilities.

The counting-on strategy can be used with the addition facts noted in Figure 8–7.

4. *Adding to 10* With the strategy of *adding to 10*, one addend is increased and the other decreased, to make one of the addends 10. It is used most easily when one of the addends is 8 or 9, although some children also find it useful when adding 6 or 7. Here is an example:

Think

$8 + 5 = \boxed{}$ $8 + 2 = 10$, and $5 = 2 + 3$
So $10 + 3 = 13$, so
$8 + 5 = 13$

Children must know the sums to 10 well in order to use this strategy. Practice with regrouping to 10 is

needed to help them become proficient. They also need to realize that it is easier to add a number to 10 than to work with some other number. Which is easier?

$$10 + 5 \quad \text{or} \quad 9 + 6$$
$$7 + 8 \quad \text{or} \quad 5 + 10$$

As another example, change this problem to an easier one:

$$9 + 6 = \boxed{}$$

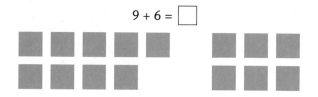

In all cases, talk the strategy through with drawings as well as objects:

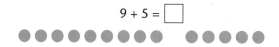

$8 + 4 = \boxed{}$ $10 + 2 = \boxed{}$

Similarly, put up objects showing 9 + 5, then remove 1:

$$9 + 5 = \boxed{}$$

Ask: "9 is close to what number that's easy to work with?" Have a child move one of the 5 objects to the group of 9:

Now,

$$10 + 4 = 14$$
$$\text{so} \longrightarrow 9 + 5 = \boxed{}$$

The adding-to-10 strategy can be used with the addition facts shown in Figure 8–8.

In many cases, more than one strategy can be used to aid in recalling a fact. This point should be made with the children. It encourages them to try

+	0	1	2	3	4	5	6	7	8	9
0										
1			2	3	4	5	6	7	8	9	10
2			3	4	5	6	7	8	9	10	11
3			4	5	6	7	8	9	10	11	12
4			5	6	7						
5			6	7	8						
6			7	8	9						
7			8	9	10						
8			9	10	11						
9			10	11	12						

Figure 8–7 • **Addition facts derived by the counting-on strategy**

+	0	1	2	3	4	5	6	7	8	9
0										
1										
2										11
3									11	12
4									12	13
5									13	14
6									14	15
7									15	16
8				11	12	13	14	15	16	17
9			11	12	13	14	15	16	17	18

Figure 8–8 • **Addition facts derived by the adding-to-10 strategy**

different ways of recalling a fact, and it may strengthen their understanding of the relationships involved. Notice from Figure 8–9 that, when the strategies for 0, 1, and doubles, counting on, and adding to 10 have been taught, only six basic facts remain. These missing facts can be derived using one of the strategies (and commutativity) or simply taught separately. Children form relationships, and almost all of the one hundred basic addition facts can be developed from relationships.

It also should be noted that children may invent strategies of their own, such as:

+	0	1	2	3	4	5	6	7	8	9
0	0	1	2	3	4	5	6	7	8	9
1	1	2	3	4	5	6	7	8	9	10
2	2	3	4	5	6	7	8	9	10	11
3	3	4	5	6	7	8	9	10	11	12
4	4	5	6	7	8	9			12	13
5	5	6	7	8	9	10	11		13	14
6	6	7	8	9		11	12	13	14	15
7	7	8	9	10			13	14	15	16
8	8	9	10	11	12	13	14	15	16	17
9	9	10	11	12	13	14	15	16	17	18

Figure 8–9 • **Addition facts derived by all thinking strategies for addition**

$$6 + 7 = \square$$

Think
6 is 5 + 1
7 is 5 + 2
So 10 + 3
13

$$6 + 8 = \square$$

Think
8 + 3 + 3
11 + 3
14

Encourage their ideas!

Thinking Strategies for Subtraction Facts For each basic addition fact, there is a related subtraction fact. In some mathematics programs, the two operations are taught simultaneously. The relationship between them is then readily emphasized, and learning of the basic facts for both operations proceeds as if they were in the same family. Even when they are not taught simultaneously, however, the idea of a fact family is frequently used (see Figure 8–10).

The addition facts form the major thinking strategy for learning and recalling the subtraction facts. Encourage children to recognize, think about, and use the relationships between addition and subtraction facts. For example,

$$15 - 7 = \square$$

Think
7 + 8 = 15
So 15 − 7 = 8

Other strategies for finding subtraction facts also can be taught: using 0 and 1, doubles, counting back, and counting on.

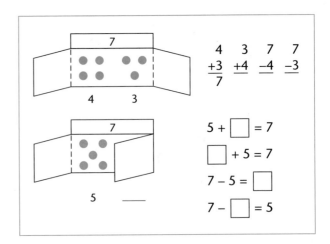

Figure 8–10 • **Examples of fact families**

1. *Using 0 and 1* As for addition, most children find it rather easy to learn the subtraction facts involving 0 and 1. They can profit from work with materials and from observing patterns similar to those used for addition facts.

2. *Doubles* The strategy for doubles may need to be taught more explicitly for subtraction facts than for addition facts. It rests on the assumption that children know the doubles for addition. Here is an example:

$$16 - 8 = \square$$

Think
$$8 + 8 = 16$$
$$16 - 8 = 8$$

3. *Counting Back* The strategy of counting back is most effectively used when the number to be subtracted is 1, 2, or 3:

$$9 - 3 = \square$$

Think
$$9 \ldots 8, 7, 6$$
$$9 - 3 = 6$$

As for other strategies, use problems and a variety of manipulative materials to help children gain facility in counting back from given numbers. Focus especially on the numbers involved in subtraction facts, as in the following examples.

Write the numbers in order backward:

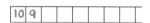

Write the numbers you say when you count back. Write the answer.

$$6 - 2 = \square$$

4. *Counting On* The strategy of counting on is used most easily when the difference is 1, 2, or 3:

$$8 - 6 = \square$$

Think
$$6 \ldots 7, 8$$
$$8 - 6 = 2$$

Activities for developing the strategy include the following:

Begin with 9. Count on until you reach 12. How many?

$$\begin{array}{c} 8 \\ -5 \end{array}$$

Begin with 5. Count on until you reach 8. How much?

The emphasis in using the counting-on strategy can also encompass adding on, "How much more would I need?" The child is encouraged to use the addition facts to reach the solution. This is particularly valuable with missing-addend situations, such as $6 + \square = 9$.

Thinking Strategies for Multiplication Facts
Multiplication is frequently viewed as a special case of addition in which all the addends are of equal size. The solution to multiplication problems can be attained by adding or counting, but multiplication is used because it is so much quicker.

Instruction on multiplication ideas begins in kindergarten as ideas about groups, numbers, and addition are developed. In grades 1 and 2, counting by twos, threes, fours, fives, tens, and possibly other numbers should be taught. Such expressions provide a basis for understanding the patterns that will occur with the basic multiplication facts. Use of the calculator as described in Chapter 6 can aid teachers in developing ideas about these patterns of multiplication. Using the constant function on calculators, children realize that two sixes equal 12, three sixes equal 18, and so on. The basic multiplication facts pair two one-digit factors with a product, as shown in Figure 8–11.

The basic multiplication facts should not be given to children in the form of a table or chart of facts until they have been meaningfully introduced. Rather, the facts should be developed through problem situations, experiences with manipulative and other materials, and the use of various thinking strategies. The table becomes the end result of this process of developing understanding of the operations and of the facts.

The thinking strategies for multiplication facts provide an efficient way for a child to attain each fact. These strategies include: commutativity, using

x	0	1	2	3	4	5	6	7	8	9
0	0	0	0	0	0	0	0	0	0	0
1	0	1	2	3	4	5	6	7	8	9
2	0	2	4	6	8	10	12	14	16	18
3	0	3	6	9	12	15	18	21	24	27
4	0	4	8	12	16	20	24	28	32	36
5	0	5	10	15	20	25	30	35	40	45
6	0	6	12	18	24	30	36	42	48	54
7	0	7	14	21	28	35	42	49	56	63
8	0	8	16	24	32	40	48	56	64	72
9	0	9	18	27	36	45	54	63	72	81

Figure 8–11 • The 100 basic multiplication facts

x	0	1	2	3	4	5	6	7	8	9
0	0	0	0	0	0	0	0	0	0	0
1		1	2	3	4	5	6	7	8	9
2			4	6	8	10	12	14	16	18
3				9	12	15	18	21	24	27
4					16	20	24	28	32	36
5						25	30	35	40	45
6							36	42	48	54
7								49	56	63
8									64	72
9										81

Figure 8–12 • Multiplication facts derived by the commutative thinking strategy

1 and 0, skip counting, repeated addition, splitting into known parts, and patterns.

1. *Commutativity* Commutativity applies to multiplication just as it does to addition. It is, therefore, a primary strategy for helping students learn the multiplication facts. Activity Cards 8–3 through 8–6 (presented earlier) emphasize this property. The calculator is also useful in reinforcing the idea. Children can multiply 4 × 6, then 6 × 4, for example, and realize that the answer to both is 24.

Here are some other examples:

$$3 \times 6 = 18 \longrightarrow 6 \times \square = 18$$

$$7 \times 5 = 35 \longrightarrow \square \times 7 = 35$$

After they have tried many combinations, they should be able to verbalize that the order of the factors is irrelevant. Figure 8–12 indicates that, as for addition, 45 of the multiplication facts remain to be learned after commutativity is applied.

2. *Using 0 and 1* The facts with zero and one are generally learned from initial work with multiplication. We want children to be able to generalize that "multiplying with 1 does not change the other number" and that "multiplying by 0 results in a product of 0." Figure 8–13 indicates the facts that can be learned with these strategies.

x	0	1	2	3	4	5	6	7	8	9
0	0	0	0	0	0	0	0	0	0	0
1	0	1	2	3	4	5	6	7	8	9
2	0	2								
3	0	3								
4	0	4								
5	0	5								
6	0	6								
7	0	7								
8	0	8								
9	0	9								

Figure 8–13 • Multiplication facts derived by strategies for 0 and 1

3. *Skip Counting* The strategy of skip counting works best for the multiples children know best, twos and fives, but it also may be applied to threes and fours (or other numbers) if children have learned to skip count by them.

Here is an example for 5:

$4 \times 5 = \square$ *Think* 5, 10, 15, 20 $4 \times 5 = 20$

The facts that can be established with the skip-counting strategy are noted in Figure 8–14.

4. *Repeated Addition* The strategy of repeated addition can be used most efficiently when one of the

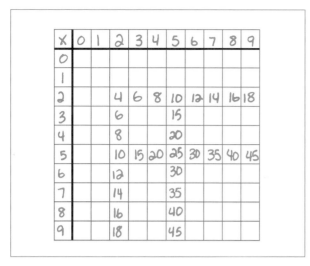

Figure 8–14 • **Multiplication facts derived by the skip-counting strategy**

factors is less than 5. The child changes the multiplication example to an addition example:

Think

$3 \times 6 = \square$ $6 + 6 + 6 = 18$
$3 \times 6 = 18$

Because this strategy is based on one interpretation of multiplication, children should have had many experiences with objects and materials. Drawings and the calculator can be used to provide additional experiences to help develop this strategy as well as the concept for the operation. Activity Card 8–7 illustrates these ideas.

In Figure 8–15, note the facts that can be learned with this strategy.

5. *Splitting the Product into Known Parts* As children gain assurance with some basic facts, they can use those facts to derive others. The strategy known as *splitting the product* is based on the distributive property of multiplication. It can be approached in terms of "one more set," "twice as much as a known fact," or "known facts of 5."

(a) The idea of *one more set* can be used for almost all multiplication facts. If one multiple of a number is known, the next multiple can be determined by adding a single-digit number:

Think

$8 \times 7 = \square$ $7 \times 7 = 49$
$8 \times 7 = 49 + 7$
$8 \times 7 = 56$

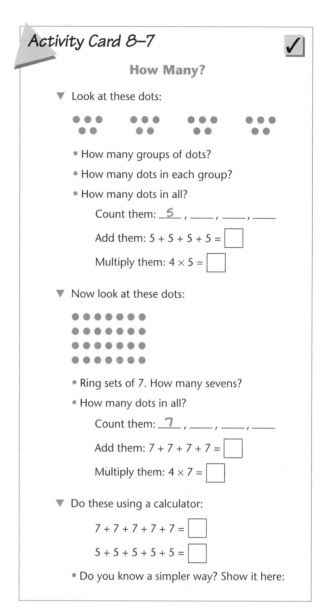

Each fact can be used to help learn the next multiple of either factor. The greatest difficulty arises when renaming is needed. Illustrating this strategy using an array model will be helpful:

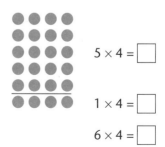

$5 \times 4 = \square$

$1 \times 4 = \square$

$6 \times 4 = \square$

X	0	1	2	3	4	5	6	7	8	9
0										
1										
2			4	6	8	10	12	14	16	18
3			6	9	12	15	18	21	24	27
4			8	12	16	20	24	28	32	36
5			10	15	20					
6			12	18	24					
7			14	21	28					
8			16	24	32					
9			18	27	36					

Figure 8–15 ● **Multiplication facts derived by the repeated addition strategy**

Ask children to name each part of the array and write the multiplication fact for the whole array.

(b) *Twice as much as a known fact* is a variation of the foregoing strategy. It can be applied to multiples of 4, 6, and 8, because an array with one of these numbers can be split in half. The product is twice as much as each half:

Think

$6 \times 8 = \square$ $3 \times 8 = 24$
6×8 is twice as much, or $24 + 24$
$6 \times 8 = 48$

Note, however, that a difficulty may arise when re-naming is needed. Again, using models will clarify this strategy:

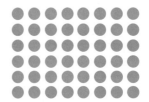

2 sevens is _____

2 sevens is _____

$4 \times 7 = \square$

In this case, children work with already-divided arrays.

As they progress, children can divide an array, such as the following; write about each part; and write the multiplication fact for the whole array.

(c) Working from *known facts of 5* also will aid children. It can be helpful for any problem with large factors but is most useful for multiples of 6 and 8. Five sixes or five eights is a multiple of 10, so it is rather easy to add on the remaining part.

For example,

Think

$7 \times 6 = \square$ $5 \times 6 = 30$
$2 \times 6 = 12$
So 7×6 is $30 + 12$, or 42.

To illustrate this strategy, the array is divided so that 5 sixes or eights (or some other number) are separated from the remaining portion:

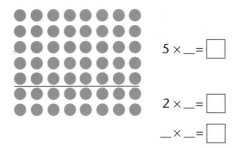

$5 \times \_\_ = \square$

$2 \times \_\_ = \square$

$\_\_ \times \_\_ = \square$

Call attention to how the array is divided. Have the children work with other arrays, determining when it seems reasonable to work with particular numbers. The facts that can be solved by splitting the product into known parts are shown in Figure 8–16.

The preceding strategies account for all the multiplication facts. One more is mentioned, however, because it can provide help with some difficult facts.

6. *Patterns* Finding patterns is helpful with a number of multiplication facts. One of the most useful aids concerns nines:

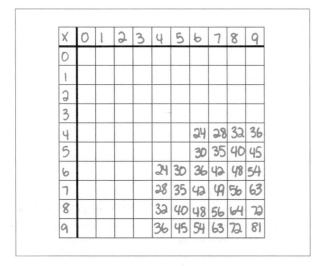

Figure 8–16 • **Multiplication facts derived by the strategy of splitting the product into known parts**

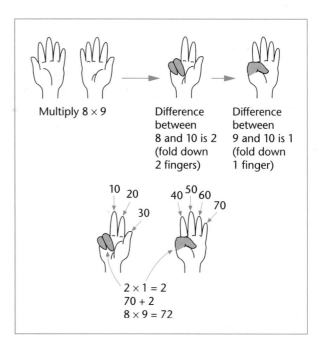

Figure 8–17 • **Finger multiplication**

$$1 \times 9 = 9 \qquad 0 + 9 = 9$$
$$2 \times 9 = 18 \qquad 1 + 8 = 9$$
$$3 \times 9 = 27 \qquad 2 + 7 = 9$$
$$4 \times 9 = 36 \qquad 3 + 6 = 9$$

The tens digit is 1 less than 4.   The *sum* of the digits of 36 is 9.

So for 5×9,

The tens digit is one less than $5 \longrightarrow 4$

The sum of the digits is 9, so $4 + \square = 9 \longrightarrow 5$

Thus, $5 \times 9 = 45$

Now try $7 \times 9 = \square$

Challenge children to find patterns in a table or chart such as the one in Figure 8–11. They should note, for instance, that the columns (and rows) for 2, 4, 6, and 8 contain all even numbers, and the columns for 1, 3, 5, 7, and 9 alternate even and odd numbers. You will probably find that children also enjoy "finger multiplication" (see Figure 8–17).

Thinking Strategies for Division Facts The teaching of division has consumed a large portion of time in the elementary school—so much that, with the increased use of calculators, some thought

has been given to reducing the attention accorded to it. Nevertheless, children will continue to need an understanding of the division process and the division facts. The facts help them to respond quickly to simple division situations and to understand better the nature of division and its relationship to multiplication.

The multiplication facts form the primary thinking strategy to aid children in understanding and recalling the division facts. Division is the inverse of multiplication; that is, a division problem seeks the unknown factor when the product and one factor are known. The multiplication table can be used for division facts.

Just as fact families can be developed for addition and subtraction, so can they be useful for multiplication and division:

$$8 \times 4 = 32$$
$$4 \times 8 = 32$$
$$32 \div 8 = 4$$
$$32 \div 4 = 8$$

Because of its relationship to multiplication, division can be stated in terms of multiplication:

$$42 \div 6 = \square \longrightarrow 6 \times \square = 42$$

Thus, children must search for the missing factor in the multiplication problem. Because multiplication facts are usually encountered and learned first, children can use what they know to learn the more difficult division facts. Moreover, division is related to subtraction, and division problems can be solved by repeated subtraction:

$$12 \div 3 = 12 - 3 - 3 - 3 - 3$$

$$12 \div 3 = 4$$

Four threes

However, repeated subtraction and the related strategies of counting backward or skip counting are confusing for many children. You may present them as ideas children might like to try, but don't be surprised if only a few children actually use them.

Think

$$15 \div 3 = \square$$

15 . . . 12, 9, 6, 3, 0
That's 5 numbers.
$15 \div 3 = 5$

Think

$$28 \div 7 = \square$$

$\left.\begin{array}{c} 28 - 7 \\ 21 - 7 \\ 14 - 7 \\ 7 - 7 \end{array}\right\}$ 4 subtractions

0
$28 \div 7 = 4$

Splitting the product into known parts relies heavily on knowledge of multiplication facts, as well as on the ability to keep in mind the component parts.

Think

$$35 \div 7 = \square$$

$2 \times 7 = 14$
$3 \times 7 = 21$
$14 + 21 = 35$
$2 + 3 = 5$
So $35 \div 7 = 5$

As with multiplication, work with arrays helps children to relate the symbols to the action.

In general, children have little difficulty in dividing by one. They need to exercise caution when zero is involved, however. Division by zero and division of zero present two different situations. We can divide 0 by 6 $(0 \div 6)$; the result is 0. We can check this by multiplying: $6 \times 0 = 0$. But division by zero cannot be checked.

For example, to solve $6 \div 0 = \square$ requires the solution of $6 = \square \times 0$. However, there is no value for $\square$ that would make this sentence true. Therefore, $6 \div 0$ has no solution, and division by zero is undefined in mathematics. Just as you may have difficulty remembering which is possible, division *of* 0 or division *by* 0, so will children have difficulty in remembering and need to be given practice.

Thus, thinking strategies for division are far more difficult for children to learn than are the strategies for the other operations. The child must remember more, and regrouping is often necessary. When skip counting, for instance, the child must keep track of the number of times a number is named even as the struggle to count backward proceeds. Therefore, the primary burden falls on the child's facility with the multiplication facts. Being able to recall those facts quickly will facilitate recall of the division facts.

Go: Mastering the Basic Facts

Consider this scene: Pairs of children are keying numbers on a calculator and passing it back and forth. Other pairs are seated at a table, some playing a card game and others playing board games. Several are busily typing numbers on computer keyboards. Still others are working individually with flashcards. What are they all doing? Probably they are practicing basic facts.

If children are to become skillful with the algorithms for addition, subtraction, multiplication, and division and proficient at estimation and mental computation, they must learn the basic facts to the level of immediate or automatic recall. When should this mastery level be attempted? As soon as children have a good understanding of the meanings of the operations and the symbols, the process of memorizing can begin. That is, as Ashlock and Washbon (1978) suggest, children should be able to:

● State or write related facts, given one basic fact

● Explain how they got an answer, or prove that it is correct

● Solve a fact in two or more ways

Research has shown that drill increases speed and accuracy on tests of basic facts (Wilson 1930). Activity Card 8–8 contains several interesting individual activities that provide drill practice for basic facts. However, drill alone will not change a child's

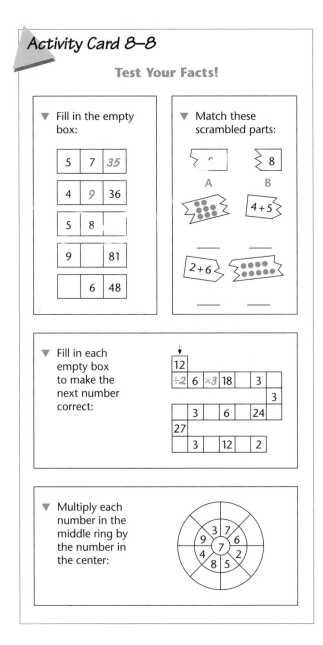

Activity Card 8–8

Test Your Facts!

▼ Fill in the empty box:

5	7	*35*

4	*9*	36

5	8	

9		81

	6	48

▼ Match these scrambled parts:

▼ Fill in each empty box to make the next number correct:

▼ Multiply each number in the middle ring by the number in the center:

---

dren should try to memorize only a few facts in a given lesson and should constantly review previously memorized facts.

- Children should develop confidence in their ability to memorize and should be praised for good efforts. Records of their progress should be kept.

- Drill activities should be varied, interesting, challenging, and presented with enthusiasm.

Computer software provides a natural complement to more traditional materials and activities, such as flashcards, games, and audiotaped practice, for establishing the quick recall of basic facts. For example, in Alien Intruder children encounter invading spaceships, each containing an addition problem. Children must provide the correct answer in order to "equalize" the spaceship before the aliens invade.

Most programs keep track of the number of exercises attempted and the number answered correctly. Some display the time taken to give correct answers, thus encouraging students to compete against their own records for speed as well as mastery. Requiring short response time (within four seconds) is very important, because it promotes efficient strategies and encourages children to memorize for quick recall.

Many children enjoy computer software that displays a cumulative record of their individual progress. This feature allows children to diagnose for themselves the basic facts they know and don't know. It also provides a source of motivation because each student can compete against himself or herself, with the goal of complete mastery always in mind.

When using flashcards, the child should go through the entire set and separate the cards into a pack of those known and a pack of those unknown. Each time the child works with the cards, he or she should review those in each pack, moving newly learned facts to the known pack. This approach makes progress evident.

Another point from research also must be taken into account: the frequency with which basic addition and multiplication facts occur in elementary school textbooks is probably a source of the difficulty. Facts with numbers larger than 5 occurred up to half as frequently as those in the range of 2 to 5; 0 and 1 occurred relatively infrequently. Thus, teachers need to assure that more practice is provided with facts involving 0, 1, and especially 6 through 9.

Several types of drill-and-practice procedures in the form of games are noted on Activity Cards 8–9

---

thinking strategies so that they become efficient. Drill will, therefore, be most effective when the child's thinking is already efficient.

Some principles for drill have been proposed, based on research with primary-grade children (Davis 1978):

- Children should attempt to memorize facts only after understanding is attained.

- Children should participate in drill with the intent to memorize. Remembering should be emphasized. This is not the time for explanations.

- Drill lessons should be short (five to ten minutes) and should be given almost every day. Chil-

Activity Card 8–9

Match Up!

▼ Use a set of at least 30 basic subtraction fact cards like these:

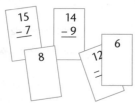

▼ Follow these rules:

- The leader deals 5 cards to each player and puts the rest of the cards in the center of the table.
- Players take turns and try to make pairs by matching an example card with an answer card. When a player has a pair, he or she puts them down during a turn.
- Each player may draw 1 card from the center during a turn. When the center cards are gone, the player may draw 1 card from the player to the right.

When all the cards are used, the player with the most pairs is the winner!

Activity Card 8–10

Addition Bingo!

▼ Each player needs a different Bingo card and some buttons or macaroni for markers.

The leader needs a pack of cards like these with all possible combinations (basic facts).

▼ It's easy to play:

- The leader draws a card and reads the addends on it.
- Each player covers the sum on his or her Bingo card.

Not all sums are given on each card.

Some sums are given more than once on a Bingo card, but a player may cover only one answer for each pair of addends.

The winner is the first person with 5 markers in a row!

Activity Card 8–11

Multig

▼ Use the playing board here or make a larger one on heavy construction paper. Each player needs some buttons, macaroni, or chips for markers.

Don't forget the spinner. You can't play this game without it!

1. Take turns. Spin twice. Multiply the 2 numbers. Find the answer on the board. Put a marker on it.

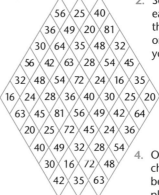

2. Score 1 point for each covered ◇ that touches a side or corner of the ◇ you cover.

3. If you can't find an uncovered ◇ to cover, you lose your turn.

4. Opponents may challenge any time before the next player spins.

5. The winner is the player with the most points at the end of 10 rounds.

through 8–13. Children in all age groups find such games an enjoyable way to practice what they know. These activities supplement the many other drill-and-practice procedures that you will find in textbooks, journals, computer software, and other sources.

▶ A Glance at Where We've Been

Skill in computation with whole numbers is developed through concrete experiences. In this chapter the prerequisites of counting, concrete experiences,

Activity Card 8–12

Zero Wins!

▼ Make two identical sets of 19 cards with a number from 0 to 18 on each!

▼ Follow these rules:

* After shuffling, the leader deals 4 cards to each player and puts the remaining cards face down in the center of the table.

* Players must add or subtract the numbers on their 4 cards so they equal 0. For example, suppose you had these cards:

6	10	2	6

$$10 - 6 = 4 \quad \text{or} \quad 6 + 6 = 12$$
$$4 + 2 = 6 \qquad\qquad 12 - 12 = 2$$
$$6 - 6 = 0 \qquad\qquad 2 - 2 = 0$$

* On each round of play, the players may exchange one card if they wish, and each player takes a turn being first to exchange a card on a round. To make an exchange, the first player draws a card and discards a card, face up. Other players can draw from either the face-down pile or the face-up discard pile.

The first player to get 0 on a round wins the round!

Activity Card 8–13

21 or Bust!

▼ Play this game with a partner:

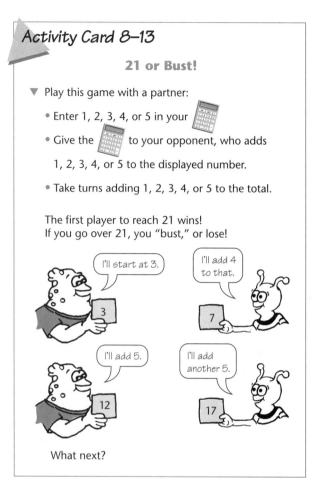

and language were considered, and models for each operation were described. Mathematical properties to be developed as part of the understanding of the operations were presented.

The remainder of the chapter focused on the basic facts for each operation. Starting from what children know, the facts are developed using experiences that range from concrete to pictorial to symbolic. Thinking strategies for the basic facts for each operation help children move from counting to more mature, efficient ways of developing the facts. Finally, ways to help children master the basic facts for quick recall were discussed, with specific suggestions for drills and activities to provide practice and promote mastery.

▶ THINGS TO DO: From What You've Read

1. What are the four or five most important guidelines you should follow in helping children learn the basic facts?

2. Discuss each of these statements:
   (a) When you teach multiplication, you begin preparation for learning division.
   (b) Children should not be allowed to count on their fingers when they start addition.
   (c) With the wide use of calculators, there is little need for children to attain prompt recall of the basic facts.

3. What prerequisites must children have before being taught the lesson that opens this chapter?

4. What properties of addition and multiplication are especially helpful in teaching the basic facts?

5. Describe the thinking strategies a child might use with the following:

$$8 + 0 = \boxed{}$$

$$18 \div 3 = \boxed{}$$

$$8 \times 5 = \boxed{}$$

$$16 - 7 = \boxed{}$$

$$7 + 8 = \boxed{}$$

6. When is counting back an effective strategy for subtraction?

▶ **THINGS TO DO:
Going Beyond This Book**

1. List the specific thinking steps a child goes through in using a doubles strategy to find the sum of 9 + 4.

2. Design an activity that provides practice on basic division facts.

3. Plan a bulletin board to help children learn about one or more thinking strategies for subtraction.

4. Find a vignette or game in *Professional Standards for Teaching Mathematics* (NCTM 1991) that focuses on basic facts. Share the ideas you find.

5. Consider the activity described in "Problem Solving with Combinations" (English 1992). How is it related to ideas presented in this chapter?

6. Select one of the books listed in the Children's Corner, and read it to some children. Describe their reactions.

▼▼▼▼▼▼▼▼▼▼▼▼▼▼▼▼▼▼▼▼▼▼▼

Children's Corner

Burningham, John. *Pigs Plus*. New York: Viking Press, 1983.

Burningham, John. *Ride Off*. New York: Viking Press, 1983.

Butler, M. Christina. *Too Many Eggs*. Boston: David R. Godine Publisher, 1988.

Calmenson, Stephanie. *Ten Furry Monsters*. New York: Parents Magazine Press, 1984.

Charosh, Mannis. *Number Ideas Through Pictures*. New York: Crowell, 1974.

Enderle, Judith Ross, and Tessler, Stephanie Gordon. *Six Creepy Sheep*. Honesdale, Pa.: Boyds Mills Press, 1992.

Gerstein, Mordicai. *Roll Over!* New York: Crown Publishers, 1984.

Gretz, Susanna. *Teddy Bears 1 to 10*. New York: Four Winds Press, 1986.

Hawkins, Colin. *Adding Animals*. New York: G. P. Putnam's Sons, 1983.

Hawkins, Colin. *Take Away Monsters*. New York: G. P. Putnam's Sons, 1984.

Hawkins, Colin, and Hawkins, Jacqui. *How Many Are in This Old Car?* New York: G. P. Putnam's Sons, 1988.

Hulme, Joy N. *Counting by Kangaroos: A Multiplication Concept Book*. New York: Scientific American Books for Young Readers, 1995.

Moerbeck, Kees, and Kijs, Carla. *Six Brave Explorers*. Los Angeles: Price Stern Sloan, 1988.

Owen, Annie. *Annie's One to Ten*. New York: Knopf, 1988.

Punnett, Dick. *Count the Possums*. Elgin, Ill.: Child's World, 1982.

Sendak, Maurice. *One Was Johnny*. New York: Harper & Row, 1962.

Srivastava, Jane Jonas. *Number Families*. New York: Crowell, 1979.

Selected References

Ashcraft, Mark H., and Christy, Kelly S. "The Frequency of Arithmetic Facts in Elementary Texts: Addition and Multiplication in Grades 1–6." *Journal for Research in Mathematics Education*, 26 (November 1995), pp. 396–421.

Ashlock, Robert B. *Error Patterns in Computation*, 6th ed. New York: Merrill, 1994.

Ashlock, Robert B., and Washbon, Carolynn A. "Games: Practice Activities for the Basic Facts." In *Developing Computational Skills*, 1978 Yearbook (ed. Marilyn N. Suydam). Reston, Va.: NCTM, 1978, pp. 39–50.

Baratta-Lorton, Mary. *Mathematics Their Way*. Reading, Mass.: Addison-Wesley, 1976.

Baroody, Arthur J., and Standifer, Dorothy J. "Addition and Subtraction in the Primary Grades." In *Research Ideas for the Classroom: Early Childhood Mathematics* (ed. Robert J. Jensen). Reston, Va.: NCTM, and New York: Macmillan, 1993, pp. 72–102.

Bruni, James V., and Silverman, Helene. "Let's Do It!: Making and Using Board Games." *Arithmetic Teacher*, 22 (March 1975), pp. 172–179.

Campbell, Melvin D. "Basic Facts Drill—Card Games." *Arithmetic Teacher*, 36 (April 1989), pp. 41–43.

Carey, Deborah A. "Students' Use of Symbols." *Arithmetic Teacher,* 40 (February 1992), pp. 184–186.

Carpenter, Thomas P.; Corbitt, Mary Kay; Kepner, Henry S., Jr.; Lindquist, Mary Montgomery; and Reys, Robert E. *Results from the Second Mathematics Assessment of the National Assessment of Educational Progress.* Reston, Va.: NCTM, 1981.

Clark, Faye B., and Kamii, Constance. "Identification of Multiplicative Thinking in Children in Grades 1–5." *Journal for Research in Mathematics Education,* 27 (January 1996), pp. 41–51.

Davis, Edward J. "Suggestions for Teaching the Basic Facts of Arithmetic." In *Developing Computational Skills,* 1978 Yearbook (ed. Marilyn N. Suydam). Reston, Va.: NCTM, 1978, pp. 51–60.

English, Lyn. "Problem Solving with Combinations." *Arithmetic Teacher,* 40 (October 1992), pp. 72–77.

Feinberg, Miriam M. "Using Patterns to Practice Basic Facts." *Arithmetic Teacher,* 37 (April 1990), pp. 38–41.

Folsom, Mary. "Operations on Whole Numbers." In *Mathematics Learning in Early Childhood,* Thirty-seventh Yearbook (ed. Joseph N. Payne). Reston, Va.: NCTM, 1975, pp. 162–190.

Funkhouser, Charles. "Developing Number Sense and Basic Computational Skills in Students with Special Needs." *School Science and Mathematics,* 95 (May 1995), pp. 236–239.

Gibb, E. Glenadine. "Children's Thinking in the Process of Subtraction." *Journal of Experimental Education,* 25 (September 1956), pp. 71–80.

Ginsberg, Herbert. *Children's Arithmetic: The Learning Process.* New York: Van Nostrand Reinhold, 1977.

Golden, Sarah R. "Fostering Enthusiasm through Child-Created Games." *Arithmetic Teacher,* 17 (February 1970), pp. 111–115.

Kouba, Vicky L., and Franklin, Kathy. "Multiplication and Division: Sense Making and Meaning." In *Research Ideas for the Classroom: Early Childhood Mathematics* (ed. Robert J. Jensen). Reston, Va.: NCTM, and New York: Macmillan, 1993, pp. 103–126.

Kouba, Vicky L., and Franklin, Kathy. "Research into Practice: Multiplication and Division: Sense Making and Meaning." *Teaching Children Mathematics,* 1 (May 1995), pp. 574–577.

Leutzinger, Larry P., and Nelson, Glenn. "Using Addition Facts to Learn Subtraction Facts." *Arithmetic Teacher,* 27 (December 1979), pp. 8–13.

Litwiller, Bonnie H., and Duncan, David R. *Activities for the Maintenance of Computational Skills and the Discovery of Patterns.* Reston, Va.: NCTM, 1980.

National Council of Teachers of Mathematics. *Curriculum and Evaluation Standards for School Mathematics.* Reston, Va.: NCTM, 1989.

National Council of Teachers of Mathematics. *Professional Standards for Teaching Mathematics.* Reston, Va.: NCTM, 1991.

Page, Anita. "Helping Students Understand Subtraction." *Teaching Children Mathematics,* 1 (November 1994), pp. 140–143.

Quintero, Ana Helvia. "Conceptual Understanding of Multiplication: Problems Involving Combination." *Arithmetic Teacher,* 33 (November 1985), pp. 36–39.

Quintero, Ana Helvia. "Children's Conceptual Understanding of Situations Involving Multiplication." *Arithmetic Teacher,* 33 (January 1986), pp. 34–37.

Rathmell, Edward C. "Using Thinking Strategies to Teach the Basic Facts." In *Developing Computational Skills,* 1978 Yearbook (ed. Marilyn N. Suydam). Reston, Va.: NCTM, 1978, pp. 13–38.

Remington, Jim. "Introducing Multiplication." *Arithmetic Teacher,* 37 (November 1989), pp. 12–14, 60.

Reys, Robert E.; Bestgen, Barbara J.; Coburn, Terrence G.; Schoen, Harold L.; Shumway, Richard J.; Wheatley, Charlotte L.; Wheatley, Grayson H.; and White, Arthur L. *Keystrokes: Calculator Activities for Young Students: Addition and Subtraction, Multiplication and Division.* Palo Alto, Calif.: Creative Publications, 1980.

Rightsel, Pamela S., and Thornton, Carol A. "72 Addition Facts Can Be Mastered by Mid-Grade 1." *Arithmetic Teacher,* 33 (November 1985), pp. 8–10.

Romberg, Thomas A.; Harvey, John G.; Moser, James M.; and Montgomery, Mary E. *Developing Mathematical Processes.* Chicago: Rand McNally, 1974–1976.

Shoecraft, Paul. " 'Equals' Means 'Is the Same As' " *Arithmetic Teacher,* 36 (April 1989), pp. 36–40.

Sowell, Evelyn J. "Effects of Manipulative Materials in Mathematics Instruction." *Journal for Research in Mathematics Education,* 20 (November 1989), pp. 498–505.

Sundar, Viji K. "Thou Shalt Not Divide by Zero." *Arithmetic Teacher,* 37 (March 1990), pp. 50–51.

Suydam, Marilyn N., and Higgins, Jon L. *Activity-Based Learning in Elementary School Mathematics: Recommendations from Research.* Columbus, Ohio: ERIC Clearinghouse for Science, Mathematics, and Environmental Education, 1977.

Suydam, Marilyn N., and Weaver, J. Fred. *Using Research: A Key to Elementary School Mathematics.* Columbus, Ohio: ERIC Clearinghouse for Science, Mathematics, and Environmental Education, 1981.

Thiessen, Diane, and Matthais, Margaret. *The Wonderful World of Mathematics: A Critically Annotated List of Children's Books in Mathematics.* Reston, Va.: NCTM, 1992.

Thompson, Charles S., and Dunlop, William P. "Basic Facts: Do Your Children Understand or Do They Memorize?" *Arithmetic Teacher,* 25 (December 1977), pp. 14–16.

Thompson, Charles S., and Van de Walle, John. "Modeling Subtraction Situations." *Arithmetic Teacher,* 32 (October 1984), pp. 8–12.

Thompson, Charles S., and Van de Walle, John. "The Power of Ten." *Arithmetic Teacher,* 32 (November 1984), pp. 6–11.

Thornton, Carol. "Strategies for the Basic Facts." In *Mathematics for the Young Child* (ed. Joseph N. Payne). Reston, Va.: NCTM, 1990, pp. 133–151.

Thornton, Carol A. " 'Look Ahead' Activities Spark Success in Addition and Subtraction Number Fact Learning." *Arithmetic Teacher,* 36 (April 1989), pp. 8–11.

Thornton, Carol A., and Smith, Paula J. "Action Research: Strategies for Learning Subtraction Facts." *Arithmetic Teacher,* 35 (April 1988), pp. 8–12.

Trafton, Paul R., and Zawojewski, Judith S. "Meanings of Operations." *Arithmetic Teacher,* 38 (November 1990), pp. 18–22.

Wills, Herbert. "Diffy." *Arithmetic Teacher,* 18 (October 1971), pp. 402–405.

Wilson, Guy M. "New Standards in Arithmetic: A Controlled Experiment in Supervision." *Journal of Educational Research,* 22 (December 1930), pp. 351–360.

9

Computational Alternatives—
The Need to Reach a Balance

 ## Snapshot of a Lesson

Third graders are working at tables in small groups. At each table paper, pencils, and calculators are available. Mr. Diggs has placed four items at the front of the room (prices also shown on the board) for all the children to see. The focus of the lesson is to provide opportunities to use different computational tools.

MR. DIGGS: "Here are some things you can buy. Please choose any two of them. Decide how much money the items you chose would cost." He waits until children have decided. He also observes how children are doing their computations. When computations are completed, Mr. Diggs says: "Make a list of the money spent in your group and then have a reporter from your group write the totals on the board.

After a few minutes, this list is compiled:

Amounts spent:	$0.50	$0.75	$1.00	$1.98
Number of Students:	8	6	9	4

MR. DIGGS: "Many of you spent $1.00. Why do you think $1 was so popular?"

WHITNEY: "Because we like apples—I'm hungry and could eat two apples."

MR. DIGGS: "I am hungry too, and wish that I had a couple of apples. Is there another reason? Justin, what do you think?"

JUSTIN: "Because it is easy to add 50 cents plus 50 cents."

WILLIAM: "I think it's easy to add 25 cents plus 25 cents. That is why I got 50 cents."

SARAH: "It is also easy to add 50 cents and 25 cents."

JUSTIN: "Easiest for me is 50 cents plus 50 cents because it makes a dollar."

This discussion provides insight into what computations are easy for the children and confirms Mr. Diggs' observation that the children did these computations mentally. He then moves the discussion to another sum that was reported.

MR. DIGGS: "Four people spent $1.98. Would someone tell me what you bought and how you decided it was $1.98?"

AARON: "I bought two pens. Each cost $0.99, so that if it was one penny more, it would be a dollar. Two of them would make two dollars—minus 2 cents, that's $1.98."

KELLY: "I did it a little differently. I knew that one more penny would make $0.99 a dollar. So I took one penny from the $0.99 and made it $0.98 and added one dollar to it to get $1.98."

ROBERT: "I couldn't hold the numbers in my head so I used paper and pencil."

MR. DIGGS: "That sounds like another good way to get the answer."

BARBARA: "I used a calculator. Is that okay?"

MR. DIGGS: "Barbara, you can use the calculator whenever you need it, but try to do it in your head first. If it is too hard to do in your head, then try doing it a different way, as Robert did."

Mr. Diggs wants to move this activity along to develop more number sense and include estimation. He asks, "Suppose I spent more than $3, what two items could I buy?"

WHITNEY: "Four pens would be almost $4."

MR. DIGGS: "That's right, Whitney, but I asked you to buy only two things."

LINDSEY: "You could buy two toys."

MR. DIGGS: "Lindsey, tell us more about how you decided two toys."

LINDSEY: "Well—I thought $1.67 is more than one and a half dollars. I know that one plus one is two and two halves make another dollar, so that makes three dollars. So it must be more than three dollars but less than four."

MR. DIGGS: "Good thinking. It often helps to decide what is the most and least that could be possible when we compute. Why do you think no one chose to buy two toys?"

Mr. Diggs anticipates an answer that the prices of the toys are hard to compute, but asks this question to refocus the discussion on how we decide what computational tools to use. He plans to ask for other possibilities, such as a pen and a toy, and observe the strategies the children use. These activities give him insight into how his students are thinking and the level of confidence, as well as skill, his students have with various tools.

 ## Introduction

Computation has evolved from using counting and calculating devices, such as piles of stones in ancient times or using a soroban in Japan, to using written computational algorithms. More recently the calculator has become available, and no computational tool has the power for greater impact on school mathematics.

The alternative computational tools of estimation, mental computation, calculator computation, and written computation are each useful and important. Historically, elementary school mathematics has emphasized written computation far more than the other tools. This, together with the fact that learners are more likely to select tools with which they are familiar, means that students will often tend to use written computation even though other more efficient computational options exist.

A better balance of instructional attention to these tools needs to be established so children can learn to make appropriate computational tool choices. In order to make this happen, we must recognize and teach that different options are available for doing computation. One insightful view of computation is shown in Figure 9–1. It illustrates that all computation begins with a problem situation involving calculation and then highlights the series of decision-making stages that must be completed

when doing computation. To summarize the diagram in Figure 9–1, in the NCTM *Standards* it is maintained that:

> when one needs to calculate to find an answer to a problem, one should be aware of the choices of methods. When an approximate answer is adequate, one should estimate. If a precise answer is needed, an appropriate procedure must be chosen. Many problems should be solved by mental calculation. Some calculations, if not too complex, should be solved by following standard paper-and-pencil algorithms. For more complex calculations, the calculator should be used. (1989, p. 8)

In every computational situation, one must decide what type of result is needed and how that result will be produced. Thus, important goals of mathematics learning related to computation are to help people:

- Develop competence with each of the computational tools

- Make wise choices among the computational tools available

- Choose tools which are consistent with the computation desired and ability to use that tool

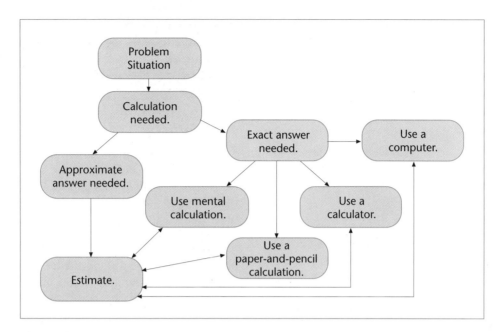

Figure 9–1 • **Decisions about calculation procedures in numerical problems**
(From *Curriculum and Evaluation Standards for School Mathematics*, NCTM 1989. Used by permission.)

- Apply the tool chosen correctly
- Use number sense to determine the reasonableness of an answer (result) for the particular problem being solved

● Computational Tools

Helping students select and use appropriate computational tools is an important goal of elementary mathematics. Furthermore, we need to think about what computations are needed and important enough to learn in school, and how instructional time should be directed. Research reports that more than eighty percent of all mathematical computations in daily life involve mental computation and estimation of numerical quantities rather than written computation. Ironically, research in the United States also shows that seventy to ninety percent of the instructional time in elementary school mathematics directed toward computation has focused on written computation procedures (Sowder 1992).

Many proposals have been made regarding computation, ranging from prohibiting calculator use to eliminating the teaching of written algorithms. NCTM recommends that:

> the availability of calculators does not eliminate the need for students to learn algorithms. Some

proficiency with paper-and-pencil computational algorithms is important, but such knowledge should grow out of the problem situations that have given rise to the need for such algorithms. (1989, p. 8)

Most people recognize the importance of each of the computational tools, and suggest that a redistribution of instructional time is needed. We strongly support a better balance of instructional time for the computational alternatives than has historically occurred in elementary schools. What percentage of time to devote to each tool remains an unanswered question and will certainly depend on the developmental levels of the students.

While we feel strongly that significant changes in the time devoted to computational alternatives are needed, we recognize that the specific percentages are open to debate. In the spirit of stimulating debate and discussion, please consider Figure 9–2; this depicts an approximation of what has happened in the past, the current situation, and our proposal for a better balance.

Any future prediction is subject to error. Thus, the percentage of time devoted to these tools is subject to question and challenge. Nevertheless, the decline in attention to standard written algorithms over the years and into the future is indisputable. Instructional time previously devoted to developing

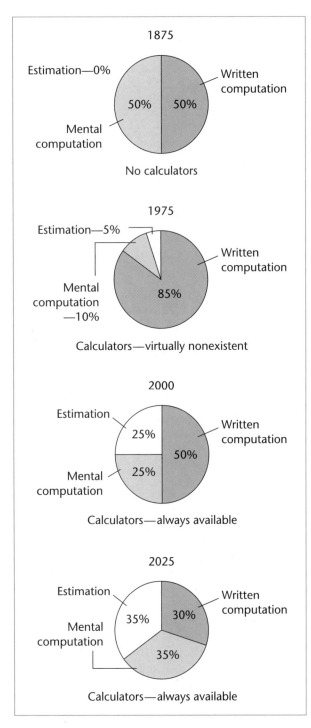

1875

Estimation—0%

Mental computation 50%

Written computation 50%

No calculators

1975

Estimation—5%

Mental computation —10%

Written computation 85%

Calculators—virtually nonexistent

2000

Estimation 25%

Mental computation 25%

Written computation 50%

Calculators—always available

2025

Estimation 35%

Mental computation 35%

Written computation 30%

Calculators—always available

Figure 9–2 • **How time devoted to computation in elementary school is spent**

proficiency with written algorithms will become available for other uses. We anticipate that much of this time will be dedicated to developing increased number sense together with greater attention to the other computational tools, calculators, mental com-

putation, and estimation. Reflecting on your experience and thinking about the future needs of your students will challenge you to develop ways of providing a proper balance in your computation instruction.

Calculators

The NCTM position statement on calculators has recommended that "appropriate calculators should be available to all students at all times." This statement suggests that, as the mathematical knowledge of students grows, their uses of calculators will change. Children outgrow calculators just as they outgrow shoes. The calculator needs of students in primary grades are different from those of students in the intermediate grades and middle school. The technology industry has anticipated these changing needs with the development of fraction calculators, scientific calculators, and graphing calculators.

Even though calculators have been in schools for over twenty years, several myths continue to exist. One myth is that calculator use does not require thinking. As teachers, we must make it clear to parents that calculators don't think—they only follow instructions. Consider the following problem:

A bus holds 36 children. If 1,000 children are being bused to a concert, how many buses are needed?

Suppose a calculator is available. Does the calculator decide which keys to press and in what order to press them? Does the calculator interpret the result? The answer to both questions is no!

Research shows this problem is difficult to solve with or without a calculator. An answer of 27.7777 buses is frequently reported with a calculator! Children intent on producing an answer without reflecting on reasonableness are likely to get answers that don't make sense. Calculators don't discourage thinking!

Neither does the use of calculators harm students' mathematics achievement, another myth that continues to linger. Research has addressed this issue and consistently reported that the use of "calculators in concert with traditional instruction . . . can improve the average student's basic skills with paper and pencil, both in basic operations and in problem solving" (Hembree and Dessart 1992). Moreover, "students using calculators possess a better attitude toward mathematics and an especially better self-concept in mathematics." Many parents and some teachers worry that students will become so dependent on calculators that they won't learn to compute. Research shows that is not the case. As teachers, we must not only make effective use of calculators in our teaching, but also help any skeptics put their fears to rest.

We recognize that computational skills must be learned, and view the calculator as a useful tool in this process. Our recommendation is that calculators be used whenever computation is needed and computational skills are not the main focus of instruction. Clearly the establishment of basic facts must remain an important goal of primary grades. Basic facts are natural stepping stones to mental computation and estimation, and to the long-term development of number sense. It is essential that rapid recall of basic facts (for example, 4×7, $8 + 6$) be an instructional goal. However, as suggested previously, calculators can be used to facilitate basic fact learning in many meaningful ways which encourage students to think.

When is calculator use appropriate? The NCTM *Standards* say that calculators should be available all the time for students in elementary school. Many teachers are unsure how to use calculators with their students. Some resort to unproductive uses of the calculator such as having students turn the calculator upside down to spell words or using the calculator to check written calculations. These activities may be somewhat motivational, but their educational value is questionable. They may communicate the message that a calculator is only for playing games or, even worse, that using a calculator is cheating and should only be used after written computation. Research shows that the more teachers use calculators in their classroom, the more they develop creative and productive ways to use them (Fey 1992). We feel that a calculator should be used as a *computational tool* when it:

1. Facilitates problem solving
2. Relieves tedious computation
3. Focuses attention on meaning
4. Removes anxiety about computational failures
5. Provides motivation and confidence

The NCTM *Standards* make an interesting analogy between using calculators for doing mathematics and word processors for writing. Both are "tools that simplify, but do not accomplish, the work at hand" (1989, p. 8). In fact, a very strong argument can be made that using a calculator actually increases student thinking. More specifically, using a calculator frees students from tedious and laborious computation and allows them to dwell on the important problem-solving processes that generally precede, and often follow, the computation.

In addition to making calculators available as a computational tool, the calculator also can be used productively as an instructional tool. Suggestions for how to do this may be found in the teacher's editions of most textbooks; there are also many resource books available that illustrate the use of the calculator as an instructional tool. Several are listed at the end of this chapter. We believe that a calculator should be used as an *instructional tool* when it:

1. Facilitates a search for patterns
2. Creates problematic situations
3. Supports concept development
4. Promotes number sense
5. Encourages creativity and exploration

Be on the lookout for examples of these types of calculator activities integrated throughout this book.

In addition to making clear and direct statements calling for the use of calculators, some recommendations also have called for helping children learn to make appropriate computational tool choices. For example, a report by the National Research Council suggests:

> Children should use calculators throughout their school work, just as adults use calculators throughout their lives. More important, children must learn when to use them and when not to do so. They must learn from experience with calculators when to estimate and when to seek an exact answer; how to estimate answers to verify the plausibility of calculator results; and how to solve modest problems mentally when neither pencil nor calculator is convenient. (1989, p. 47)

When introducing the calculator to our students we can provide experiences that will help them make appropriate use of the tool. As with any new manipulative, we should provide time for students to explore with the calculator on their own and discuss rules for handling and caring for them. We can demonstrate that:

1. Calculators do not think for themselves
2. Not all problems can be solved with a calculator
3. It is sometimes faster to compute mentally

Communicating with parents, so that they understand what is happening and why, is important. Often a simple note to parents (see Figure 9–3) is

Dear Parents:

We are using calculators in our second grade class this year in many different ways. Sometimes we use them to develop skills in counting and recognizing patterns; other times to explore new topics, such as decimals; and often when solving problems that require tedious computations. Research suggests that a variety of early experiences with calculators will help young children make wise use of calculators both in and out of school.

If you have questions about how we are using calculators, please ask your child to share some things they have been doing with this tool. If you have further questions, please let me know.

Figure 9–3 ● **A sample note to parents about calculators in primary grades**

effective. This note serves several useful purposes. It establishes communication between teacher and parents. It also lets parents know that calculators will be used in their child's classroom and tells why they are being used. Learning how and when to use calculators as well as other computational alternatives, such as estimation, mental computation, and written computation, is an important goal for every mathematics program.

Mental Computation

Mental computation is done without the aid of external tools. This sounds simple enough, and it certainly is a natural way to do many computations. The naturalness of "doing it in your head" is demonstrated in the Snapshot at the beginning of this chapter as well as by the fact that many young children (before being able to write) have already developed ways of computing. In fact, research has documented a wide variety of creative mental computation techniques that children have constructed (Cobb and Merkel 1989; Kamii et al. 1993).

Doing mental computation builds onto and naturally extends thinking strategies used to develop basic facts that were discussed in the previous chapter. Extending basic facts is an early step in developing more powerful mental computation strategies and skills. For example, the basic fact 4×6 could serve as a foundation or stepping stone for many mental computations, such as:

4×600 is 4×6 hundreds, which is 24 hundreds, or 2,400.

$4 \times 6,000$ is 4×6 thousand, which is 24 thousands, or 24,000.

These extended facts build on basic facts, place-value concepts, and suggest different patterns and relationships in the process. Mental computation together with calculators can be used to explore a range of patterns that suggest different relationships and may stimulate conjectures and discoveries. As patterns emerge, students can explore relationships between:

4×6 and 4×60 and 4×600 and $4 \times 6,000$

Students can tell how these results are alike and how they are different. A slightly different exploration can be generated by challenging students to

"Tell why these are the same."

$4 \times 600 \quad 40 \times 60 \quad 400 \times 6 \quad 4,000 \times 0.6$

Doing mental computation encourages flexible thinking and rewards thoughtful analysis that often uses very different techniques. Consider for example Activity Card 9–1.

Notice the range of strategies used in Activity Card 9–1. Each strategy is meaningful to the student using it. However, that strategy may not be known by everyone and may even seem strange to others. Talking over ways different children compute mentally encourages freedom of thought and flexibility of strategies. Children often can learn new strategies by hearing their classmates' explanations. In fact, encouraging students to share and explain how they did it in their heads is an important part of instructional activities promoting mental computation.

As children develop their mental computation abilities, it is important that they encounter a range of activities that encourage and reward the wide variety of skills used when doing mental computation. Rather than have everyone use the same strategy to solve a problem, the goal of mental computation instruction is to encourage individual students to use strategies that make sense to them. Here are some things children should be encouraged to do:

● Always try mental computation before written methods or calculator use.

Activity Card 9–1

Choose Your Strategy

▼ How many cubes in this building?

- Tell how you did it.

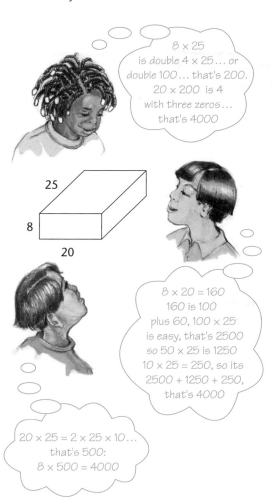

8 × 25 is double 4 × 25... or double 100... that's 200. 20 × 200 is 4 with three zeros... that's 4000

25

8

20

*8 × 20 = 160
160 is 100 plus 60, 100 × 25 is easy, that's 2500 so 50 × 25 is 1250 10 × 25 = 250, so its 2500 + 1250 + 250, that's 4000*

20 × 25 = 2 × 25 × 10... that's 500: 8 × 500 = 4000

- Describe the thinking that each student used.

- Which method do YOU think is the easiest? Tell why.

• Use numbers that are easy to work with:

	One way to think
397 × 4 = ?	400 × 4 = 1600
	3 × 4 = 12
	1600 − 12 = 1588
$6.98 + $7.98 + $9.98 = ?	7 + 8 + 10 = 25
	3 × 2¢ = 6¢
	$25 − 6¢ = $24.94

• Look for an easy way:

2 × 3 × 7 × 5 = ?	2 × 3 = 6
	6 × 5 = 30
	30 × 7 = 210
	or
	2 × 5 = 10
	3 × 7 = 21
	10 × 21 = 210

65 × 8 × 19 × 0 = ?   0 is a factor, which means the product is zero.

• Use logical reasoning

15 × 120   That's halfway between 10 × 120 and 20 × 120 . . . halfway between 1200 and 2400 . . . that's 1800
or
That's 10 × 120 plus half of 10 × 120 . . . 1200 + 600 that's 1800

• Use knowledge about the number system

56 − 24 = ?   50 − 20 = 30
6 − 4 = 2
30 + 2 = 32
or
54 − 24 = 30
so 56 − 24 = 32

Why emphasize mental computation? Here are several reasons for helping students develop mental computation:

• Mental computation is very useful. An overwhelming majority (more than three-fourths) of all calculations by adults are done mentally. Encouraging, developing, and rewarding mental computation early is an important step toward developing this practical and life-long skill.

• Mental computation provides a direct and efficient way of doing many calculations. For example, research has shown that the computation 200 − 5 is easier to do mentally than in a written form. Student are more likely to make sensible judgments about the results and less likely to report 205 (a common error for the written form). Likewise in the middle grades, computations such as $\frac{3}{4} - \frac{1}{2}$ are easier to compute mentally than in a written form (McIntosh et al. 1995).

● Mental computation is an excellent way to develop critical thinking and number sense and to reward creative problem solving. Students must choose (invent) a strategy and use it. In this process, they become aware that there is more than one way to perform most calculations mentally and are encouraged to seek simple and economical methods that make sense to them (Cobb and Merkel 1989).

● Proficiency in mental computation contributes to increased skill in estimation. Mental computation provides the cornerstone for all estimation processes, offering a variety of alternative algorithms and nonstandard techniques for finding answers.

Advocates argue that mental computation encourages flexible thinking, promotes number sense, and encourages creative work with numbers in an efficient manner. Thus, 165 + 99 might be solved in several different ways, such as:

> "I subtracted 1 from 165 and added it to 99. Then I added 164 + 100 to get 264."

> "I added 165 plus 100 and got 265, then I subtracted 1 and got 264."

Research has documented many insightful techniques. However, the dominant strategy among children above grade 2 was applying written algorithms mentally when doing the computation (McIntosh, Reys and Reys 1997). Thus when asked to compute 165 + 99 mentally, the typical description was:

> "I added 5 plus 9 and got 14. I carried the ten, and 5 + 9 plus 1 is 15. I carried that 1 and got 2. It's two-six-four or 264."

For many students, mental computation is thought of as applying written algorithms in their heads (Reys and Barger 1994). This notion of mental computation is far different than the mental computation we have in mind and is often very difficult and impractical.

Research suggests that practice with written computational algorithms increases the likelihood of students trying to apply written methods mentally. This phenomena is an international dilemma. Although the range of different mental computation strategies in Canada and the United States was

far greater than in Japan, in each country a learned "paper/pencil" strategy was the dominant strategy reported by students. It appears that the application of written algorithms mentally most likely reflects the emphasis given to written algorithms in school and appears to inhibit the development of flexible and more efficient mental computation strategies (Hope and Sherrill 1987; Shigematsu et al. 1994; Reys, Reys, Nohda, Emori 1995; Reys and Yang, in press). Increasing the acceptance of an emphasis on flexible, student-generated strategies will enable students to compute mentally without relying on written algorithms to do so.

Many useful mental computation strategies have been documented and identified. Just as teachers can help children develop a repertoire of problem-solving strategies, they also can help them develop a collection of mental computation strategies. In Figure 9–4, several common strategies for whole number addition are presented. As you examine these examples, see if you have ever used any of these strategies. Chances are, you have!

Among the guidelines you should follow when developing mental computation are these:

● Encourage students to do computations mentally. Make it clear that mental computation is not only acceptable but desired when possible. Students report that mental computation is not encouraged and often discouraged in school (Sowder 1992). It has been suggested that when teachers say, "Show your work," that students interpret this to mean that mental computation is unacceptable. Thus, instead of doing $1,000 \times 945$ mentally, a student might write:

$$
\begin{array}{r}
945 \\
\times\ 1000 \\
\hline
000 \\
000 \\
000 \\
945 \\
\hline
945000
\end{array}
$$

Applying this written algorithm is both unnecessary and inefficient, yet is often preferred by students, presumably because they think it is required.

● Check to learn what computations students prefer to do mentally. Research suggests that, when given the choice, students from grade four and up prefer to use written computations rather than calculators or mental computation. For ex-

Problem	Strategy	How I did it
43 + 48	Adding from the left	40 plus 40 is 80, 3 plus 8 is 11, 80 plus 11 is 91
43 + 48	Counting on	I'll count by tens. 48 . . . 58 . . . 68 . . . 78 . . . 88 Then I'll count by ones. 89 . . . 90 . . . 91
43 + 48	Making tens	48 plus 2 is 50, 50 plus 40 is 90, 90 plus 1 more is 91
43 + 48	Doubling	48 plus 48 is 96. Since 43 is 5 less than 48, 96 minus 5 is 91.
43 + 48	Making compatibles	43 and 7 are compatible because they make 50, 50 plus 40 is 90, 90 plus 1 more is 91
43 + 48	Bridging	I'll break up a number and add the parts. 43 plus 8 is 51, add 40 more is 91

Can you think of any other ways to solve this problem?

Figure 9–4 • Some examples of flexible mental computation strategies for whole number addition

ample, a majority of fifth graders chose to do 1000 × 945 with either a calculator or paper/pencil. Although this is not a wise choice, research suggests that such choices typically reflect the student's lack of experience and confidence in doing computations mentally. Activity Cards 9–2 and 9–3 illustrate one way to explore the computational preferences of students with whole numbers and with fractions. These cards include a range of computations. Some look easy, such as $1 - \frac{1}{3}$, yet only about 15 percent of fifth graders could produce a correct result (Reys et al. 1993).

- Check to learn if students are applying written algorithms mentally. Ask students to tell how they did a computation in their head. When students tell how it was done, the strategies and thinking used become clear.

- Plan to include mental computation systematically and regularly as an integral part of your instruction. Systematic attention and practice will improve your students' mental computation performance. Experiences should focus on development of strategies and thinking patterns that make sense to students. These may be self-generated strategies as well as those learned from others.

- Keep practice sessions short—perhaps 10 minutes at a time. Many teachers use activities such as "Follow Me" while children are waiting in

Activity Card 9–2

How Would You Do It?

	In your head	With a calculator	With paper/pencil
60 × 60	☐	☐	☐
945 × 1000	☐	☐	☐
450 × 45	☐	☐	☐
24 × 5 × 2	☐	☐	☐
16,000/2,000	☐	☐	☐
450/45	☐	☐	☐
4 × 15	☐	☐	☐
50 × 17 × 2	☐	☐	☐

Follow Up

▼ Write a computation YOU would solve with a calculator _____

▼ Write a computation YOU would solve mentally _____

▼ Write a computation YOU would solve with paper/pencil _____

Activity Card 9–3 ✓

How Would You Do It?

	In your head	With a calculator	With paper/pencil
½ + ¼	☐	☐	☐
1 − ⅓	☐	☐	☐
¾ + ¾	☐	☐	☐
⅕ + ⅙	☐	☐	☐
½ + ⅚	☐	☐	☐
1½ + 2¾	☐	☐	☐
2 − ¾	☐	☐	☐
½ − ⅓	☐	☐	☐

Follow Up

▼ Write a computation YOU would solve with a calculator _____

▼ Write a computation YOU would solve mentally _____

▼ Write a computation YOU would solve with paper/pencil _____

Activity Card 9–4 ✓

Today's Target Is ☐

Try to make today's target in these ways:

1. adding three numbers
2. finding the difference between two numbers
3. multiplying two numbers
4. adding and subtracting
5. using a fraction
6. doing it an unusual way

Activity Card 9–5 ✓

Compatible Numbers

▼ Find two numbers with a sum of 100.

17	46	15	39
83	61	54	43
92	85	8	75
25	57	80	20

Activity Card 9–6 ✓

Compatible Numbers

▼ Find two fractions with a sum of 1.

¼	⅔	⅞	⅝
½	¹⁄₁₀	¾	⁵⁄₁₀
⅜	⅛	⁵⁄₁₂	⁹⁄₁₀
⁷⁄₁₂	³⁄₁₀	⅓	⁷⁄₁₀

line: "3 + 7 + 10 − 4 + 20 . . ." or Today's Target (see Activity Card 9–4) which can be varied by changing target numbers or asking different questions. For example, you might say, "Today's target is 10." Then ask students different ways to make 10. Next time, change the target number to 100 and ask the same questions.

- Develop children's confidence. Pick numbers that are easy to work with at first (such as 3 × 99 or ½ of 84) then increase the difficulty (for example, try 5 × 75 or ⅔ of 96). Experiences with compatible numbers (numbers easy to compute) such as those shown in Activity Cards 9–5 and 9–6 help develop confidence, number sense, and promote a valuable skill.

- Encourage inventiveness. There is no one right way to do any mental computation, but there may be certain ways that are more efficient and interesting. Asking students, "How did you do that?" can reveal highly ingenious mental computation strategies. For example, 60 × 15 was

given to students in an interview (Hope 1987). Among the strategies reported were:

"10 times 60 is 600. 5 times 60 is 300. 600 plus 300 is 900."

"60 times 10 is 600 and half of 600 is 300, so it is 600 plus 300 or 900."

"60 is 4 times 15, so that is 4 times 15 times 15. 15 squared is 225 times 4 is 900."

The latter strategy was reported by an eighth grader and is a reminder of the "interesting" techniques employed by students when doing mental computation. Many mental computational strategies are self-developed; and the power of self-learned out-of-school mental computation techniques has been reported (Carraher et al. 1985, 1987).

- Make sure children are aware of the difference between estimation (in which answers are approximations) and mental computation (in which answers are exact).

Computational Estimation

Computational estimation is a process of producing answers that are close enough to allow for good decisions without making elaborate or exact computations. Real world situations utilizing estimation are diverse and plentiful. Computational estimation is typically done mentally, but there are circumstances which may require recording some results. Figure 9–5 illustrates how estimation serves as a monitoring function at three different places in the problem-solving process.

Estimation *prior to starting exact computation* (A) helps build a general sense of what to expect. Estimation *while doing computation* (B) provides an immediate or intermediate check to determine if the computation is moving in the right direction. *After the computation is completed* estimation provides an opportunity to reflect on an answer and helps determine if the result is reasonable (C). As children become aware of different uses of estimation, they develop a greater respect for its power and view it as an essential part of the total computational process.

Research has confirmed that good mental computation skills and number sense provide the foundation for the successful development of computational estimation techniques. Systematic attention to computational estimation can significantly improve performance. Students must be given the opportunity to estimate; and, although some dramatic improvements can occur quickly, the development of good computational estimation skills is a lengthy process that will be accomplished only over a period of years (Sowder and Kelin 1992).

The NCTM *Standards* highlight estimation in all elementary grades. Estimation provides the first mathematical encounter that is not exact, yet is nonetheless a natural part of mathematics. As young children talk about mathematics, their language and vocabulary include words such as *about, almost, just over,* and *nearly*. As children grow older,

A. Before computing

B. During computing

C. After computing

Figure 9–5 • **Different times to estimate**

additional vocabulary is added to describe mathematical answers, including *approximate, reasonable,* and *unreasonable,* as well as phrases such as *in the ball park*. Developing comfort and confidence in using language to describe the inexactness found in the real world not only contributes to developing number sense but also prepares them for computational estimation.

Instruction should begin with making students aware of what estimation is about, so they develop a tolerance for error. Estimation involves a mind set different from that used to compute an exact answer. The "exact-answer mentality" must be changed before specific estimation strategies are developed. This change begins when students recognize that estimation is an essential and practical skill. That's why teachers must consistently emphasize computational estimation within different problem situations and along with computation procedures.

Immediate feedback to students on how well they have done in providing estimates is important. Be lenient in accepting responses initially. Ask students to explain how they obtained their estimates, because the discussion will help clarify procedures and may even suggest new approaches to estimating in a given problem. However, beware of letting them confuse estimation, which produces an answer that is close, with mental computation, which produces an exact answer.

One of the keys to developing good estimation strategies is to help children be flexible when thinking about numbers. Suppose you wanted students to evaluate 418 + 349. One child might think, "400 + 300 is 700, and 49 + 18 is less than 100, so the

sum is between 700 and 800." This approach uses the leading digits. Another child might think, "418 is about 400 and 349 is almost 350, so the sum is about 750." This child rounded to numbers that are easy to compute. As with mental computation, it is important that children develop different strategies, and it is critical that they think about the problem, the operations, and the numbers involved and not rely on a fixed set of rules to produce an estimate. When estimation is mentioned, many adults think of rounding. However, as in mental computation, several strategies can be developed with children so they possess a repertoire of strategies from which to choose. A few of these will now be discussed.

Front-End Estimation

The front-end strategy for estimation is a very basic, yet powerful approach that can be used in a variety of situations. Two important things must be checked: (1) the leading, or front-end digit in a number, and (2) the place value of those digits. To help students understand this strategy, Figure 9–6 shows a three

Figure 9–6 ● Illustrating the power of front-end estimation

▼ What are the most important digits? Why?

▼ Now what is your estimated answer?

Figure 9–7 • Front-end estimation in action

digit number hidden behind a sheet of paper on the board. Give students the opportunity to see one digit of their choosing. Some students choose the ones digit, but others choose the hundreds digit and find that this gives the most useful information. A few exercises such as this help students begin to grasp the power of the leading, or front-end, digits.

Figure 9–7 shows how the front-end digits are used to obtain an initial estimate. The unique advantage of the front-end strategy is that all of the numbers to be operated on are visible in the original problem. Thus students can reach an estimate quickly and easily. The strategy also encourages students to use number sense as they think about the computations.

To extend front-end estimation further, "hide" some digits as shown on Activity Card 9–7. Students are encouraged to consider the value of the leading digits and the number of digits in the results. Using these two factors wisely helps produce reasonable estimates.

Adjusting or Compensating

Number sense has many dimensions, one of which is recognizing when something is a little more or a little less. As students use the front-end or leading digits to make an estimate, it becomes natural to begin refining their initial estimate by making adjustments or compensating. Figure 9–8 illustrates one way that adjusting is accomplished. This process of adjustment or compensation cuts across all estimation strategies and all operations.

Activity Card 9–7

Estimate the Possibility!

▼ Some digits are missing in these problems, but you can use what is shown.

• Decide how many digits are possible in the result.

• Use triangles to indicate the number of digits in your estimate.

A. $\begin{array}{r} 5\,\triangle\,\triangle \\ +\ 2\,\triangle\,\triangle \\ \hline \triangle\,\triangle\,\triangle \end{array}$

B. $\begin{array}{r} 4\,\triangle\,\triangle\,\triangle \\ \times\ 2\ \triangle \\ \hline \end{array}$

C. $\begin{array}{r} 0.6\,\triangle\,\triangle \\ -\ 0.29\ \triangle \\ \hline \end{array}$

D. $\frac{2}{3}$ of $2\,\triangle\,\triangle$ _____

E. $\begin{array}{r} 4\,\triangle\,\triangle\,\triangle \\ -\ 1\,\triangle\,\triangle\,\triangle \\ \hline \end{array}$

F. $7)\overline{4\,\triangle\,\triangle\,\triangle\,\triangle}$

G. $\begin{array}{r} 4.7\,\triangle\,\triangle \\ \times\ 3.\triangle \\ \hline \end{array}$

H. $4\frac{\triangle}{5} \times 21.\triangle\,\triangle$ _____

• Which three problems could have two different possibilities for the number of correct digits? _____

Flexible Rounding

Rounding is more sophisticated than front-end estimation, because the numbers are changed or reformulated. Rounding is appropriate for all operations with all types of numbers, but is particularly well-suited for multiplication. Children should be adept at the process of rounding to reform a number, as illustrated in Figure 9–9. Problems like the one shown in Figure 9–9 need to be accompanied by questions that go beyond those asking what the estimate is to those that encourage children to think about the process:

> How has the problem changed?
> Why was the problem changed?

The key to the effective use of rounding in estimation is to round to compatible numbers, which involves substituting numbers that are close to the original numbers but are more manageable to compute mentally. Children should be encouraged to think of possible substitutions and to reason about their choice from among them. The choices illustrated in the following example lead naturally to such questions as "Which pair would you choose to make the estimate?" and "Why?"

Adjusting is often done to compensate for how the numbers were rounded, as in the following example in which an initial estimate is made by rounding:

Next the student makes an adjustment to refine the initial estimate:

Figure 9–8 • Example of front-end estimation with adjustment

Where did the $4 estimate come from?

What digits were not used to formulate the $4 estimate?

How will they affect the actual cost?

Can the bill be paid with only $4? How about $5? Explain how you decided?

Here are some other examples:

	Think	Result
42×61	$40 \times 60 = 2400$	A little more than 2400
39×78	$40 \times 80 = 3200$	A little less than 2400
27×32	$30 \times 30 = 900$	About 900

For the first two examples, the rounding procedure makes clear whether the result is an underestimate or an overestimate. But in the last example, it is not so obvious. Students must think about the numbers used to produce their estimate.

It is important for students to realize that they have the freedom to choose strategies, as illustrated on Activity Card 9–8. This activity should be accompanied by discussion of the different strategies that were used.

As students' mental computation skills progress, the rounding procedures they use to produce estimates reflect more flexibility. That's one of the reasons why the NCTM *Standards* suggest less attention to "rounding numbers out of context." When estimating, people always round to numbers that are easy for them to compute mentally. This means that traditional rounding rules (such as if the digit is more than 5, round the preceding digit up) are not necessarily followed, and common sense is the hallmark. It also means that different people may round the same numbers in a problem differently, depending on what is easiest to them. Notice in Figure 9–10 that, although the students rounded to different numbers, each approach produced a good estimate.

Compatible Numbers

The *compatible numbers strategy* uses nice, friendly numbers that are easy to compute mentally and that seem to go together naturally. Work with the ten-frame helps children recognize that 6 and 4 are compatible with 10. This experience extends naturally to help them recognize that 60 and 40 are compatible with 100. These compatibles aid the development of other pairs, such as 65 and 35, that are also compatible with 100, and should be extended to other numbers as was done earlier with Activity Cards 9–5 and 9–6. Activity Card 9–9 illustrates how students can use compatible numbers to make computations easier.

When the compatible numbers strategy is used, the numbers in the problem are rounded to numbers that are easier to work with. Figure 9–11 shows

Figure 9–9 • **Example of rounding to reformulate numbers for mental computation**

Figure 9–10 • **Example of flexible rounding and the different estimates which result**

Activity Card 9–8

What Would You Do?

▼ Look at the strategies for estimating the sum of these prices:

● Describe each of the strategies.

● Which would you use? Tell why.

Activity Card 9–9

What Are Compatible Numbers?

▼ Compatible numbers are sets of numbers that are easily computed.

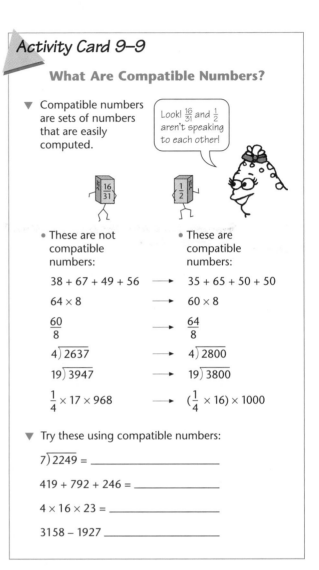

● These are not compatible numbers:

$$38 + 67 + 49 + 56$$

$$64 \times 8$$

$$\frac{60}{8}$$

$$4\overline{)2637}$$

$$19\overline{)3947}$$

$$\frac{1}{4} \times 17 \times 968$$

● These are compatible numbers:

$$35 + 65 + 50 + 50$$

$$60 \times 8$$

$$\frac{64}{8}$$

$$4\overline{)2800}$$

$$19\overline{)3800}$$

$$(\frac{1}{4} \times 16) \times 1000$$

▼ Try these using compatible numbers:

$7\overline{)2249}$ = _____

$419 + 792 + 246$ = _____

$4 \times 16 \times 23$ = _____

$3158 - 1927$ _____

how the strategy works for division, with which it is particularly powerful. Given these problems, children need to be encouraged to think about why 7 and 2800 are compatible numbers for the problem $6\overline{)2775}$ or what different pairs of numbers could be used to estimate the answer to $18\overline{)371}$. Activity Card 9–10 provides students with experience in first recognizing compatible numbers and then choosing the "best" pairs from a set.

Although compatible numbers can be applied to all types of computations, they are often used in addition. In the following example, the student first used the front-end strategy and then compatible numbers to adjust the initial estimate:

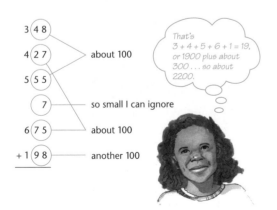

Clustering

The *clustering*, or *averaging*, *strategy* uses a mean for an estimate. Whenever a group of numbers cluster around a common value, this two-step process is used:

● First estimate the average value of the numbers.

● Then multiply by the number of values in the group.

Figure 9–12 gives a glimpse of this strategy in action. For problems like the ones shown in Figure 9–12, questions such as the following can help give meaning to this strategy:

What number do all the values cluster around?

Why is the average estimated?

Why is the estimated average multiplied by 6 (or by 5)?

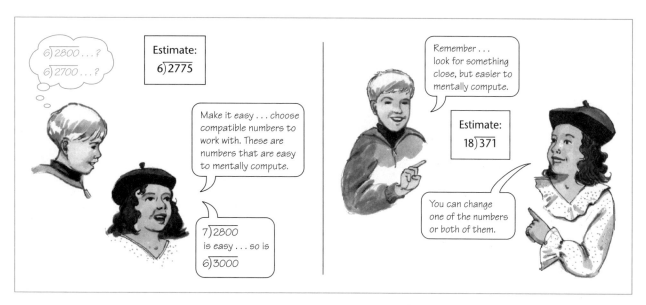

Figure 9–11 • **Examples of the compatible numbers strategy for division**

Asking what the estimated total is for these and a range of similar problems helps children become adept at using this strategy.

Clustering is a limited strategy but a useful one. It is appropriate for estimating sums of groups of numbers quickly. A strength of this strategy is that it eliminates the mental tabulation of a long list of front-end digits or rounded numbers.

• Choosing Estimation Strategies

Estimation strategies take many different forms, often for the same problem. In fact it is rare that a single strategy is used. Figure 9–13 illustrates how several different strategies might be applied to different situations. The choice of strategies depends on the situation, as well as on the numbers and operations involved. A challenge for us as teachers is to help our students become aware of the wide array of estimation strategies that exist and to help our students develop confidence in their ability to engage in estimation.

Among the guidelines we think are useful when developing computation estimation are these:

- Provide situations that encourage and reward computational estimation. For example, 78 + 83 should be computed mentally to produce an exact answer, but 78,342 + 83,289 is more likely to promote estimation. Thus, make sure the numbers are messy enough so that students want to estimate, rather than use a different alternative.

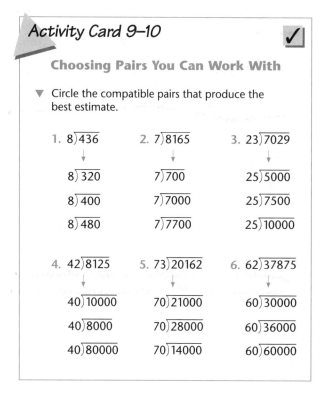

Activity Card 9–10

Choosing Pairs You Can Work With

▼ Circle the compatible pairs that produce the best estimate.

1. 8)436
   ↓
   8)320
   8)400
   8)480

2. 7)8165
   ↓
   7)700
   7)7000
   7)7700

3. 23)7029
   ↓
   25)5000
   25)7500
   25)10000

4. 42)8125
   ↓
   40)10000
   40)8000
   40)80000

5. 73)20162
   ↓
   70)21000
   70)28000
   70)14000

6. 62)37875
   ↓
   60)30000
   60)36000
   60)60000

- Check to learn if students are computing exact answers and then "rounding" to produce estimates. Research has documented the popularity of this technique (Sowder 1992) and unfortunately these approaches often go undetected. Talking with students and observing their approaches to estimation provides checks to ensure that they are truly engaging in the process of estimating.

Figure 9–12 • Examples of the clustering strategy for addition

- Ask students to tell how their estimates were made. Research suggests that students often develop individual and unique approaches to computational estimation processes (Sowder 1992). By sharing them, students develop an appreciation of different estimation processes.

- Destroy the one-right-answer syndrome early. Help students realize that several different yet acceptable estimates might be made for the same problem. One way to do this is to invite students to identify acceptable intervals for good estimates. Their discussion will generally reveal different strategies and help everyone learn about other strategies. Such experiences help students become more comfortable with the notion that several different but correct estimates exist.

- Encourage students to think carefully about real-world applications where estimates are made. Critical thinking skills can be sharpened in deciding when to overestimate and underestimate.

Activity Card 9–11 illustrates several situations to encourage such thinking.

 ## A Glance at Where We've Been

As teachers we must help students develop confidence and skill in using computational alternatives. This should include ready access to, and appropriate use of, calculators. As basic facts are established mental computation becomes an important tool for many computations. When the computations be-

---

Activity Card 9–11

Over or Under

▼ Read each of these situations.

▼ Then decide whether you would over- or underestimate. Tell why.

1. Your car usually gets about 25 miles per gallon on the highway. Your gas tank is about one-quarter full and it is 100 miles to the next gas station. Is this a good time to over- or underestimate your gas mileage?

2. You are talking with a car dealer about buying a car, and you ask about the gas mileage. Do you think the car dealer will over- or underestimate the gas mileage of the car?

3. You have $20 to spend on groceries for a group picnic. As you place each item in the grocery cart, is this a good time to over- or underestimate the cost of each item?

4. You are forecasting the lava speed of an active volcano. As the lava is moving down the mountainside toward a town, a decision needs to be made when to evacuate the town. Should you over- or underestimate the speed of the lava?

5. Your plane is scheduled to leave at 4:00 and it usually takes about one hour to get to the airport. Should you over- or underestimate the time needed to get to the airport when deciding what time to leave?

6. YOUR TURN. Make up an estimation problem for when you would want to overestimate. Underestimate.

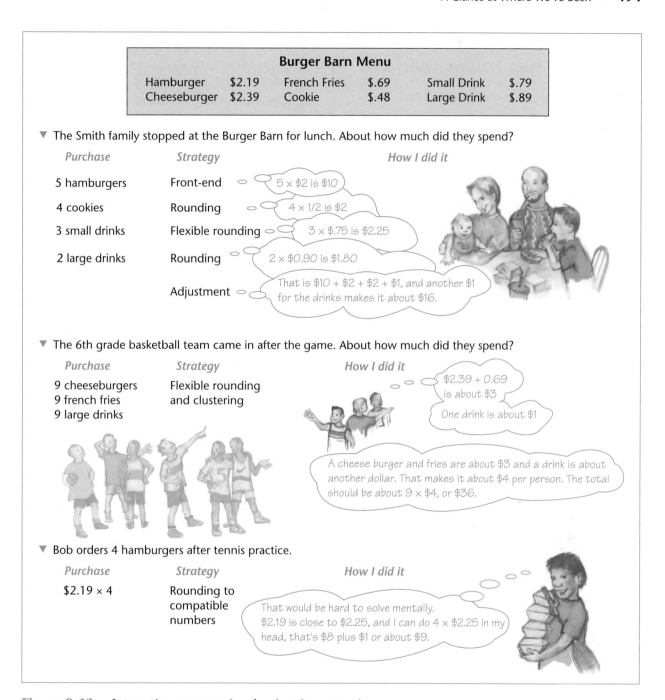

Burger Barn Menu

Hamburger	$2.19	French Fries	$.69	Small Drink	$.79
Cheeseburger	$2.39	Cookie	$.48	Large Drink	$.89

▼ The Smith family stopped at the Burger Barn for lunch. About how much did they spend?

Purchase	Strategy	How I did it
5 hamburgers	Front-end	5 × $2 is $10
4 cookies	Rounding	4 × 1/2 is $2
3 small drinks	Flexible rounding	3 × $.75 is $2.25
2 large drinks	Rounding	2 × $0.90 is $1.80
	Adjustment	That is $10 + $2 + $2 + $1, and another $1 for the drinks makes it about $16.

▼ The 6th grade basketball team came in after the game. About how much did they spend?

Purchase	Strategy	How I did it
9 cheeseburgers 9 french fries 9 large drinks	Flexible rounding and clustering	$2.39 + 0.69 is about $3 One drink is about $1

A cheese burger and fries are about $3 and a drink is about another dollar. That makes it about $4 per person. The total should be about 9 × $4, or $36.

▼ Bob orders 4 hamburgers after tennis practice.

Purchase	Strategy	How I did it
$2.19 × 4	Rounding to compatible numbers	That would be hard to solve mentally. $2.19 is close to $2.25, and I can do 4 × $2.25 in my head, that's $8 plus $1 or about $9.

Figure 9–13 • Integrating computational estimation strategies

come too tedious to compute exact answers via mental computation, then estimation is a natural next step. Is the answer more than . . . Should it be less than . . . are questions encouraging estimation and number sense. When exact answers are too tedious to obtain mentally, calculators and written algorithms are the appropriate tools. However, in our judgment, care needs to be taken to develop confidence and proficiency with mental computation and estimation prior to introducing and practicing formal written algorithms. Such a plan will challenge each of us to reflect on the worth of different computational tools and strive to provide the balance of the instructional time that each deserves.

▶ THINGS TO DO: From What You've Read

1. What are some goals related to computation that involve computational tools?

2. How would you respond to the following statement by a parent? "Calculators should not be used in school, because if students use them, they will never have to think."

3. Do you agree with the proposal in Figure 9–2 regarding percent of instructional time devoted to developing computational alternatives? If not, choose a grade level and decide how you think instructional time devoted to computation should be allocated, and be prepared to defend your proposal.

4. Distinguish between mental computation and estimation.

5. Describe some situations when a calculator should be used.

6. Several uses of the calculator as an instructional tool and a computational tool were discussed. Are these two uses mutually exclusive? Explain and give an example to illustrate what you mean.

7. What do you think are the strongest reasons for encouraging and developing good mental computational skills?

8. A fifth-grader described this solution to 7 × 499 in her head: "I put the 499 on top and the 7 on bottom, then I get 3 and carry the 6 and 9 carry the 6 and 7 times 4 is 28 plus 6 is 34. . . ." Would you say this student was successfully doing mental computation? Explain why. Describe some other strategies that might be explored.

9. Discuss why it is important for students to develop a tolerance for an acceptable range of answers when doing computational estimation.

10. Tell why compensation and adjustment are an integral part of making estimates.

11. Identify several different estimation strategies and give an example of how each strategy might be used.

12. Why is the following not a good assignment? "I want you to estimate the answers to these problems, then compute the correct answers, and see how far off your estimate was."

13. Consider this question: "How much money was needed to play 60 video games at 25¢ a game?" Do you think this is a good candidate to do mentally? Tell why? Describe a strategy you would use. Ask another person to solve this problem mentally and to share their strategy.

14. Figure 9–3 shows a possible letter to parents about calculator use in second grade. Prepare a letter to sixth grade parents telling them that calculators will be used in your class and can be used on homework. Briefly explain why you are allowing and encouraging calculator use.

15. Here is an actual quote from a fourth grader telling what she thinks her teacher wants:

   I think she doesn't like us to use mental (computation) because she thinks we might just be copying because she can't see the writing. And she doesn't like us to use the calculator a whole lot because then we'll get too used to it and we won't want to learn and stuff. . . . And she likes us to use written (computation) because she can see what we're doing and if we're having problems she can see what we're doing wrong.

   How would you respond to this student? Suppose you had an opportunity to talk with the student's teacher. What would you tell her teacher?

▶ THINGS TO DO: Going Beyond This Book

1. Keep a log of the computational tools (mental computation, estimation, calculator, written computation) that you use for one day. Estimate what percent of your computations made use of each tool.

2. Use exercises from one of the activity cards and survey students to determine which method (calculator, mental, written) they would prefer to use. Ask students which computations they think are the easiest? Most difficult? Summarize your results and share them with your class.

3. Ask several students in primary grades how to compute 99 + 165 mentally and to tell how they did it. Ask several middle grade students how they did the same computation. Describe the strategies you observed at each level. Did you find evidence that "written algorithms" were applied mentally?

4. Review one of the mental math books by Hope et al. (1987, 1988). Select a lesson and highlight the key ideas for your classmates.

5. Review one of the *Computation Estimation* books by Reys et al. (1987). Select a lesson and highlight the key ideas for your classmates.

6. Examine one of the Keystrokes book by Reys et al. (1980) or CAMP-LA books. For the grade level of your choice, select an activity that illustrates a calculator activity you would like to use and tell why you chose the activity.

7. Examine the NCTM Yearbooks *Estimation and Mental Computation* (Schoen 1986) or *Calculators in Mathematics Education* (Fey 1992), for an article which you think will help you better develop com-

putational alternatives with your students. Summarize this article and tell why you found it useful.

8. Select a standardized achievement test. Review the test and determine the attention given to assessing mental computation and computational estimation. Discuss the strengths and weakness of test items that you found addressing mental computation or estimation.

9. Check the article by Harries and Dobson or McIntosh, et al. for a summary of different ways students do computations orally and on paper. Do you agree with the summary? Tell why.

Selected References

CAMP-LA: *Activities Enhanced by Calculator Use.* Book 1, Grades K–2, Book 2, Grades 3–4; Book 3, Grades 5–6. Orange, Calif.: Cal State Fullerton Press, 1991.

Clayton, John C. Encouraging Estimation, *Mathematics Teaching,* 157 (pp. 23–27), December 1996.

Cobb, P., and Merkel, G. "Thinking Strategies: Teaching Arithmetic Through Problem Solving." In *New Directions for Elementary School Mathematics* (eds. P. R. Trafton and A. P. Shulte). Reston, Va.: National Council of Teachers of Mathematics, 1989, pp. 70–81.

Carraher, T. N.; Carraher, D. W.; and Schliemann, A. D. "Mathematics in the Streets and in Schools." *British Journal and Developmental Psychology,* 3 (1985), pp. 21–29.

Carraher, T. N.; Carraher, D. W.; and Schliemann, A. D. "Written and Oral Mathematics." *Journal for Research in Mathematics Education,* 18 (1987), pp. 83–97.

Fey, James. (Ed.) *Calculators in Mathematics Education,* 1992 Yearbook of the National Council of Teachers of Mathematics. Reston, Va.: National Council of Teachers of Mathematics, 1992.

Harries, Tony, and Dobson, Alan. Oral and Written Methods of Calculation" *Mathematics Teaching,* 154 (pp. 32–35), March 1996.

Hembree, Ray, and Dessart, Donald J. "Research on Calculators in Mathematics Education." In *Calculators in Mathematics Education,* 1992 Yearbook of the National Council of Teachers of Mathematics (ed. James Fey). Reston, Va.: National Council of Teachers of Mathematics, 1987, pp. 23–32.

Hope, J. A. "A Case Study of a Highly Skilled Mental Calculator." *Journal for Research in Mathematics Education,* 18 (1987), pp. 331–342.

Hope, Jack A.; Leutzinger, Larry; Reys, Barbara J.; and Reyes, Robert E. *Mental Math in the Primary Grades,* Palo Alto, Calif.: Dale Seymour Publications, 1988.

Hope, Jack A.; Reys, Barbara J.; and Reys, Robert E. *Mental Math in the Middle Grades,* Palo Alto, Calif.: Dale Seymour Publications, 1987.

Hope, J. A., and Sherrill, J. M. "Characteristics of Unskilled and Skilled Mental Calculators." *Journal for Research in Mathematics Education,* 18 (1987), pp. 98–111.

Kamii, Constance; Lewis, Barbara A.; and Livingston, Sally Jones. "Primary Arithmetic: Children Inventing Their Own Procedures," *Arithmetic Teacher,* 41 (December 1993), 200–203.

McIntosh, Alistair; Nohda, Nobuhiko; Reys, Barbara J.; and Reys, Robert E. "Mental Computation Performance in Australia, Japan and the United States." *Educational Studies in Mathematics* 29 (1995), pp. 237–258.

McIntosh, Alistair; Reys, Robert E.; and Reys, Barbara J. Mental Computation in the Middle Grades: The Importance of Thinking Strategies, *Teaching Mathematics in the Middle School,* 2(322–327), March–April, 1997.

National Council of Teachers of Mathematics. *Curriculum and Evaluation Standards for School Mathematics.* Reston, Va.: National Council of Teachers of Mathematics, 1989.

National Research Council. *Everybody Counts: A Report to the Nation on the Future of Mathematics Education,* Washington, D.C.: National Academy Press, 1989.

Rathmell, Edward, and Trafton, Paul R. "Whole Number Computation." *Mathematics for the Young Child* (ed. Joseph N. Payne), Reston, Va.: NCTM, 1990, pp. 153–174.

Reys, R. E. "Testing Mental-Computation Skills." *Arithmetic Teacher,* 33 (1985), pp. 14–16.

Reys, R. E. "Estimation." *Arithmetic Teacher,* 33 (February 1985), pp. 37–41.

Reys, R. E.; Bestgen, B. J.; Coburn, T. G.; Schoen, H. L.; Shumway, R. J.; Wheatley, C. L.; Wheatley, G. H.; and White, A. L. *Keystrokes: Calculator Activities for Young Students* (Series) Palo Alto, Calif.: Creative Publications, 1980.

Reys, B. J., and Barger, R. "Mental Computation: Evaluation, Curriculum, and Instructional Issues from the United States Perspective." In *Computational Alternatives for the Twenty-First Century: Cross-Cultural Perspectives from Japan and the United States* (Eds. R. E. Reys and N. Nohda). Reston, Va.: National Council of Teachers of Mathematics, 1994, pp. 31–47.

Reys, R. E.; Reys, B. J.; Nohda, N.; and Emori, H. (1995). Mental computation performance and strategy use of Japanese students in grades 2, 4, 6, and 8, *Journal for Research in Mathematics Education,* 26(4), 304–326.

Reys, B. J.; Reys, R. E.; and Hope, J. A. "Mental Computation: A Snapshot of Second, Fifth, and Seventh Grade Student Performance." *School Science and Mathematics,* 93 (1993) pp. 306–315.

Reys, R. E., and Yang, D. C. "Relationship between Computational Performance and Number Sense among Sixth and Eighth Grade Students in Taiwan." *Journal for Research in Mathematics Education.*

Schoen, Harold (Ed.) *Estimation and Mental Computation,* 1986 Yearbook of the National Council of Teachers of Mathematics. Reston, Va.: National Council of Teachers of Mathematics, 1986.

Shigematsu, K.; Iwasaki, H.; and Koyama, M. "Mental Computation: Evaluation, Curriculum, and Instructional Issues from the United States Perspective." In *Computational Alternatives for the Twenty-First Century: Cross Cultural Perspectives from Japan and the United States* (eds. R. E. Reys and J. Nohda). Reston, Va.: National Council of Teachers of Mathematics, 1994, pp. 19–30.

Sowder, J. T. "Mental Computation and Number Sense." *Arithmetic Teacher,* 37 (1990), 18–20.

Sowder, J. T. Estimation and Related Topics. In *Handbook for Research on Mathematics Teaching and Learning* (ed. D. Grouws). New York: Macmillan, 1992, pp. 371–389.

Sowder, J. T., and Kelin, J. "Number Sense and Related Topics." In *Research Ideas for the Classroom: Middle School Mathematics* (ed. D. T. Owns). New York: Macmillan, 1992, pp. 41–57.

Extending Whole-Number Operations: Algorithms

 ## Snapshot of a Lesson

On the chalkboard, the teacher has drawn a problem:

136 boxes in all

How many boxcars are needed?

TEACHER: As you can see, I've put a problem on the board. Can your group solve it using the materials in front of you? [Each group has a different type of material.] After you've had a chance to try, we'll share the ways we attacked it.

After seven or eight minutes, all the groups are ready to tell how they solved the problem:

We changed 136 to 13 tens and 6 ones, because we couldn't work well with 1 hundred. We took 8 from each one of the tens in our minds, but that got too mixed up. So we said, 10 boxcars would hold 80 boxes — that's 8 tens. 5 tens left. 5 more boxcars would hold 40 boxes. There's 1 ten and 6 ones left. That's 2 more eights. So you'd need 10 + 5 + 2 boxcars.

H	T	O

We laid out 136 cubes, and then separated them into groups of 8.

We keyed 8 on the calculator, then the division sign, then 136 — but the answer was less than 1! So we knew we'd used the wrong order. We had to key 136, then the division sign, then 8 — 136 divided by 8.

TEACHER: Good work! Now, how would you write this problem?

Several children write each of these formats:

$$136 \div 8 \qquad \frac{136}{8} \qquad 8\overline{)136}$$

TEACHER: Yes, all show 136 divided by 8. We will use the third way when we work with paper and pencil. We know now that the answer is 17—will you put the answer in place, Karen?

Karen writes:

$$\overset{17}{8\overline{)136}}$$

Several other children say "No!" They are asked why.

CHILDREN: The answer has 1 ten and 7 ones, so it must be written in those places.

TEACHER: Good. I hope you'll always remember that. Now, suppose you didn't know what the answer was. Can you find it using just the numbers?

We know there are at least 10 eights in 136, because 10 x 8 = 80. When I subtract, there are 56 left. 56 ÷ 8 is 7.

TEACHER: Great! Now try: 259 ÷ 6.

Introduction

For hundreds of years, computational skill with paper-and-pencil procedures, called *algorithms*, has been viewed as an essential component of children's mathematical achievement. The teaching of computation has become more exciting in the past few years. Instead of teachers merely presenting a stream of algorithms, showing children just what to do, step by step by step, we've begun to incorporate what children can construct or develop for themselves. Computation has become a problem-solving process, one in which children are encouraged to reason their way to answers, rather than merely memorizing procedures that the teacher says are correct.

This change also means that children can explore alternative algorithms. The algorithms that teachers usually present have been refined over the centuries. They are highly efficient, but they do not necessarily reflect the way children think as they compute. We still want accuracy and efficiency, but the latter is of lesser importance. The focus is on reasoning and thinking.

Although calculators are readily available to relieve the burden of computation, the ability to use algorithms is still considered essential. The NCTM *Standards* (1989) stress the need for children to "select and use computation techniques appropriate to

specific problems and determine whether the results are reasonable" (p. 44). To develop such an enhanced ability, revisions in the teaching of computation include the following:

- Fostering a solid understanding of, and proficiency with, simple calculations

- Abandoning the teaching of tedious calculations using paper-and-pencil algorithms in favor of exploring more mathematics

- Fostering the use of a wide variety of computation and estimation techniques—ranging from quick mental calculation to those using computers—suited to different mathematical settings

- Developing the skills necessary to use appropriate technology and then translating computed results to the problem setting

- Providing students with ways to check the reasonableness of computations (number and algorithmic sense, estimation skills). (NCTM 1989, p. 95)

The *Standards* suggest that decreased emphasis should be given to performing paper-and-pencil calculations with numbers of more than two digits.

Performing two-digit computations ... aids students in understanding connections between computation and numeration. Even though students can explore paper-and-pencil computations with numbers of any size and with various systems, they should not be expected to become proficient with paper-and-pencil computations with several digits. (NCTM 1989, p. 96)

Many parents and some teachers have worried that students will become so dependent on calculators that they will forget how to compute. This concern is not supported by research. Hembree and Dessart (1986) reported from an analysis of a large number of research studies that the use of "calculators in concert with traditional instruction ... can improve the average student's basic skills with paper and pencil, both in basic operations and in problem solving" (p. 96).

Over the years, we have learned much about teaching computation. Key ideas that help to shape the role of computational skills in the curriculum, along with the belief that children are and must be actively involved in constructing their own mathematical learning, will guide our discussion. Of central importance is the need to teach children to choose an appropriate calculation procedure, depending primarily on whether an exact or approximate answer is needed.

Role of Materials in Learning Algorithms

The use of manipulative materials in developing understanding of the algorithms is essential. In the Snapshot Lesson that opened this chapter, the use of materials was the basis on which work with symbols was formed. Materials form a bridge between the real-life problem situation and the abstract algorithm, helping to forge the recognition that what is written down represents real objects and actions. Children must be given sufficient time to handle the materials and make the transition to pictures and symbols (Thompson 1991). Unifix cubes, base-ten blocks, rods, popsicle sticks, beansticks and loose beans, buttons, and myriad other materials, either derived from the problem setting or representative of that setting, help children to construct understanding of when and how an algorithm works.

Importance of Place-Value Ideas

Each of the algorithms for whole-number computation is based on place-value ideas, many of which were discussed in Chapter 7. Children need to have a firm understanding of these ideas before they can work effectively with the algorithms. Linking place-value ideas directly with renaming ideas is a necessary step as the algorithms for each operation are explored and developed. Providing numerous trading activities is accompanied by renaming activities.

Regroup 138 ones into tens and ones:

138 is _____ tens _____ ones

Show 46 with bundles of tens and ones:

46 is _____ tens _____ ones

Rename: 7 tens 16 ones = 8 tens _____ ones
35 is 2 tens _____ ones

Rename 5 tens 3 ones to show more ones:

Tens	Ones
5	3

T	O
4̶5̶	1̶3̶3̶

Write 6 tens 5 ones in five different ways.

Write 37 in all the different ways you can.

Don't be surprised at the ideas that arise in response to this last activity and that you thought were "beyond them"!

Developing the algorithms that work with multidigit numbers has to evolve from students' understanding of place value, which

... involves building connections between key ideas of place value—such as quantifying sets of objects by grouping by ten and treating the groups as units—and using the structure of the written notation to capture this information about groupings. (Wearne and Hiebert 1994, p. 273)

● Addition

You've just walked into a first-grade classroom. After a brief activity to review renaming (for example, renaming 52 as 5 tens 2 ones, and so on), a problem is posed to the children:

Jill and Jeff both collected baseball cards. Jill had 27 cards and Jeff had 35. How many did they have together?

To focus attention on the reasonableness of the answers they will find, you might begin with such questions as

Would they have more than 50 cards?

More than 100 cards?

How do you know?

Then, actual cards or slips of paper to represent cards are given to each group of four or five children, with the direction to figure out an answer, show it on paper, and be ready to tell why it's right. At other times the children are asked to solve the problem individually and write an explanation of what they did. They then need time to explore and invent strategies and to make connections between different ways of thinking about or doing the same process. After each group has reached an answer, the whole class meets to share the ways in which they solved the problem.

● Group 1 counted 27 cards and 35 cards together:

$$27 + 35 = 62$$

● Group 2 made 2 piles of ten cards, with 7 extras and 3 piles of ten cards, with 5 extras:

$$\begin{array}{r} 2 \text{ tens} + 7 \\ + 3 \text{ tens} + 5 \\ \hline \end{array}$$
5 tens + 12, which is renamed as 6 tens + 2, or 62

● Group 3 recognized that 20 and 30 make 50, and 7 and 5 make 12:

$$\begin{array}{r} 20 + 7 \\ + 30 + 5 \\ \hline 50 + 12, \text{ or } 62 \end{array}$$

● Group 4 relied on what Kim's older brother had shown her:

$$\begin{array}{r} 27 \\ + 35 \\ \hline 12 \\ 50 \\ \hline 62 \end{array}$$

● Group 5 did almost the same thing, but a little differently:

$$\begin{array}{r} 27 \\ + 35 \\ \hline 50 \\ 12 \\ \hline 62 \end{array}$$

● Group 6 decided to work with a "tens" number, and then compensated. They checked their answer, too!

$$\begin{array}{r} 27 + 3 = 30 \\ + 35 - 3 = 32 \\ \hline 62 \end{array} \qquad \begin{array}{r} 27 - 5 = 22 \\ + 35 + 5 = 40 \\ \hline 62 \end{array}$$

Everyone was sure they were right, and could tell why—and they were sure that the other groups were right, too! Is 62 correct just because it is the answer every group reached? No! retorted a number of children. It is a reasonable answer because 27 is almost 30, and 35 more would make it 65, but 27 is 3 less than 30, so 62 is right. Frequently, they worked from left to right, as research has indicated children frequently do when constructing their own algorithms (Kamii et al. 1993; Madell 1985). Not all used the manipulative materials, but those who did wrote an algorithm that modeled what they had done with the materials. Or they used procedures that they had "invented" outside of school.

Perhaps it has occurred to you that some of the procedures the children used were as plausible for mental computation as for paper-and-pencil computation. We want children to recognize this, too, as well as that much addition involving one- and two-digit numbers can and should be done mentally. Lots of activities with renaming have given these children a good base from which to tackle addition algorithms. However, none of the groups came up with the "standard" algorithm:

Think

$$\begin{array}{r} \overset{1}{2}7 \\ + 35 \\ \hline 62 \end{array}$$
7 + 5 = 12
Write 2 in the ones column and 1 in the tens column.
2 + 3 + 1 = 6 tens

That they did not use this algorithm should not surprise us. It is the result of centuries of refinement. It is commonly used because it's efficient, but it is also less obvious in that someone probably needs to tell you about placing the one ten from 12 in the tens column. As groups share their different ways of working, children learn from each other. At some point, the teacher will probably want to share "her" way—noting that it's shorter than some of theirs, but that they should work with the procedure they find easiest to understand. There is no reason why all children should end up using the same algorithm.

The next problem the teacher posed to the children involved the addition of 13 and 54. Up until recently, teachers would have introduced this problem, which does not involve renaming, far earlier than the one involving 27 and 35, which does involve renaming. We have finally come to realize, however, that this type of split leads to misconceptions about the operation and the algorithm.

The addition of

$$\begin{array}{c} 437 \\ +\ 25 \end{array} \text{ or } \begin{array}{c} 437 \\ +521 \end{array} \text{ or } \begin{array}{c} 254 \\ +283 \end{array} \text{ or } \begin{array}{c} 672 \\ +188 \end{array}$$

is simply an extension of the procedure to the hundreds place. We want children to have enough experience with numbers with more than two digits so they realize that there are no hidden difficulties; if they had no calculators, they could do the computation. But most of the practice will focus on two-digit numbers, with which we do want them to become proficient.

Adding multiples of 10, 100, and so on is another simpler case:

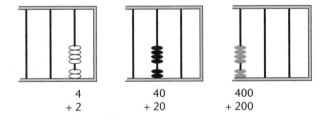

4	40	400
+ 2	+ 20	+ 200

As children work with addition (as well as the other operations), they should be encouraged to estimate in order to ascertain whether the answer they reach is approximately correct. Activity Card 10–1 illustrates how an estimation activity provides practice with adding multiples of 10.

Use of *compatible numbers*—numbers that are easy to compute mentally—is a powerful estimation strategy. Some problem-solving activities to practice

Activity Card 10–1

Compatible Numbers

▼ Look at these numbers. You can use compatible numbers to help add them.

$3.09
$4.99
$5.15
$7.05
$17.95
$13.11

I see many pairs of compatible numbers — which should I take?

Compatible numbers basket

▼ Name 2 numbers

• That add to about $10 _____

• That add to about $20 _____

• That add to about $30 _____

▼ See how many different pairs of compatible numbers you can find.

mental computation and sharpen estimation skills, as well as deepen understanding of addition algorithms, are found on Activity Card 10–2.

Column Addition

Column addition with three or more one-digit addends is often introduced after some of the basic addition facts are learned, so it may be used to provide varied practice. One new skill is required—adding an unseen addend. In this example, the 4 resulting from the addition of 3 + 1 must be added mentally to 2:

Think

$$\left.\begin{array}{r} 3 \\ 1 \end{array}\right\} 3 + 1 = 4$$
$$\begin{array}{r} +2 \end{array} \quad 4 + 2 = 6$$

As with other topics, column addition is introduced through a problem situation:

Sasha bought a lollipop for 3¢, a jellybean for 1¢, and a gumdrop for 2¢. How much did he spend?

Activity Card 10–2

Starters

▼ Find each missing digit:

$$
\begin{array}{cccc}
52 & 29 & \square 8 & 452 \\
+16 & +36 & +21 & +\square 7 \\
\hline
6\square & \square 5 & 79 & 489
\end{array}
$$

▼ Use only the digits given in the cloud to make a problem with the sum shown:

$$
\begin{array}{ccc}
\begin{array}{c} \cancel{4}\ \cancel{4} \\ +\ \cancel{4}\ 6 \\ \hline 9\ 0 \end{array} (4, 6) &
\begin{array}{c} -\ - \\ +\ \_\ \_ \\ \hline 8\ 8 \end{array} (3, 5) &
\begin{array}{c} -\ - \\ +\ \_\ \_ \\ \hline 7\ 0 \end{array} (7, 3)
\end{array}
$$

▼ Use 2, 4, 6, and 8 for these problems:

- Use each digit once to make the smallest sum possible.

$$\begin{array}{c} \square\square \\ +\square\square \\ \hline \end{array}$$

- Use each digit once to make the largest sum possible.

$$\begin{array}{c} \square\square \\ +\square\square \\ \hline \end{array}$$

- Use each digit once to make a sum as near 100 as possible.

$$\begin{array}{c} \square\square \\ +\square\square \\ \hline \end{array}$$

▼ Use only these numbers:

| 24 | 40 | 22 | 15 | 31 | 14 |

- Name two numbers whose sum is 64. _____
- Name two numbers whose sum is more than 70. _____
- Name two numbers whose sum ends in 8. _____
- Name three numbers whose sum is 93. _____

Using manipulative materials, flannelboard objects, or drawings will help children to visualize the situation:

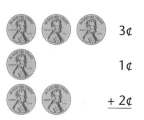

The materials or pictures help the children to bridge from the situation to the solution with symbols.

Is it better to teach children to add down, to add up, or to group numbers that add to 10 (using the associative property)?

Research has indicated that adding either up or down (and using the opposite to check) is better than grouping (Wheatley and Wheatley 1978). Fewer errors of omitting numbers or using a number more than once are likely to occur. "Be consistent" is the best rule.

Higher-Decade Addition

Combinations such as 17 + 4 or 47 + 8 or 3 + 28, called *higher-decade combinations,* are used in a strategy sometimes referred to as "adding by endings." Note that the two-digit number may come either before or after the one-digit number.

The need for higher-decade addition arises in many real-life problems; for instance, adding 6¢ tax to a purchase of 89¢. The skill is also necessary in column addition and in multiplication. To help children learn how to do such addition readily, experiences with manipulative materials, place-value charts, and the abacus are useful. The strategy of counting on will probably occur to some children, and it's clearly a way of solving this type of problem. In Activity Card 10–3, attention is focused on the relationship of 9 + 5, 19 + 5, 29 + 5, and so on. As a result of this activity, we want children to realize the following:

- In each example, the sum has a 4 in the ones place because 9 + 5 = 14, and the tens place has 1 more ten.

Activity Card 10–3

Look for Patterns

▼ Complete the sums in these addition problems:

$$3 + 6 = 9$$
$$13 + 6 = 19$$
$$23 + 6 = 29$$
$$53 + 6 = \boxed{}$$
$$83 + 6 = \boxed{}$$

Find a pattern in the answers!

▼ How does 4 + 8 help you to add 14 + 8?

$$\begin{array}{cc} 4 & 14 \\ +8 & +8 \\ \hline 12 & 22 \end{array}$$

▼ Your turn:

$$\begin{array}{cccccc} 9 & 19 & 29 & 39 & 79 & 89 \\ +5 & +5 & +5 & +5 & +5 & +5 \end{array}$$

$$\begin{array}{cccccc} 7 & 17 & 27 & 37 & 47 & 87 \\ +3 & +3 & +3 & +3 & +3 & +3 \end{array}$$

- The sum of 9 + 5 is more than 10, so the sum of 19 + 5 is more than 20, and the sum of 29 + 5 is more than 30.

- For 59 + 5, there is 4 in the ones place and 6 (5 + 1) in the tens place.

Children need to learn to perform such additions automatically, without adding ones and then tens as they do with examples such as 27 + 32. Such experiences not only encourage mental computation but also greatly increase this skill.

● Subtraction

Subtraction poses a bit more difficulty for most children. Because subtraction of multidigit numbers requires only knowledge of the basic subtraction facts and of place value, as does addition, renaming seems more confusing to many children.

The standard algorithm for subtraction, which has been taught in recent years, is the *decomposition algorithm*. It involves a logical process of "decomposing" or renaming the sum. In the following example, 9 tens and 1 one is renamed as 8 tens and 11 ones:

Think

$$\begin{array}{ll} \overset{8\ \ 1}{9\,1} & 11 - 4 = 7 \text{ ones} \\ -2\,4 & 8 - 2 = 6 \text{ tens} \\ \hline 6\,7 & \end{array}$$

Before the decomposition algorithm gained prominence in this country, the *equal-additions algorithm* was taught. Both the sum and the known addend are renamed. In this example, 1 ten is added to each as 10 ones or 1 ten:

Think

$$\begin{array}{ll} \overset{1}{9}\,1 & 11 - 4 = 7 \text{ ones} \\ \underset{3}{-2}\,4 & 9 - 3 = 6 \text{ tens} \\ \hline 6\,7 & \end{array}$$

Research has confirmed that both are effective in terms of speed and accuracy when taught meaningfully (Brownell 1947), with a problem setting, manipulative materials, and clear rationale.

But children often develop different algorithms for subtraction, just as they did for addition. They may try to work from left to right, and perhaps it is at this point that some confusion begins. But, when they think about the numbers, they construct alternatives such as the following:

$$\begin{array}{ccccc} 74 & & 74 & & 74 \\ -58 & = & -(58+2) & = & -60 \\ & & & & \overline{14 + 2 = 16} \end{array}$$

or

$$\begin{array}{rl} 70 - 50 = & 20 \\ 4 - 8 = & -4 \\ \hline 20 - 4 = & 16 \end{array}$$

or

$$\begin{array}{r} 70 + 4 \\ -50 - 8 \\ \hline 20 - 4 = 16 \end{array}$$

or

$$\begin{array}{rl} 70 - 50 = & 20 \\ 20 - 8 = & 12 \\ 12 + 4 = & 16 \end{array}$$

Some algorithms that children construct are related to the *complement technique*, which has been used in some other countries as the primary algorithm for subtraction. This method relies on replacing the subtrahend with a related number—its complement—and then adding to the minuend. The complement of any single digit number is the difference of that number and nine.

Digit: 0 1 2 3 4 5 6 7 8 9
Complement: 9 8 7 6 5 4 3 2 1 0

Here is an example:

   2384 Align the numbers vertically.
  − ~~1695~~ Cross out the subtrahend,
   8304 replacing it below with the
        complement of each digit.

   2384 Add this new number to
  − ~~1695~~ the minuend.
  + 8304
  10688

  10688 Cross out the left-most digit
  + 1 of this sum (it will be a 1)
   689 and add one for the answer.

If your students are having difficulty, you might want to show some of them this algorithm or similar algorithms for the other operations (see Meiring 1982). You might also have them conjecture about *why* it "works."

Children need to connect the steps that are used to solve a problem with manipulatives to the steps in the symbolic solution of an algorithm. Questions that encourage children to focus on the connections between manipulatives and symbols are very important. Consider the following example using a problem posed by Rathmell and Trafton (1990, p. 168):

There were 61 children who did not sign up for hot lunch. There were 22 of these who went home for lunch. The rest brought a cold lunch. How many brought a cold lunch?

What are we trying to find?

Do you think it will be more than 60?

How many did not sign up for hot lunch?

How many went home?

How can we show this?

What do we subtract first?

Are there enough ones to subtract 2?

How can we get more ones?

If we trade in a 10 for ones, how many ones do we get?

How many ones are there now?

How much is 5 tens and 11 ones?

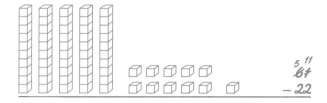

Now are there enough ones to subtract 2?

What is 11 − 2?

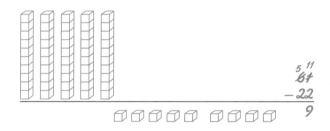

Now what do we subtract?

What is 5 tens minus 2 tens?

How many children are eating a cold lunch?

Does this answer make sense? Why?

Experiences with regrouping from tens to hundreds or in both places are also helpful. Activity Card 10–4 presents two activities that provide practice with estimation as well as computation. To focus attention on higher-decade combinations like 17 − 4 and 59 − 6 is the goal of Activity Card 10–5. Subtracting a one-digit number from another number is facilitated by focusing attention on the pattern.

Activity Card 10–4

Mentally Calculate!

▼ Use only these numbers to answer each question:

78	27	39	43	46	15

- What two numbers have a difference of
  35?_____ 31?_____ 39?_____
- What two numbers have a difference of
  more than 50?_____ of less than 5?_____
- What number minus 39 gives 7?_____
- What number minus 27 gives 16?_____
- What two numbers have a difference that
  ends in 19?_____ 7?_____

▼ Find the missing weights:

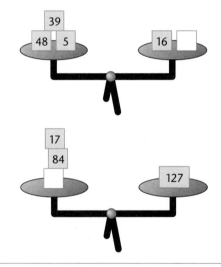

Activity Card 10–5

Pattern Search

▼ Write the answer to the last problem in this group:

Can you find a pattern in the answers?

$$
\begin{array}{ccccc}
16 & 26 & 46 & 56 & 36 \\
-\ 4 & -\ 4 & -\ 4 & -\ 4 & -\ 4 \\
\hline
12 & 22 & 42 & 52 &
\end{array}
$$

▼ Try these:

1.
$$
\begin{array}{ccccccc}
18 & 28 & 48 & 38 & 68 & 58 & 98 \\
-\ 2 & -\ 2 & -\ 2 & -\ 2 & -\ 2 & -\ 2 & -\ 2
\end{array}
$$

2.
$$
\begin{array}{ccccccc}
18 & 28 & 68 & 38 & 48 & 78 & 58 \\
-\ 9 & -\ 9 & -\ 9 & -\ 9 & -\ 9 & -\ 9 & -\ 9
\end{array}
$$

▼ Complete these subtraction problems:

$$
\begin{array}{cccc}
60 & 60 & 60 & 60 \\
-27 & -47 & -17 & -57
\end{array}
$$

- What is alike about each example?
- What is alike about each answer?
- Use the pattern to do these mentally:

$60 - 37 = \square$ $60 - 7 = \square$

▼ Now try these:

$43 - 13 = \square$ $153 - 13 = \square$
$73 - 13 = \square$ $123 - 13 = \square$
$93 - 13 = \square$ $273 - 13 = \square$

Zeros in the Sum

The presence of zeros in the sum demands special attention. If the zero is in the ones place, it causes little difficulty. Thus, in this example, 50 is renamed as 4 tens and 10 ones:

$$
\begin{array}{r}
850 \\
-\ 287 \\
\hline
\end{array}
$$

Zero in the tens place is slightly more difficult, especially when regrouping in the ones place is also necessary. The steps are shown in Figure 10–1.

The biggest difficulty lies with numbers having more than one zero. One alternative is multiple renaming, from hundreds to tens, then from tens to ones:

$$
\begin{array}{cccc}
500 & \overset{4\ 10}{5\ 0\ 0} & \overset{9\ 10}{4\ \cancel{10}\ 0} & \overset{9\ 10}{4\ \cancel{10}\ 0} \\
-257 & -257 & -257 & -257 \\
\hline
 & & & 243
\end{array}
$$

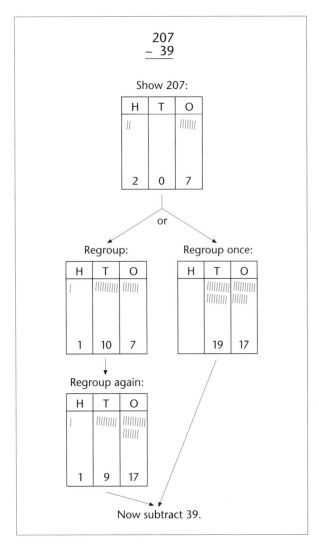

Figure 10–1 • **Subtraction model**

Place-value experiences are important in preparing children to cope with these problems. They must clearly understand that 500 can be renamed as 4 hundreds and 10 tens, or as 4 hundreds, 9 tens, and 10 ones. They will then find it easier to recognize the need for multiple regrouping when they see multiple zeros and will be able to do all the renaming at once:

$$
\begin{array}{cc}
500 & \overset{4\ 9\ 1}{\cancel{5}\cancel{0}\cancel{0}} \quad 500 = 49 \text{ tens } 10 \text{ ones} \\
-283 & -283
\end{array}
$$

In the example 207 − 39, children can similarly rename 207 as 19 tens and 17 ones in one step. However, the need to do this is not readily recognizable to all children; those who need to do the double renaming should be allowed to do so.

● Multiplication

Before children tackle the multiplication algorithms, they must have a firm grasp on place value, expanded notation, and the distributive property, as well as the basic facts of multiplication. As with the other operations, it is wise to review each of these prerequisites before beginning work with the multiplication algorithms. And it is also wise to develop situations or problems for which children compute mentally, without concern for the paper-and-pencil forms.

Multiplication with One-Digit Multipliers

Children should be encouraged to talk about what they think, as the meaning of multiplication is reinforced with materials:

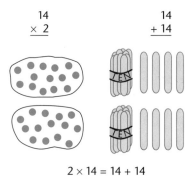

$$2 \times 14 = 14 + 14$$

Use of the distributive property is pointed out:

$$2 \times 14 = 2 \times (10 + 4) = (2 \times 10) + (2 \times 4)$$
$$= 20 + 8 = 28$$

Arrays are also used to develop meaning:

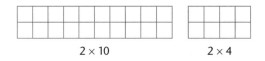

Place-value ideas are noted along with materials:

Expanded algorithms can be developed or constructed by the children easily:

$$\begin{array}{r} 14 \\ \times\ 2 \end{array}$$

1 ten 4 ones		4	$2 \times 10 = 20$
$\times$	2	$\times\ 2$	$2 \times 4 = \underline{\ 8}$
2 tens 8 ones		$\underline{8}$	$20 + \ 8 = 28$
		$\underline{+20}$	
		28	

One algorithm that children probably won't discover for themselves is the lattice method, which is illustrated in Figure 10–2. This centuries-old procedure avoids the use of renaming in multiplication (although it does involve renaming in addition), and it may be helpful to children having difficulty. Or it may be presented to children with an invitation to see if they can figure it out!

The distributive property helps children understand the algorithm. Activity Card 10–6 illustrates one way of using the property in providing mental computation and serves to sharpen estimation skills. The calculator also promotes a focus on estimation, while decreasing the amount of time spent

Activity Card 10–6

Use What You Know!

▼ Rename the larger factor, and multiply it by the smaller factor. Then subtract the smaller one.

1. 3×99 *Think*

     3 hundreds – 3 = 300 – 3 = 297

2. 7×104 *Think*

     7 hundreds + 7 fours =

3. 6×49 _____

4. 5×95 _____

5. 4×24 _____

on computation. Some activities with that focus are found on Activity Card 10–7. Also aided by calculator use is the exploration and discovery of patterns. One of the most useful of these is the focus of Activity Card 10–8.

Multiplication with Two-Digit Multipliers

As children work with two-digit multipliers, the use of manipulative materials becomes cumbersome. Grids provide one means of bridging the gap from concrete materials to symbols. As shown in Figure 10–3, a grid can also provide entirely new ways of

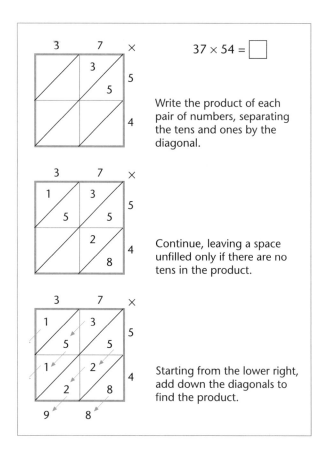

Figure 10–2 • Lattice method for multiplication

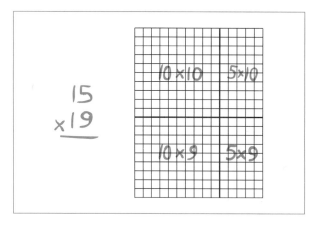

Figure 10–3 • Use of a grid to solve multiplication with two-digit multiplier

Activity Card 10–7

What's Missing?

▼ Guess the numbers that will go into the circles and boxes.

Write your number and then check it on a .
Score 2 points if correct on the first try and
1 point if correct on the second try.

(④ ⑥ ⑦ ⑧ 32 | 48 | 68 | 82)

◯ × ☐ = 408   ◯ × ☐ = 272

◯ × ☐ = 476   ◯ × ☐ = 336

◯ × ☐ = 384   ◯ × ☐ = 492

▼ Try these using only 2, 3, and 4:

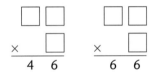

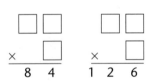

▼ Now use only 4, 6, 8, and 9.

• Make the largest product.

☐ ☐ ☐
× ☐
‾‾‾‾‾‾

• Make the smallest product:

☐ ☐ ☐
× ☐
‾‾‾‾‾‾

Activity Card 10–8

Nines, Nines, Nines . . .

Use your ▯ to solve these equations.

Write your answers in the blanks.

9 × 1 = _____   99 × 1 = _____

9 × 2 = _____   99 × 2 = _____

9 × 3 = _____   99 × 3 = _297_

9 × 4 = _____   99 × 4 = _____

9 × 5 = _45_   99 × 5 = _____

9 × 6 = _____   99 × 6 = _____

9 × 7 = _____   99 × 7 = _693_

9 × 8 = _____   99 × 8 = _____

9 × 9 = _____   99 × 9 = _____

• What is the sum of the digits in each product?_____

• What is the sum of the first and last digits in each product? _____

• What number is the middle digit in each product?_____

▼ Use your ▯ to solve these equations. When you see the pattern, try to predict the remaining answers.

Then use your ▯ to check.

3 × 9 = _27_   5 × 9 = _45_

3 × 99 = _297_   5 × 99 = _____

3 × 999 = _____   5 × 999 = _____

3 × 9999 = _____   5 × 9999 = _____

3 × 99999 = _____   5 × 99999 = _____

6 × 9 = _____   7 × 9 = _____

6 × 99 = _____   7 × 99 = _____

6 × 999 = _5994_   7 × 999 = _____

6 × 9999 = _____   7 × 9999 = _69993_

6 × 99999 = _____   7 × 99999 = _____

viewing and writing about a multiplication example. Some other materials are used to tie the work to previously learned procedures, but increasingly the emphasis shifts to working with symbols, as shown in Figure 10–4. This approach is possible because of the earlier base built on the use of materials.

Two activities for using calculators with multi-digit multipliers can be found on Activity Cards 10–9 and 10–10. One aids in strengthening the meaning of the algorithms, and the other presents a problem-solving situation. Another natural blend of calculators and written algorithms is shown in Activity Card 10–11. This computation might be broken into 47 × 5280 and 56 × 5280 so that each of these computations could be done on a calculator and the products recorded. Students can then mentally multiply the first product by one million and sum the two products. Such computational approaches illustrate how the calculator, mental computation, and paper-and-pencil recording may be integrated to solve a single problem.

Multiplying by 10 and Multiples of 10

Multiplying by 10 comes easily to most children, and it is readily extended to multiplying by 100 and 1000 as children gain understanding of larger numbers. The children can be shown a series of examples, after which they are asked to discuss and generalize, noting that, when there is a zero in the ones place, each digit moves one place to the left in the product. Activity Card 10–12 shows how a calculator can help children develop ideas about the effect of zero.

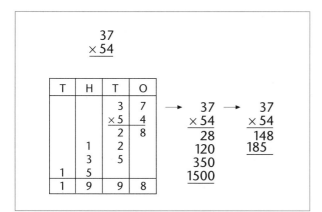

Figure 10–4 • **Symbolic approach to multiplication with two-digit multiplier**

Activity Card 10–9

Analyzing Multiplication

▼ Use the partial product from the completed problems to help you find the missing numbers *mentally*.

```
    387
  × 264
   1548
  23220
  77400
 102168
```

387 × 60 = _____

2640 × 70 = _____

200 × 387 = _____

2640 × _____ = 79200

```
    264
  × 387
   1848
  21120
  79200
 102168
```

264 × 80 = _____

264 × 300 = _____

I know I can do these mentally!

▼ Check your mental answers with a . Score one point for each correct answer.

Activity Card 10–10

Making Conjectures

▼ Use your calculator:

• Multiply some 2-digit numbers by 99. Record your results and make a conjecture.

• Multiply some 3-digit numbers by 999. Record your results and make a conjecture.

• Multiply some 2-digit numbers by 999. Record your results and make a conjecture.

▼ Now try these. Find the pattern.

11 × 11
111 × 111
1111 × 1111

Hmmm — con·jec·ture: a hypothesis . . .

▼ Predict 11111 × 11111 and check!

Activity Card 10–11

How Large Is a Large Number?

▼ Use your to find the answer to this large-number problem:

47000056 × 5280 = _____

- Can you get an exact answer on your calculator in one step? Tell why.

- How can you use your calculator to help you get an exact answer? Show your method.

Activity Card 10–12

Zeros Count

▼ Use your  to find the product:

8 × 10 = _____

- How many 0's in 10? _____
- How many 0's in the product? _____

6 × 100 = _____

- How many 0's in 100? _____
- How many 0's in the product? _____

9 × 1000 = _____

- How many 0's in 1000? _____
- How many 0's in the product? _____

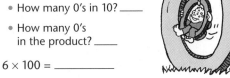

▼ Complete this multiplication table. Use your to check your answers.

×	10	100	1000
7			
14		*1400*	
28			*28000*
247			
989			

Multiplying by 20, 30, 200, 300, and so on is an extension of multiplying by 10 and 100. The emphasis is placed on comparing what happens across examples and generalizing from the pattern. For example, have children consider 3×50:

$$3 \times 5 = 15$$
$$3 \times 5 \text{ tens} = 15 \text{ tens} = 150$$
$$3 \times 50 = 150$$

Then have them consider 4×50:

$$4 \times 5 = 20$$
$$4 \times 5 \text{ tens} = \underline{\quad} \text{ tens} = \underline{\quad}$$
$$4 \times 50 = \underline{\quad}$$

After several more examples, they are given other examples for which they are to find the pattern:

20	70	90		36	52
× 7	× 6	× 8	. . .	×20	×30

A similar sequence is followed for examples with hundreds, such as 2×300:

$$2 \times 3 = 6$$
$$2 \times 3 \text{ hundreds} = \underline{\quad} \text{ hundreds} = \underline{\quad}$$
$$2 \times 300 = \underline{\quad}$$

Finally, examples such as these might be given:

273	418
× 50	× 80

It is tremendously useful for children to be able to use multiplication by rounded numbers in making estimates. Consider one child's thinking when asked to make an estimate:

Think

427   That's about 20 × 400.
× 19   2 × 4 = 8.
     2 × 400 = 800.
     So 20 × 400 would be 8000.

Another child's thinking will differ:

Think

427   That's about 20 × 425.
× 19   2 × 425 = 850.
     20 × 425 = 8500.
     So 19 × 427 is about 8500.

Both 8000 and 8500 are good estimates. When making estimates, students should round to numbers that are easy for them to compute. Consequently, different estimates are not only to be expected, but also encouraged. In conjunction with estimation, students also need to answer questions such as these:

- How do I know how many zeros will be in the product?
- How is the number of zeros in the estimate related to the factors?
- How many digits will be in the estimated product?

Multiplying with Zeros

When zeros appear in the factor being multiplied, particular attention needs to be given to the effect on the product or partial product. Many children are prone to ignore the zero. Thus, for 9×306, their answer may be

$$\overset{5}{306} \\ \underline{\times \quad 9} \\ 324$$

When an estimate is made first, children have a way of determining whether their answer is "in the ballpark." Use of a place-value chart may help them to understand what the correct procedure must be, as will expanded notation:

Estimate

$$\begin{array}{ll} 306 & 9 \times 3 = 27 \\ \underline{\times \quad 9} & 9 \times 300 = 2700 \end{array}$$

T	H	T	O
	3	0	6
			9
2	7	5	4

$$\begin{aligned} 9 \times 306 &= 9 \times (300 + 6) \\ &= (9 \times 300) + (9 \times 6) \\ &= 2700 + 54 \\ &= 2754 \end{aligned}$$

Multiplication with Large Numbers

How can the calculator be used to solve computations involving numbers that appear too big for the calculator? As children experiment with using a calculator for multiplication, there will come a time when they overload the calculator. Sometimes the number to be entered will contain more digits than the display will show. At other times the product will be too big for the display. For instance, if this ex-

ample is entered in a four-function calculator, an error message will result:

$$2345678 \\ \underline{\times \qquad 4003}$$

When this happens, children should be encouraged to estimate an answer and then use the distributive property plus mental computation along with the calculator.

Estimate:

$$4000 \times 2000000 = 8000000000$$
$$4003 = 4000 + 3$$
$$\qquad = (4 \times 1000) + 3$$

Calculate:

$$4 \times 2345678 = 9382712 \quad \text{(with the calculator)}$$
$$9382712 \times 1000 = 9382712000 \quad \text{(mentally)}$$
$$3 \times 2345678 = 7037034$$

Add:

$$7037034 \\ \underline{+ \; 9382712000}$$

Such examples show how an understanding of multiplication, plus problem-solving skills, can be used with calculators to reach a solution. They also remind us that calculator algorithms differ from the currently used paper-and-pencil algorithms.

● Division

Division is without doubt the most difficult of the algorithms for children to master, for a number of reasons:

- Computation begins at the left, rather than at the right as for the other operations.
- The algorithm involves not only the basic division facts, but also subtraction and multiplication.
- There are a number of interactions in the algorithm, but their pattern moves from one spot to another.
- Trial quotients, involving estimation, must be used and may not always be successful at the first attempt—or even the second.

Teachers struggle to teach division, and children struggle to learn division; it is little wonder that the use of calculators is posed as a means of resolving the dilemma of the division algorithm. As *An Agenda for Action* (NCTM 1980, p. 6) indicates:

> For most students, much of a full year of instruction in mathematics is spent on the division of whole numbers—a massive investment with increasingly limited productive return. . . . For most complex problems, using the calculator for rapid and accurate computation makes a far greater contribution to functional competence in daily life.

On the national mathematics assessments, some exercises were given with and without the use of calculators. On the fourth assessment, third graders were given the problem $3\overline{)42}$. When calculators were not used, about 20 percent of the answers were correct; when calculators were used, about 50 percent were correct (Lindquist et al. 1988). On one item on the sixth assessment, students who reported using a calculator scored 82 percent correct, and those who reported they did not use a calculator scored only 35 percent (Kenney and Silver 1997). Even more dramatic were results from the second assessment (Carpenter et al. 1981). One exercise, $23\overline{)3052}$, was given only to thirteen- and seventeen-year-olds when calculators were not used, because nine-year-olds had not yet been taught division with a two-digit divisor. Thirteen-year-olds scored 46 percent and seventeen-year-olds scored 50 percent without calculators. With calculators, the scores rose dramatically, to 82 percent and 91 percent, respectively. And 50 percent of the nine-year-olds attained the correct answer when they used calculators. Considering that half of the seventeen-year-olds could not perform the division even after years of practice, is it not reasonable to let them use the tool with which they are successful—and which they will use anyway for the rest of their lives?

The NCTM Standards stress that "our technological age requires us to rethink how computation is done today" (NCTM 1989, p. 44). We strongly recommend that division with one-digit divisors should be the focus of instruction, followed by some work with two-digit divisors so that students understand how such division is done. Performing more complex division—perhaps any that takes over 30 seconds to do—with paper and pencil is a thing of the past for adults. Thus, schools should not demand that children spend countless hours mastering an antiquated skill. Teachers can't afford the instructional time for this. Instead, estimation skills should be used to define the bounds of the quotient, so that the reasonableness of calculator answers can be determined—just as such estimates should be used with division with one-digit divisors and, in fact, with all addition, subtraction, and multiplication too.

Division with Remainders

Children encounter remainders from the time they begin to work with division. As long as problems remain on a concrete level, the concept of remainder is rather easy. Here are some examples of varied situations:

- Separate a class of 31 into 2 teams. The 1 left over is scorekeeper.
- Pass out 17 pieces of paper to 5 children. Each receives 3 sheets with 2 left over.
- How much change would you get when you buy some pencils for 24 cents each and give the clerk 75 cents?
- Four children can ride in each car. If 30 children are going on the class trip, how many cars are needed?

The "part left over" is given a different task, discarded, saved, or rounded up. In other cases, it is expressed as a fraction or decimal. With calculators, the results of inexact division are expressed in decimal form, and children need to learn how to interpret the remainder when it is not an integer (see Chapter 12).

Initially, children are taught to write the remainder in one of the following ways:

$$
\begin{array}{r}
2 \\
6\overline{)13} \\
12 \\
\hline
1
\end{array}
\quad \text{with 1 left over}
$$

$$
\begin{array}{r}
5 \\
5\overline{)27} \\
25 \\
\hline
2
\end{array}
\quad
\begin{array}{l}
\text{remainder 2} \\
\text{(later shortened to R2 or r2)}
\end{array}
$$

It is important to emphasize the real-life situations from which examples arise and to decide whether a "remainder of 2" makes sense in that situation. Activities such as the game in Activity Card 10–13 provide practice in identifying the remainder.

Calculators can be used to solve problems with remainders, but the correct answer depends on the thinking a child does. Consider this problem:

> A bus holds 36 children. If 1000 children are being bused to a concert, how many buses are needed?

Does the calculator decide which keys to punch and in what order to punch them? Does the calculator interpret the result? Calculators don't solve problems—people do. Research shows the previous problem to be difficult for children to solve with or without a calculator. An answer of 27 remainder 28 is often reported without a calculator, and 27.777 buses is reported with a calculator. The children seem more intent on producing an answer than on deciding if their answer makes sense.

Some activities have been developed for calculators with "integer division" capabilities so that any remainder is displayed as a whole number. These activities were designed to help students develop conceptual understanding of division and the relationships among the dividend, divisor, and remainder. They involve estimation skills, so students have a better chance of success if they are reasoning as they work. An example is given in Activity Card 10–14.*

Division with One-Digit Divisors

Children clearly need a good understanding of place value as they work with the division algorithm, and understanding of the distributive property is also essential. Two algorithms have been used for division most frequently; both are effective (Van Engen

---

Activity Card 10–13

The Remainder Game
(A game for 2 to 4 players)

For this game, you will need

- A copy of this gameboard on heavy paper
- Four cards of each numeral 0 to 9
- A counter for each player

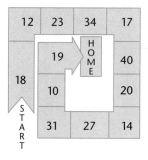

Game Rules

1. Place the cards face down in a pile.

2. The first player draws a card.

   - For a player's first turn, divide the first number on the board by the number drawn.

   - For a player's additional turns, the dividend is the number on the space where his or her counter landed on the previous turn.

3. Move the counter forward by the number of spaces indicated by the *remainder*. If the remainder is 0, no move is made.

4. Each of the other players go in turn.

5. To get "home," a player must be able to move the exact number of spaces left.

   The first person home wins!

Activity Card 10–14

Number Net

▼ Work with a partner or in a small group to determine the missing values:

Dividend	Divisor	Quotient	Integral Remainder
632	73	____	____
345	____	____	45
____	34	____	27
____	____	____	18
____	746	89	____
7439	____	274	____
____	____	56	73

▼ If the solutions are not unique, explain why not. If no solution is possible, explain why.

- Which combinations result in unique solutions?

- Given any two numbers in a row, can a solution always be found? Why or why not?

- Given only one number in a row, can a solution always be found? Why or why not?

- Which combinations make finding a solution easy? Difficult? Why?

---

*Activity Card 10–14 is adapted from Usnick and Lamphere (1990).

and Gibb 1956). The *distributive algorithm* is most common:

$$
\begin{array}{r}
94\ \text{r}3 \\
4\overline{)379} \\
36 \\
\hline
19 \\
16 \\
\hline
3
\end{array}
$$

Think

How many fours in 37?

How many fours in 19?

The *subtractive algorithm* is, however, easier for most children to learn because correction of the quotient is seldom needed. The child can take out any number of the divisor, but the process may take longer.

$$
\begin{array}{r}
4\overline{)379} \\
200 \quad 50 \times 4 \\
\hline
179 \\
160 \quad 40 \times 4 \\
\hline
19 \\
16 \quad 4 \times 4 \\
\hline
3 \quad \overline{94\ \text{r}3}
\end{array}
$$

$$
\begin{array}{r}
4\overline{)379} \\
40 \quad 10 \times 4 \\
\hline
339 \\
40 \quad 10 \times 4
\end{array}
$$

Sometimes the quotient is written above the dividend:

$$
\begin{array}{r}
40 \\
50 \\
4\overline{)379} \\
200 \\
\hline
179 \\
\vdots
\end{array}
$$

Although we will help children to understand such algorithms, we also need to let them explore. As with the other operations, children develop their own algorithms. Some are closely allied with manipulative materials, as shown in Figure 10–5. Others make use of number sense, reasoning in terms of the numbers involved, as the following examples indicate:

52 ÷ 7   52 divided by 7 is close to 49 divided by 7, or 7. But there are 3 left over. So the answer is 7 remainder 3.

85 ÷ 5   20 divided by 5 is 4. There are four 20's in 80, so 4 × 4 = 16, and then there's one more 5. So the answer is 17.

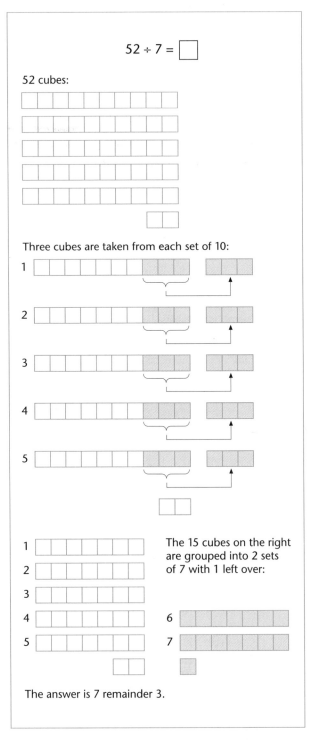

Figure 10–5 • Alternative algorithm for division using manipulative materials (Adapted from Harel and Behr 1991.)

69 ÷ 4   69 = 60 + 9. 60 divided by 4 is 15, and 9 divided by 4 is 2, with a remainder of 1. So the answer is 17 remainder 1.

Burns (1991) posed problems and had third-grade students explain their answers and the methods they used to reach them. For instance, one problem called for four children to divide fifty-four marbles equally. One group counted out fifty-four cubes (to represent the marbles), divided them into four groups, and wrote:

> We think we get 13 each. We think this because we took the cubes and "dealed" out them one by one. We had two left. Bryce was sick so we gave the extra to him. (Burns 1991, p. 16)

Other groups wrote:

> We had 54. We gave each person 10 because we "thout" if there was 40 there would be 4 tens and 14 would be left. Each person gets 3 "witch" "leves" 2. Each person gets 13.

> We drew 54 marbles and then I numbered them 1, 2, 3, 4 and then we counted the ones and then we knew that each child gets 13 marbles and we lost the other two.

> I write down 54. I took away 12. I got 42. I took "anther" 12 away. I got 18. I took another 12 away. I got 6. Then I took away 4. I got 2. I "chiped" each of them into "halfs" that made 4 "halfs." Each person got 13 and a half. (Burns 1991, pp. 16–17)

Burns noted that, from listening to each others' methods, the children not only heard different approaches to solving division problems, but they also learned that division can be done in a variety of ways.

Have you begun to believe that the possibilities for constructing ways to find an answer are myriad? Just when you think you've seen all the possible algorithms, another student will probably come up with a new one. Enjoy this process. Be an explorer right along with the children. But you also have another role. Just because all the algorithms we've displayed here are correct doesn't mean that children never come up with incorrect algorithms. They do.

You need to watch for this possibility—and you need to make children aware of the need to "prove" that a procedure really works across examples. You also need to be aware of consistent error patterns that crop up in children's work—error patterns that usually indicate some difficulty such as lack of knowledge about place value, or a lack of mastery of some basic facts, and some other misunderstanding. Fortunately, there are sources of information, such as Ashlock (1994), to which you can turn. This source not only helps you identify the patterns, but

also provides specific suggestions for how to help the child get onto the right track. For additional help in working with children with learning problems, you could turn to such articles as Moyer and Moyer (1978) or Sears (1986).

As with the other operations, it is important that children work with manipulative materials as well as place-value charts. They need to keep in mind the problem situation, and not forget that it is the process of sharing that is of concern, not merely working their way through the algorithm. A variety of experiences, such as those on Activity Cards 10–15 and 10–16, may help children to gain facility with the division algorithm.

There is evidence from research that students also need to be encouraged to do more reasoning

---

Activity Card 10–15

The Missing Digits Game

▼ Try this game with several friends who have been divided into two teams.

- Teams take turns selecting the leader for a round of the game.

- The leader starts a round by working out a division problem and putting the pattern on the board.

- Players on each team take turns asking about the digits that go in the boxes. For example, a player on Team A might ask if there are any boxes containing 2's; then a player on Team B might ask if there are any containing 7's.

- If a digit appears in the problem, the leader writes it in the appropriate box(es).

- A team scores a point for each box that gets filled in during its turn. If there are no boxes for a digit, the team scores 0 for that turn.

- The winner for the round is the team with the highest score. (If a team guesses the problem before all the boxes are filled in, it wins the round and gets bonus points for the number of boxes that are still empty.)

▼ Play several rounds to determine which team wins the game!

Activity Card 10–16

Making Examples

▼ Make a division example with

• A dividend of 47 and a divisor of 3

• A dividend of 81 and a divisor of 5

▼ Now make a division example with

I know I can do this . . .

• A quotient of 6 r2

• A quotient of 10 r4

• A quotient of 23 r5

▼ Try these:

• A divisor of 6 and a quotient of 15 r3

• A divisor of 3 and a quotient of 25 r2

• A dividend of 83 and a quotient of 11 r6

about their work. In particular, middle-school students were found to have a very difficult time providing written explanations of their reasoning about division problems with remainders (Silver et al. 1993). They did not associate "sense-making" with the solution of school mathematics problems. Some students assess their results by spurious criteria, such as whether a number "divides evenly" (Garofalo and Bryant 1992). We need to keep students aware of the real-world applications of the mathematics they are learning, but we also need to make them aware of how "reason-able" it is.

Determining a reasonable answer can be particularly difficult with the division algorithms, but questions can help students make sense of them. A necessary first step in determining a quotient is to estimate the number of places in the quotient:

$$6 \overline{)839}$$

Are there as many as 10 sixes in 839? [Yes, 10 sixes are only 60.]

Are there as many as 100 sixes? [Yes, 100 sixes are 600.]

Are there as many as 200 sixes? [No, 200 sixes are 1200.]

So the quotient is between 100 and 200—and probably closer to 100.

An alternative to this is the following sequence:

$$3 \overline{)187}$$

Are there enough hundreds to divide? [No.]

Are there enough tens? [Yes—18 tens.]

So the quotient has two digits, and we decide that there are 6 tens.

So we know the answer is between 60 and 70.

Such procedures help to develop an early recognition of the range for a quotient. They help to provide meaning to the algorithm while developing valuable estimation skill.

Division with Two-Digit Divisors

Work with two-digit divisors should be aimed toward helping children to understand what the procedure involves, but not toward mastery of an algorithm. The calculator does the job for most adults, and there is little reason to have children spend months and years of time mastering multi-digit division. Other mathematics is of more importance for children to learn.

Both procedures discussed in the preceding section are readily extended to multidigit examples. In work with multidigit divisors, there are two other procedures used in many textbooks that involve using an estimate as a trial divisor. Neither method works with all examples, but both the apparent method and the rounding-off method are widely taught.

• *Apparent Method.* Only the first digit of the divisor is used as the trial number:

$$34 \overline{)876} \quad \text{How many 3's in 8?}$$

$$57 \overline{)472} \quad \text{How many 5's in 47?}$$

• *Rounding-Off Method.* When the second digit from the left in the two-digit divisor is 4 or less, the rounding-off method is the same as the apparent method. When that digit is 5, 6, 7, 8, or 9, the tens digit is increased by 1 and used as the trial divisor.

$$34 \overline{)876} \quad \text{How many 3's in 8?}$$

$$57 \overline{)472} \quad \text{How many 6's in 47?}$$

Because 57 is closer to 60 than to 50, using 60 will lead to a more accurate estimate.

Either method needs corrections. When the tens digit is 5 or greater, the trial quotient (if incorrect) will be too small by rounding off and too large by the apparent method. When the tens digit is less than 4, the trial quotient (if incorrect) will be too large by both methods.

Activity Card 10–17 suggests one idea for making estimates for division to determine whether the calculator answer is "in the right ball park." The calculator is used to judge the successfulness of estimates necessary for performing the algorithm.

The development of division with two-digit divisors proceeds through stages from concrete to abstract, paralleling the work with one-digit divisors. Much practice is needed with the symbolic form;

but, if children have had the procedure developed with materials, they are likely to attain proficiency sooner. Use of the calculator is interwoven in the activities, as indicated on Activity Card 10–18, where the calculator is used to strengthen understanding of the relationships between numbers.

● Checking

Just as it is important to estimate before computing, it is important to check after computing. Ordinarily, addition and subtraction are used to check each other, as are multiplication and division. Unfortunately, checking does not always achieve its purpose of ascertaining correctness; research has indicated that children frequently "force the check"—that is, make the results agree without actually performing the computation (Grossnickle 1938). Obviously, children must come to understand the purpose of check-

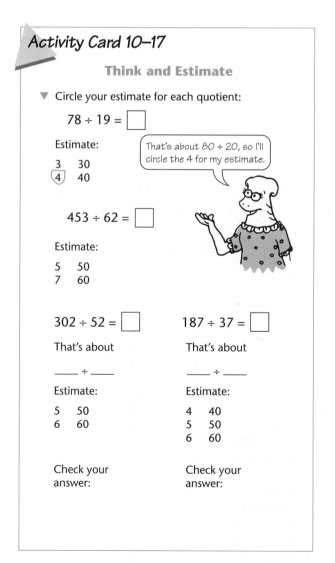

Activity Card 10–17

Think and Estimate

▼ Circle your estimate for each quotient:

78 ÷ 19 = ☐

Estimate:

    3   30
   ④)   40

That's about 80 ÷ 20, so I'll circle the 4 for my estimate.

453 ÷ 62 = ☐

Estimate:

    5   50
    7   60

302 ÷ 52 = ☐   187 ÷ 37 = ☐

That's about   That's about

___ ÷ ___   ___ ÷ ___

Estimate: Estimate:

    5   50   4   40
    6   60   5   50
                           6   60

Check your   Check your
answer: answer:

Activity Card 10–18

Easy Does It!

▼ Use your calculator to find the missing numbers:

$$45\overline{)}\;^{159\ r13}$$

$$23\overline{)69783}\;^{r\_}$$

$$\_\overline{)7683}\;^{98\ r39}$$

$$37\overline{)16972}\;^{r\_}$$

$$\_\overline{)4745}\;^{46\ r7}$$

$$73\overline{)}\;^{89\ r13}$$

ing, as well as what they must do if the solution in the check does not agree with the original solution.

Although checks by other procedures (such as casting out nines) are possible, the existence of calculators has made teaching them less important, except for enrichment. The calculator can serve many other functions, but its use in checking has not been overlooked by teachers.

Nevertheless, we do not recommend that the calculator be used primarily to have children check paper-and-pencil computation. It insults students to ask them to spend large amounts of time on a computation and then use a machine that does the computation instantly. We do recommend that estimation be used extensively, both as a means of identifying the "ballpark" for the answer *and* as a means of ascertaining the correctness of the calculator answer. The words "use your calculator to check" appear in some activity cards, but almost always when the calculator is to perform the computation following an estimate.

● Choosing Appropriate Ways

As the NCTM *Standards* and the discussion in Chapter 9 make very clear, children must learn to choose an appropriate means of calculating. Sometimes paper and pencil is better; sometimes mental computation is more efficient. Other times use of a calculator is better than either, and sometimes only an estimate is needed. Activity Card 10–19 illustrates one way of getting students to think about which method of calculation is most appropriate.

Encouraging students to defend their answers often yields valuable insight into their thinking. Children need to discuss when each method or tool is appropriate, and they need practice in making the choice, followed by more discussion, so that a rationale for their choice is clear. They need to realize that this is a personal decision. A problem that one child chooses to do with a calculator may be done with mental computation by another. Figure 9–1, from the *Standards*, should be helpful as you guide this decision-making process.

▶ A Glance at Where We've Been

Although computational skill is viewed as an essential component of children's mathematical achievement, its role in the curriculum and the methods of teaching it are changing. The development of algo-

---

Activity Card 10–19

Deciding How YOU Would Do It

▼ Decide how you would do these computation exercises, and write your answers in the column that shows the method you decided to use. Explain your decisions.

Mentally   Calculator

	Mentally	Calculator
$999 \times 4 =$	_____	_____
$500 + 85 =$	_____	_____
$4200 \div 60 =$	_____	_____
$365 \times 24 =$	_____	_____
$600 \times 1000 =$	_____	_____

▼ Follow up:

• Write a computation YOU would use a calculator with. _____

• Write a computation YOU would do mentally. _____

• Write a computation YOU would use a paper and pencil with. _____

---

rithms for each operation emphasizes the use of manipulative materials, place-value ideas, and estimation. Suggestions for developing the algorithms have been provided, and many alternative algorithms are presented. The use of calculators has been interwoven with many activities that use calculators as well as activities using other materials.

▶ THINGS TO DO: From What You've Read

1. What prerequisites must the child have in order to succeed in the chapter's opening lesson?

2. Consider the decomposition and equal-addition algorithms for subtraction. What are the advantages and disadvantages of each?

3. List at least five ways to help children who are having difficulty subtracting two two-digit numbers with regrouping.

4. Discuss: "All students should be able to divide a seven-digit number by a three-digit number using a paper-and-pencil algorithm."

5. Select an algorithm for one operation. List ways in which you could help children to master it.

6. Consider each example. Describe what a child would think as he or she worked. What questions might you ask to develop or explain the procedure? How could manipulative materials be used?

a.
$$
\begin{array}{r}
\overset{1}{5}36 \\
279 \\
+\ \ 83 \\
\hline
8
\end{array}
$$

b.
$$
\begin{array}{r}
\overset{2}{\cancel{3}}\overset{14}{4}9 \\
-1\ 84 \\
\hline
5
\end{array}
$$

c.
$$
\begin{array}{r}
73\overset{14}{\cancel{4}} \\
-2\overset{7}{\cancel{6}}9 \\
\hline
5
\end{array}
$$

d.
$$
\begin{array}{r}
\overset{5}{7}9 \\
\times\ \ 6 \\
\hline
4
\end{array}
$$

e.
$$
\begin{array}{r}
45 \\
\times\ \ 3 \\
\hline
15 \\
120
\end{array}
$$

f.
$$
38\overline{)291}^{\ \ \ 9}
$$

▶ THINGS TO DO: Going Beyond This Book

1. Choose a textbook for grade 3 or 4. Trace the development of multiplication algorithms. How are they introduced? What steps do children go through?

2. Choose a textbook series. Trace the development of division algorithms. What phases of development have been or should be modified because of the use of calculators?

3. Choose a textbook for grade 2 and analyze a lesson plan on computation in the teacher's guide. What stages from concrete to abstract are involved in the lesson?

4. Design an activity card to provide experience with materials for multiplication with zero.

5. Plan a lesson to teach children how to multiply 9876543×99.

6. Read the article by Merseth (1978). How are trading games helpful in teaching addition and subtraction? How do trading games help to bridge the gap between materials and the symbolic representation for $37 + 95$?

7. Develop three evaluation items that would assess students' understanding of adding two two-digit numbers with regrouping.

8. Several educators have proposed the use of "transition boards" in work with addition and subtraction. Read the article by Sutton and Urbatsch (1991) and develop a report for your class.

9. Becca investigating a multiplication problem is the focus of the article by Whitin (1993). After you have read about her investigation, write an evaluation of her work.

▼▼▼▼▼▼▼▼▼▼▼▼▼▼▼▼▼▼▼▼▼▼▼▼

Children's Corner

Anno, Mitsumasa. *Anno's Math Games*. New York: Philomel Books, 1987.

Anno, Mitsumasa. *Anno's Magic Seeds*. New York: Philomel Books, 1995.

Anno, Mitsumasa, and Anno, Masaichiro. *Anno's Mysterious Multiplying Jar*. New York: Philomel Books, 1983.

Froman, Robert. *The Greatest Guessing Game: A Book about Dividing*. New York: Crowell, 1978.

Trivett, John V. *Building Tables on Tables: A Book about Multiplication*. New York: Crowell, 1975.

Selected References

Ashlock, Robert B. *Error Patterns in Computation,* 6th ed. New York: Merrill, 1994.

Baroody, Arthur J., and Standifer, Dorothy J. "Addition and Subtraction in the Primary Grades." In *Research Ideas for the Classroom: Early Childhood Mathematics* (ed. Robert J. Jensen). Reston, Va.: NCTM, and New York: Macmillan, 1993, pp. 72–102.

Brandau, Linda, and Easley, Jack. *Understanding the Realities of Problem Solving in Elementary School, with Practical Pointers for Teachers.* Columbus, Ohio: ERIC Clearinghouse for Science, Mathematics, and Environmental Education, 1979.

Brownell, William A. "An Experiment on 'Borrowing' in Third-Grade Arithmetic." *Journal of Educational Research,* 41 (November 1947), pp. 161–171.

Burns, Marilyn. "Introducing Division through Problem-Solving Experiences." *Arithmetic Teacher*, 38 (April 1991), pp. 14–18.

Burns, Marilyn. *Math and Literature (K–3)*. White Plains, N.Y.: Cuisenaire Company of America, 1992.

Carpenter, Thomas P.; Corbitt, Mary Kay; Kepner, Henry S., Jr.; Lindquist, Mary Montgomery; and Reys, Robert E. *Results from the Second Mathematics Assessment of the National Assessment of Educational Progress*. Reston, Va.: NCTM, 1981.

Driscoll, Mark J. "Algorithms in Elementary School Mathematics." In *Research within Reach: Elementary School Mathematics*. Reston, Va.: NCTM, 1981.

Dubitsky, Barbara. "Making Division Meaningful with a Spreadsheet." *Arithmetic Teacher*, 36 (November 1988), pp. 18–21.

Folsom, Mary. "Operations on Whole Numbers." In *Mathematics Learning in Early Childhood*, Thirty-seventh Yearbook (ed. Joseph N. Payne). Reston, Va.: NCTM, 1975, pp. 162–190.

Garofalo, Joe, and Bryant, Jerry. "Assessing Reasonableness: Some Observations and Suggestions." *Arithmetic Teacher*, 40 (December 1992), pp. 210–212.

Graeber, Anna O., and Tanenhaus, Elaine. "Multiplication and Division: From Whole Numbers to Rational Numbers." In *Research Ideas for the Classroom: Middle Grades Mathematics* (ed. Douglas T. Owens). Reston, Va.: NCTM, and New York: Macmillan, 1993, pp. 99–117.

Grossnickle, Foster E. "The Effectiveness of Checking Subtraction by Addition." *Elementary School Journal*, 38 (February 1938), pp. 436–441.

Hamic, Eleanor J. "Students' Creative Computations: My Way or Your Way?" *Arithmetic Teacher*, 34 (September 1986), pp. 39–41.

Harel, Guershon, and Behr, Merlyn. "Ed's Strategy for Solving Division Problems." *Arithmetic Teacher*, 39 (November 1991), pp. 38–40.

Hazekamp, Donald W. "Teaching Multiplication and Division Algorithms." In *Developing Computational Skills*, 1978 Yearbook (ed. Marilyn N. Suydam). Reston, Va.: NCTM, 1978, pp. 96–128.

Hembree, Ray, and Dessart, Donald J. "Effects of Hand-Held Calculators in Precollege Mathematics Education: A Meta-Analysis." *Journal for Research in Mathematics Education*, 17 (March 1986), pp. 83–99.

Huinker, DeAnn M. "Multiplication and Division Word Problems: Improving Students' Understanding." *Arithmetic Teacher*, 37 (October 1989), pp. 8–12.

Kamii, Constance; Lewis, Barbara A.; and Livingston, Sally Jones. "Primary Arithmetic: Children Inventing Their Own Procedures." *Arithmetic Teacher*, 41 (December 1993), pp. 200–203.

Kenney, Patricia Ann, and Silver, Edward A. (eds.). *Results from the Sixth Mathematics Assessment of the National Assessment of Educational Progress*. Reston, Va.: NCTM, 1997.

Kouba, Vicky L., and Franklin, Kathy. "Multiplication and Division: Sense Making and Meaning." In *Research Ideas for the Classroom: Early Childhood Mathematics* (ed. Robert J. Jensen). Reston, Va.: NCTM, and New York: Macmillan, 1993, pp. 103–126.

Lindquist, Mary M.; Brown, Catherine A.; Carpenter, Thomas P.; Kouba, Vicky L.; Silver, Edward A.; and Swafford, Jane O. *Results from the Fourth Mathematics Assessment of the National Assessment of Educational Progress*. Reston, Va.: NCTM, 1988.

Madell, Rob. "Children's Natural Processes." *Arithmetic Teacher*, 32 (March 1985), pp. 20–22.

Meiring, Steven P. *Computation: A Changing Perspective*. Columbus, Ohio: Ohio Department of Education, 1982.

Merseth, Katherine Klippert. "Using Materials and Activities in Teaching Addition and Subtraction Algorithms." In *Developing Computational Skills*, 1978 Yearbook (ed. Marilyn N. Suydam). Reston, Va.: NCTM, 1978, pp. 61–77.

Miller, Don. *Calculator Explorations and Problems*. New Rochelle, N.Y.: Cuisenaire Company of America, 1979.

Moyer, John C., and Moyer, Margaret Bannochie. "Computation: Implications for Learning Disabled Children." In *Developing Computational Skills*, 1978 Yearbook (ed. Marilyn N. Suydam). Reston, Va.: NCTM, 1978, pp. 78–95.

National Council of Teachers of Mathematics. *Curriculum and Evaluation Standards for School Mathematics*. Reston, Va.: NCTM, 1989.

National Council of Teachers of Mathematics. *Professional Standards for Teaching Mathematics*. Reston, Va.: NCTM, 1991.

Phillipp, Randolph A. "Multicultural Mathematics and Alternative Algorithms." *Teaching Children Mathematics,* 3 (November 1996), pp. 128–133.

Rathmell, Edward, and Trafton, Paul. "Whole Number Computation." In *Mathematics for the Young Child* (ed. Joseph N. Payne). Reston, Va.: NCTM, 1990, pp. 153–172.

Reys, Robert E.; Bestgen, Barbara J.; Coburn, Terrence G.; Schoen, Harold L.; Shumway, Richard J.; Wheatley, Charlotte L.; Wheatley, Grayson H.; and White, Arthur L. *Keystrokes: Calculator Activities for Young Students: Addition and Subtraction, Multiplication and Division*. Palo Alto, Calif.: Creative Publications, 1980.

Sawada, Daiyo. "Mathematical Symbols: Insight through Invention." *Arithmetic Teacher*, 32 (February 1985), pp. 20–22.

Sears, Carol J. "Mathematics for the Learning Disabled Child in the Regular Classroom." *Arithmetic Teacher*, 33 (January 1986), pp. 5–11.

Silver, Edward A.; Shapiro, Lora J.; and Deutsch, Adam. "Sense Making and the Solution of Division Problems Involving Remainders: An Examination of Middle School Students' Solution Processes and Their Interpretations of Solutions." *Journal for Research in Mathematics Education*, 24 (March 1993), pp. 117–135.

Stanic, George M. A., and McKillip, William D. "Developmental Algorithms Have a Place in Elementary School Mathematics Instruction." *Arithmetic Teacher*, 36 (January 1989), pp. 14–16.

Sutton, John T., and Urbatsch, Tonya D. "Transition Boards: A Good Idea Made Better." *Arithmetic Teacher*, 38 (January 1991), pp. 4–8.

Suydam, Marilyn N., and Dessart, Donald J. *Classroom Ideas from Research on Computational Skills*. Reston, Va.: NCTM, 1976.

Thompson, Frances. "Two-Digit Addition and Subtraction: What Works?" *Arithmetic Teacher*, 38 (January 1991), pp. 10–13.

Trafton, Paul R., and Zawojewski, Judith S. "Implementing the Standards: Meanings of Operations." *Arithmetic Teacher*, 38 (November 1990), pp. 18–22.

Tucker, Benny F. "The Division Algorithm." *Arithmetic Teacher*, 20 (December 1973), pp. 639–646.

Usnick, Virginia E., and Lamphere, Patricia M. "Calculators and Division." *Arithmetic Teacher*, 38 (December 1990), pp. 40–43.

Van de Walle, John A. "Implementing the Standards: Redefining Computation." *Arithmetic Teacher*, 38 (January 1991), pp. 44–51.

Van de Walle, John, and Thompson, Charles S. "Partitioning Sets for Number Concepts, Place Value, and Long Division." *Arithmetic Teacher*, 32 (January 1985), pp. 6–11.

Van Engen, Henry, and Gibb, E. Glenadine. *General Mental Functions Associated with Division. Educational Service Studies,* No. 2. Cedar Falls: Iowa State Teachers College, 1956.

Wearne, Diana, and Hiebert, James. "Place Value and Addition and Subtraction." *Arithmetic Teacher*, 41 (January 1994), pp. 272–274.

Wheatley, Grayson H., and Wheatley, Charlotte L. "How Shall We Teach Column Addition? Some Evidence." *Arithmetic Teacher*, 25 (January 1978), pp. 18–19.

Whitin, David J. "Becca's Investigation." *Arithmetic Teacher*, 41 (October 1993), pp. 78–81.

11

Exploring Geometry

 ## Snapshot of a Lesson

Students are grouped in interest centers in a kindergarten. Several of the groups are building with blocks and decorating their structures with wooden geometric solids. Mrs. Pedro moves to a small group of children who are disagreeing about the use of some of the solids. She uses the opportunity to engage them in an activity she uses frequently to develop familiarity with the properties of solid three-dimensional objects.

MRS. PEDRO: Jonathan, what seems to be the problem?

JONATHAN: We want these (pointing to some of the solids)—the ones we have won't stack.

MRS. PEDRO: Let's all solve a puzzle. Whoever can solve it, gets those solids. We need two of each solid and the mystery box.

MARIA: Oh, I remember this game. We have to find out what's in the box.

Turning around so the children cannot see her, Mrs. Pedro puts one solid in the box.

MRS. PEDRO: Right. I put one solid in the mystery box and the rest away so we can't see them. One solid from one of these three pairs is in the box.

JONATHAN: Can we shut our eyes and feel?

MRS. PEDRO: No, this time we must only listen. Anthony, you may try listening to the box first. But all of you listen because you may be able to tell.

ANTHONY: It's not rolling like a ball.

JONATHAN: Let me hear. You're right, so it can't be the ball.

MRS. PEDRO: Does everyone agree? Joanne, could you hear?

JOANNE: No, let me try. Yeah, it sort of rolls, but not like a ball.

MRS. PEDRO: Let's put this one aside, since everyone agrees it isn't the ball. Now, it must be one of these two.

MARIA: This one (pointing to the cube) would just slide—slunk, slunk—and wouldn't roll at all.

EARL: This one (pointing to the cone) would roll if it was like this.

ANTHONY: Not if you shook the box. It might not roll.

JONATHAN: Right, so maybe it isn't this one.

MRS. PEDRO: So, which is it?

ALL: This one! Let us see.

Mrs. Pedro opens the box to let them see it was the cone.

JOANNE: Let's try again.

MRS. PEDRO: Yes, here's one that will really make all of you think.

They play several more rounds.

EARL: Let us try to stump you.

MRS. PEDRO: All right. I'll be back in a minute.

Mrs. Pedro hears talking and laughing. They hand her the box.

MRS. PEDRO: Oh, you rascals. You filled the box. You really stumped me.

 ## Introduction

You may find yourself working with some teachers who respond to geometry in the following ways:

"Oh, I could never do proofs."

"The children don't understand it, so why do it?"

"We do it if we finish everything else."

There are many reasons for such responses. Some are based on past personal experiences such as an unsatisfactory geometry course in high school or no geometry in elementary school. Some are based on inappropriate geometry curriculum materials that use, for example, an abstract, definitional approach. Some are based on a historical emphasis on computation—even though geometry has been recommended by various professional groups for over a hundred years.

You may find that you are working with some teachers who respond like this:

"It amazes me who is good in geometry; it's not always my best arithmetic students."

"What a joy it is to see a child's eyes light up as she discovers. . . ."

"Some of my students could work on a geometry problem for hours."

"Geometry gives me an opportunity to work on communication skills and to help children follow instructions."

"The change in the spatial ability of children after they work with geometric shapes always surprises me."

"I love to learn with my students; I never liked geometry before."

The second group of teachers is in concert with the vision of the role of geometry in the elementary curriculum advocated in the *Curriculum and Evaluation Standards for School Mathematics* (NCTM 1989).

The first paragraph of the discussion of the K–4 geometry standard summarizes some of the reasons why geometry is important:

> . . . because geometric knowledge, relationships, and insights are useful in everyday situations and are connected to other mathematical and school subjects. Geometry helps us represent and describe in an orderly manner the world in which we live. Children are naturally interested in geometry and find it intriguing and motivating; their spatial capabilities frequently exceed their numerical skills, and tapping these strengths fosters an interest in mathematics and improves number understandings and skills. (NCTM 1989, p. 48)

You will enjoy including geometry in your teaching if you adopt the philosophy of the teacher who said, "I love to learn with my students." As you read this chapter, begin the process of learning. You may meet many new ideas, but by trying the activities and brushing up on some things you may have once learned, you will begin to extend your knowledge of how to help children learn geometry.

• Solid Geometry

We live in a three-dimensional world that can be represented and described geometrically; this is the world of the young child, along with the flat, two-dimensional world of pictures. It is important that children explore their world in the geometric sense. In this section, we will consider some of the three-dimensional aspects of our surroundings.

Studying geometric properties of three-dimensional objects also provides an opportunity to emphasize the process goals of geometry. This section is built around some of these processes: describing and classifying, constructing, exploring and discovering, and relating three-dimensional shapes to two-dimensional shapes. We will often refer to a three-dimensional shape in this section as a *solid,* although the object may be hollow.

Models play an important role in solid geometry. If wooden or plastic solids are not available, you can make models as suggested later in this section. You and your students should also collect real objects that have particular geometric shapes, including spheres (balls), cylinders (cans), prisms (boxes), and cones, as well as shapes that may not have geometric names.

Describing and Classifying Objects

Children need to be able to describe properties of three-dimensional objects to see how two or more objects are alike or different according to geometric properties. Describing and classifying are processes that should be extended over time as new and more complex properties are added.

In the activities that follow, we suggest vocabulary and properties appropriate for beginning, intermediate, and more advanced students. Older children who have not been exposed to three-dimensional activities will benefit from activities such as the ones described in the beginning activities. Their responses, of course, will be more sophisticated.

Beginning Activities Often children are taught the names of the geometric shapes, but they do not develop the discriminating power they need in order to use the names with meaning. In these beginning activities you should build on the children's own vocabulary, adding new words as appropriate. Although the names of the solids can be used, they need not be formally introduced until children have done activities like these.

1. *Who Am I?* Put out three objects (such as a ball, a cone, and a box). Describe one of them (it is round all over, it is flat on the bottom, its sides are all flat), and have the children guess which one you are describing.

2. *Who Stacks?* Provide a collection of solids for children to sort according to which will stack, which will roll, and which will slide. A more sophisticated sorting is one that requires three groups: solids that can be stacked no matter what face is down, solids that can be stacked if placed in some ways but not in other ways, and solids that cannot be stacked in any way.

3. *How Are We Alike or Different?* Hold up two solids such as the following:

Ask children to tell how they are alike or different. For example, children may compare the two solids shown as follows:

"They are both flat all over."

"One is tall."

"One has bigger sides."

"They have some square faces."

"They have six faces."

4. *Who Doesn't Belong?* Put out three solids such as these:

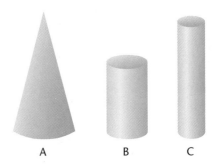

A   B   C

Ask children which does not belong with the other two. Since there are many ways to solve this problem, be ready to encourage lively discussion. For example, some children may say A doesn't belong because it has a point. Others may say B doesn't belong because it's short, or C doesn't belong because it's skinny or has a smaller bottom.

5. *How Many Faces Have I?* A *face* is a flat side of a solid object. Have children count the number of faces on solids of various shapes. Then ask children to collect objects with six faces (boxes, books), with two faces (cans), and with zero faces (balls). You will be surprised at what they find.

6. *Can You Find an Object Like Me?* Put out a solid and see if children can find real objects that have the same shape. You may get disagreement about which are alike.

Intermediate Activities The following activities introduce the names of some solids and consider sizes (or measure properties) as well as edges, faces, and vertices.

1. *Using Edges, Vertices, and Faces.* After introducing *edge* (a straight segment formed by two faces) and *vertex* (a point at which three or more edges come together), have children solve these riddles:

> I am a solid with . . . :
> - eight edges—who am I?
> - six edges and four faces—who am I?
> - five corners—who am I?
> - the same number of corners as faces—who am I?
> - no faces (no corners)—who am I?
> - one face and no corners—who am I?

2. *Classifying Solids.* Introduce each type of solid—cube, cone, pyramid, cylinder, and sphere—by putting out solids that are examples and nonexamples; then compare the properties of each to decide whether it belongs to the group. Then use activities like the one in Activity Card 11–1, which focuses on a particular group using pictorial models. Ask children to tell why the solid belongs to its group.

3. *Searching for Solids.* Make up a set of activity cards that have children search out solids according to the size and shape of the faces and the length of the edges. The clues you give will depend on the solids you use, but here are some samples to get you started:

> Search for a solid with . . . :
> - exactly two faces that are the same size and shape (*congruent*)
> - exactly three faces that are the same size and shape
> - all edges the same length
> - edges of three different lengths

Advanced Activities These activities focus on the properties of parallel and perpendicular faces and edges as well as more careful definition and classification of the solids.

1. *Parallel Faces.* This activity can be done after parallel faces have been introduced. It consists of questions about real objects and why faces are parallel. A few sample questions are given here to start you thinking:

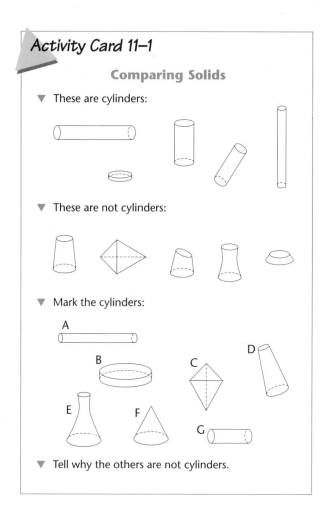

Activity Card 11–1

Comparing Solids

▼ These are cylinders:

▼ These are not cylinders:

▼ Mark the cylinders:

A

B

C

D

E

F

G

▼ Tell why the others are not cylinders.

Why are the top and bottom of soup cans parallel?

Why are shelves parallel to the floor?

Why are roofs of houses in cold climates usually not parallel to the ground?

Why is the front side of a milk carton parallel to the back side?

2. *Perpendicular Edges.* Activity Card 11–2 provides clues about particular solids focused on perpendicular edges and asks students to construct the solids from sticks and connectors. See the "stick" models section which follows for a variety of materials. Students enjoy making their own mysteries for other students to solve. This provides excellent experience in writing descriptions that are clear, precise, and noncontradictory.

3. *Right Prisms.* This activity introduces the definition of right prisms and how to name prisms. Show examples and nonexamples of right prisms (as in the second of the intermediate activities), and ask students to describe the bases and faces, ultimately

Activity Card 11–2

Solid Mystery

▼ Solve each of these mysteries by constructing a "suspect" from sticks and connectors. If you think there is more than one suspect, look at Clue 2.

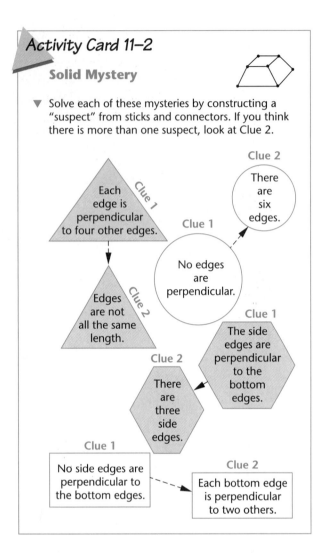

Constructing and Then Exploring and Discovering

One of the difficulties that children have with three-dimensional geometry is visualizing the solids. It is essential to have models. If models are not available, there are many ways in which children can make them.

As children are making the models, they often discover many things about the solids. There are, however, other properties or relationships that they may not discover and other ways to explore the solids. The following activities provide examples of ways to structure their investigations.

Paper Tubes Some of the easiest and most versatile models can be made from heavy construction paper. Activity Card 11–3 shows how open-ended tube

Activity Card 11–3

How Many Prisms Can You Make?

▼ Use construction paper and masking tape to construct these tubes. Fold and tape each as shown.

• Prism with three congruent faces:

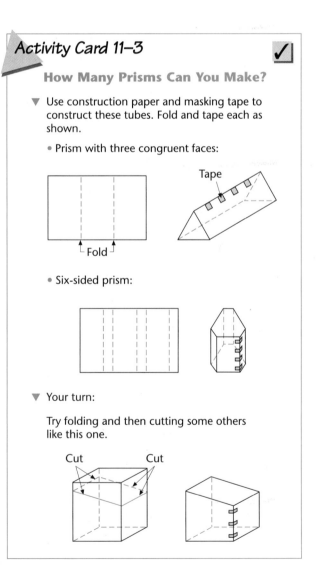

• Six-sided prism:

▼ Your turn:

Try folding and then cutting some others like this one.

encouraging them to come up with the definition of *prism*—a solid that has congruent and parallel bases (top and bottom) joined by rectangular faces. Then have students discuss how prisms are named. See if they can determine a way to distinguish between prisms. For example, if the base is a triangle it is a triangular prism.

These activities are only suggestions to help children construct their knowledge of geometric ideas. By the end of the eighth grade, children should have developed the ability to identify solids (cones, prisms, cylinders, spheres, and pyramids) and name special ones. More importantly, they should be able to contrast the different solids with respect to the properties mentioned in this discussion. The activities in the rest of this section on solid geometry reinforce and extend these ideas.

models of cylinders and prisms can be made. The top and bottom faces may be added to these models by tracing the top of the tube, cutting out the shape, and taping it to the tube. As Activity Card 11–3 suggests, many variations of prisms can be made, and these can be cut to create many strange shapes.

The exploration in Activity Card 11–4 is a variation of a famous formula, Euler's (pronounced "oilers") formula, which relates the number of edges (E), faces (F), and vertices (V) to each other: $V + F = E + 2$. Because the tubes used for the activity have no top or bottom face, the formula here is $V + F = E$, which is more readily evident. Several other patterns can be found for these paper tubes; have four students look for these.

"Stick" Models Models can be made from straws, pipe cleaners, toothpicks, or other "sticks" that can be connected with clay, small marshmallows, or tape. There are also reasonably priced, commercial materials that are designed for this purpose. Activity Card 11–5 illustrates how to make a three-dimensional figure from newspaper sticks and tape.

When building three-dimensional objects with newspaper sticks, the children can investigate the rigidity of triangles, squares, or other polygons.

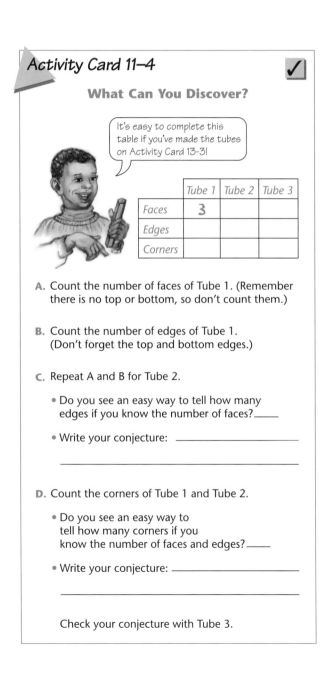

Activity Card 11–4 ✓

What Can You Discover?

It's easy to complete this table if you've made the tubes on Activity Card 13-3!

	Tube 1	Tube 2	Tube 3
Faces	3		
Edges			
Corners			

A. Count the number of faces of Tube 1. (Remember there is no top or bottom, so don't count them.)

B. Count the number of edges of Tube 1. (Don't forget the top and bottom edges.)

C. Repeat A and B for Tube 2.

• Do you see an easy way to tell how many edges if you know the number of faces?_____

• Write your conjecture: _____

_____

D. Count the corners of Tube 1 and Tube 2.

• Do you see an easy way to tell how many corners if you know the number of faces and edges?_____

• Write your conjecture: _____

_____

Check your conjecture with Tube 3.

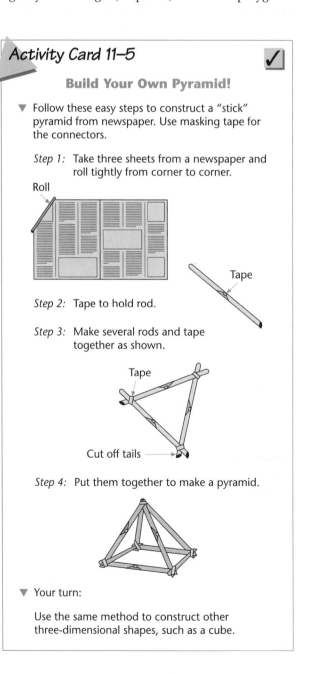

Activity Card 11–5 ✓

Build Your Own Pyramid!

▼ Follow these easy steps to construct a "stick" pyramid from newspaper. Use masking tape for the connectors.

Step 1: Take three sheets from a newspaper and roll tightly from corner to corner.

Roll

Tape

Step 2: Tape to hold rod.

Step 3: Make several rods and tape together as shown.

Tape

Cut off tails

Step 4: Put them together to make a pyramid.

▼ Your turn:

Use the same method to construct other three-dimensional shapes, such as a cube.

They should find that the pyramid built with Activity Card 11–5 is a rigid structure, but the cube needs bracing to be sturdy.

Networks A network is the pattern of a solid given so that, when edges are attached, the solid will be created. Some networks can be "folded" to create a solid; others cannot be. Activity Card 11–6 gives students a chance to see if they can tell whether or not a solid can be constructed from a network. Children can verify their answers by cutting out the network and folding.

Activities such as the one on Activity Card 11–6 enable children to make connections between two- and three-dimensional geometry. Other suggestions follow that focus on different ways to visualize and represent solids or parts of solids. The sixth mathematics assessment of the National Assessment of Educational Progress included an item about networks and cubes for students in grades 4 and 8 (Strutchens and Blume 1997). Given the network of a cube shown here, they were asked what face would be on top if the cube was folded and rested on the face marked X. More fourth-grade students chose D (30 percent) than chose the correct answer, face A (22 percent). Eighth-grade students (55 percent) chose A, but D remained an attractive distracter. Look and see why D might have distracted the students. Do you think it is because of spatial ability or because of a lack of considering the conditions of the problem?

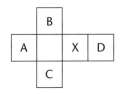

Relating Three Dimensions to Two

Because three-dimensional objects often must be pictured in two dimensions, children must be able to relate the objects to pictures. They also need to be able to analyze a three-dimensional object in terms of its two-dimensional parts. Constructing solids from networks and other materials assists in this skill, but you can help focus directly on the two-dimensional aspect by the activities you choose and the questions you ask.

Matching Imprints of Faces with the Solid Make imprints in playdough (home-made works great) of

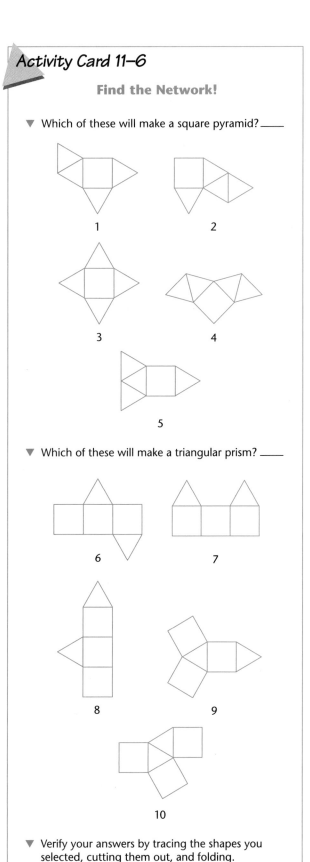

Activity Card 11–6

Find the Network!

▼ Which of these will make a square pyramid? _____

1 2 3 4 5

▼ Which of these will make a triangular prism? _____

6 7 8 9 10

▼ Verify your answers by tracing the shapes you selected, cutting them out, and folding.

the faces of wooden geometric solids. Have children match each solid with a face. The faces can be traced instead of making imprints, but younger children can work easily with imprints. Activity Card 11–7, which provides a similar matching activity with pictorial models, also can be used.

Identifying Different Views of a Solid Provide several two-dimensional views of solids, and have children choose which are possible and which are not. Activity Card 11–8 gives two variations of this type of matching activity. Have examples of the solids available and ask children to show how the views are possible or tell why the view is not possible.

Visualizing Cross Sections of Solids Cross sections of solids are often difficult for children to visualize. Cutting tubes in the process of construction helps children to see the cross sections. If you have other objects that can be cut (oranges, carrots shaped in cones, or zucchini shaped in different solids), you can help the children see the cross sections.

Next time you are eating cheese, cut small cubes of cheese, then try slicing each cube so the slice shows different geometric shapes. Can you slice the cube to see a triangle? a different triangle? How can you slice the cube to make a rectangle that is not a square? Try a pentagon and hexagon.

Working with Drawings of Solids Many children need help in drawing three-dimensional objects. As illustrated in Activity Card 11–9, isometric paper can be used to draw numerous views of prisms. (A master sheet of isometric paper can be found in Appendix B.) Activity Card 11–9 also provides experience in interpreting two-dimensional drawings to construct the three-dimensional structures.

Experiences such as these will help children understand the concept of volume. As children build various shapes with a given number of cubes, they will be investigating the relationship of volume and shape. How many rectangular prisms can you build

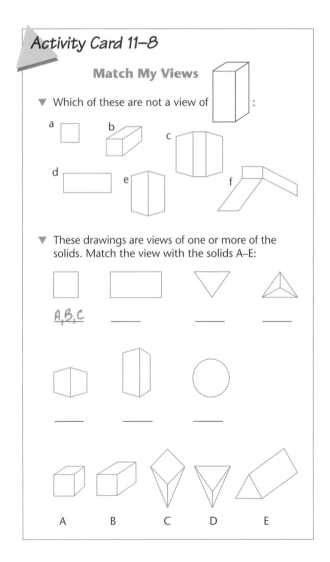

Activity Card 11–7

Which Solid Am I?

▼ I only have two different faces:

▼ Which solid could I be?

A B C

D E

▼ Why can I not be the others?

Activity Card 11–8

Match My Views

▼ Which of these are not a view of ☐ :

a b c

d e f

▼ These drawings are views of one or more of the solids. Match the view with the solids A–E:

A,B,C _____   _____   _____

_____

A   B   C   D   E

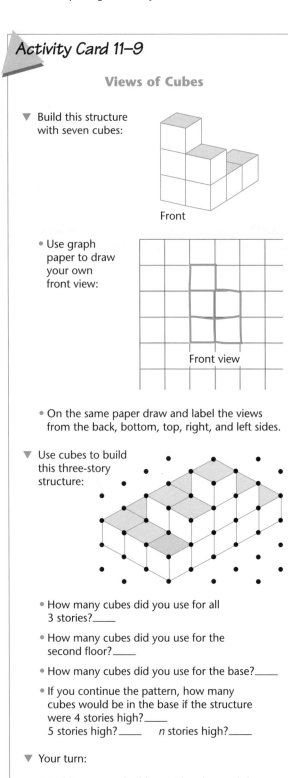

Activity Card 11–9

Views of Cubes

▼ Build this structure
with seven cubes:

Front

- Use graph
paper to draw
your own
front view:

Front view

- On the same paper draw and label the views
from the back, bottom, top, right, and left sides.

▼ Use cubes to build
this three-story
structure:

- How many cubes did you use for all
3 stories?____

- How many cubes did you use for the
second floor?____

- How many cubes did you use for the base?____

- If you continue the pattern, how many
cubes would be in the base if the structure
were 4 stories high?____
5 stories high?____   *n* stories high?____

▼ Your turn:

- Build your own building with cubes and draw
two views on isometric paper.

- See if a friend can build your building from
the drawings. If the friend is having difficulty,
draw all the views of the building.

that have a volume of 24 cubes? Look at the pictures in Figure 11–1 these fifth-grade students drew of a prism made with 12 cubes. What concepts are being developed?

● Plane Geometry

In this section, we consider properties of two-dimensional shapes, relationships among shapes, and classification schemes. The ideas mainly are presented through sample activities involving many types of physical materials, such as geoboards, pattern blocks (Figure 11–2), and paper strips. Many engaging geometric activities also can be done with paper and pencil, and computer programs provide a rich environment for geometric exploration.

In examining three-dimensional shapes, we often focus on the faces (two- dimensional); similarly, in examining two-dimensional shapes, we often focus on the sides or vertices (one-dimensional). We will build these one-dimensional concepts as they occur naturally within a two-dimensional context.

Properties of a Shape

Children first recognize shapes in a holistic manner—that is, a triangle is a triangle because it looks like a shape that someone has called a triangle. If an equilateral triangle with its base parallel to the bottom of the page is always used, then this shape will be children's image of a triangle. It is important to provide many examples and nonexamples of shapes in order for children to have rich images of the different shapes.

Children naturally have an intuitive feel for the differences among shapes, but they need ways to describe these differences. By considering the properties of shapes, you can help develop children's ability to describe and extend their knowledge of particular shapes. For example, think of how you would describe a rectangle to someone who had never seen one. Draw a strange shape that has no special name to you, and try to describe it to someone. Consider the properties of the shape that you used.

There are many ways of describing geometric shapes, as illustrated in the activities that follow. The different properties are discussed separately but should be combined in activities similar to the ones given. Realize that keeping two or more properties in mind is more difficult than just focusing on one. For example, creating a figure with four sides on a geoboard is at a much simpler level than creating a

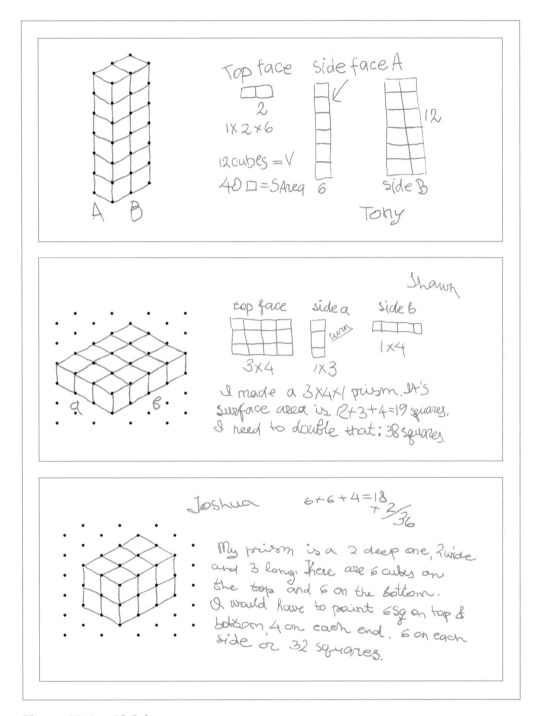

Figure 11–1 ● **12 Cubes**

figure with four sides that has two right angles and one side longer than the other.

Number of Sides One of the first properties children focus on is the number of sides. They readily count the number of sides (line segments) of a shape, unless a shape has many sides. Then, they may need to mark the place where they begin counting. As you have children participate in activities such as the ones that follow, they will begin to make many conjectures about shapes and learn vocabulary.

1. *How Many Sides?* This simple activity uses pattern blocks (see Figure 11–2). If you do not have pattern

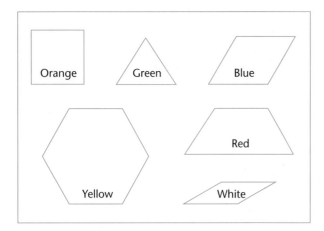

Figure 11–2 • Pattern blocks

blocks, you can use other shapes or cut shapes with different numbers of sides from construction paper. Each child needs only one shape for this activity.

- Call a number and ask children who have a shape with that number of sides to stand. (Be certain to call numbers such as two and seven, for which no one will stand.)

- Then have a search for all the different shapes that have three sides, four sides, five sides, six sides, and zero sides (the circle).

- Put a sample of each different shape somewhere within view of all children, and call on children to tell how the four-sided shapes differ (some are bigger than others, some are skinny, and some are slanty—accept their everyday words at this point). It is important for them to realize that the number of sides does not determine the shape.

2. *Can You Make _____ ?* In this challenging activity, children make a figure of a given number of sides on a geoboard. (See Appendix B for a geoboard model.) Give each child a geoboard and one rubber band. Begin by asking them to make simple shapes, and gradually add other conditions. For example,

Can you make a four-sided figure?

Can you make a four-sided figure that touches only four pegs?

Can you make a four-sided figure that touches six pegs?

Can you make a four-sided figure that has two pegs inside (not touching) it?"

3. *Less Is Best.* Activity Card 11–10 provides a more advanced activity in which children put pattern

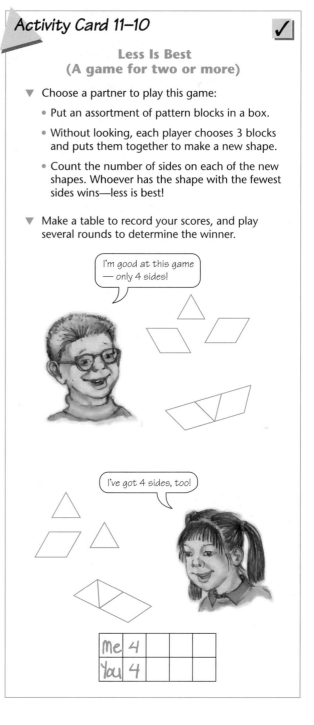

blocks together to make new shapes with as few sides as possible. Two or more children "blindly" choose three pattern blocks. They can play several rounds to determine the winner.

Number of Corners Closely related to counting the numbers of sides is counting the number of corners. Children will soon realize that any polygonal figure has the same number of sides as corners if they count both on each shape. The activities suggested for counting the number of sides can be modified for counting corners.

Symmetry Two types of symmetry—line or reflectional symmetry and rotational symmetry—may be used to describe geometric shapes as well as objects in the real world.

To introduce line symmetry, ask children to compare two snowmen:

When they say one looks lopsided, show them how they can fold the drawings in the center to see if the sides match. A child's first perception of symmetry is visual. Use this visual perception to help build the idea of "folding" to match the sides or edges. You may also want the children to explore with mirrors or miras to bring in the idea of reflection. A figure has line or reflectional symmetry if, when reflected over a line, the resulting image coincides with the original figure.

Have students find the line(s) of symmetry of geometric shapes. Be sure to let them try folding a square (four lines of symmetry), an equilateral triangle (three lines of symmetry), and a circle (an infinite number) to find lines of symmetry before moving to activities such as the one in Activity Card 11–11. Older children can often see the lines of symmetry without folding, but some shapes are misleading. One of these is a parallelogram. Many children will say at first glance that a parallelogram has two lines of symmetry. (Try it yourself.)

It is important that children also see symmetry in things around them. You might have them make a bulletin board of pictures of things that are symmetric. They also enjoy making symmetric shapes. One way is to fold a piece of paper and cut the folded piece, leaving the fold intact. (Can you figure out how to make a shape with two lines of symmetry?)

An unusual children's book to help establish the basic concepts of symmetry is *Reflections* (Jonas

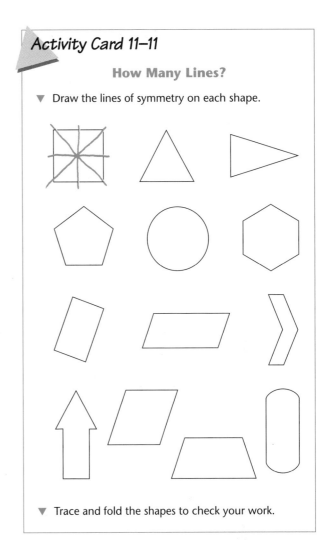

1987). This book allows students to examine images in a variety of ways.

Length of Sides Many of the definitions of geometric shapes as well as classification schemes for them depend on the length of sides. Help children focus on the length by having them find the shape with the longest side, find the shortest side of a given shape, and measuring lengths of sides. Activity Card 11–12 presents an example of a more advanced activity in which children make shapes on a geoboard according to certain specifications about the lengths of the sides. Try the items yourself, and classify each as to whether it is easy, medium, or challenging.

Size of Angles There are many ways to examine the angles of geometric figures. A more complete introduction to angles may be found in Chapter 12

Activity Card 11–12

Show My Sides

▼ Use a geoboard to show these figures:

1. Can you make a 4-sided figure with exactly two equal sides?

2. Can you make a 12-sided figure with all sides equal?

3. Can you make a 3-sided figure with three equal sides?

4. Can you make an 8-sided figure with four sides of one length and the other four of another length?

5. Can you make a 5-sided figure with exactly four equal sides?

6. Can you make a 4-sided figure with two pairs of equal sides that is not a parallelogram?

7. Can you make a 3-sided figure with two equal sides?

8. Can you make a 7-sided figure with no equal sides?

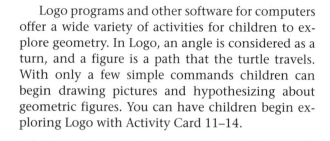

Here are some of the properties related to angles that children may discover:

- The sum of the angles of a triangle is 180.
- The sum of the angles of a quadrilateral is 360.
- The base angles of an isosceles triangle are equal.
- Opposite angles of a parallelogram are equal.
- A polygon with more than three sides can have equal sides without having equal angles.
- The angle opposite the longest side of a triangle is the largest.

A guided activity such as the one in Activity Card 11–13 will help students discover for themselves that the angles of a quadrilateral sum to 360°. Can you think of a similar activity for discovering the sum of the angles of a triangle?

Logo programs and other software for computers offer a wide variety of activities for children to explore geometry. In Logo, an angle is considered as a turn, and a figure is a path that the turtle travels. With only a few simple commands children can begin drawing pictures and hypothesizing about geometric figures. You can have children begin exploring Logo with Activity Card 11–14.

Parallel and Perpendicular Sides In addition to examining parallel and perpendicular sides in geometric shapes, children need to be able to identify parallel lines and perpendicular lines in a plane and, later, in space. Two lines in a plane are parallel if they never intersect. (Remember, a line can be extended indefinitely in either direction.) Another useful definition states that two lines are parallel if they are always the same distance (perpendicular distance, that is) apart. Two lines are perpendicular if they intersect at right angles. Activity Card 11–15 is straightforward in asking children to identify parallel lines.

It is important that children recognize perpendicular and parallel lines in the world around them. Have them search for them in the room. You might together start a list on the board, letting children add to it as they find other examples. Here is a start:

Parallel Lines

- Opposite sides of a book
- The horizontal lines in E
- The top and bottom of the chalkboard

Perpendicular Lines

- Adjacent sides of a book
- The vertical and horizontal lines in E

You may also have the children identify parallel and perpendicular sides on the pattern blocks (Figure 11–2). Begin by asking them to find all the pieces that have one pair of perpendicular sides, next all the pieces with more than one pair of perpendicular sides, and then a piece with one pair of parallel sides. You also can use Activity Card 11–16, which challenges children to arrange two pieces to make shapes with a specified number of parallel sides.

Convexity and Concavity Often children are exposed only to convex shapes (any polygon with all angles less than 180°). Many of the activities suggested thus far have included concave shapes. When children are making shapes, concave examples will often give interesting variety.

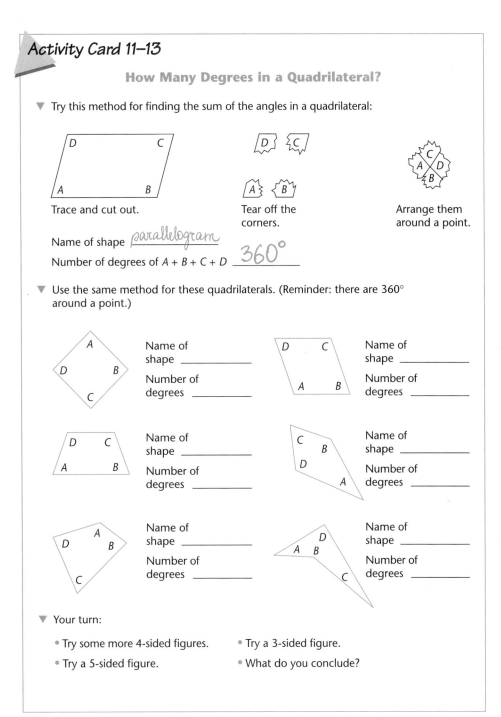

Activity Card 11–13

How Many Degrees in a Quadrilateral?

▼ Try this method for finding the sum of the angles in a quadrilateral:

Trace and cut out.

Tear off the corners.

Arrange them around a point.

Name of shape _parallelogram_

Number of degrees of A + B + C + D ___360°___

▼ Use the same method for these quadrilaterals. (Reminder: there are 360° around a point.)

Name of shape _____
Number of degrees _____

Name of shape _____
Number of degrees _____

Name of shape _____
Number of degrees _____

Name of shape _____
Number of degrees _____

Name of shape _____
Number of degrees _____

Name of shape _____
Number of degrees _____

▼ Your turn:

• Try some more 4-sided figures.
• Try a 5-sided figure.
• Try a 3-sided figure.
• What do you conclude?

Show children two shapes such as these and have them describe how they are alike and different:

A   B

They will probably express the idea that shape A "comes back" on itself or "caves in" (concave). Introduce the terms *concave* and *convex*. After children classify shapes as convex or concave, you might have them investigate questions such as the following:

Can you draw a four-sided (five-sided, six-sided, seven-sided) figure that is concave?

Activity Card 11–14

Exploring with Logo

▼ Use a Logo program. You will need to know the following commands before trying this activity. If you do not, explore these first.

```
FORWARD (FD), RIGHT (RT), HOME,
SHOW TURTLE (ST), CLEARSCREEN (CS)
```

▼ Identify each of these figures. Write your guess and then draw the figure. Don't forget to CS after each figure is identified.

A _____ B _____ C _____ D _____

HOME	HOME	HOME	HOME
FD 40	FD 40	FD 40	RT 120
RT 90	RT 60	RT 120	FD 40
FD 20	FD 40	FD 40	RT 120
RT 90	RT 60	RT 120	FD 40
FD 40	FD 40	RT 40	RT 120
RT 90			FD 40
FD 20			

▼ Try the following:

1. REPEAT 4 [FD 40 RT 90]

   • What did you draw? _____

2. RT 45 REPEAT 4 [FD 40 RT 90]

   • What is the difference between 1 and 2? _____

3. REPEAT 3 [FD 40 RT 120]

   • Have you drawn this one before? _____

▼ See if you can draw a hexagon.

   • What did you tell the turtle to do? _____

▼ For fun try these:

```
TO BOX
REPEAT 4 [FD 40 RT 90]
END
BOX
CS

TO BOXES
REPEAT 8 [BOX RT 45]
END
BOXES
```

Activity Card 11–15

Parallel Pairs

▼ Which of the pairs 1–6 show parallel lines?

Pair 1 — a — b
Pair 2 — c — d
Pair 3 — e — f
Pair 4 — g — h
Pair 5 — i — j
Pair 6 — k — l

▼ Challenge:

There are 7 other pairs of parallel lines on this card beside the ones you indicated.

• See if you can find them, and write the letters of the lines in each pair:

Pair 7 _____   Pair 8 _____

Pair 9 _____   Pair 10 _____

Pair 11 _____   Pair 12 _____

Pair 13 _____

Can you draw a five-sided (six-sided, seven-sided) figure that is concave in two places (or that has two angles greater than 180)?

Can you draw a six-sided (seven-sided, eight-sided) figure that is concave in three places?

It is challenging to try these with Logo on the computer. Have the children keep a record of the steps it takes to make each figure.

Altitude The altitude (or height) of a geometric shape depends on what is specified as the base. Iden-

Activity Card 11–16

Piezles

▼ Solve these *piezles* (puzzles) using pattern blocks. Draw a sketch of the shape you made.

1. Use two different pieces; make a shape with

   • Exactly 2 pairs of parallel sides.

   • Exactly 1 pair of parallel sides.

   • No parallel sides.

2. Use three different pieces; make a shape with

   • Exactly 3 pairs of parallel sides.

   • Exactly 2 pair of parallel sides.

   • Exactly 1 pair of parallel sides.

   • No parallel sides.

3. What is the largest number of pairs of parallel sides of a shape you can make from

   • 2 pieces?

   • 3 pieces?

   • 4 pieces?

4. Can you put all the pieces together to make a shape with no parallel sides?

Activity Card 11–17

What's My Altitude?

▼ Make a triangle from a stiff piece of paper. Cut a strip 2 cm by 20 cm. Mark off segments of 9 cm, 4 cm, and 7 cm and label them A, B, and C, respectively. Fold and tape as shown:

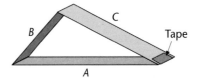

1. Set the triangle on side A. This is the base.

   • How long is the base? ___9 cm___

   • What is the altitude? _____

   • How long is the altitude? _____

2. Set the triangle on side B. This is the base now.

   • How long is the base? _____

   • What is the altitude? _____

   • How long is the altitude? _____

3. Set the triangle on side C. This is the base now.

   • How long is the base? _____

   • What is the altitude? _____

   • How long is the altitude? _____

▼ On a large sheet of paper: Trace the triangle and show the altitude for each of the bases.

Names of Geometric Shapes

Often children are taught the geometric names without being given much opportunity to explore the properties or to solve problems. This approach is in direct contrast to the Japanese curriculum. Teachers in Japan use the names in context as the children are exploring and using the shapes rather than providing isolated lessons on the names. The sixth national assessment shows that students in the United States know the names of geometric shapes, but have difficulty with complex geometric properties (Strutchens and Blume 1997).

Children should begin to recognize types of shapes through examples and nonexamples, not through definitions. By experiencing examples and

tifying and measuring the altitude is essential in finding the area of geometric figures. The first part of Activity Card 11–17 is designed to help children realize that a geometric object has different heights or altitudes. The second part is designed to transfer the idea of height to altitude (or from a geometric object to a drawing or piece of paper).

discussing the properties, they can begin to realize what properties define a shape. Activity Card 11–18 gives examples and nonexamples of triangles. Do you see why the different shapes were included? If a child says that C, B, F, or G is a triangle, what property of triangles do you think is being ignored in each case? If a child fails to realize that D is a triangle, what do you think may be the reason?

Children also need to be able to recognize geometric shapes as models for real objects. For example, you might have young children write a "book" about circles. What is shaped like a circle? Let them find examples and draw pictures. Older children can be challenged to tell why certain objects are shaped in a certain way:

Why are most buttons shaped like a circle?

Why is paper rectangular?

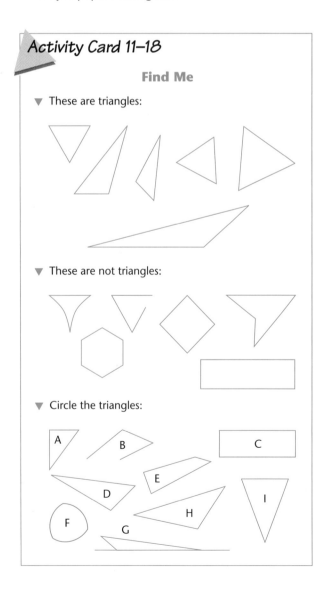

Activity Card 11–18

Find Me

▼ These are triangles:

▼ These are not triangles:

▼ Circle the triangles:

A B C E D I F H G

Why are walls rectangular?

Why are support braces triangular?

Children should know the names of the most common shapes: triangle, square, rectangle, circle, and parallelogram. They also should be aware of other words that are used with shapes; for example, children should be able to identify the center, radius, diameter, and circumference of a circle. The most important thing with all vocabulary is that, after it is introduced, it is used.

Relationships between Shapes

In the preceding section we looked at properties of individual shapes. To emphasize those properties, it is often helpful to compare two or more shapes. When considering two or more shapes, you can examine two relationships, congruence and similarity, central to the study of geometry. After we look at these two relationships, we will consider how children at different levels might respond to comparing two shapes on all the properties we have mentioned so far.

Congruence Two shapes are said to be *congruent* if they have the same size and the same shape. Young children grasp this idea when they see that one shape can be made to fit exactly on the other. If the two shapes are line segments, they are congruent if they have the same length. If the two shapes are two-dimensional, and if they are congruent, then they have the same area. The converse is not true. Two shapes with the same area may not be congruent. Children have difficulty with this concept, and many middle-school students will respond that the parallelogram shown here is congruent to the rectangle:

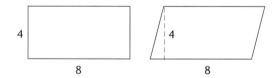

This difficulty may be more a function of the word *congruence* than of the concept. Young children have little difficulty identifying figures with the same shape and size. Thus, the task becomes one of asking young children to match figures to see if they are the same size and shape and gradually introducing and using the word *congruence*.

You may have children begin to investigate the relationship of same area but different shape through activities such as that on Activity Card 12–9. Congruence can be examined through matching activities, such as the one on Activity Card 11–19.

Congruence is often investigated through motion geometry. If two shapes are congruent, they can be made to fit by one or more of the three motions illustrated in Figure 11–3. It sometimes takes more than one motion, as shown by the glide.

Similarity Children have some idea of similarity, but some shapes are misleading, as illustrated in Figure 11–4. Intuitive notions about similarity have to be refined to a mathematical definition: Two figures are *similar* if corresponding angles are equal and corresponding sides are in the same ratio.

This definition is too formal for a beginning. Instead you can begin by using a geoboard and geopaper. Children can make a design on the geoboard and transfer it to smaller geopaper, or they can copy designs from one size of graph paper to another.

After students have been introduced to ratio, they can investigate similarity in a more rigorous

way. (The use of similar triangles is discussed in Chapter 14.)

Comparing Two Figures As children at all grade levels are learning about the properties of geometric figures, they should be given many opportunities to compare figures. As illustrated in Figure 11–5, children's understanding of geometric properties

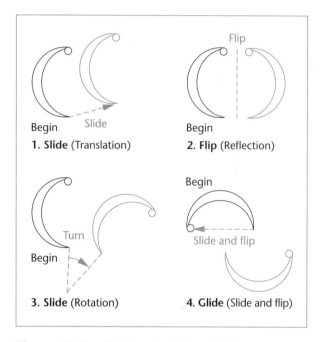

Figure 11–3 • Motions for determining congruence

Activity Card 11–19 ✅

The Triangle Experiment

▼ Follow these directions:

Step 1: Draw a triangle.
Cut it out.

Step 2: Find, by folding, the midpoint of each side.

Step 3: Join the midpoints.

Step 4: Cut apart the 4 triangles.

• What did you find? _____

▼ Try another triangle.

• Did the same thing happen? _____

▼ Try an isosceles triangle.

• What are the small triangles? _____

▼ Try an equilateral triangle.

• What are the small triangles? _____

• What is your conjecture? _____

Similar Triangles

Rectangles That Are Not Similar

Similar Rectangles

Figure 11–4 • Examples of figures for developing the concept of similarity

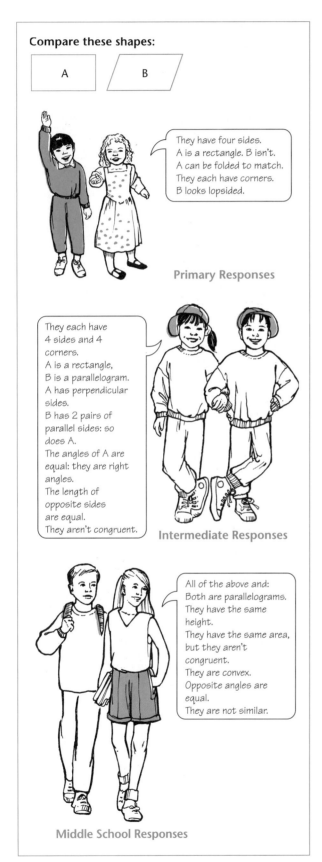

Compare these shapes:

A   B

They have four sides.
A is a rectangle. B isn't.
A can be folded to match.
They each have corners.
B looks lopsided.

Primary Responses

They each have
4 sides and 4
corners.
A is a rectangle,
B is a parallelogram.
A has perpendicular
sides.
B has 2 pairs of
parallel sides: so
does A.
The angles of A are
equal: they are right
angles.
The length of
opposite sides
are equal.
They aren't congruent.

Intermediate Responses

All of the above and:
Both are parallelograms.
They have the same
height.
They have the same area,
but they aren't
congruent.
They are convex.
Opposite angles are
equal.
They are not similar.

Middle School Responses

Figure 11–5 ● **Examples of children's responses that reflect their understanding of relationships between figures at various stages**

varies as they construct their knowledge through experiences.

Classification Schemes

We have examined many properties of, and relationships among, geometric figures. Now we will look in more detail at the defining properties of two-dimensional shapes. What makes a parallelogram a parallelogram? When is a rhombus a square? What is a regular polygon?

Triangles   Triangles are classified either by sides or by angles:

By Sides	By Angles
Equilateral	Acute
three congruent sides	all angles less than 90°
Isosceles	Right
at least two congruent sides	one angle equal to 90°
	Obtuse
Scalene	one angle greater than
no sides congruent	90°

After children have learned to identify triangles by sides and by angles, the two properties may be put together, as on Activity Card 11–20.

Quadrilaterals   There are many special names for quadrilaterals; the most common are parallelograms, rectangles, squares, rhombuses, trapezoids, and kites. These classes are not disjoint; one shape may be in several categories. For example, a rectangle is also a parallelogram. This type of classifying process is more difficult for children than partitioning the whole set into disjoint classes, as is the case with triangles. It requires more than just recognizing examples of figures; it requires understanding the defining properties. For example, a parallelogram is a quadrilateral with two pairs of parallel sides. Assuming you know that a quadrilateral is a four-sided, closed, simple figure, can you identify which of the following are parallelograms? What other names do they have?

You are correct; they all are. Thus, a square, a rhombus, and a rectangle are all special types of parallelograms.

See if you can answer these questions, and discuss them with a colleague. What is a rhombus? A *rhombus* is a parallelogram with all sides congruent. Does that mean that a square is a rhombus? What is a rectangle? A *rectangle* is a parallelogram with right angles. Does that mean a square is a rectangle? Figure 11–6 shows these relationships.

How do you begin to teach such relationships? Children must first begin to verbalize many properties of the figure. For example, they must be able to describe a square:

As a closed, four-sided figure (property 1)
with opposite sides parallel (property 2),
all right angles (property 3), and
all sides congruent (property 4).

Properties 1 and 2 make it a parallelogram; properties 1, 2, and 3 make it a rectangle; properties 1, 2, and 4 make it a rhombus; properties 1, 2, 3, and 4 make it a square. Activity Card 11–21 helps children with this idea.

Polygons Polygons are named according to the number of sides:

3 sides: triangles
4 sides: quadrilaterals
5 sides: pentagons
6 sides: hexagons

Activity Card 11–20

Is There Such a Thing?

▼ Seven of these triangles exist.

• Draw a sketch of each of the seven:

1. Scalene, right
2. Scalene, acute
3. Scalene, obtuse
4. Isosceles, right
5. Isosceles, acute
6. Isosceles, obtuse
7. Equilateral, right
8. Equilateral, acute
9. Equilateral, obtuse

• Which two are not possible? _____

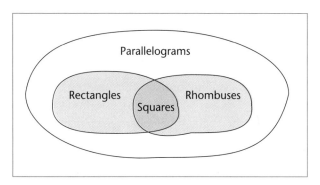

Figure 11–6 • Relationship of quadrilaterals

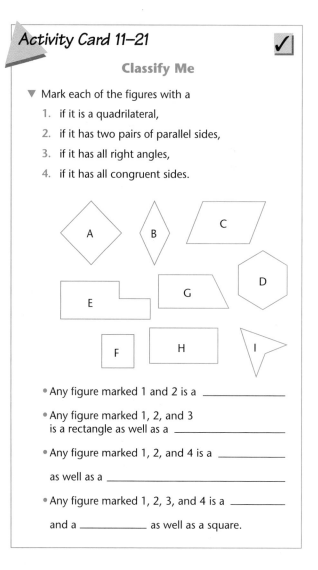

Activity Card 11–21

Classify Me

▼ Mark each of the figures with a

1. if it is a quadrilateral,

2. if it has two pairs of parallel sides,

3. if it has all right angles,

4. if it has all congruent sides.

• Any figure marked 1 and 2 is a _____

• Any figure marked 1, 2, and 3 is a rectangle as well as a _____

• Any figure marked 1, 2, and 4 is a _____

as well as a _____

• Any figure marked 1, 2, 3, and 4 is a _____

and a _____ as well as a square.

7 sides: heptagons
8 sides: octagons
9 sides: nonagons
10 sides: decagons

This classification scheme is not difficult, but often children are shown only regular polygons. Thus, among the shapes shown here, a child sees only the first as a hexagon, instead of realizing they are all hexagons.

Activity Card 11–22

Can You Find It?

▼ See if you can find each of these in the design. Fill in the shape, and mark it with the matching letter.

A. triangle—isosceles

B. triangle—scalene

C. quadrilateral—not symmetric

D. quadrilateral—4 lines of symmetry

E. pentagon—concave

F. pentagon—convex

G. hexagon—exactly 2 pairs of parallel sides

H. hexagon—symmetric

I. heptagon (7 sides)—symmetric

J. heptagon—not symmetric

K. octagon

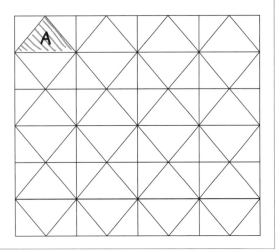

Children should be encouraged to think of real objects that are shaped like these.

The names *heptagons, nonagons,* and *decagons* are not widely used, so in doing activities you may have to remind children of these names. Activity Card 11–22 uses the names as well as other properties.

A Glance at Where We've Been

Geometry is a topic that is often neglected in elementary school, yet it has many benefits for children if presented in an intuitive, informal manner. This chapter presented a variety of examples of activities that provide this type of informal experience. These activities can be modified in many ways to suit the topic and the level of your students. In the section on solid geometry we looked at processes that you also can use with plane figures. The solid figures also can be considered in terms of their properties, relationships among them, and classification schemes, as was emphasized in the plane geometry section.

We have touched on only a few things you can do to help children build concepts and skills in geometry, as well as only a few ways to present problems and apply geometry. There are many other fascinating topics and activities that you can use. Begin to collect these and use them in your teaching.

THINGS TO DO: From What You've Read

1. Give four reasons why geometry should be included in an elementary mathematics program. Explain, in your own words, what one of these reasons means to you.

2. Construct three solids using at least two of the different methods suggested in this chapter.

3. Name three properties of solids that children should learn at each of these levels: beginning, intermediate, and advanced.

4. Defend spending time on constructing models of solids.

5. List eight geometric properties of plane shapes that children can describe.

6. Give the reason for including each example and nonexample of a triangle on Activity Card 11–18.

7. Design a classifying activity for intermediate students based on one of the ideas in the beginning activities.

8. Explain how quadrilaterals can be classified. Why are squares a type of rectangle? How could rectangles be defined so that squares would not be rectangles?

9. Try the Logo activity on Activity Card 11–14. What did you discover?

10. A fellow teacher says that he cannot start to teach any geometry until the students know all the terms and definitions and that his fifth graders just cannot learn them, so he does not do any geometry. What misconceptions about teaching geometry does this teacher hold?

▶ THINGS TO DO: Going Beyond This Book

1. Make a list of ten questions like the ones on Activity Card 11–12 and find a solution for each.

2. Find an activity involving students in an art project that deals with symmetry.

3. Design a discovery lesson for one of the properties of angles on page 232.

4. Try one of the geometry activities in this chapter with children. Describe your plan, the children's reactions, and what you learned about children's understanding of geometry.

5. Suppose you have a student in your class who cannot manipulate a compass. Describe materials you could have him or her work with in order to make geometric figures.

6. Try some of the Logo activities for yourself. Write a guided discovery lesson for children using Logo.

7. Look at the geometry in a textbook at a given grade level. Make a list of the activities from this chapter that would complement the text.

8. Read about the use of geometry in everyday life in another country or culture. Describe how it is different and how you could use this in your teaching.

9. Ask children of different ages to draw three different triangles. If they are successful with three, ask for another one. Keep asking those who are successful for other variations until you have a good idea of their view of triangles. What do you notice?

10. Find a vignette involving geometry in *Professional Standards for Teaching Mathematics* (NCTM 1991). Share and discuss it with your classmates.

▼▼▼▼▼▼▼▼▼▼▼▼▼▼▼▼▼▼▼▼▼▼

Children's Corner

Ada, Alma Flor. *El Reino de la Geometria.* Laredo, Tex.: Laredo Publishing Co, 1993.

Allen, Pamela. *A Lion in the Night.* New York: Putnam, 1986.

Ehlert, Lois. *Color Zoo.* New York: Lippincott, 1989.

Ehlert, Lois. *Color Farm.* New York: Lippincott, 1990.

Flournoy, Valerie. *The Patchwork Quilt.* New York: Dial Books, 1985.

Hoban, Tana. *Look! Look! Look!* New York: Greenwillow Books, 1988.

Hoban, Tana. *Shadows and Reflections.* New York: Greenwillow Books, 1990.

Hutchins, Pat. *Changes, Changes.* New York: Macmillan, 1987.

Isaacson, Philip M. *Round Buildings, Square Buildings, and Buildings That Wiggle Like a Fish.* New York: Knopf, 1988.

Jonas, Ann. *Reflections.* New York: Greenwillow Books, 1987.

Rogers, Paul. *The Shapes Game.* New York: Holt, 1989.

Selected References

Battista, Michael T., and Clements, Douglas H. "Research into Practice: Constructing Geometric Concepts from Logo." *Arithmetic Teacher,* 38 (November 1990), pp. 15–17.

Battista, Michael T., and Clements, Douglas H. "Using Spatial Imagery in Geometric Reasoning." *Arithmetic Teacher,* 39 (November 1991), pp. 18–21.

Battista, Michael T., and Clements, Douglas H. *Investigations in Number, Data, and Space: Seeing Solids and Silhouettes.* Palo Alto, Calif.: Dale Seymour, 1995.

Bradley, Claudette. "Making a Navajo Blanket Design with Logo." *Arithmetic Teacher,* 40 (May 1993), pp. 520–523.

Clements, Douglas H.; Russell, Susan Jo; Tierney, Cornelia; Battista, Michael T.; and Meredith, Julie Sarama. *Investigations in Number, Data, and Space: Flips, Turns, and Area.* Palo Alto, Calif.: Dale Seymour, 1995.

Confer, Chris. *Math by All Means: Geometry Grade 2.* Sausalito, Calif.: Math Solutions Publications, 1994.

Craig, Bill. "Polygons, Stars, Circles, and Logo." *Arithmetic Teacher,* 33 (May 1986), pp. 6–11.

Crowley, Mary L. "The van Hiele Model of the Development of Geometric Thought." In *Learning and*

Teaching Geometry, K–12, 1987 Yearbook (ed. Mary Montgomery Lindquist). Reston, Va.: NCTM, 1987, pp. 1–16.

Dana, Marcia E. "Geometry—A Square Deal for Elementary School." In *Learning and Teaching Geometry, K–12,* 1987 Yearbook (ed. Mary Montgomery Lindquist). Reston, Va.: NCTM, 1987, pp. 113–125.

Dana, Marcia E., and Lindquist, Mary Montgomery. "The Surprising Circle." *Arithmetic Teacher,* 25 (January 1978), pp. 4–11.

Dana, Marcia E., and Lindquist, Mary Montgomery. "Let's Try Triangles." *Arithmetic Teacher,* 26 (September 1978), pp. 2–9.

DeGuire, Linda J. "Geometry: An Avenue for Teaching Problem Solving." In *Learning and Teaching Geometry, K–12,* 1987 Yearbook (ed. Mary Montgomery Lindquist). Reston, Va.: NCTM, 1987, pp. 59–68.

Del Grande, John J. "Spatial Perception and Primary Geometry." In *Learning and Teaching Geometry, K–12,* 1987 Yearbook (ed. Mary Montgomery Lindquist). Reston, Va.: NCTM, 1987, pp. 126–135.

Evered, Lisa J. "Folded Fashions: Symmetry in Clothing Designs." *Arithmetic Teacher,* 40 (December 1992), pp. 204–206.

Friedlander, Alex, and Lappan, Glenda. "Similarity: Investigations at the Middle School Level." In *Learning and Teaching Geometry, K–12,* 1987 Yearbook (ed. Mary Montgomery Lindquist). Reston, Va.: NCTM, 1987, pp. 136–145.

Geddes, Dorothy; Bove, Julianna; Fortunato, Irene; Fuys, David J.; Morgenstern, Jessica; and Welchman-Tischler, Rosamund. *Geometry in the Middle School.* Reston, Va.: NCTM, 1992.

Giganti, Paul, Jr., and Cittadino, Mary Jo. "The Art of Tesselation." *Arithmetic Teacher,* 37 (March 1990), pp. 6–16.

Heukerott, Pamela Beth. "Origami: Paper Folding—the Algorithmic Way." *Arithmetic Teacher,* 35 (January 1988), pp. 4–9.

Leidtke, Walter W. "Developing Spatial Abilities in the Early Grades." *Teaching Children Mathematics,* 2 (September 1995), pp. 12–18.

Lindquist, Mary Montgomery; Brown, Catherine A.; Carpenter, Thomas P.; Kouba, Vicky L.; Silver, Edward A.; and Swafford, Jane O. *Results from the Fourth Mathematics Assessment of the National Assessment of Educational Progress.* Reston, Va.: NCTM, 1989.

Lindquist, Mary Montgomery, and Dana, Marcia E. "Strip Tease." *Arithmetic Teacher,* 25 (March 1980), pp. 4–9.

Morrow, Lorna J. "Geometry through the Standards." *Arithmetic Teacher,* 38 (April 1991), pp. 21–25.

National Council of Teachers of Mathematics. *Curriculum and Evaluation Standards for School Mathematics.* Reston, Va.: NCTM 1989.

National Council of Teachers of Mathematics. *Professional Standards for Teaching Mathematics.* Reston, Va.: NCTM, 1991.

Pohl, Victoria. "Visualizing Three Dimensions by Constructing Polyhedra." In *Learning and Teaching Geometry, K–12,* 1987 Yearbook (ed. Mary Montgomery Lindquist). Reston, Va.: NCTM, 1987, pp. 144–154.

Rectanus, Cheryl. *Math by All Means: Geometry Grade 3.* Sausalito, Calif.: Math Solutions Publications, 1994.

Silverman, Helene. "Ideas." *Arithmetic Teacher,* 37 (May 1990), pp. 18–24.

Strutchens, Marilyn E., and Blume, Glendon W. "What Do Students Know about Geometry?" In *Results from the Sixth Mathematics Assessment of the National Assessment of Educational Progress* (eds. Patricia Ann Kenney and Edward A. Silver). Reston Va.: NCTM, 1997, pp. 165–193.

Taylor, Lyn. "Activities to Introduce Your Class to Logo." *Arithmetic Teacher,* 39 (November 1991), pp. 52–54.

Theissen, Diane, and Matthias, Margaret. "Selected Children's Books for Geometry." *Arithmetic Teacher,* 37 (December 1989), pp. 47–51.

Zaslavsky, Claudia. "People Who Live in Round Houses." *Arithmetic Teacher,* 37 (September 1989), pp. 18–21.

Zaslavsky, Claudia. "Symmetry in American Folk Art." *Arithmetic Teacher,* 38 (September 1990), pp. 6–13.

12

Measuring

Snapshot of a Lesson

Orientation

A sixth-grade class of 29 students is studying area of rectangles. In the previous lesson, the class learned to use the base and the altitude to find areas of rectangles. In this lesson, small groups of three or four will find the area of rectangular objects in the room. Mr. Katz circulates to help groups or to ask questions of those who need challenging.

PAT: This card wants us to find which is larger, the desk top or the top of the bookcase? That's easy. The bookcase is much longer.

KIM: But it says "area," Pat. We need to find the area and I think the desk is larger.

WES: I think it's the bookcase. Let's see.

MR. KATZ: Well, what did you find?

PAT: The desk was larger in area even though the bookcase was longer. When we covered them with squares the other day, the desk took more squares.

KIM: Unless I remember that I'm trying to find how many squares, I forget why I'm measuring the lengths and whether to add or multiply.

WES: It really helps me to think of the number of rows and the number of squares in each row. All you have to do is to count the number of squares, and multiplying is an easy way to count.

MR. KATZ: Why don't you try a challenge card instead of the next task card?

KIM: Oh, let's try this one. I've always wanted to cover the science table with a rug!

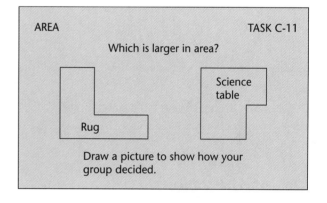

WES: These aren't rectangles.

PAT: Look, we can make them into two rectangles. Remember when we cut those shapes apart? Let's cut the rug!

WES: Funny, but you're right. Let's mark where we would cut them. Then we can find the area of each rectangle and add them.

MR. KATZ: (Approaching another group) What's the problem?

SASHA: We don't know where to begin.

MR. KATZ: What are you trying to do?

SASHA: We have to find something in the room that is about 120 square centimeters. That's awfully large. Are you sure there is something?

SUE: No, it isn't. A square centimeter is awfully small.

JANE: Well, I just can't imagine 120 square centimeters. What can we do?

MR. KATZ: Do you know how large your name card is?

SUE: Let me measure. It's about 7 centimeters by 11 centimeters. That means it's about 77 square centimeters. We need something larger.

SASHA: How about this sheet of paper?

JANE: That's way too much. It's about four times larger. We need something in between.

Across the room, two students seem to be struggling with another type of problem.

MAUREEN: Mr. Katz, can you help us?

MR. KATZ: We'll see. What are you doing?

TOMAS: Well, we were talking and Maureen said the reading table was larger than this table. How can we tell?

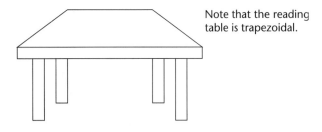

Note that the reading table is trapezoidal.

MR. KATZ: Is the reading table a rectangle?

TOMAS: No, but can't we just measure the length and width?

MR. KATZ: What would be the length?

MAUREEN: Isn't it the longest side?

Mr. Katz observes during the time the groups take to complete their tasks.

MR. KATZ: Let's get back together and see what all of you have found.

SUE: We found three things that were about 120 square centimeters. One was the task card itself—that was pretty sneaky.

KIM: The science table is larger than the rug. Even if we could cut the rug, it wouldn't cover the table. Guess we won't have an easy-on-your-elbows table after all.

TOMAS: We finally figured out the reading table. How about other shapes? How do you find the areas without covering them with squares?

MR. KATZ: Tomas, what do you mean you "figured out" the reading table?

TOMAS: Well, it isn't a rectangle, so we had to do some cutting. We cut off this triangle and put it there to make a rectangle.

MR. KATZ: Right. When things aren't rectangles, we need other ways to find the area. Tomorrow, we'll look at another shape. Some of you might wish to explore other shapes on your own. The task cards in the area packet have some ideas.

 ## Introduction

The snapshot gave us a glance into a sixth-grade classroom. What experiences should the children have before this lesson? What concepts and skills are important for the children to learn? How do you help children to have these experiences? Before examining these and other questions that we should consider as teachers, we will discuss why measuring should be taught.

Stop and think about how you have used numbers in the past few days. Did you tell someone how long it took you to drive to school, how many calories are in a piece of chocolate cake, how far it is to the nearest store, or how many cups of coffee you drank? All of these are measurements. Measurement is the topic from the elementary curriculum that we use the most in our daily lives. Thus, one of the main reasons to include measuring is that it has

many practical applications. As the *Curriculum and Evaluation Standards for School Mathematics* (NCTM 1989, p. 51) points out, "Measurement is of central importance to the curriculum because of its power to help children see that mathematics is useful in everyday life."

A second reason is that measurement can be used in learning other topics in mathematics. It is apparent that children need many of the other topics of mathematics to help them with measuring. For example, they may count the number of grams it takes to balance a scale, multiply to find a volume, divide to change minutes to hours, subtract to see how close an estimate was, or add to find the perimeter of a triangle. To report the number of units, children may use whole numbers, common fractions, decimals, and negative numbers.

Although not quite as apparent, measurement can help teach about operations or numbers. Many of the numeration models we use have a measurement base. For example, the number line is based on length. One model for multiplication is an area model. Also, there are concepts and procedures that underlie both measurement and number ideas. As shown in Figure 12–1, measuring to the nearest unit is similar to rounding to a given unit. Thus, measurement ideas may be used to complement numerical ideas.

Not only is measurement useful in everyday life, but it also is useful in other areas of the curriculum. If you are trying to think of ways to connect mathematics with other subjects, think of measurement and consider the ways in which measurement is used in other areas such as art, music, science, social studies, and language arts.

Another reason why measurement is an important part of the mathematics curriculum is not so much mathematical as pedagogical. Measurement is an effective way to involve students in activities that are often a change of pace from other mathematics topics. Look again at the Snapshot at the beginning of this chapter. Were you fortunate enough to have similarly lively math classes when you were in sixth grade?

Measurement provides an excellent way to present problem-solving experiences at every level. Activity Card 12–1 gives samples of some problems at various levels. Each could be used at the grade level suggested or could be modified for use with students at another grade level.

Research from international studies has often shown that measurement and geometry are the two topics on which students in the United States perform less well than their counterparts in other countries. Through the years, the data from the mathematics assessments of the National Assessment of Educational Progress (NAEP) have given reason for concern about the performance of students in this country. As you read about these results in this chapter, think about your responsibility to help students become more proficient in measuring.

In summary, measurement should be an integral part of the mathematics curriculum for several important reasons:

- It provides many applications to everyday life.
- It can be used to help learn other mathematics.
- It can be related to other areas of the school curriculum.
- It involves the students in active learning.
- It can be approached through problem solving.

The NCTM *Standards* call for measurement to be a continuing part of the mathematics program, rather than being presented in a few isolated lessons.

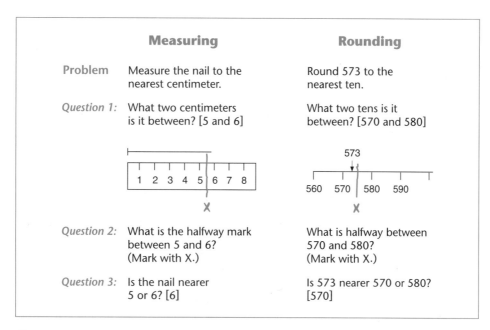

Figure 12–1 • **The similarity between measuring and rounding**

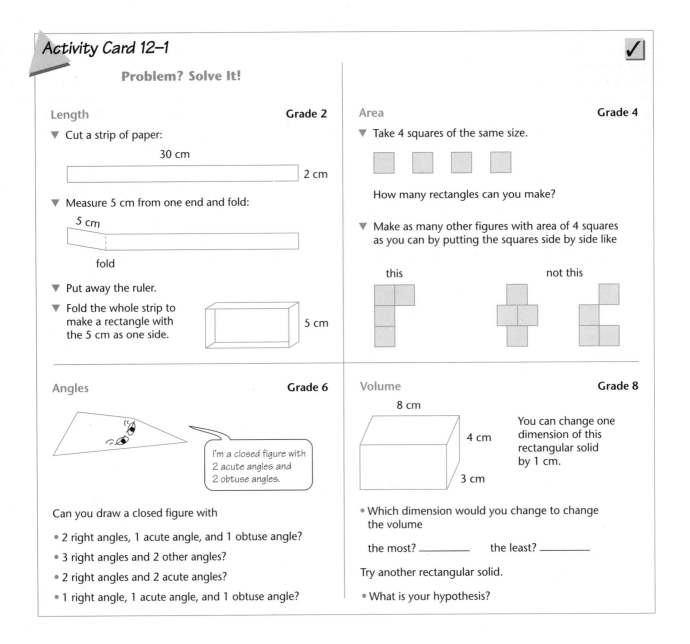

● Teaching Measurement

Most of the research about how children measure and think about measurement does not indicate specifically and directly how the teacher should plan for instruction. Rather, research has focused on what children can do and understand. For example, Wilson and Osborne (1988, p. 109) suggest the following based on their study:

● Children must measure frequently and often, preferably on real problems rather than on text-book exercises.

● Children should encounter activity-oriented measurement situations by doing and experi-

menting rather than passively observing. The activities should encourage discussion to stimulate the refinement and testing of ideas and concepts.

● Instructional planning should emphasize the important ideas of measurement that transfer or work across measurement systems.

Measuring is a process by which a number is assigned to an attribute of an object or event. Length, capacity, weight, area, volume, time and temperature are the measurable attributes considered in most elementary mathematics programs. Although each of these attributes is different, there are some overall commonalities in how to help children learn about measuring them. The following outline is based on the measuring process and can be used to plan instruction:

I. Identify the attribute by comparing objects
   A. Perceptually
   B. Directly
   C. Indirectly through a reference

II. Choose a unit
   A. Arbitrary
   B. Standard

III. Compare the object to the unit

IV. Find the number of units
   A. Counting
   B. Using instruments
   C. Using formulas

V. Report the number of units

If a new attribute is being introduced, one recommended approach is to cycle through I–V several times: the first time using only arbitrary units and counting, the next time using standard units and counting, and only then introducing instruments or formulas. This cycling may take place over several years for the first attributes studied, but after several attributes have been introduced, the length of the cycling should be shortened.

Identifying Attributes

To measure with understanding, children should know what attribute they are measuring. Take, for example, a measure of attitude. What are we actually measuring? Because we do not fully understand the attribute being measured, scores on attitude tests are often difficult to interpret. For young children, measuring the area of an object also can be difficult if they do not understand the concept of area. Thus, one of our first tasks is to build an understanding of measurable attributes.

Children's literature provides an excellent source for developing an understanding of attributes. For example, in the Children's Corner listing, the book *More Spaghetti, I Say!* (Gelman 1977) can be used to help develop an understanding of length and weight by using pasta as a unit of measurement. We also encourage comparing and estimating lengths as a way to build understanding of length concepts.

Three types of comparisons can build understanding of attributes: comparing objects perceptually, comparing them directly, and comparing them indirectly. As children make these types of comparisons, not only are they gaining an understanding

of the particular attribute and the associated vocabulary, but they are also learning procedures that will help them in assigning a number to a measurement. We will examine each attribute separately because of the importance of having children participate in such experiences. As you read, see if you can tell the differences among the three types of comparison, and how each can be used to develop an understanding of that attribute.

Length Length is one of the most easily perceived attributes of objects. Children come to school with some concept of length and some vocabulary associated with it. However, they often have what adults may consider misconceptions about length. For example, they may say that a belt is shorter when it is curled up than when it is straight. These misconceptions disappear as children develop cognitively and are given constructive experiences.

Lesson Cards 12–1, 12–2, and 12–3 illustrate comparison activities that are appropriate for kindergarteners, first graders, or older children who need a review. Lesson Card 12–1 involves comparisons made perceptually. In the beginning of this activity, all irrelevant perceptual attributes have been masked—that is, the objects are the same except for length.

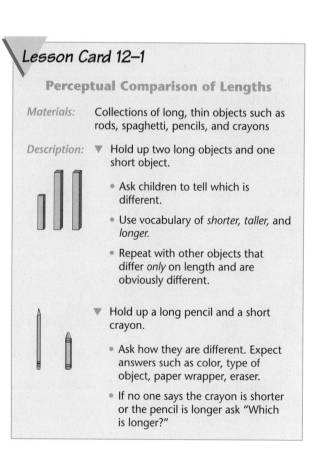

Lesson Card 12–1

Perceptual Comparison of Lengths

Materials: Collections of long, thin objects such as rods, spaghetti, pencils, and crayons

Description:
▼ Hold up two long objects and one short object.

- Ask children to tell which is different.
- Use vocabulary of *shorter, taller,* and *longer.*
- Repeat with other objects that differ *only* on length and are obviously different.

▼ Hold up a long pencil and a short crayon.

- Ask how they are different. Expect answers such as color, type of object, paper wrapper, eraser.
- If no one says the crayon is shorter or the pencil is longer ask "Which is longer?"

Lesson Card 12–2

Direct Comparison of Length

Materials: A box of long, thin objects, some of which are about the same length, and sheets of construction paper (one of each labeled "shorter," "same," and "longer"):

Description:

Ask a child to choose a reference object and place it on a baseline. Then ask the child to compare each of the other objects with the reference object and put them on the appropriate piece of labeled construction paper.

Baseline

SHORTER

SAME

LONGER

Lesson Card 12–3

Indirect Comparison of Length

Materials: A piece of string and a pair of scissors for each child, index cards, tape, and a pen

Description:

▼ Choose two objects that cannot be moved and that are about the same length (or two dimensions of the same object—for example, the height and width of your desk).

  • Ask which is longer and how you could show which is longer.

  • Show the children the process of cutting pieces of string the same length as each object to be compared.

  • Compare the string representations to show which length is longer.

▼ Give each child a string and let them choose an object you've marked on an index card.

  • Ask each to make a string representation of the object and then compare it with several others.

  • Make a "graph" of all the lengths for comparison:

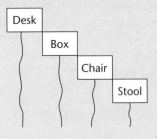

This allows children to build the concept of length as an attribute of long, thin things. As the activity progresses and vocabulary is reviewed and extended, the objects compared differ on several attributes, but the focus remains on length.

Lesson Card 12–2 uses the procedure of making direct comparisons. This type of comparison of length involves taking two objects and placing them side by side on a common baseline. This activity may be extended to seriating objects by length—that is, arranging them from shortest to tallest. For the young child, this task is more difficult because multiple comparisons must be made.

Lesson Card 12–3 presents the problem of indirectly comparing two objects when they cannot be placed side by side. Children must use a third object to help them make the comparison. This activity is what we do when we use a ruler to assign measurements: The ruler is the third object that assists us in making a comparison. Young children can work with string, strips of paper, erasers, or other items as the third object.

Through activities such as these, children begin to develop an understanding of length as an attribute of long, thin objects. However, length is used in other ways. For example, length is the distance around your waist. Young children can use string to compare their waists or to compare their wrists with their ankles. Older children can guess whether the height or the distance around a variety of cylindrical cans is longer and then check their guess by using string.

The distance between two points is also measured by length. In this case, words such as *nearer* and *farther* may be used when comparing two distances. Distance is often more difficult to perceive than the length of a long, thin object, so it should be introduced later.

Perimeter—the distance around a region—is a special type of length. Children should be given the opportunity to measure the distance around a region with string or a measuring tape. Later they can add the lengths of the various sides of the region to find the perimeter.

Capacity Capacity is an attribute of containers that can be introduced to young children by asking, "Which holds more?"

Although perceptual comparisons can be made between two containers, young children often make the comparisons based on length (height) rather than on capacity. When asked which holds more—a tall container or a short container—most children will choose the taller container even if the shorter one may actually hold more. Thus, it is probably best to begin the study of capacity by using direct comparisons.

Some type of filler is needed to make direct comparisons. Water and sand are easy for young children to use. Given a variety of containers, children can fill one and pour it into the other to see which holds more. After children have done some experimenting with direct comparison, activities involving perceptual comparisons are possible. For example, children greatly enjoy guessing contests in which they guess which container holds more, and then you can check the results together. You also can use drawings of pairs of containers that are lettered and ask children to circle the letter of the container in each pair that holds more.

Indirect comparisons are used when two containers cannot be compared perceptually or directly. For example, suppose you have two containers with small openings that make it difficult to pour from one into another. By pouring each into a pair of identical large-mouth containers, the capacities can be compared. Note that this activity is similar to what we do when we use graduated cylinders.

Weight To compare weights perceptually, we need to be able to lift the two objects. Children should be given a variety of pairs of objects (one of which is much heavier than the other) and asked to hold one in each hand. Children often think that a larger object weighs more. Thus, some of the objects should be small and heavy and others large and light. For children to understand that to find which is heavier, they must do more than look at the object; they may need experiences in comparing two objects that look the same but weigh different amounts. An easy way to provide this experience is by having children compare identical containers with lids (such as cottage-cheese containers) filled to weigh a different amount.

When you cannot feel the difference between the weight of two objects, you need a balance scale to assist in the comparison. To introduce the balance, choose two objects that differ greatly in weight so children can see that the heavier object "goes down" on the balance.

Many activities may be set up in which children compare the weights of two objects. One challenging activity is to compare five identical containers, with lids secured and filled with different amounts of weight, and put them in order from lightest to heaviest.

Indirect comparisons are not necessary until units of weight are introduced because, whenever each of two objects could be compared to a third on the balance, it would be much simpler to compare the two directly.

Area Area is an attribute of plane regions that can be compared by sight if the differences are large enough and the shapes similar enough. That is, it is easy to tell this page is larger than a driver's license, but it may be difficult to compare the areas of the three regions A, B, and C.

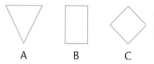

If the regions can be cut out, it is fairly easy to compare regions B and C by placing one on top of the other. It is more difficult to compare either B or C with A. Only when children have some idea of *conservation of area*—that a region can be cut and rearranged without changing the area—can this experience be meaningful. Thus, the first direct comparisons should be made with two regions, one of which fits within the other.

If objects cannot be moved to place one on top of the other, children can trace one object and use this representation to make an indirect comparison. For example, to compare the area of a desk to the area of a bulletin board, you could ask them to cut a piece of paper the size of the desk and put it on the bulletin board.

To help children understand that regions can be rearranged and not affect the area, geometry activities, such as the shape search on Activity Card 12–2, are helpful.

Volume If volume is considered as "how much space a three-dimensional object takes up," then it is difficult to make anything but perceptual comparisons before units are introduced. Thus, volume should receive little attention until fourth or fifth grade. However, because there is a close connection between volume and capacity, some background can be provided if containers are filled with nonliquids, such as blocks, balls, or other objects.

Activity Card 12–2

Shape Search

▼ Take 2 triangles:

▼ Put them together by matching sides:

How many different shapes can you make? (Trace your answers on your paper.)

▼ Now see how many different shapes you can make with 3 triangles:

Temperature We can certainly sense great differences in temperatures. Before introducing thermometers, you can have children compare to see which of two objects is colder (or hotter). You can also talk about things (or times) that are hot or cold; however, there are few other comparisons you can make without an instrument to help.

Time There are two attributes of events that can be measured: *time of occurrence* and *length of duration*. You can begin describing the time of occurrence by giving a time span. It happened today, in the morning, in October. Young children need to develop the vocabulary of days, months, and seasons of the year.

Children can tell which of two events takes longer (duration) if their lengths are greatly different. Does it take longer to brush your teeth or read a story? If the events are similar in duration, children can tell which lasts longer if they both begin at the same time (note the similarity to deciding which object is longer when both are placed on a baseline). You can think of many contests that use this idea: whose paper plane flew longer; whose eyes were shut longer; who hopped for a longer time.

Units of Measure

After children have begun to develop a firm concept of an attribute through comparison activities, it is important to help them move through the remaining steps of the measurement process (steps II–V) described on page 247. Before instruments or formulas are introduced, children should be able to count the number of units that describe a given attribute.

To answer the question, "How long is the pencil?" we can say, "It's longer than my thumb" or "It's

shorter than my arm." These are relative statements that give a range of possibilities for length but do not do a very accurate job of describing it. To be accurate, we need to compare the pencil to a unit. We can use an arbitrary unit such as a paper clip and say that the pencil is 7 paper clips long, or we can use a standard unit and say it is 16 centimeters long. Once we have described the length, we can compare it to other lengths. That is, we use the symbolic description to assist us in indirectly comparing. The unit of measurement gives us much power; we can communicate with others and we can make comparisons that were previously difficult to make.

The unit of measurement is one of the most important aspects of measurement. Research results from the second national mathematics assessment show that children do have some knowledge of units and can apply "this knowledge in simple tasks, but appear to abandon this knowledge in more complex settings" (Hiebert 1981, p. 42). For example, over three-fourths of nine-year-olds could find the volume of this rectangular solid:

When the solid was more complicated, they counted the faces of the cubes that were visible rather than the number of cubes.

Concepts Related to Units There are many concepts related to units of measurement that teachers need to help children develop. The concepts described here are developed over time. A single activity will not suffice; you need to be aware of the concepts, include similar activities with other attributes, and look for opportunities within any measurement activity to further the development of the concepts.

1. *A measurement must include both a number and the unit.* (How many times do you remember a teacher telling you to be certain to write inches? And how many times did you not see the necessity—probably because you were only measuring in inches for the entire lesson?) When children measure the same object with many different arbitrary units, research indicates that they are more likely to see the need to report the unit. Having children measure the length of a book with paper strips, erasers, or cubes, or weigh an object with washers, pennies, or paper clips, is the type of task that will encourage younger children to write (or draw) the unit. Lesson Card 12–4

Lesson Card 12–4

Measuring Length with Arbitrary Units

Materials: Erasers, paper clips, books, boxes, and other objects that can be used as arbitrary units of measure

Description:

▼ Ask children to measure objects in the room in specific units; for example,

- Length of desk — erasers
- Height of door — your shoe
- Distance around globe — chains
- Cabinet drawer — paper clips
- Wastebasket height — hands
- Distance across room — book

▼ Record the lengths; for example,

- Desk: 15 erasers
- Door: 10 shoes
- Globe: 8 chains
- Drawer: 32 paper clips
- Basket: 18 hands
- Room: 36 books

▼ Ask children to use the information to tell which is longest.

▼ Choose pairs of objects that are close in length; for example, the cabinet drawer or the distance around the globe.

- Ask children which object in each pair is longer and which is shorter.
- Check by measuring each object with the same unit.

provides examples of activities that encourage children to focus on the importance of reporting the unit.

2. *Two measurements may be easily compared if the same unit is used.* Young children often rely on only the number or possibly only the unit to make a comparison. For example, if one pencil is 6 paper clips long and another pencil is 2 strips long, a child will say that the one that measures 6 is longer. They have not yet reached the stage where they can coordinate the number with unit.

3. *One unit may be more appropriate than another to measure an object.* The size of the unit chosen depends on the size of the object and on the degree of accuracy desired. If children are allowed to choose

the unit, the idea of the unit's size depending on the size of the object will be clearer. Activity Card 12–3 provides an example of this type of activity.

4. *There is an inverse relationship between the number of units and the size of the unit.* When measuring the same object with different units, children soon realize that the larger the unit, the fewer are required. For example, you could ask each child to weigh a different object with pennies, washers, and cubes. If each child makes a graph of the results, a pattern becomes apparent when all the graphs are compared.

5. *Standard units are needed to communicate effectively.* Many concepts about units can be well developed with arbitrary units. At the same time you will be teaching procedures of measuring with units (how to line up units, use a balance, cover a region, keep track of how many units, and so on).

At some point, depending on the attribute, you will begin using standard units. Standard units are either customary (inch, pint, pound, etc.) or metric (meter, gram, liter, etc.). Children already have heard of standard units but may not realize why we use them.

Activity Card 12–3

Choose a Unit

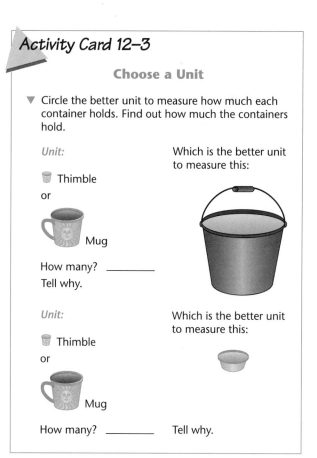

▼ Circle the better unit to measure how much each container holds. Find out how much the containers hold.

Unit:

🥃 Thimble

or

☕ Mug

How many? _____
Tell why.

Which is the better unit to measure this:

Unit:

🥃 Thimble

or

☕ Mug

How many? _____   Tell why.

Which is the better unit to measure this:

Stories and activities that demonstrate the difficulty in communicating sizes when there is no standard of measurement are one way to present the necessity of a standard unit. The book *How Big Is a Foot?* (Myller 1991) is an interesting and amusing source to use in helping children see the necessity for a standard unit. Another enjoyable activity for children is making a recipe of Kool-Aid—using a very large cup for the water and a very small spoon for the Kool-Aid powder. (Be sure to have enough Kool-Aid so the children can make it tasty.)

6. *A smaller unit will give a more exact measurement.* First, children need to realize that all measurements are approximate. If you have had them do a lot of measuring of real objects, they will have been reporting approximate measurements but perhaps without being fully aware of it. A practice of saying "about 6 inches," "more than 6 inches," or "between 6 and 7 inches" will help.

To set up the need for a more precise measurement, give each of two children, sitting far apart, a paper strip between 2 and 3 decimeters long (say, 26 and 27 centimeters) and decimeter strips. Have each measure the paper strip and tell its length in decimeters. Then ask the class which strip is longer (no fair comparing the strips directly). Next, have them measure with centimeters. Discuss with the class why a smaller unit was needed.

Measuring in Units Length is the first attribute that most children measure. They take an arbitrary unit and copies of that unit and put them end to end until the units are as long as the object they are measuring. From previous direct comparisons of two objects, children should know when the lengths are the same. However, they have not lined up the units in a straight line with no gaps in between and no overlaps, nor have they counted the units. Units that connect, such as Unifix cubes or Lots-a-Links, are good to begin with because they are easy to handle and line up readily without gaps or overlaps.

After an example or two, you need only set up objects to be measured and supply the units, then observe and help. Later, children can take one unit and move it (an *iteration*). This more advanced skill is needed for proper use of a ruler when measuring objects longer than the ruler. It is a skill that should not be pushed too early. If you find children who cannot move, mark, and count, postpone introducing it until later.

If children have been measuring with arbitrary units, then the move to using standard units should be easy. They will have a good understanding of the

process of measuring, so the purpose should be to give them a feel for the standard unit. Let us take the decimeter as an example and consider some ways to build the feel for it as a standard unit.

Give each child a paper strip that is 10 centimeters by 2 centimeters. Do a variety of activities that have the children compare things to the decimeter strip. Some are suggested here.

- *Decimeter List-Up:* Put a list on the board of objects children can find in the room that are the same length as a decimeter. Be sure to include things on them such as fingers, pockets, soles of shoes.

- *Decimeter Hold-Up:* Pair the children and have one child try to hold two forefingers a decimeter apart, vertically, horizontally, and obliquely. The partner should check each time; then roles should be reversed.

- *Decimeter Stack-Up:* Set up stations with pennies, chips, clips, beans, cubes, and the like. At one station, children should try to stack the chips a decimeter high. At another station they should try to make a line of chips a decimeter long. Then they should use their decimeter strip to see how close they were.

After children are somewhat familiar with the length of a decimeter, they can begin to measure with decimeters. A good way to begin is by asking them to estimate the lengths of objects and then check. As children are measuring with decimeter strips, they (and you) should notice that putting down strip after strip is not the easiest way to measure. Have them tape their strips together, end to end, alternating colors if two colors are available. Now they have a "decimeter ruler," except they still have to count the units. After they have done some counting, see if anyone will suggest numbering the strips. This activity will help children understand how rulers are made and that they are counting units.

Once children are familiar with the decimeter measurement of small objects, the next stage is measuring something very long. Have each child make a ten-decimeter ruler. Tell the children that this unit is called a *meter* and is used to measure longer distances. Activities similar to those suggested with decimeters will help them become familiar with meters. New units should be related to those children have already used to help them understand the new unit and to assist them in making conversions from one unit to another.

Children become familiar with standard units through comparing, measuring, estimating, and constructing. The experiences you provide should include all these processes. It is also important that not too many standard units are introduced at one time, that the unit is not too small or too large for a child of that age to handle, and that the numbers generated are not too large. Table 12–1 is a guide to the most common standard units used in elementary school and the approximate grade levels at which it is appropriate to introduce them.

Instruments for Measuring

Instruments are used to measure some attributes. In elementary school, the more common instruments are rulers, scales, graduated containers, thermometers, protractors, and clocks. Other attributes (such as area and volume) are assigned a measurement by the use of a formula after an instrument has been used to measure some dimensions. Later, other attributes are derived from measurements of more than one attribute (for example, speed is derived from distance and time).

Table 12–1 • **Standard units for elementary students (with approximate grade level)**

Attribute	Metric Units	Customary Units
Length	Decimeter (1–2) Centimeter (2–3) Meter (2–3) Millimeter (3–4) Kilometer (4–5)	Inch (1–2) Foot (2–3) Yard (2–3) Mile (4–5)
Weight	Kilogram (2–3) Gram (4–5)	Ounce (2–3) Pound (2–3)
Capacity	Liter (1–2) Milliliter (4–5)	Quart (2–3) Cup (1–2) Gallon (2–3)
Area	Square centimeter (4–5) Square meter (5–6)	Square inch (4–5) Square foot (4–5) Square yard (4–5)
Volume	Cubic centimeter (5–6) Cubic meter (5–6)	Cubic inch (5–6) Cubic foot (5–6) Cubic yard (5–6)
Temperature	Celsius degree (2–3)	Fahrenheit degree (2–3)
Time		Hour (1–2) Minute (1–2) Second (3–4) Day (K–1) Week (1–2) Month (K–1)

Much of the emphasis in the elementary curriculum is on instruments and formulas, and some children encounter difficulty with both. One probable source of difficulty is that the children do not understand what they are measuring and what it means to measure. The activities and suggestions presented so far in this chapter have dealt with building this understanding. Here we will look at some common problems children have with particular instruments and some ways to assist in developing the correct skills.

Ruler A ruler automatically counts the number of units, but children must realize what unit they are using and line up the ruler properly. Children will focus on the unit being used if the scale on the ruler has only that unit. For example, if the unit is centimeters, choose a ruler marked in centimeters, not in centimeters and millimeters. Or if the unit is inches, choose a ruler without the markings of fourths or eighths.

It is important that children measure real objects with the ruler. Make certain that you include activities in which children measure objects longer than one ruler. Can they move the ruler (iterate), and do they have the addition skills to add the units? For example, suppose the children have a 25-centimeter ruler and they are to measure something that is 43 centimeters long. Can they add 25 and 18? Of course, they could use counting or techniques that rely on their place value and counting background: 25, 35, 36, 37, . . . , 43. Let them try; they will surprise you if they are given a problem to solve. Your role is to ask questions to assist.

Children may have difficulty in measuring to the nearest fourth, eighth, or sixteenth of a unit. For example, 47 percent of the thirteen-year-olds in a national assessment had difficulty measuring to the nearest one-fourth inch (Carpenter et al. 1981). One cause of this difficulty may be the smallness of the unit (there is more room for error), but more probably it is their lack of confidence and understanding of fractions, their lack of understanding of the unit (fourths), and their lack of consciousness of how to measure to the nearest unit. In measuring to a unit, they tend to decide by simply looking at the nearest larger unit. The example of measuring in Figure 12–1 gives you some idea of how to make this process more explicit. It also will be helpful to emphasize the units by asking, "What two units is the nail between—two-fourths and three-fourths or three-fourths and four-fourths?" Children must be able to answer this question before deciding which it is nearer. A firm foundation of fractions, and especially fractions as they relate to length, will help with measuring to the nearest unit.

Figure 12–2 illustrates an exercise for using a ruler similar to a question from the fourth national mathematics assessment. What do you think was the most common answer of nine-year-olds? Most said the segment was 5 inches long. Almost half of the thirteen-year-olds also gave this response. Results from the sixth national mathematics assessment of the NAEP also indicate these patterns of responses. Children must be helped to see that the 1 on a ruler means that one unit has already been used. A review of direct comparison would help a child who was having difficulty using a ruler. You also could use separate units, or just mark the inches on the segment and count.

Although we have concentrated on the difficulties some children have in learning to use a ruler, do not be discouraged. Children love to use rulers, and overall they do quite well with them. Make certain you have children not only measuring objects but also constructing line segments or objects of a given length.

Scaled Instruments Instruments such as bathroom scales, graduated cylinders, and thermometers cause children some trouble because each unit is not marked. On national assessments, students have always had difficulty reading thermometers on which the markings represent 2 degrees. Over half of the fourth-grade students on the sixth national mathematics assessment chose a distractor based on thinking the marking represented one rather than two units (Kenney and Kouba, 1997).

One way to help children become more aware of the markings on a scale is to show to them and read with them many scales with different markings, but a more powerful way is to have them make their own instruments. They can make graphs, for example, using different scales (see Chapter 15), or they can mark their own graduated cylinders. Activity

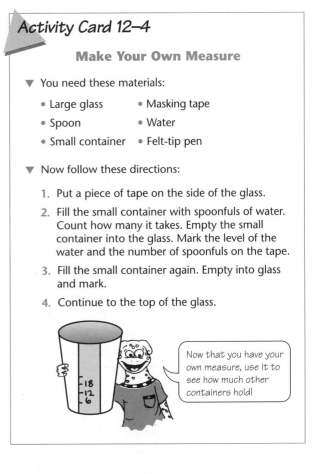

Card 12–4 gives children instructions on how to make the "cylinder." After they have made it, have them measure the amounts other containers hold. Note that this activity is also good practice for finding multiples of a number.

Clocks The ordinary dial clock or watch is one of the most complicated instruments to read—and yet it is often one of the first to be taught. Not only are there two or more ways to read the scale on it (hour, minute, and second), but the hands (indicators of

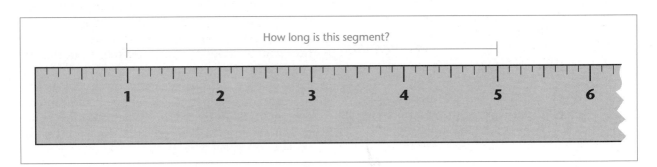

Figure 12–2 • **An exercise assessing understanding of a ruler**

the measures) move in a circular fashion. There is no set age at which children appear ready to learn how to tell time; you will often notice a wide range of ability within a class. The following list of skills associated with telling time is not necessarily in the order in which children may develop them.

● Identify the hour hand and the minute hand and the direction they move.

● Orally tell time by the hour (noting that the minute hand is on the 12) and moving the hands of a clock to show the hourly times.

● Identify the hour that a time is "after" (for example, it's after 4 o'clock).

● Count by fives to tell time to the nearest 5 minutes and report it orally (for example, as 4 o'clock and 20 minutes after).

● Count on by ones from multiples of 5 to tell time to the nearest minute (for example, 25, 26, 27).

● Identify the hour that a time is "before" (for example, it's before 10) and count by fives and ones to tell about how many minutes before the hour.

● Write the time in digital notation (4:20).

● Match the time on a digital clock to a regular clock.

These skills need to be developed over a long period of time, and children need to have clocks with movable hands. To give you some idea of what nine-year-olds, in general, are able to do, let's examine the results of the second national assessment (Carpenter et al. 1981, p. 92):

> Ninety-three percent could tell time on the hour, 86 percent could tell time at 15-minute intervals (e.g., 8:15, 6:45), 69 percent could tell time at 5-minute intervals (e.g., 6:25, 11:55), and 59 percent could tell time at one-minute intervals (e.g., 2:53). [However] only about one-third could solve problems involving time, such as telling the time 8 hours after a given time.

You can begin problem solving with young children if they have clocks or watches. For example, as soon as children can tell time on the hour, you can ask questions such as, "What time will it be in 2 hours?" As the children become more familiar with the clock, you can give more challenging questions, such as those on Activity Card 12–5.

Although reading digital clocks is easier than reading regular clocks, solving the types of problems given in Activity Card 12–5 is more difficult with a

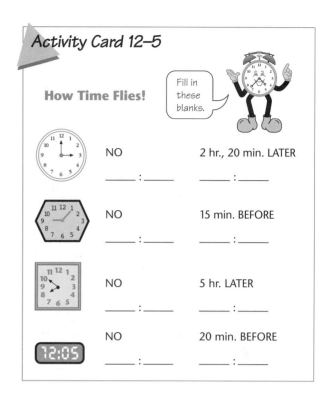

Activity Card 12–5

How Time Flies!

Fill in these blanks.

NO	2 hr., 20 min. LATER
____:____	____:____
NO	15 min. BEFORE
____:____	____:____
NO	5 hr. LATER
____:____	____:____
NO	20 min. BEFORE
____:____	____:____

12:05

digital clock. In learning to read a regular clock, a child learns the relationship of the minutes and hours and has a model to use in solving such problems. If all clocks were digital, teachers would need to spend less time on reading time but more on how our time system works.

To integrate math and history, an interdisciplinary unit on the history of time and clocks could prove to be interesting to older students. Students might be amazed to see how the measurement of time has evolved through the years. Students could make sand clocks or other primitive instruments.

Formulas for Measuring

Formulas for area, perimeter, volume, and surface area usually are introduced in the upper grades. Although formulas are necessary in many measurement situations, they should not take the place of careful development of measurement attributes and the measuring process. The skill of using formulas needs to be developed—but not at the expense of helping students see how formulas are derived. The main emphasis in this section will be on ways to build meaning of the area formulas. The formulas for the other attributes may be developed similarly.

Before formulas are considered, students should be given the opportunity to compare regions of area with and without units. We have already discussed comparing areas without the aid of units by placing one region on top of the other and by cutting one region in order to make the comparison.

When introducing units of area, provide students with experiences in covering a region with a variety of types of units—squares, triangles, rectangles. To find the area of a region, they should count the number of units. Covering many different shapes will help students see the need to approximate and to use smaller units. For example, this region was first covered by one size of squares and then by smaller squares:

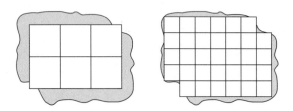

When students are thoroughly familiar with counting units covering different shapes, especially rectangles, it is time to introduce the formula for area of a rectangle. In this section, we examine steps for developing this formula and then show how to use it to develop the formulas for parallelograms, triangles, trapezoids, and other figures. After learning how to use these formulas, children need experiences such as those on Activity Card 12–6, in which they have to combine formulas for different shapes.

Rectangle The formula for the area of a rectangle is often the first formula children encounter. Use of the rectangle is appropriate because it can be developed easily, building on models that children may have used for multiplication.

Figure 12–3 shows a sequence of steps that can be used to develop instructional activities that lead to the formula for the area of a rectangle, $A = b \times a$ (where A is area, b is base, and a is altitude). This form of the formula generalizes better than $A = l \times w$. Recall in the Snapshot at the beginning of this chapter that the length-and-width interpretation led to initial confusion with the trapezoidal table.

When children measure with square units, the base and altitude will not be an exact number of units. You may have them begin by estimating how many squares it would take to cover the shape. Later you can develop the idea of using smaller units or fractional parts of the unit.

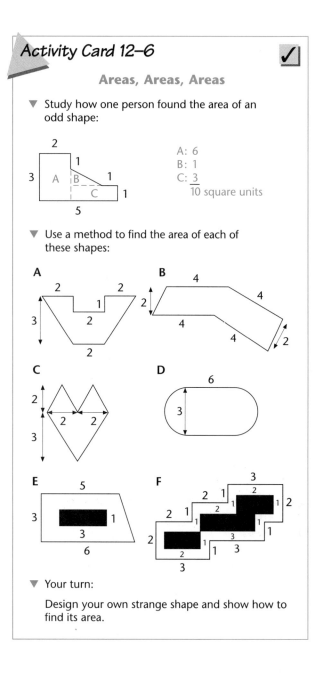

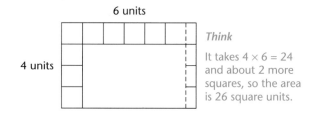

We are not suggesting that you teach the steps as listed in Figure 12–3. It is given as an outline to help you sequence experiences and assess students' understandings. Although some of the steps could be

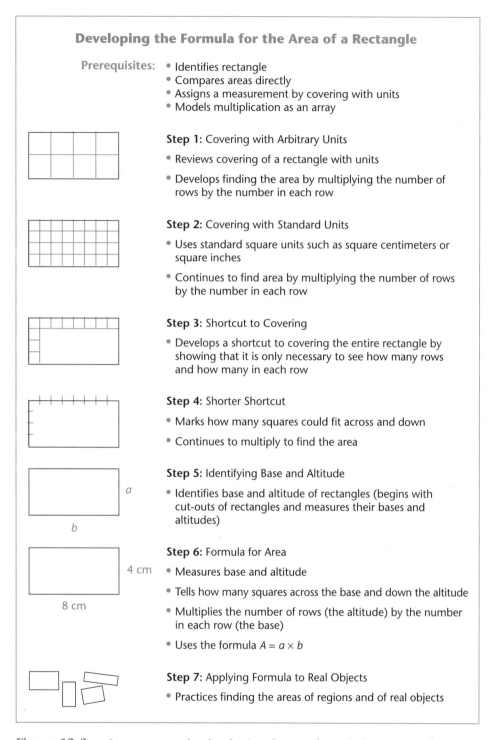

Developing the Formula for the Area of a Rectangle

Prerequisites:
- Identifies rectangle
- Compares areas directly
- Assigns a measurement by covering with units
- Models multiplication as an array

Step 1: Covering with Arbitrary Units
- Reviews covering of a rectangle with units
- Develops finding the area by multiplying the number of rows by the number in each row

Step 2: Covering with Standard Units
- Uses standard square units such as square centimeters or square inches
- Continues to find area by multiplying the number of rows by the number in each row

Step 3: Shortcut to Covering
- Develops a shortcut to covering the entire rectangle by showing that it is only necessary to see how many rows and how many in each row

Step 4: Shorter Shortcut
- Marks how many squares could fit across and down
- Continues to multiply to find the area

Step 5: Identifying Base and Altitude
- Identifies base and altitude of rectangles (begins with cut-outs of rectangles and measures their bases and altitudes)

Step 6: Formula for Area
- Measures base and altitude
- Tells how many squares across the base and down the altitude
- Multiplies the number of rows (the altitude) by the number in each row (the base)
- Uses the formula $A = a \times b$

Step 7: Applying Formula to Real Objects
- Practices finding the areas of regions and of real objects

Figure 12–3 • **One sequence for developing the area formula for a rectangle**

combined into a single activity, step 3 should not be done until children have the experiences listed in step 1. In addition, problems may arise when children are doing step 7 if they have not had prior experience in covering real objects.

One difficulty that children often have with area of a rectangle is that they may learn, by rote, that the area is the length times the width (or base times altitude) but not develop the underlying concepts. Thus, when they are faced with finding the area of a square, they run into difficulty. (It has no side that is longer than the others!) The results of the fourth national assessment (Kouba et al. 1988) showed that seventh-grade performance dropped from 50 percent correct for rectangles to 10 percent correct for squares.

Parallelogram After children have worked with the area formula for a rectangle, the area formula for a parallelogram can be developed. Children need background in geometric experiences in which they have compared parallelograms with rectangles and have tried to cut the parallelograms to rearrange them into rectangles. Next, they should identify the base and altitude of parallelograms. Note that any side can be designated as a base, and the altitude depends on what side was chosen.

The next stage in developing the formula is seeing the relationship of the area of a parallelogram with base b and altitude a and the corresponding rectangle. From exercises such as those on Activity Card 12–7, children should see the area of a parallelogram is the same as the corresponding rectangle:

$$A = b \times a$$

Triangle Children's understanding of the area of a triangle can be developed from the realization that a triangle is always half of a parallelogram. This development depends on a strong background of geometry, experiences like those described in Chapter 11 and activities such as Activity Card 12–8. Even when students see that the area of a triangle is half that of a corresponding parallelogram, or

$$A = \tfrac{1}{2}(b \times a)$$

they have difficulty identifying the altitude, especially in triangles like E in Activity Card 12–8.

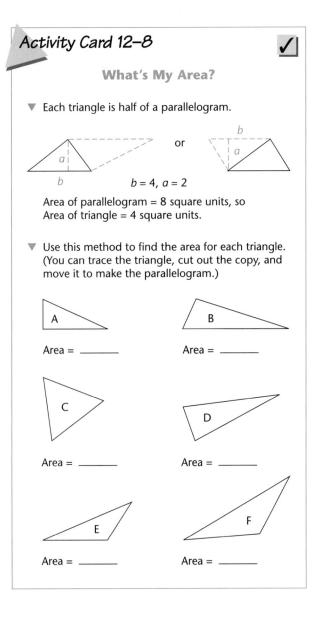

Activity Card 12–8

What's My Area?

▼ Each triangle is half of a parallelogram.

or

$b = 4, a = 2$

Area of parallelogram = 8 square units, so
Area of triangle = 4 square units.

▼ Use this method to find the area for each triangle. (You can trace the triangle, cut out the copy, and move it to make the parallelogram.)

A Area = _____

B Area = _____

C Area = _____

D Area = _____

E Area = _____

F Area = _____

Activity Card 12–7

How Are We Alike?

If areas are the same, show how you can cut the parallelogram and move it to make a rectangle.

Do we have the same . . .

base? _yes, 6cm_

altitude? _yes, 4cm_

area? _yes_

base? _____

altitude? _____

area? _____

base? _____

altitude? _____

area? _____

Trapezoid There are many ways to develop the formula for the area of a trapezoid. One of the easiest is to rely again on the area of a parallelogram. Consider the example of finding the area of the following trapezoid.

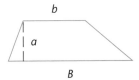

Students can be instructed to make a copy of the trapezoid and place it adjacent to the original:

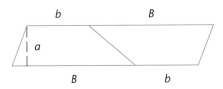

The area formula can now be developed through a series of questions.

What figure have you formed? [a parallelogram]

What is its base? [$B + b$]

What is its altitude? [a]

What is its area? [$A = a(B + b)$]

How does the area of the trapezoid compare to the area of the parallelogram? [half as much]

Therefore, how might we write a formula for area of a trapezoid? [$A = \frac{1}{2}a(B + b)$]

Circle The circle is the one common geometric figure whose area is not directly related to the previous procedures. Students may discover that the formula is logical by cutting a circle into segments and rearranging them to form a pseudo-parallelogram, as shown in Figure 12–4. This activity depends on their knowledge of the circumference being $2\pi r$.

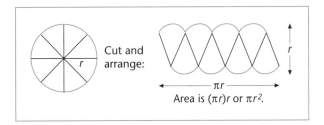

Figure 12–4 • **An activity that relates the area of a circle to a parallelogram**

● Comparing Measurements

After making a measurement, we often use it to solve a problem involving a comparison or an arithmetic operation. In so doing, we may need to change from one unit to another *(conversion),* which relies on the *equivalence* relation of the two units.

In this section, we will examine equivalences and conversions within the customary or the metric system. Students should become conversant in each system and not rely on converting between systems.

Equivalences

As you introduce new standard units, you should relate them to the others. For example, suppose you are introducing the millimeter; you should relate it to a centimeter by showing that it is smaller and that it is one-tenth of a centimeter.

After using different units and being given the equivalences, children should learn certain equivalences. Some of these, such as seven days = one week, sixty minutes = one hour, and twelve inches = one foot, will become known through repeated use. Children need to know that they are expected to know other equivalences.

Although children are no longer required to memorize long tables of equivalences, you should expect them to memorize the ones that are commonly used. The task is easier with metric system because of the standard prefixes and tens relationship between units as indicated in Table 12–2. Be-

Table 12–2 • **Most commonly used metric units**

	1000 kilo (k)	*100 hecto (h)*	*10 deka (da)*	*Base unit*	$^5{}_8$ *deci (d)*	$^1{}_{100}$ *centi (c)*	$^1{}_{1000}$ *milli (m)*
Length	kilometer (km)			meter (m)		centimeter (cm)	millimeter (mm)
Capacity				liter (l)			milliliter (ml)
Mass	kilogram (kg)			gram (g)			

cause not all equivalences will be memorized, children must become familiar with using a table of equivalences. You will need to help them develop the different skills related to a table.

The following table and questions illustrate these skills:

Unit	Equivalent
1 day	24 hours
1 hour	60 minutes
1 minute	60 seconds

How many hours in a day?

(This answer is a straightforward reading from the table.)

What part of a day is one hour?

(This answer involves knowledge of fractional relations of the units in the table.)

How many seconds in an hour?

(This answer involves conversion of units in the table.)

Area and volume equivalences can be difficult for many children because they are often derived from the linear equivalences. For example, knowing that $1 \text{ m} = 10 \text{ dm}$ allows you to derive $1 \text{ m}^2 = 100 \text{ dm}^2$ and $1 \text{ m}^3 = 1000 \text{ dm}^3$. Children need experiences in seeing these basic relationships through models, drawings, and questions such as on Lesson Card 12–5.

Conversions

To change from one unit to another, children must know the equivalence or relation between the two units. However, by itself, this information is not sufficient to make conversions. Let's look at an example of a class discussion.

MR. BANE: It seems that several of you are stumped on the assignment. Devon, please read the first exercise and let's look at it together.

DEVON: Blank dm equals 5 m.

Mr. Bane writes on the board: _____ dm = 5 m.

MR. BANE: Who can tell me what we are looking for?

Lesson Card 12–5

Solving Conversion Problems with Square Units

▼ Take 1 square decimeter. Draw on the board 1 square meter. Ask the students how many square decimeters it would take to cover 1 square meter.

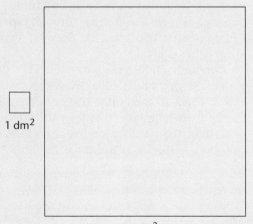

1 dm²

1 m²

▼ Establish that it would take 100 square or 1 m² = 100 dm². Show that each row would have 10 and that there would be 10 rows.

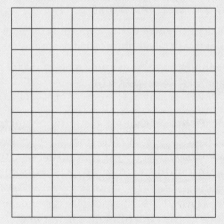

10 × 10 = 100 squares

▼ Solve some area problems drawing sketches and using the model.

• Conrad has a piece of cloth that is 3m² or 3 m × 1 m. How many dm² is that?

• Maria has a blanket that is 15 dm × 10 dm. How many m² is it?

GEORGE: How many decimeters there are in 5 meters.

MR. BANE: What do you know about decimeters and meters?

ALANA: A decimeter is about this big and a meter is about this big.

MR. BANE: That's right. Could everyone see Alana's hands? Which unit is larger, the meter or the decimeter? . . . Right, so will it take more than 5 decimeters or less than 5 to make 5 meters?

KARINA: It'll take more. It takes 10 decimeters to make 1 meter.

Mr. Bane draws this on the board:

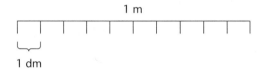

MR. BANE: If 1 meter is 10 decimeters, then what would 5 meters be?

DEVON: I see, it's 5 groups of the 10 decimeters or 50 decimeters.

MR. BANE: Good. Let's try another:

$$20 \text{ cm} = \underline{\hspace{1cm}} \text{ dm.}$$

LEON: Centimeters are smaller, they take more; so it won't be as many as 20 dm.

MR. BANE: Good. We know our answer must be less than 20.

RANDY: Let's draw a picture like this. Oh, there's no use drawing in all 20 marks. We know 10 cm makes 1 dm. So we want to know how many tens in 20.

MR. BANE: Right, in this case we can just look at the picture and see that it is 2 decimeters. But what if it was 184 centimeters?

DAVE: We still need to know how many tens in 184—we divide.

JIM: There are 18 decimeters.

MR. BANE: What about the 4 left over?

PAULA: Those are centimeters. We have 18 full decimeters and 4 left-over centimeters.

MR. BANE: Let's write that down:

$$184 \text{ cm} = 18 \text{ dm } 4 \text{ cm}$$

OK. Try some on your own and I'll help you if you have questions.

This discussion, although not an initial presentation to the class, points out many good techniques to use in developing conversions. First, Mr. Bane had the children decide whether their answer would be larger or smaller than the number given. This relies on children's knowing the relative sizes of the units and their understanding that the smaller the unit, the more it takes. Second, Mr. Bane tried to have the children visualize the relationship between the units. Third, he related the operation to be used to their understanding of what multiplication and division mean.

If one is doing a lot of metric conversions, there are shortcuts. These depend on the facility to estimate and to multiply and divide by powers of ten. These shortcuts are helpful but should not replace a careful building of the process.

● Estimating Measurements

Estimating is the mental process of arriving at a measurement without the aid of measurement instruments. There are many reasons to include estimating in the development of measurement. It helps to reinforce the size of units and the relationships among units. It is a practical application—think of all the times you want to know approximately how long, how heavy, or how much something holds.

There are two main types of estimation. In the most common type, the attribute and object are named and the measurement is unknown. For example, about how long is your arm? In the other type, the measurement is known and the object is to be chosen. For example, what piece of furniture in your room is about one meter long?

By keeping the two classes of estimation in mind, you will be able to expand your repertoire of estimation activities. Several common strategies can be used with either type. You can help children develop these strategies by talking through the various methods that different children use to make an estimation and by presenting the following strategies.

One strategy is to *compare to a referent*. If you know that you are 1 m 70 cm tall, then you can estimate the height of a child who comes up to your waist. Or, if you have to choose a board that is 2 m long, you will have some idea of the size.

Another strategy is that of *chunking*. In this process, you break the object into subparts and estimate each part. For example, you want to know about how far you walked from your home to the library and the store and then back to your home. If you know that from your home to the library is about a mile, that it's about that same distance from the library to the store, and twice as far from the store back to your home, you walked about four miles altogether.

A refinement of chunking is *unitizing*. In this case, you estimate one part and see how many parts are in the whole. For example, someone asks you to cut a piece of string that is about three meters long. You estimate one meter and take three of these. This strategy is a good one to emphasize when you are teaching multiplication because it provides an application of multiplication.

When including estimation in your program, you should try to make it a natural part of measurement activities.

1. Encourage children to see if they can tell about how long or heavy the object they are going to measure is.

2. Look for ways to include estimation in other subject areas:

   About how far did you jump?

   What size paper do you need?

   About how long did it take you?

3. Plan estimating activities for their own sake or use brief ones as daily openers for several weeks throughout the year.

The activities in Figure 12–5 give some ideas to get you started. Once you begin thinking about the things in your room, you will be able to come up with a lot of variations.

One thing to remember: do not mark an estimation as right or wrong. Help children develop ways to make better estimates (the strategies and practice will help), but do not discourage them. Let them check their estimates by measuring. They will know whether they were close or not. You may be surprised to find out who are the good estimators in your class.

● Connecting Attributes

Activities involving two attributes can help children see how the attributes are related or how one attribute is not dependent on the other. For example, by doubling the dimensions of a rectangle, children may see how the area is changed. By examining figures with the same area but different shape, children may see that area is independent of shape. We have included sample activities with suggestions of other

variations or extensions. If you do not know the answer, you will be able to find it by doing the activity.

Area and Shape

Activity Card 12–9 encourages children in grades two through four to investigate the different shapes they can make using two to four squares. For older children, you can extend this activity to more squares and place the restrictions that the squares must have touching sides (not corners) and that two

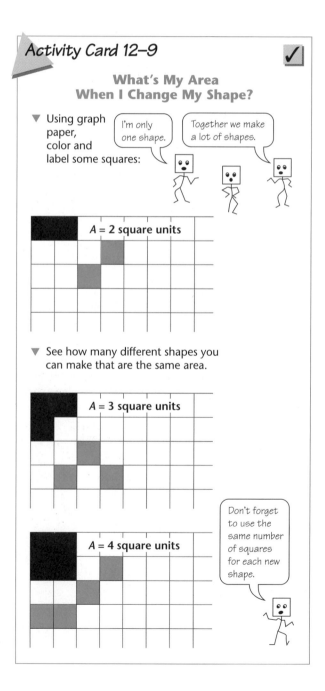

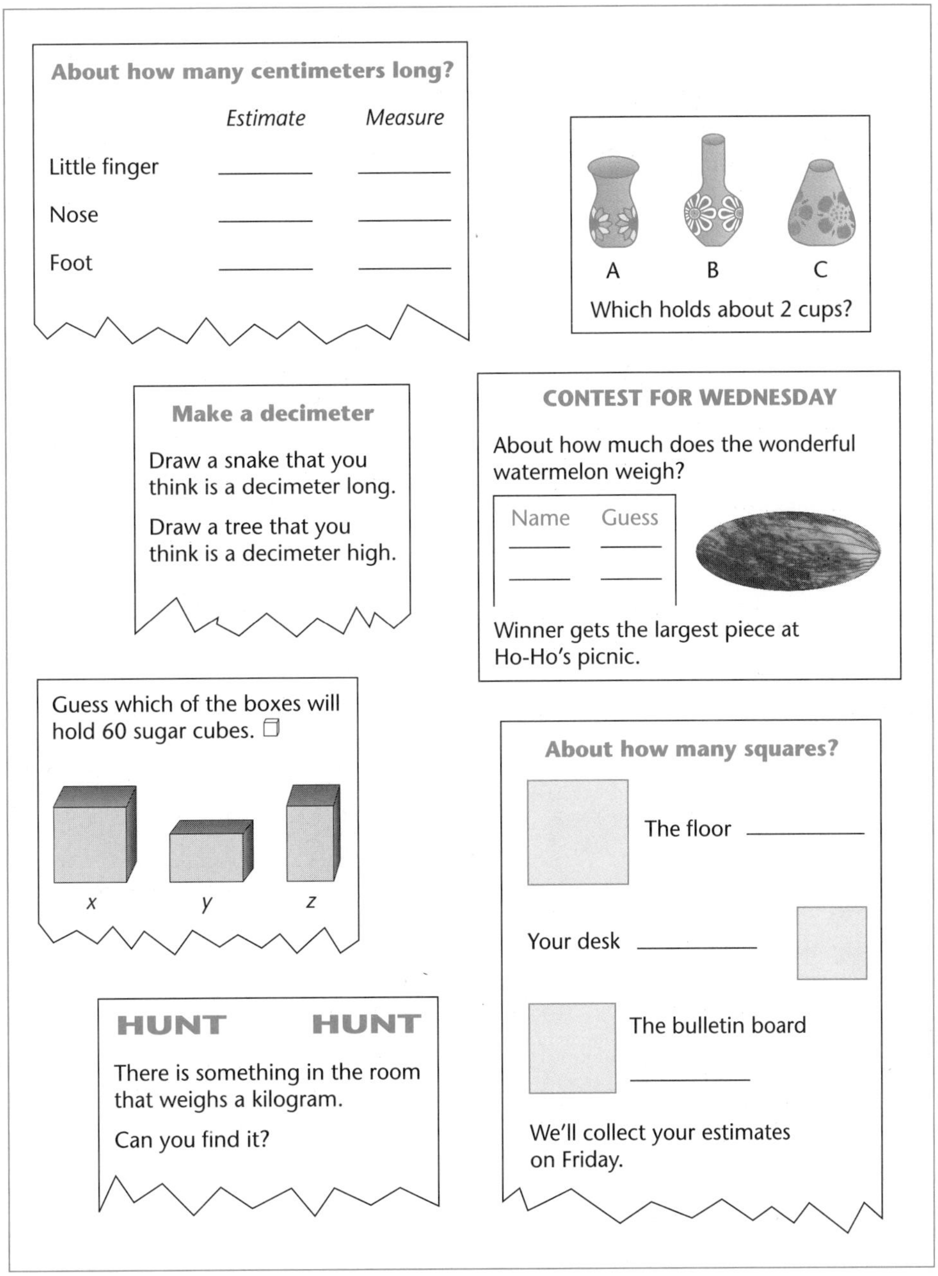

About how many centimeters long?

	Estimate	Measure
Little finger	_____	_____
Nose	_____	_____
Foot	_____	_____

A   B   C

Which holds about 2 cups?

Make a decimeter

Draw a snake that you think is a decimeter long.

Draw a tree that you think is a decimeter high.

CONTEST FOR WEDNESDAY

About how much does the wonderful watermelon weigh?

Name	Guess
_____	_____
_____	_____

Winner gets the largest piece at Ho-Ho's picnic.

Guess which of the boxes will hold 60 sugar cubes.

x   y   z

About how many squares?

The floor _____

Your desk _____

The bulletin board

_____

We'll collect your estimates on Friday.

HUNT   HUNT

There is something in the room that weighs a kilogram.

Can you find it?

Figure 12–5 • **Ideas for developing estimation skills**

shapes are the same if one is a reflection or rotation (see Chapter 11) of the other. A variation is to use triangular graph paper rather than the square. You also can have children look at figures with the same shapes but different areas.

Volume and Shape

An activity such as the one on Activity Card 12–9 can be done with cubes. For older children, Activity Card 12–10, not only has them examine different shapes with constant volume, but also ties their investigation to number theory (primes and composites).

Perimeter and Area

Children are often confused about perimeter and area. This confusion may be due partly to a lack of understanding of area and partly to premature in-

Activity Card 12–10 ✓

Same Volume, Different Shape

I'm 8 cubes — 8 by 1 by 1.
My volume is
8 square units.

I'm 8 cubes — 2 by 2 by 2
My volume is
8 square units, too!

▼ See how many different rectangular solids you can make with 12 cubes. Record the dimensions and volume of each.

▼ Now try some of these:

7, 9, 16, 11, 13, 18, 15 cubes

▼ How many different solids can you make if the number of cubes is

• prime? _____

• a product of two primes? _____

• a perfect square? _____

▼ How many solids can you make with

24 cubes? _____

Activity Card 12–11 ✓

Do You Know How to Connect Perimeter and Area?

▼ Cut a string 14 cm long, and use stick pins to attach it to graph paper.

▼ How many different rectangles can you make with a perimeter of 14 cm? Find the area of each.

Here's one that I made.

I see you followed the rules and made each side a whole number.

Now try 20 cm. What about 13 cm? What about 17 cm? What about . . .

$P = 14$ cm
$A = 10$ cm^2

troduction of the formulas. There are many activities that can help children see that a figure with a given perimeter may have many different areas. One is found on Activity Card 12–11. (Activity Card 12–13 also touches on these concepts.) Children also should realize that figures with the same area can have different perimeters. You can modify Activity Card 12–9 for older children by asking them to find the perimeter of each of the shapes or by challenging them to take five squares and see what shape they can make that has the largest perimeter or the smallest perimeter.

Volume and Surface Area

Just as the area of a figure does not depend on the perimeter, the volume does not depend on the surface area. The experiment on Activity Card 12–12 looks at the relation of lateral surface area to volume. You can vary this activity by having children fold the papers into thirds (sixths) both ways or

make cylinders (a long, thin one and a short, fat one). In middle school, after developing the formula for rectangular solid, students could calculate the volume of each of the tubes on Activity Card 12–12.

Perimeter and Dimensions

On Activity Card 12–13, children may expect the pattern that emerges relating the length of each side to the number of sides, but be surprised by the pattern of the number of sides and the height.

Metric Relations

Activity Card 12–14 helps children find some of the important relationships among different metric units. These relationships make the metric system convenient to use because it gives an easy translation from solid measures to liquid measures.

Activity Card 12–12

What Is the Connection between Volume and Area?

▼ Use construction paper to make two tubes:

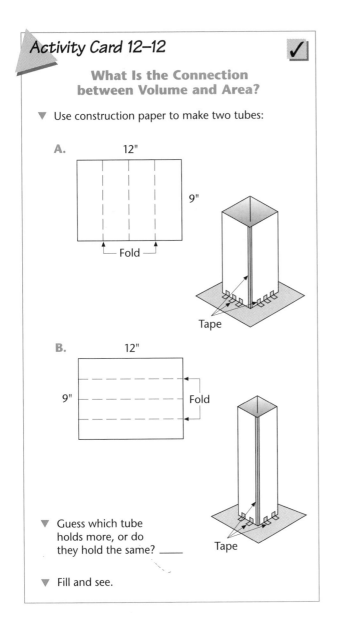

A. 12"

9"

⌐ Fold ⌐

Tape

B. 12"

9"

Fold

Tape

▼ Guess which tube holds more, or do they hold the same? _____

▼ Fill and see.

Activity Card 12–13

What Is the Connection between Perimeter and Height?

▼ Cut 6 strips (2 cm by 21 cm) from stiff paper.

▼ Fold one strip into thirds, and tape together to make a fence triangle:

Tape

▼ Fold the other strips into fourths, fifths, sixths, sevenths, and eighths to make additional fences.

▼ Fill it in the chart:

Number of sides	Length of each side in mm	Height (stand it on one side and see how tall)
3	_____ mm	_____ mm
4	_____	_____
5	_____	_____
6	_____	_____
7	_____	_____
8	_____	_____

• Which has the largest area?
• Which has the smallest area?

▶ A Glance at Where We've Been

Measuring is a process that may be used for many attributes. Basically each attribute is measured in the same way, but the unique characteristics of each make the actual steps differ. Most important in these steps is knowing the attribute that is being measured. This chapter has given many suggestions about ways to develop premeasurement ideas by comparing perceptually, directly, and indirectly.

These ideas are built on as children begin to use units. Children may first assign a number by counting and later by using instruments or formulas. Other suggested ways to help children learn about measuring are estimating and relating two attributes.

By including measuring in your program, you have the opportunity to show how mathematics is practical, to develop problem-solving skills, to develop other mathematical ideas, to relate mathematics to other topics, and to make mathematics fun for many children.

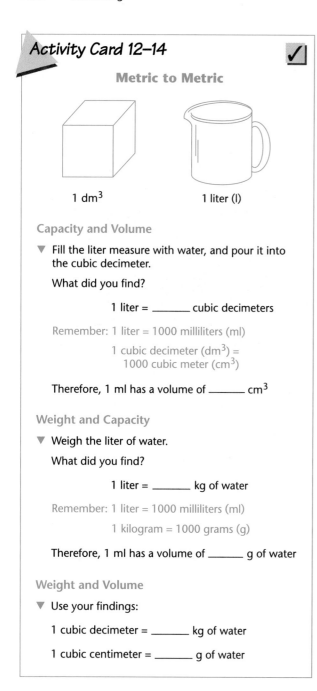

Activity Card 12–14

Metric to Metric

1 dm³   1 liter (l)

Capacity and Volume

▼ Fill the liter measure with water, and pour it into the cubic decimeter.

What did you find?

1 liter = _____ cubic decimeters

Remember: 1 liter = 1000 milliliters (ml)

1 cubic decimeter (dm³) = 1000 cubic meter (cm³)

Therefore, 1 ml has a volume of _____ cm³

Weight and Capacity

▼ Weigh the liter of water.

What did you find?

1 liter = _____ kg of water

Remember: 1 liter = 1000 milliliters (ml)

1 kilogram = 1000 grams (g)

Therefore, 1 ml has a volume of _____ g of water

Weight and Volume

▼ Use your findings:

1 cubic decimeter = _____ kg of water

1 cubic centimeter = _____ g of water

THINGS TO DO: From What You've Read

1. What are the five steps in the measuring process?

2. What attributes, units, and instruments are included in most elementary mathematics programs?

3. Why should you include measurement in your mathematics program? Choose one reason and give examples of how measurement fulfills that reason.

4. What concepts related to units need to be developed as children have experiences with measurements?

5. List three difficulties children have with measuring instruments.

6. Why do students need to be able to convert from one unit to another?

7. Give three examples of connections that can be made between different attributes. Include at least one connection between time and another attribute.

THINGS TO DO: Going Beyond This Book

1. You have a child in your class who physically cannot handle a ruler. What would you do in this situation? Give at least two solutions.

2. Describe a set of activities that you could use to introduce a centimeter, a kilogram, a liter, or a square decimeter.

3. Design an activity card that investigates a fixed area to varying perimeters; for example, a fixed area of four square units made with four square tiles. Include the answer to the investigation.

4. Describe how you could help convince a student that these triangles have the same area.

5. Design three task cards for the chapter Snapshot Lesson, one of which is an extension for gifted students.

6. Critique the video, "Pencil Box Staining," from the series: *Teaching Math: A Video Library, K–4.* What strategies did the students use to find the area?

7. Check the scope-and-sequence chart of a textbook series to see how the introduction of units corresponds to Table 12–1.

8. Try the activity on Activity Card 12–8 with students. What difficulties did they encounter? How did you help them? How would you change the activity?

9. Examine upper-level textbooks to see how they introduce the formula for the area of a rectangle. Contrast this with the sequence suggested in Figure 12–2.

10. For a grade level of your choice, design five estimation activities that include both types of estimation (estimating measurement for a known object and choosing an object that fits a known measurement).

11. Try one of the activities in the section on connections between attributes with students. Describe your experience, including whether or not the children could make the connections expected.

12. Outline a series of steps for developing the volume formula for rectangular solids, similar to those for developing the area formula for a rectangle.

▼▼▼▼▼▼▼▼▼▼▼▼▼▼▼▼▼▼▼▼▼▼

Children's Corner

Allen, Pamela. *Who Sank the Boat?* New York: Putnam, 1990.

Anno, Mitsumasa. *All in a Day.* New York: Putnam, 1990.

Gelman, Rita Golden. *More Spaghetti, I Say!* New York: Scholastic, 1977.

Hutchins, Pat. *Happy Birthday, Sam.* New York: Penguin, 1985.

Myller, Rolf. *How Big Is a Foot?* New York: Dell Publishing, 1991.

Pluckrose, Henry. *Capacity.* New York: Franklin Watts, 1982.

Youldon, Gillian. *Sizes.* New York: Franklin Watts, 1982.

Selected References

Benswanger, Richard. "Discovering Perimeter and Area with Logo." *Arithmetic Teacher,* 36 (September 1988), pp. 18–25.

Burns, Marilyn. *Math and Literature (K–4).* Sausilto, Calif.: Math Solutions Publications, 1992.

Carpenter, Thomas P.; Corbitt, Mary Kay; Kepner, Henry S., Jr.; Lindquist, Mary Montgomery; and Reys, Robert E. *Results from the Second Mathematics Assessment of the National Assessment of Educational Progress.* Reston, Va.: NCTM, 1981.

Cook, March. "Ideas." *Arithmetic Teacher,* 36 (March 1989), pp. 27–32.

Fry, Nancy, and Tsarides, Catherine. "Metric Mall." *Arithmetic Teacher,* 37 (September 1989), pp. 6–11.

Harrison, William R. "What Lies Behind Measurement?" *Arithmetic Teacher,* 34 (March 1987), pp. 22–23.

Hawkins, Vincent J. "Applying Pick's Theorem to Randomized Areas." *Arithmetic Teacher,* 36 (October 1988), pp. 47–49.

Hiebert, James. "Units of Measure: Results and Implications from National Assessment." *Arithmetic Teacher,* 28 (February 1981), pp. 38–43.

Jensen, Robert J. (ed.). *Research Ideas for the Classroom: Early Childhood Mathematics.* Reston, Va.: NCTM, and New York: Macmillan, 1993.

Johnson, Gretchen L. "Using a Metric Unit to Help Preservice Teachers Appreciate the Value of Manipulative Materials." *Arithmetic Teacher,* 35 (October 1988), pp. 14–20.

Kenney, Patricia Ann, and Kouba, Vicky L. "What Do Students Know about Measurement"? In *Results from the Sixth Mathematics Assessment of the National Assessment of Educational Progress* (eds. Edward A. Silver and Patricia Ann Kenney). Reston Va.: NCTM, 1997, pp. 141–163.

Kliman, Marlene. "Integrating Mathematics and Literature in the Elementary Classroom." *Arithmetic Teacher,* 40 (February 1993), pp. 318–321.

Kouba, Vicky L.; Brown, Catherine A.; Carpenter, Thomas P.; Lindquist, Mary Montgomery; Silver, Edward A.; and Swafford, Jane O. "Results of the Fourth NAEP Assessment of Mathematics: Measurement, Geometry Data Interpretation, Attitudes, and Other Topics." *Arithmetic Teacher,* 35 (May 1988), pp. 10–16.

Lindquist, Mary Montgomery. "Estimation and Mental Computation." *Arithmetic Teacher,* 34 (January 1987), pp. 16–17.

Lindquist, Mary Montgomery. "Implementing the Standards: The Measurement Standards." *Arithmetic Teacher,* 37 (October 1989), pp. 22–26.

Lindquist, Mary Montgomery, and Dana, Marcia E. "The Neglected Decimeter." *Arithmetic Teacher,* 25 (October 1977), pp. 10–17.

National Council of Teachers of Mathematics. *Curriculum and Evaluation Standards for School Mathematics.* Reston, Va.: NCTM, 1989.

Owens, Douglas T. (ed.). *Research Ideas for the Classroom: Middle Grades Mathematics.* Reston, Va.: NCTM, and New York: Macmillan, 1993.

Payne, Joseph N. (ed.). *Mathematics for the Young Child.* Reston, Va.: NCTM, 1990.

Silverman, Helene. "Ideas." *Arithmetic Teacher,* 37 (March 1990), pp. 26–32.

Teaching Math: A Video Library, K–4. South Burlington, VT: The Annenberg/CPB Math and Science Collection, 1995.

Wilson, Patricia S., and Osborne, Alan. "Foundational Ideas in Teaching about Measure." In *Teaching Mathematics in Grades K–8* (ed. Thomas R. Post). Toronto: Allyn and Bacon, 1988, pp. 78–110.

Young, Sharon, "Ideas." *Arithmetic Teacher,* 38 (September 1990), pp. 23–34.

Young, Sharon, "Ideas." *Arithmetic Teacher,* 38 (November 1990), pp. 23–30.

13

Developing Fractions and Decimals

▶ Snapshot of a Lesson

Orientation

A fifth-grade class has reviewed ways to model fractions given a whole object or a set of objects. When we join the class, the teacher, Mrs. Benson, is making the transition from review to the lesson for today, in which a fractional part of a whole is given and the whole must be constructed.

MRS. BENSON: Good, you know a lot about fractions. Today, we are really going to test our brains. You found that it is fairly easy to show a fractional part of a whole. What if I give you a fractional part and you have to show me the whole?

JUSTIN: I'm not certain what you mean.

MRS. BENSON: Well, if I told you that this picture represents three-fifths of a cake, could you draw the whole cake?

$\frac{3}{5}$ of the cake

ROSA LEE: It sure would be a skinny cake.

CAMILLE: That depends on how the two-fifths was cut off.

MRS. BENSON: You are both right; you won't be able to tell exactly what the shape of the cake was before it was cut unless I tell you where it was cut. Let's pretend you can see that it was cut right here (pointing to the right side). What do you know?

GILBERT: You have three of the 5 equal pieces. If we divide this into 3 equal parts, we know how large one-fifth is.

MRS. BENSON: Let's do that. Who can tell me how to finish the problem?

$\frac{3}{5}$ of the cake

OLAV: All you have to do now is add the missing two-fifths. Rosa Lee, you are right, it is a skinny cake. It would look like this. [Coming to the board, he draws two more parts.]

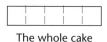

The whole cake

MRS. BENSON: How about another one? I have two-sevenths of a piece of licorice. How long was the licorice to begin with? Each of you draw a small line segment and label it two-sevenths.

JUSTIN: Does it matter how long it is?

MRS. BENSON: No, Justin, but we'll each be doing a slightly different problem. How long did you draw yours?

JUSTIN: About 5 centimeters.

MRS. BENSON: Do each one of you have a picture something like this?

$\frac{2}{7}$ of the licorice

What do you do next?

WINIFRED: That must be two of the seven parts, so one part would be about this long (holding up her fingers). Now, we need seven of those.

MRS. BENSON: Suppose I know that the twelve pieces of candy in a box are three-fifths of the original amount. How many pieces were in the box?

DENISE: I drew twelve pieces, but then I don't know what to do.

MRS. BENSON: Let's think, what does this picture tell you?

$\frac{3}{5}$ of the candy

DENISE: I think it means that three of five parts are in the box; this is three equal parts. Oh, there are twelve pieces so there must be four in each part.

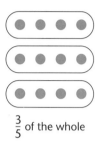

$\frac{3}{5}$ of the whole

MRS. BENSON: Good, let's circle the three sets of four.

DENISE: You need two more sets of four. So there must have been twenty pieces to begin with.

MRS. BENSON: Does that make sense? Is twelve three-fifths of twenty?

After a few more examples using improper fractions and mixed numbers, the students do the exercises Mrs. Benson had ready for them.

▶ Introduction

Fractions and decimals have long been a stumbling block for many students. One reason may be that teachers tend to rush to symbolization and operations without developing strong conceptual underpinnings for these numbers and operations on them. Thus, much of this chapter is devoted to concept development and the processes underlying the operations.

As you will see in examining the concepts associated with fractions and decimals, they are complex. However, two rather simple but powerful ideas—*partitioning* and *equivalence*—can help tie many of the ideas together (Kieren 1980). Partitioning is the process of sharing equally, and equivalence focuses on different ways to represent the same amount.

One idea related to equivalence that you should keep in mind is that decimal fractions are another notation for common fractions. For example, 0.5 and $^5/_{10}$ are just two different ways to represent the same fractional part. Each of these fractions is equivalent to one-half.

Both common fractions and decimal fractions can represent fractional parts. However, decimal fractions represent only partitionings of tenths, hundredths, and so on; common fractions can represent any partitionings. We have chosen to begin with common fractions in this chapter, because they are more general than decimal fractions.

Although we first concentrate on common fractions (simply called *fractions* from here on), we do not mean to imply that the entire study of fractions should be done before decimals. After a beginning foundation has been built with fractions, decimal notation can be introduced. In fact, many of the operations with decimals are easier than the corresponding operations with fractions and can be taught meaningfully before the entire study of operations with fractions is completed.

● Conceptual Development of Fractions

The *Curriculum and Evaluation Standards for School Mathematics* (NCTM 1989) emphasize that students should be given the opportunity to develop concepts as well as number sense with fractions and decimals. A careful examination of the items on the fourth national assessment reveals that concepts and models underlying fractions are not well developed by age nine and that although older students can relate fractions to a pictorial model, they do not realize that these models can be helpful in solving problems (Kouba et al. 1988).

Mathematics literature can serve as an excellent basis for a conceptual development of fractions. For example, one book, *Ed Emberleys Picture Pie, A Circle Drawing Book* (Emberley 1984), allows students to see and make colorful pictures and patterns from fractional parts of a circle. Another book, *The Doorbell Rang* (Hutchins 1987), is an excellent source to use when introducing the concept of partitioning. Often books can help lay the groundwork for an understanding of mathematical concepts, and according to the NCTM *Standards* (1989, p. 17):

> A conceptual approach enables children to acquire clear and stable concepts by constructing meanings in the context of physical situations and allows mathematical abstractions to emerge from empirical evidence.

Three Meanings of Fractions

Three distinct meanings of fractions—part–whole, quotient, and ratio—are found in most elementary mathematics programs. Most fraction work is based on the part–whole meaning, often with little development of the other two meanings. Ignoring these other two may be one source of students' difficulty.

Part–Whole The part–whole interpretation of a fraction such as ⅗ indicates that a whole has been partitioned into five equal parts and three of those parts are being considered. This fraction may be shown with a region model:

The whole

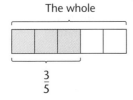

$$\frac{3}{5}$$

Quotient The fraction ⅗ may also be considered as a quotient, 3 ÷ 5. This interpretation also arises from a partitioning situation. Suppose you had some big cookies to give to five people. You could give each person one cookie, then another, and so on until you had distributed the same amount to each. If you had twenty cookies, then you could represent this process mathematically by 20 ÷ 5; each person would get four cookies.

Now consider this problem:

> You have three big cookies and you want to give them to five people; that is, you want to divide the three cookies among five people, or 3 ÷ 5.
>
> How much would each person get?
>
> Would anyone get a whole?

One way to solve the problem using pictures of the cookies is shown in Figure 13–1. This interpretation of fractions is used when a remainder in a division problem is expressed as a fraction. It is also the interpretation that is needed to change a fraction to decimal notation.

Ratio The fraction ⅗ may also represent a ratio situation, such as there are three boys for every five girls. Here is a model for this situation:

Begin with 3 cookies. Cut each into 5 parts.

Each person gets $\frac{1}{5}$ of each cookie.

Thus, each person gets

$$\frac{1}{5} + \frac{1}{5} + \frac{1}{5} \quad \text{or} \quad \frac{3}{5} \quad \text{or} \quad 3 \div 5 = \frac{3}{5}$$

Figure 13–1 • An example of a quotient interpretation of fractions

You can see that this interpretation is conceptually quite different from the other interpretations of fractions. In this chapter, we will consider only the other two interpretations; the ratio interpretation is discussed in Chapter 14.

Models of the Part–Whole Meaning

We will concentrate on four models for the part–whole meaning: region, length, set, and area. Any of these models may also be used for the quotient interpretation; however, the region model is most often used because it is the simplest. Other attributes, such as capacity, volume, or time, also can be used as models.

Region The region model is the most concrete form and is most easily handled by children. The *region* is the whole (the unit), and the parts are *congruent* (same size and shape). The region may be any shape, such as circle, rectangle, square, or triangle. A variety of shapes should be used when presenting the region model, so that the children do not think that a fraction is always a "part of a pie."

As Figure 13–2 indicates, the rectangle is probably the easiest region model for children to draw and to partition. (Try partitioning each of the shapes shown into three equal parts to see which is easiest.) The circle does have one advantage; it is easy to see as a whole. Because the region is the most common model, we will give many uses of it throughout this chapter.

Length Any unit of length can be partitioned into fractional parts with each part being equal in length. Children can fold a long, thin strip of paper

(*partition* it) into halves, fourths, and so on. Later this activity should lead to indicating fractions as points on a number line. That is, by partitioning a unit, or the distance between two points such as 4 and 5, into thirds, children can find one-third of the unit and will see that it is more than 4. If the children understand that each unit has been partitioned into thirds, they will realize that the point is $4 + \frac{1}{3}$, or $4\frac{1}{3}$, as shown in Figure 13–3.

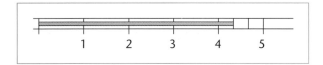

| 1 | 2 | 3 | 4 | 5 |

Figure 13–3 • **Length model of $4\frac{1}{3}$**

Set The set model uses a set of objects as a whole (the unit). This model sometimes causes difficulty, partly because students have not often considered a set of, say, twelve objects as a unit. The more likely reason for difficulty is that the students have not physically partitioned objects; furthermore, the symbolization is often rushed for this model.

Without mentioning fractions, children should be given experiences partitioning sets, which provides a background for division as well as for fractions. For example, a child may be asked to give twelve toys to four children. Later, attention should be focused on whether or not a given number of objects can be partitioned equally among a given number of people:

Can 15 toys be partitioned equally among 5 people? [yes]

4 people? [no]

3 people? [yes]

2 people? [no]

With this understanding, the set model can be related to fractions; for example, finding fifths by partitioning the set into five equal parts. Figure 13–4 shows a set of fifteen marbles that have been partitioned into five equal parts. Each part is one-fifth of the whole set. From this modeling, children can answer questions such as these:

What is one-fifth of 15? [3]

Two-fifths of 15? [6]

Three-fifths of 15? [9]

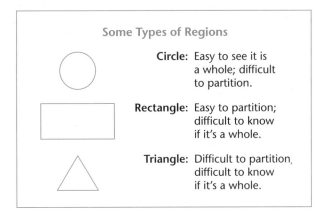

Some Types of Regions

Circle: Easy to see it is a whole; difficult to partition.

Rectangle: Easy to partition; difficult to know if it's a whole.

Triangle: Difficult to partition, difficult to know if it's a whole.

Figure 13–2 • **Types of regions for concrete models**

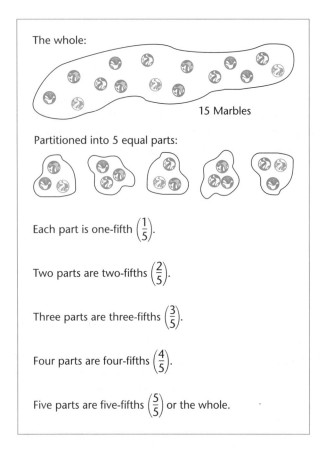

The whole:

15 Marbles

Partitioned into 5 equal parts:

Each part is one-fifth $\left(\frac{1}{5}\right)$.

Two parts are two-fifths $\left(\frac{2}{5}\right)$.

Three parts are three-fifths $\left(\frac{3}{5}\right)$.

Four parts are four-fifths $\left(\frac{4}{5}\right)$.

Five parts are five-fifths $\left(\frac{5}{5}\right)$ or the whole.

Figure 13–4 • An example of a set model

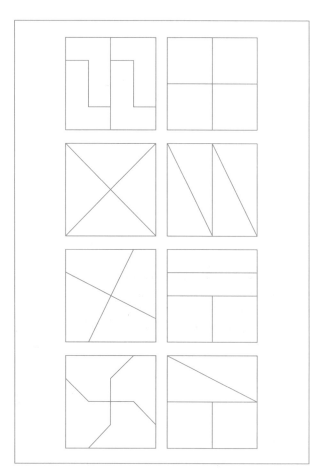

Figure 13–5 • Ways to partition an area model

Experience of this type allows children to solve many practical problems and gives background for multiplication of fractions.

Area The area model is a sophisticated one that encompasses the region model. We remove the restriction that the parts must be the same shape; they must only be equal in area. Before using this model, children must have some idea of when two different shapes have equal areas. Figure 13–5 shows eight squares partitioned into fourths in different ways. This model is more appropriate for older children (about third and fourth grade) than for younger ones.

One Way to Introduce Fractions

Explaining, in order, all the meanings and models, as done so far in this chapter, is not the way to teach fractions. You want to begin with the simplest meaning and model—something that can be made meaningful for children. The part–whole meaning and the region model provide a good starting place. After introducing this model and the language and symbols associated with fractions, you can intro-

duce other part–whole models. The other meanings of fractions can be introduced after children become more familiar with fractions through ordering and finding equivalent fractions and as they are introduced to improper fractions and mixed numbers.

Partitioning Underlying the idea of part–whole is the meaning of *part* and of *whole*. The whole is whatever is specified as the unit. At first, the whole should be obvious. Children must learn to partition the whole into equal parts, then to describe those parts with fractional names.

Let the children do the partitioning. For example, each child could be given a "candy bar" (a piece of paper the size of a large candy bar) to share with a friend. Have them fold the "candy bar" to show how they would share. Talk about whether a fold like the one sketched here would be a "fair share" for two people.

Through other examples, develop sharing equally among 4, 3, 6, and 5 people. For some of the more difficult sharing such as 5, you may want to use a strip of paper already marked.

Words As soon as you have developed the idea of equal parts, introduce the words *halves, thirds, fourths,* and so on. Be sure to ask such questions as, "How many equal parts would I have if each part was a fifth? an eighth?" (and even a twenty-fourth).

Counting Once children are familiar with the fractional part words, it is time to begin counting parts. This process should not be any more difficult than counting apples, but the children need to know what they are counting. An example of an activity to practice counting is given on Lesson Card 13–1.

Symbols Both symbols and written words should be used together or alternately until students understand the meaning of the symbol.

> Using the written fraction symbol is appropriate only after children can name, count, and compare using oral language with facility. . . . Written symbols are developed in the same way as oral language. The same kind of questioning can be used, but now the model and the oral language are connected with the symbol. (Payne, Towsley, and Huinker 1990, p. 185)

We can depict these connections as follows:

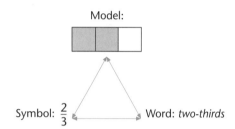

When children can match the words with the model, it is time to tell them that we write the symbol ⅔ for the word *two-thirds*. Then, they need to have many opportunities to connect different representations:

1. Given a model, the child writes the symbol.
2. Given a symbol, the child chooses the model.
3. Given a symbol, the child says the word.
4. Given a word, the child writes the symbol.

Textbooks usually concentrate on tasks like 1 and 2, so you will find plenty of examples of these. Tasks 3 and 4 require oral work, so you need to provide opportunities to read problems and answers.

Drawing a Model In this developmental sequence, children have modeled fractions by folding paper or by choosing a picture. You also want them to be able to draw a picture. The rectangle is probably the easiest shape to use to show a "good approximation" to a fractional part. Encourage the children to be as accurate as possible, but do not worry if their drawings are not perfect. For example, which of these two drawings would you accept as a picture of two-thirds?

Lesson Card 13–1

Fraction Bars

Materials: 4 construction paper strips (3" × 9") of 4 different colors for each child

Preparation of Fraction Bars: Each child should fold a blue strip into halves, mark the fold with a dark line, and write halves on the back.

Make fraction bars for thirds, fourths, and sixths in other colors in the same way.

Activities:

▼ Ask each child to take the fourths bar, and count the parts: 1, 2, 3, 4 fourths

▼ Ask each to count the parts of other bars; for example, 1 sixth, 2 sixths, 3 sixths, . . .

▼ Ask a pair of children to count the fourths in two bars:

1, 2, 3, 4   5, 6, 7, 8 fourths

▼ See that 8 fourths is 2 wholes, 6 fourths is 1 whole and 2 fourths, and so on.

▼ Ask each to count all the sixths in the class.

▼ Challenge all children to tell how many strips it would take to show 11 sixths or 23 sixths. Let them experiment in groups of 4.

Bob's work   Marilyn's work

Bob's work is neater than Marilyn's, but he seems to have missed the point that the three parts must be equal. You might help Marilyn be a little neater, but she does seem to have the idea of two-thirds.

Extending the Model   The results of a national assessment question are given in Table 13–1. There is no doubt that this model is more complicated than the ones we have been using, but it is a very useful one for introducing equivalent fractions and for ordering fractions.

You also can use paper folding to introduce the model in Table 13–1 and to introduce equivalent fractions. For example, give each child a fourth of a sheet of plain paper. Have each child fold the paper into thirds and shade two-thirds. Now fold the paper in half the other way. Ask how many parts and what kind of parts [6, sixths]. Then, ask what part is shaded. Encourage both ²⁄₃ and ⁴⁄₆. Tell the children that we call ²⁄₃ and ⁴⁄₆ *equivalent fractions* because they represent the same amount.

After more examples and practice with folding paper, children should be ready to understand what happens with the paper folding through drawings.

Table 13–1 ● Results of national assessment question using the region model

What fractional part of the figure is shaded?

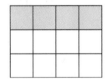

	Percent Responding	
Responses	*Age 9*	*Age 13*
Acceptable responses	20	82
¹⁄₃, ⁴⁄₁₂, .33		
Unacceptable responses		
¹⁄₄, .25	5	4
Top 4, top part 4/8	36	6
Other	15	6
I don't know	17	1
No response	7	1

● Begin by drawing a picture of the paper folded in thirds and shade ²⁄₃:

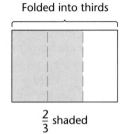

Folded into thirds

$\frac{2}{3}$ shaded

● Now draw the fold made when partitioning it into halves, making certain the children can identify the way the paper was "folded" in both directions.

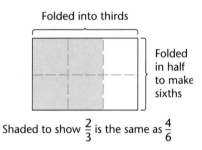

Folded into thirds

Folded in half to make sixths

Shaded to show $\frac{2}{3}$ is the same as $\frac{4}{6}$

● Ask children to show ¹⁄₃, ²⁄₃, ⁴⁄₆, and so on and to name an equivalent fraction for each.

Next, move to pictures showing only the folded paper, such as the representation below:

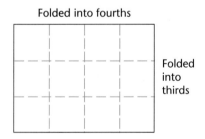

Folded into fourths

Folded into thirds

Make certain the students can identify the way the paper was "folded" in both directions. Have them show

$$\frac{1}{3}, \quad \frac{2}{3}, \quad \frac{1}{4}, \quad \frac{3}{4},$$

and so on and give an equivalent fraction. This sequence, along with activities such as those in this chapter's Snapshot of a Lesson, provides a strong background for further development of fractions and the operations.

Ordering Fractions

Part of understanding fractions is realizing that they are numbers and can be ordered, added, subtracted, multiplied, and divided. The instructional goal is to have children order fractions symbolically, but you can build a bridge from the concrete to the symbolic. Not only will this bridge help children realize what they are doing when they are ordering fractions, but it also will give another context in which to practice relating fractions and the models. Many problems involving ordering capture children's interest because they want to know which is more, which is shorter, which is larger, and so on.

Concrete Models If children have made concrete models, it is not difficult for them to order fractions using various models. For example, children can make fraction bars, as described in Lesson Card 13–1, then use them to find out which is larger, ⅔ or ¾. Folding the thirds strip so that it is ⅔ long and the fourths strip so that it is ¾ long provides a concrete model for the comparison.

Pictorial Models Children are able to order fractions if given pictures of the models, such as the fraction strips in Figure 13–6. (A more complete set of fraction strips is given in Appendix B.) The accurate scale of these models allows children to compare lengths to decide which is larger, ¾ or ⅔.

Children also can construct or draw their own pictorial models to represent fractions. Activity Card 13–1 illustrates an activity in which they create the model, identify fractions, and order them. The model in this type of activity does not depend on the accuracy of the size of the parts, as the model in Figure 13–6 does.

Symbolic Representation It is easier to compare two measurements given in the same unit (78 meters and 20 meters) than two measurements given in different units (83 meters and 4,318 centimeters). Similarly, it is easier to compare two fractions that are symbolically represented by the same subunit (⅗ and ⅖) than two fractions that are represented by different subunits (⅔ and ⁵⁄₇). In mathematics, we often try to turn a more difficult situation into a simpler case—that is, representing the things to be compared in the same unit. With fractions, simpler means expressing each fraction as an equivalent

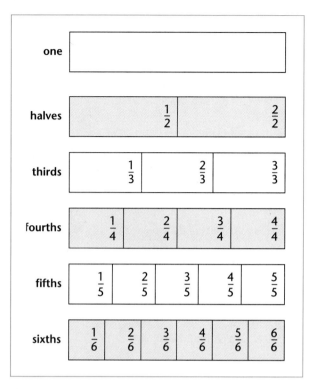

Figure 13–6 • **Pictorial model of fraction strips**

fraction in the same subunit, or common denominator. The pictorial model shown in Activity Card 13–1 can be extended to develop this idea. Once the rectangle has been partitioned into both thirds and sevenths, it is partitioned into twenty-firsts so that ⅔ is 14 of the 21 parts or $^{14}/_{21}$, and ⁵⁄₇ is 15 of the 21 parts or $^{15}/_{21}$. Thus, 21 is the common denominator for comparing the fractions ⅔ and ⁵⁄₇:

$$\frac{2}{3} = \frac{14}{21}$$

and

$$\frac{5}{7} = \frac{15}{21}$$

Therefore,

$$\frac{5}{7} > \frac{2}{3}$$

When children can order fractions symbolically, they may enjoy the quick and easy game in Activity Card 13–2. If they have difficulty playing, they may need to return to a concrete or pictorial representation.

Activity Card 13–1

How Many Parts?

▼ Partition this rectangle into thirds one way and sevenths the other way:

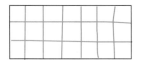

▼ Try these:

$\frac{1}{3}$ is __7__ parts of the whole

$\frac{2}{7}$ is ____ parts of the whole

• Which is larger, $\frac{1}{3}$ or $\frac{2}{7}$? ____

$\frac{2}{3}$ is ____ parts of the whole

$\frac{5}{7}$ is ____ parts of the whole

• Which is larger, $\frac{2}{3}$ or $\frac{5}{7}$? ____

$\frac{1}{3}$ is ____ parts of the whole

$\frac{3}{7}$ is ____ parts of the whole

• Which is larger, $\frac{1}{3}$ or $\frac{3}{7}$? ____

Activity Card 13–2

Whole Hog

▼ Choose a partner, and each of you make your own gameboard by tracing the H (for Hog):

▼ Cut ten squares of paper. Write one of these fractions on each square:

$\frac{1}{2}$ $\frac{1}{3}$ $\frac{1}{6}$ $\frac{2}{6}$ $\frac{1}{9}$ $\frac{2}{9}$ $\frac{3}{9}$ $\frac{1}{18}$ $\frac{2}{18}$ $\frac{3}{18}$

▼ Be sure each of you has a crayon.

Now you are ready to go Whole Hog!

Game Rules

1. Put the fraction cards in a pile face down.

2. Each of you pick a card from the top of the pile.

3. Turn your cards over and decide who has the larger fraction.

4. The player with the larger fraction must color that fractional part of her or his H.

5. Put both cards at the bottom of the pile.

6. Choose two or more cards and play as before.

7. If a player with the larger fraction cannot color the fractional part shown on the card, both players must put their cards back and pick two more.

8. Continue playing until one person colors the whole H. That person is the first to go Whole Hog and loses the game.

▼ Trace two more H's and play again.

Although we have considered ordering fractions before we examined equivalent fractions, the two ideas build on each other. Before children can become proficient with ordering fractions symbolically, they must be familiar with how to find equivalent fractions.

Equivalence of Fractions

We have looked at models that represent fractional parts in more than one way, such as by $\frac{2}{3}$ and $\frac{3}{4}$. Students with this background are familiar with the concept of equivalent fractions, but they may not have developed many of the skills associated with finding equivalent fractions symbolically. Finding an equivalent fraction rests on the generalization that both the numerator and denominator may be multiplied (or divided) by the same number.

Finding an Equivalent Fraction with a Model To develop the generalization for finding an equivalent fraction, you can again begin with the paper-folding model and symbolically describe what is happening.

- Make a model of ¾ by folding a piece of paper in fourths (A); then fold it in half the other way (B).

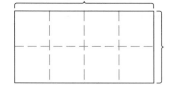

(A) Fold into fourths.

(B) Fold in half to make eighths.

- Ask what happened to the fourths when the paper was folded in half.
- Use shading to confirm that you created twice as many equal parts (or 2 × 4) and twice as many shaded parts (or 2 × 3).

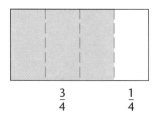 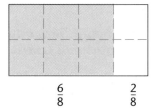

$$\frac{3}{4} \qquad \frac{1}{4} \qquad \frac{6}{8} \qquad \frac{2}{8}$$

- Express the model symbolically:

$$\frac{2 \times 3}{2 \times 4}$$

or

$$\frac{3 \times 2}{4 \times 2} = \frac{6}{8}$$

After more examples such as these, children should be able to make the generalization that both numerator and denominator may be multiplied by the same number and the resulting fraction is equivalent.

Conversely, you could begin with the model of eight parts and describe how to get to four parts. In this case, you begin with the eight parts and group them by two, or 8 ÷ 2, which is 4. You also group the number of parts under consideration by two, or 6 ÷ 2. Thus,

$$\frac{6}{8} = \frac{6 \div 2}{8 \div 2} = \frac{3}{4}$$

Again, this type of example should lead to the generalization that the numerator and denominator may be divided by the same number.

Finding an Equivalent Fraction Given Its Denominator After the students have made the generalization that both the numerator and denominator may be multiplied or divided by the same number, then they are ready to move to exercises such as these:

$$\frac{2}{3} = \frac{\square}{12}$$

$$\frac{4}{6} = \frac{\square}{3}$$

In this example, students need to think "What is 3 multiplied by to get 12?" Once they have established it is 4, they should think and write:

$$\frac{2 \times 4}{3 \times 4} = \frac{8}{12}$$

In the second example, they should realize that 6 was divided by 2 to obtain 3, so 4 would also have to be divided by 2:

$$\frac{4 \div 2}{6 \div 2} = \frac{2}{3}$$

The first example is the type of thinking needed in finding a common denominator; the second is the type needed in simplifying many problems.

Children also should be helped to see that a common fraction cannot always be changed to an equivalent one with a certain specified denominator if the numerator must be a whole number. For example, ⁵⁄₁₂ cannot be changed to thirds even though you can divide 12 by 4 to get 3. When you divide 5 by 4, you do not get a whole number. Similarly, you cannot change ⅔ to fifths:

$$\frac{2}{3} = \frac{\square}{5}$$

There is no whole number that you can multiply 3 by to get 5. Exercises such as those in Activity Card 13–3 focus on these skills.

Finding a Common Denominator In the past there has been much emphasis on finding the *least common denominator*. With a decreased emphasis on fractions, this skill is not as essential as it once was. However, to add or subtract fractions one often finds a common denominator.

For example, given the fractions ⅖ and ¾, finding a common denominator requires finding a frac-

Activity Card 13–3

Can You Divide It?

Draw lines to divide the fractional parts into smaller parts if possible.

▼ These regions have been divided into halves. Change

- To fourths:
- To tenths:

- To sixths:
- To eighths:

▼ These regions have been divided into thirds. Change

- To twelfths:
- To tenths:

- To ninths:
- To sixths:

▼ These regions have been divided into fifths. Change

- To tenths:
- To fifteenths:

- To twelfths:
- To twentieths:

tion equivalent to $\frac{2}{5}$ and a fraction equivalent to $\frac{3}{4}$ with the same denominator. That is, you must find a number for the denominator that both 5 and 4 will divide.

The product of two denominators will always give a common denominator. As shown in Figure 13–7, the same modeling that we showed for ordering fractions indicates why the product method works.

At times, however, the product of the denominators is not the least common denominator. For example, a common denominator of $\frac{5}{6}$ and $\frac{3}{4}$ is 6×4, or 24, but the least common denominator is 12. The least common denominator is the smallest number that both 6 and 4 will divide. With small denominators, the least common denominator can often be found by inspection, which is probably a more beneficial approach than learning a routine.

Mixed Numbers and Improper Fractions

Through models, you can lead naturally into mixed numbers and improper fractions. For example, the most natural representation of the following model is the mixed number $2\frac{1}{4}$.

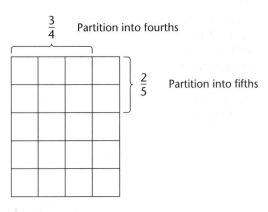

Figure 13–7 • **A model for finding a common denominator**

Adding partitions in the model to show all the fourths leads to the initial counting of 9 fourths and to the representation by the improper fraction ⁹⁄₄.

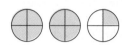

To help children gain experience with mixed number and improper fractions, use models as much as possible and ask them to write *both* types of numbers to represent the models. When children become familiar with the process, they need practice in changing from one form to the other without the use of models. However, do not rush to a routine, but encourage students to think problems through, as in the examples on Activity Card 13–4. Then they can learn the shortcut you probably use. They can think:

Activity Card 13–4 ✔️

Think, Think, Think!

To find equivalent mixed numbers and fractions without using pictures, you can think of whole numbers that are equivalent to fractions:

$$1 = \frac{3}{3}, \text{ so } 8 = \frac{24}{3}$$

$$8\frac{2}{3} = \frac{24}{3} + \frac{2}{3} = \frac{26}{3}$$

$$\frac{8}{8} = 1, \text{ so } \frac{24}{8} = 3$$

$$\frac{27}{8} = \frac{24}{8} + \frac{3}{8} = 3\frac{3}{8}$$

▼ Try these. (Remember, no pictures allowed.)

1.
$$1 = \frac{\Box}{4}, \text{ so } 5 = \frac{\Box}{4}$$
$$5\frac{3}{4} = \frac{\Box}{4}$$

2.
$$\frac{\Box}{5} = 1, \text{ so } \frac{40}{5} = \Box$$
$$\frac{43}{5} = \Box\frac{\Box}{5}$$

3.
$$1 = \frac{\Box}{6}, \text{ so } 7 = \frac{\Box}{6}$$
$$7\frac{5}{6} = \frac{\Box}{6}$$

4.
$$\frac{\Box}{9} = 1, \text{ so } \frac{18}{9} = \Box$$
$$\frac{20}{9} = \Box\frac{\Box}{9}$$

5.
$$1 = \frac{\Box}{3}, \text{ so } 4 = \frac{\Box}{3}$$
$$4\frac{1}{3} = \frac{\Box}{3}$$

6.
$$\frac{\Box}{7} = 1, \text{ so } \frac{21}{7} = \Box$$
$$\frac{22}{7} = \Box\frac{\Box}{7}$$

7.
$$1 = \frac{\Box}{10}, \text{ so } 7 = \frac{\Box}{10}$$
$$7\frac{6}{10} = \frac{\Box}{10}$$

8.
$$\frac{\Box}{5} = 1, \text{ so } \frac{15}{5} = \Box$$
$$\frac{18}{5} = \Box\frac{\Box}{5}$$

8 is 8 groups of 3 thirds, or 24 thirds.

8⅔ is 24 thirds and 2 thirds, or 26 thirds.

Thus, 8⅔ = ²⁶⁄₃.

● Operations with Fractions

The key to a meaningful presentation of the operations with fractions is to establish a firm background in fractions, especially equivalent fractions and modeling fractions. Then, problem situations that involve fractions and operations should be presented. Whenever possible, the meanings given to operations with whole numbers should be extended to fractions. There are, however, meanings of operations that do not extend directly. For example, for the multiplication of two fractions, multiplication is not repeated addition. Other differences also must be kept in mind, such as when multiplying two whole numbers, the product is always larger than either factor; but in multiplying two proper fractions, the product is always less than either factor.

Children gain a better understanding of operations with fractions if they learn to estimate answers by using whole numbers and fractions such as one-half or one-tenth. For example, before actually computing the answer to 3⅔ + 4⅚, they should be able to realize that the answer is more than 7. In fact, since ⅔ and ⅚ are each more than ½, the answer is more than 8. Developing this type of number and operation sense will make it easier to establish what are reasonable answers to problems. Many calculators will perform operations with fractions. It is important that the conceptual underpinnings be firmly established so that answers can be checked for reasonableness.

Addition and Subtraction

Instead of beginning addition and subtraction with fractions with a symbolic sentence such as ⅔ + ¼, begin with joining and separating situations. Problems involving these situations, together with pictorial models, can:

- Help children see that adding and subtracting of fractions solve problems similar to those with whole numbers
- Give children an idea of what a reasonable answer will be
- Help children see why a common denominator is necessary when adding or subtracting

Let's look at how you could introduce these ideas. You will need blank transparencies and one with a copy of the fraction strips in Appendix B, a transparency marker, and an overhead projector.

1. Show the transparency with strips and ask questions to make certain the children are able to tell what kind of strips are shown (halves, thirds, fourths, etc.).

2. Present a joining situation that uses whole numbers:

   If I had eight whole strips and you gave me three more, how many would I have altogether?

   They will think this task is easy, but make the point that you are now going to look at fractions as they look at whole numbers.

3. Now give the same situation using fractions:

   If I have ¼ of a strip and you give me ⅓ more of a strip, how much do I have altogether?

   Discuss their ideas to see if anyone suggests putting together with . You can then confirm (or introduce) this idea in the next step.

4. Using a blank transparency, first draw a copy of ¼ and then "add" to it a copy of a strip ⅓ long in order to show how long a strip you have altogether.

5. Now help children try to find a name for this length. You will find that it matches the ⁷⁄₁₂ strip.

6. Then, write on the transparency where you "added":

$$\frac{1}{4} + \frac{1}{3} = \frac{7}{12}$$

7. Continue with other joining situations that lead to sentences such as the following:

$$\frac{3}{12} + \frac{4}{12} \quad \text{Like denominators}$$

$$\frac{1}{6} + \frac{5}{12} \quad \text{Unlike denominators}$$

Now, move to separating, or take-away, situations:

1. Again begin with a situation involving whole numbers:

   If I had ¾ of a strip and I gave you ⅓ of a strip, how much would I have left?

Accept children's ideas and solutions; they are more likely to suggest drawing on the blank transparency, now that they have seen it used for addition.

2. Draw a strip that is $\frac{3}{4}$ long, then from one end cross out a strip that is $\frac{1}{3}$ long and check to show what is left.

3. Help children find a strip that shows $\frac{5}{12}$ is left.

4. Write:

$$\frac{3}{4} - \frac{1}{3} = \frac{5}{12}$$

5. Continue with other separating situations, including at least one in which the subtraction is impossible; for example:

   I have $\frac{1}{3}$ of a strip and I give you $\frac{7}{12}$.

   How much do I have left?

After this kind of introduction, children need to begin solving such problems on their own. A challenging set of problems is given on Activity Card 13–5, where children have to first find each of the fractions in the picture.

Adding Symbolically The teaching sequence for developing fraction concepts given thus far pro-

Activity Card 13–5

✓

Painting Problems

▼ Several artists were painting unusual pictures. Use their pictures to help you answer the questions.

Untitled #1

This painter painted $\frac{1}{4}$ of his painting. He rested and then painted $\frac{3}{8}$ more. How much did he paint altogether? $\frac{5}{8}$

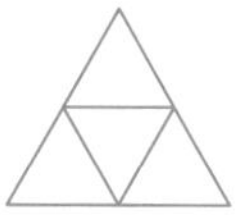

Untitled #2

This painter carefully painted $\frac{2}{4}$ of the painting. Then she painted $\frac{1}{2}$ more of it. How much did she paint altogether? ______

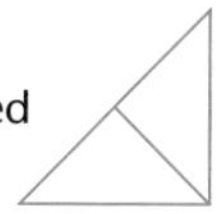

Untitled #3

After this painter had done $\frac{2}{3}$ of this painting, he found he had made a mistake and had to scrape off $\frac{2}{6}$. How much was still painted? ______

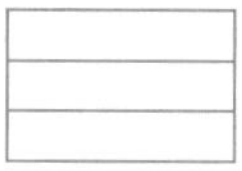

Untitled #4

This painter painted $\frac{3}{4}$ of her canvas yellow. She then scraped the paint off $\frac{1}{2}$ of her canvas. How much was still painted? ______

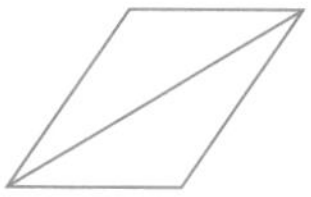

Untitled #5

First, $\frac{3}{8}$ of this lovely canvas was painted. Then $\frac{3}{8}$ more was painted. How much was painted altogether? ______

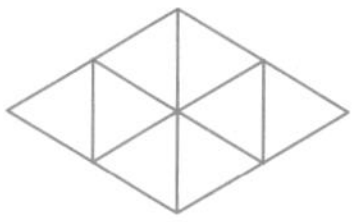

Untitled #6

After this artist finished $\frac{1}{3}$ of the painting, he decided that he didn't like it, so he scraped the paint off $\frac{2}{9}$ of it. How much was left painted? ______

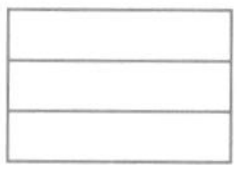

Untitled #7

This painter painted $\frac{3}{10}$ of her canvas upside down and $\frac{2}{5}$ of it right side up. How much did she paint altogether? ______

Untitled #8

This painting was damaged by a low-flying bird when $\frac{2}{3}$ of it was done. So $\frac{4}{6}$ had to be repainted. How much of the painted part was not damaged? ______

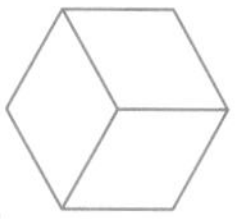

vides children with much *oral* experience in adding and subtracting fractions with like denominators, but they have not been given the problems symbolically. If children have any difficulty in adding or subtracting like fractions, use the fraction words to help:

$$\frac{1}{5} \quad \text{one-fifth}$$

$$+\frac{3}{5} \quad \text{three-fifths}$$

$$\overline{\frac{4}{5}} \quad \text{four-fifths}$$

It also will help to have children read the problem orally. The main idea to be developed when adding or subtracting fractions with unlike denominators is that they cannot be added or subtracted symbolically without first changing them to like denominators. In order to help children see that fractions with unlike denominators cannot be added or subtracted without changing them to like denominators, it may help to return to the following:

1. *Return to the Words.* Introduce the fractions in the problem using words:

What is one-*fourth* plus one-*third*? Is it thirds, fourths, or some other fraction?

2. *Return to Measurement.* Use examples involving familiar measurements. If we measured one thing in inches and another in feet, how long would the two be together? Before adding, we usually change both to the same unit. Similarly, if we measure something in thirds and something in fourths, we must change both of them to the same unit.

3. *Return to the Transparency of the Strips.* Use the transparencies for the joining and separating situations to help children see that when you add (subtract) fractions with unlike denominators, the result is a fraction with a denominator different from at least one of the two:

$$\frac{1}{3} + \frac{1}{4} = \frac{7}{12}$$

$$\frac{1}{3} + \frac{1}{6} = \frac{1}{2}$$

$$\frac{1}{3} + \frac{5}{6} = \frac{7}{6}$$

Now use the strips to show adding $\frac{1}{3}$ and $\frac{1}{4}$ by adding $\frac{4}{12}$ and $\frac{3}{12}$, or

$$\frac{1}{3} = \frac{4}{12}$$

$$+\frac{1}{4} = \frac{3}{12}$$

Even when children know why it is necessary to first change fractions to like fractions or to find a common denominator, you will need to continue to work with children on how to do this (see the discussion of equivalent fractions).

Figure 13–8 gives examples that show how to add mixed numbers and indicates two additional skills that are needed. (See if you can identify the new skills before reading on.)

Subtracting fractions greater than one or mixed numbers is often more difficult, partly because children have not changed a mixed number to another mixed number or because they lack understanding of regrouping.

The subtraction example in Figure 13–9 requires regrouping $6\frac{3}{7}$ to $5\frac{10}{7}$. Help children understand that

$$2\frac{3}{4} \qquad \text{Are the denominators the same?}$$
$$+5\frac{2}{3} \qquad \text{No, change to like fractions.}$$

$$2\frac{9}{12} \qquad \text{Are the denominators the same?}$$
$$+5\frac{8}{12} \qquad \text{Yes, add the fractions; then add the whole numbers.}$$
$$7\frac{17}{12} \qquad \text{Is the fraction more than a whole?}$$
$$\qquad\qquad \text{Yes; then you may want to change to}$$
$$7\frac{17}{12} = 8\frac{5}{12} \qquad \text{a mixed number.}$$

Figure 13–8 • Adding mixed numbers

$$6\frac{3}{7} \qquad \text{Are the denominators the same?}$$
$$-2\frac{4}{7} \qquad \text{Yes. (If not, change them to like fractions.)}$$
$$\qquad\qquad \text{Can I take } \frac{4}{7} \text{ from } \frac{3}{7}?$$
$$5\frac{10}{7} \qquad \text{No, I must regroup } 6\frac{3}{7}.$$
$$-2\frac{4}{7} \qquad (1 = \frac{7}{7}, \text{ so } \frac{3}{7} + \frac{7}{7} = \frac{10}{7}.)$$
$$3\frac{6}{7} \qquad \text{Now subtract the fraction parts, then the whole parts.}$$

Figure 13–9 • Subtracting mixed numbers

1 is $\frac{7}{7}$ and 6 is $5 + 1$, or $5 + \frac{7}{7}$

Thus,

$$6\frac{3}{7} \text{ is } 5 + \frac{7}{7} + \frac{3}{7}, \text{ or } 5\frac{10}{7}$$

If children are having difficulty with regrouping fractions, the following model can help them see, for example, that $6\frac{3}{7} = 5\frac{10}{7}$.

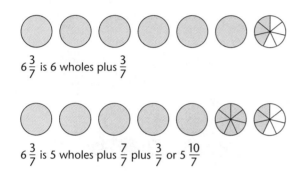

$6\frac{3}{7}$ is 6 wholes plus $\frac{3}{7}$

$6\frac{3}{7}$ is 5 wholes plus $\frac{7}{7}$ plus $\frac{3}{7}$ or $5\frac{10}{7}$

Multiplication

The algorithm for multiplication of fractions is one of the simplest. Multiply numerators to find the numerator, multiply denominators to find the denominator.

This algorithm can be taught in minutes (and forgotten in seconds unless a great amount of practice is provided). However, simply teaching this algorithm does not provide insight into why it works or when to use it. We suggest a development that gives the underlying meanings of multiplication, an idea of the size of an answer, and the reason why the algorithm works before the algorithm itself is presented.

We will look at four different cases: a whole number times a fraction or mixed number, a fraction times a whole number, a fraction times a fraction, and a mixed number times a mixed number. In each case, we will tie the multiplication to a meaning of multiplication of whole numbers. We will use the knowledge that 3×4 means three groups of four and 3×4 is the area of a 3-by-4 rectangle.

Whole Number Times a Fraction Let's begin with a problem:

You have 3 pans each with $\frac{4}{5}$ of a pizza. How much pizza do you have?

How is this problem like having three bags each with four marbles? See if this sketch helps you to see the similarity between multiplying whole numbers and multiplying a whole number times a fraction:

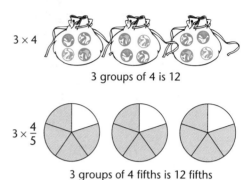

3×4

3 groups of 4 is 12

$3 \times \frac{4}{5}$

3 groups of 4 fifths is 12 fifths

If we consider three groups of four to be 3×4, it makes sense to consider three groups of $\frac{4}{5}$ to mean $3 \times \frac{4}{5}$. How did we first find three groups of four? We could have put out three groups of four marbles and counted them. Similarly, if we want to find three groups of $\frac{4}{5}$, we can put out three pans of pizza, each having $\frac{4}{5}$ in it, and count the number of fifths. Or, to find 3×4, we can consider repeated addition:

$$4 + 4 + 4 = 12$$

Thus,

$$3 \times \frac{4}{5} \text{ is } \frac{4}{5} + \frac{4}{5} + \frac{4}{5} = \frac{12}{5}$$

After the students have solved problems like this one with pictures, see if they can solve them without pictures or repeated addition. Be sure to place strong emphasis on the words. Have them listen carefully as you read:

$5 \times \frac{2}{3}$ is 5 groups of two-thirds,
which is *5 groups of 2 or 10* (thirds),
or $\frac{10}{3}$

Fraction Times a Whole Number Again let's begin with a problem:

You have $\frac{3}{4}$ of a case of twenty-four bottles. How many bottles have you?

If children have worked with the set model, they have the background to solve this problem with physical objects. Here, we want to move to solving it symbolically and tying it to multiplication.

First, let's look at why it makes sense to consider this problem as a multiplication problem. If we had 5 cases with 24 bottles in each, what would we do to find out how many? We would multiply 5×24. Similarly, 20 cases would be 20×24, 53 cases would be 53×24, and, thus, $\frac{3}{4}$ case would be $\frac{3}{4} \times 24$.

Now let's review how we find $\frac{3}{4}$ of 24. We first partition the set into 4 equal parts (each part would have 6), or, in other words, we first find $\frac{1}{4}$ of 24. Thus, $\frac{3}{4}$ would be 3 times as many, or $3 \times 6 = 18$.

$$\frac{3}{4} \times 24 = \square$$

Think

$$\frac{1}{4} \times 24 = 6$$

$\frac{3}{4}$ is 3 times as many,

or $3 \times 6 = 18$

At first glance, this procedure looks slightly different from the algorithm for multiplying numerators and multiplying denominators. Actually, the results are the same:

$$\frac{3}{4} \times 24 = \frac{3}{4} \times \frac{24}{1} = \frac{3 \times 24}{4} = \frac{72}{4} = 18$$

One way to approach these problems is to use commutativity. Since $3 \times 4 = 4 \times 3$, then we want

$$\frac{3}{4} \times 24 = 24 \times \frac{3}{4}$$

We can then find $\frac{3}{4} \times 24$ by the procedures discussed in multiplying a whole number by a fraction. Although this approach may be easier, the opportunity to present the "of" meaning of multiplication is lost.

Fraction Times a Fraction Here's another problem:

If you own $\frac{3}{4}$ of an acre of land and $\frac{5}{6}$ of this is planted in trees, what part of the acre is planted in trees?

Why is this problem a multiplication problem? Let's begin solving the problem by drawing pictures. Consider first the acre partitioned into fourths and the amount you own, which is $\frac{3}{4}$:

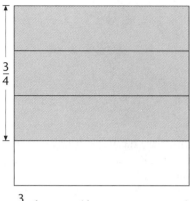

$\frac{3}{4}$ of an acre (the amount you own)

Partitioning the acre into sixths, we can now focus on the $\frac{5}{6}$ that you have planted:

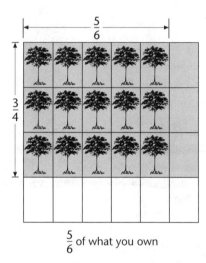

$\frac{5}{6}$ of what you own

What we have is a tree-planted rectangle that is $\frac{3}{4}$ by $\frac{5}{6}$, and its area is found by multiplying $\frac{3}{4} \times \frac{5}{6}$.

This model will need to be developed slowly, and only after children have had experience with finding areas of rectangles. Find out whether any children can see a shorter way to find the product. Make a list of multiplication exercises and products (do not reduce the answers). See if the children notice the multiplication pattern.

If children have had experience with finding area, this model can be used to see the procedure for multiplying fractions (multiply the numerators, multiply the denominators). You can refer to the diagrams to show why the procedure works. You have partitioned the acre into fourths one way and sixths the other way, thus creating 4×6, or 24, equal parts (the denominator). Trees were planted in three rows of five, or fifteen of these parts, so 3×5 is the numerator. Symbolically, we write

$$\frac{3}{4} \times \frac{5}{6} = \frac{3 \times 5}{4 \times 6} = \frac{15}{24}$$

At this point, return to earlier examples and let children know that this process holds for those cases also. A word of caution: do not rush to canceling. Be sure that children can do multiplication this way, reducing answers only if necessary and applying multiplication to problems, before introducing canceling.

Mixed Number Times a Mixed Number Problems that involve multiplication of mixed numbers also can be solved with models. Consider the following problem:

> You have a piece of cloth that is 2¼ yards by 1½ yards. How many square yards do you have?

Part A in Figure 13–10 presents a model showing how to change both mixed numbers in this problem to improper fractions, and the model in part B shows how to multiply the mixed numbers without first changing them to improper fractions.

Division

As with multiplication, many division situations can be modeled. The models get rather complicated,

however, so we present only one model and then show how the division algorithm can be developed symbolically. If you are presenting the division algorithm to children who are not ready for a symbolic treatment, you will need to find other models for other situations.

Consider this problem:

> Suppose you have ¾ of a square pizza and you want to share it equally among five people. How much of the pizza would each person receive?

This problem can be solved by division:

$$\frac{3}{4} \div 5 = \boxed{}$$

You know how you would solve this with a pizza—by drawing a picture:

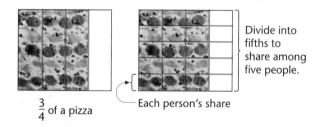

Divide into fifths to share among five people.

$\frac{3}{4}$ of a pizza — Each person's share

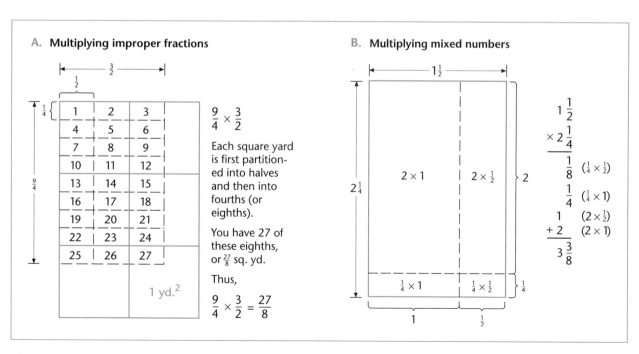

A. Multiplying improper fractions

$\frac{9}{4} \times \frac{3}{2}$

Each square yard is first partitioned into halves and then into fourths (or eighths).

You have 27 of these eighths, or $\frac{27}{8}$ sq. yd.

Thus,

$$\frac{9}{4} \times \frac{3}{2} = \frac{27}{8}$$

B. Multiplying mixed numbers

$$
\begin{array}{rl}
& 1\frac{1}{2} \\
\times & 2\frac{1}{4} \\
\hline
& \frac{1}{8} \quad (\frac{1}{4} \times \frac{1}{2}) \\
& \frac{1}{4} \quad (\frac{1}{4} \times 1) \\
& 1 \quad (2 \times \frac{1}{2}) \\
+ & 2 \quad (2 \times 1) \\
\hline
& 3\frac{3}{8}
\end{array}
$$

Figure 13–10 • Multiplication models

Each person gets three of twenty pieces, or $\frac{3}{4} \div 5 = \frac{3}{20}$. You notice that this is the same picture as:

$$\frac{1}{5} \times \frac{3}{4} \text{ or } \frac{3}{4} \times \frac{1}{5}$$

This problem thus begins to develop the rule that:

$$\frac{3}{4} \div 5 = \frac{3}{4} \times \frac{1}{5}$$

There are several ways to show why the algorithm for dividing fractions works. Here, we will consider only one way, which depends on knowing that $a \div b = \frac{a}{b}$ and that if the numerator and denominator of a fraction are multiplied by the same number, the resulting fraction is equivalent.

Suppose you want to solve: $\frac{3}{4} \div \frac{5}{8} = \square$. You could talk through the problem in this way:

$$\frac{3}{4} \div \frac{5}{8} = \boxed{}$$

$$\frac{3}{4} \div \frac{5}{8} = \frac{\frac{3}{4}}{\frac{5}{8}}$$ We rewrite $\frac{3}{4} \div \frac{5}{8}$ just as $5 \div 6$ can be rewritten as $\frac{5}{6}$.

$$= \frac{\frac{3}{4} \times \frac{8}{5}}{\frac{5}{8} \times \frac{8}{5}}$$ We multiply the numerator and denominator by the same number.

$$= \frac{\frac{3}{4} \times \frac{8}{5}}{1}$$ We chose $\frac{8}{5}$ because we wanted the denominator to be 1.

$$= \frac{3}{4} \times \frac{8}{5}$$ We know that a number divided by one is the number

Thus,

$$\frac{3}{4} \div \frac{5}{8} = \frac{3}{4} \times \frac{8}{5}$$

When children understand this process, let them verbalize the rule: to divide two fractions, invert the divisor and multiply.

Do not forget that students can check a division problem by multiplying:

$$15 \div 5 = 3 \quad \text{because} \quad 3 \times 5 = 15$$

$$\frac{3}{4} \div \frac{5}{8} = \frac{6}{5} \quad \text{because} \quad \frac{6}{5} \times \frac{5}{8} = \frac{30}{40} = \frac{3}{4}$$

It is a good idea to take some time to talk about the answers, particularly in cases like the last example. Notice that the quotient ($\frac{6}{5}$) is larger than either of the other two numbers. This result is quite different from whole numbers, and students should realize it is possible to obtain a larger quotient when dividing fractions. You can give a logical explanation using models and a problem such as $6 \div \frac{3}{4}$.

● Development of Decimals

In introducing decimals, you should link them to other knowledge—in particular, to common fractions and to place value. Although you will need to interweave both of these ideas in your teaching, we have separated them for ease of discussion.

Relationship to Common Fractions

Decimal fractions are just another notation for tenths, hundredths, and other powers-of-ten parts of a unit. Thus, basic to decimals is understanding of these fractional parts. Hopefully, that understanding has been built in introducing common fractions. We will assume so.

Tenths Before introducing the decimal notation for tenths, let's review what students know about tenths from their background with fractions. They should know that, to partition a unit into tenths, there must be ten equal parts. They also should be able to make the connection between the model, the oral name, and the fraction. And they should know that ten tenths make a whole, that seven tenths is less than a whole, and that twenty-seven tenths is more than a whole.

With this background, the children should be ready to learn that 0.3 is a new symbol for $\frac{3}{10}$. At this point, you should link the place-value ideas to the new notation (see the discussion on place value). You also need to stress that 0.3 is read just like $\frac{3}{10}$. Also look at $\frac{27}{10}$, or $2\frac{7}{10}$. This amount is written 2.7 and read as "two and seven-tenths." Note that the word *and* is said for the decimal point. Reading decimals in this way helps to connect decimal and fraction ideas. A quick game to play that practices writing decimal and fraction notation is described on Lesson Card 13–2. Before introducing hundredths, you should make certain that the students have made all the connections in this triangle.

Model:

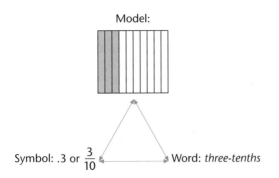

Symbol: .3 or $\frac{3}{10}$ ← → Word: *three-tenths*

Hundredths To begin extending decimals to hundredths, provide each child with a copy of the model or grid of hundredths, shown in Figure 13–11 (and in Appendix B) and also ten strips that are one square by twenty squares. Make certain that the children know that the unit (entire square or grid) is one, and that each part (small square) is one hundredth. Using the model, ask them to show $\frac{3}{100}$, $\frac{7}{100}$, $\frac{10}{100}$, $\frac{21}{1000}$. . . .

Figure 13–11 • **Model of hundredths**

Lesson Card 13–2

Can You Beat the Toss?

Materials: Paper and pencil for children; a penny for the teacher

Directions:

▼ The teacher reads a number.

▼ Each child writes the number in either decimal or fraction notation.

▼ Each child receives 1 point if he or she writes the number correctly.

▼ The teacher tosses a coin.

• If it's *heads,* then those who wrote a *decimal* receive one more point.

• If it's *tails,* then those who wrote a *fraction* receive one more point.

Suggested Numbers:

two-tenths	one and three-tenths
seven-tenths	twenty-two and five-tenths
five and seven-tenths	thirty-four and no-tenths
eleven and four-tenths	

Challenge Numbers:

sixteen-tenths	five and eleven-tenths

Then develop the idea that one strip is of the hundredths model. Ask the children to use two strips to cover the tenths column and to lightly mark three more squares. Ask what part of the whole is covered. Elicit both responses, $\frac{2}{10} + \frac{3}{100}$ as well as $\frac{23}{100}$. Then write

$$\frac{23}{100} = \frac{2}{10} + \frac{3}{100}$$

Now connect the place-value interpretation and the decimal notation 0.23. You can also use the model to show that 0.2 = 0.20. Continue having children make the connections shown in the triangle—that is, by connecting the model, the symbol, and the word.

Thousandths and Other Decimals One national assessment reported that

. . . although thirteen- and seventeen-year-olds appeared to have facility with tenths and hundredths, their competency was less developed for thousandths and smaller decimal numbers. [Carpenter et al. 1981, p. 39]

This deficiency is partly because there is less emphasis on these decimals, but also because teachers often expect children to generalize after hundredths to all the other places. Most of the work with smaller decimals should be done primarily through the place-value interpretation because the fractions become unwieldy. However, thousandths should be developed as one-tenth of a hundredth, and the understanding that ten thousandths is $\frac{1}{100}$ should be developed through a model.

Decimals and Other Common Fractions One skill that needs to be developed is the ability to relate fractions to decimals. Hopefully, if decimals have been introduced carefully, students will be able to write the fraction notation for a decimal and the decimal notation for any fraction expressed in tenths, hundredths, and so on.

Activity Card 13–6 provides practice in changing various common fractions into tenths, hundredths,

and thousandths, which then can be expressed in decimal notation.

The ability to relate fractions to decimals when expressed in tenths, hundreds, and so on does not ensure that students can express other fractions as decimals. Table 13–2 shows two exercises from a national assessment as well as the responses of thirteen-year-olds. In each case, less than 30 percent responded correctly. Analyze the errors made in both examples and consider what they indicate about students' grasp of fractions and decimals. Would you not hope that more students would realize that $\frac{5}{8}$ is just a little more than one-half and thus could not equal 0.85, which is almost a whole?

Activity Card 13–6

More Tenths, Hundredths, and Thousandths

▼ Can you write an equivalent fraction in tenths, hundredths, or thousandths for each kind of fractional part? If not, write "no." If you can, write "yes," and then fill in the box to complete the sentence.

Kind of Fractional Part	Tenths	Hundredths	Thousandths
Thirds	<u>NO</u> $\frac{1}{3} = \frac{\Box}{10}$	_____ $\frac{1}{3} = \frac{\Box}{100}$	_____ $\frac{1}{3} = \frac{\Box}{1000}$
Fourths	_____ $\frac{1}{4} = \frac{\Box}{10}$	<u>YES</u> $\frac{1}{4} = \frac{\boxed{25}}{100}$	_____ $\frac{1}{4} = \frac{\Box}{1000}$
Fifths	_____ $\frac{1}{5} = \frac{\Box}{10}$	_____ $\frac{1}{5} = \frac{\Box}{100}$	_____ $\frac{1}{5} = \frac{\Box}{1000}$
Sixths	_____ $\frac{1}{6} = \frac{\Box}{10}$	_____ $\frac{1}{6} = \frac{\Box}{100}$	_____ $\frac{1}{6} = \frac{\Box}{1000}$
Eighths	_____ $\frac{1}{8} = \frac{\Box}{10}$	_____ $\frac{1}{8} = \frac{\Box}{100}$	_____ $\frac{1}{8} = \frac{\Box}{1000}$
Twentieths	_____ $\frac{1}{20} = \frac{\Box}{10}$	_____ $\frac{1}{20} = \frac{\Box}{100}$	_____ $\frac{1}{20} = \frac{\Box}{1000}$
Twenty-fifths	_____ $\frac{1}{25} = \frac{\Box}{10}$	_____ $\frac{1}{25} = \frac{\Box}{100}$	_____ $\frac{1}{25} = \frac{\Box}{1000}$
Fortieths	_____ $\frac{1}{40} = \frac{\Box}{10}$	_____ $\frac{1}{40} = \frac{\Box}{100}$	_____ $\frac{1}{40} = \frac{\Box}{1000}$

Table 13–2 • Results of national assessment items on equivalence of decimals and fractions

Exercise	Percent Responding Age 13
A. Which decimal is equal to $\frac{1}{5}$?	
○ .15	12
● .2	38
○ .5	38
○ .51	3
○ I don't know.	6
B. Which decimal is equal to $\frac{5}{8}$?	
○ .6	7
● .625	27
○ $.\overline{714285}$	3
○ .85	30
○ I don't know.	30

When you have established that many fractions can be written as decimals, you can turn to the meaning of a fraction as division. Begin with an example that can be easily changed to a decimal, for example, $\frac{4}{5}$. Children should know that $\frac{4}{5} = \frac{8}{10} = 0.8$.

Then proceed to the idea that $\frac{4}{5}$ means $4 \div 5$. In order to divide 4 by 5, a child needs to be able to divide decimals and to realize that 4 is also 4.0:

$$\frac{4}{5} = 4 \div 5, \text{ which is } 5\overline{)4},$$
$$\text{or } 5\overline{)4.0}^{.8}$$

Therefore,

$$\frac{4}{5} = .8$$

Make certain you encourage the children to tell first whether the answer is more or less than one to help them place the decimal point.

Once you have introduced the procedure, the children can explore many interesting patterns that occur when converting fractions to decimals. Some of these can be investigated with a calculator. For example, look at the decimal equivalents for ninths:

$$\frac{1}{9} = .11111 \ldots$$

$$\frac{2}{9} = .22222 \ldots$$

$$\frac{3}{9} = .33333 \ldots$$

You should do a few of these calculations by hand to show that the pattern continues forever. If you use only the calculator, students may think that $\frac{1}{9} = 0.11111111$ (or the number of places on their calculator screen).

Students can also be helped to see that $\frac{1}{3}$ does not equal 0.33, 0.333, or 0.3333 by looking at the meaning of $\frac{1}{3}$. If $\frac{1}{3} = 0.33$, then each of three equal parts of a whole would be 0.33. Thus, the whole would be 0.33 + 0.33 + 0.33, or 0.99, which is not one. Similarly, $1 \neq 0.3333$, even though this is a better approximation.

Relationship to Place Value

The place-value interpretation of decimals is most useful in understanding computation with decimals. We look now at a way to develop this interpretation and how to use it in ordering and rounding decimals.

Interpretation Return to whole numbers and think about what children know about place value. Take, for example, the number 2,463. Children can identify the places (ones, tens, hundreds, and thousands) as well as what number is in each (3, 6, 4, and 2). They know, for example, that the four means four hundreds. They also have learned how the places were formed: beginning with ones as a unit, grouping ten of these to form a new unit (tens), grouping ten of these to form a new unit (hundreds), and so forth.

In introducing place-value ideas with decimals, begin with ones as the unit. Instead of grouping by tens, take one-tenth of the one to form the new unit of tenths. To indicate this new unit in our place-value system, we use a decimal point after the ones place. Children also should be helped to realize that ten of the tenths make a one (just like ten of any unit make the next larger unit). They also should be able to identify the tenths place in a number. This interpretation should be integrated with the interpretation of decimals as fractions.

Again, when introducing hundredths, the place-value interpretation should be made. Given a number such as 51.63, a child should be able to tell what number is in the tenths place and the hundredths place as well as the relationships between the places (hundredths is $\frac{1}{10}$ of the tenths, or ten hundredths is one tenth). After introducing thousandths in a similar way, the children should be able to generalize to any decimal place.

Let us see how a place-value mat, or grid, can assist with decimals. When learning about decimals, it is most important that a decimal such as 24.09 be read as twenty-four *and* 9 hundredths—not "two, four, point, zero, nine." The words tenths and hundredths help students keep the tie between fractions and decimals. Consider 32.43, for example:

T	O	tth	hth
3	2 •	4	3

32 *and* 43 hundredths
or
32 *and* 4 tenths, 3 hundredths

Now let's use the grid for writing other decimals. (Remember to use models when first developing place value, as described in Chapter 7.)

Write 8 hundredths:

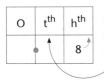

Children should realize there are 0 tenths.

What is 29 hundredths?

O	tth	hth
•	2	9

What is 29 tenths?

O	tth	hth
2 •	9	

Now look at 4.3 on the grid:

How many tens? [0]

T	O	tth	hth
	4 •	3	

You could write a zero in the tens place, but this is not customary. However, sometimes it is helpful to write a zero in the hundredths place:

How many hundredths? [0]

What does that tell you?

T	O	tth	hth
	4 •	3	0

4.3 is the same as 4.30.

Children who are well acquainted with the models and the grid for place value should be able to handle decimals with ease.

Ordering and Rounding Decimals

The ordering and rounding of decimals should follow directly from an understanding of decimals and the ability to order and round whole numbers. This understanding must include being able to interpret the decimals in terms of place value and being able to think of, for example, 0.2 as 0.20 or 0.200.

Here is an example of a discussion you might use in ordering two decimals:

Which is larger—23.61 or 23.9?

Questions	Expected Responses
What do we do first?	Compare the numbers in the largest place.
What is the largest place?	Tens.
Those numbers are the same, what do we do next?	Compare the numbers in the ones place.
Those are the same, what do we do?	Compare the numbers in the tenths place.
Which is larger?	The 9.
Therefore, which is larger—23.61 or 23.9?	23.9
Can anyone tell us another way to look at this?	23.9 is 23.90, and 90 hundredths is more than 61 hundredths.

In rounding a decimal such as 24.78 to the nearest tenth, you need to ask the same types of questions as you do with whole numbers, but children must also understand that 24.7 = 24.70.

Questions	Expected Responses
What "tenths" is 24.78 between?	It's between 24.7 and 24.8 (or 24.70 and 24.80).
Is it nearer 24.7 or 24.8?	Looking at 24.70 and 24.80, it's nearer 24.80.
How will you round it?	To 24.8.

● Decimal Operations

Certainly one advantage of decimals over fractions is that computation is much easier and basically follows the same rules as for whole numbers. In teaching the algorithms for decimals, you should build on the place-value interpretations and the corresponding whole-number algorithms. Given the wide availability of calculators, it is important that you spend as much time seeing whether answers are reasonable as on the algorithms. Thus, estimation skills (described in Chapter 9) become crucial.

Activity Card 13–7 combines estimation skills and operations with decimals. In activities of this type, you may need to encourage some students who are unsure of their skills when doing these types of activities, but accepting any reasonable answer will help build their confidence.

Addition and Subtraction

If your students have done a lot of estimation with whole numbers, you might begin the study of adding and subtracting decimals with finding approximate answers to problems. This approach, of course, depends on the students' understanding of decimals. After estimating with decimals has been developed in problem situations, children need to construct algorithms for adding and subtracting. These are the same as algorithms for whole numbers, but you need to stress the following:

- Adding or subtracting like units
- Regrouping in the decimal places

Activity Card 13–7

What's Your Answer?

▼ Use the data in this table:

Country	Area (Thousands of km²)	Population (Millions)
England	50.363	46.351
N. Ireland	5.452	1.537
Scotland	30.415	5.196
Wales	8.019	2.768

▼ Answer these questions:

- About how much larger is England than Scotland? _____
- About how large is Great Britain? _____
- About what is the population of Great Britain? _____
- Do twice as many people live in Wales as live in N. Ireland? _____
- Is England more than six times larger than Wales? _____

A few examples with models will usually allow children to generalize from the whole-number algorithms.

Difficulty with adding or subtracting decimals arises mainly when the values are given in horizontal format or in terms of a story problem and the decimals are expressed in different units; for example, 51.23 + 0.4 + 347. To deal with this difficulty, it is wise to have children first focus on an approximate answer. Will it be more than 300? More than 500? More than 1000? It is a help for some children to use a grid:

H	T	O	tth	hth
	5	1 • 2	3
		• 4	0
+3	4	7 • 0	0

After the algorithms have been introduced and understood, you should continue to use them in problem-solving situations to approximate answers and to practice adding and subtracting (it's a good way to keep these skills sharp). Let children use calculators as they solve problems and encourage estimation as a way to check reasonableness.

Multiplication and Division

Before we examine how to multiply or divide two decimals, let's consider multiplying and dividing a decimal by a whole number. These operations are conceptually easier to explain and allow for some development that will be helpful when multiplying or dividing two decimals. They also build the understandings needed for effective use of calculators.

Consider the following problem:

Six tables are lined up end-to-end. Each table is 2.3 meters long. How long is the line of tables?

Students should be able to solve this problem by adding decimals; and from their previous work with multiplication, they also should realize it is a multiplication problem. Thus, they should see that:

$$6 \times 2.3 = 2.3 + 2.3 + 2.3 + 2.3 + 2.3 + 2.3 = 13.8$$

However, just as children moved away from repeated addition to find the product of two whole numbers, they need to do so with this type of problem. Here is another way to think about it: multiplication depends on a firm foundation of the place-value interpretation of decimals.

Think

2.3	23	tenths
× 6	× 6	
	138	tenths, which is 13.8
2.37	23	hundredths
× 6	× 6	
	1422	hundredths, which is 14.22

Working with the grid will help students remember that 138 tenths is 13.8. In using this method, you should first have the students decide on a reasonable answer. For example, is 6 × 2.37 more than 12? As much as 18? They can also check by repeated addition.

The distributive algorithm that was used for dividing whole numbers may be used for dividing a decimal by a whole number. Consider this problem:

A vinegar company distributed 123.2 million liters of vinegar equally to eight customers. How much vinegar did each customer receive?

First, ask for reasonable answers.

Did each customer get more than ten million liters? [Yes, that would only be eighty million liters.]

Did each get more than twenty million liters? [No, that would be 160 million liters.]

What is the answer? [Between ten and twenty million liters]

Talk through the division as follows:

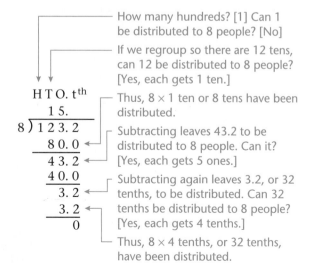

After this method is introduced, do some problems with remainders and then develop division to a specified number of places:

```
      15.4
 8)123.8
     80.0
     43.8
     40.0
      3.8
      3.2
       .6   Remainder is .6
```

Note that keeping the decimal in the algorithm helps one see that the remainder is 0.6, not 6.

Now try the same problem carrying out the division to two places (123.8 − 123.80):

```
      15.47
 8)123.80
     80.0      123.8 = 123.80
     43.8
     40.0
      3.8
      3.2
       .60
       .56
       .04   Remainder is .04
```

There are **several ways to teach multiplication of a decimal by a decimal.** If all teachers do is give students a rule for counting off decimal places, they will not help them develop a sense of decimals. Children can discover the rule by using calculators and examining patterns. Another way is to change the decimals to fractions and develop the rule through multiplication of fractions. Another method is to use place value and the knowledge that tenths times tenths is hundredths as shown here:

Think

3.2	32	tenths
× 1.6	× 16	tenths
	512	hundredths or 5.12

No matter which method you choose to teach multiplication of decimals, the important thing for the children is that they be able to check to see that their answer is reasonable.

To divide a decimal by a decimal, children can essentially turn the problem into one they already know how to do. That is, make the divisor a whole number by multiplying the divisor by a power of ten, such as 10, 100, 1,000. In order not to change the problem, the dividend must also be multiplied by that same number:

$$.5\overline{)1.25} \quad \text{Change to} \quad 5\overline{)12.5}$$

Multiply
by 10

There is a shortcut for this procedure: Move the decimal point the number of places in the divisor needed to make it a whole number, then do the same in the dividend.

Although this rule can be quickly learned, there is still the question of why it works. Students can easily be told why to turn the problem into one they can already do and convinced that it works (using the calculator or multiplying to check). However, what would you say to the inquisitive child who

asks why it works? One way is to appeal to fractions. We know that:

$$1.25 \div .5 = \frac{1.25}{.5}$$

And we know that we can multiply the numerator and denominator by the same number. Thus,

$$\frac{1.25}{.5} = \frac{1.25 \times 10}{.5 \times 10} = \frac{12.5}{5}$$

or

$$1.25 \div .5 = 12.5 \div 5$$

Students need more practice with multiplication and division of decimals than with addition and subtraction. The reason is partly because multiplication and division of whole numbers is not as firmly fixed as addition and subtraction. It is also because new rules are needed. You will find a great variation in skill level among children in your class. You might want to begin collecting some challenging activities such as the one on Activity Card 13–8 as well as games and other practice materials.

▶ A Glance at Where We've Been

This chapter has examined how to approach fractions and decimals in a meaningful way. This goal can be done through thoughtful teaching that first develops an understanding of the numbers through models and appropriate language. It involves careful sequencing and a pace that does not rush to the symbols alone. The operations with these numbers also can be developed in a meaningful way, instead of through rules learned by rote. A firm foundation of fractions and decimals and the operations will assist students in using these numbers to solve problems. Thus, throughout the development in this chapter, applications have been included to let students see how these numbers are used and to give meaning to the numbers and operations.

Ages or grade levels have not been given because we have found that often older children will profit from some of the beginning concepts. It will be your job to realize what pieces of this topic your students are missing. This task will not be as difficult as it sounds if you are familiar with the background and how the concepts and skills interweave.

Activity Card 13–8 ☑️

Plug-In Puzzles

▼ Use these decimal fractions to fill in the blanks.

| 8.3 | 4.2 | 5.5 | 3.1 | 7.6 | 6.7 |

Do each multiplication or division. In the division problems, divide to the hundredths place. Sum the four answers.

____ × ____ = _____

____ ÷ 5 = _____

____ × ____ = _____

____ ÷ 3 = _____

Total _____

• What is the largest total you can get? _____

• Can you get a total greater than 50? _____

• Can you get one greater than 100? _____

▼ Arrange these four decimals in the boxes so that the sentence is true. (Remember to do the parts in the parentheses first.)

5.13　　4.24　　3.84　　3.16

$$\left(\underline{\quad} \times 5\right) + \underline{\quad} = \left(4 \times \underline{\quad}\right) + \underline{\quad}$$

▼ Pick the two decimals from those listed that will make the sentence true.

21.21　　42.42　　36.36　　63.63　　27.27

$$\left(\underline{\quad} \div 7\right) \times 8 = \left(\underline{\quad} \div 9\right) \times 6$$

THINGS TO DO:
From What You've Read

1. Show four different part–whole models for ¾.

2. Illustrate three different meanings of ¾.

3. What concepts related to fractions need to be developed?

4. What is partitioning? How is this process related to division and to fractions?

5. Illustrate how two fractions may be ordered pictorially. Does your pictorial representation relate to the usual symbolic method? If so, how? If not, find one that does and explain how it relates to the symbolic method.

6. Why is equivalence of fractions a difficult concept for some students?

7. Show, with pictures, why $2\frac{3}{5}$ is equivalent to $\frac{13}{5}$; show why $2\frac{3}{5}$ is equivalent to $1\frac{8}{5}$.

8. How is multiplication of fractions different from multiplication of whole numbers?

9. Describe how decimal and common fractions are alike and different.

10. Describe how to explain, with meaning, that 2.8×3.7 is 10.36.

THINGS TO DO:
Going Beyond This Book

1. Create five story problems that ask children to order fractions.

2. Design a worksheet that would be a good follow-up to the chapter Snapshot. Include three models—region, length, and area—and a couple of challenging problems.

3. Make up a worksheet that follows the introduction to adding and subtracting fractions. Use halves, fourths, fifths, tenths, and twentieths, providing the appropriate picture of strips similar to Figure 13–6.

4. Make up five story problems that can be solved by multiplying fractions, and draw the area model to find the solution.

5. Examine two elementary mathematics textbook series to see how they introduce division of fractions, and contrast each to the methods in this book.

6. Experiment with a calculator that has a fraction key. What fraction skills and understanding would be important if such calculators were used?

7. Illustrate (using the hundredths model in Figure 13–11) the steps in the algorithms for each of these problems:

$$
\begin{array}{cc}
5.69 & 15.2 \\
+\,9.35 & -\,7.9
\end{array}
$$

8. Develop five tasks to ascertain a child's understanding of fractions (or of decimals). Interview at least three children on the tasks. Discuss what you observed and learned.

9. Design an assessment task that will help you understand whether or not your students understand operations with fractions.

▼▼▼▼▼▼▼▼▼▼▼▼▼▼▼▼▼▼▼▼▼▼▼▼▼

Children's Corner

Dennis, J. Richard. *Fractions Ar   ts of Things.* New York: Crowell, 1971.

Emberly, Ed. *Ed Emberley'   cle Drawing Book.* Boston: Little, Br

Hutchins, Pat. *The Doorbell Rang.* New York: Greenwillow, 1987.

Matthews, Louise. *Gator Pie.* New York: Dodd, Mead, 1979.

Pomerantz, Charlotte. *The Half-Birthday Party.* New York: Clarion, 1984.

Silverstein, Shel. *A Giraffe and a Half.* New York: Harper and Row, 1964.

Selected References

Baker, Kay M., and Graeber, Anna O. "Little into Big Is the Way It Always Is." *Arithmetic Teacher,* 39 (April 1992), pp 18–21.

Bezuk, Nadine S. "Fractions in the Early Childhood Mathematics Curriculum." *Arithmetic Teacher,* 35 (February 1988), pp. 56–61.

Bezuk, Nadine, and Cramer, Kathleen. "Multiplication of Fractions: Teaching for Understanding." *Arithmetic Teacher,* 39 (November 1991), pp. 34–37.

Bright, George W., and Harvey, John G. "Using Games to Teach Fraction Concepts and Skills." In *Mathematics for the Middle Grades (5–9)* 1982 Yearbook (ed. Linda Silvey). Reston, Va.: NCTM, 1982, pp. 205–216.

Carpenter, Thomas P.; Corbitt, Mary Kay; Kepner, Henry S., Jr.; Lindquist, Mary Montgomery; and Reys, Robert E. *Results from the Second Mathematics Assessment of the National Assessment of Educational Progress.* Reston, Va.: NCTM, 1981.

Goldenberg, E. Paul. "A Mathematical Conversation with Fourth Graders." *Arithmetic Teacher,* 38 (April 1991), pp. 38–43.

Groff, Patrick. "It Is Time to Question Fraction Teaching." *Mathematics Teaching in the Middle School,* 1 (January–February 1996), pp. 604–607.

Houbner, Mary Ann. "Percents: Developing Meaning Through Models." *Arithmetic Teacher,* 40 (December 1992), pp. 232–234.

Kieren, Thomas E. "Knowing Rational Numbers: Ideas and Symbols." In *Selected Issues in Mathematics Education* (ed. Mary Montgomery Lindquist). Berkeley, Calif.: McCutchan Publishing, 1980, pp. 69–81.

Kouba, Vicky L.; Brown, Catherine A.; Carpenter, Thomas P.; Lindquist, Mary M.; Silver, Edward A.; and Swafford, Jane O. "Results of the Fourth NAEP Assessment of Mathematics: Number, Operations, and Word Problems." *Arithmetic Teacher,* 35 (April 1988), pp. 14–19.

Kouba, Vicky L.; Zawojewski, Judith S.; and Strutchens, Marilyn E. "What Do Students Know about Numbers and Operations?" In *Results from the Sixth Mathematics Assessment of the National Assessment of Educational Progress* (eds. Patricia Ann Kenney and Edward A. Silver). Reston, Va.: NCTM, 1997, pp. 87–140.

Langford, Karen, and Sarullo, Angela. "Introductory Common and Decimal Fraction Concepts." In *Research Ideas for the Classroom: Early Childhood Mathematics* (ed. Robert J. Jensen). Reston, Va.: NCTM, 1992, pp. 223–247.

National Council of Teachers of Mathematics. *Curriculum and Evaluation Standards for School Mathematics.* Reston, Va.: NCTM, 1989.

Ott, Jack M. "An Unified Approach to Multiplying Fractions." *Arithmetic Teacher,* 37 (March 1990), pp. 47–49.

Payne, Joseph N., and Towsley, Ann N. "Implications of NCTM's Standards on Teaching Fractions and Decimals." *Arithmetic Teacher,* 37 (April 1990), pp. 23–26.

Payne, Joseph N.; Towsley, Ann N.; and Huinker, DeAnn M. "Fractions and Decimals." In *Mathematics for the Young Child* (ed. Joseph N. Payne). Reston, Va.: NCTM, 1990, pp.175–200.

Pothier, Yvonne, and Daiyo, Sawada. "Partitioning: An Approach to Fractions." *Arithmetic Teacher,* 38 (December 1990), pp. 12–16.

Romberg, Thomas A.; Harvey, John G.; Moser, James M.; and Montgomery, Mary E. *Developing Mathematical Processes* (DMP). Chicago: Rand McNally, 1974–1976.

Steffe, Leslie, and Olive, John. "The Problem of Fractions in the Elementary School." *Arithmetic Teacher,* 38 (May 1991), pp. 22–24.

Thompson, Charles S., and Walker, Vicki. "Connecting Decimals and Other Mathematical Content." *Teaching Children Mathematics,* 2 (April 1996), pp. 496–502.

Wentworth, Nancy M., and Monroe, Eula Ewing. "What Is the Whole?" *Mathematics Teaching in the Middle School,* 1 (April–May 1995), pp. 356–360.

Williams, Susan E., and Copley, Juanita. "Promoting Classroom Dialogue: Using Calculators to Discover Patterns in Dividing Decimals." *Mathematics Teaching in the Middle School,* 1 (April 1994), pp. 72–75.

14

Ratio, Proportion, and Percent

 Snapshot of a Lesson

Orientation

Mr. Flores and his students have been working on percents, a very important and often misunderstood concept. He wants to help them appreciate the power of percents and recognize some of the difficulties in making interpretations and judgments based solely on percents. For today's lesson, Mr. Flores has collected the results from the first four basketball games for the sixth-grade team.

Mr. Flores has prepared the following data to be entered into a spreadsheet and projected the computer screen on the overhead projector.

	A	B	C	D
1				
2	Player's	Shots	Shots	Percent
3	Name	Made	Taken	
4				
5	Billy	12	25	48%
6	Doug	8	17	47%
7	Harlan	1	8	13%
8	Bryan	3	5	60%
9	Rustin	15	43	35%
10	Eric	1	1	100%
11	Whitney	0	2	0%
12	Nick	0	0	#####

Mr. Flores begins by entering only the names and the middle column (shots taken) and asks:

Which students have taken the most shots?

Which students have taken the least shots?

Would this information help you decide who is the "best" shot? Tell why.

After some discussion, he also enters the first column of data (shots made) and asks:

What if you wanted to find the best shooters, which students would you check? Why?

Is it easy to compare $^{15}/_{43}$ with $^{12}/_{25}$? Why? Why not?

Is it easy to compare $^{12}/_{25}$ with $^{8}/_{17}$? Why? Why not?

Before calculating Column D, the students share what they notice. Joe thinks Billy and Doug shot about the same because 12 is about half of 25 and 8 is about half of 17. He predicts both percents will be a little less than 50 percent. Susan notices that Rustin made about a third of his shots so he wasn't as accurate as Billy and Doug. She predicts his percent will be close to 33 percent. After more discussion, Mr. Flores has the spreadsheet calculate Column D and asks:

How does the percent column help us compare shooters? Do these results support what we noticed earlier?

How can Nick and Whitney have the same shooting percentage?

What if you looked only at the shooting percentages? Of all the players, who would be the best shot? Do you agree that person is the best shot?

The class also noticed how the spreadsheet handled Nick's data by placing ##### in the percent column. This provided Mr. Flores with an opportunity to introduce how dividing Column B12 by C12 results in division by zero, which is undefined. They also talked about how in the real world 0 percent would still be reported.

After discussing each of the next two questions, Mr. Flores reenters Columns B and C and the class examines the results.

What if each player took one more shot and missed it—which percents would change the most? The least? Tell why.

	A	B	C	D
1				
2	Player's	Shots	Shots	Percent
3	Name	Made	Taken	
4				
5	Billy	12	26	46%
6	Doug	8	18	44%
7	Harlan	1	9	11%
8	Bryan	3	6	50%
9	Rustin	15	44	34%
10	Eric	1	2	50%
11	Whitney	0	3	0%
12	Nick	0	1	0%

What if each player took one more shot and hit it—which percents would change the most? The least? Tell why.

	A	B	C	D
1				
2	Player's	Shots	Shots	Percent
3	Name	Made	Taken	
4				
5	Billy	13	26	50%
6	Doug	9	18	50%
7	Harlan	2	9	22%
8	Bryan	4	6	67%
9	Rustin	16	44	36%
10	Eric	2	2	100%
11	Whitney	1	3	33%
12	Nick	1	1	100%

The class continues to interpret the data, generate other "what if" questions, and use the spreadsheet to answer those questions. As the discussion continues, Mr. Flores also asks questions designed to help students gain a greater understanding of percents.

Introduction

- "Family income this year increased by 10 percent."
- "Ian did only half the work Angela did."
- "Her salary is three times my salary."
- "The cost of living tripled during the last eight years."
- "Your chances of winning the lottery are less than one in a million."

Frequently heard statements like these reflect the fact that much of our quantitative thinking is relational. In such thinking, what is important is the relationship between numbers, rather than the actual numbers themselves.

Students in the elementary and middle school grades learn to represent number relationships by using ratios, proportions, and percents. In the NCTM *Curriculum and Evaluation Standards* (1989, p. 87) it is recommended that students ". . . understand, represent, and use numbers in a variety of equivalent forms. . . ."

For example, consider the prices of three carpets.

CARPET SALE

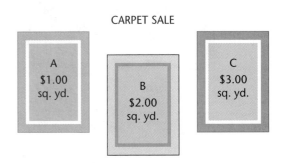

The difference in price between these carpets (A and B or B and C) is $1 per square yard. Yet B is twice as expensive as A and C is 50 percent more expensive than B. In comparing relative cost, the ratio relationship of the prices rather than the prices themselves are important.

● Ratios

Ratios involve comparing things, and some of children's earliest experiences with comparisons involve rates. For example, if a child pays one dime for three stickers, the rate is three stickers for one dime.

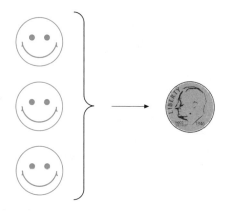

This ratio may be read as "three to one" and recorded as 3 to 1 or 3:1 or $\frac{3}{1}$. Any of these forms is acceptable.

Ratios also can be formed to report the number of stickers to nickels as 3 to 2 or stickers to pennies as 3 to 10:

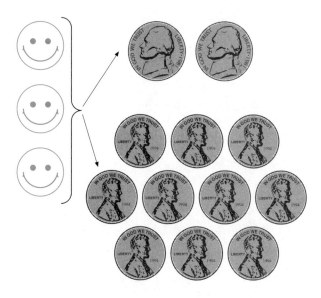

This ratio can also be expressed as ten pennies for every three stickers, which can be written as 10 to 3 or as the quotient 10 ÷ 3. The latter form provides a per-sticker cost of over three pennies and illustrates a powerful application of ratios.

Early experiences with ratios should stimulate children to think of two related numbers simultaneously. As children use manipulatives such as coins or draw pictures they should be encouraged to think about ordered pairs of numbers, such as (3 stickers, 2 pennies). The models help link the operation of multiplication directly to ordered pairs and ratios.

Using facts about money (the number of pennies in a nickel, nickels in a quarter, and so on) provides natural and meaningful experiences with ratios. Activity Card 14–1 shows how organizing such information not only visually displays many ratios, but also helps students realize that a ratio is a multiplicative comparison of two or more numbers in a given order. The activity also provides patterns that encourage students to explore relationships, generate formulas, and engage in algebraic thinking.

The money model also provides a natural extension of ratio to more than two numbers. For example, the ordered triple (2, 10, 50) relates 2 quarters, 10 nickels, and 50 pennies. Using a calculator to skip count by 5's or 25's or a spreadsheet to extend patterns would be appropriate uses of technology. The children's book *If You Made a Million* (Schwartz 1989) also provides photographs and explanations of ratios using coins.

Children encounter ratios in many different forms: "three video games for a dollar," "twice as long," "half as much," and so on. Real-world examples of ratios help develop a greater awareness and understanding. Prices such as two cans for 99¢, three pounds for $1.99, and 88¢ a dozen are frequently encountered and illustrate ratios in action. The statement of values (8–12–20, for example) on a sack of lawn fertilizer uses a ratio to report the percents of phosphorus, nitrogen, and potash the fertilizer contains.

This example is a reminder of the importance of the order of the entries and the need to understand what each entry represents. An ordered pair from Activity Card 14–1, such as (5, 25), could represent 5 quarters and 25 nickels or 5 nickels and 25 pennies. Whether a ratio has two, three, or more entries, it has little meaning until the nature of the entries is known.

Although multiplication problems provide opportunities to discuss ratio informally, the concept of ratio is typically not studied until fifth grade. Although the concept of ratio is closely linked to multiplication, it is often difficult for students to make the necessary connections. For example, research shows that students often base their intuitive thinking about ratio on counting, adding, and combining. Many of these students have a fundamental misconception of ratio.

When asked to find the length of the side *L*, students frequently report 9 rather than 15:

$$\begin{array}{cc} & 5 \\ 2\ \square & \end{array} \qquad \begin{array}{c} L \\ 6\ \boxed{} \end{array}$$

Such students tend to add an amount rather than multiplying by a scale factor. Research shows that this error reflects students' cognitive function level and is not simply the result of carelessness (Cramer et al. 1993).

Suppose you are ready to extend some ideas on multiplication to develop the concept of ratio. After the students use models and complete and discuss Activity Card 14–1, you might consider how some of those tasks lead directly toward writing ratios, as presented on Activity Card 14–2.

Students are sometimes confused with the different symbols used to record ratios. This confusion can be minimized by linking the symbols to appropriate models and promoting class discussion. Chips or cut-out wheels could be used to model these tasks before ratios are written. A table might be made to help organize the information. After the ratios are recorded, guided discussion centering on the information and the situation helps children talk about the mathematics.

For example, questions such as the following will provide early practice in verbalizing and describing some of the mathematics surrounding the concept of ratio:

If I have three bicycles and six wheels, the ratio is three to six or (3, 6).

If the ratio is four to eight, how many bicycles do I have?

If the ratio is five to ten, how many wheels do I have?

If I have six bicycles, how many wheels are there? What is the ratio?

It is important that ratios be correctly applied to all types of numbers. In elementary school, however, the emphasis is typically on smaller numbers such as 1-to-2, 2-to-3, and 3-to-4. These ratios are the most frequently used and much easier to model and conceptualize than 7-to-9 or 11-to-14. Several real life examples may be examined in the counting book, *Each Orange Had 8 Slices: A Counting Book* (Giganti, 1992).

Far more important than how the ratio is expressed is the understanding of the relationship. Young children with a good understanding of num-

Activity Card 14–1

Know Your Coins

▼ Use patterns to help complete this table:

Number of

Quarters	1	2		4	5	6	□
Nickels	5	10	15	20		30	△
Pennies	25	50	75		125	150	○

- Describe a pattern you found in each row.
- Write a ratio for the number of quarters to nickels. _____
- Write a ratio for the number of nickels to pennies. _____
- Write a ratio for the number of quarters to pennies. _____

▼ Try these:

- How many nickels will be needed for 8 quarters? ____ Tell two different ways to decide.
- How many pennies will be needed for 10 quarters? ____ Tell two different ways to decide.
- Give three numbers (not shown in the table) that could go

  in the △ row _____

  in the ○ row _____
- Give three numbers that could *not* go

  in the △ row _____

  in the ○ row _____
- How many quarters would you have

  when □+△+○ first exceeds $50? _____

bers use "twice as much" just as often and as comfortably as "half as much." Instruction should take advantage of these different expressions to develop further reversible thinking.

Activity Card 14–2

Ratios, Ratios, Ratios, . . .

▼ Write a ratio to compare three bicycles with wheels.

• There are ____ bicycles and ____ wheels.

• We can write this ratio as _____ or _____ .

▼ Write a ratio to compare four bicycles with wheels.

• There are ____ bicycles and ____ wheels.

• We can write this ratio as _____ or _____ .

▼ Write another ratio comparing bicycles with wheels.

_____

▼ Choose a tricycle or wagon.

• Write an appropriate ratio. _____

▼ Suppose you chose a unicycle.

• Write the ratio. _____

• Tell what makes this ratio special.

▼ Write a ratio to compare the number of wheels

• on a bicycle and a wagon _____

• on a tricycle and a wagon _____

● Proportions

Proportions are two or more equal ratios and are frequently used in problem situations. Consider, for example, this problem:

SALE

Hot Cross Buns
3 for 49¢

About how much will a dozen cost?

In approaching such a problem, using words along with numerical symbols helps children not only organize the information but also understand it more clearly. It is helpful, too, to get students to think and talk about reasonable answers before getting into specific computation. For example, children might think:

$\frac{1}{4}$ dozen is almost 50¢, so

$\frac{1}{2}$ dozen is almost \$1, so

1 dozen will be almost \$2

Such thinking is very productive. It should be both encouraged and rewarded. It uses estimation along with ratios to produce ballpark answers. Frequent experiences similar to this will improve students' judgment, making them less likely to fall victim to unreasonable answers resulting from indiscriminate number crunching.

Students also should realize that a single situation can be represented by several proportions. For example, here are some ways of writing proportions for the hot cross buns:

$$\frac{3}{49} = \frac{12}{\Box} \qquad 3{:}49 = 12{:}\Box$$

$$\frac{3}{12} = \frac{49}{\Box} \qquad 3{:}12 = 49{:}\Box$$

$$\frac{49}{3} = \frac{\Box}{12} \qquad 49{:}3 = \Box{:}12$$

$$\frac{12}{3} = \frac{\Box}{49} \qquad 12{:}3 = \Box{:}49$$

Although students should recognize the equivalence of these statements, they should feel free to use the form of their choice.

The pennies–nickels comparisons shown in Activity Card 14–1 contain many equivalent ratios (1:5 = 2:10, 2:10 = 3:15, and so on). The concept of equivalent ratios is very important and can be anchored in different ways. For example, Activity Card 14–3 provides practice exercises that a child could model with objects or solve using technology to promote and reward the discovery of patterns.

After equivalent ratios are established, they can be used in a variety of ways. For example, comparative shopping relies heavily on determining which of two (or more) ratios is lower. Suppose the same product is packaged in two different sizes:

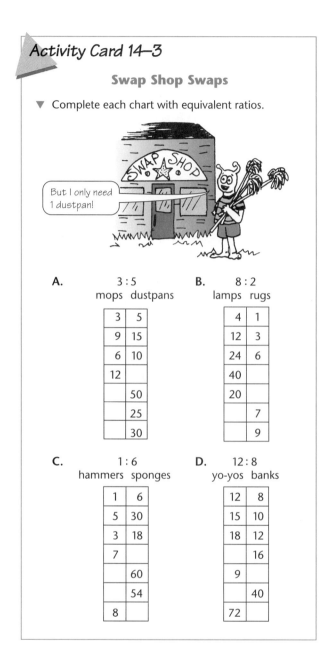

Activity Card 14–3

Swap Shop Swaps

▼ Complete each chart with equivalent ratios.

But I only need 1 dustpan!

A. 3 : 5
mops   dustpans

mops	dustpans
3	5
9	15
6	10
12	
	50
25	
30	

B. 8 : 2
lamps   rugs

lamps	rugs
4	1
12	3
24	6
40	
20	
	7
	9

C. 1 : 6
hammers   sponges

hammers	sponges
1	6
5	30
3	18
7	
	60
	54
8	

D. 12 : 8
yo-yos   banks

yo-yos	banks
12	8
15	10
18	12
	16
9	
	40
72	

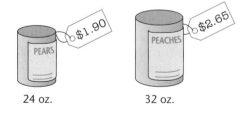

PEARS $1.90   PEACHES $2.65
24 oz.   32 oz.

Do the two cans have the same unit price?

Although this question can be solved in different ways, it involves ratios. More specifically, are these ratios equal?

$$\frac{\$1.90}{24} \overset{?}{=} \frac{\$2.65}{32}$$

This problem can be solved several ways, but one of the most natural is by finding equivalent ratios:

$$\frac{\$1.90 \times 4}{24 \times 4} = \frac{\$7.60}{96} \qquad \frac{\$2.65 \times 3}{32 \times 3} = \frac{\$7.95}{96}$$

Ratios are not equal

A calculator also could be used to demonstrate that $1.90 \div 24 \neq 2.65 \div 32$, so the ratios are unequal. Because the ratios are not equal, the prices are not equivalent.

Many problems involving proportions are solved mentally without any paper-and-pencil computation. This approach should be encouraged whenever possible. However, when the computation becomes too messy, the proportion can be solved algorithmically. Activity Card 14–4 highlights two different mental strategies. Providing two ways of solving proportions mentally encourages students to analyze the problem situation before choosing an approach to use. Figure 14–1 illustrates how some students solved the first two proportion problems on Activity Card 14–4. Notice that, although not all solutions are correct, the students tried to make sense of the problem and approached it in a way that was meaningful to them. See what you can learn about their thinking.

Consider using other real life applications such as recipes, photographs and their negatives, maps, and scale drawings or models. Activity Card 14–5 provides opportunities for students to use measurement skills along with ratios in some practical problem solving.

The concepts of ratio and proportionality can be naturally connected to geometry problems. One natural and powerful connection to geometry uses similarity. Two figures are similar if their respective sides are in the same ratio—that is, proportional. Thus, all squares are similar, but all rectangles are not.

Look for some patterns in the similar triangles in Figure 14–2. Triangle A is similar to triangle B because the extended ratios 1:2:4 and 2:4:8 are equal. Likewise, triangles B and C are similar. Now let's use triangles D and E for some additional problem solving. If triangle D is similar to A, describe how to find the length of the longest side of D. If triangle E is also similar to A, describe how the lengths of its other two sides can be found. Because the resulting ratios for E involve multiples of five, these values could be related to the ratios for coins on Activity

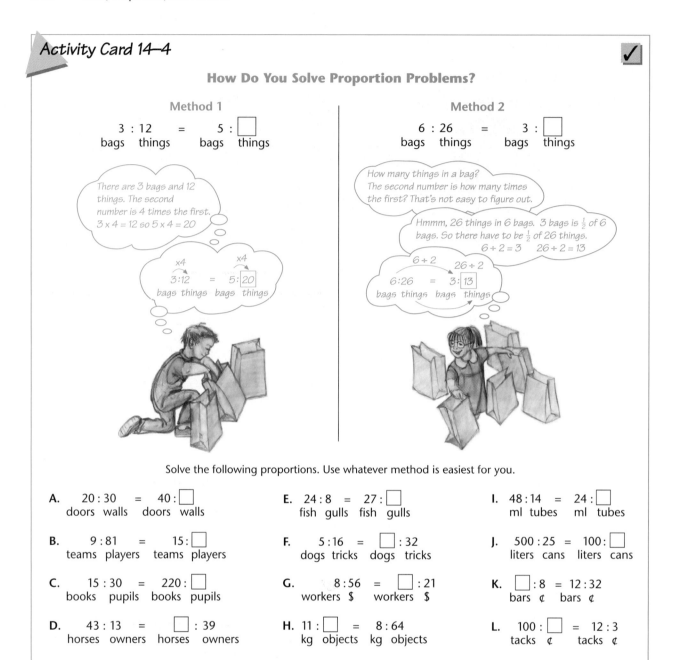

Activity Card 14–4

How Do You Solve Proportion Problems?

Method 1

$$3 : 12 \;=\; 5 : \square$$
bags things bags things

There are 3 bags and 12 things. The second number is 4 times the first. 3 × 4 = 12 so 5 × 4 = 20

×4   ×4
$$3:12 \;=\; 5:\boxed{20}$$
bags things bags things

Method 2

$$6 : 26 \;=\; 3 : \square$$
bags things bags things

How many things in a bag? The second number is how many times the first? That's not easy to figure out.

Hmmm, 26 things in 6 bags. 3 bags is ½ of 6 bags. So there have to be ½ of 26 things.
6 ÷ 2 = 3   26 ÷ 2 = 13

6 ÷ 2   26 ÷ 2
$$6:26 \;=\; 3:\boxed{13}$$
bags things bags things

Solve the following proportions. Use whatever method is easiest for you.

A. $20 : 30 \;=\; 40 : \square$
doors walls doors walls

B. $9 : 81 \;=\; 15 : \square$
teams players teams players

C. $15 : 30 \;=\; 220 : \square$
books pupils books pupils

D. $43 : 13 \;=\; \square : 39$
horses owners horses owners

E. $24 : 8 \;=\; 27 : \square$
fish gulls fish gulls

F. $5 : 16 \;=\; \square : 32$
dogs tricks dogs tricks

G. $8 : 56 \;=\; \square : 21$
workers $ workers $

H. $11 : \square \;=\; 8 : 64$
kg objects kg objects

I. $48 : 14 \;=\; 24 : \square$
ml tubes ml tubes

J. $500 : 25 \;=\; 100 : \square$
liters cans liters cans

K. $\square : 8 \;=\; 12 : 32$
bars ¢ bars ¢

L. $100 : \square \;=\; 12 : 3$
tacks ¢ tacks ¢

Card 14–1. This activity illustrates multiembodiment and reminds students that the same numerical patterns can occur in very different settings.

An interesting application of ratio and proportion appears in architectural designs. The ratio of the sides of the rectangle varies, but one ratio, known as the golden ratio, has occurred in many architectural structures and works of art.

Children's books such as *Anno's Math Games* (Anno 1987) provide different yet interesting contexts to explore ratio and proportions and connect them to percent. Other books such as *In One Day* (Parker 1984) encourage students to think about different ways of relating numbers.

● Percents

One need only read a newspaper or watch television to be reminded that percent is one of the most widely used mathematical concepts:

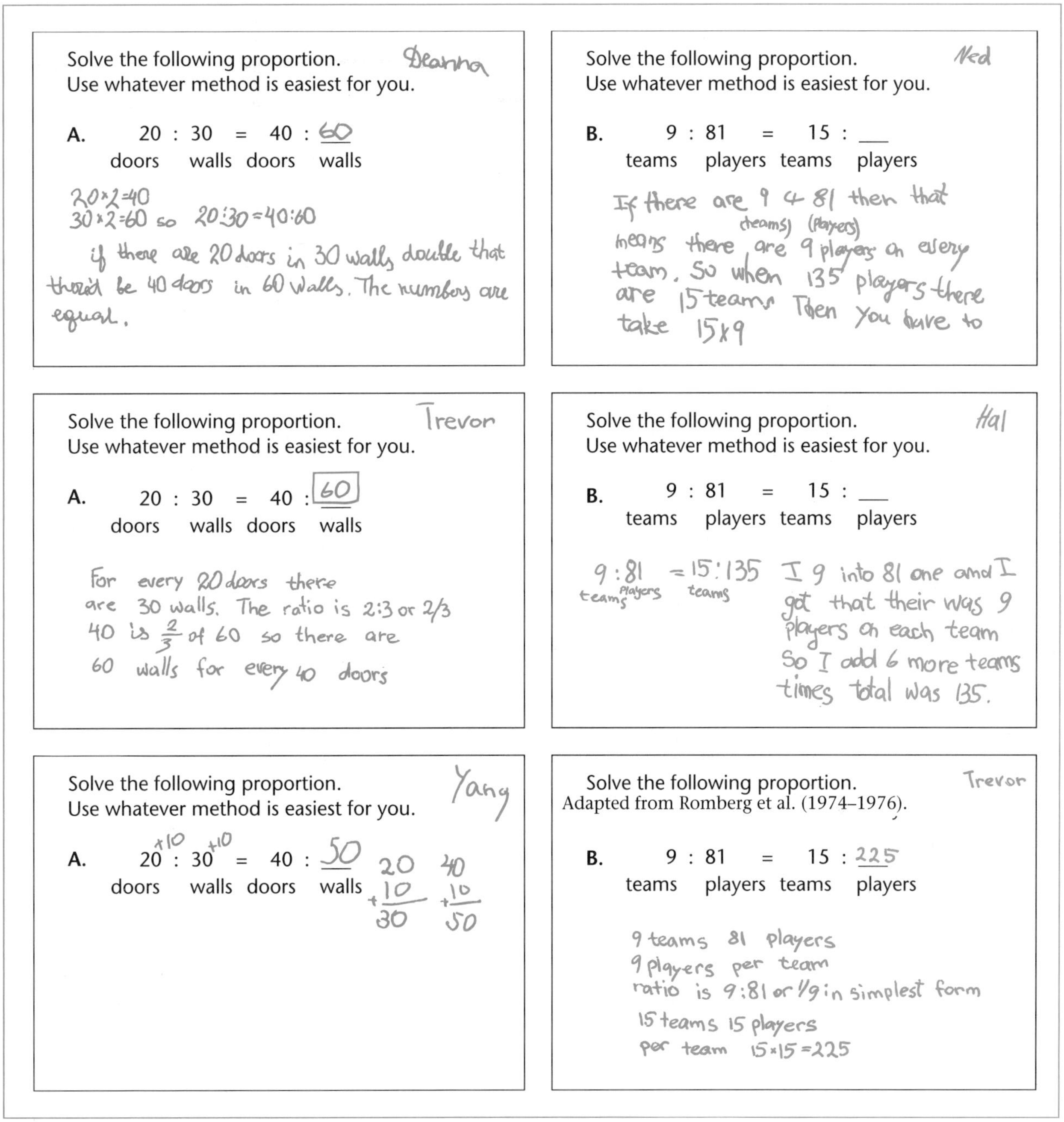

Solve the following proportion. *Deanna*
Use whatever method is easiest for you.

A.   20 : 30   =   40 : 60
      doors   walls   doors   walls

20×2=40
30×2=60 so   20:30 = 40:60

if there are 20 doors in 30 walls. double that there'd be 40 doors in 60 Walls. The numbers are equal.

Solve the following proportion. *Ned*
Use whatever method is easiest for you.

B.   9 : 81   =   15 : ___
      teams   players   teams   players

If there are 9 & 81 then that
            (teams) (players)
means there are 9 players on every team. So when 135 players there are 15 teams. Then you have to take 15×9

Solve the following proportion. *Trevor*
Use whatever method is easiest for you.

A.   20 : 30   =   40 : 60
      doors   walls   doors   walls

For every 20 doors there are 30 walls. The ratio is 2:3 or 2/3
40 is $\frac{2}{3}$ of 60 so there are 60 walls for every 40 doors

---

Solve the following proportion. *Hal*
Use whatever method is easiest for you.

B.   9 : 81   =   15 : ___
      teams   players   teams   players

9 : 81 = 15 : 135   I 9 into 81 one and I
teams players   teams   got that their was 9 players on each team So I add 6 more teams times total was 135.

Solve the following proportion. *Yang*
Use whatever method is easiest for you.

A.   20 : 30   =   40 : 50
      doors   walls   doors   walls

$\begin{array}{cc} 20 & 40 \\ +10 & +10 \\ \hline 30 & 50 \end{array}$

Solve the following proportion. *Trevor*
Adapted from Romberg et al. (1974–1976).

B.   9 : 81   =   15 : 225
      teams   players   teams   players

9 teams 81 players
9 players per team
ratio is 9:81 or 1/9 in simplest form
15 teams 15 players
per team   15×15 = 225

Figure 14–1 • Samples of students' solutions to proportion problems

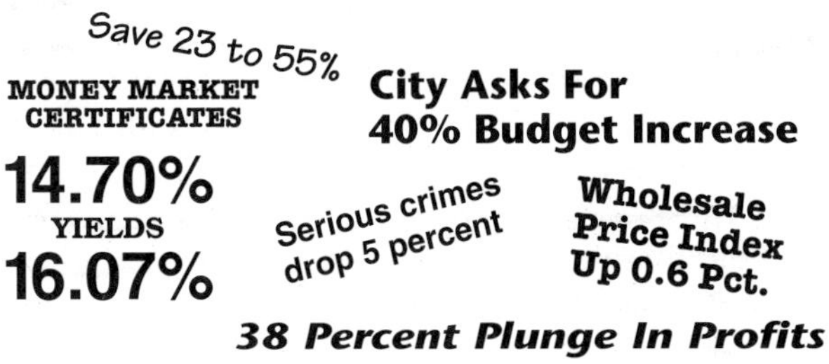

Understanding of percent is taken for granted, even though there is plenty of evidence to the contrary. Incorrect usage of percent is frequent among both secondary students and adults. Flagrant errors abound, suggesting that often the most basic ideas are unclear. For example, consider the following question (Carpenter et al. 1978):

If 5% of the students are absent today, then 5 out of how many are absent?

Activity Card 14–5

Draw Your Classroom

▼ First measure your classroom.

▼ Next decide on a scale to use.

▼ Now make a scale drawing of the room.

• Show where doors, windows, tables, and desks are located.

• Be sure to put your scale on your drawing, such as 1 in. : 5 ft   or   1 cm : 1 m

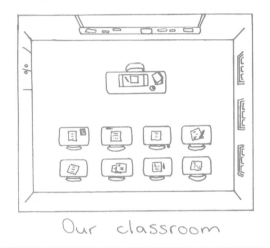

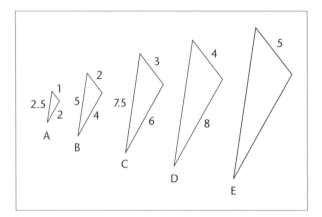

Figure 14–2 • **Some similar triangles**

Carpenter et al. (1978) reported that about one-third of the seventeen-year-olds and adults missed this question; apparently they did not know that 100 is the comparison base for percent. Low performance is found in other countries also. About half

of the sixth graders tested in Japan correctly reported 100% of 48 (Reys and Reys 1993).

Misconceptions, distortions, and confusion surrounding percent are surprisingly easy to find. Here are examples:

1. "Prices reduced 100%." If this advertisement were correct, the items would be free. Probably the prices were reduced 50%. If an item that originally cost $400 was on sale for $200, then the ad based the 100% on the sale price, when it should have been based on the original price.

2. "Of all doctors interviewed, 75% recommended our product." This type of claim could be an effective advertisement for a company. If, however, the ad said "3 out of the 4 doctors we interviewed recommended our product," the consumer reaction might be different. Percents can often be used to disguise the number involved. Thus, they can be misused. Percents allow for easy comparisons because of the common base of one hundred, but they may appear to represent a larger sample than actually exists.

Discussing the following questions and providing real-life examples can help students develop a number sense for percents.

• Can you eat 50% of a cake?
• Can you eat 100% of a cake?
• Can you eat 150% of a cake?

• Can a price increase 50%?
• Can a price increase 100%?
• Can a price increase 150%?

• Can a price decrease 50%?
• Can a price decrease 100%?
• Can a price decrease 150%?

Ironically, the understanding of percent requires no new skills or concepts beyond those used in mastering fractions, decimals, and ratios. In fact, percent is not really a mathematical topic, but rather the application of a particular type of notational system. The justification for teaching percent in school mathematics programs rests solely on its social utility. Consequently, percent should be taught and learned in application situations similar to the one given in the Snapshot of a Lesson at the beginning of this chapter. Because the primary objective is to solve problems involving percent, the use of calculators would be appropriate and would allow students to focus on the concepts of percents rather than get bogged down in the written algorithm for multiplication. Special function keys such as the percent key and the memory keys also could be introduced.

As is true with decimals and fractions, percents express a relationship between two numbers. Percents are special ratios based on 100 and without a doubt are the most widely used of all ratios. Percent is derived from the Latin words *per centum,* which mean "out of a hundred" or "for every hundred." Thus, the origin of percent and its major uses are more closely associated with ratio than with either decimals or fractions.

When is percent understood? Students understand percent when they can use it many different ways. For instance, if a child understands 25%, he or she can do the following.

1. Find 25% in various contexts:

   Cover 25% of a floor with tiles.

   Determine 25% off the price of a given item.

   Survey 25% of the students in class.

In many such situations, estimates of 25% are not only appropriate but essential.

2. Identify characteristics of 25%:

   25% of the milk in a glass is less than half.

   If 25% of the milk in a glass is spilled, then 75% remains.

3. Compare and contrast 25% with a range of other percents and numbers such as 5%, 50%, 100%, one-fourth, one-half, and 0.25.

   25% is half as much as 50%, one-fourth as much as 100%, five times as much as 5%, less than one-half, and the same as one-fourth and twenty-five hundredths.

Understanding Percents

Percents should be introduced only after students thoroughly understand fractions and decimals and have had experiences with ratios. Percent is not studied extensively in elementary school, although it is typically introduced in fifth or sixth grade.

Initially, students need a variety of experiences with the fundamental concepts of percent, and these experiences should be connected to various concrete models. Computation applying percent in problem-solving situations is generally reserved for later. Lembke found that students naturally use benchmarks to make initial judgments about percent situations (Lembke and Reys 1994). Those students who understood that percent means parts out of one hundred and had a good pictorial representation of percent were more successful in solving percent problems than those who did not. Helping students develop the concepts for common percent benchmarks and their fraction and decimal equivalents such as 10%, 25%, 33%, 50%, and 75% will help them apply their percent number sense to problem-solving situations.

Initial instruction should build on familiar models. A dollar is made up of one hundred cents; therefore, it provides a natural connection among percents, fractions, and decimals. For example, 25 cents is $0.25, one-fourth of a dollar, and also 25% of a dollar.

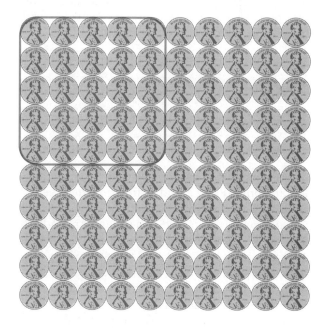

This model should be expanded to illustrate a wide range of percents, such as 50 percent, 90 percent, 5 percent, 100 percent, 99 percent, 1 percent, and 200 percent. These percents should be illustrated with a variety of different situations and models. For example, a meter stick provides an easily accessible and effective model. Cover part of the meter stick with blue paper and ask children to estimate the percent of the meter stick that is covered.

Students could be shown the meter stick face down (if the scale is on both sides, cover one side with masking tape) and then asked:

Estimate what percent of the meter stick is blue.

About what percent of the meter stick is not blue?

How can we check our estimate? [Turn the stick over.]

This model allows many different situations (25%, 50%, 1%, and so forth) to be presented and discussed quickly. Patterns may also emerge as students realize that the sum of the covered and uncovered portions will always total 100 percent. Shaded fraction circles (Appendix B) also can be used to provide multiembodiment and help students see connections between fractions and percents.

A related activity involving area could have students using a stack of twenty cards with the B side down. On the A side, specific percents of the card are colored blue (0%, 10%, 20%, . . . , 100%), with the remainder (100%, . . . , 0%) white.

Side A

Side B
30%

Ask students to take turns trying to win cards by looking only at side A and trying to predict the percents shown on side B. Eleven-peg geoboards or four five-peg geoboards placed in a square (Appendix B) also may be used to model percents. Lesson Card 14–1 provides some additional tasks that use models to develop important concepts about percent. Each of these tasks provides ideas that can be used to relate percents and fractions.

These early experiences with percent should be followed by activities that center around direct translation experiences involving 100. The national assessment data revealed that only 68 percent and 31 percent of seventh graders correctly wrote the decimals 0.42 and 0.9, respectively, as percents. These data remind us of the fragile nature of students' understanding and the importance of connecting percents with decimals and fractions. Having students use base-ten blocks or share decimal paper (Appendix B) provides another concrete model for percents and helps students see the connections between decimals and percents. Figure 14–3 illustrates how the same diagram can be repre-

Lesson Card 14–1

Using Percent Models

Materials: Several different models, each of which displays clearly the 100 parts in a whole.

Activity: Pose additional questions to accompany the following teacher-led discussions.

1. Construct a model that has 100 parts but at the same time has the potential of displaying equivalent subsets of these 100 elements. Here are two models:

Rope with 100 discs arranged 10 black, 10 red, 10 black, 10 red, ...   Rectangle 5 × 20 with all small squares as shown.

2. Find representations of various percents on each model. For example, when representing 50 percent, help students realize that any 50 of the parts could be chosen — for example, in either of the two ways shown here:

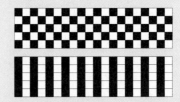

3. Have students consider the model as a whole and ask for all the fractions that show the same amount as 50 percent. Write the results on the board:

Fifty percent — 50%

$\frac{1}{2}$ $\frac{50}{100}$ $\frac{5}{10}$

4. Repeat step 3 using 20 percent:

Twenty percent — 20%

$\frac{2}{10}$ $\frac{1}{5}$ $\frac{20}{100}$

5. Compare the representations for 50 percent and 20 percent on each model. Ask questions such as

● Which is greater, 50 or 20 percent?

● What fractional part is covered by 20 percent?

● What fractional part remains uncovered?

6. Any multiple of 10 can be illustrated easily with these models. Continue to model different percents and their corresponding fractions until generalizations of these relationships are established.

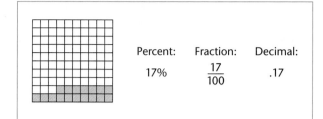

Figure 14–3 • Model and symbolizations of 17%

sented symbolically by a fraction, a decimal, and a percent. It should be emphasized that each small square represents 1% and the large square represents 100%. Practice activities using this model to convert percents to fractions and decimals, and vice versa, should be plentiful. Calculators which convert fractions, decimals, and percents are useful when students are discovering patterns and relationships.

For example, Figure 14–3 provides a visual reminder that 17% can also be thought of as $17 \times \frac{1}{100}$, so the symbol % can be thought of as equivalent to the fraction $\frac{1}{100}$. Also, 17% can be thought of as $\frac{17}{100}$, so the concept of ratio is reinforced. This helps students feel comfortable with different interpretations of percent.

The importance of establishing 100 as the base for percent cannot be overemphasized, and 50% should be recognized as the fraction $\frac{50}{100}$ or the product $50 \times \frac{1}{100}$. However, it is also important that students know that an infinite number of equivalent fractions ($\frac{1}{2}$, $\frac{2}{4}$, $\frac{3}{6}$, . . . , $\frac{50}{100}$, . . .) also represent 50%.

Activity Card 14–6 provides a natural means of developing some important ideas in an informal and yet meaningfully structured way. Each of the four activities should further develop children's concept of percent. Activities B, C, and D require some collection and recording of data prior to reporting the percents. The use of three different base numbers (10 logs, 100 pennies, and 20 chips) will strengthen the link between ratio and percent. Even though answers on each activity depend on the data recorded, some patterns will emerge. A few questions from the teacher should trigger some stimulating discussion. For example, do the percents in each item total 100%? Why does this happen? Can you think of a time when it would not?

One particularly troublesome aspect of percents involves small percents between 0 percent and 1 percent. For example, $\frac{1}{2}$ percent, as in "$\frac{1}{2}$ percent milk fat," is not well understood. A visual representation, as in Figure 14–4, can help show that $\frac{1}{2}$ per-

Activity Card 14–6

Using Percents

A. Color this circle:
- 25% red
- 50% blue

What percent is uncolored? ____

B. Use 3 colors:
- Blue
- Green
- Yellow

Color each log with only one color. Color all logs.

	Number Colored	Percent Colored
Blue	____	____
Green	____	____
Yellow	____	____

C. Take 100 pennies, shake, and toss them in a box. Count the number of heads.

	Number	Percent
Heads	____	____
Tails	____	____

Did you need to count the tails? ____

D. Here are 20 poker chips. Count the number of each color.

	Number	Percent
Blue	____	____
Black	____	____
White	____	____

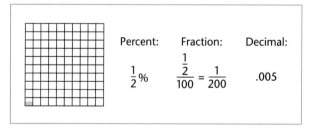

Figure 14–4 • Model and symbolizations of $\frac{1}{2}$%

cent is indeed less than 1 percent. Understanding rests on the earlier agreement that each small square represents 1 percent, which cannot be mentioned too often. As is true with all percents, this percent also can be shown symbolically as a fraction or a decimal. However, it is more important in elemen-

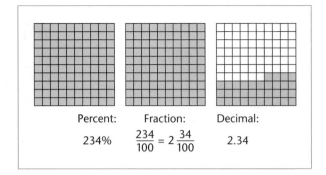

Figure 14–5 • **Model and symbolizations of 234%**

tary school to establish the intuitive notion of relative size of small percents than to devote extensive time to the algebraic gymnastics of showing the fraction and decimal equivalents.

Development of percents greater than 100 percent also is challenging and should be illustrated with models. Once the idea is established that a given region represents 100 percent, more than one such region can be used to represent percents greater than 100 percent. For example, 234 percent could be represented by two completely shaded large squares and a partially shaded one (see Figure 14–5). Using every opportunity to show equivalence of percents, fractions, and decimals helps establish and maintain these relationships.

Applying Percents

In elementary school, students should solve percent problems meaningfully and avoid rushing toward symbolic methods. As mentioned in Chapter 9, children develop number sense when encouraged to think flexibly about numbers and solve problems using strategies that are meaningful to them. Whenever possible, students should be asked to discuss how to solve percent problems mentally using what they know about common percent benchmarks. Even when a formal method is required, using informal methods first to obtain an estimate will help students focus on the reasonableness of results obtained by formal methods.

Although percents are regularly encountered in many real-life problem-solving situations, only three basic types of problems involve percents. Several different formal methods can be used to solve percent problems, and we will illustrate two of them typically found in elementary and middle school textbooks—equation and ratio. The effective use of

these methods requires a firm understanding of the concepts of percent and ratio as well as the ability to solve simple equations and proportions. Such skills are developed over a period of several years and need not be rushed.

In the equation method, the following equation is used:

$$\text{percent} \times \text{total} = \text{part}$$

The two known values are placed in the equation and one solves the equation for the third, unknown value.

In the ratio method, we know that a (part) is b (percent) of c (total). The variables are set up as equal ratios or a proportion:

$$\frac{b \ (\text{percent})}{100} = \frac{a \ (\text{part})}{c \ (\text{total})}$$

The three known values are placed into the proportion and one solves for the fourth, unknown value.

Now let's take a brief look at each of the three types of percent problems and how they may be solved using both informal and formal methods:

1. **Finding the percent of a given number.**

   Lucas receives $60 a month for a paper route, and next month he will get a 10 percent raise. How much will his raise be?

The context of this problem suggests that the raise will be something considerably less than $60. The situation might be solved mentally or modeled as shown in Figure 14–6.

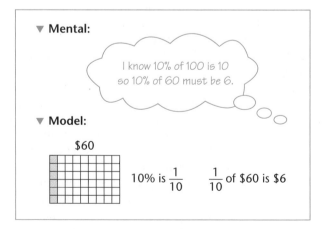

Figure 14–6 • **Use of mental strategy or model for finding a percent of a number**

This problem could also be solved in these ways:

Ratio method: $\dfrac{10\%}{100\%} = \dfrac{R}{60}$ $R = \$6$

Equation method: $R = 10\%$ of $\$60$
$$R = .1 \times \$60$$
$$= \$6$$

The computation is simple and may disguise the level of difficulty this type of problem presents. Only about one-third of the seventh graders were successful at solving this type of problem on the fourth national assessment.

2. Find what percent one number is of another number.

The Cardinals won 15 of their 20 games. What percent did they win?

Intuitively, it is clear that the Cardinals did not win all their games, so the answer must be less than 100 percent. Similarly, they won more than half their games, so it must be more than 50 percent. The situation could be solved mentally or modeled as shown in Figure 14–7.

Here are two other ways to find the solution:

Ratio method: $\dfrac{P\%}{100\%} = \dfrac{15}{20}$ $P = 75\%$

Equation method: $P \times 20 = 15$
$$P = \dfrac{15}{20} \times 5$$
$$= \dfrac{75}{100} = 75\%$$

Once again the computation is easy, but the national assessment provides a reminder of the difficulty students have with percent. For example, 43 percent of seventh graders correctly answered "30 is what percent of 60?" but only 20 percent correctly answered "9 is what percent of 225?"

3. Find the total (100%) when only a percent is known.

The sale price on a coat was $40, and it was marked down 50%. What was its original price?

Common sense suggests that the original price should be more than $40. Guess-and-test is often a very effective strategy in solving this type of problem. For example, if children guess an original price of $60, then the sale price of $30 is too low. Still, they are on the right track; and, if this approach is continued, it will eventually lead to the correct price of $80. The problem could be solved mentally or modeled as shown in Figure 14–8. The model provides a base for either of these solutions, where *OP* is the original price:

Ratio method: $\dfrac{50\%}{100\%} = \dfrac{\$40}{OP}$ $OP = \$80$

Equation method: 50% of $OP = \$40$
$$OP = \dfrac{\$40}{50} \times 2$$
$$= \dfrac{80}{100} = 80\%$$

This type of problem is typically more difficult to solve, as was confirmed by results from the fourth

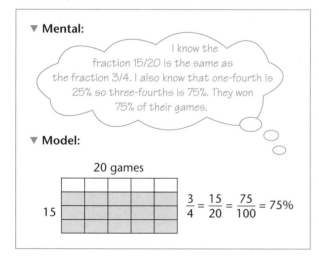

Figure 14–7 • Use of mental strategy or model for finding what percent one number is of another number

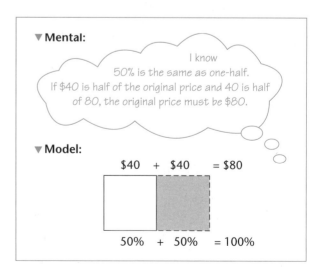

Figure 14–8 • Use of mental strategy or model for finding the total when only a percent is known

national mathematics assessment (Lindquist et al. 1988). Less than 22 percent of the seventh graders correctly answered a question of this type.

The consistently poor performance on percent problems means that instruction must become more meaningful. If emphasis is placed on a particular method before the problem is thought through and well understood, the result will probably be confusion and poor performance. Instructional emphasis in elementary school must be on thinking aloud and talking about what should be done and what would be a reasonable answer. These teacher-led discussions should occur before any serious efforts are made to solve the problem with pencil and paper. Early emphasis on writing a solution to a percent problem forces many students to operate mechanically (without any conscious thinking) on the numbers to produce an answer.

Students should be encouraged to think quantitatively in solving problems involving percent. Research does not support the teaching of a single method (such as ratio or equation) to solve such problems. Instruction, therefore, should be flexible and not locked into a single method. It is recommended that a variety of problems involving percent be presented and then student leads followed flexibly toward solutions. More specifically, some verbalization of the solution should accompany the actual problem-solving process. This helps clarify what was done (either right or wrong) and provides some closure to the process. It also promotes consideration of the reasonableness of an answer.

This less formal, intuitive approach lacks the structure and security of emphasizing a particular method. Yet it has several important advantages. In particular, it encourages students to understand the problem in their own minds along with possible solutions, and it decreases the likelihood of their applying a method blindly.

▶ A Glance at Where We've Been

Ratios compare two or more numbers. They take different forms and have many applications—money (pennies for nickels), measurements (12 inches in a foot), consumer purchases (3 for 29¢), scale drawings, and blueprints are but a few. Together with proportion, ratios provide an opportunity to practice many computational skills as well as strengthen problem-solving skills. Ratios also provide a natural means of studying percent, which has a comparison base of 100. Since few mathematical topics have more practical usage than percents, it is essential

that meaningful and systematic development of percent be provided. Instruction should include the use of concrete models that support the development of number sense.

▶ THINGS TO DO: From What You've Read

1. Give a real-life example of a ratio and a proportion. How could you help children distinguish between them?

2. Describe how estimating the number of heartbeats in an hour or in a lifetime uses ratios. How could you use a calculator or a spreadsheet to solve the problem?

3. Describe how you could use a meter stick, graduated in millimeters, to illustrate each of the following percents:
   a. 35 percent
   b. 3.5 percent
   c. 0.35 percent

4. Make up a story for each of these sentences:
   a. $\dfrac{5}{12} = \dfrac{x}{\$1.80}$
   b. 40% of 95 = ☐

5. Rose was making $26,000 a year. She received a 10 percent raise. Later in the year, the company started losing money and reduced all salaries 10 percent. Rose said, "I'm making less money than last year." Is her thinking correct? Tell why.

6. In our discussion of percent problems, we emphasized the importance of talking or thinking through a solution before setting up equations to solve. Is this in the spirit of communication advocated in the *Curriculum and Evaluation Standards for School Mathematics* (NCTM 1989)? Tell why.

7. Here is a partially completed chart:

Decimal	Fraction	Percent
—	—	5%
.1	¹⁄₁₀	10%
—	¹⁄₄	—
.333 . . .	—	—
.5	—	—
—	²⁄₃	—
—	—	75%

Explain why it would be helpful to have students learn these popular percents and their related fraction and decimal forms.

8. Describe how you would think through a solution to this problem: the population of a city increased from 200,000 to 220,000. What is the percent increase?

9. Suppose you ask a student to enlarge the 1×2 rectangle shown here, and a 2×4 rectangle is correctly produced. Then you ask the student to enlarge it again so the base is 6. The student draws a 4×6 rectangle and says, "If I doubled it, the base would have been 8, so I added 2 on and the other side is 4." Would you say this student is an "adder" or a "multiplier"? Describe some additional questions you might ask to gain more insight into this student's understanding of ratio.

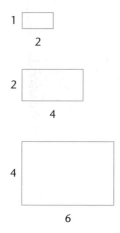

THINGS TO DO: Going Beyond This Book

1. Examine an elementary textbook series. Identify the grade level at which ratios are first introduced. Describe the models used to help students develop the concept of ratio. Check the next grade level of the same series, and describe how the concept of ratio is extended.

2. Many excellent articles on ratio, proportion, and percent appear in *Arithmetic Teacher, Teaching Children Mathematics,* and *Mathematics Teaching in the Middle School.* Conduct an ERIC search, select an article, then prepare an activity card based on it to help children learn a particular concept.

3. Examine *Similarity and Equivalent Fractions* from the Middle Grades Mathematics Project (Lappan et al. 1986). Choose a lesson that you think would help students develop the concept of ratio. Try it with a group of students and share your experiences.

4. Ratios may be used to determine the best buy. Use local newspaper advertisements to find information and set up ratios to compare prices for different sizes of the same product. Can you refute the claim "the larger the quantity, the lower the unit price"?

5. Read the article, "Our Diets May Be Killing Us" by Shannon (1995) or "Integrating Mathematics and Literature in the Elementary Classroom" by Kliman (1993). Describe how you could use ideas like those to make a ratio or percent lesson.

6. Describe how the white, red, purple, and brown Cuisenaire rods could be used to develop ratios. Describe several different equivalent ratios that could be made with these rods.

7. Read the article, "Let's Do It! From Blocks and Model Making to Ratio and Proportion" by Bruni and Silverman (1977). Describe some of the activities that could be used to develop ratio and proportion concepts with young children.

8. Examine some of the material in *Ratio, Proportion and Scaling* (Mathematics Resource Project 1977). Summarize and share some ideas you find for lessons.

9. Review *The Wonderful World of Mathematics* (Thiessen and Matthias 1992). Several books focus on multiplication and division and use these concepts to develop ratio or proportion. Choose one of the books to read with some children and describe how they reacted.

10. Read one of the research articles related to ratio and proportion listed in the reviews by Cramer et al. (1993) or Behr et al. (1992). Discuss the nature of the research. Also identify an instructional idea or activity suggested by the research that you think would be effective in helping children learn a particular concept.

11. In an elementary textbook series, examine a lesson which involves solving percent problems. What formal method is introduced? Identify problems in the lesson which can be solved using the informal methods discussed in this chapter.

12. Read the counting book, *Each Orange Had 8 Slices: A Counting Book* by Giganti listed in the Children's Corner. Design some ratio problems children could solve for some of the pages. Try out the lesson with some children.

13. Develop a spreadsheet similar to those in the article by Hoeffner et al. (1990) which will allow children to solve some real-life ratio and percent problems.

14. Read the articles, "Toys 'R' Math" by Tracy & Hague (1997) or "Children's Literature: Impetus for a Mathematical Adventure" by Gibbons (1996). Create a lesson using toys and try it out.

▼▼▼▼▼▼▼▼▼▼▼▼▼▼▼▼▼▼▼▼▼▼▼▼

Children's Corner

Anno, Mitsumasa. *Anno's Math Games.* New York: Philomel Books, 1987.

Anno, Mitsumasa. *Anno's Math Games II.* New York: Philomel Books, 1989.

Banks, Lynne Reid. *The Indian in the Cupboard.* New York: Avon Books, 1980.

Burns, Marilyn. *The I Hate Mathematics! Book.* Boston: Little, Brown, 1975.

Diagram Group. *Comparisons.* New York: St. Martin's Press, 1980.

Giganti, Jr., Paul. *Each Orange Had 8 Slices: A Counting Book.* New York: Greenwillow Books, a division of William Morrow & Co., 1992.

Laithwaite, Eric. *Size: The Measure of Things.* New York: Franklin Watts, 1988.

Lipscomb, Susan Drake, and Zuanich, Margaret Ann. *BASIC Fun: Computer Games, Puzzles, and Problems Children Can Write.* New York: Avon Books, 1982.

Parker, Tom. *In One Day.* Boston: Houghton-Mifflin, 1984.

Schwartz, David M. *If You Made a Million.* New York: Lothrop, Lee and Shepard Books, Division of William Morrow, 1989.

Selected References

Allinger, Glenn D., and Payne, Joseph N. "Estimation and Mental Arithmetic with Percent." *Estimation and Mental Computation,* 1986 Yearbook (ed. Harold L. Schoen). Reston, Va.: NCTM, 1986, pp. 141–155.

Behr, Merlyn J.; Harel, Guershon; Post, Thomas; and Lesh, Richard. "Rational Number, Ratio, and Proportion." In *Handbook of Research on Mathematics Teaching and Learning* (ed. Douglas A. Grouws). New York: Macmillan, 1992, pp. 296–333.

Behr, Merlyn J.; Post, Thomas R.; and Wachsmuth, Ipke. "Estimation and Children's Concept of Rational Number Size." In *Estimation and Mental Computation,* 1986 Yearbook (ed. Harold L. Schoen). Reston, Va.: NCTM, 1986, pp. 103–111.

Bennet, Albert B., and Nelson, Ted. "A Conceptual Model for Solving Percent Problems." *Mathematics Teaching in the Middle School,* 1 (April 1994), pp. 20–25.

Brown, Gerald W., and Kinney, Lucien B. "Let's Teach Them about Ratio." *Mathematics Teacher,* 66 (April 1973), pp. 352–355.

Bruni, James V., and Silverman, Helene J. "Let's Do It! From Blocks and Model Making to Ratio and Proportion." *Arithmetic Teacher,* 24 (March 1977), pp. 172–180.

Carpenter, Thomas P.; Coburn, Terrence G.; Reys, Robert E.; and Wilson, James W. *Results from the First Mathematics Assessment of the National Assessment of Education Progress.* Reston, Va.: NCTM, 1978.

Carpenter, Thomas P.; Corbitt, Mary Kay; Kepner, Henry S., Jr.; Lindquist, Mary Montgomery; and

Reys, Robert E. *Results from the Second Mathematics Assessment of the National Assessment of Educational Progress.* Reston, Va.: NCTM, 1981.

Cole, Blaine L., and Weissenfluh, Henry S. "An Analysis of Teaching Percentage." *Arithmetic Teacher,* 21 (March 1974), pp. 226–228.

Cramer, Kathleen; Post, Thomas; and Currier, Sarah. "Learning and Teaching Ratio and Proportion: Research Implications." In *Research Ideas for the Classroom: Middle Grades Mathematics* (ed. Douglas T. Owens). Reston, Va.: NCTM, and New York: Macmillan, 1993, pp. 159–178.

Gay, Susan, and Aichele, Douglas B. "Middle School Students' Understanding of Number Sense Related to Percent." *School Science and Mathematics,* 97 (January 1997), pp. 27–36.

Gibbons, Estelle. "Children's Literature: Impetus for a Mathematical Adventure." *Teaching Children Mathematics,* 3 (November 1996), pp. 142–147.

Glatzer, David J. "Teaching Percentage: Ideas and Suggestions." *Arithmetic Teacher,* 31 (February 1984), pp. 24–26.

Haubner, Mary Ann. "Percents: Developing Meaning Through Models." *Arithmetic Teacher,* 40 (December 1992), pp. 232–234.

Hauch, Eldon. "Concrete Materials for Teaching Percentage." *Arithmetic Teacher,* 1 (December 1954), pp. 9–12.

Hoeffner, Karl; Kendall, Monica; Stellenwerf, Cheryl; Thames, Pixie; and Williams, Patricia. "Problem Solving with a Spreadsheet." *Arithmetic Teacher,* 38 (November 1990), pp. 52–56.

Hoffer, Alan R. "Ratio and Proportional Thinking." In *Teaching Mathematics in Grades K–8* (ed. Thomas R. Post). Boston: Allyn and Bacon, 1988.

Kliman, Marlene. "Integrating Mathematics and Literature in the Elementary Classroom." *Arithmetic Teacher,* 40 (February 1993), pp. 318–321.

Lappan, Glenda; Fitzgerald, William; Winter, Mary Jean; and Phillips, Elizabeth. *Similarity and Equivalent Fractions.* Menlo Park, Calif.: Addison-Wesley, 1986.

Lembke, Linda O., and Reys, Barbara J. "The Development of, and Interaction between, Intuitive and School-Taught Ideas about Percent." *Journal for Research in Mathematics Education,* 25 (May 1994), pp. 237–259.

Lindquist, Mary M.; Brown, Catherine A.; Carpenter, Thomas P.; Kouba, Vicky L.; Silver, Edward A.; and Swafford, Jane O. *Results from the Fourth Mathematics Assessment of the National Assessment of Educational Progress.* Reston, Va.: NCTM, 1988.

Mathematics Resource Project. *Ratio, Proportion and Scaling.* Palo Alto, Calif.: Creative Publications, 1977.

National Council of Teachers of Mathematics. *Curriculum and Evaluation Standards for School Mathematics.* Reston, Va.: NCTM, 1989.

Quintero, Ana Melvia. "Helping Children Understand Ratios." *Arithmetic Teacher,* 34 (May 1987), pp. 17–21.

Reys, Barbara J., and Reys, Robert E. *Mental Computation Performance and Strategy Use of Japanese Students in Grades 2, 4, 6 and 8.* Final Report NSF Int9000203. Columbia, Mo.: University of Missouri, 1993.

Romberg, Thomas A.; Harvey, John G.; Moser, James M.; and Montgomery, Mary E. *Developing Mathematical Processes* (DMP). Chicago: Rand McNally, 1974–1976.

Shannon, Brenda K. "Our Diets May Be Killing Us." *Mathematics Teaching in the Middle School,* 1 (April–May 1995), pp. 376–382.

Thiessen, Diane, and Matthias, Margaret. *The Wonderful World of Mathematics: A Critically Annotated List of Children's Books in Mathematics.* Reston, Va.: NCTM, 1992.

Tracy, Dyanne M., and Hague, Mary S. "Toys 'R' Math." *Mathematics Teaching in the Middle School,* 2 (January 1997), pp. 141–145+.

Wiebe, James H. "Manipulating Percentages." *Mathematics Teacher,* 79 (January 1986), pp. 23–26.

15

Using Data

 ## Snapshot of a Lesson

Key Ideas

1. Construct graphs.

2. Promote graph-reading skills.

3. Increase awareness and importance of different scales on graph.

Necessary Materials

Several different colors of blocks, sheets of graph paper, and markers or crayons.

Orientation

Children need opportunities to build and construct graphs. This second-grade lesson provides some valuable experiences and, while doing so, moves naturally from concrete toward symbolic representation of data. Graphs trigger many questions that help develop graph-reading skills and lead to better understanding of data. The teacher knows that involving students in collecting data and formulating questions is an important part of problem solving.

> TEACHER: We have been keeping track of the children absent from our classroom. These blocks show the number absent each day last week. Let's graph this information on grid paper.

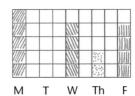

Daily absences in our class last week

Look at our graph carefully. I want you to ask a question that could be answered from this graph. Bob, your hand was up first.

BOB: How many students were sick in our school?

GLORIA (after a long wait): The graph doesn't answer that question. It only shows information about our room.

TEACHER: That's right, Gloria. This graph only shows what happened in our room. Also, it doesn't tell us how many were sick, only how many were absent. That reminds us to read the title of the graph so that everyone will know what it represents. Now, let's hear another question. Aaron?

314

AARON: How many people were absent Wednesday?

SHARON: Four.

TEACHER: Doug, let's hear your question.

DOUG: On which day was everyone in class?

SHARON: Tuesday.

DOUG: That's right, because no one was absent.

TEACHER: Do you have a question, Kelly?

KELLY: Which day had the most absences?

SHARON: Monday had the most. There were five students absent.

JANE: Would next week look like this?

Other questions are posed and discussed. A bit later in the lesson, the teacher continues.

TEACHER: Let's look at the absences for the last two weeks. Here are tallies of the absences for each day.

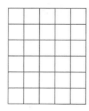

Let's make a graph of them on this paper.

SANDY: Our graph paper isn't tall enough!

TEACHER: What do you mean?

SANDY: We can only show six absences on the paper, but there were eight absences on Monday.

TEACHER: Could we do any trading here?

SANDY: What do you mean?

TEACHER: In place value, when we get ten ones we trade for one ten.

SANDY: But we don't have ten.

TEACHER: Maybe we can make other trades. For example, we trade five pennies for a nickel or. . . .

SANDY: Two nickels for a dime.

SHARON: I got it—we can trade two absences for one square on the grid.

TEACHER: That's a nice idea, let's try it. We would color four squares for Monday. How many for Tuesday?

SHARON: One. And two for Wednesday.

SANDY: Two and one-half for Thursday and five for Friday.

Daily absences in our class for the last two weeks

TEACHER: This graph is almost finished.

SANDY: It looks done to me . . . what else could we do?

TEACHER: We need to show on the graph what each box represents.

The code is recorded in a highly visible place beside the graph:

Code:
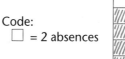 = 2 absences

Daily absences in our class for the last two weeks

Introduction

Probability and statistics are now highly visible topics in elementary school mathematics programs. The shift of attention to these areas has been dramatic and reflects the growing importance of knowing about probability and statistics in our daily lives. These topics provide a context for promoting critical thinking, developing number sense, and applying computation. The *Curriculum and Evaluation Standards for School Mathematics* (NCTM 1989) also identifiers statistics and probability as "important links to other content areas, such as social studies and science."

The *Standards* reported earlier in Figures 1–1 and 1–2 in Chapter 1 show specific standards related to statistics and probability that are introduced (for example, Standard 11 in Grades K–4) and followed by continuous exploration throughout elementary school (Standard 11 in Grades 5–8). In addition, statistical topics are reflected in several other standards, including Standard 8 on Patterns and Functions and Standard 9 on Algebra.

The NCTM *Agenda Series* includes a number of books, such as *Making Sense of Data* (Lindquist et al. 1992) and *Dealing with Data and Chance* (Zawojewski et al. 1991), which provide many valuable and exciting ideas for developing probability and statistics. Textbooks are also increasing attention on developing probability and statistics.

Let's look at some reasons for including the study of probability and statistics in elementary and middle school. Children encounter ideas of probability and statistics outside of school everyday. For example, news reports present national economic and social statistics, opinion polls, and medical, business, and financial data. As these examples suggest, data are not merely numbers, but numbers with a context. The number 12 in the absence of a context carries no information; but saying that a baby weighed twelve pounds at birth makes it easy to comment about its size. Data provide many opportunities to think, use, understand, and interpret numbers, rather than simply carrying out arithmetical operations. Using data helps further develop number sense.

Statistics and probability provide opportunities for computational activity in a meaningful setting, usually requiring judgment in choosing methods and interpreting results. Thus, statistics and probability are not taught in elementary school for their own sake, but because they provide an effective way to develop quantitative understanding and mathematical thinking.

For example, calculating the mean price of six videotapes is a routine exercise in arithmetic. However, noticing that the prices of six videotapes vary, then deciding which is the best buy, and determining how much can be saved help develop mathematical thinking, as well as further promoting respect for the power and usefulness of mathematics.

Many decisions are based on market research and sales projections, and, if these data are to be understood and used widely, every educated person must be able to process such information effectively and efficiently.

Data are often presented in a graphical, statistical, or probabilistic form:

Graphical: Where are the jobs?

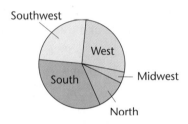

Statistical: The mean salary of professional baseball players is $1,350,000 a year.

Probabilistic: The probability of rain today is 0.35.

Each of these statements needs to be understood if meaningful interpretations are to be made.

The context and format of the way such information is presented vary greatly, but correct interpretation of the information often requires the application of a variety of mathematics. Consider, for example, the mathematical concepts involved in weather reports (decimals, percents, and probability), public opinion polls (sampling techniques and errors of measurement), advertising claims (hypothesis testing), and monthly government reports involving unemployment, inflation, and energy supplies (percentages, prediction, and extrapolation).

All the media rely on techniques of summarizing information. Radio, television, and newspapers bombard us with statistical information. The current demand for information-processing skills is much greater than it was twenty-five years ago, and technological advances will place a far greater premium on such skills in the years ahead.

Graphing, statistics, and probability are closely intertwined. Consider, for example, the life-

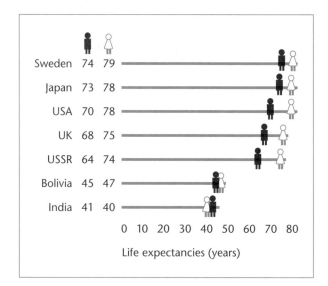

Figure 15–1 • **A graph of life expectancies**

expectancy information shown in Figure 15–1, which visually summarizes much information. Questions such as these can be answered quickly from the graph in the figure:

Which country has the longest life expectancy?

Which country has the shortest life expectancy?

In which countries do females live longer than males?

Extending this discussion to questions such as these involves statistics:

What is the life expectancy in Sweden for females?

How much longer can women in the United States expect to live than men?

How is life expectancy determined?

Further extensions might include these questions:

If I am born in the United States, what are my chances of living to be 75?

If my spouse and I are both 23 years old, what is the probability that we will both be alive at age 40?

These questions not only require additional data, but also provide direct applications of probability. Such questions related to life expectancy are answered regularly by insurance companies.

Graphing, statistics, and probability should not be viewed or treated in isolation. Their study provides numerous opportunities to review and apply much mathematics in a variety of real-world situations. For example, understanding of whole numbers, fractions, decimals, percents, ratios, and proportion is essential and is often called upon. Many computational skills are reviewed and polished as they are applied in graphing or doing statistics and probability.

• Graphing

Graphing skills include constructing and reading graphs as well as interpreting graphical information. They should be introduced early in the primary grades.

Here is a way of getting started. First, ask each child to choose one piece of his or her favorite fruit from a basket and position this piece of fruit on a table, as shown in Figure 15–2A. The resulting rows of fruit represent the children's preferences in a concrete fashion. Next, ask each child to draw the fruit he or she chose on an index card, then have the children use the cards to build a picture-bar graph, as in Figure 15–2B. Although this graph is a less concrete means of showing the information, most children still find it a very meaningful way to represent their preferences.

Finally, this same information can be expressed more symbolically in the bar graph in Figure 15–2C. Regardless of how the data are presented, pertinent questions can be asked to encourage thoughtful interpretation of the graphs. Such questions might include the following:

How many children prefer apples?

What is the favorite fruit?

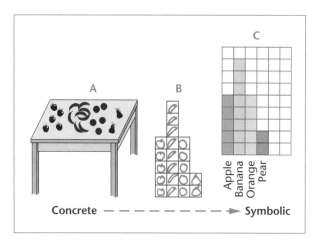

Figure 15–2 • **One method for introducing graphs**

How many different fruits are shown?

How many children contributed to the graph?

These types of questions result naturally from the data and provide valuable opportunities for students to ask as well as answer questions.

Survey data result from collecting information. These data may range from a national public opinion poll to simply tallying the ages of students in a class. The actual data used depends on student interest and maturity, but survey data collected by students provides a freshness that increases student interest and sustains persistence in related problem-solving activities. Here are a few kinds of survey data that could be collected in the classroom:

- *Physical characteristics*—heights, weights, color of eyes, shoe sizes
- *Sociological characteristics*—birthdays, number in family, amount of allowances
- *Personal preferences*—favorite television shows, favorite books, favorite sports, favorite color, favorite drinks

Each of these examples gives students the opportunity to collect data themselves. A lesson built around Activity Card 15–1 will sharpen data-gathering techniques, and a host of other idea starters is available (Lindquist et al. 1992; Pagni 1979; Zawojewski et al. 1991). In completing Activity Card 15–1, students are required to refine and polish their questions to get whatever information they are seeking, which in itself is an important and valuable experience.

After information has been collected, graphs are often used to present information and help others digest the results. Many different types of graphs exist. Skills related to constructing and interpreting the various types of graphs are an important part of mathematics instruction. We will examine the four most popular types of graphs introduced in elementary school. For each type, we'll show an example typical of those found in elementary programs as well as one that demonstrates how the same graphical form is used in real life.

Picture Graphs

In *picture graphs,* data are represented by pictures. A picture can represent one object (Figure 15–3) or several (Figure 15–4). In order to properly interpret picture graphs, children must know how much each object represents. Research shows that students

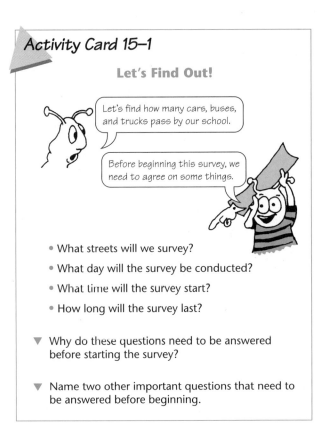

Activity Card 15–1

Let's Find Out!

Let's find how many cars, buses, and trucks pass by our school.

Before beginning this survey, we need to agree on some things.

- What streets will we survey?
- What day will the survey be conducted?
- What time will the survey start?
- How long will the survey last?

▼ Why do these questions need to be answered before starting the survey?

▼ Name two other important questions that need to be answered before beginning.

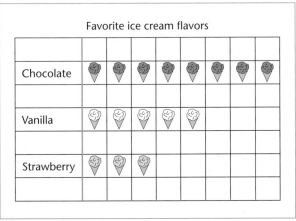

Favorite ice cream flavors

Figure 15–3 ● **A picture graph in which each picture represents one object**

often ignored such coding information when interpreting graphs (Bright and Hoeffner 1993). This is why coding was highlighted in the opening Snapshot of a Lesson.

Pie, or Circle, Graphs

A *pie graph* is a circle representing the whole, wedges reporting percentages of the whole, as illustrated in

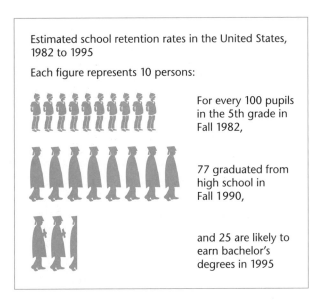

Estimated school retention rates in the United States, 1982 to 1995

Each figure represents 10 persons:

For every 100 pupils in the 5th grade in Fall 1982,

77 graduated from high school in Fall 1990,

and 25 are likely to earn bachelor's degrees in 1995

Figure 15–4 • **A picture graph in which each picture represents several objects** (From surveys, estimates, and projections of the National Center for Education Statistics.)

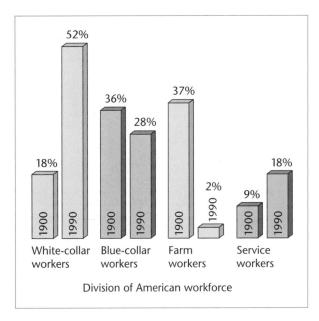

Figure 15–6 • **A bar graph with values shown directly on the bars**

Figure 15–5. The pie graph is popular because it is easy to interpret. It has major limitations in that it represents only a fixed moment in time, and it cannot exceed 100 percent.

Bar Graphs

Bar graphs are used mostly for discrete data; the bars represent this data. Figure 15–2 showed that values can be read from the axis. Figure 15–6 shows that other times the values are reported directly on the graph. Bar graphs are often used for quick visual comparisons of categories of data, but line graphs are effective for showing trends over time.

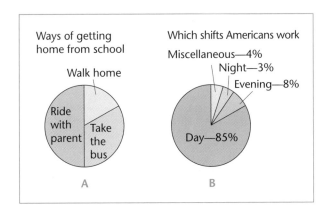

Figure 15–5 • **Pie graphs**

Line Graphs

In *line graphs*, points on a grid are used to represent continuous data. Each axis is clearly labeled, so the data shown can be interpreted properly. A wide variety of line graphs exist and are used, but two basic assumptions are inherent:

1. The data are continuous rather than discrete.
2. Change is accurately represented with linear functions (that is, by lines) rather than some other curve.

As Figure 15–7 shows, line graphs are particularly good for showing variations, such as hours of daylight, temperatures, rainfall, and so on. They are also an effective visual means of comparing several sets of data, as illustrated in Figure 15–8. Constructing or interpreting line graphs requires children to examine both horizontal and vertical axes, which is good preparation for coordinates.

Stem-and-Leaf Plots and Box Plots

In recent years, stem-and-leaf plots have been used frequently in magazines and newspapers because they provide efficient ways of showing information, as well as comparing different sets of data. Suppose, for example, you wanted to explore some questions related to the height of students in a fourth-grade

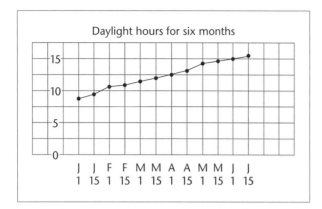

Figure 15–7 • **A line graph of a single set of varying data**

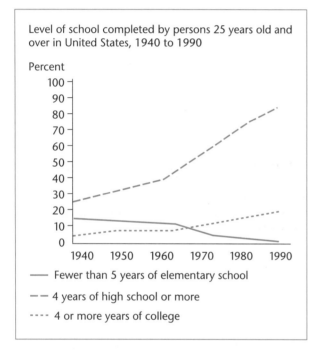

Figure 15–8 • **A line graph comparing several sets of data**

Boys				Girls			
118	132	135	137	122	155	114	125
120	125	147	129	155	137	136	137
133	148	153	125	134	130	133	145
				148	148	147	

Rather than use a traditional frequency distribution, the values are organized in a stem-and-leaf plot, shown in Figure 15–9. The stem represents the hundreds and tens places of the data on student height, and the leaves represent the ones place. Thus, in the last row of Figures 15–9, |11| 4 means one girl had a height of 114 cm. The stem-and-leaf plot preserves the individual measures while revealing the general shape of the organized data. Thus, it presents all of the information, in this case for both groups, and provides a clear visual picture of it.

A box plot summarizes data and provides a visual means of showing variability, that is, the spread of data. The box plot shown in Figure 15–10 summarizes the data on heights very succinctly. The median is a key reference point; more will be said about the median in the next section. The lower hinge is the median of the lower half of the data, and the upper hinge is the median of the upper half. These are found by computing the medians of the data in the lower and upper halves, respectively. The midspread is a measure of variability and is the difference between the upper and lower hinges. In Figure 15–10, the midspread for the boys is 17 (142 – 125) and that for the girls is 16.5 (148 – 131.5). The smallest and largest heights represent the lower extreme and the upper extreme. The lines (also called whiskers) extending from the top of the upper hinge to the largest value and then from the bottom of the lower hinge to the smallest value provide another visual indication of variability.

class. Comparing the heights of the boys and girls will generate some interesting discussion. Questions such as "Which group is tallest?" and "Which group has the most variability?" are naturals. After some conjectures have been made, it is time to have students measure their heights and begin to analyze those data.

Here are some steps that lead to stem-and-leaf plots as well as box plots. The heights of the twenty-seven fourth-grade students (fifteen girls and twelve boys) are reported in centimeters in the following table:

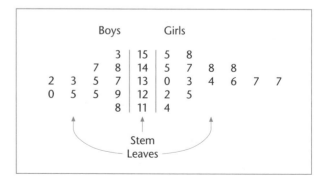

Figure 15–9 • **Stem-and-leaf plot of heights of boys and girls**

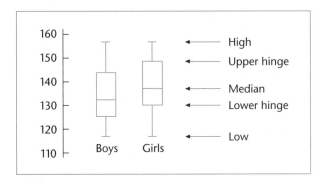

Figure 15–10 • Box plot for heights of boys and girls

The box plot shows many things. For example, it shows the median height for the girls is greater than that for the boys. Although the groups have about the same midspread, the boys are a bit more evenly distributed throughout the box than the girls are. (Why? Because the median of the boys is closer to the middle of the box than is the median of the girls.) The box plot is derived naturally from a stem-and-leaf plot. The box plot shows many important characteristics of a group visually and, when two or more groups are shown on the same graph, it allows comparisons to be made easily.

Graphical Roundup

Each of these graphs deserves instructional attention. Children need experience constructing them and interpreting information that is represented. The availability of graphing calculators and spreadsheets with accompanying graphing packages (such as Claris Works and Microsoft Works) allows for the construction of a variety of graphs easily. This availability of different graphs via technology places a greater premium on interpreting and understanding the graphs that are so easily produced. As children become familiar with different graphs they should recognize some characteristics associated with them. Figure 15–11 highlights specific characteristics of graphs that are encountered in elementary school. The focus here is not on memorizing characteristics of these graphs, but rather on becoming aware that each type has strengths and the selection

Type of Graph	Characteristics
Picture	Frequently encountered in newspapers and reports Generally easy to use and interpret but visuals may be misleading Codes/keys which accompany graph need to be understood
Circle	Frequently encountered in newspapers and reports Shows fractional parts, which are based on a whole or 100% Easy to use and interpret Difficult to construct by hand, easy with technology
Bar	Mostly used for discrete data Frequently encountered in newspapers and reports Easy to interpret Uses scales/codes that need to be understood
Line	Frequently encountered in newspapers and reports Used for continuous data Effective to show patterns, trends, comparisons and change over time Uses vertical and horizontal scales that need to be understood Provides good readiness for coordinate graphs
Stem & Leaf	Efficient way to show detailed data Provides similar visual patterns as a bar graph but more detailed information Uses stem and leaf coding that needs to be understood Technology has facilitated its use
Box Plot	Provides useful information about the variability of data Requires knowledge of range, median and quartiles to interpret Technology has facilitated its use

Figure 15–11 • Characteristics of graphs

of a particular graph should capitalize on these strengths, while recognizing any of its limitations.

Teaching Tips

Interpreting graphs and answering specific questions from them can help students better understand and appreciate their value. In addition, these activities can lead students toward recognition of the strengths and limitations of the different types of graphs.

Showing the same data in different graphs can be both useful and effective. For example, the data shown in the bar graph in Figure 15–2 can be easily shown in a circle graph. Cubes of different color to match the fruits could be strung together as shown here:

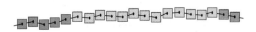

Then the string can be placed in a circle:

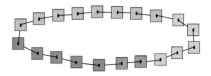

This experience helps make a connection between bar and circle graphs. It also provides a natural context for fractions and percents. For example, the circle graph suggests that $\frac{1}{4}$ of the fruits are oranges.

This model can be extended by placing a meter tape, or a 100-cm strip of paper marked with similar units, around the circle of blocks to form concentric circles, as shown in Figure 15–12A. Comparing the sections suggested by the different groups of colored blocks with the markers on the strip or meter tape will identify percents that can be easily read.

As a more concrete visualization, twenty children can be arranged in a circle, and the "wedges" of a circle graph duplicated with string, as is illustrated in Figure 15–12B. Both of the models in Figure 15–12 make it easy to estimate or read the percentages and conclude, for example, that over 50 percent of the children chose apples or bananas.

Similar observations might have been made directly from the bar graph in Figure 15–2, but conclusions involving fractions and percents are much more obvious from the circle graph. The process of moving from a bar graph to a circle graph also provides different perspectives for the same set of data, and research suggests that developing such multiple perspectives helps promote greater understanding (Shaughnessy 1992).

An important component in developing graphing skills is the ability to critically examine graphs and correctly interpret the data presented. Sometimes even simple graphs may be misleading. For example, consider the graph shown in Figure 15–13. Eighth-graders were asked to explain why this graph was misleading.

Although the data in the graph indicate that the amount of trash has doubled in two decades, the visual elements reflect a doubling of both the width and height to produce a figure whose area is four

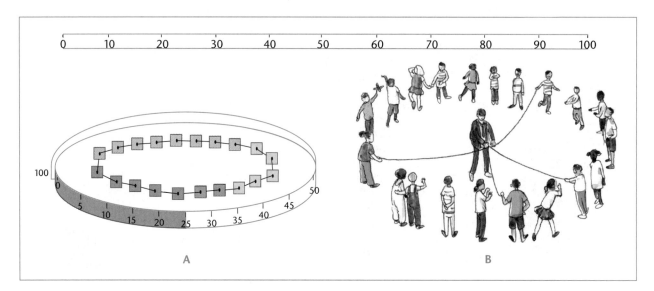

Figure 15–12 • **Models for interpreting circle graph data**

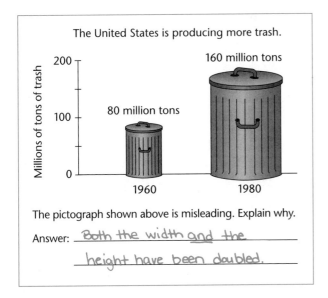

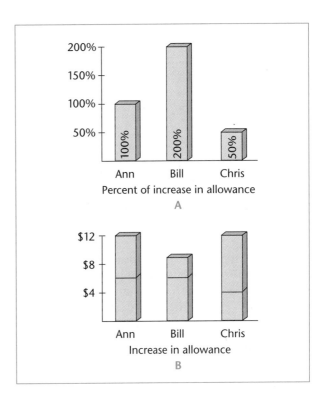

Figure 15–13 • **Eighth-grade national assessment question on interpreting graphs**

Figure 15–14 • **Example of distortion of data in graphs**

times greater. People may focus on the visual graph and ignore the numerical data that accompany the graph. In fact, less than 10 percent of eighth graders identified the critical problem associated with the graph in Figure 15–13, which suggests that instructional attention needs to be given to helping children examine graphs with a careful and suspecting eye.

Graphs also may be deceptive in other ways. For example, the graph in Figure 15–14A reports changes in allowances for three children. It shows that Ann's allowance was doubled, Bill's tripled, and Chris's increased by one-half. Based on this information, we may imagine Bill feeling philanthropic and Chris complaining of hard times. What is wrong with the graph? Technically it is correct, but it doesn't tell the entire story because the original allowances were not the same.

Let's look at the data:

	Size of Increase	Amount of Increase	New Allowance
Ann	Double	$6.00	$12.00
Bill	Triple	6.00	9.00
Chris	Half	4.00	12.00

As Figure 15–14B shows, a graph with a labeled vertical axis reflects the situation more accurately. These different graphs of the same data demonstrate how graphs can distort and sometimes misrepresent

information. Developing a healthy skepticism of graphical displays is an important part of developing graphing skills.

It takes many years to develop the graphing skills necessary to cope with the wide variety of real-life needs, and school provides many opportunities. Here are a few specific suggestions to guide graphing experiences:

- Use information that interests students.

- Provide opportunities for students to collect their own data and decide how to best represent those data graphically.

- Consider alternate ways of graphically representing the same data. This includes changing the scales as well as the kinds of graphs.

- Present some data that are hard to digest or at least difficult to grasp without a graph.

- Pose questions that go beyond direct reading of graphs, and encourage students to both describe and interpret the information.

- Encourage students to think about the characteristics of various types of graphs, including their strengths and weaknesses.

● Statistics

Statistics is the collection and organizing of data. So much information exists today that it must be simplified or reduced in ways other than by graphs. The collection, organization, presentation, and interpretation of data is called *descriptive statistics*. Here are some familiar examples:

> "Most children in the fifth grade are twelve years old."
>
> "The median family income is $25,250."
>
> "The average temperature today was 29°."

Each of these statements uses statistics to describe a current situation or condition. Descriptive statistics are in common use. They are introduced in the primary grades through data collection and graphs, then extended with further exploration and practice activities in the intermediate grades.

Averages

As statistical knowledge grows more specific, descriptive statistical measures should be discussed. For example, *average* is a popular statistical term that many children have heard. It is used to report such things as average temperature, average family income, test averages, batting averages, and average life expectancy.

Any number that is used to represent a series of values is called an average of those values. Many different averages exist, but only three—mean, median, and mode—are commonly encountered in elementary school. Each of these can be developed meaningfully through concrete activities before computation is introduced. Such experiences will provide greater understanding of the concept of average. Furthermore, they will help the later acquisition and development of symbolic formulas in secondary school.

Care must be taken to ensure that statistics is viewed as more than a series of skills or techniques. How to find an average is an important skill that should be developed. However, the teaching of statistics must not stop with the "how to"; rather, it must raise questions such as, "When is an average useful?"

For example, the ice cream survey in Figure 15–3 reports eight students like chocolate, five like vanilla, and three like strawberry. This picture graph clearly and accurately shows student ice cream preferences. A mean of these data could be computed, but it would be inappropriate. In fact, a mean is meaningless for these data! Before any statistics are computed, challenge students to decide what questions are to be answered and discuss what statistics, if any, are needed to answer them.

Additional questions might include "Why should the average be reported?" "What average is most appropriate?" "Why?" "What degree of precision is needed?" These questions are essential and must be asked regularly. The teaching of statistics in elementary school must aim higher than skill development. Students should know how to "get" a statistic, but must also know what they have "gotten."

The Mean

The *mean,* the arithmetic average, is determined by adding all the values involved and dividing by the number of addends. Figure 15–15 shows one way to model the mean. Test scores are returned to children on pieces of adding machine tape, and the length of each strip is determined by the score. That is, a score of 88 is 88 cm long, and a score of 64 is 64 cm long. Scores can be physically compared using the tapes; for example, it is clear that the score on Test 2 was higher. To show the mean score, simply tape the two strips of paper together and then fold the resulting strip in half. This technique is very appealing and enlightening.

A somewhat different but similar concrete approach can be taken to find the mean. The blocks in Figure 15–16A show the number of absences in a

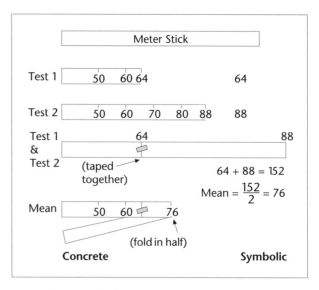

Figure 15–15 ● **Model for finding the mean using lengths of adding machine tape to indicate test scores**

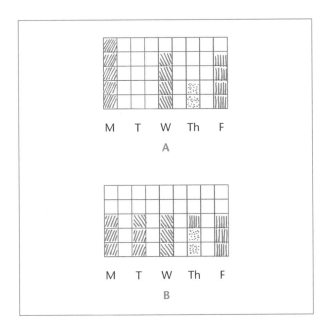

M   T   W   Th   F
A

M   T   W   Th   F
B

Figure 15–16 • **Model for finding the mean number of absences using blocks**

Akira read from a book on Monday, Tuesday, and Wednesday. He read an average of 10 pages per day. Circle whether each of the following is possible or not possible.

Possible	Not Possible		Pages Read Monday	Tuesday	Wednesday
A	Ⓐ	**(a)** 4 pages	4 pages	2 pages
Ⓑ	B	**(b)** 9 pages	10 pages	11 pages
Ⓒ	C	**(c)** 5 pages	10 pages	15 pages
D	Ⓓ	**(d)** 10 pages	15 pages	20 pages

Figure 15–17 • **Eighth-grade national assessment question on interpreting an average (Correct responses are circled.)**

class for one week. If children are asked to "even out" the blocks as much as possible, this evening-out process produces a mean of three blocks per day (Figure 15–16B).

The mean also could have been determined by computing:

$$\text{mean} = \frac{5 + 0 + 4 + 2 + 4}{5}$$

$$= \frac{15}{5} = 3$$

For some children, manipulating the physical model not only helps them understand the formula, but also promotes greater retention.

These types of experiences help students understand some fundamental notions related to the mean; namely, that the mean must be somewhere between the values averaged. The fourth national assessment reported that only about 40 percent of seventh graders responded that the average of two numbers must be halfway between the numbers (Lindquist et al. 1989).

Difficulties in interpreting the mean were also shown on another national assessment (Educational Testing Service 1992). Figure 15–17 shows a question that required eighth graders to determine what data would be reasonable for a given mean. Less than 40 percent answered all four choices correctly.

These assessment results illustrate the findings from research that many middle-grade students are able to calculate averages when asked to do so, but the depth of their understanding of the concept of average is shallow (Shaughnessy 1992).

Grasp of "average" is a powerful tool in estimation and problem solving. Problems such as the one in Figure 15–18 provide opportunities to apply averages and estimation in everyday situations.

The Median

The *median* is the middle value in a set of data. Thus the same number of values are above as below the median. The median is easy to illustrate. Consider the ages of five children: 2, 3, 7, 9, 9. The middle age or median is 7 years. Reference to a highway median will remind students that a median in statistics is a middle position.

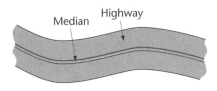

The median is another measure of central tendency, although one that is generally unfamiliar to most elementary students. It, too, can be modeled. For example, consider the five test scores shown on cards in Figure 15–19(a). Ordering them from lowest to highest, as in Figure 15–19(b) provides practice in using greater than, less than, and ordering skills. To find the middle score, or median, simply remove the highest and lowest cards simultaneously, as shown

Figure 15–18 ● Example problem for developing averaging and estimating skills

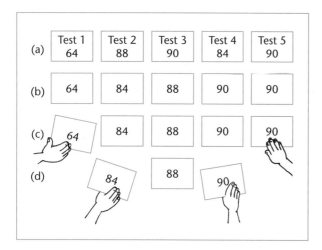

Figure 15–19 ● Model for finding the median of five test scores

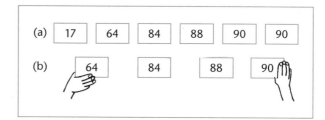

Figure 15–20 ● Model for finding the median of six test scores

in Figures 15–19(c) and (d). Continue this process until the middle card remains. This score, 88, is the median.

There are five scores in Figure 15–19. Suppose a sixth score of 17 was made. A new arrangement could be made by ordering the six test scores, as shown in Figure 15–20(a). Again remove the highest and lowest cards simultaneously until two cards remain. In this case, as shown in Figure 15–20(b) the median is the middle point between these two scores, or 86.

The following table provides a summary of the test scores reported in Figures 15–19 and 15–20:

	Mean	Median
Five tests	83	88
Six tests	72	86

This summary illustrates that the median was affected very little by the extreme low score on the last test, but the mean dropped greatly. One characteristic of the mean is that its value is affected by extreme scores.

Suppose you are preparing a report of average incomes and you want to present the fairest picture. Should the mean—which would be affected by the extremely high salaries of movie stars, professional athletes, and corporate heads—be used? Many governmental agencies handle this problem by reporting median family incomes.

The Mode

The *mode* is the value that occurs most frequently in a collection of data. In physical terms, this is the tallest column in a bar graph, for example. In Figure 15–19a the most frequently occurring test score is 90 (it occurred twice), so the mode is 90. The mode is easy to find and is affected very little by extreme scores.

Students' ages within a class provide an excellent application of mode, because, within a given class, a large number of children will be the "same" age. Businesses also frequently rely on the mode to select merchandise. Suppose, for example, that you own a shoe store. The mean and/or median size of shoe you sell has no practical value for restocking, but the modal shoe size holds clear implications because you want to stock the sizes most people wear.

Finding the mean, median, and mode for the same data can generate discussion about when certain averages should be used. For example, look at Activity Card 15–2. Calculating the mean, median, and mode provides practice in computational skills. More important, however, is deciding which of these averages to report. The median salary of $500,000 or the modal salary of $480,000 seems more representative than the mean salary of $1,030,000. If salary negotiations were taking place, the players might cite one "average" and the owners a very different "average." Discussing which averages are appropriate for what purpose helps students better understand why different ones exist and are used.

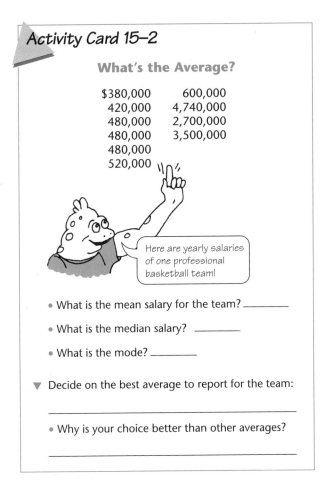

Activity Card 15–2

What's the Average?

$380,000	600,000
420,000	4,740,000
480,000	2,700,000
480,000	3,500,000
480,000	
520,000	

Here are yearly salaries of one professional basketball team!

• What is the mean salary for the team? _____

• What is the median salary? _____

• What is the mode? _____

▼ Decide on the best average to report for the team:

_____

• Why is your choice better than other averages?

_____

The fourth national mathematics assessment shows that students' performance on mean, median, and mode varies (Lindquist et al. 1989). For example, 40 percent, 38 percent, and 26 percent of seventh graders could find the mean, median, and mode, respectively, for a set of data that included fifteen values. This suggests that instruction should be designed to provide a balance of experiences with "averages." Each of the averages can be modeled and developed in ways that are appealing, interesting, and meaningful. No new mathematics is required, yet learning about averages provides a vehicle for applying many mathematical concepts and skills that students are developing.

● Probability

Probability is encountered daily. Here are some examples of common probabilistic statements:

"The chance of rain today is 40 percent."

"The Cards are a 3-to-1 favorite to win."

"The probability of an accident on the job is less than 1 in 100."

"The patient has a 50–50 chance of recovering."

"If I study, I will probably pass the test."

"I am sure we will have a test Friday."

"We will have milk at the cafeteria today."

The first three statements are commonly heard and relate directly to probability. The last four illustrate a subtle but frequent use of probability in many everyday situations. In all these cases it is the utilitarian role of probability that makes it an important basic skill. One way to increase awareness that probability surrounds us is to have students make a daily or weekly list of probability statements they have seen (in newspapers, magazines, or on television) or heard (on radio and television).

Probability will not, and should not, be learned from formal definitions; rather, the presentation of varied examples will help illustrate and clarify its important concepts. At all stages of instruction, teachers must use correct language to describe what is happening. This language serves as a model for children as they begin developing probability concepts and simultaneously add new probabilistic terms to their vocabulary. Let's look at appropriate ways for elementary students to experience some key concepts and terms.

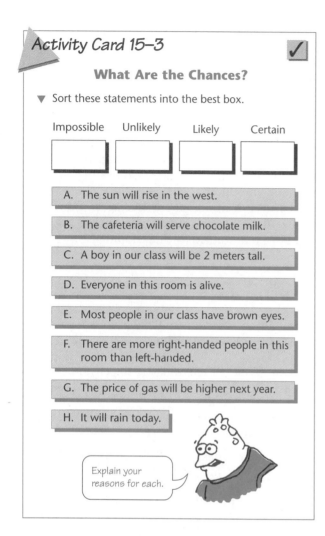

Probability of an Event

Look at these statements that involve probability:

The probability of tossing a head is $\frac{1}{2}$.

The probability of rolling a four on a die is $\frac{1}{6}$.

The probability of having a birthday on February 30 is 0.

In these examples, "tossing a head," "rolling a four," and "having a birthday on February 30" are *events* or *outcomes*. Probability assigns a number (from zero to one) to an event. The more likely an event is to occur, the larger the number assigned to it, and so the probability is 1.0 when something is certain to happen. For example, the probability of students in an elementary class having been born in the twentieth century is 1. On the other hand, the probability of something impossible happening is zero. For example, the probability of students in the class having been born in the nineteenth century is zero.

Long before probabilities of specific events are calculated, it is important that terms such as *certain, uncertain, impossible, likely,* and *unlikely* be introduced and discussed. Most students, even in primary grades, are familiar with the terms *impossible* and *certain* and can give meaningful examples. Although *likely* and *unlikely* will be less familiar and will require more careful development, Activity Card 15–3 provides a good start. As each card is sorted, an explanation or argument for placing it in the specific box should be given. This rationale is essential in refining and developing a clear understanding of these important terms.

An excellent follow-up to Activity Card 15–3 is to have students write statements to be sorted into the same categories. Each should write several original statements and then exchange papers so that someone else classifies them. Once these general probabilistic terms become familiar, more specific probabilities can be determined.

Sample space is a fundamental concept that must be established, or at least understood, before the probabilities of specific events can be determined. The sample space for a probability problem represents all possible outcomes.

Activity Card 15–4 is designed to help children think about what outcomes are possible for a particular event. Consider, for example, the situation in which cups are tossed. Some children may realize that a cup will not land on its edge, nor will it float. Thus only three outcomes can happen, and these possible outcomes comprise the sample space. Likewise, when a coin is being flipped, it will neither float nor land on its edge, so only two outcomes are possible.

Once the sample space is known, the calculation of specific probabilities usually follows naturally. When a coin is flipped, as described in Table 15–1, the probability of a head is the number of ways a head can occur divided by the total number of outcomes (head or tail), or $\frac{1}{2}$. Specific probabilities rest heavily on fractions, which provide a direct and convenient means of reporting and interpreting probabilities.

Discussion of possible outcomes helps identify the sample space and clarify notions of probability. Questions along these lines might get the discussion started:

> Can the spinner shown on Activity Card 15–4 stop in region C if there is no area marked C?
>
> Can the spinner stop on a line?

Even though this outcome is unlikely, it can happen, and a plan of action should be specified if it does. (Maybe you spin again.) See Appendix B for spinner masters

Consider the sample space for tossing cups, as shown on Activity Card 15–4. Is a cup equally likely to land on its top, its side, or its bottom? Without additional information, it would be foolhardy to decide.

Activity Card 15–5 provides a possible start. In addition to helping children decide which outcomes are more or less likely, this exploration may lead to more precise statements. For example, one reasonable conclusion from Activity Card 15–5 is that the probability of the cup landing on its side is about one-half.

Activity Card 15–6 involves collecting data, graphing results, and exploring patterns. It uses several valuable ideas of probability (sample space and probability of an event) in a natural and interesting setting. As children are involved in this process, they are developing and practicing basic facts. Such

Table 15–1 • **Sample spaces of some events and their probabilities**

Questions	Sample space	Number of successes	Probability
What is the probability of getting a head on a single toss of a coin?	H,T	1	$\frac{1}{2}$
What is the probability of getting two heads when two coins are tossed?	HH, HT, TH, TT	1	$\frac{1}{4}$
What is the probability of getting a five on a single roll of a die?	1, 2, 3, 4, 5, 6	1	$\frac{1}{6}$
What is the probability of drawing a spade from a deck of 52 playing cards?	52 cards	13	$\frac{13}{52}$ or $\frac{1}{4}$
If each letter of the alphabet is written on a piece of paper, what is the probability of drawing a vowel?	26 letters of the alphabet	5 (a, e, i , o, u)	$\frac{5}{26}$

Activity Card 15–5

What's the Probability?

▼ Toss a cup to see how it lands:

▼ Before you toss it again, circle how you think it will land:

▼ Toss your cup 20 more times, and tally how it lands!

Bottom	Top	Side

• I have decided that _____ is most likely.

• I have decided that _____ is least likely.

You can make some more tosses if it will help.

▼ Here are some results from tossing the cup:

A. | 2 | 0 | 3 | B. | 15 | 10 | 25 |

C. | 32 | 17 | 51 |

• Is it possible that all these tallies are results of tossing the same cup? _____ Explain.

• Which of these tables would you feel best about using? _____ Explain.

Decision time:

The probability of landing on the side is

about _____ .

Activity Card 15–6

Rolling and Recording

▼ Try this:

1. Choose a partner, and each of you make a chart like the one shown.

2. Each of you take turns rolling two dice.

3. On a turn, find the sum of the spots on the two dice, and check that column on your chart.

4. Continue rolling and recording until one of you has 10 tally marks in one column.

2	3	4	5	6	7	8	9	10	11	12
			/							

Putting it together:

• Why doesn't the chart need a ones column? A thirteens column?

• In which column did you or your partner reach 10?

• Compare your results, and tell how they are similar. Different.

• Tell why you would expect more sums of 7 than 2.

• Complete the following: "I would expect about the same number of sums of 4 as . . . ."

• Would you expect to get about the same number of even sums as odd sums? Tell why.

Extending this activity:

Suppose you multiplied the numbers on the dice instead of adding them.

• How would the values along the base of the chart change?

• How many values (that is, different products) would be needed?

• Which values would be least likely?

• Would you expect to get about the same number of even values as odd values? Tell why.

---

an activity further illustrates how mathematical topics are interrelated and how important connections can be made.

Another perspective of Activity Card 15–6 can be obtained by examining Table 15–2 which summarizes the results when two dice are added. The diag-onal of Table 15–2A shows all the ways that a sum of 7 can be obtained. Table 15–2 also shows the different ways that each of the other sums can result. Is the sum of two dice more likely to be even or odd? An examination of Table 15–2A shows the even sums will occur 18 out of 36 times, or half the time.

Table 15–2 • Results of operations with two dice

+	1	2	3	4	5	6
1	2	3	4	5	6	7
2	3	4	5	6	7	8
3	4	5	6	7	8	9
4	5	6	7	8	9	10
5	6	7	8	9	10	11
6	7	8	9	10	11	12

a

×	1	2	3	4	5	6
1	1	2	3	4	5	6
2	2	4	6	8	10	12
3	3	6	9	12	15	18
4	4	8	12	16	20	24
5	5	10	15	20	25	30
6	6	12	18	24	30	36

b

Is the product of two dice more likely to be even or odd? The shaded cells in Table 15–2B shows the even products much more likely. In fact, an even product would be expected to occur 27 times out of 36, or three-fourths of the time. Analyzing and discussing why this happens helps connect probability to properties and relationships between numbers and operations.

Randomness

Randomness is an important concept underlying all learning in probability. When something is random, it means that it is not influenced by any factors other than chance. Activity Card 15–7 builds on Activity Card 15–3 and provides an opportunity to discuss randomness in a specific context. Here students are encouraged to think about events based on their classmates and decide about where these events would be placed on a probability number line that shows 0 and 1. Here are some starter questions:

Why is it important that the "name will be randomly picked"?

Activity Card 15–7

Our class is having a drawing. Each person gets to place their name in the drawing one time. One name will be randomly picked, and that person will be the winner.

▼ Read each of the following statements.

▼ Think about the people in our class.

▼ Then, check the number line below and decide about where the following statements should be placed:

A. The winner will be left handed.

B. The winner will be a girl.

C. The winner will be someone in our class.

D. The number of letters in the first name of the winner will be less than the number of letters in their last name.

E. The winner's first name will begin with a vowel.

F. The winner will wear glasses.

G. You will be the winner.

H. The winner will be wearing socks.

I. You will not be the winner.

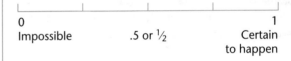

0
Impossible   .5 or ½   1
                              Certain
                              to happen

Should the names be seen by the person doing the drawing?

Would it matter if some people wrote their names on large pieces of paper an others on small pieces of paper?

If the names are seen, or if people don't all write their name on the same size of paper, the drawing might not be random. When this happens, some people would have an advantage and the notions of *fair* and *unfair* become important.

The term *fair* is often used in describing a situation. For example, to say "a fair coin" or "fair dice" makes it clear that no inherent biases exist that would affect randomness. A person may be asked to toss (not scoot) a die to ensure that one face is not favored. If ping-pong balls are drawn from a bowl, it is important that the balls be thoroughly mixed and the person doing the drawing be blindfolded to ensure both randomness and fairness.

Discussions on the consequences of unfairness and absence of randomness should be a regular part of developing probability. For example, would it be fair if two dice are rolled and player A wins if the product is even and player B wins if the product is odd? Table 15–2B shows that A will win much more than B, so this game is not fair. On the other hand, if the game is based on the sum of two dice (Table 15–2A), each player has an equal chance of winning and the game is fair. Suppose you modify the sum-of-two-dice game to play with three players:

Player A wins if the sum is 1, 2, 3, or 4

Player B wins if the sum is 5, 6, 7, or 8

Player C wins if the sum is 9, 10, 11, or 12.

Is this game fair for each of the players? Does each player have the same chance of winning? An analysis of Table 15–2A, suggests that Player B will win more often than either of the other players. As children explore this game, you might challenge them to tell how the game might be modified to make it fair for everyone.

Independence of Events

Independence of events is an important concept in probability, but one that does not develop naturally from intuition. If two events are independent, one event in no way affects the outcome of the other. Thus if a coin is tossed, lands heads, and then is tossed again, it is still equally likely to land heads or tails. This sounds simple enough, but consider this question:

> Suppose four consecutive sixes have occurred on four rolls of a fair die. What is the probability of getting a six on the next roll?

Research shows that a majority of middle-grade students miss this question (Shaughnessy 1992). Many students suggested that the die had a "memory," and things would "even out." Most did not conclude that the probability was unchanged, regardless of what had already happened. If an event has occurred a number of times in a row, most people falsely presume that the "law of averages" makes it unlikely that the event will occur on the next trial. This basic misunderstanding contradicts the notion of independence of certain events.

Having children collect data and discuss the results can help dispel some of this erroneous thinking. Activity Card 15–8 will produce different results

Activity Card 15–8

Can You Make Predictions?

▼ Roll a die six times and record the results:

1	2	3	4	5	6

- Did each face appear once? _____
- Does knowing what happened on the first roll

  help predict the second? _____

  the third? _____

▼ Roll a die 24 times and record the results.

1	2	3	4	5	6	7	8	9	10	11	12

13 14 15 16 17 18 19 20 21 22 23 24

- Did each face appear once? _____

  the same number of times? _____
- What face appeared most? _____

  Does this mean the die is unfair? _____

  Does this record tell you
  what will occur on the next roll? _____

for different students, yet the answers to the questions will be very similar. Why? Because these events, the rolls of a die, are independent of one another.

Tossing a coin and recording the outcomes in sequence will likely generate some long runs of an occurrence even though each outcome is independent of the others. Although the probability of a head is ½, children might flip a coin ten times and get 8, 9, or even 10 heads in a row. Consider this record of 20 tosses of a coin:

T T T T T H T H H H H T T H H T H H H H

There are two sequences of four consecutive heads and one of five consecutive tails. Overall, eleven heads appeared. Such analysis and discussion helps

Activity Card 15–9

Check Your Probability Knowledge

This bag has three red balls, one white ball, and one black ball.

Sample space:

- How many balls are in the bag?

- What color balls could be drawn?

- Must a ball be returned to the bag after it has been drawn? (This, of course, depends on the questions being asked.)

Probability of an event:

- What is the probability of drawing a red ball?

- What is the probability of drawing a ball that is not red?

- What is the probability of drawing a black or white ball?

- What is the probability of drawing a green ball?

- What is the probability of drawing a red, black, or white ball?

Randomness:

- Should the red balls be placed at the bottom of the bag and the black and white balls placed on top of them?

- Should the bag be shaken before each draw?

- Should people be allowed to choose their favorite color?

- Should people be allowed to pick several balls and then choose their favorite?

- Should the person choosing be blindfolded?

- Should a transparent bag be used?

Independence:

- If a white ball has just been drawn and returned to the bag, what is the probability the next ball will be white?

- If four consecutive red balls have been drawn and returned each time to the bag, what is the probability the next ball will be red?

children understand that things don't even out on each flip. However, as the number of flips gets very large, the ratio of heads to the total number of flips will get closer and closer to the theoretical expected

value of $\frac{1}{2}$. This latter point is very important, but it often baffles elementary students.

There are, of course, times where one event may depend on another. For example, suppose you wanted to roll two dice and obtain a sum of 8. If a 1 is shown on the first die, it is impossible to get a sum of 8. This leads toward notions of *conditional probability*.

Activity Card 15–9 provides a single setting that will address each of several key probability concepts that should be established in the elementary school. The questions direct attention to these concepts and should produce valuable discussion. The interrelatedness of these concepts is also illustrated.

Instruction is needed to develop the necessary techniques to solve simple probability problems. There are, of course, other very complicated situations for which probabilities are difficult to calculate. What is the probability of New York winning the World Series? Of a woman being elected president? Such questions do not lend themselves to simple solutions, but their probabilities can be approximated by experts. Regardless of who determines the numerical probabilities, the knowledge and interpretative skills developed in simpler probability situations can be successfully applied.

A Glance at Where We've Been

Using data to organize, analyze, and interpret information develops critical thinking. In addition, using data provides many opportunities to apply fractions, decimals, and ratios as well as practice computational skills and problem solving. Also, the elements of uncertainty inherent in working with probability and statistics present situations that require critical thinking skills.

Meaningful learning is always important. It is difficult to imagine any mathematical topic that allows for more involvement and stimulates more enthusiasm than probability and statistics. The importance of probability and statistics is unchallenged, yet performance on these topics leaves much to be desired. Contemporary elementary school mathematics programs are giving much more attention and emphasis to all forms of data analysis at all grade levels. The NCTM *Standards* have made a strong push toward relating school mathematics to real-world mathematics, and no area lends itself better to this linkage than using data.

▶ THINGS TO DO: From What You've Read

1. Suppose you have opened some Nutty Bars to check the company's claim of an "average" of 8 peanuts per bar.

Bar	Number of Peanuts
1st	5
2nd	8
3rd	8
4th	8
5th	11
6th	7
7th	8
8th	6
9th	6
10th	6

   a. What is the mean number of nuts?
   b. What is the median number?
   c. What is the modal number?
   d. Which average did the company probably use?

2. Here are the results on three tests: 68, 78, 88. What are the mean and the median? Explain why the mode is of little value. What score would be needed on the next test to get an average of 81? Describe two different ways this could be done.

3. Arrange interlocking cubes together in lengths of 3, 6, 6, and 9.

   a. Describe how you could use the blocks to find the mean, median, and mode.
   b. Suppose you introduce another length of 10 cubes. Has the mean changed? The median? The mode?

4. Describe how the activities in Activity Card 15–4 could be used to discuss probabilities of zero and one.

5. Pick five questions from Activity Card 15–8 that you would include in an introductory fifth-grade lesson on probability. Tell why you picked those questions.

6. Ten cards are marked 0, 1, 2, 3, . . . , 9 and placed face down. If the cards are shuffled then one card drawn, tell why the following statements are true:

   a. The sample space has 10 events.
   b. The probability of drawing the 6 is $^{7}/_{10}$.
   c. The probability of drawing the 3 is the same as the probability of drawing the 7.

7. Many of the state lotteries advertise with a slogan, "If you don't play, you can't win." Does that mean if you do play, you will win? Explain.

8. The chances of picking six numbers correctly in a state lottery depends on the numbers from which you select. Explain why you would rather pick from the set of numbers 1 through 10 than from the set of numbers 1 through 20. About how much better are your chances of winning with the smaller set of numbers than with the larger set of numbers?

9. Answer each of the following questions, and tell why you answered as you did.

   a. Is it possible for a set of data to have more than one mode? Give an example.
   b. Is it easier to find the median of 25 or 24 student scores?
   c. Could the mean be as large as the largest value in a set of data? Tell how.

▶ THINGS TO DO: Going Beyond This Book

1. Review the NCTM books *Making Sense of Data* (Lindquist et al. 1992) and *Dealing with Data and Chance* (Zawojewski et al. 1991). Select an activity. Decide where and how you would use it in teaching a lesson.

2. Examine a newspaper or magazine. Make a list of the different kinds of graphs used. Tell why you think a particular graph (picture graph, circle graph, bar graph) was used in each situation.

3. Examine the scope-and-sequence chart for an elementary textbook series. At what level is graphing first introduced? What kinds of graphing skills are highlighted? What important statistical topics are included? At what levels are they taught?

4. Review the *Wonderful World of Mathematics* (Thiessen and Matthias 1992). Find a book related to statistics or probability that is highly recommended. Read the book with some children and describe how they reacted.

5. Select one of the activities from *Probability* (Phillips et al. 1986). Develop the materials needed and demonstrate the lesson.

6. Examine the 1981 yearbook of the National Council of Teachers of Mathematics, entitled *Teaching Statistics and Probability* (Shulte 1981). Select an article to read and use as a basis for preparing a lesson plan.

7. Examine *Exploring Data and Exploring Probability* (Landwehr and Watkins 1986) and identify several different stem-and-leaf plots and box plots that are illustrated. Describe how those presentations help simplify the data.

8. Games are fun and can help develop a better understanding of probability. Play the game "Montana Red Dog," described in *Dealing with Data and*

Chance (Zawojewski et al. 1991), play one of the games from "Fair Games, Unfair Games" (Bright et al. 1981), *What Are My Chances?* (Shulte & Choate, 1996) or the "Cover Up Game" from *Chance Encounters: Probability in Games and Simulation* (Brutlag, 1996). Identify some of the mathematics learned in these games. Tell how you might use these games with students.

9. Read one of the research articles related to probability or statistics listed in Bright and Hoeffner (1993) or Shaughnessy (1992). Discuss the nature of the research. Also identify an instructional idea or activity suggested by the research that you think would be effective in helping children learn a particular concept.

10. Examine one of the following books from *Used Numbers: Real Data in the Classroom* (Friel and Corwin 1990):

    Counting: Ourselves and Our Families (K–1)
    Sorting: Groups and Graphs (2–3)
    Measuring: From Paces to Feet (3–4)
    Statistics: The Shape of the Data (4–6)
    Statistics: Prediction and Sampling (5–6)
    Statistics: Middles, Means, and In-Betweens (5–6)

    Choose an activity and discuss how it might be presented to a group of students. Better yet, present it to an appropriate group of students. Discuss what happened.

▼▼▼▼▼▼▼▼▼▼▼▼▼▼▼▼▼▼▼▼▼▼

Children's Corner

Arnold, Caroline. *Charts and Graphs: Fun, Facts, and Activities.* New York: Franklin Watts, 1984.

Carle, Eric. *Rooster's Off to See the World.* Natick, Mass.: Picture Book Studio, 1972.

Cushman, Jean. *Do You Wanna Bet? Your Chance to Find Out about Probability.* New York: Clarion Books, 1991.

Diagram Group. *Comparisons.* New York: St. Martin's Press, 1980.

Gardner, Beau. *Can You Imagine . . . ? A Counting Book.* New York: Dodd, Mead and Co., 1987.

Linn, Charles F. *Probability.* New York: Thomas Y. Crowell Publishers, 1972.

Mori, Tuyosi. *Socrates and the Three Pigs.* New York: Philomel Books, 1986.

Parker, Tom. *In One Day.* Boston: Houghton Mifflin, 1984.

Spier, Peter. *People.* New York: Thomas Y. Crowell Publishers, 1975.

Srivastava, Jane Jonas. *Averages.* New York: Thomas Y. Crowell Publishers, 1975.

Winthrop, Elizabeth. *Shoes.* New York: Harper & Row, 1986.

Ziefert, Harriet. *Where's the Halloween Treat?* New York: Puffit Books, 1985.

Selected References

Bestgen, Barbara J. "Making and Interpreting Graphs and Tables: Results and Implications from National Assessment." *Arithmetic Teacher,* 28 (December 1980), pp. 26–29.

Bright, George W., and Hoeffner, Karl. "Measurement, Probability, Statistics and Graphing." In *Research Ideas for the Classroom: Middle Grades Mathematics* (ed. Douglas T. Owens). Reston, Va.: NCTM, and New York: Macmillan, 1993, pp. 78–98.

Bright, George W.; Harvey, John G.; and Wheeler, Margarette Montague. "Fair Games, Unfair Games." In *Teaching Statistics and Probability,* 1981 Yearbook (ed. Albert Shulte). Reston, Va.: NCTM, 1981, pp. 49–59.

Browning, Christine A., and Channell, Dwayne E. "A 'Handy' Database Activity for the Middle School Classroom." *Arithmetic Teacher,* 40 (December 1992), pp. 235–238.

Bruni, James V., and Silverman, Helen J. "Developing Concepts in Probability and Statistics—and Much More." *Arithmetic Teacher,* 33 (February 1986), pp. 34–37.

Brutlag, Dan. "Choice and Chance in Life: The Game of 'Skunk'." *Mathematics Teaching in the Middle School,* 1 (1), (April 1994), pp. 28–33.

Brutlag, Dan. *Chance Encounters: Probability in Games and Simulation.* Palo Alto, Calif.: Creative Publications, 1996.

Burrill, Gail. "Implementing the Standards: Statistics and Probability." *Mathematics Teacher,* 83 (February 1990), pp. 113–118.

Carpenter, Thomas P.; Corbitt, Mary Kay; Kepner, Henry S., Jr.; Lindquist, Mary; and Reys, Robert E. "What Are the Chances of Your Students Knowing Probability?" *Mathematics Teacher,* 74 (May 1981), pp. 342–344.

Corwin, Rebecca, and Friel, Susan. *Used Numbers—Statistics: Prediction and Sampling, Grades 5–6.* Menlo Park, Calif.: Dale Seymour Publications, 1990.

Curcio, Frances R. *Developing Graph Comprehension: Elementary and Middle School Activities.* Reston, Va.: NCTM, 1989.

Dickinson, J. Craig. "Gather, Organize, Display: Mathematics for the Information Society." *Arithmetic Teacher,* 34 (December 1986), pp. 12–15.

Dixon, Juli K., and Falba, Christy J. "Graphing in the Information Age: Using Data from the Worldwide

Web." *Mathematics Teaching in the Middle School,* 2 (March–April 1997), pp. 298–304.

Easterday, Kenneth E.; Henry, Loren I.; and Simpson, F. Morgan. *Activities for Junior High School and Middle School Mathematics.* Reston, Va.: NCTM, 1981.

Educational Testing Service. *NAEP 1992 Mathematics Report Card for the Nation and the States.* Princeton, N.J., ETS, 1992.

Friel, Susan N., and Corwin, Rebecca B. "Implementing the Standards: The Statistics Standards in K–8 Mathematics." *Arithmetic Teacher,* 38 (October 1990), pp. 35–39.

Friel, Susan N., and Corwin, Rebecca B. *Used Numbers: Real Data in the Classroom* (series of six books). Palo Alto, Calif.: Dale Seymour Publications, 1990.

Green, David. "From Thumbtacks to Inference." *School Science and Mathematics,* 83 (November 1983), pp. 541–551.

Hofstetter, Elaine B., and Sgroi, Laura A. "Data with Snap, Crackle, and Pop." *Mathematics Teaching in the Middle School,* 1 (4), (March–April 1996), pp. 760–764.

Ihor, Charischak, and Berkman, Robert. "Looking at Random Events with Logo Software." *Mathematics Teaching in the Middle School,* 1 (4), (January–March 1995), pp. 318–322.

Kader, Gary, and Perry, Mike. "Learning Statistics with Technology" *Mathematics Teaching in the Middle School,* 1 (2), (September–October 1994), pp. 130–136.

Landwehr, James M., and Watkins, Ann E. *Exploring Data and Exploring Probability.* Palo Alto, Calif.: Dale Seymour Publications, 1986.

Landwehr, James M., and Watkins, Ann E. "Stem and Leaf Plots." *Mathematics Teacher,* 78 (October 1985), pp. 528–538.

Lappan, Glenda, and Winter, Mary J. "Probability Simulation in Middle School." *Mathematics Teacher,* 73 (September 1980), pp. 446–449.

Lindquist, Mary M.; Brown, Catherine A.; Carpenter, Thomas P.; Kouba, Vicky L.; Silver, Edward A.; and Swafford, Jane O. *Results from the Fourth Mathematics Assessment of the National Assessment of Educational Progress.* Reston, Va.: NCTM, 1989.

Lindquist, Mary M.; Lauquire, J.; Gardner, A.; and Shekaramiz, S. *Making Sense of Data.* Reston, Va.: NCTM, 1992.

Mathematics Resource Project. *Statistics and Informational Organization.* Palo Alto, Calif.: Creative Publications, 1978.

National Council of Teachers of Mathematics. *Curriculum and Evaluation Standards for School Mathematics.* Reston, Va.: NCTM, 1989.

Pagni, David L. "Applications in School Mathematics: Human Variability." In *Applications in School Mathematics,* 1979 Yearbook (ed. Sidney Sharron). Reston, Va.: NCTM, 1979, pp. 43–58.

Paull, Sandra. "Not Just an Average Unit." *Arithmetic Teacher,* 38 (December 1990), pp. 54–58.

Paulos, John Allen. *Innumeracy.* New York: Hill and Wang, 1989.

Phillips, Elizabeth; Lappan, Glenda; Winter, Mary Jane; and Fitzgerald, William. *Probability.* Menlo Park, Calif.: Addison–Wesley, 1986.

Quinn, Robert J. "Having Fun with Baseball Statistics." *Mathematics Teaching in the Middle School,* 1 (10), (May 1996), pp. 780–785.

Shaughnessy, J. Michael. "Research in Probability and Statistics: Reflections and Directions." In *Handbook of Research on Mathematics Teaching and Learning* (ed. Douglas Grouws). New York: Macmillan, 1992, pp. 495–514.

Shulte, Albert P. "Learning Probability Concepts in Elementary School Mathematics." *Arithmetic Teacher,* 34 (January 1987), pp. 32–33.

Shulte, Albert P. (ed.) *Teaching Statistics and Probability,* 1981 Yearbook. Reston, Va.: NCTM, 1981.

Schulte, Albert P., and Choate, Stuart A. *What Are My Chances?* Palo Alto, Calif.: Creative Publications, 1996.

Shulte, Albert P., and Swift, Jim. "Plotting and Predicting from Pairs." *Mathematics Teacher,* 77 (September 1984), pp. 442–447.

Silverman, Helene. "Ideas." *Arithmetic Teacher,* 37 (April 1990), pp. 27–32.

Thiessan, Diane, and Matthias, Margaret (eds.). *The Wonderful World of Mathematics: A Critically Annotated List of Children's Books in Mathematics.* Reston, Va.: NCTM, 1992.

Uccellini, John C. Teaching the Mean Meaningfully. *Mathematics Teaching in the Middle School,* 2(2), (November–December 1996), pp. 112–115.

Vissa, Jeanne M. "Probability and Combinations for Third Graders." *Arithmetic Teacher,* 36 (December 1988), pp. 33–37.

Vissa, Jeanne M. "Sampling Treats from a School of Fish." *Arithmetic Teacher,* 34 (March 1987), pp. 36–37.

Wilson, Melvin R. (Skip), and Krapfl, Carol M. "Exploring Mean, Median, and Mode with a Spreadsheet" *Mathematics Teaching in the Middle School,* 1 (6), (September–October 1995), pp. 490–495.

Young, Sharon. "Ideas." *Arithmetic Teacher,* 38 (September 1990), pp. 23–34.

Zawojewski, Judith S. "Research into Practice: Teaching Statistics: Mode." *Arithmetic Teacher,* 35 (March 1988), pp. 25–27.

Zawojewski, Judith S.; Brooks, G.; Dinkelkamp, L.; Goldberg, E.; Goldberg, H.; Hyde, A.; Jackson, T.; Landau, M.; Martin, H.; Nowakowski, J.; Paull, S.; Shulte, A.; Wagreich, P.; and Wilmot, B. *Dealing with Data and Chance.* Reston, Va.: NCTM, 1991.

Zawojewski, Judith S.; Nowakowski, J.; and Boruch, Robert. "Romeo and Juliet: Fate, Chance, or Choice?: An English Lesson Using Probability." *Teaching Statistics,* 10 (May 1988), pp. 37–42.

16

Searching for Patterns and Relationships

 ## Snapshot of a Lesson

Orientation

An eighth-grade class is studying number theory; the students have learned to identify primes and to express composite numbers as products of primes. The lesson has just begun, and they are reviewing previous work.

MISS BELL: Yesterday we looked at prime factors. Who can tell how to find the prime factors of 429?

HANS: That one is easy, because you can look at 429 and see that 3 is a factor, since 429 = 3 · 143.

MISS BELL: That's quick, but why did you stop with the 143?

HANS: 143 is prime, I think.

MISS BELL: How would we check?

LEE: Use the calculator and start dividing.

MISS BELL: That's fine. What would you try first?

NICOLE: Begin with two and try every prime afterward. What happens if we accidentally use a composite?

LAURIE: That wouldn't matter. If it did divide 143, then you could just factor it. Just like we did with the factor tree.

JESSE: OK, but it seems like you could be trying a lot of numbers before you get to 143.

MISS BELL: That's what we all thought, but yesterday when you were absent we found a shortcut. Who can tell Jesse what we found?

ANDRA: You can stop when you get halfway there.

MISS BELL: Andra, what do you mean by halfway?

ANDRA: Well it's not really half—it is sort of a funny half. You know [going to the board], when we found all the factors of 28 we listed them:

$$1 \quad 2 \quad 4 \quad 7 \quad 14 \quad 28$$

When you get to 4 you have them all. That's what I mean by half.

MISS BELL: You have the right idea, but how do we know where to stop trying if we don't list all the factors?

HANS: You can stop when you get to the square root of the number. That's what we found out yesterday.

ANDRA: That's what I meant by halfway.

MISS BELL: Okay. Now what numbers do we have to try for 143?

LEE: The calculator says that the square root of 143 is 11.95.

HANS: So we need to try 2, 3, 5, 7 and—let's see . . . 11.

LAURIE: But we don't have to try 2 and 5, we know they don't divide 143.

▶ *Introduction*

> Mathematics is an exploratory science that seeks to understand every kind of pattern—patterns that occur in nature, patterns that are invented in the human mind, and even patterns created by other patterns. To grow mathematically, children must be exposed to a rich variety of patterns appropriate to their own lives, through which they can see variety, regularity, and interconnections. (Steen 1990, p. 8)

The author of this quote, a mathematician, presents a view of mathematics consistent with the description in Chapter 1 of this book. Throughout this book, you have encountered many patterns: patterns in the mathematics, patterns in ways children learn mathematics, and patterns in methods for instruction. In this chapter, we turn our attention to patterns and relationships in mathematics that are both numerical and nonnumerical. The first part of the chapter focuses on recognizing, describing, extending, and creating patterns, and on representing and describing relationships as called for in the *Curriculum and Evaluation Standards for School Mathematics* (NCTM 1989) for grades K–4 and grades 5–8. The second part of the chapter focuses on number theory as a search for special whole-number patterns and relationships.

● Patterns and Relationships

> We encounter patterns all the time—every day in the spoken and written word, in musical forms and video images, in ornamental designs and natural geometry, in traffic patterns, and in objects we build. Our ability to recognize, interpret, and create patterns is the key to the world around us. (Senegal 1990, p. 139)

Many possibilities for instruction open when a broad view of patterns is taken. Patterns provide a method to help children connect many ideas in mathematics and to use mathematics in a variety of ways. You can build on the background children have in describing patterns and relationships with everyday language to help them represent those patterns and relationships with mathematical symbols. For example, if children have described a pattern as "each term is 2 more than the last one," they can describe the term after the *n*th term as *n* + 2. Thus, patterns and relationships can be a natural way to lead to an understanding of functions and to algebra. In the sections that follow, we will examine only a few

of the different types of patterns and relationships and ways to describe them. The more you help your students describe patterns and relationships with pictures, words, tables, and variables, the more power they will have with mathematics.

Repeating Patterns

Repeating patterns can be simple or puzzling; of course, with young children you should begin with patterns that they can grasp. A pattern that has only two repeating elements in its core, known as an *ab* linear repeating pattern, is a good beginning.

Before doing patterns with pictures, begin with ideas such as those illustrated in Figure 16–1. You

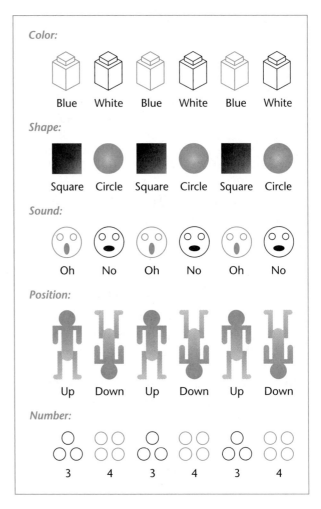

Figure 16–1 • Repeating patterns, *ab* core

may not want to start by having children stand on their heads, but do use the children themselves: one sits, one stands, one sits, one stands. Have the first few children do what you say (sit, stand, sit, stand) and ask "What should the next child do?" It will help some children to hear the pattern: "sit, stand, sit, stand, ..."

Color is a very visual attribute for children. Ask them to describe the pattern shown in Figure 16–1 (use Unifix cubes or other blocks), and then continue that pattern. You can use geometric shapes, sounds, numbers, and many other materials. When children become familiar with patterns such as these, they can extend other patterns that are begun or make their own patterns.

There are many variations of linear repeating patterns in which the core, the part that repeats, is not *ab*. For example, how would you describe the core in each of the following patterns?

A: ¿¿ □ ¿¿ □ ¿¿ □

B: # * # * * # * # * * # * # * *

C: □ $ □ $ $ □ $ □ $ $ □ $ □ $ $

The core in A may be described as *aab* or something similar. Although the core in B may be described as *ababb,* some children may see that pattern as having two cores, *ab* followed by *aab* and then repeated, or as a pattern of single *a*'s with one *b* then two *b*'s in between. The pattern in C may be described the same way as the pattern in B. It is important that children verbalize a pattern (not necessarily with *a* and *b*) and tell how it is like and different from other patterns.

Remember that children think about a pattern in a way that differs from you and that there is often more than one correct way to extend a pattern. Children's explanations of why they chose the next element of a pattern will help you understand their thinking and perhaps help you look at a pattern in a different way. Research from the Sixth Mathematics Assessment of NAEP indicates that fourth-grade students often have more difficulty inserting a missing element in a pattern than identifying the next element (Blume and Heckman 1997). Perhaps this is because they have been asked to continue patterns more than fill in the missing parts. Your curriculum should include both types of experiences.

You could do a different linear repeating pattern each day because of the variety, but do not forget geometric patterns. Figure 16–2 shows a few simple variations. Look for the use of geometric patterns by

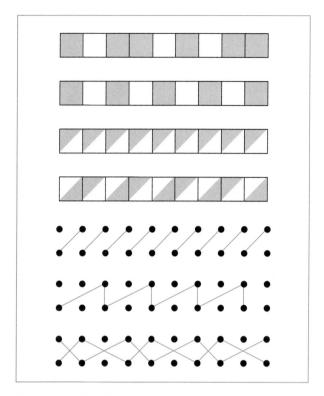

Figure 16–2 • Examples of simple geometric patterns

different cultures of the world. Quilts, fabrics, rugs, pottery, and other arts and crafts often use repetition or other intriguing patterns.

Activity Cards 16–1 and 16–2 provide activities that integrate geometric concepts with patterns. Be sure to build to Activity Card 16–2 by beginning with simpler examples. The cores of the patterns, which vary from one to four squares, may be more difficult for children to see. (Can you tell which patterns have one, two, or four squares as their core?)

Repeating patterns do not have to be linear; they can be two-dimensional or even three-dimensional. The designs on Activity Card 16–2 are two-dimensional. In some, linear patterns have been put together; in others, the pattern repeats in two directions. Can you distinguish between them?

An obvious two-dimensional pattern that is in every classroom is the calendar. Figure 16–3 shows the calendar for March 1999 as an example. Younger children may recognize that every other day has an even date or that the date of the next Friday after March 12th is 7 more, or the 19th. These observations can lead to activities involving other patterns

Activity Card 16–1

Create a Design!

▼ Color one to three triangles of the top left square in each Design A–D.

Design A   Design B

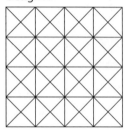 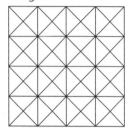

Design C   Design D

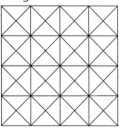 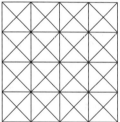

- For Design A, color each square the same way you did the first square.

- For Design B, color each square in the first row the same way. Color the next row the opposite way. Repeat.

- For Design C, color the first square in the first row. Color the second square the opposite way. Repeat for rows and columns.

- For Design D, make up your own pattern.

with squares in the calendar. Have students find the sum of all the numbers in a square. After finding the sum of the numbers in this square and several other squares of the same size, students may observe that the sum is 9 times the number in the center. Older students should be able to see why this result is true; often using letters to define the 9 numbers in the square helps. If the middle number is represented by m, then the number a week later is m + 7. Note that the sum of all these expressions is 9m. These activities with the calendar patterns are a nice way to ease into algebra.

Activity Card 16–2

Square Designs

▼ Look at these designs made by sixth-grade students. The students began with the segmented square shown, colored part of it, and then flipped, turned, or slid it to the next square.

- For each pattern, tell which motion was used and the number of squares in the core (that is, the number of squares before the pattern repeats).

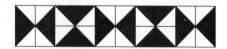

A. Motion: _____ Number of squares in core: ____

B. Motion: _____ Number of squares in core: ____

C. Motion: _____ Number of squares in core: ____

D. Motion: _____ Number of squares in core: ____

E. Motion: _____ Number of squares in core: ____

F. Motion: _____ Number of squares in core: ____

▼ Your turn:
- Begin with this square:
- Color part of it.
- Flip, turn, or slide.

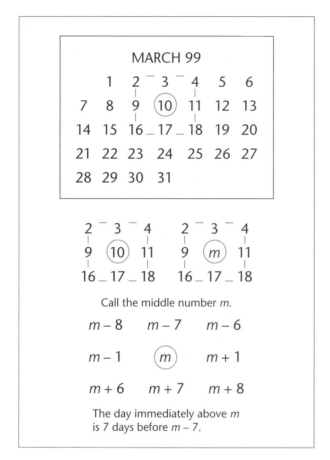

Figure 16–3 • **Calendar patterns**

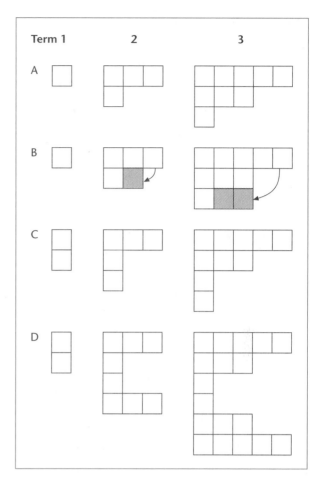

Figure 16–4 • Growing squares

Growing Patterns

Another type of pattern, often called a growing pattern, may be linear as in patterns like these:

□ ○ ○ □ □ ○ ○ ○ □ □ □ ○ ○ ○ ○ □ □ □ □ ○ ○ ○

H H T H H H H T T H H H H H H T T T T T T

Y B B Y B B B B Y B B B B B B Y B B B B B B B

Notice that only the B's are growing in the last pattern.

Growing patterns may also be two-dimensional, such as the ones formed with squares in Figure 16–4. One way to help students see these growing patterns is to have them model a pattern with square tiles then move the tiles as shown by the shaded squares in the pattern in Figure 16–4B to see what shape is formed and how it relates to the term number. For pattern A, you can ask questions such as these:

How many squares are in each of the terms, 1, 2, and 3?

Can you tell how many squares the 4th term will take?

How many squares will the 5th term take?

If you were to extend this pattern to the 100th term, how many squares would it take?

How can you describe growing pattern A?

We can describe the pattern with squared numbers. The 3rd term has 3^2 squares, the 100th term has 100^2 squares, and the nth term has n^2 squares.

See if you can see how patterns C and D are like pattern A. Do you see that each term in C has one more square than the corresponding term in A? The numbers of squares in the terms of C are 2, 5, 10, ... This sequence of numbers may not be easy for some children to represent. Yet, if you think about how A and C relate, you can see that the nth term of C has $n^2 + 1$ squares. See if you can describe the nth term of pattern D.

Relationships

Relationships abound in mathematics; here we will touch on only a few. You can look at other chapters of this book for many other examples of relationships. We will focus on describing relationships with numbers and variables.

Young children can be asked how the number of boys in a group is related to the number of hands:

If multiplication symbols have been introduced, B boys and $2 \times B$ hands describe this simple relationship. Begin by describing the number of hands of three boys as 2×3, of four boys as 2×4, and of ten boys as 2×10, writing the results for each in a table:

Number of Boys	1	2	3	4		10	B
Number of Hands	2	4	6	8		20	$2 \times B$

Consider the relationship of girls to triangles if girls make triangles from string as shown in the following figure:

Although this relationship may seem very similar to the one in the preceding example, it is a 3-to-1 relationship rather than a 1-to-2 relationship. Some children may have difficulty describing the general

Table 16–1 • **NAEP: Fourth-grade students performance on relation item**

Item	Percent Responding	
	Grade 4	*Grade 8*
1ª. In 1990 a school had 125 students. Each year the number of students in the school increases by 50. Fill in the table to show the number of students expected for each year.		

Year	Number of Students
1990	125
1991	___
1992	___
1993	___

	Grade 4	Grade 8
All three answers correct (175, 225, 275)	51	—
One or two correct answers	12	—
Incorrect or incomplete responses for all three years	30	—
Omitted	7	—

terms in this case because the relationship calls for division rather than multiplication. Again begin slowly and write the results in a table:

Number of Girls	3	6	9	12		45		N
Number of Triangles	1	2	3	4		?		$N \div 3$

At times, you may want a relationship to be established by a "function machine," which outputs a number for every number input. The challenge for the students is to decide what the function machine did and how to describe it. These machines can be simple, such as one that always gives an output of one more than the number put in, twice as much as the number put in, or two less than the number put in. For a more complicated machine, inputs and outputs might be as follows:

In	3	5	12	25		53		N	
Out	7	11	25	51	29		163		S

Be sure to ask questions about specific values that go in each direction:

Given the input _____ , what is the output?

Given the output _____ , what is the input?

In responding to the output of 64, some students will say it is impossible because it is even and all the other outputs are odd. Others will give a fraction as an input. Discuss with the students why each could be a correct interpretation. If the machine will take only whole numbers, then 64 is not a possible output. But if the machine will take fractions, $31\frac{1}{2}$ is the input for 64.

Before talking about the general rule, describe many of the outputs in terms of the inputs or what the function machine is doing in words and numbers; then try the more abstract symbols. Students may generalize as follows: "you add the number twice and then add one more" or "double the number, and add one." When the students reach this stage, have them see that a way to write each of these is $N + N + 1$ and $(2 \times N) + 1$.

Exploring relationships such as the ones discussed here can be enhanced by letting children use calculators. On the Sixth Mathematics Assessment of NAEP, fourth-grade students were asked the problem shown in Table 16–1. In this problem, the students had to find the amount of students in school

if the number increased by a constant amount each year for three years. Students who said they used a calculator did significantly better than those who said they did not make use of the available calculator. Try this problem with some fourth-grade students and observe how they approach it.

A fun way to slip into representing relationships is through number puzzles such as the one shown in Table 16–2. As a first activity, have children do the puzzle with various numbers. After using many different numbers chosen by the children, let them use materials to model the steps. You can observe whether they have strongly developed concepts

Table 16–2 • A number puzzle

Numbers	Modeling Materials	Algebra
	Pick a number:	
11	Call it ◯	Call it N
	Add 4:	
11 + 4 = 15	● ◯◯◯◯	N + 4
	Double it:	
$2 \times (11 + 4) =$ $2 \times 15 =$ 30	● ◯◯◯◯ / ● ◯◯◯◯	$2 \times (N + 4)$ or $2N + 8$
	Subtract 6:	
30 – 6 = 24	● ⊗⊗⊗⊗ / ● ⊗⊗◯◯	$2N + 8 - 6$ or $2N + 2$
	Divide by 2:	
24 ÷ 2 = 12	● ◯ / ● ◯	$\dfrac{2N + 2}{2}$ or $N + 1$
	Subtract 1:	
12 – 1 = 11	● ⊗	$N + 1 - 1$
	Answer: The original number	
11	●	N

about the operations. If you discover, for example, that some children do not know how to model "multiply by two" or "divide by two," then you can reinforce the meanings. After the students are able to model, they will enjoy describing the steps with algebra. Notice the concepts they can gain by doing this with simple algebraic representations. For example, it is easy to see that $2 \times (N + 4)$ is the same as $2N + 8$ because it is two ways to describe the same picture.

● Number Theory

Number theory is the branch of mathematics concerned mainly with the natural numbers. Odd and even numbers, primes, prime factorization, number patterns, least common multiples, and greatest common divisors are some of the typical topics included in elementary and middle school curricula. After considering why number theory should be included, we will look at a sampling of topics and ideas for teaching those topics.

Benefits of Teaching Number Theory

There are at least five reasons to include number theory in the elementary school curriculum. Read through this section and try the activities; then decide for yourself why number theory should be included.

Fascination with Numbers and Number Patterns From the time of ancient civilizations, people have been fascinated with numbers and number patterns. Ancients often thought numbers had mystical qualities, and the branch of mathematics called numerology was studied in great depth by some. Others were fascinated by patterns of numbers, such as those that occur in the 100-triangle chart on Activity Card 16–3. Many of your students, given an opportunity, will also be fascinated by numbers and some of their unusual properties. Thus, one reason to study number theory is to awaken and encourage a fascination for numbers in settings that require looking for relationships and solving problems.

A Chance to Discover Mathematics Many conjectures in number theory are easy to state, even though some may be difficult to prove. For example, the famous conjecture by Goldbach is easy enough for fourth and fifth graders to understand. In 1742, Goldbach conjectured that any even number greater than 2 could be written as the sum of two primes.

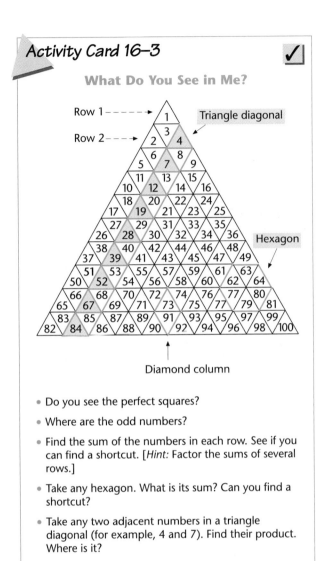

Activity Card 16–3

What Do You See in Me?

- Do you see the perfect squares?
- Where are the odd numbers?
- Find the sum of the numbers in each row. See if you can find a shortcut. [*Hint:* Factor the sums of several rows.]
- Take any hexagon. What is its sum? Can you find a shortcut?
- Take any two adjacent numbers in a triangle diagonal (for example, 4 and 7). Find their product. Where is it?

For example, $8 = 3 + 5$, $18 = 11 + 7$, and $162 = 79 + 83$. After children have shown that this conjecture is reasonable for the first hundred even numbers, they can explore some conjectures of their own. See Activity Card 16–4 for some starting places. It is important that each child keep a record of conjectures that fail, or you can keep a class record. It is just as important to know what will not work as it is to know what will work. Be sure to emphasize that students have not proved a conjecture by trying examples; they have only found out that it works for the examples chosen. In fact, no one has ever proved or disproved Goldbach's conjecture.

A chance to discover some pattern in the 100-triangle chart, a conjecture, or a divisibility test maybe as close as many students will come to doing original mathematics. Although some of the things

Activity Card 16–4

Do You Believe That?

▼ Try one of these conjectures about positive whole numbers. See if you can find examples that disprove each.

- *Tinbach's Conjecture:* Every number can be expressed as the difference of two primes.

  Examples: $14 = 17 - 3$ $5 = 7 - 2$ $28 = 31 - 3$

- *Zinbach's Conjecture:* Every number can be expressed as the sum of 3 squares (0 is permitted).

  Examples: $3 = 1^2 + 1^2 + 1^2$ $14 = 1^2 + 2^2 + 3^2$
  $9 = 3^2 + 0^2 + 0^2$

- *Aluminumbach's Conjecture:* Every odd number can be expressed as the sum of 3 primes.

  Examples: $15 = 5 + 5 + 5$ $11 = 3 + 3 + 5$

- *Brassbach's Conjecture:* Every square number has exactly 3 divisors.

  Example: $2^2 = 4$, 4 has 3 divisors 1, 2, and 4

- *Copperbach's Conjecture:* The product of any number of primes is odd.

  Examples: $5 \times 3 \times 7 = 105$ (3 primes)
  $7 \times 3 \times 3 \times 5 = 315$ (4 primes)

Activity Card 16–5

Am I Abundant, Deficient, or Perfect?

▼ How to tell:

- Find all the divisors of the number, except itself, and add those divisors.
- If the sum is *greater* than the number, then the number is **abundant**.
- If the sum is *less* than the number, then the number is **deficient**.
- If the sum is *equal* to the number, then the number is **perfect**.

▼ Examples:

35	$1 + 5 + 7 = 13$	$13 < 35$ deficient
18	$1 + 2 + 3 + 6 + 9 = 21$	$21 > 18$ abundant
28	$1 + 2 + 4 + 7 + 14 = 28$	$28 = 28$ perfect

▼ Your turn:

Classify the numbers 1–20.

Find 5 abundant numbers.

▼ Challenge:

What is 496?

▼ Superchallenge:

What is 8128?

your students discover may not be original, they can still feel the joy of their own ideas or realizations.

Extension and Practice Teachers often need ways to help individualize within a topic. For example, suppose you need to review multiplication and division with some children in a fifth-grade class. Even though all of the children would probably benefit from some review, they all will not need the same amount. What do you do with those students who do not need as much review? Number theory often provides an extension. In this case, you might have them use Activity Card 16–5 to investigate abundant, deficient, and perfect numbers. This activity will give a lot of practice with multiplication and division.

Recreation Did you ever think of mathematics as a recreation? Number theory provides many puzzle-type activities that many children will find recreational. Just as not all children enjoy the same sports

or games, not all will find puzzles enjoyable. However, if you begin with simple puzzles and treat them as games, many children will become interested.

In solving puzzles, students are practicing skills, developing number sense, and using problem-solving strategies. For example, in the magic square shown in Figure 16–5, children soon learn that the two largest numbers cannot go in the same row, column, or diagonal. This activity can be done solely with paper and pencil, but it is suggested that you use cards. First, the use of cards makes the activity more like a puzzle to many children. Second, it saves erasing wrong tries until holes appear in the paper. The disadvantage of the cards is that children have

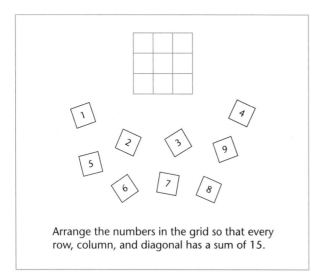

Arrange the numbers in the grid so that every row, column, and diagonal has a sum of 15.

Figure 16–5 • A magic square

no records of their tries and may repeat the same attempt over and over. You can help them solve this problem by encouraging them to create a table to record their attempts.

Use in Other Mathematics Topics Number theory can be used for practice in the four operations and in problem solving, but it also can be used in other mathematics topics. For example, the least common multiple can be used in finding common denominators, or greatest common divisors can be used in reducing fractions. At one time, many of the number-theory topics were of assistance in doing or checking computation. For example, the divisibility tests were a quick way to see if a number was a factor of another, and "casting out nines" was a quick check on long computations. Although none of these uses retain their former importance, these topics can be justified if they also fulfill some of the other reasons to study number theory.

Specific Number Theory Topics

Certain skills related to number theory are expected of most students. In this section, we will examine some ways to develop these skills. As is true with any skills after they are developed, they need to be maintained. To teach children what a prime number is in fourth grade and then never use primes again assures that primes will be forgotten. Only about 58 percent of thirteen-year-olds could choose the definition of a prime number (Carpenter et al. 1981). Beyond the skills to be developed, it is important to keep in mind the reasons for studying number the-

ory. If all teachers do is have children learn definitions and rules, they have missed the real power of number theory.

Odds and Evens Classifying numbers as odd or even is one of the first number-theory topics that children encounter. As children count by twos—2, 4, 6, 8, 10—they learn that there is something different about these numbers; these are the even numbers, and the others are the odds. More precisely, an even number is a number that is a multiple of 2.

You can begin the study of odds and evens by having young children model the natural numbers with square tiles. Give each child a number (two through twenty) of square tiles. Young children may pretend they are making candy bars that are two squares wide. If a number of squares can be arranged in a rectangle that is two squares wide, then that number is even. If not, it is odd. Why is that last statement true?

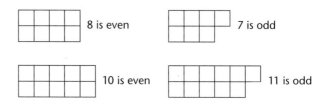

Have the children list all the odd and even numbers. They should see the pattern that every other number is even and that the even numbers end in 0, 2, 4, 6, or 8.

Children can use this candy-bar model to investigate the sum of two evens or two odds or the products of evens and odds. For example, as shown in Figure 16–6, two odds can always be put together to make an even; the sum of two odds is even. Similarly, the product of an even and an odd will always be even.

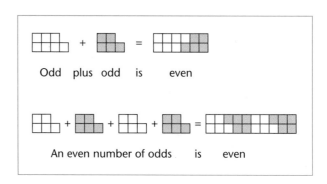

Figure 16–6 • Models for summing odd numbers

Evens and odds arise on many occasions, and you should look for experiences in which the ideas of odds and evens are used. For example, students might find the sum of the first 50 odd numbers (see Activity Cards 2–2 and 2–3), find the probability of throwing an even number with two dice, or find the first odd number that is divisible by 11.

Factors, Primes, and Prime Factorization As children are learning about multiplication and division, they are also beginning to learn about multiples and factors. In this section, we will examine how to extend and use these ideas.

Factors. Each of two numbers multiplied together to give a product is called a *factor* of that product. For example, 3 and 4 are factors of 12 because 3 times 4 is 12.

Children can begin exploring factors by using materials. For example, begin with 12 objects. See if they can group the 12 objects by ones, twos, threes, . . . , twelves. There are 12 groups of ones, 6 groups of twos, 4 groups of threes, 3 groups of fours, 2 groups of sixes, and 1 group of twelves, but 12 cannot be grouped by fives, sevens, eights, nines, tens, or elevens.

The 12 Story

$$12 = 12 \times 1$$
$$12 = 6 \times 2$$
$$12 = 4 \times 3$$
$$12 = 3 \times 4$$
$$12 = 2 \times 6$$
$$12 = 1 \times 12$$

Later, children should be able to find all the factors of a given number. For example, what are all the factors of 84? One place to begin is to see what numbers will divide 84. Have the children begin with the simplest divisor. You might lead them through a process such as this:

We know that 1 will divide 84, so 1 and 84 are factors. Write:

1   84

Now try 2 (in your head). [2 × 42 = 84, so 2 and 42 are factors.] Write:

1, 2   42, 84

How about 3? (Use your calculator.) [3 × 28 = 84, so 3 and 28 are factors.] Write:

1, 2, 3   28, 42, 84

How about 4? [4 × 21 = 84, so 4 and 21 are factors.] Write:

1, 2, 3, 4   21, 28, 42, 84

How about 5? No, so try 6. [6 × 14 = 84, so 6 and 14 are factors.] Write:

1, 2, 3, 4, 6   14, 21, 28, 42, 84

How long do we continue? Do you see that we are closing in on it? At this point you can conclude that we don't need to try anything beyond 14 because anything larger than 14 would have to be multiplied by something smaller than 6 and we've tried that. So, let's try 7. [7 × 12 = 84, so 7 and 12 are factors.] Write:

1, 2, 3, 4, 6, 7   12, 14, 21, 28, 42, 84

How about 8? 9? Do you need to try 10?

Children will need to try 10, 11, and perhaps some more numbers before they realize that, if they divide 84 by 10, 11, and so on, they always get a quotient smaller than 9, and they have checked each one of these.

This process is the one on which the students in the Snapshot Lesson at the beginning of this chapter were working. Activity Card 16–6 is a game that requires children to find the factors of the numbers 2 through 36 and to use some strategy. (Try it with a friend. It's not as easy to win as you may think!)

Multiples. A multiple of a number is the product of that number and any natural number. For example, 36 is a multiple of 4 because 36 is 4 times 9. In looking at multiples, we usually begin with the number and generate multiples of it. Here are the positive multiples of 4:

4, 8, 12, 16, 20, 24, 28, . . .

Activity Card 16–6

Factor Me Out

▼ Choose a partner and make a chart to play this game:

●	2	3	4	5	6
7	8	9	10	11	12
13	14	15	16	17	18
19	20	21	22	23	24
25	26	27	28	29	30
31	32	33	34	35	36

▼ Rules:

• Player 1 chooses a number. He or she gets that many points. The opponent gets points equal to the sum of all the factors.

• Make a table to record scores:

Player 1	Player 2
10	7 (2 + 5)

• Mark out the number and the factors; these cannot be used again.

• Repeat with Player 2 choosing the number.

• Alternate turns until no numbers are left.

The player with the most points wins.

How did we generate this list? (We multiplied 4 by 1, 2, 3, 4, and so forth.)

Many different materials can be used to illustrate multiples such as the number line, Cuisenaire rods, and the hundred chart. Children should be familiar with the smaller multiples of the numbers 1 through 10 through the multiplication facts.

The concept of a multiple is not difficult—remember, it is a product. It is simply a new word, and children often confuse it with another new word, factor, or divisor. Confusion also arises when teachers ask, "What is 36 a multiple of?" They are actually asking children to find the factors of 36. Then when they ask, "What is 4 a factor of?" they are actually asking the children to find the multiples of 4. Children need to be able to think in both directions—for example, to list all the multiples of 7 and to find what 42 is a multiple of. But when you are first beginning the study of multiples and factors, keep the language consistent.

Primes and Composites. A whole number greater than one is prime if it has exactly two factors: one and itself. Otherwise, it is composite. There are several concrete models that you may use to introduce the idea of primes. The activity on Lesson Card 16–1 illustrates one model.

After children have been introduced to primes, develop the definition with them. Then, have them identify which numbers are primes and which are composites. The chapter opening Snapshot Lesson illustrates a procedure they may use to classify numbers as prime or composite.

There are other explorations that focus on primes, such as the sieve of Eratosthenes, described later. One can also investigate twin primes (pairs of primes that are two apart, such as 11 and 13), reversal primes (pairs of primes such as 79 and 97), or the infinitude of primes.

Prime Factorization. The fundamental theorem of arithmetic says that every composite number may be expressed as a product of primes in only one way. Many patterns and formulas in number theory, as well as some algorithms for finding the greatest common factor and the least common multiple, depend on expressing a number as a product of primes (prime factorization).

How would you begin to find the prime factors of 3190?

Two methods are commonly used to find the prime factorization of a number. One is the *factor tree method:*

```
            3190
           /    \
         10      319
        /  \    /  \
       2    5  11   29
```

The other is the *division method,* in which the number is divided by primes:

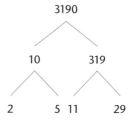

What is the difference between the two methods? In the factor tree method, the first step is to factor the number into any two factors. In the division method, you must divide by a prime. If, in the factor tree method, you made the rule that one factor must always be a prime, then the two methods would be the same except for notation.

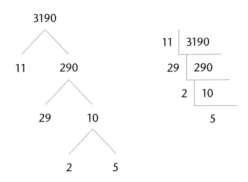

No matter which method students use, make certain that they write the prime factorization. For example, they should express 3190 as $2 \times 5 \times 11 \times 29$.

Greatest Common Factor and Least Common Multiple   We have looked at factors and multiples of individual numbers; now we will examine pairs of numbers to find the greatest common factor (GCF) and the least common multiple (LCM) by asking

> What is the largest number that is a factor of both numbers?
>
> What is the smallest number that is a multiple of both numbers?

Understanding these concepts depends mainly on knowing how to find factors and multiples and keeping straight which is which. Algorithms for finding the GCF and the LCM are very similar. Often teachers develop GCF and LCM right after the other and then do not use them. Or, if they develop the two ideas at separate times, they never bring them back together to compare and contrast them. If taught at all, these two concepts should be presented in a meaningful manner. Several algorithms are available for finding the GCF and LCM; the listing algorithm and the factorization algorithm are commonly used. Because the listing algorithm is the more concrete of the two, we will present it here. This would be a good time to let children develop their own algorithm. After seeing different ways that they found the GCF for two numbers, discuss the efficiency of some of the ways.

To find the GCF with the listing algorithm, you first list all the factors of the two (or more) numbers. For example, to find the GCF of 18 and 24, list the following:

Factors of 18:   1   2   3   6   9   18

Factors of 24:   1   2   3   4   6   8   12   24

Then we look for the common factors—1, 2, 3, 6—and choose the largest. Thus, 6 is the GCF.

Similarly, to find the LCM, list the multiples of each number until you find common multiples. For example, to find the LCM of 18 and 24, list the following:

Multiples of 18:   18   36   54   72   90 . . .

Multiples of 24:   24   48   72   96 . . .

By inspection, 72 is the smallest number common to both sets. Thus, the LCM is 72.

Children may use the LCM as they find the least common denominator of two fractions, and they may use the GCF when they reduce fractions. Yet often we fail to teach them what they are using. For example, to reduce $^{18}/_{24}$, children may first reduce it to $^{9}/_{12}$ and then to $^{3}/_{4}$. If they see that the GCF of 18 and 24 is 6, then they can do the reduction in one step. However, the time saved by finding the GCF first is probably not worth the effort.

Similarly, at times it is important to find the least common denominator, but often it is sufficient to find a common denominator. Today, with the prevalence of calculators and decreased emphasis on complicated fractions, finding GCFs and LCMs is not as crucial as it once was. If you do teach these concepts, however, develop them carefully and at a stage in the students' maturity when they can grasp what they are doing.

Divisibility Tests   At one time the divisibility rules were important. Today, they are an interesting sidelight in mathematics. It is the discovery of some of the rules or the investigation to see why they work that makes them a topic worth the study.

Many children discover on their own the rules for 2 and 5 through observing patterns in the multiplication and division facts for those numbers. The rules for other numbers are not quite as evident. Activity Card 16–7 provides a guided discovery activity for the divisibility rules for 3 and 9. It is important to discuss the results in the table with the class and to give more examples if the students don't answer

Lesson Card 16–1

Materials: A copy of the worksheet: The Hip-Hoppers Hop

Directions: Have the children do the worksheet after introducing the terms *prime* and *composite*. (The primes have two hopper stoppers; the composites have more than two hopper stoppers; and one is neither.)

When they have completed the chart, discuss the following questions with them:

- What numbers had two hopper stoppers? [2, 3, 5, 7, etc.]

- What numbers had more than two hopper stoppers? [4, 6, 8, 9, etc.]

- What number had only one hopper stopper? [1]

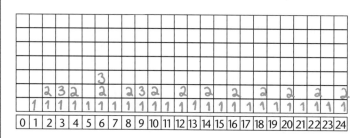

The Hip-Hoppers Hop

The hoppers are strange characters that can only hop a certain length. For example, the 5-hopper hops 5 spaces each time. They all begin at 0.

See where each hopper will land. The 1-hopper and the 2-hopper have been done for you.

Be a 3-hopper. You will land at 3 (write a 3 above the 3), you will land at 6 (write a 3 above the 6). Keep going. (You should have 3's above 9, 12, 15, 18, 21, 24).

Do the same for the 4-hopper, the 5-hopper, all the way to a 24-hopper. Then, answer the questions your teacher has.

---

the questions clearly. Here are some good questions to raise:

Does this divisibility test work for larger numbers?

Is this a test only for 3 and 9?

Why does this work?

You can help students reason through the last question by examining a model of a different way to divide, say, 456 by 3. Figure 16–7 shows one way to think about dividing 456 by 3 so that the divisibility test makes sense.

You can look at other divisibility tests in a similar manner. For example, the divisibility test for 4 depends only on the tens boxes and the ones. The hundreds boxes, thousands boxes, and so on can always be divided or shared by 4, but a ten cannot be broken into four equal whole number parts. Thus, a

Activity Card 16–7

Divisibility Discovery

▼ Use your [calculator]. Fill in the chart and look for patterns.

Number	Divisible by 3?	9?	Sum of digits	Sum divisible by 3?	by 9?
456	yes	no	4 + 5 + 6 = 15	yes	no
891					
892					
514					
37					
78					
79					
1357					
1358					
1359					
1360					
1361					
1362					

▼ What do you think?

- A number is divisible by 3. Is it always divisible by 9?

- A number is divisible by 9. Is it always divisible by 3?

- What does the sum of the digits tell you?

- What did you notice about the sequence of numbers 1357, 1358, 1359, . . . 1362?

TIP: DISCUSS THESE IN YOUR GROUP!

number's divisibility by 4 depends on how many tens and ones it has. For example, 526 is not divisible by 4 because 26 is not, but 536 is divisible by 4 because 36 is.

Other Ideas to Investigate There are many other topics in number theory that you can have students investigate. Some ideas are given here, but only as a starter. These topics are suitable for middle school students with your guidance.

Pascal's Triangle. Pascal's triangle is most closely associated with probability. However, there are many number patterns in it. Some are suggested on Activity Card 16–8.

Pythagorean Triples. A Pythagorean triple is a triple of numbers, (a, b, c), such that $a^2 + b^2 = c^2$. For example, $(3, 4, 5)$ is a Pythagorean triple. There are many ways to generate Pythagorean triples and many patterns in the triples. The chart on Activity Card 16–9 gives a way to generate such triples and looks at some patterns.

Fibonacci's Sequence. Fibonacci's sequence of numbers is

$$1 \quad 1 \quad 2 \quad 3 \quad 5 \quad 8 \quad 13 \quad 21 \quad 34 \ldots$$

Do you know the next number in the sequence? Can you tell how the sequence is formed? Many patterns in nature follow this sequence. A computer

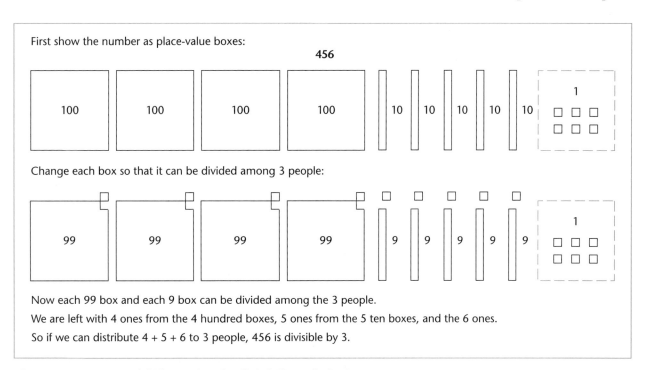

First show the number as place-value boxes:

456

Change each box so that it can be divided among 3 people:

Now each 99 box and each 9 box can be divided among the 3 people.

We are left with 4 ones from the 4 hundred boxes, 5 ones from the 5 ten boxes, and the 6 ones.

So if we can distribute 4 + 5 + 6 to 3 people, 456 is divisible by 3.

Figure 16–7 • **A model illustrating the divisibility rule for 3**

Activity Card 16–8

Pascal's Triangle

▼ Finish row 7 of this triangle.

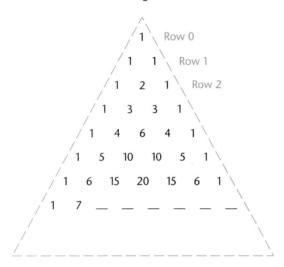

▼ Write rows 8 and 9.

• What patterns do you see?

▼ Find the sum of each row, by filling in the table:

Row	Sum
0	1
1	1 + 1 = 2
2	1 + 2 + 1 = 4
3	
4	
5	

▼ Guess before you calculate:

• What do you think the sum of the eighth row is?

• How about the twentieth row?

▼ Look at the numbers in any odd row (ignore the ones):

• What do you notice?

• Do you think this will be true in row 9?

Activity Card 16–9

Pythagorean Patterns

▼ Here is a table of Pythagorean triples:

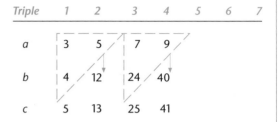

Triple	1	2	3	4	5	6	7
a	3	5	7	9			
b	4	12	24	40			
c	5	13	25	41			

▼ Use a calculator and check to see if (3, 4, 5), (5, 12, 13), (7, 24, 25), and (9, 40, 41) are Pythagorean triples. (See if $a^2 + b^2 = c^2$).

▼ Create the fifth triple.

• What would a be?

• To find b, look at the three numbers in the dotted triangle. What do you do with the three numbers to get the b marked with an arrow?

• If you know b, how do you get c?

• Did you get (11, 60, 61)?

▼ Create the sixth, seventh, and eighth Pythagorean triples. Check each with the calculator.

Sieves. The most famous of the sieves is the sieve of Eratosthenes, in which the numbers are arranged in ten columns. The sieve shown on Activity Card 16–12 gives an easy method for generating the primes. At first the process will seem long, but children will soon realize how quickly the primes can be generated. The beauty of the arrangement of the sieve in columns of six is that after 2 and 3, all the primes occur in the first or the fifth column. Do you see why?

▶ A Glance at Where We've Been

This chapter has considered some reasons for including patterns and relationships in the elementary mathematics curriculum. From the very beginning of schooling, children can describe, extend, and create patterns in a variety of ways. As they progress through school, both the types of patterns

can help generate Fibonacci numbers and other sequences, as illustrated by Activity Card 16–10.

Number Patterns in Geometry. Many patterns in geometry lead to interesting number patterns. A sample is given on Activity Card 16–11.

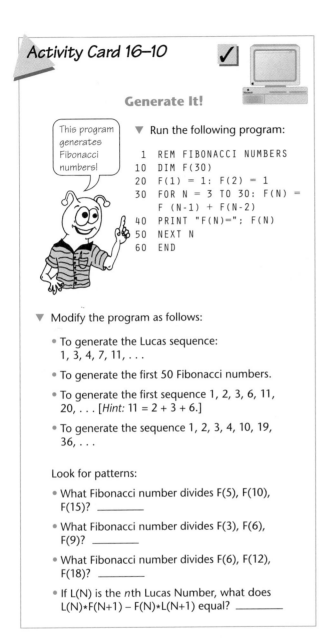

Activity Card 16–10

Generate It!

This program generates Fibonacci numbers!

▼ Run the following program:

```
 1 REM FIBONACCI NUMBERS
10 DIM F(30)
20 F(1) = 1: F(2) = 1
30 FOR N = 3 TO 30: F(N) =
   F (N-1) + F(N-2)
40 PRINT "F(N)="; F(N)
50 NEXT N
60 END
```

▼ Modify the program as follows:

• To generate the Lucas sequence:
  1, 3, 4, 7, 11, . . .

• To generate the first 50 Fibonacci numbers.

• To generate the first sequence 1, 2, 3, 6, 11,
  20, . . . [*Hint:* 11 = 2 + 3 + 6.]

• To generate the sequence 1, 2, 3, 4, 10, 19,
  36, . . .

Look for patterns:

• What Fibonacci number divides F(5), F(10),
  F(15)? _____

• What Fibonacci number divides F(3), F(6),
  F(9)? _____

• What Fibonacci number divides F(6), F(12),
  F(18)? _____

• If L(N) is the *n*th Lucas Number, what does
  L(N)*F(N+1) – F(N)*L(N+1) equal? _____

Activity Card 16–11

Count Those Rectangles!

▼ How many rectangles in this figure?

▼ If you want some hints, try this.

▼ Begin with a smaller problem:

☐ 1 square
   0 nonsquare rectangles
   1 total

☐☐ 2 squares
   1 nonsquare rectangles
   3 total

☐☐☐ 3 squares
   3 nonsquare rectangles
   6 total

▼ Continue with 4 squares, 5 squares, and on.

▼ Complete the table:

• Fill in Row A of the table with the
  number of squares.

• Fill in Row B with the number of
  rectangles that are not squares.

• Find the total for each column and fill in
  Row C.

  Look for a pattern to help you!

A	1	2	3	4	5	6						
B	0	1	3									
C	1	3	6									

and their descriptions can become more sophisticated. In describing patterns and relationships, variables can be used in a natural way.

This chapter also has presented some reasons for studying number theory. At this level, number theory is a topic that can be used to illustrate for students what it means to do mathematics. Number theory offers an abundance of ideas suitable for students to investigate; thus, it provides many problem-solving situations and ways to extend other topics in mathematics.

The use of topics concerning patterns, relationships, and number theory will enliven your classroom and help your students make sense of mathematics.

▶ THINGS TO DO: From What You've Read

1. Why should children study patterns in mathematics?

2. What are two common types of patterns? How do they differ? How are they alike?

3. Give three ways that children can describe relationships.

4. Try the number puzzle in Table 16–2 with friends. Can they explain why it worked? Can you show

Activity Card 16–12

Sieve 6

▼ Do it:

- Circle 2, then mark out every second number.

- Circle 3, then mark out every third number (6, 9, 12, . . .) Some may already be marked out.

- Circle 5 (since 4 is marked out) and mark out every fifth number. Continue to 96.

②	3	4̶	5	6̶
7	8̶	9	10	11	12
13	14	15	16	17	18
19	20	21	22	23	24
25	26	27	28	29	30
31	32	33	34	35	36
37	38	39	40	41	42
43	44	45	46	47	48
49	50	51	52	53	54
55	56	57	58	59	60
61	62	63	64	65	66
67	68	69	70	71	72
73	74	75	76	77	78
79	80	81	82	83	84
85	86	87	88	89	90
91	92	93	94	95	96

▼ Talk about it:

- What numbers are circled? _____

- In what columns are they? _____

them with materials why it worked? Make up one of your own and try that one.

5. List four reasons for teaching number theory. Give an example of an activity, other than the ones in the text, to illustrate one of your four reasons.

6. Explain with a picture like that in Figure 16–7 why the divisibility test for eight works.

7. Use the picture method of Figure 16–7 to discover a divisibility test for 11.

8. Show how one can develop the concept of multiples with Cuisenaire rods, a number line, or any other concrete model.

9. Try one of the conjectures on Activity Card 16–4 with a student. Record the student's procedure, comments, and hints that you provided.

▶ THINGS TO DO: Going Beyond This Book

1. Examine the treatment of patterns in an elementary mathematics textbook at a grade level of your choice. How does it differ from what is shown here?

2. Find examples of patterns in everyday life. Write about them or illustrate them with drawings. Which of them have a connection with mathematics?

3. Find a number theory activity that provides practice with one of the four operations.

4. Examine *Patterns and Functions* (Phillips et al. 1991). Choose one of the patterns presented and describe how you would share it with children.

5. In a middle school textbook, locate the factoring algorithm for finding the GCF or the LCM. Compare that method with the listing algorithm presented here with respect to level of difficulty in developing meaning and ease of use.

6. Make a worksheet that uses materials and encourages the discovery of each of the following: the product of two even numbers is even, the sum of two odds is even, the sum of an even and an odd is odd, and the sum of any number of even numbers is even.

7. Write a lesson plan for one of the following:
   a. Finding all the factors of a number.
   b. Finding the prime factors of a number.
   c. Finding the least common multiple.

8. Collect activities that you can use in teaching one of these topics: Pascal's triangle, Pythagorean triples, sieves, divisibility tests, magic squares, geometric number patterns, Fibonacci's sequence, or number patterns.

▼▼▼▼▼▼▼▼▼▼▼▼▼▼▼▼▼▼▼▼▼▼▼▼▼

Children's Corner

Burningham, John. *The Shopping Basket*. New York: Crowell Jr. Books, 1980.

Gelman, Rita Golden. *More Spaghetti, I Say!* New York: Scholastic, 1977.

Kent, Jack. *The Twelve Days of Christmas*. New York: Scholastic, 1971.

Masaichiro, Anno, and Mitsumasa, Anno. *Anno's Mysterious Multiplying Jars*. New York: Philomel Books, 1983.

Randell, Beverly. *At the Zoo*. New York: Nelson (Joining-in Books), 1986.

Selected References

Avital, Shmuel. "Don't Be Blue, Number Two." *Arithmetic Teacher*, 34 (September 1986), pp. 42–45.

Bezuszka, Stanley J. "A Test for Divisibility by Primes." *Arithmetic Teacher*, 33 (October 1985), pp. 36–39.

Blume, Glendon W., and Heckman, David S. "What Do Students Know about Algebra and Functions." In *Results from the Sixth Mathematics Assessment of the National Assessment of Educational Progress* (eds. Patricia Ann Kenney and Edward A. Silver). Reston Va.: NCTM, 1997, pp. 225–277.

Boyd, Barbara Vogel. "Learning about Odd and Even Numbers." *Arithmetic Teacher*, 35 (November 1987), pp. 18–20.

Bright, George W. "Using Tables to Solve Some Geometry Problems." *Arithmetic Teacher*, 25 (May 1978), pp. 39–43.

Brown, G. W. "Searching for Patterns of Divisors." *Arithmetic Teacher,* 32 (December 1984), pp. 32–34.

Burton, Grace M., and Knifong, J. Dan. "Definitions for Prime Numbers." *Arithmetic Teacher*, 27 (February 1980), pp. 44–47.

Carpenter, Thomas P.; Corbitt, Mary Kay; Kepner, Henry S., Jr.; Lindquist, Mary Montgomery; and Reys, Robert E. *Results from the Second Mathematics Assessment of the National Assessment of Educational Progress*. Reston, Va.: NCTM, 1981.

Coburn, Terrence G.; Bushey, Barbara J.; Holtan, Liana C.; Latozas, Debra; Mortimer, Debbie; and Shotwell, Deborah. *Addenda Series, Grades K–6: Patterns*. Reston, Va.: NCTM, 1992.

DiDomenico, Angelo. "Eureka! Pythagorean Triples from the Multiplication Table." *Mathematics Teacher,* 76 (January 1983), pp. 48–51.

Duncan, David R., and Litwiller, Bonnie H. "Number–Lattice Polygons and Patterns: Sums and Products." *Arithmetic Teacher*, 37 (January 1990), pp. 14–15.

Hoffman, Nathan. "Pascal's Triangle." *Arithmetic Teacher,* 21 (March 1974), pp. 190–198.

Howden, Hilde. "Implementing the Standards: Patterns, Relations, and Functions." *Arithmetic Teacher,* 37 (November 1989), pp. 18–25.

Jensen, Robert J. "Teaching Mathematics in Technology: Common Multiples Activities On and Off the Computer." *Arithmetic Teacher,* 35 (December 1987), pp. 35–37.

Kuczkowski, Joseph. "Sneaking in Basic Drill with Sneaky Squares." *Arithmetic Teacher*, 30 (December 1982), pp. 32–34.

Litwiller, Bonnie H., and Duncan, David R. "Polygons on a Number Lattice: Sums, Products, and Differences." *Arithmetic Teacher*, 37 (November 1989), pp. 39–43.

National Council of Teachers of Mathematics. *Curriculum and Evaluation Standards for School Mathematics*. Reston, Va.: NCTM, 1989.

Norman, F. Alexander. "Figurate Numbers in the Classroom." *Arithmetic Teacher*, 38 (March 1991), pp. 42–45.

Omejc, Eve. "A Different Approach to the Sieve of Eratosthenes." *Arithmetic Teacher,* 19 (March 1972), pp. 192–196.

Parker, Janet, and Widmer, Connie Carroll. "Patterns in Measurement." *Arithmetic Teacher,* 40 (January 1993), pp. 292–295.

Phillips, Elizabeth; Gardella, Theodore; Kelly, Constance; and Stewart, Jacqueline. *Addenda Series, Grades 5–8: Patterns and Functions*. Reston, Va.: NCTM, 1991.

Senegal, Majorie. "Shape." In *On the Shoulders of Giants: New Approaches to Numeracy* (ed. Lynn A. Steen). Washington, D.C.: National Academy Press, 1990, pp. 139–182.

Sherrill, James M. "Magic Squares and Magic Triangles." *Arithmetic Teacher*, 35 (October 1987), pp. 44–47.

Steen, Lynn A. "Pattern." In *On the Shoulders of Giants: New Approaches to Numeracy* (ed. Lynn A. Steen). Washington, D.C.: National Academy Press, 1990, pp. 1–10.

Tierney, Cornelia C. "Patterns in a Multiplication Table." *Arithmetic Teacher*, 33 (March 1985), pp. 36–40.

Whitin, David J. "Bring on the Buttons." *Arithmetic Teacher*, 37 (January 1989) pp. 4–6.

Whitin, David J. "More Magic with Palindrones." *Arithmetic Teacher*, 33 (January 1985), pp. 25–26.

Wills, Herbert, III. "Magic with Magic Squares." *Arithmetic Teacher*, 36 (April 1989), pp. 44–49.

Summary of NCTM Recommendations

Summary of Changes in Content and Emphasis in K–4 Mathematics

Increased Attention

Number
- Number sense
- Place-value concepts
- Meaning of fractions and decimals
- Estimation of quantities

Operations and Computation
- Meaning of operations
- Operation sense
- Mental computation
- Estimation and the reasonableness of answers
- Selection of an appropriate computational method
- Use of calculators for complex computation
- Thinking strategies for basic facts

Geometry and Measurement
- Properties of geometric figures
- Geometric relationships
- Spatial sense
- Process of measuring
- Concepts related to units of measurement
- Actual measuring
- Estimation of measurements
- Use of measurement and geometry ideas throughout the curriculum

Probability and Statistics
- Collection and organization of data
- Exploration of chance

Decreased Attention

Number
- Early attention to reading, writing, and ordering numbers symbolically

Operations and Computation
- Complex paper-and-pencil computations
- Isolated treatment of paper-and-pencil computations
- Addition and subtraction without renaming
- Isolated treatment of division facts
- Long division
- Long division without remainders
- Paper-and-pencil fraction computation
- Use of rounding to estimate

Geometry and Measurement
- Primary focus on naming geometric figures
- Memorization of equivalencies between units of measurement

Summary of Changes in K–4 Mathematics—continued

Increased Attention

Decreased Attention

Patterns and Relationships
- Pattern recognition and description
- Use of variables to express relationships

Problem Solving
- Word problems with a variety of structures
- Use of everyday problems
- Applications
- Study of patterns and relationships
- Problem-solving strategies

Problem Solving
- Use of clue words to determine which operation to use

Instructional Practices
- Use of manipulative materials
- Cooperative work
- Discussion of mathematics
- Questioning
- Justification of thinking
- Writing about mathematics
- Problem-solving approach to instruction
- Content integration
- Use of calculators and computers

Instructional Practices
- Rote practice
- Rote memorization of rules
- One answer and one method
- Use of worksheets
- Written practice
- Teaching by telling

Changes in Content and Emphasis in 5–8 Mathematics

Increased Attention

Decreased Attention

Problem Solving
- Pursuing open-ended problems and extended problem-solving projects
- Investigating and formulating questions from problem situations
- Representing situations verbally, numerically, graphically, geometrically, or symbolically

Problem Solving
- Practicing routine, one-step problems
- Practicing problems categorized by types (e.g., coin problems, age problems)

Communication
- Discussing, writing, reading, and listening to mathematical ideas

Communication
- Doing fill-in-the-blank worksheets
- Answering questions that require only yes, no, or a number as responses

Reasoning
- Reasoning in spatial contexts
- Reasoning with proportions
- Reasoning from graphs
- Reasoning inductively and deductively

Reasoning
- Relying on outside authority (teacher or an answer key)

Connections
- Connecting mathematics to other subjects and to the world outside the classroom
- Connecting topics within mathematics
- Applying mathematics

Connections
- Learning isolated topics
- Developing skills out of context

Summary of Changes in 5–8 Mathematics—continued

Increased Attention

Number/Operations/Computation
- Developing number sense
- Developing operation sense
- Creating algorithms and procedures
- Using estimation both in solving problems and in checking the reasonableness of results
- Exploring relationships among representations of, and operations on, whole numbers, fractions, decimals, integers, and rational numbers
- Developing an understanding of ratio, proportion, and percent

Patterns and Functions
- Identifying and using functional relationships
- Developing and using tables, graphs, and rules to describe situations
- Interpreting among different mathematical representations

Algebra
- Developing an understanding of variables, expressions, and equations
- Using a variety of methods to solve linear equations and informally investigate inequalities and nonlinear equations

Statistics
- Using statistical methods to describe, analyze, evaluate, and make decisions

Probability
- Creating experimental and theoretical models of situations involving probabilities

Geometry
- Developing an understanding of geometric objects and relationships
- Using geometry in solving problems

Measurement
- Estimating and using measurement to solve problems

Instructional Practices
- Actively involving students individually and in groups in exploring, conjecturing, analyzing, and applying mathematics in both a mathematical and a real-world context
- Using appropriate technology for computation and exploration
- Using concrete materials
- Being a facilitator of learning
- Assessing learning as an integral part of instruction

Decreased Attention

Number/Operations/Computation
- Memorizing rules and algorithms
- Practicing tedious paper-and-pencil computations
- Finding exact forms of answers
- Memorizing procedures, such as cross-multiplication, without understanding
- Practicing rounding numbers out of context

Patterns and Functions
- Topics seldom in the current curriculum

Algebra
- Manipulating symbols
- Memorizing procedures and drilling on equation solving

Statistics
- Memorizing formulas

Probability
- Memorizing formulas

Geometry
- Memorizing geometric vocabulary
- Memorizing facts and relationships

Measurement
- Memorizing and manipulating formulas
- Converting within and between measurement systems

Instructional Practices
- Teaching computations out of context
- Drilling on paper-and-pencil algorithms
- Teaching topics in isolation
- Stressing memorization
- Being the dispenser of knowledge
- Testing for the sole purpose of assigning grades

Appendix A is from *Curriculum and Evaluation Standards for School Mathematics*. Reston, Va.: NCTM, 1989, pp. 20–21, 70–73. Used by permission.

Appendix B

Blackline Masters

- B–1   Ten Frames
- B–2   Hundred Charts
- B–3   Variations of Hundreds Charts
- B–4   Base-Ten Model
- B–5   Powers of Ten
- B–6   Trading Mat
- B–7   Decimal Paper
- B–8   Decimal or Percent Grids
- B–9   Fraction Bars
- B–10   Fraction Models
- B–11   Rulers
- B–12   Geoboard Template
- B–13   Geoboard Recording Paper
- B–14   Centimeter Dot Paper
- B–15   Isometric Paper
- B–16   Centimeter Grid Paper
- B–17   Inch Grid Paper
- B–18   Half-Inch Grid Paper
- B–19   Quarter-Inch Grid Paper
- B–20   Spinners
- B–21   Attribute Pieces
- B–22   Tangram

B–1 Ten Frames

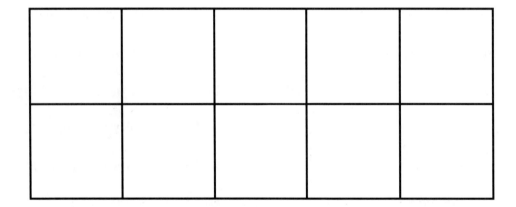

B–2 Hundred Charts

0	1	2	3	4	5	6	7	8	9
10	11	12	13	14	15	16	17	18	19
20	21	22	23	24	25	26	27	28	29
30	31	32	33	34	35	36	37	38	39
40	41	42	43	44	45	46	47	48	49
50	51	52	53	54	55	56	57	58	59
60	61	62	63	64	65	66	67	68	69
70	71	72	73	74	75	76	77	78	79
80	81	82	83	84	85	86	87	88	89
90	91	92	93	94	95	96	97	98	99

B–3 Variations of Hundreds Charts: A

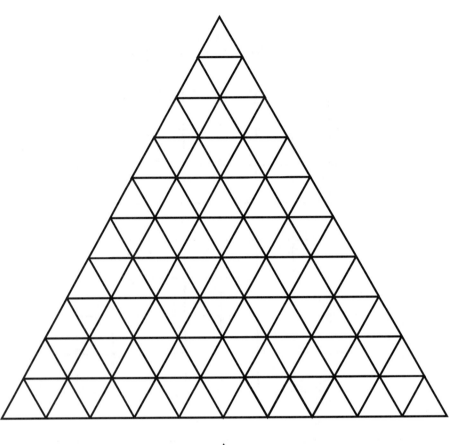

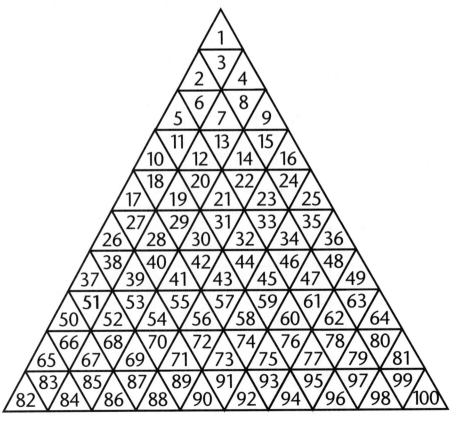

B–3 Variations of Hundreds Charts: B

0	1	2	3	4	5	6	7	8	9
10	11	12	13	14	15	16	17	18	19
20	21	22	23	24	25	26	27	28	29
30	31	32	33	34	35	36	37	38	39
40	41	42	43	44	45	46	47	48	49
50	51	52	53	54	55	56	57	58	59
60	61	62	63	64	65	66	67	68	69
70	71	72	73	74	75	76	77	78	79
80	81	82	83	84	85	86	87	88	89
90	91	92	93	94	95	96	97	98	99

B–3 Variations of Hundreds Charts: C

1	2	3	4	5	6	7	8	9	10
11	12	13	14	15	16	17	18	19	20
21	22	23	24	25	26	27	28	29	30
31	32	33	34	35	36	37	38	39	40
41	42	43	44	45	46	47	48	49	50
51	52	53	54	55	56	57	58	59	60
61	62	63	64	65	66	67	68	69	70
71	72	73	74	75	76	77	78	79	80
81	82	83	84	85	86	87	88	89	90
91	92	93	94	95	96	97	98	99	100

B–3 Variations of Hundreds Charts: D

.01	.02	.03	.04	.05	.06	.07	.08	.09	.10
.11	.12	.13	.14	.15	.16	.17	.18	.19	.20
.21	.22	.23	.24	.25	.26	.27	.28	.29	.30
.31	.32	.33	.34	.35	.36	.37	.38	.39	.40
.41	.42	.43	.44	.45	.46	.47	.48	.49	.50
.51	.52	.53	.54	.55	.56	.57	.58	.59	.60
.61	.62	.63	.64	.65	.66	.67	.68	.69	.70
.71	.72	.73	.74	.75	.76	.77	.78	.79	.80
.81	.82	.83	.84	.85	.86	.87	.88	.89	.90
.91	.92	.93	.94	.95	.96	.97	.98	.99	1.00

B–3 Variations of Hundreds Charts: E

10	20	30	40	50	60	70	80	90	100
110	120	130	140	150	160	170	180	190	200
210	220	230	240	250	260	270	280	290	300
310	320	330	340	350	360	370	380	390	400
410	420	430	440	450	460	470	480	490	500
510	520	530	540	550	560	570	580	590	600
610	620	630	640	650	660	670	680	690	700
710	720	730	740	750	760	770	780	790	800
810	820	830	840	850	860	870	880	890	900
910	920	930	940	950	960	970	980	990	1000

B–4 Base-Ten Model

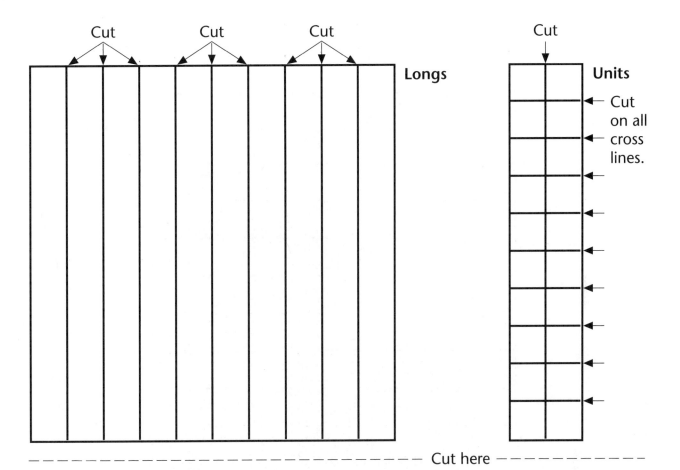

Cut   Cut   Cut   Cut

Longs

Units

← Cut on all cross lines.

– Cut here – – – – – – – – – –

Flats

B–5 Powers of Ten

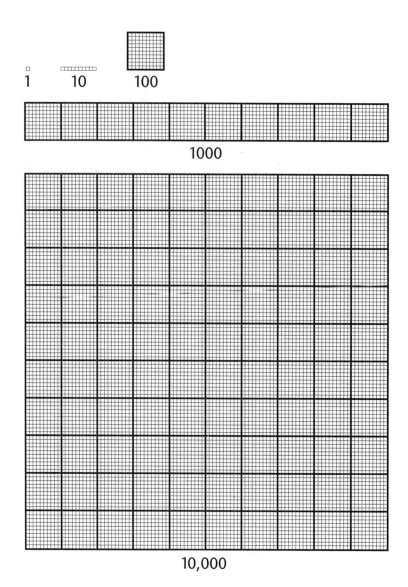

B–6 Trading Mat

Green	Blue	Yellow

B–7 Decimal Paper

B–8 Decimal or Percent Grids

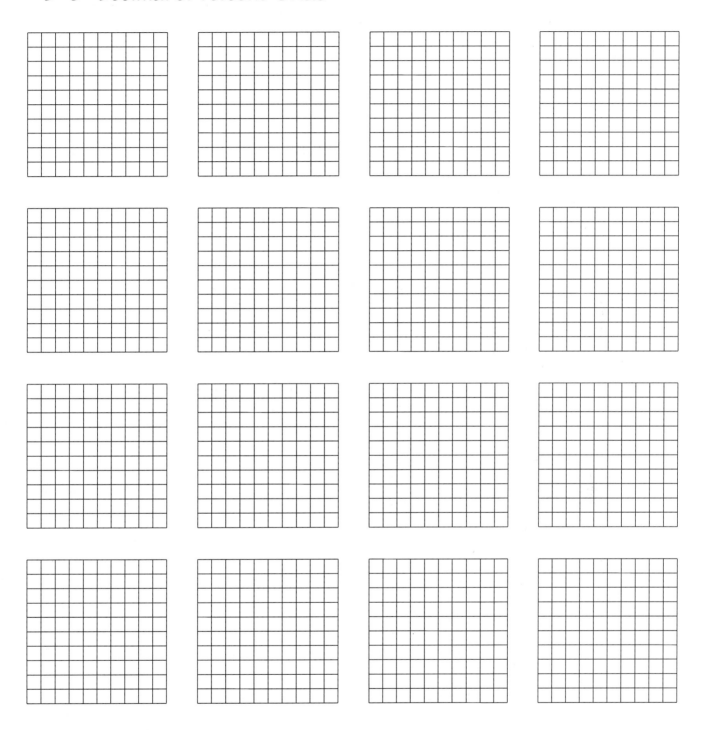

B–9 Fraction Bars

one	

| halves | $\frac{1}{2}$ | $\frac{2}{2}$ |

| thirds | $\frac{1}{3}$ | $\frac{2}{3}$ | $\frac{3}{3}$ |

| fourths | $\frac{1}{4}$ | $\frac{2}{4}$ | $\frac{3}{4}$ | $\frac{4}{4}$ |

| fifths | $\frac{1}{5}$ | $\frac{2}{5}$ | $\frac{3}{5}$ | $\frac{4}{5}$ | $\frac{5}{5}$ |

| sixths | $\frac{1}{6}$ | $\frac{2}{6}$ | $\frac{3}{6}$ | $\frac{4}{6}$ | $\frac{5}{6}$ | $\frac{6}{6}$ |

| eighths | $\frac{1}{8}$ | $\frac{2}{8}$ | $\frac{3}{8}$ | $\frac{4}{8}$ | $\frac{5}{8}$ | $\frac{6}{8}$ | $\frac{7}{8}$ | $\frac{8}{8}$ |

| ninths | $\frac{1}{9}$ | $\frac{2}{9}$ | $\frac{3}{9}$ | $\frac{4}{9}$ | $\frac{5}{9}$ | $\frac{6}{9}$ | $\frac{7}{9}$ | $\frac{8}{9}$ | $\frac{9}{9}$ |

| tenths | $\frac{1}{10}$ | $\frac{2}{10}$ | $\frac{3}{10}$ | $\frac{4}{10}$ | $\frac{5}{10}$ | $\frac{6}{10}$ | $\frac{7}{10}$ | $\frac{8}{10}$ | $\frac{9}{10}$ | $\frac{10}{10}$ |

| twelfths | $\frac{1}{12}$ | $\frac{2}{12}$ | $\frac{3}{12}$ | $\frac{4}{12}$ | $\frac{5}{12}$ | $\frac{6}{12}$ | $\frac{7}{12}$ | $\frac{8}{12}$ | $\frac{9}{12}$ | $\frac{10}{12}$ | $\frac{11}{12}$ | $\frac{12}{12}$ |

B–10 Fraction Models: A

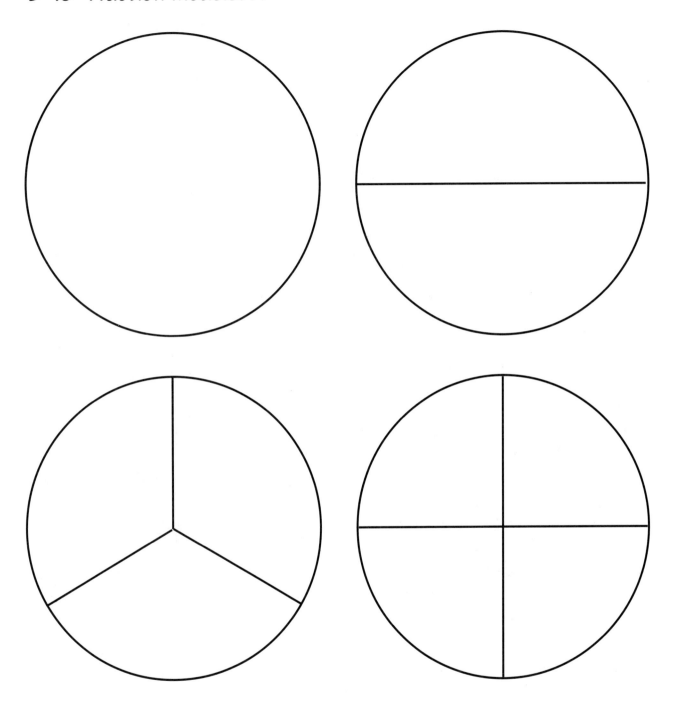

B–10 Fraction Models: B

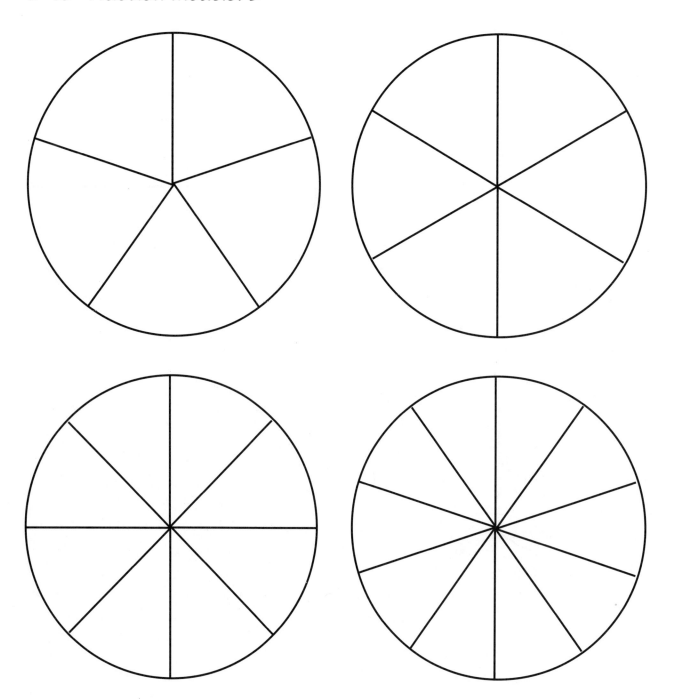

B–11 Rulers

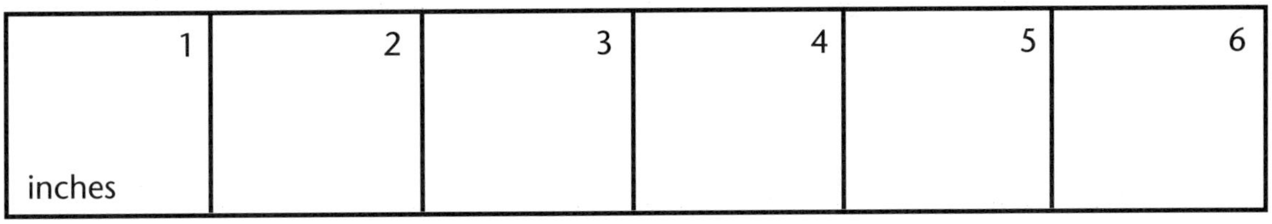

inches

Primary-inch ruler

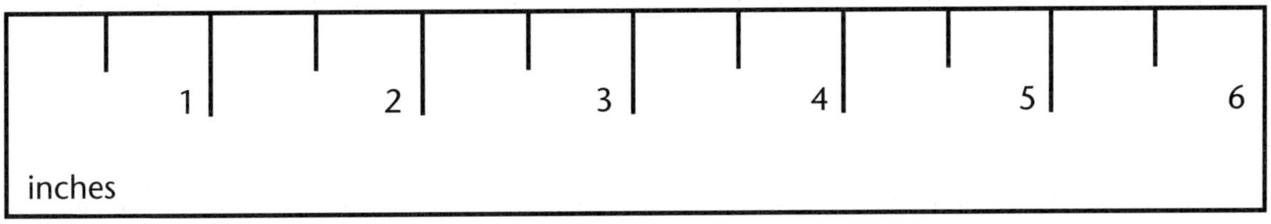

inches

Half-inch ruler

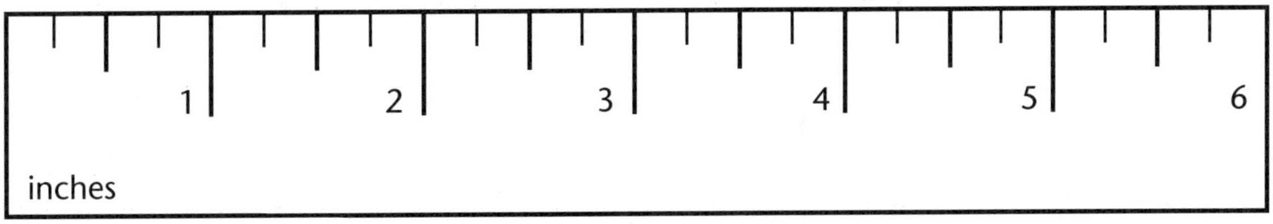

inches

Fourth-inch ruler

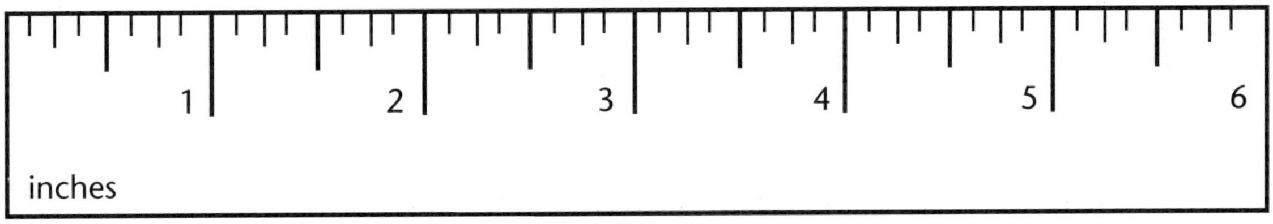

inches

Eighth-inch ruler

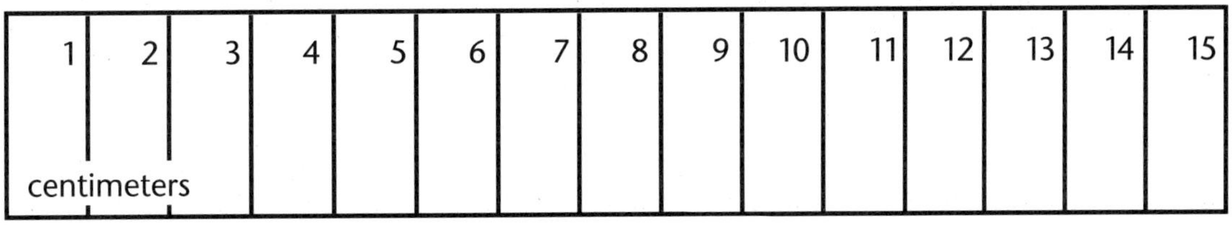

centimeters

Primary centimeter ruler

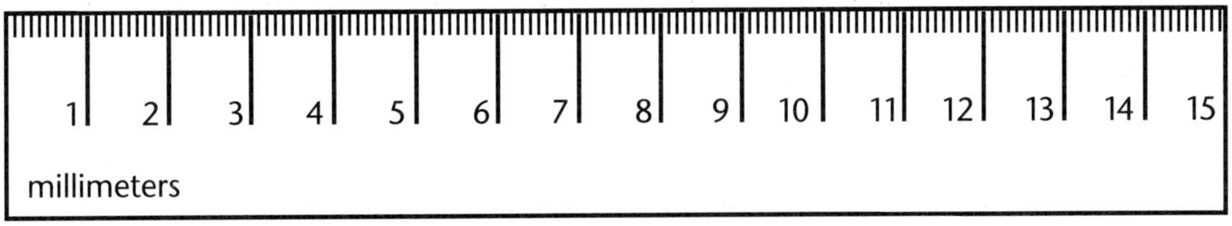

millimeters

Millimeter ruler

B–12 Geoboard Template

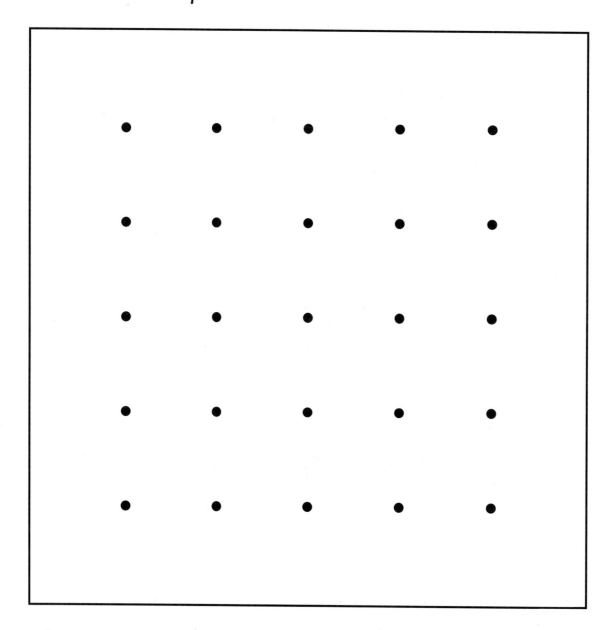

B–13 Geoboard Recording Paper

B–14 Centimeter Dot Paper

B–15 Isometric Paper

B–16 Centimeter Grid Paper

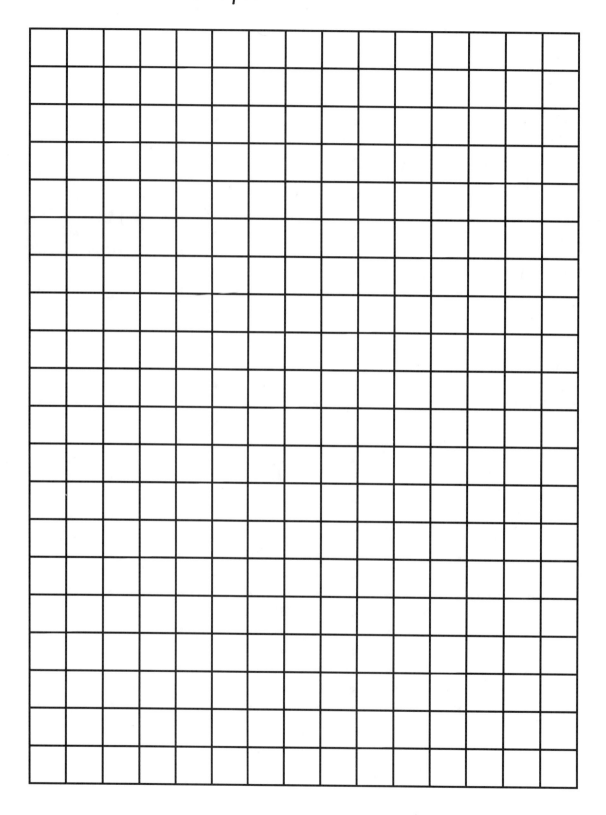

B–17 Inch Grid Paper

B–18 Half-Inch Grid Paper

B–19 Quarter-Inch Grid Paper

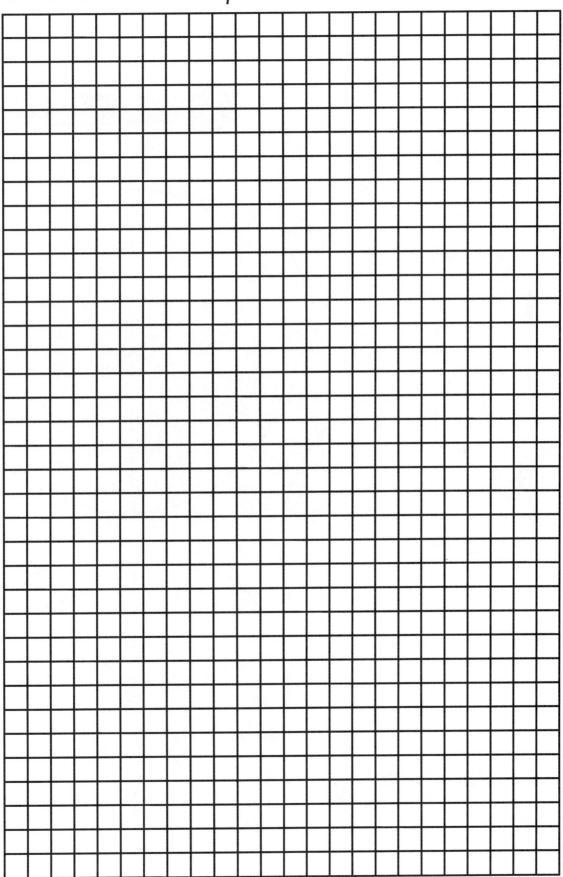

B–20 Spinners

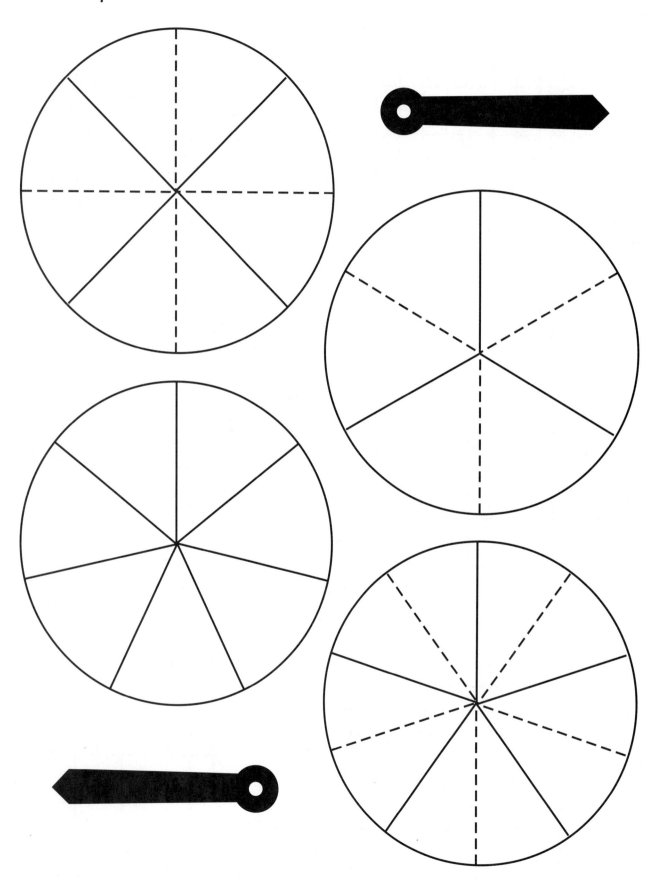

B–21 Attribute Pieces

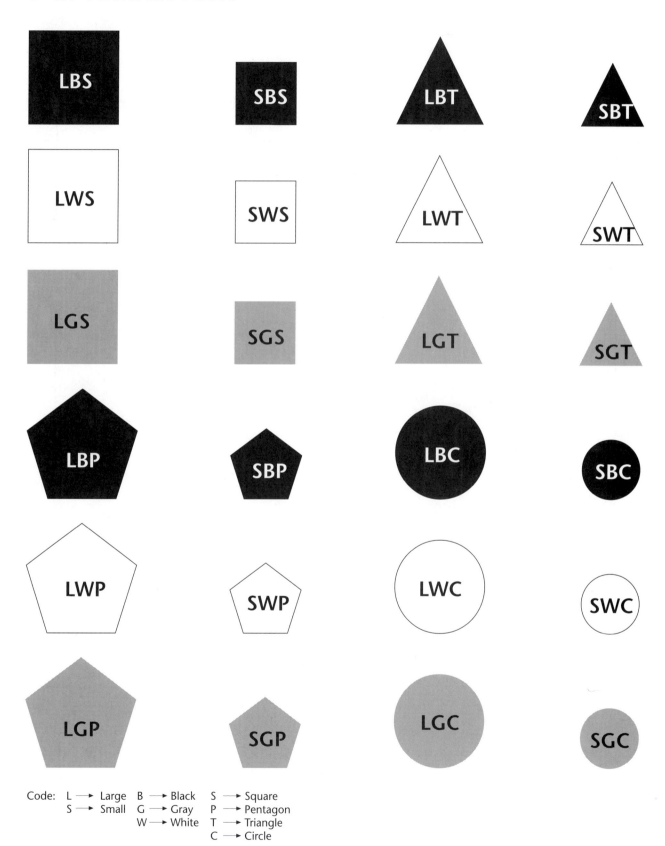

Code:
L → Large	B → Black	S → Square
S → Small	G → Gray	P → Pentagon
	W → White	T → Triangle
		C → Circle

LBS = Large Black Square

B–22 Tangram

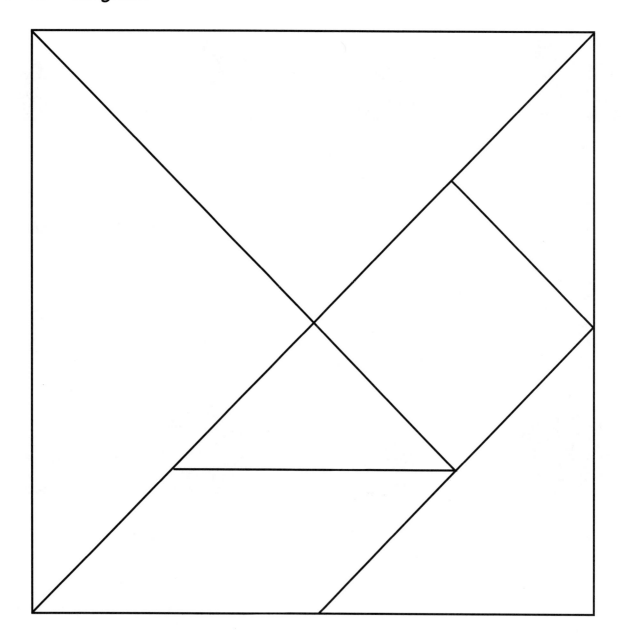

Appendix C

Publishers and Distributors

Instructional Materials

Activities Resources
P.O. Box 4875
Hayward, CA 94540
510-782-1300
info@activityresources.com

Creative Publications
Customer Service
5623 W. 115th St.
Worth, IL 60432-9931
800-624-0822
http://www.mathland.com

Cuisenaire Company of America, Inc.
P.O. Box 5026
White Plains, NY 10602-5026
800-237-3142
http://www.cuisenaire.com

Dale Seymour Publications
P.O. Box 5026
White Plains, NY 10602-5026
800-USA-1100
http://www.aw.com/dsp/

Delta Education, Inc.
P.O. Box 3000
Nashua, NH 03061-3000
800-442-5444
http://www.delta-ed.com

Didax, Inc.
Education Resources
395 Main Street
Rowley, MA 01969-9007
800-458-0024
http://www.Didaxinc.com

Education Teaching Aids (ETA)
620 Lakeview Parkway
Vernon Hills, IL 60061-9923
800-445-5985
info@etauniverse.com

GEMS
Lawrence Hall of Science #5200
University of California
Berkeley, CA 94720-5200
510-642-7771

Heinemann
361 Hanover Street
Portsmouth, NH 03801-3912
800-541-2086
http://www.heinemann.com

Ideal School Supply Company
11000 South Lavergne Street
Oak Lawn, IL 60453
800-323-5131
http://www.instructionalfair.com

Key Curriculum Press
2512 Martin Luther King Jr. Way
P.O. Box 2304
Berkeley, CA 94702-0304
800-995-MATH
http://www.keypress.com

Math Learning Center
P.O. Box 3226
Salem, OR 97302
503-370-8130

National Council of Teachers
   of Mathematics
1906 Association Drive
Reston, VA 22091-1593
800-235-7566
nctm@nctm.org
http://www.nctm.com

Nasco Math
901 Janesville Avenue
Fort Atkinson, WI 53538-0901
800-558-9595
http://www.nascota.com

Scott Resources
P.O. Box 2121
Ft. Collins, CO 80522
800-289-9299

Summit Learning
P.O. Box 493C
Ft. Collins, CO 80522
800-777-8817

Tricon Publishing
2150 Enterprise Drive
Mt. Pleasant, MI 48858
512-772-2811

USA Today Teaching Guides
Mathematics Science Education
   Board
2101 Constitution Ave., NW HA 476
Washington, DC 20418
800-USA-0001
http://www.usatoday.com

Index

Addition
with decimals, 291
with fractions, 280–283
with whole numbers, 198–201
basic facts, 153
column addition, 199–200
higher-decade, 200–201
models, 147–149
thinking strategies, 155–160
Additive property, 117
Adjusting, 184, 185
Agenda for Action, An, 9, 11, 69, 210
Algebra, 8, 12, 13, 338, 344
Algorithms, 5
with decimals, 290–293
with fractions, 280–286
manipulative materials and learning, 197
place-value ideas and, 197
with whole numbers, 195–219
addition, 198–201
checking, 215–216
choosing appropriate means of calculating, 215
division, 209–215
greatest common factor and least common multiple, 349
importance, 196–197
multiplication, 204–209
subtraction, 201–204
Altitudes, 234–235
Analysis of teaching/learning, 38, 39
Angles of geometric figures, 231–232
Anxiety, 28–29, 32
Applications, 4, 13, 72, 308–310
Area, 243–244, 249, 262–265
formulas, 255–259
Assessment, 47, 52–67
major shifts in practice, 53–54
national, 71, 117, 126, 133, 139, 210, 250, 306, 309, 327
standards, 6, 9, 52–53
ways to gather evidence
achievement tests, 60–61
interviewing, 55, 84
inventories and checklists, 84
observation, 54, 83–84
performance tasks, 55–56
portfolios, 57
questioning, 45, 54–55
self-assessments, 56–57

work samples, 57
writings, 57–58
written tests, 58–60, 84
ways to record and communicate, 61–65
Associative property, 153
Attitudes, 1, 11, 27–28, 57, 221
Attribute blocks, 92, 93
Averages, 324
Averaging strategy, 188

Bar graph, 319, 321
Base of ten, 117
Basic facts, 144–171
mastery, 166–168
models for operations, 147–151
prerequisites, 146–147
properties, 151–152, 153
thinking strategies, 155–166
addition, 155–160
division, 165–166
multiplication, 161–165
subtraction, 160–161
Basic (or essential) skills, 4, 12–14
Behaviorism, 18–19
Blackline masters, 359–386
Box plot, 319–321

Calculators, 4, 5, 9, 10, 14, 74, 126, 128–129, 131, 132, 176–178
Cardinal number, 109, 110
Checking, 82, 180–181, 215–216
Checklists, 61, 62–63, 84
Circle, area formula for, 259
Circle (pie) graph, 318–319, 321
Classification, 90–94
Class records, 61
Clocks, 254–255
Clustering, 188
Column addition, 199–200
Common denominator, 277–278
Communication, 5, 7, 24–25, 32, 57, 63–65, 92. *See also* Language
Commutative property, 153, 155–156, 162
Comparisons, 95–97, 261
Compatible numbers, 187–189
Compensation, 184, 185
Complement technique, 201–202
Computational alternatives, 173–194. *See also* Algorithms
estimation strategies, choosing, 189–190, 191

tools, 175–189
adjusting or compensating, 184, 185
calculators, 4, 5, 9, 10, 14, 74, 126, 128–129, 131, 132, 176–178
clustering, 189
compatible numbers, 187–189
computational estimation, 183–184
flexible rounding, 184–187
front-end estimation, 184, 185
mental computation, 123, 125–126, 178–183
Computers, 4, 5, 10, 14, 74, 129–130, 131–132, 133
Concavity, 232–234
Conceptual knowledge, 21
Connectionism, 3
Connections, 5, 6, 7, 14, 21, 30–31, 106–109, 262–265
Conservation, 97–98, 249
Constructivism, 3, 17, 19
Conversions, 259, 260–261
Convexity, 232–234
Cooperative learning, 44
Counting, 98–104, 128–130, 146, 273
practice, 102–105
principles, 99–100
stages, 100
strategies, 100–102
Curriculum change, 1–16
essential content, 12–14
forces affecting, 8–11
influences, 2–4
needs of child, 3
needs of society, 4
needs of subject, 2–3
ongoing concerns, 14
what mathematics to teach, 4–8

Data, use of. *See* Graphs; Probability; Statistics
Decimals, 6, 286–293
development, 286–290
ordering and rounding, 290
relation to common fractions, 286–289
relation to place value, 289–290
operations, 290–293
addition and subtraction, 291
multiplication and division, 291–293
Decomposition algorithm, 201
Diagnosis, 47
Discourse, 37–38

Distributive algorithm, 212
Distributive property, 153
Divisibility tests, 349–351
Division
  with decimals, 291–293
  with fractions, 285–286
  models, 149–151
  with whole numbers, 149–151,
    209–215
    basic facts, 153
    one-digit divisor, 211–214
    remainders, 210–211
    thinking strategies, 165–166
    two-digit divisor, 214–215
Division method to find prime
    factorization, 348–349
Drill and practice, 3, 12, 46–47,
    102–105, 166–168
Dyslexia, 123

Equity, 27, 32, 48
Equivalences, 259–260
Estimation, 5, 8, 13, 103–104, 136–137,
    183–184
  adjusting, 184–185
  clustering, 189
  compatible numbers, 187–189
  flexible rounding, 184–187
  front-end, 184
  measurement, 261–262
  strategies, choosing, 189–190, 191
Evaluation. *See* Assessment; National
    assessment

Factors, 347
Factor tree method, 348–349
Fibonacci's Sequence, 351–352, 353
Field (Gestalt) theory, 3
Flexible rounding, 184–187
Formulas, measurement, 255–259
Fractions, 6, 268–286
  conceptual development, 269–280
    equivalence, 276–278
    meanings, 270–271
    mixed numbers and improper
      fractions, 278–280
    models of part–whole, 271–272
    ordering, 275–276
  introduction, 269, 272–275
  operations, 280–286
    addition and subtraction, 280–283
    division, 285–286
    multiplication, 283–285
  relation to decimals, 286–289
Front-end estimation, 184

Gender aptitudes, equality of, 27,
    29–30, 32. *See also* Equity
Generalizing, 82
Geometry, 5, 8, 13, 220–242
  number patterns in, 352
  plane, 228–240
    classification scheme, 238–240
    names of shapes, 235–236
    properties of shapes, 228–235
    relationships between shapes,
      236–238
    ratio and proportionality and, 301
  solid, 221–228
    constructing, exploring,
      discovering, 224–226

describing and classifying, 222–224
relating three dimensions to two,
    226–228
Gestalt theory, 3
Goals, 1, 39–40, 41
Government influence, 10–11
Graphs, 316, 317–323
  bar, 319, 321
  box plot, 319–321
  characteristics of, 321–322
  for comparisons, 96–97
  line, 319, 321
  picture, 318, 321
  pie (circle), 318–319, 321
  stem-and-leaf plot, 319–321
  teaching tips, 322–323
Greatest common factor, 349
Grouping, 32, 42–44, 74–75
Group recognition, 98

Higher-decade addition, 200–201

Identity property, 153
Improper fractions, 278–280
Incidental learning, 3
Individual differences, 1, 33, 71, 75, 155
Instructional tool, calculator used as, 177
Interviewing, 55, 84

Language, 2, 24–25, 92, 123, 147
Learned helplessness, 29
Learning environment, 38
Learning theories
  behaviorism, 18–19
  constructivism, 17, 19
  how children learn mathematics,
    17–20
  levels of development, 19–20, 23
  metacognition, 26–27, 32
  procedural vs. conceptual knowledge,
    21
  recommendations for teaching, 31–32
  spiral approach, 23–24, 40
  teaching principles, 31–32
Least common denominator, 277
Least common multiple, 349
Lesson planning
  components, 41–42
  evaluation, 47–48
  grouping, 42–44
  importance, 39–40
  levels, 40–41
  standards, 37–39
  strategic moment, 48–49
  student response, 44–45
Lessons, examples of, 68, 88–89,
    115–116, 144–145, 173–174,
    195–196, 220–221, 243–244,
    268–269, 296–297, 314–315, 337
Line graph, 319, 321
Line symmetry, 231
Literature, Children's, 32, 85, 102,
    112–113, 133, 170–171, 217, 241,
    267, 294, 311–312, 335, 354
Logic blocks, 92, 93

Manipulative materials, 6, 22, 25–26,
    32, 45–46, 120–121, 197, 212.
    See also Models
Mastery learning approach, 40
Mathematics, definition of, 2

Mean, 324–325
Meaningful learning, 19, 30, 89, 155
Measurement, 5, 8, 13, 243–267
  area, 243–244, 249, 262–265
  capacity, 249
  connections between attributes,
    262–265
  definition, 246
  equivalences and conversions,
    259–261
  estimation, 261–262
  formulas, 255–259
  identifying attributes, 247–250
  importance, 244–245
  instruments, 253–255
  length, 247–248
  perimeter, 248, 263–264, 265
  process, 246–247
  temperature, 250
  time, 250
  units, 250–253
  volume, 249, 263, 264, 265
  weight, 249
Median, 325–326
Mental computation, 123, 125–126,
    178–183
Metacognition, 26–27, 32
Metric relations, 264, 266
Mixed numbers, 278–280
Mode, 326–327
Models, 25–26, 32, 117, 120–121, 127,
    130, 132, 147–151, 224–226,
    271–275, 305–306. *See also*
    Manipulative materials
Multi-embodiment, 26
Multiples, 347–348
Multiplication
  algorithms for, 204–209
  with fractions, 283–285
  models, 149–151
  with whole numbers, 204–209
    basic facts, 153
    with large numbers, 209
    with one-digit multiplier, 204–205
    by tens, 207–209
    thinking strategies, 161–165
    with two-digit multiplier, 205–207
    with zeros, 209

National Advisory Committee on
    Mathematical Education
    (NACOME), 9
National assessment, 71, 117, 126, 133,
    139, 210, 250, 306, 309, 327
National Assessment of Educational
    Progress, 10
National Council of Teachers of
    Mathematics (NCTM), 1, 175
  Agenda for Action, An, 9, 11, 69, 210
  NCTM *Addenda Series*, 19, 90
  NCTM *Agenda Series*, 316
  NCTM *Assessment Standards for School
    Mathematics*, 52–53
  NCTM *Curriculum and Evaluation
    Standards*, 4–8, 9, 10, 14, 18, 19,
    23, 41, 57, 69, 83, 89, 117, 132,
    139, 147, 174, 177, 183, 186,
    196–197, 210, 216, 221, 244, 245,
    269, 297, 316, 338
  Summary of recommendations,
    356–358

National Council of Teachers of
Mathematics (NCTM), *(cont'd)*
NCTM *Professional Standards,* 6, 12,
19, 22, 31, 37–39, 41, 42, 43, 45,
48, 56
position statement on calculators, 176
*Nation at Risk: The Imperative for
Educational Reform, A,* 9
Nominal numbers, 109–110
Nonexamples, 26
Number sense and concepts, 5, 88–114.
See also Numeration system; Place
value
cardinal, ordinal, and nominal
numbers, 109–110
counting, 98–104, 128–130, 146, 273
practice, 102–105
principles, 99–100
stages, 100
strategies, 100–102
early number development,
104–109
benchmarks, 104–105
connections, 106–109
prenumber concepts, 90–98
classification, 90–94
comparisons, 95–97
conservation, 97–98
group recognition, 98
patterns, 94–95
writing numerals, 110–111
Number theory, 7, 344–352
benefits of teaching, 344–346
divisibility tests, 349–351
factors, primes, and prime
factorization, 347–349
greatest common factor and
least common multiple,
349
odds and evens, 346–347
Numeration system, 117–121

Observation, 54, 83–84
One-right-answer syndrome, 190
Ordinal number, 109, 110

Paper-and-pencil tests. *See* Written
tests
Parallel lines, 232
Parallelogram, area formula for, 258
Parents, communicating assessments to,
64
Partitioning, 150–151, 272–273
Pascal's Triangle, 351, 352
Patterns, 2, 6, 7–8, 94–95, 104, 128–130,
164–165, 201, 338–344
growing patterns, 341
relationships, 342–344
repeating patterns, 338–341
Percents, 302–310
applying, 308–310
understanding, 305–308
Performance test, 55–56
Perimeter, 248, 264, 265
area and, 263–264
Perpendicular lines, 232
Picture graph, 318, 321
Pie (circle) graph, 318–319, 321
Place value, 56, 197
with decimals, 289–290
developing, 121–132

estimation, 136–137
numeration system, 117–121
grouping (trading), 117–118
modeling, 120–121
nature of place value, 118–120
properties, 117
thinking place value, 117
reading and writing numbers,
132–135
regrouping and renaming, 130–132
rounding, 137–139
Plane geometry, 228–240
Polygons, 239–240
Prenumber concepts, 90–98
classification, 90–94
comparisons, 95–97
conservation, 97–98
group recognition, 98
patterns, 94–95
Prime factorization, 348–349
Primes, 348
Probability, 5, 8, 13, 316, 317, 327–333
of an event, 328–331
independence of events, 332–333
randomness, 331–332
Problem solving, 1, 4, 5, 7, 9, 13, 14, 27,
29, 30, 68–87
assessment, 83–84
definition, 70–71
effective teaching, 71–75
class management, 74–75
planning, 72–73
resources, 73–74
technology, 74
time, 72
metacognition, 26–27
opportunities, using, 82–83
strategies, 75–81
Procedural knowledge, 21
Properties, 151–152, 153
Proportions, 300–302, 303
Pythagorean Triples, 351, 352

Quadrilaterals, 238–239
Questioning, 25, 45, 54–55

Randomness, 331–332
Rational counting, 100
Ratios, 297, 298–300, 301
Reading numbers, 132–135
Reasoning, 5, 7, 13
Records, assessment, 61–63
Rectangle, formula for area of, 256–258
Regrouping and renaming, 130–132
Relationships, 342–344
Remediation, 47–48
Research, 10, 17, 19, 21, 26, 27, 31,
32–33, 37, 43, 46, 48, 74, 80, 103,
109, 127, 136, 154, 155, 166, 167,
180, 183, 190, 200, 201, 213, 245,
246, 250, 298
Retention, 30
Rote counting, 100, 101
Rounding, 137–139, 184–187, 190, 245,
290
Rulers, 253–254

Scaled instruments, 254
School administration, communicating
assessments to, 65
Self-assessments, 56–57

Shape
area and, 262–263
volume and, 263, 264
Skip counting, 101–102, 162
Social utility, 4
Software, 74, 167, 232
Solid geometry, 221–228
Spatial sense, 5
Spiral approach to learning, 23–24, 40
Standards, assessment, 6, 9, 52–53. *See
also* National Council of Teachers
of Mathematics (NCTM)
Statistics, 5, 8, 12, 13, 316, 317,
324–327
averages, 324
mean, 324–325
median, 325–326
mode, 326–327
Stem-and-leaf plot, 319–321
Strategies
basic facts, thinking strategies for,
155–166
counting, 100–102
problem solving, 75–81
Student files, 61
Students, communicating assessment
to, 64
Subtraction
algorithms for, 201–204
basic facts, 153
thinking strategies for,
160–161
with fractions, 280–283
models, 147–149
with whole numbers, 160–161
zeros in sum, 203–204
Subtractive algorithm, 212
Surface area, volume and, 264, 265
Symmetry of geometric shapes, 231

Tasks, 37
Technology, 1, 3, 6, 10, 14, 74
Ten frame, 108, 360
Temperature, 250
Testing, 3, 9, 10, 11, 47, 58–61, 84
Textbooks, 2, 11, 17, 22, 40–41, 42, 46,
72, 73, 76, 78, 80
Third International Mathematics
and Science Study (TIMSS), 10,
23, 40
Time
measuring, 250
use of, 41–42, 72
Time-on-task, 39–40, 44
Trapezoid, area formula for, 259
Triangles, 238
area formula for, 258

Unitizing, 262
USMES Guide, The, 80

Volume, 249, 263, 264, 265

Weight, measuring, 249
Whole-number operations. *See*
Algorithms; Basic facts
Workbooks and worksheets, 46
Writing numbers, 132–135
Written tests, 56–60, 84

Zero, use of, 117